②

will ~~it~~ know what we don't know — namely how
well we did with those problems? In short they will
be living in the world we helped to shape.

Will they read the letter with gratitude in their
hearts for what we did or will they be bitter because
~~miserable~~ the heritage we left them was one of human
misery?

Oh I wrote of the problems we face here in 1976.
The choice we face between continuing the policies of
the last 40 yrs. that have led to bigger & bigger govt.
less & less liberty, redistribution of earnings through
confiscatory taxation or trying to get back on the original
course set for us by the Founding Fathers. Will we
choose fiscal responsibility, limited govt. and freedom of
choice for all our people? Or will we let an irresponsible
Congress ~~take the road~~ set us on the road our English cousins
have already taken? The road to ec. ruin and state control of our
very lives? On the international scene two great super powers
face each other with nuclear missiles at the ready —
poised to bring Armageddon to the world.

Those who read my letter will know whether those
missiles were fired or not. Either they ~~they~~ will be surrounded by
the same beauty ~~we know~~ ~~as I wrote the letter~~ or they
will wonder sadly what it was like when the world
was still beautiful ~~before that awful day when civilization broke down~~

If we here today ~~in this election year of our Lord~~ 1976
meet the challenge confronting us — those who open that
time capsule ~~in~~ 100 yrs from now will do so in ~~a place of~~ beauty,
~~having~~ peace, prosperity and the ultimate in personal
freedom ~~consistent with an orderly civilized society~~.

If we don't ~~meet~~ keep our rendezvous with destiny,
the letter probably will never be read — because
~~they will live in the world which we had a hand in shaping~~
~~both of individual freedom will not be permitted~~
we left them
~~in that world 100 yrs from now which we are shaping~~
a world ~~and~~ in which no one is allowed to read of individual liberty
~~terms or~~ freedom of choice. ~~or individual liberty~~

fP

Well that's all the desk clearing for today
~ as I indicated ~~~~~~~~ when I began
has been my last such chore. This is ~
~al commentary. I'm going to miss these w~
~l all of you. I've enjoyed every one. Even wri~
~n has been a lot of fun. I've scratched th~
~ on a yellow tablet in airplanes, riding ~
~s, and at the ranch when the sun was ~
~n.

Some time later today if you happen to ~
~ on television you'll understand why I can ~
~ a bring you these commentaries.

Well that's all the desk clearing for today
~ as I indicated ~~~~~~~~ when I began
has been my last such chore. This is ~
~al commentary. I'm going to miss these w~
~l all of you. I've enjoyed every one. Even wri~
~n has been a lot of fun. I've scratched th~
~ on a yellow tablet in airplanes, riding ~
~s, and at the ranch when the sun was ~

THE WRITINGS OF RONALD REAGAN THAT REVEAL HIS REVOLUTIONARY VISION FOR AMERICA

Reagan, In His Own Hand

EDITED, WITH AN INTRODUCTION AND COMMENTARY BY

Kiron K. Skinner
Annelise Anderson
Martin Anderson

with a Foreword by George P. Shultz

THE FREE PRESS
New York London Toronto Sydney Singapore

*f*P

THE FREE PRESS
A Division of Simon & Schuster, Inc.
1230 Avenue of the Americas
New York, NY 10020

Designed by Kim Llewellyn

Manufactured in the United States of America

10   9   8   7   6   5   4   3   2   1

Library of Congress Cataloging-in-Publication Data

Reagan, Ronald.
    Reagan, in his own hand : The writings of Ronald Reagan that reveal his revolutionary vision
for America / edited, with an introduction and commentary by Kiron K. Skinner, Annelise
Anderson, Martin Anderson ; with a foreword by George P. Schultz.
        p. cm.
Includes index.
    1. Reagan, Ronald—Political and social views.   2. United States—Politics and
government—1981–1989.   I. Skinner, Kiron K.   II. Anderson, Annelise Graebner.
III. Anderson, Martin.   IV. Title.

E838.5.R432 2001a
973.927—dc21   00-066304

ISBN 0-7432-0123-X

For Ronald Reagan

Who wrote the documents

Contents

Part Four

OTHER WRITINGS NOV. 6, 1925–NOV. 5, 1994 421

Foreword

I was surprised when I first saw some examples of Ronald Reagan's hand-written essays and heard of the large number of them that had just been found. I had no idea that they existed. But when I thought it over, I was really not surprised at all.

I have logged many hours with Ronald Reagan, advising him during the 1980 presidential campaign, then serving as his secretary of state for nearly seven years. Sometimes I would listen to him in conversations with fellow heads of governments or with the officials of our government. Sometimes I would listen as he talked policy and politics with members of the Congress, but perhaps the most important comments I heard him make occurred during our biweekly private meetings in the White House.

I was always struck by his ability to work an issue in his mind and to find its essence, and by his depth of conviction. Thinking back on all the time we spent together, I remembered his intense interest and fondness for the spoken word, for caring very deeply about how to convey his thoughts and ideas to people—not only to the American people, but to people living all over the world.

I recall one incident vividly. I was to deliver the Reagan administration's position on an important foreign policy issue. I brought the text of my proposed speech with me to our private meeting and I asked him to look it over to be sure that I had it the way he wanted it.

He nodded, took the speech draft, read it through carefully, then looked up at me and pronounced it to be "perfectly satisfactory."

Then there was a slight pause and he said, "Of course, if I were giving that speech, it would be different."

That got my attention. I asked, what did he mean?

"Well," he said, "you've written this so it can be read. It can be reprinted in the *New York Times* or in your *State Department Bulletin* that goes around the world. That's perfectly appropriate. But I talk to people—when they are in front of me, or at the other end of a television camera or a radio microphone—and that's different.

"I'll show you what I mean."

He took the text of my speech, flipped it open at random, took out a pen and quickly began to edit the page. He made four or five edits and put a caret in the margin and wrote "story." Then he handed it back to me.

As I read what he had done, I saw that he had changed the tone of my speech completely.

Reading through the essays in this book, I thought about all the times I had been with him when he spoke without notes or briefings, forcefully and clearly spelling out what would be the policy positions of the United States. Somehow he always seemed to know what to say.

To many people, President Reagan was a mystery. How did he know what to say? Who was handing him notes and whispering in his ear? Who was writing his speeches? Even some of his close aides were puzzled. I remember his national security adviser, Bud McFarlane, just a few months before Bud resigned, shaking his head and saying in bewilderment, "He knows so little and accomplishes so much."

The answer to that mystery may lie in these essays, which were written well before he became president. Apparently, even then, he knew quite a bit.

I remember when I accompanied the president to the Geneva Summit meeting in 1985, where he and Mikhail Gorbachev, whom he would meet there for the first time, were scheduled to talk about the full range of issues confronting the United States and the Soviet Union. On the second morning, the subject was strategic nuclear arms. Donald Regan, Bud McFarlane, Paul Nitze, Roz Ridgway, and Arthur Hartman joined the president and me on our side of the table, facing our Soviet counterparts.

Mikhail Gorbachev suddenly began to harangue us about our Strategic Defense Initiative, our plans for missile defense.

President Reagan exploded. The two leaders went back and forth, interrupting each other and expressing their views with vehemence.

Then Ronald Reagan got the floor. He spoke passionately about how much better the world would be if we were able to defend ourselves against nuclear warheads on ballistic missiles. He was intense as he expressed his abhorrence at having to rely on the ability to "wipe each other out" as the only means of keeping the peace. "We must do better, and we can," Reagan declared.

The depth of President Reagan's belief in missile defense was vividly apparent. Ronald Reagan was talking from the inside out. Translation was simultaneous. Gorbachev could connect what Reagan was saying with his facial expressions and body language.

When the president finished, there was total silence.

After what seemed an interminable time, Gorbachev said, "Mr. President, I don't agree with you, but I can see that you really mean what you say."

Ronald Reagan had made an immense impression on Mikhail Gorbachev, who must have realized that he could not talk, con, bully, or in any other way manipulate Ronald Reagan into dropping his missile defense research program. Ronald Reagan had personally nailed into place an essential plank in our negotiating platform.

On another occasion, I accompanied Reagan to a meeting of NATO heads at a particularly tense time. As always at such meetings, each leader was allotted a limited amount of time to speak. Questions were raised about the importance of NATO and the U.S. commitment to its success.

Sitting beside Ronald Reagan, I could see him become increasingly restive and agitated. He had some prepared notes in his hand, but when his turn to speak came, he ignored the notes and virtually exploded into the meeting. He talked intensely and extemporaneously about the importance of NATO and its role, and his complete commitment to its mission.

Nobody had written that talk for him, and he had not written it himself beforehand. He just knew what he wanted to say, and it showed how crisply and clearly he had thought through this important matter in our foreign and defense policy.

I could tell dozens of stories about specific times when Ronald Reagan displayed detailed knowledge about policy issues, and when he took decisive action based on that knowledge—without the benefit of someone whispering in his ear or sliding a note into his hand. But so ingrained is the belief that he was an amiable man—not too bright, the willing captive of his aides—that it would probably not make much difference.

And that is the reason why this book is so important. It provides a key to unlocking the mystery of Reagan that has baffled so many for so long. How could a man of supposedly limited knowledge and limited intelligence accomplish so much? How did he get elected and reelected the governor of our largest state? How did he get elected and reelected president of the United States? How did he preside over a time of unprecedented prosperity, the winning of the cold war, and the demise of communism worldwide? How?

Well, maybe he was a lot smarter than most people thought.

This book is devoted to the hundreds of policy essays that Reagan wrote from 1975 to 1979. The essays cover an extraordinary range of foreign policy, defense and domestic policy issues, reflecting Reagan's personal views. Once written, they were recorded and broadcast by radio to an audience of millions.

They were written to be listened to, to be broadcast once into the air, and then to disappear. But luckily, about 670 of the original handwritten drafts were saved, hidden away for over 20 years. Now they have been found and they force us to reflect on the light they shed on the mind and the capability of the man, Ronald Reagan.

I can't say enough about the dedicated scholarship and care with which the editors listed on the front of this book, and others, have resurrected those essays from their dusty storage boxes and presented them to us.

But with all due respect, this is the book that Ronald Reagan wrote—and in his own hand.

George P. Shultz

Introduction

He wasn't a complicated man. He was a private man, but he was not a complicated one. But he was a very sentimental one. And he was a very, very good writer. All of his ideas and thoughts were formulated well before he became governor or certainly president.

Nancy Reagan, in an interview with the editors

Ronald Reagan wrote, in his own hand, from his high school years right through his presidency and on into retirement—until Alzheimer's disease wreaked its gradual destruction. He wrote not only letters, short fiction, poetry, and sports stories, but speeches, newspaper articles, instructions to his cabinet and staff, and radio commentary on public policy issues, both foreign and domestic.

Nevertheless, many of the writings under his name—including the two books, *Where's the Rest of Me?* and *An American Life*—were partially written by ghostwriters. A few of his presidential speeches were drafted personally, but most were written in interaction with White House speechwriters. Most of his original writings—those we are absolutely sure are his—were pre-presidential. As Nancy Reagan recalls, "He continued to write in the White House. He wrote speeches in the Oval Office, and he had his own desk in the living quarters of the White House. He was always sitting at his desk in the White House, writing. He was so used to writing his own speeches that it took him a while to realize that, as president, he just wasn't going to have the time to write, though he could go over a speech draft and edit and correct. But to take the time to write a whole speech? He soon realized he wasn't going to have that time."

From his high school and college years, seventeen handwritten manuscripts (and a French quiz) written between 1925 and 1931 have been preserved, mostly short stories. The high school yearbook (on which he worked) has a story and a poem he wrote. In college, he wrote for the weekly newspaper. Reagan wrote a weekly sports column for the *Des Moines Dispatch* while he worked as a radio announcer at WHO. When he went to Hollywood, he wrote, with the cooperation of Warner Bros. but not, according to Reagan himself, with their help, a series of seventeen articles about his experiences for the *Des Moines Sunday Register.*

Nothing has thus far been found in his own hand of the speeches he gave to employees at General Electric's 135 plants between September 1954 and 1962 (although he often used a question-and-answer format on these occasions) or the many other speeches he gave during this time. It is quite possible that they were his own creations, but we cannot be sure. A number of these speeches appeared in print in various publications with titles such as *A Time for Choosing, Encroaching Control,* and *Losing Freedom by Installments.* We have excluded them from this book in order to focus on the substantive writings from the immediate pre-presidential years that exist in his own handwritten drafts.

We know that Reagan wrote extensively during 1975–79, between his years as governor of California and his inauguration as president. He spent these years giving speeches, writing a newspaper column, and giving over a thousand radio addresses. The idea of the radio broadcasts and newspaper columns was developed in 1974 during Reagan's final months as governor of California. Peter Hannaford, assistant to the governor and director of public affairs during Reagan's final year, conferred with Ed Meese, then Reagan's chief of staff, and Michael Deaver, and suggested that the governor consider the offer of Harry O'Connor, the head of O'Connor Creative Services in Hollywood, to produce "a five-day-a-week, five-minute RR [radio] commentary program, to be syndicated nationally." *

One weekend in October 1974, Hannaford and Deaver presented a comprehensive plan to Reagan—including newspaper columns, radio commentary, and several speeches a month. Reagan agreed to do it under the management of a new firm, Deaver & Hannaford, Inc.* *

On December 30, 1974, Governor Reagan announced his plans at the Los Angeles Press Club. The radio broadcasts were produced by Harry O'Connor and titled "Viewpoint." Though Reagan relied on Hannaford to draft

---

*Hannaford's memo is titled "RR, 1975." A radio program is also proposed in two memos dated November 4, 1974. See "Ronald Reagan: Building a National Organization," and "Ronald Reagan: A Program for the Future." Deaver and Hannaford collection, Box 1. Hoover Institution Archives.
* *Editors' interviews with Peter Hannaford, February 11, 2000, and with Harry O'Connor, August 18, 2000.

most of the newspaper columns, he enjoyed writing the radio broadcasts himself, and eventually wrote most of those essays.

In a letter dated September 19, 1978, Reagan explained to a private citizen how his radio broadcasts were written: "I write many of my commentaries while I'm traveling and this [the one requested by the citizen] was done on a cross country plane trip." * Reagan taped the broadcasts in batches of fifteen at a recording studio. O'Connor Services would distribute them with suggested airing dates, but radio stations would broadcast them according to their schedules. The dates used here are taping dates, except as noted.

In a memo to Reagan on May 23, 1975, five months after the commentaries and columns began, Peter Hannaford reported that the broadcasts were being heard on 286 radio stations, and the columns were being printed in 226 newspapers. Similar numbers were reported by Hannaford two years later. In correspondence on October 30, 1978, Reagan estimated that through his daily radio broadcasts and biweekly newspaper columns he was in touch with "20 million Americans each week." * *

The radio broadcasts began in January 1975. Reagan suspended the broadcasts when he ran for the presidency in the late fall of 1975. The broadcasts were resumed by Reagan after he lost the Republican Party's nomination to President Gerald Ford in the summer of 1976. He ended his broadcasts in October 1979 as he was preparing to announce his 1980 presidential aspirations.

Only a few people who worked with or were close to Reagan, like Nancy Reagan, knew that the governor wrote most of the radio broadcasts. "He worked a lot at home," Nancy recalled in an interview. "I can see him sitting at his desk writing, which he seemed to do all the time. Often he'd take a long shower because he said that was where he got a lot of his thoughts. He'd stand in the shower and think about what he wanted to write. And then, when he got out, he'd sit down and write. . . . Nobody thought that he ever read anything either—but he was a voracious reader. I don't ever remember Ronnie sitting and watching television. I really don't. I just don't. When I picture those days, it's him sitting behind that desk in the bedroom, working."

Martin Anderson recalls traveling with Reagan in 1976. On airplanes,

*Pre-Presidential Papers, Box 4; K RR Correspondence 1978. Ronald Reagan Presidential Library.
* *Pre-Presidential Papers, Boxes 6 and 12, and Citizens for Reagan, Box 106, Hoover Institution Archives.

Reagan always sat by the window, and whoever was traveling with him took the aisle seat next to him as a "blocker." As soon as the airplane lifted off the runway, he would reach for his briefcase. The briefcase contained articles to read, stacks of 4- by 6-inch cards that contained speech drafts written in his shorthand, pens and pencils, and a supply of writing paper, which was almost always lined, yellow, legal-size paper.

When Reagan wrote, he didn't scribble or scrawl, he wrote in a clear script. He rarely stopped to cross things out or edit. When he reached the bottom of the legal pad, he carefully flipped the page over, tucked it in on the back side of the pad, and proceeded on to the second page. The desired length of one of his radio essays was two full legal pages, and his words almost always just filled that second page—rarely shorter or longer.

Dennis LeBlanc, a young member of the California State Police, was assigned to the security detail of Governor Reagan in 1971. After Reagan left office, LeBlanc stayed on with Reagan to do all his scheduling and advance work, and became the only man to travel continually with Reagan for the next three years, often traveling alone with him.

"He was constantly writing," declared LeBlanc; "a lot of the time it was on a legal pad, where he'd write things out longhand. Other times it would be taking speeches that he wrote out longhand, and then putting it on 4 by 6 cards in an abbreviated way, using the special shorthand he had developed.

"But all the time he was writing. He would always fly first class. He'd sit by the window, and I'd sit in the aisle seat next to him. It didn't matter whether or not there was a movie being shown and all the lights were out— he'd turn on his reading lamp and would constantly be writing."

Beginning in early 1975, Reagan, with the help of LeBlanc and Barney Barnett, a retired California highway patrolman who had been Reagan's driver when he was governor, spent a lot of time rebuilding the ranch property he had recently bought.

"We drove up to the ranch from Los Angeles and back down the same day many, many times for the next two years," recalls LeBlanc. "Either Barney or I would drive, and Reagan would sit in the backseat with his legal pad, writing.

"The car we used was a red 1969 Ford station wagon, because Mrs. Reagan's favorite color was red. Barney and I and Reagan would leave Los Angeles at seven o'clock in the morning, and it would take us about two and a half hours to get to the ranch. All the way up Reagan would be writing.

"When we got to the ranch, we'd put in eight or nine hours of work. We ripped out walls and really gutted the place, so you couldn't stay overnight there. Then we'd drive back. He would be writing in the backseat when we drove back. There was some idle chitchat and stuff, but he never fell asleep and he never read—he was just always writing.

"What was amazing to me," said LeBlanc, "was the fact that Ronald Reagan never slept on planes when he was traveling. It was the same way when I was with him in the station wagon. It was like—you're wasting time if you are sleeping. You know, everyone's got things to do. And his thing to do when I was with him was his writing."

David Fischer, Reagan's executive assistant in 1978 and 1979, had similar memories. "The minute the meal service was done, he'd whip out the legal pad and start writing. He wrote to fit the exact time he needed to record. I was always amazed at how hard he worked. I'd be exhausted from traveling with him; I could start reading something and quickly fall asleep, and when I woke up he'd still be working, just writing away."

Michael Deaver and Ed Meese, his two top advisers since the mid-1960s, both confirm the same story. In addition to the broadcasts, Ed Meese remembers that he wrote many of his own speeches, at home on weekends. "He would come in on Monday morning with six, eight, or ten pages from his legal pad, all in his own handwriting. One day we found him in his office checking the typed copy of one of his speeches against his written copy to make sure it was accurate, and then he took the written pages, tore them up and put them in the wastebasket. I'm afraid a lot of his handwritten documents ended up that way."*

It may partly be luck that so many handwritten drafts of the policy essays Reagan wrote for his radio broadcasts survived. William P. Clark, who served as chief of staff to Governor Reagan in California and later followed him to Washington and became his national security adviser, recalled the difficulty his staff had in preserving documents while he was governor.

"Yes, he was a writer," said Clark about Reagan, but "unfortunately, he maintained one habit we were unable to ever break other than by scouring his trash basket.

"He threw away his longhand notes. Insisting that the top of his desk must be clear at the end of each day, he would carefully place a paper or two in his top desk drawer to age for the morrow's review and action. Then, a few informational items would go into a folder or small leather briefcase for completion at the residence. But then his longhand notes would go into the wastebasket unless intercepted. With our admonition that these could be important to historians some day, he would respond, 'Well, OK, OK.' Helene or Kathy (his secretaries) would take possession of our catch as he moved to-

*Telephone interview with Edwin Meese, August 11, 2000.

ward the door, giving his own cheery admonition, 'All right, you good people, goodnight and get home to your families.'

"Nodding, we always remained."

As Hannaford recalls, Reagan would write large numbers of radio addresses at a time. "I can still see him coming into the office in Los Angeles after these trips, often with a sheaf of yellow pages in his hand and a big grin on his face. He would hand the handwritten pages triumphantly to Elaine Crispen [at the time our chief administrative assistant], saying: 'There you are, Elaine, three weeks' worth of radio scripts for typing.' "

Elaine Crispen (now Elaine Sawyer) was the person who took the handwritten drafts that Reagan produced and typed them for his recording sessions. She worked for Reagan during the five years he had his radio program. "As I remember it," recalled Elaine, "he would go to the recording studio on a Saturday. He had written a lot of the radio scripts while he was out on the road. When he came back to the Los Angeles office, he would give them to us. We had to have a hard copy that you could read from, because sometimes his handwriting was not that easy to read. We typed every one of his handwritten yellow sheets so that he could go to the studio and read them in clear print. . . . We had devised a system so that his handwritten yellow sheets were never to be thrown out. We were supposed to save them and file them. Probably some of us knew that maybe someday they would be valuable historically."

We have included very few speeches in this book, because apparently few survive in his own hand. We do know that he wrote many of his pre-presidential speeches. His use of notecards for their delivery became famous, although the details of how he did it have not been widely shared.

Over the years Ronald Reagan wore either eyeglasses or contact lenses for reading, and felt that any serious policy speech—with its myriad facts and numbers—had to be written out in advance and read to avoid errors. But as he once explained, he didn't like to wear eyeglasses; when he wore contact lenses, he could see the audience but could not read his speech because the writing blurred, and finally, he felt the audience did not like anyone to read a speech.*

Reagan's solution to this problem was twofold. First, he figured out how to read a speech draft without wearing his glasses. En route to his speech, he wore his long-distance contact lenses. They were the older, fairly small, hard plastic lenses. Just before he arrived at the speech site, while sitting in a car or

*Conversation with Martin Anderson during the 1976 presidential campaign.

in an airplane, he would lean forward, bring both hands to his face, and then with his forefinger and thumb pluck out the lens that was in his right eye. After popping the lens in his mouth for a quick wash, he carefully placed the lens into a small case and dropped it into his coat pocket.

Now Reagan had one long-vision eye and one near-vision eye, and he had learned how to use them separately. With his naked right eye, he could read. But when he looked out at the audience, he focused on them with his lens-

One of Reagan's speech cards. When Reagan had finished with this card, he folded it in two and threw it in the trash. Martin Anderson retrieved it.

clad left eye. Throughout his speech he would go back and forth, reading with one eye, watching the audience with the other.

As for the text, he disliked reading speeches typewritten on regular letter-sized paper. Carrying a speech when he walked up to the lectern was obvious, and on a windy day at an outside lectern it was difficult to hold and turn the pages—and more than one presidential candidate has lost pages of a speech in this situation. What he settled on were index cards, medium size, 4- by 6-inch cards that would fit into the side pocket of his suit coat.

He would take the speech draft he had written out longhand, and transfer it directly to the cards for reading. The problem was that the speeches were written on yellow legal pads, 14 by 8½ inches in size—five times bigger than those 4- by 6-inch cards that fitted so nicely in his suit coat pocket.

So Reagan invented his own shorthand.

He would spend hours changing the penned words into this shorthand. Some words in the original draft were left out. Other words he shortened by dropping vowels or using special abbreviations. Every now and then he would make coded letters to represent words. All the shorthand writing was block printed on the cards, in capital letters—usually in black ink. Once he had rewritten a sentence of his original writing into shorthand, he would draw a line above and below the new writing so it would stand out. To further pack even more text onto a card, he eliminated all indentations and paragraphs. One sentence followed another, separated only by the thick black lines.

Using this technique, Reagan could copy much of the writing that filled one page of a legal pad onto a 4-by-6 card. Each card was then numbered in the upper right-hand corner so he could keep track of them. Finally, the finished pack of cards was bound together with an elastic band. A major speech filled twenty-five to thirty cards.

Reagan's speech system gave the appearance of being casual and spontaneous, while in reality his speeches had the cold precision of any carefully researched and typed speech manuscript.

He would walk across the stage to the lectern to address his audience, both arms swinging back and forth, often waving to the audience, giving no sign whatsoever of a prepared text. After he reached the lectern, only those seated behind him could notice, if they watched very closely, his left hand drop into his jacket pocket and pull out a packet of those cards. Laying the cards on top of the lectern, he would glance down, read the top card, and begin to speak.

It helped a lot that he had a gift for remembering all that was on that card.

e sorting the cards, slipping the top card to the
naked eye glanced down every now and then to
speech was over, he quickly scooped the cards
opped them back in his coat pocket his other
nce.

asy to edit and prepare new speeches. To cut
ed some cards. To add something, he prepared
the deck. To prepare a new speech, Reagan
o or more speech card decks, producing a
terial.

esident, he did not have time to prepare
n speechwriters to prepare drafts, which he
ad them. But while he was writing his own
ll.

book is drawn were discovered by acci-
holar since Edmund Morris to be granted
sident Ronald Reagan. She found several
radio broadcasts, speeches, and correspon-
by Reagan, and with Annelise Anderson and Martin Anderson, under-
took to prepare a selection of these documents for publication, with Skinner
focusing on the foreign and defense policy essays and the Andersons on domestic and economic policy. Together, the editors realized that they had a
treasure trove of documents that showed Reagan grappling with the major
policy issues of the time.

Although the handwritten broadcasts and other pre-presidential papers
are stored at the Reagan Library, the National Archives does not have authority over them because they are President Reagan's private papers and not
those of the U.S. government. The president's personal papers have been
kept in boxes for many decades. Some boxes contain archival folders that
separate documents by subject or chronology; others contain hundreds of
disorganized pieces of paper. The index to the collection is incomplete, but a
database of the radio broadcasts developed by Annelise Anderson is produced here in the Appendix.

Reagan's work is presented as he wrote it. The book offers Reagan's own
words in his own hand, including personal edits and even a few errors.
Everything here, including the marginal comments, is Reagan's own. The
Note on Editorial Methods (page xxv) explains the conventions used to display his handwritten drafts in type.

In reading these first rough drafts it should be kept in mind that they *are* first rough drafts. They were never intended to be published. They were written to be edited and typed, and Reagan took shortcuts while writing.

When Reagan wrote he often used abbreviations and some of the shorthand he used on his speech cards. This was especially true when he was writing something that would be typed before he recorded it as a radio broadcast or gave it as a speech. His secretaries knew his abbreviations and shorthand and turned them into clean English as they typed.

For example, he would write "nat." for nation, "ec. & pol." for economics and politics, "burocracy" for bureaucracy. He was often casual about where he placed apostrophes, if he used them at all, and they can be found hovering over a word that needed one. After writing the teaser with which he began all his radio essays, he usually wrote "I'll be right back." But sometimes he wrote "I'll be rite back."

If you look back at his speech card on page xix, you can see the full use of this technique: "Ending" becomes "Endng"—and "fight" becomes "fite."

Reagan's essays and other writings constitute many hundreds of pages of original first drafts. We have tried to select documents so that they represent a fair sampling of Reagan's views on a wide variety of specific issues over the five-year period he was broadcasting the radio commentaries.

In writing these daily essays on almost every national policy issue during the 1970s, Reagan was acting as a one-man think tank. He drew upon hundreds of sources, and his drafts contain thousands of facts and figures. Sometimes he lists his sources in accompanying documents. In one case, for an essay on oil, he appended them. At times he cites his sources in the text. And in many cases he simply does not mention the specific sources.

Because he was writing on topical subjects in the 1970s, it is sometimes difficult, many years later, to determine sources. We have checked dozens of references in his writings and, in virtually all cases, Reagan correctly cited or quoted his sources.

In Martin Anderson's experience, while advising Reagan during his presidential campaigns and in the presidency, whenever aides challenged him on some fact he had used, Reagan produced a source for his statements. In rare cases the source itself might not have been entirely accurate.

As our memory of events in the 1970s recedes, some of the events that Reagan reports might seem questionable. For instance, in one of his radio commentaries he writes about the plan of the People's Republic of China to "liberate Taiwan," as presented in a private speech given by Foreign Minister Huang Hua on July 30, 1977. After considerable searching, we found a copy of Huang Hua's speech, "Report on the World Situation," in a Taiwanese journal, *Issues and Studies: A Journal of China Studies and International Affairs*.

We have not fact-checked everything that Reagan writes about in his radio commentaries, but we have checked numerous events he cites—and they are discussed in our footnotes.

The bulk of the original handwritten documents reproduced in this volume are stored at the Reagan Presidential Library in Simi Valley, California, in the "Pre-Presidential Papers, 1921–1980" (PPP) collection of papers. The original handwritten drafts of radio broadcasts are mainly found in boxes 12, 14, 15, and 21. Typescripts of the radio broadcasts are found in these boxes and others throughout the PPP collection. Typescripts are also found at the Hoover Institution Archives in the Citizens for Reagan (CFR) Collection, the Peter Hannaford (PH) Collection, and the Ronald Reagan Subject Collection (RRSC). The main boxes for locating typescripts of the radio broadcasts at Hoover are CFR 35, 39, 104, and 105; PH 2 and 3; and RRSC 8.

In addition to the radio scripts, we have included examples of the other kinds of documents that exist in his handwriting. Most of these documents are found in the President's private papers at the Ronald Reagan Library. A few of Reagan's other writings included in this book come from private collections.

The last document he wrote, a letter Edmund Morris calls "a masterly piece of writing" with "the simplicity of genius," is of course the 1994 letter to the nation about his Alzheimer's. Nancy recalls that she "had somebody ask me just the other day about the Alzheimer's letter. 'Did he just sit down and write it? Or did he do some drafts?' I said, 'No, he just sat down and wrote it.' "

A Note on Editorial Methods

In producing a printed version of what Reagan wrote in his own hand, we have shown his own inserts in small italic capital letters when he used them, or italics when he added in script rather than capitals. His deletions are shown with a single strike-through except where we could not read what he struck out; unreadable strike-outs are shown with only a single symbol, a ⚡.

We have not corrected spelling or punctuation, nor have we expanded the abbreviations he often used. His placement of apostrophes in contractions, however, was as casual as the dotting of an i, and so we have often located them at their conventional place.

In the rare cases where editorial changes were made by someone other than Reagan, we present those edits in brackets.

Reagan's marginal comments are indicated by daggers (†) and are printed at the end of the document on which they appear. Asterisks are used to indicate editors' footnotes, and are at the bottom of the page.

The titles of the documents are the titles Harry O'Connor of O'Connor Creative Services used in distributing them, rather than the even briefer identifiers Reagan used when he wrote them. The dates given are taping dates, each of which is the closest known date to the time of writing. The taping date of course preceded the distribution date and can be estimated in those cases where it is unknown. Radio broadcasts were usually taped in batches of fifteen, although at first fewer were taped at a time. Sometimes more than fifteen would be taped, and the extras held for distribution during a time when Reagan was traveling abroad and couldn't do a taping. The air dates can therefore be two to five weeks and sometimes more after the taping date.

Reagan wrote his radio commentaries in two parts. First, he used a brief introduction or "teaser" to entice the radio audience to stay tuned to the station. He would always finish this part by saying, "I'll be right back." Then, after the radio commercials, he would read his essay for the day. Each of his radio commentaries ended with: "This is Ronald Reagan. Thanks for listening."

Three different versions of most of the radio commentaries can be found in the archives. One is Reagan's handwritten draft. The typed version of Reagan's draft prepared by his staff is also in the archives. The third version is the transcript of Reagan's taping session prepared by O'Connor Creative Services. O'Connor's transcripts were distributed to radio stations so that they would know what was on the tapes or records being sent to them. The O'Connor version does not include Reagan's teaser or his sign-off.

Part One

REAGAN'S PHILOSOPHY

"The ideological struggle

dividing the world is

between communism and

our own belief in freedom

to the greatest extent

possible consistent with

an orderly society."

*T*he eight radio addresses in this section express concepts and themes found in many of Reagan's handwritten manuscripts for radio commentaries and speeches given in his pre-presidential years. Taken together, the essays state the political and philosophical views on which his policies as president, both foreign and domestic, were based.

As we look back on what he wrote in the late 1970s from the perspective of the post-Communist era, in a time of economic vitality and with the United States as the world's only superpower, it is easy to forget how at odds his views were with the accepted wisdom of the day. The late 1970s was a period of high inflation, low economic growth, relatively high unemployment, and questions about the influence of the United States on the world scene. Many believed that the political systems of the United States and the Soviet Union were gradually converging. Some doubted that a political system based on individual freedom and free markets could compete effectively with a centrally controlled command economy that could override and repress political dissent.

Reagan had no such doubts. In spite of the economic and political problems, he found America's strength in its political system—in liberty, in the system that freed, as he put it, the individual genius of man—a system that, he said, has given the country political stability, the creativity of private enterprise, advanced technology, and a generosity of spirit. He also considered virtue fundamental to representative government and argued against expediency rather than principle in foreign policy.

His condemnation of communism, in words written in 1975, is powerful.

Communism, he wrote, is neither an economic nor a political system, but a form of insanity, an aberration. He wonders "how much more misery it will cause before it disappears." In comparing the statements of past and present leaders of the two systems, he quotes, as he often did, John Winthrop's 1630 statement on the deck of the Arbella: *"We shall be as a city upon a hill." But as the complete quotation Reagan uses makes clear, the significance of the city's location on a hill is not only that it is blessed, but that it is open to observation and judgment by the entire world.*

The great challenge of the world situation was, Reagan says in 1975, maintaining peace and avoiding the catastrophe of nuclear war, and doing so not through surrender but through military strength backed by economic vitality and credibility. In a radio address that is an elaboration of his extemporaneous speech at the Republican National Convention in 1976 after losing the nomination to Gerald Ford, he tells of writing a letter for a time capsule to be opened one hundred years later. He turns again to the question of nuclear Armageddon, of the potential of the two superpowers to fire missiles at one another. The challenge is not only preserving the beauty he sees as he travels the Pacific Coast Highway, but of preserving a world of peace, prosperity, and freedom of choice.

Reagan reiterated the same themes and concepts of these eight essays in his farewell speech from the Oval Office on January 11, 1989. Not even he had known how far-reaching his philosophy and policies would be, for, he says, "We meant to change a nation, and instead, we changed a world."

Peace
April 1975

How much is it worth to not have WWIII
   I'll be right back.

While in London I had an opportunity to visit with various govt. officials including those concerned with foreign affairs. Inevitably the conversation turned to the world situation & how to maintain peace. ~~in the world.~~ And just as inevitably the Soviet U. was automatically accepted as the possible threat to peace just as 40 yrs. ago it was Nazi Germany that loomed as the storm cloud on the horizon. And of course that storm cloud did *eventually* fill the sky & ~~raining~~ *rain* fire & ~~brimstone~~ on all the world.

The leaders of that generation saw the growing menace & talked of it but reacted to the growing mil. might of Germany with anguished passiveness. Will it be said of todays world leaders ~~th~~ as it was of the pre W.W.II. leaders "they were better at surviving the catastrophe than they were at preventing it?

Peace

1

How much is it worth to not have W W III
     I'll be right back.

_____

While in London I had an opportunity to visit with
various govt. officials including those concerned with foreign affairs.
Inevitably the conversation turned to the world situation & how
to maintain peace. ~~in the truth~~. And first as inevitably the Soviet U.
was automatically accepted as the possible threat to peace just as 40 yrs.
ago it was Nazi Germany that loomed as the ~~storm~~ cloud on the
horizon. And of course that storm cloud did "eventually" fill the sky &
~~rain~~ fire & ~~~~ on all the world.

     The leaders of that generation saw the growing menace &
talked of it but reacted to the growing mil. might of Germany
with anguished passiveness. Will it be said of todays world
leaders ~~the~~ as it was of the pre W.W.II. leaders" they were better at
surviving the catastrophe than they were at preventing it?

~~Several times in the discussion at Whitehall~~

     W.W.II did not happen because the Nat's. of the free world
engaged in a massive mil. buildup. ~~The opposite is true~~. In
most countries including our own, "too little too late" described ~~was~~ the
reaction to the Nazi mil. colossus.

     What does it take for us to learn? On every hand here &
abroad when the suggestion is made that we strengthen the
mil. capability of Nato the reply is that it's not politically
expedient to incr. spending for armaments because the people
are against it. Our own Congress which is willing to run an
80 Bil. deficit for every kind of social experiment screams
long & loud for reduction of the budget for defense. But have
any of the pol. leaders laid the facts out for the people?
Of course the over taxed citizenry in Europe & America
want govt. spending reduced. But if we are told the
truth, namely that enough evidence of weakness or lack

2

of will power ~~on any front~~ could tempt ~~even~~ the Soviet U. ~~it~~ as it once ~~did tempted~~ Hitler & the mil. rulers of Japan & believe our decision would be in favor of an ounce of prevention. Certainly we havent forgotten that after W.W II the Japanese told us ~~they~~ they ~~decided on war~~ when they saw our army staging war games with wooden guns. A ~~few~~ month before Pearl Harbor Cong. came within ~~one~~ a single vote of abolishing the draft & sending the ~~entity of our army home.~~

It has recently been revealed that for 12 yrs. a behavioral scientist at the U. of Hawaii has headed up a team of distinguished colleagues in a Federally-Funded, computerized study of International behavior. Summed up in one sentence They have learned that "to abdicate power is to abdicate the right to maintain peace."

The study focused mainly upon Red China, Russia & the US. Every bit of data from trade to terrain — from threats to treaties was fed into the computers. The findings prove conclusively that what Lawrence Beilenson wrote in his book "The Treaty Trap" is true "Nations that place their faith in treaties & fail to keep their hardware up dont ~~stick around long enough to~~ ~~write very~~ many pages in history."

(quote) "It is not equality in power ~~(according to the report)~~" that reduces hostility & conflict. Rather it is power dominance or submission. Peace is purchased by making yourself stronger than your adversary — or by dismantling power & submitting to ones enemies." (unquote)

Power is not only sufficient mil. strength but ~~it also~~ a sound economy, a reliable energy supply and credibility — the belief by any potential enemy that you will not choose surrender as the way to maintain peace. Thomas Jefferson said "the American people wont make a mistake if they

3

are given all the facts.

~~It's time we were given the facts about~~
Perhaps Cong. should be given some facts about
us, namely that we'd rather prevent a war by
being well armed than by surrendering.

this is Ronald Reagan. thanks for listening.

~~Several times in the discussions at Whitehall~~
W.W.II did not happen because the Nat's. of the free world engaged in a massive mil. buildup. ~~The opposite is true.~~ In most countries including our own, "too little too late" described ~~our~~ *the* reaction to the Nazi mil. colossus.

What does it take for us to learn? On every hand here & abroad when the suggestion is made that we strengthen the mil. capability of Nato the reply is that it's not politically expedient to incrs. spending for armaments because the people are against it. Our own Congress which is willing to run an $80 Bil. deficit for every kind of social experiment screams long & loud for reduction of the budget for defense. But have any of the pol. leaders laid the facts out for the people? Of course the overtaxed citizenry in Europe & America want govt. spending reduced. But if we are told the truth, namely that enough evidence of weakness or lack of willpower ~~on our part~~ could tempt ~~≠~~ the Soviet U. ~~into~~ as it once ~~did~~ *tempted* Hitler & the mil. rulers of Japan I believe our decision would be in favor of an ounce of prevention. Certainly we havent forgotten that after W.WII the Japanese told us ~~they~~ they ~~were tempted~~ *decided on war* when they saw our army staging war games with wooden guns. *They also took note that* One month before Pearl Harbor Con*gress* came within ~~one~~ *a single* vote of abolishing the draft & sending the bulk of our army home.

It has recently been revealed that for 12 yrs. a behavioral scientist at the U. of Hawaii* has headed up a team of distinguished colleagues in a Federally-Funded, computerized study of International behavior. Summed up in one sentence they have learned that "to abdicate power is to abdicate the right to maintain peace."

The study focused mainly upon Red China, Russia & the US. Every bit of data from trade to tourism—from threats to treaties—was fed into the computers. The findings prove conclusively *that* what Laurence Beilenson wrote in his book "The Treaty Trap" is true.** "Nations that place their faith in treaties & fail to keep their hardware up don't ~~hang around to~~ *stick around long enough* to write many pages in history."

According to the report *(quote)* "It is not equality in power," "that reduces hostility & conflict. Rather it is power dominance or submission."— Peace is purchased by making yourself stronger than your adversary—or by dismantling power & submitting to ones enemies." *(unquote)*.

*Professor Rudolph Rummel, Department of Political Science.
**Laurence W. Beilenson, *Treaty Trap: A History of the Performance of Political Treaties by the United States and European Nations* (Washington, D.C.: Public Affairs Press, 1969). Beilenson was the legal counsel for the Screen Actors Guild when Reagan was president of the organization. Reagan considered him an old friend.

Power is *not only* sufficient mil*itary* strength but ~~it's also~~ a sound economy, a reliable energy supply and credibility—the belief by any potential enemy that you will not choose surrender as the way to maintain peace. Thomas Jefferson said "The American people won't make a mistake if they are given <u>all</u> the facts."

~~It's time we were given the facts about~~

Perhaps Cong. should be given some facts about us, namely that we'd rather prevent a war by being well armed than by surrendering.

This is Ronald Reagan. Thanks for listening. ❖

Shaping the World for 100 Years to Come
September 1, 1976

In this election year many of us talk about the world *of* tomorrow but do we really think about it? I'll be right back.

Sometimes it's *very* easy to get ~~very~~ glib about how the decisions we are making will shape the world for a hundred years to come. *Then* A few weeks ago I found myself faced with having to really think about ~~it.~~ *what we are doing today & what people (not history)* PEOPLE LIKE OURSELVES *will say about us.*

I'd been asked to write a letter for a "time capsule" which would be opened ~~in Los Angeles~~ 100 yrs. from now. ~~It will be~~ The occasion will be the Los Angeles Bicentennial & of course our countrys tri-centennial. It was suggested that I mention some of the problems confronting us in this election year. Since I've been talking about those problems for ~~about~~ *some* 9 months that didn't look like too much of a chore.

So riding down the coast highway from Santa Barbara—a yellow tablet on my lap (someone else was driving) I started to write my letter to the future.

It was a beautiful summer afternoon. The Pacific stretched out to the horizon on one side of the highway and on the other the Santa Ynez mt's. were etched against a sky as blue as the Ocean.

I found myself wondering if it would look the same 100 yrs. from now. Will there still be a coast highway? Will people still be travelling in automobiles, or will they be looking down at the mountains from aircraft or moving so fast the beauty of all ~~I saw~~ *this* would be lost?

Suddenly the simple drafting of a letter became a rather complex chore. Think about it for a minute. What do you put in a letter that's going to be read 100 yrs. from now—in the year 2076? What do you say about our problems when those who read the letter will ~~alr~~ know what we dont know—namely how well we did with those problems? In short they will be living in the world we helped to shape.

Will they read the letter with gratitude in their hearts for what we did or will they be bitter because ~~miserable~~ the heritage we left them was one of human misery?

Oh I wrote of the problems we face here in 1976—The choice we face between continuing the policies of the last 40 yrs. that have led to bigger & bigger govt, less & less liberty, redistribution of earnings through confiscatory taxation or trying to get back on the original course set for us by the Founding Fathers. Will we choose fiscal responsibility, limited govt, and freedom of choice for all our people? Or will we let an irresponsible Congress ~~take the final~~ set us on the road our English cousins have already taken? *The road to ec. ruin and state control of our very lives?*

On the international scene two great superpowers face each other with nuclear missiles at the ready—poised to bring Armageddon to the world.

Those who read my letter will know whether those missiles were fired or not. ~~They~~ *Either they* will be surrounded by the same beauty ~~I knew as I wrote the letter~~ *we know* or they will wonder sadly what it was like when the world was *still* beautiful. ~~before that awful day when civilization broke down.~~

If we here ~~in this election year of our Lord 1976~~ *today* meet the challenge confronting us,—those who open that time capsule ~~in 2076~~ *100 yrs. from now* will do so in ~~a place of~~ beauty ~~knowing~~ peace, prosperity and the ultimate in personal freedom. ~~consistent with an orderly, civilized society.~~

If we dont ~~meet~~ keep our rendezvous with destiny, the letter probably will never be read—because ~~talk of individual freedom will not be permitted in that world 100 yrs. from now which we are shaping and~~ they will live in the world ~~which we had a hand in shaping and~~ *we left them, a world* in which no one is allowed to read ~~or hear such terms as~~ *of individual liberty or* freedom of choice. ~~& individual liberty.~~ ❖

Communism, the Disease
May 1975

Mankind has survived all ~~maner~~ *manner* of evil diseases & plagues—~~let's hope he can~~ [*but, can it*] survive Communism?

I'll be rite back.

When a disease like communism hangs on as it has for a half century or more it's good, now & then, to be reminded of just how vicious it really is. Of course those who have the disease use all kinds of misleading terms to de-

scribe it's symptoms and it's effects ~~on the human system One We should re-~~
~~member one of the characteristics of the ailment is~~ <u>double</u> ~~talk beginning~~ For
example if you and I in America planted ~~land~~ mines on our borders, ringed the
country with barb wire and machine gun toting guards to keep anyone from
leaving the country we'd hardly describe that as "liberating" the people.

But we've grown so used to communist doubletalk I sometimes think
we've lost some of our fear of the disease. We need ~~a~~ frequent vaccination to
guard against being infected until ~~one~~ *the* day *when* this health threat will be
eliminated as we eliminated the black plague.

How many of us are aware of some of the differences between those ~~of us~~
who have the sickness & we who ~~are well~~ [*don't?*] Right now there are a
number of Russian women who fell in love & married Americans & other
foreigners who happened to be stationed in the Soviet U. for a time.

Now falling in love isn't something you set out to do, and among well
people it isn't considered a criminal act. But these Russian women are separated from their husbands, some of them for several years. When their Am.
husbands ~~for example~~ finished ~~whatever~~ [*their*] assignments ~~they were on~~ *in*
Russia and came home their wives had to get [*Soviet government*] permission to ~~leave~~ *go with them.* ~~from the Soviet govt.~~ *And* The Soviet govt. plays
a heartless game of burocratic paper shuffling—never coming right out &
saying "no," but just keeping them filling out papers, renewing applications
etc.—sometimes for years.

There is the case of a young teacher who married an American. During the
application process she was fired from her job.—Reason?—she fell in love
with an American—that's reason enough *where the Soviet is concerned.* Her
students all loved her. They presented her with a farewell gift of flowers. A Soviet official ~~visited~~ *dropped in on* the class to tell them *that* ~~for doing so they~~
~~giving the teacher~~ [*that for giving the*] *flowers* none of them would be permitted to go on to college. They ~~were all~~ *would all be* assigned to ~~the~~ *a* labor force
upon graduation!

Now the Associated Press brings another story from Berlin illustrating
how the communist sickness ~~≠~~ looks upon human life—even the life of ~~an~~
~~innocent~~ *a* child.

Berlin is divided, as ~~we~~ [*you*] know, ~~between~~ into the East or sick-with-
communism ~~Berlin~~ *side* and the well or ~~Free Berlin~~ Western *side.* Between the
two flows the Spree river. Around noon on ~~the 11th of~~ May *11,* a 5-year-old
boy fell into the river. ~~at the point where the entire stream is in East Berlin.~~
Firemen from W. Berlin started to *go to* his rescue. An East German patrol
boat barred them from entering the water because at that point the stream
flows wholly on East Berlin territory. The 5 yr. old boy drowned.

The Mayor of W. Berlin described the refusal of the E. German guards to ~~either~~ permit the Westerners to come to his rescue as "an incomprehensible and frightful act—placing pol. considerations before the saving of a human life." Which is exactly what they did. Remember they were in a patrol boat—they chose to prevent the W. Germans from ~~setting foot~~ [*entering*] in their Eastern water rather than go to the child's rescue themselves. But they did tidy things up—3 hrs. later E. German frog men recovered the body.*

Communism is neither an ec. or a pol. system—it is a form of insanity—a temporary aberration which will one day disappear from the earth because it is contrary to human nature. I wonder how much more misery it will cause before it disappears. ❖

America's Strength
December 22, 1976

Every once in a while it's important that we look at the balance sheet so we'll know what it is we're trying to save. I'll be right back.

I know that I've used these broadcasts to criticize those who have lost faith in our system; those who would make fundamental changes on the premise that what we've done in the past is all wrong and those (~~who seem to be~~ increasing in number) who think we are over the hill & headed for the dustbin of history.

Therefore it is important every once in a while to remind ourselves of our accomplishments ~~before~~ *lest* we let someone talk us into throwing out the baby with the bathwater. I intend to go on talking about our problems because in the main they are problems that truly need solving. I'm also going to go on resisting those who would have us believe the problems ~~are the result of~~ *are proof that our* system isn't working. Put another way it's time we recognize the system has never let us down—we've let the system down now & then because we're only human.

Compared to the world at large we are politically stable. A few years ago when we had the unprecedented resignation of a President there were no knots of people gathered on street corners, no boarding up of storefronts, no people ~~took to~~ *marching in* the streets nor screaming sirens hearalding the round up of cabinet officers and officials. Americans just went about their business, took in a ball game and watched their favorite TV shows. And that's why foreign money invested in America has increased about 50% in the last 5 yrs.

---

* "Berlin Drowning Increases Tension," *New York Times,* May 18, 1975.

Last year ~~was~~ in spite of govt. confiscating our earnings at an unprecedented rate for a lot of unproductive ~~go~~ social reforms we managed to raise $217 Bil. to finance new & existing private enterprise projects.

Our productivity is phenomenal. We raise 37% more wheat per acre than the national average. We are 6% of the worlds population on only 7% of the worlds land but we produce almost half the worlds corn, 2/3 of the soy beans, 1/3 or more of the worlds paper, electrical power, college graduates and almost 1/3 of the farm machinery. Just to round it off we make more than 2/3 of the computers & 80% of all the passenger aircraft.

We lead the world in advanced technology; in telecommunications, drilling & mining equipment, medical science & agri-science.

All of this is because our system freed the individual genius of man. Released him to fly as high & as far as his own talent & energy would take him. We allocate resources not by govt. decision but by the mil's. of decisions customers make when they go into the mkt. place to buy. If something seems too high priced we buy something else. Thus resources are steered toward those things the people want most at the price they are willing to pay. It may not be a perfect system but it's better than any other that's ever been tried.

Sure we have an unemployment problem—7½ mil. people looking for jobs. If we are going to deal with the problem we should look at it. To start with, only half are people who lost their jobs. The others ~~quit~~ quit or are looking for their 1st job. Only 2.8 mil. are the head's of familys and only 2.4 mil. have been unemployed 15 weeks or longer, meaning the unemployed are an ever changing group not a body of permanent ~~ly un~~ jobless. And since 82 mil. are employed—most in productive private industry ~~lets~~ *why dont we* see what roadblocks have been thrown in the way of ~~the private industry to keep it from expanding~~ *our tried & true system* and remove them. This is RR—Thanks for listening. ❖

Two Worlds
August 7, 1978

The ideological struggle dividing the world is between communism and our own belief in freedom to the greatest extent possible consistent with an orderly society. I'll be right back.

I was going through a ~~collection~~ *bundle* of quotations I've collected over the years looking for something appropriate for ~~an speech~~ upcoming speech. I keep them on cards & they aren't indexed or catalogued so I literally have to shuffle through the whole stack.

While doing that ~~an~~ a thought came to me appropos of the present world situation where we continue to believe we can maintain a detente with the Soviet U. and that ~~they want~~ *their leaders down* underneath must be pretty much like us. ~~This tho~~ I was shuffling through statements of great Americans & mixed in with them were quotes by the past & present greats of the Soviet U.

There was that poetry ~~inscribed~~ *from whence comes the inscription* on ~~the~~ *our* statue of liberty: "Her name—Mother of Exiles. From her beacon hand glows worldwide welcome; her mild eyes command the air bridged harbor that twin cities frame. Keep your ancient lands, your storied pomp! cries she with silent lips. Give me your tired, your poor, your huddled masses yearning to breathe free, the wretched refuse of your teeming shore. Send these, the homeless, tempest ~~tossed~~ TOST to me. I lift my lamp beside the golden door."

How that contrasts with these words of the Soviet U's founding father— Nicolai Lenin*: "It would not matter if ¾ of the human race perished; the important thing is that the remaining ¼ be communist." ** And his invitation; "The communist party ENTERS into bourgois institutions not to do constructive work but in order to direct the masses to destroy from within the whole bourgois state machine & the parliament itself."

John Winthrop on the deck of the tiny Arbella in 1630 off the coast of Mass. said to the little band of pilgrims: "We shall be as a city upon a hill. The eyes of all people are upon us, so that if we shall deal falsely with our God in this work we have undertaken & so cause him to withdraw his present help from us, we shall be made a story & a byword throughout the world."

The oath of the Communist Party U.S.A. written in 1930 says nothing of a city upon a hill. ~~It says:~~ "I pledge myself to rally the masses to defend the Soviet U. the land of victorious socialism. I pledge ~~to~~ myself to remain at all times a vigilant & firm defender of the Leninist line of the party, the <u>only</u> line that insures the triumph of Soviet power in the U.S." ***

Thomas Jefferson said, "The policy of the Am. govt. is to leave their citizens free, neither restraining nor aiding them in their pursuits." And he added, "The God who gave us life gave us liberty—can the liberties of a Nat. be secure when we have removed a conviction that these liberties are the gift of God."

---

*Vladimir Ilyitch Lenin.

**This statement was attributed to Lenin by Nicholas T. Goncharoff in congressional testimony. U.S. Congress. Senate. Subcommittee to Investigate the Administration of the Internal Security Act and Other Internal Security Laws of the Committee on the Judiciary. 83rd Congress. 2d sess. July 15, 1954, 207.

***This statement was read to Communist Party members in New York in 1935. See J. Peters, *The Communist Party: A Manual on Organization* (New York: Workers Library Publishers, 1935), 104.

Pravda responds with these inspiring words: "The world wide nature of our communist program is not mere talk <u>but</u> all embracing & all blood soaked reality."

There were dozens more and from our Founding Fathers to present day leaders the plea was for social justice, decency & adherence to the highest standards man has evolved in his climb from the swamp to the stars. From the Soviet leaders came calls for treachery, deceit, destruction & bloodshed.

Détente—isn't that what a farmer has with his turkey—until thanksgiving day?

This is RR   Thanks for listening. ❖

Letters to the Editor
June 1975

Letters to the editor don't get picked up by ~~associated press~~ [*the news wires.*]—Maybe sometimes they should.

I'll be right back.

In these times when so many of us have a tendency to lose faith in ourselves its good now and then to be reminded of the good natured, generous spirit that has been an American characteristic for as long as there has been an America.

Not too long ago such a reminder came in the form of a letter to the editor. I thought ~~ma~~ you might like to ~~hear it~~ [*hear*] about it.

The writer was a refugee from S.V.N., but he was American not Vietnamese, a clergyman ~~and~~—I suppose a missionary; although I can't vouch for that.

The Rev. described a 20 ft. craft ~~in~~ *adrift in* the gulf of Thailand with no fuel, no food, no water, barely afloat & sinking with its cargo of 82 refugees. Towering over it was the aircraft carrier the U.S.S. Midway. The Rev. described the Midway as tired. It had already deposited some 2000 refugees on other ships, refugees who had arrived in more than 500 flights. One flight was ~~an~~ *a* light observation plane not designed for carrier landings. The Midway had moved up to top speed to enable the pilot to land with an entire family ~~crammed~~ [*jammed*] inside the tiny fuselage. There were 40 choppers on the deck, brand new F5E fighters and A37s that had carried people who preferred not to be "liberated" by the communists. The Midway also carried a sign the crew had made that said "Welcome Refugees." So they picked up the 82 who were begging to be taken aboard.

Once on board they had one question; would they be handed over to an unfriendly govt. [*perhaps*] to be eventually murdered? ~~by the new govt. in Saigon.~~ The exec. officer of the ship ~~informed~~ ~~*answered*~~ [*told*] them this would not happen. He said "Our job is to make you as comfortable as possible, heal the sick and feed you to your hearts content."

That was the official policy of our ~~Nat.~~ [*nation*] & therefore of the Midway. How was it carried out? Well according to the Rev., the sick *were* cared for. A tiny baby with double pneumonia was cured. People without clothes were given American clothing. Sailors took the old clothing and washed them for their guests. Pretty soon homeless children were being given ~~horse back~~ [*piggyback*] rides on the shoulders of ~~Am.~~ [*American*] seamen, and Navy T-shirts bearing the Midway decal began appearing on the little ones.

The tragedy they'd been through hung heavily on the adults of course so the sailors planned entertainment for them.—But let the Rev. tell it, *(QUOTE)* "Different Navy groups collected money.—Ads went into the ships paper asking for toys. Charity begat more charity. There is a motto on the Midway—'Midway puts it together.' For the grateful refugees that is the understatement of the year." ~~end of quote~~ *(UNQUOTE)*

In the dark days right after WWII when our industrial power and mil. might were all that stood between a war-ravaged world and a return to the dark ages Pope ~~Pius~~ Pius the 12th said "~~The~~ America has a genius for great and unselfish deeds. Into the hands of Am. God has placed the destiny of an afflicted mankind." ~~I don't think God has given us a job we cant handle.~~

I think those young men on the Midway have reassured God that he hasn't given us more of an assignment than we can handle.

This is RR ❖

Nigeria
July 9, 1979

We know we are paying a high price in dollars for imported oil—how much are we paying in loss of independence & self respect? I'll be right back.

Someone once said that every form of govt. has one characteristic peculiar to it and if that characteristic ~~were~~ *is* lost the govt. ~~would~~ *will* fall. In a monarchy it is affection & respect for the royal family. If that is lost the ~~kingdom~~ *monarch* is lost. In a dictatorship it is fear. If the people stop fearing the dictator he'll lose power. In a representative govt. such as ours it is virtue. If virtue goes the govt. falls.

Are we choosing paths that are politically expedient and morally questionable? Are we in truth losing our virtue?

Our govt. has refused to recognize the ~~newly elected~~ *new* govt. of Rhodesia claiming it is bound by the U.N. sanctions against that country. Our ambassador to the U.N. has hinted we may have other reasons for holding off. It seems that we received a gentle warning from General Obasanjo RULER of Nigeria that serious consequences might follow if we recognized the regime of Bishop Muzorewa who has been elected Prime Minister of Rhodesia legally & legitimately.*

Now ~~what~~ *how* could Nigeria possibly threaten our nation and by so doing dictate our foreign policy? General Obasanjo rules not by any vote of his people. There hasn't been an election in Nigeria in 13 yrs. ~~B~~ Yet he calls the Rhodesian election a "mockery of democracy" and his govt. run Nigerian newspaper ~~accuses~~ *charges* Rhodesia ~~of~~ *with* practicing "political fraud."

Our U.N. ambassador says we must take the Generals threats seriously. ~~because~~ *You see* Nigeria has oil wells ~~Indeed we~~ *which produce* one out of 8 barrels of the oil we import. ~~comes from Nigeria. Therefore this~~ ~~our~~ ~~great and powerful nation must bow and say "yes sir" to the unelected mil. dictatorship of a small~~ Oh it's ~~also~~ true that Nigeria ALSO buys from ~~us~~ *our country* but not enough to balance the oil they sell us. Still isn't our ambassador overlooking the fact that General Obasanjos principle cash crop is oil and without our cash for that oil his entire country could become another clearing in the jungle?

But isn't there another argument—one having to do with virtue—which our ambassador has completely overlooked? ~~Rhodesia-Zimbabwe~~ Zimbabwe-Rhodesia has taken a great stride toward the kind of democratic values we have always endorsed. Indeed in this case it is the stride we pressured them to take. But instead of holding out our hand to them in friendship we turn our back because ~~a~~ *the* dictator of a country that has no democratic values at all might decide to do without our money and keep his oil.

Are we as Americans so thirsty for oil that we'll forget the traditions upon which our country is founded and let our foreign policy be dictated by anyone who has oil for sale? If so we may be nearer the dustbin of history than we realize.

This is RR Thanks for listening. ❖

---

*Olusequn Obasanjo and Abel Tendekai Muzorewa.

Looking Out a Window
January 27, 1978

It's nightfall in a strange town a long way from home. I'm watching the lights come on from my hotel room window on the 35th floor.

I'll be right back.

I'm afraid you are in for a little bit of philosophizing if you dont mind. Some of these broadcasts have to be put together while I'm out on the road traveling what I call the mashed potato circuit. In a little while I'll be speaking to a group of very nice people in a banquet hall.

Right now however I'm looking down on a busy city at rush hour. The streets below are ~~two colored~~ *twin* ribbons of sparkling red & white. ~~The colored ones~~ *Tail lights on the cars* moving away from my vantage point provide the red and *the headlights of* ~~those on the opposite side of the street~~ *those coming toward me* the white. It's logical to assume all or most are homeward bound at the end of ~~the~~ *a* days work.

I wonder why some social engineer hasn't tried to get them to trade homes. The traffic is equally heavy in both directions so if they all lived in the end of town where they worked it would save a lot of travel time. Forget I said that ~~or~~ *&* dont even think it or some burocrat will *try* do it.

But ~~you~~ *I* wonder about the people in those cars, who they are, what they do, what they are thinking about as they head for the warmth of home & family. Come to think of it I've met them—oh—maybe not those particular individuals but still ~~I~~ *I feel I* know them. Some of our social planners refer to them as "the masses" which only proves they <u>dont</u> know them. I've been privileged to meet people all over this land in the special kind of way you meet them when you are campaigning. They are not "the masses," ~~They are individuals.~~ *or as the elitists would have* it—"the common man." They are very uncommon. ~~individuals who make this system work.~~ *Individuals each with his or her own hopes & dreams, plans & problems and the kind of quiet courage that makes this whole country run better than just about any other place on earth.*

~~Now~~ By now, thinking of their homecoming I'm counting how many more hotel room windows I'll be looking out of before I'm in the rush hour traffic heading home. And yes I'm feeling a little sorry for myself and envious of the people in those cars down below. ~~There have been~~ *It seems I've said* a thousand goodbyes, each one harder than the one before.

Someone very wise once wrote that if we were all told one day that the end was coming; that we were living our last day, every road, every street &

all the telephone lines would be jammed with people trying to reach someone to whom ~~they~~ *we* wanted *simply* to say, "I love you."

~~It seems kind of foolish to wait for such a final day dosen't it? I'll have to
stop now—I have a phone call to make.~~

~~This is RR Thanks for listening.~~

But dosen't it seem kind of foolish to wait for such a final day and take the
chance of not getting there *in time? And speaking of time* I'll have to stop
now—~~I have to make a phone call.~~ *OPERATOR I'D LIKE TO MAKE A PHONE
CALL—LONG DISTANCE.*

This is RR. Thanks for listening. ❖

Part Two

FOREIGN
POLICY

"We want to avoid a war

and that is better achieved

by being so strong

that a potential enemy

is not tempted

to go adventuring."

*T*hirty percent of the 670 handwritten drafts of Reagan's radio broadcasts tackle defense or foreign policy issues. There is considerable thematic overlap in these writings, but in general they fall into one of the following categories: communism, defense policy, foreign policy double standards, and Third World politics. Reagan's main concern throughout the broadcasts is the cold war. It is the prism through which he analyzes and understands most defense and foreign policy issues. He discusses his understanding of the sources and symptoms of the cold war; he criticizes the foreign policy of the Ford and Carter administrations; he provides policy prescriptions; and he interprets various episodes in U.S. foreign policy. To make his case, Reagan relies heavily on the speeches and writings of certain scholars and policy experts. He identifies what he sees as enduring American preferences and supports those preferences. He never blames the American people for policy failures; he blames those in power and other elites, including some members of his own party.

According to Reagan, the main goal of the United States' cold war policy should be to hasten the end of communism. Communism will not survive, he writes, because it lays the groundwork for its own destruction by suppressing economic, political, and social freedom, which is contrary to the needs and desires of mankind. Given the opportunity, those in captivity will seek freedom. In Reagan's view, transforming the Soviet political system to one that allows freedom and is representative of the people would constitute cold war victory.

A first step toward hastening the demise of Soviet communism, Reagan *writes, is to distinguish the symptoms of the cold war from its sources. He views the arms race as a symptom of the cold war, and thus concludes that arms control negotiations will neither end the conflict nor improve bilateral relations. The only reason to sign an arms control treaty, he writes, is to en-hance the security interests of the United States. And even then, the United States should be vigilant because the causes of the cold war—the internal and external policies of the Soviet Union—still remain. Reagan is concerned deeply about avoiding nuclear war but thinks American leaders have failed to situate properly the arms race in the overall context of the cold war.*

Reagan also argues that the popular idea that a "Vietnam Syndrome" ex-ists in the United States should be abandoned. Even though the fall of Saigon punctuated a painful period of American military failure, Reagan contends that America is not unwilling or unable to fight the cold war. America's des-tiny is to be a shining example and defender of freedom; it is a destiny that transcends the temporary setback of Vietnam, he says. The American people will accept the responsibilities of their country's destiny if the requirements of freedom and the nature of internal and international challenges are ex-plained to them, but, Reagan charges, American leaders failed to do this dur-ing the Vietnam War.

Although he thinks communism will not survive, Reagan does not think that cold war victory is inevitable in the short-term. There are two choices for the superpowers in the cold war: surrender or victory. The only way for the United States to avoid surrender is to elect leaders who understand the re-quirements of victory; who explain the requirements of victory to the Amer-ican people; and who have the courage to do what is necessary for the United States to be the victor.

Another step toward this goal, Reagan writes, it to abandon superpower détente. Under détente, he says, the Ford and Carter administrations have treated the Soviet Union like a normal state. But the Soviet Union, like any communist state, is not and cannot be normal, he writes, because its supreme foreign policy goal is domination of others; imperialism is the essence of So-viet foreign policy. Internal oppression is a necessary condition for the sur-vival of its political system, and détente has been one-sided. Instead of reciprocity, Reagan says, the United States made most of the concessions and the Soviet Union reaped most of the benefits. Reagan repeatedly asserts that the great shame of the Ford and Carter administrations is appeasement.

He prefers peace through strength. Americans desire mutual cooperation and peace, but this will be possible only if the Soviet Union abandons its po-litical system and joins the community of free states. America can help make this come about through economic and military strength (a military build-up), a morality-based foreign policy, and political resolve.

Reagan says that U.S. foreign policy leaders have failed to appreciate that clearly delineated defense perimeters are central to international credibility and sound strategic doctrine, and they will help bring an end to communism. Much of Reagan's analysis of crises in the Third World is framed in terms of his concern for the United States' defense perimeters.

Reagan also writes about the internal conditions of Third World countries. In some of his commentaries on Africa and Asia, he expresses concern that the internal political structures of those countries do not represent the people and are not responsive to them or to the rule of law.

Human rights, intelligence policy, and international organizations are some of the other international issues covered in Reagan's commentaries.

Throughout his campaign for the presidency in 1980, Reagan was criticized for lacking knowledge of international relations. Yet the commentaries show that he was thinking and writing about a wide variety of foreign and defense policy issues before his presidency.

Many of the policy positions he took in the 1970s (and in some cases earlier) became policy during his presidency. His rejection of the Nixon-Kissinger idea of "linkage" helped inform what became known as his administration's "four-part agenda." Recognizing an intrinsic link among all issues in superpower relations, under the four-part agenda, arms control, regional crises, human rights, and bilateral contacts were treated separately. The United States tried to act with strength in each area. Elements of the so-called "Reagan Doctrine" of supporting "freedom fighters" in the Third World can be found in some of the radio commentaries. Reagan's broadcasts on South Africa likewise presaged future policies. He insists that although morally repugnant, apartheid in South Africa cannot be ended by imposing sanctions on the country. He made similar arguments as president, and apartheid and sanctions became some of the most controversial foreign policy issues in the United States in the 1980s. In 1986 the U.S. Congress overrode his veto of sanctions legislation.

A few issues that became central during his presidency are scarcely mentioned here. Missile defense and the Middle East peace process receive little coverage in Reagan's commentaries and other pre-presidential writings.

Taken together, the essays reveal that Reagan not only wrote and thought about a broad range of issues but show that he read a variety of sources, from the conservative journal National Review, *to government documents such as NSC-68, to essays and speeches by leading foreign policy experts.*

COMMUNISM, ASIA, EUROPE, AND THE SOVIET UNION

The commentaries in this section constitute a stark statement of Reagan's views about the Soviet Union and its satellites, communism, and the cold war. The Soviet Union is the culprit in the cold war, Reagan says, because it continually seizes territory, and lacks a moral base and internal legitimacy. According to Reagan, these are the seeds of destruction of the Soviet Union. Victorious at the end of World War II, the United States did not seize any territory. The United States, Reagan writes, is not imperialistic and is guided by a strong moral compass. Yet, the United States betrays itself and threatens its security when it is lulled into a false sense of friendship, as with the People's Republic of China, or when it excuses the evil deeds of communist states.

In the essay below, Reagan argues that there are only two outcomes for the Soviet Union: collapse or voluntary abandonment of its political system. Also, he weighs the pros and cons of a grain embargo. On April 24, 1981, President Reagan fulfilled his campaign pledge to reverse the partial grain embargo that President Jimmy Carter had imposed on the Soviet Union in the wake of its invasion of Afghanistan.

The Russian Wheat Deal
October 1975

How many sides are there to the Russian Wheat Deal & which side should we be taking? I'll be right back.

Radio The Russian Wheat Deal   1

How many sides are there to the Russian Wheat Deal
& which side should we be taking? I'll be right back.

The Russians want to buy American wheat & Am.
farmers want to sell their wheat. Anti-communist
water front workers don't want to load the wheat on
foreign ships to carry it to Russia. ~~I'm not sure it's because they
are world communist or because they think the wheat
should be carried in American ships. In which case
they are on these anti-communist feelings.~~

Am. Consumers with the experience of the
previous wheat sale ~~and its effect~~
and high food prices in mind ~~prices gently considerably~~ are alarmed & The Sec of
Agriculture says ~~it~~ this sale shouldn't have that
effect. ~~and~~ | With all these points & counter points
maybe we still aren't getting to the heart of the problem

Please don't think I'm leading up to a pat
answer to all these questions – It first isn't that
easy. ~~Philosophically my view is that~~ If we
                                                   shouldn't
believe in a free mkt. ~~then~~ our farmers ~~should~~
                                      anywhere in the world
be allowed to sell their produce ~~on the world mkt.~~
for the best price they can get. ~~To not allow them~~
~~from doing~~ this is to subsidize and make available
to ~~the~~ our own consumers lower priced food at the
expense of our own farmers.

                                                    however
Not inconsistent with that philosophy ~~however~~
                                        in the
is our own ~~mkt.~~ interest ~~having to do with the~~
matter of nat. security. ~~If~~ we believe the Soviet
U. is ~~a~~ hostile to the free world and we must
                                   a nuclear defense
or we wouldn't be maintaining ~~our defenses &~~ &
continuing in Nato then are we not adding to our own
danger by helping the troubled Soviet economy? ~~Then) &~~
~~this context~~ But isn't there also a moral issue? Are we not
helping a Godless tyranny maintain its hold on ~~millions~~
millions of helpless people? Wouldn't ~~these~~ those

2

helpless victims have a better chance of becoming
free if their slave masters regime collapsed economically?
One thing is certain, the threat of hunger to the
Russian people is due to the Soviet obsession with
mil. power.

Nothing proves the ~~thing~~ failure of Marxism more
than the Soviet Unions inability to produce weapons
for its mil. ambitions and at the same time provide
~~of defense and provide~~ for their peoples every day needs.
~~The~~ ~~world~~ Only ~~it~~ takes about 4% of our labor force ~~is in farming~~
~~the U.S. feeds~~ to provide for 211 mil. Americans and provide 80% of all the
food shipped to the worlds underdeveloped nations.

A full ⅓ of Russias workers are in agriculture & still
they'd starve without our wheat. And the failure is not
Russian it is communist, for every other country that has
collectivized its agriculture has gone down hill in farm
production.

The moral question then is ~~could~~ Am. alone force
the change to peaceful pursuits on Russia by refusing to
sell ~~it~~ or would we have to persuade the other free nations
to do the same. Following such a course what would
we do then about our farmers and the surplus they'd
have on their hands? ~~And said it is it then is an~~
~~empty it seems.~~

The Wheat deal is beneficial to us economically. Right
now ~~maybe~~ in our time of ec. dislocation & imbalance
of trade · maybe it benefits us enough to outweigh the strategic
~~the most~~ factor. In other words it strengthens us more than we'd
be benefitted by weakening them. But the moral question
in the long run wont go away. The Soviet U. is an
aggressor & a threat to world peace. ~~It~~ can remain so only
by denying its people freedom & the basic commoditys that
make life worth living, ~~and~~ which we take for granted.
~~Why shouldnt we study~~ the problem and consider
~~Have we the right to ask~~
buying the wheat ~~ourselves~~ ~~even~~ if only to give it away — to as to
be fair to our farmers; counting this as a part of our defense
as we let them choose between ec. collapse or abandonment of their arms

3

The Russians have told us over & over again their goal is to impose their incompetent and ridiculous system on the world. We invest in armaments to hold them off, ~~Sudes~~ but what do we envision as the eventual outcome? Either that they will see the fallacy of their way & give up their goal or their system will collapse or ─ (and we don't let ourselves think of this) we'll have to use our weapons one day.

Maybe there is an answer ─ We ~~simply do~~ what's morally right. Stop doing business with them. Let their system collapse but in the mean time buy our farmers wheat ourselves & have it on hand to feed the Russian people when they finally become free. ─ This is RR Thanks for listening

The Russians want to buy American wheat & Am. farmers want to sell their wheat. Anti-communist waterfront workers dont want to load the wheat on ~~to~~ *foreign* ships *to carry it to Russia.* ~~and personally I'm not sure it's because they are anti-communist or because they think the wheat should be carried in American ships~~ *vessels.* ~~In which case they'd overcome their anti-communist feelings.~~

Am. Consumers with the experience of the previous wheat sale *~~fresh in mind and the fact that it~~* which ~~jumped domestic food prices quite considerably~~ *and high food prices in mind* are alarmed & The Sec. of Agriculture says ~~it~~ ≠ this sale shouldn't have that effect. ~~and~~

~~w~~With all these points & counterpoints maybe we still aren't getting to the heart of the problem.

Please dont think I'm leading up to a pat answer to all these questions. It just isn't that easy. ~~Philosophically my view is that~~ If we believe in a free mkt. ~~then~~ *shouldn't* our farmers ~~should~~ be allowed to sell their produce ~~on the world mkt.~~ *anywhere in the world* for the best price they can get. ~~To prevent them from doing~~ *To not allow* this is to subsidize and make available to ~~the~~ our own consumers low priced food at the expense of our own farmers.

Not inconsistent with that philosophy ~~however~~ *however* is our own ~~Nat.~~ interest ~~having to do with the~~ *in the* matter of Nat. security. If we believe the Soviet U. is ~~a~~ hostile to the free world and we must or we wouldn't be maintaining ~~our defenses at~~ *a nuclear defense* & continuing in Nato then are we not adding to our own danger by helping the troubled Soviet economy? ~~There~~

~~In this context~~ *But* isn't there also a moral issue? Are we not helping a Godless tyranny maintain its hold on ~~milions~~ millions of helpless people? Wouldn't ~~their~~ those helpless victems have a better chance of becoming free if their slave masters regime collapsed economically? One thing is certain, the threat of hunger to the Russian people is due to the Soviet obsession with mil. power.

Nothing proves the ~~fallacy idiocy of their whole~~ *failure of Marxism more* than the Soviets Unions inability to produce weapons ~~of defense and provide~~ *for its mil. ambitions and at the same time provide* for their peoples everyday needs *~~at the same time.~~ It Only takes* about 4% of our labor force ~~is in farming yet that 4% feeds~~ *to grow food for* 211 mil. Americans ~~& provides~~ *and provide* 80% of all the food shipped to the worlds underdeveloped nations.

A full ⅓ of Russias workers are in agriculture & still they'd starve without our wheat. And the failure is not Russian it is communist, for every other country that has collectivized it's agriculture has gone downhill in farm production.

The moral question then is ~~could~~ *can* Am. alone force the change to peaceful pursuits on Russia by refusing to sell ~~to~~ or would we have to persuade the other free Nations to do the same. Following such a course what would we do then about our farmers and the surplus they'd have on their hands? ~~As I said it isn't there is no easy, pat answer.~~

The Wheat deal is beneficial ~~≠~~ *to us* economically. Right now ~~maybe~~ in our time of ec. dislocation & imbalance of trade *maybe* it benefits us enough to outweigh the strategic ~~or the moral~~ factor. In other words it strengthens us more than we'd be benefitted by weakening them. But the moral question in the long run wont go away. The Soviet U. is an aggressor & a threat to world peace. ~~It's system is so incompetent~~ *It can remain so only by denying* its people freedom & the basic commoditys that make life worth living ~~and~~ which we take for granted.

~~Have we ever really studied~~ *Why shouldn't we study* ~~the~~ the problem and ~~considered~~ *consider* ~~buying the wheat ourselves even if only to give~~ *it* ~~away so as to be fair to our farmers; counting this as a~~ ~~cost of~~ *part of our Nat. defense* ~~as we let them choose between ec. collapse or abandonment of their arms.~~

The Russians have told us over & over again their goal is to impose their incompetent and ridiculous system on the world. We invest in armaments to hold them off, ~~Either~~ but what do we envision as the eventual outcome? Either that they will see the fallacy of their way & give up their goal or their system will collapse or—(and we dont let ourselves think of this) we'll have to use our weapons one day.

Maybe there is an answer.—~~by doing~~ *We simply do* what's morally right. Stop doing business with them. Let their system collapse but in the meantime buy our farmers wheat ourselves & have it on hand to feed the Russian people when they finally become free.—This is RR   Thanks for listening. ❖

Katyn Forest
November 2, 1976

Not all memories are pleasant but we shouldn't put the unpleasant ones out of our mind. At least not all of them. I'll be right back.

In a tiny cemetery in Gunnersbury Eng. on Sept. 18th 7000 people from all over the world gathered for the unveiling of a monument. ~~It was a 21 ft. pyramid. Carved on it one side is the Polish~~ ~~egle~~ *eagle* ~~wearing a crown of barbed wire~~ *and inscribed on the* ~~≠~~ ~~monument~~

It is a 21 ft. pyramid bearing the inscription "Katyn 1940" and a carved Polish eagle with a crown of barbed wire. Katyn is a ~~word~~ *name* we should all remember. It is the name of a forest in Poland. But the monument does not memorialize a place. It is dedicated to 14,500 Polish officers who served in the defense of Poland when the Nazis were invading from the West & the Russians from the East. The officers disappeared when the invading forces met and divided Poland.*

A few years later a mass grave was found in the Katyn forest. It contained the bodies of forty five hundred of those Polish officers who had been executed and buried there. What of the other 10,000? It is believed they were put on barges that were towed out into icy ~~arctic water~~ *arctic* waters and sunk drowning all on board.

For a time this massacre was thought to be just another Nazi atrocity but with the Nuremberg trials the truth was finally revealed. The 14,500 officers ~~were~~ *had been* captured by the Russians and murdered in 1940—the date now inscribed on the memorial. As a matter of fact the Germans had found the grave in 1943 in what had been Russian occupied territory following the partition of Poland. *The 4,500 had dug the grave and then standing on the pits edge had been machine gunned.*

The selection of Gunnersbury cemetery is an interesting sidelight on relations between the free world and the Soviet U. Maybe we need to be reminded there is still a Polish govt. in exile in London. In 1971 the movement to honor the murdered officers was started & because London is the home of that exiled Polish govt. it was decided London should be the site of the memorial.

The British govt. was subjected ~~by~~ *to* bitter and constant pressure from Moscow to prevent the raising of such a monument. Year after year ~~they blocked~~ *the British Govt. Blocked* every location selected by the memorial commission. Finally ~~the tiny~~ *in some way the tiny,* obscure Gunnersbury cemetery *was found &* ended up as the only possible location for the memorial.

Lord Oswald** vice chairman of the commission spoke at the dedication but let it be known there was no official representative of the British govt. nor of the Church of Eng. present. He declared: "Intrinsic also, and essential is the date 1940 engraved upon the face, because that relates in stone another

---

*For analysis of and documents about the Katyn massacre see Louis Fitzgibbon, *Unpitied and Unknown: Katyn . . . Bologoye . . . Dergachi* (London: Bachman and Turner, 1975), and *The Katyn Memorial* (London: SPK-GRYF Publications LTD, 1977); Wojciech Materski, ed., *Katyn: Documents of Genocide* (Warsaw: Institute of Political Studies, Polish Academy of Sciences, 1993); Brian Crozier, "Remembering Katyn," *Hoover Digest*, No. 2, 2000; and Archives of the Soviet Communist Party and Soviet State, Fond 89, Communist Party of the Soviet Union on Trial, Katyn Forest Massacre, Opis' 14, Dela 1–20.
**Rowland Denys Guy Winn St. Oswald.

element of the truth, which only the guilty, the ignorant, and the ignoble still crave to deny."

A member of Parliament and former Conservative Cabinet Minister, Julian Amery made known that he had invited representatives of other countries in letters to 42 embassies. Only seven sent representatives to the *little cemetery for* the ~~dedication~~ *memorial* ceremony ~~in the little cemetery~~ *& only one* WAS A *major power. There was* Bolivia, Brazil, Colombia, Liberia, South Africa, Uruguay & you'll be proud I'm sure to know—the United States of America.

This is R.R.—Thanks for listening. ❖

Russians
May 25, 1977

Standing in the Athenian mkt. place 2000 yrs. ago Demosthenes asked, "What sane man would let another mans words rather than his deeds tell him who is at ~~peace~~ *war &* who is at ~~war~~ *peace* with him?" I'll be right back.

When I was a young boy our nation fought a ~~world~~ war to, "make the world safe for democracy." And in less than 2 decades we had a Hitler, a Mussolini & a Joseph Stalin abroad in the world.

When I was a young adult we fought a ~~world~~ war to end all wars. And we've known hardly one day of peace in the world in the more than 30 yrs. since that war ended.

The other day a young man, R. Emmett Tyrrell Jr., ~~who publishes a fine~~ *editor of a fine* paper called "The Alternative: An American Spectator," wrote in that paper, "Throughout the last 3 decades I cannot think of one threat to world peace that would not have paled into, at worst, a regional altercation, were it not for the eager presence of the Soviet U. or one of it's clients. Nor would international terrorism, hijackings, kidnapings, and other assorted barbarities peculiar to our time be such vexed questions were it not for the Soviet U. the worlds arsenal of anarchy." *

That, in my opinion is a blunt but extremely accurate ~~summing up of the record~~ *summation of the biggest single* problem we face ~~in the world and its cause.~~ *as a nation.* Now, I'm well aware those words will be dismissed as utter nonsense in our state dept., which is why that dept. is referred to as "foggy bottom." ~~Those~~ *They will be sneered at by those* in the entertainment world who are writing fiction about quote the McCarthy era, unquote and calling it history ~~or who glorify~~ *make* ~~movies & TV specials in which noble~~

---

* "A World Without Russians," Vol. 10, No. 8, May 1977.

souls were ~~are apparently blacklisted in the Hollywood of yesteryear when their only sin was~~

~~I wonder what Demosthenes would~~ say about our ~~attitude toward someone who has by deed & word~~

I think if Demosthenes were standing in <u>our</u> mkt. place today he'd have a low opinion of diplomats, pundits & enthusiastic disarmament buffs who ignore the Soviet effort ~~build~~ to build the most powerful mil. force the world has ever seen. He'd be surprised that we slumbered while our lead in technology was *being* wiped out. Apparently the Russians have a laser beam capable of blasting our missiles from the sky if we should ever try to use them. And apparently we had no inkling such a weapon was being added to their arsenal.

He might even be surprised that the American Communist Party was on the ballot in our last election. And, he'd be dumfounded to know, that in Calif., an effort was made to excuse that one party from obeying the election laws, with regard to identifying campaign contributors by name, *because* ~~Someone thought~~ it might be embarrassing ~~to those who gave money to the cause~~ *to them.*

~~His sur surprise should be understandable. In 1930 the Am. Communist Party U.S.A. adopted a pledge that read "I pledge myself to rally the masses to defend the Soviet U. the land of victorious socialism." Th Members also pledged to "insure the triumph of Soviet power in the U.S."~~

~~But Demosthenes while not a fan of rhetoric would have had to recognize the eloquence of the Communist cand. for U.S. Pres. in 1976 who delivered the funeral oration for the party chmn in 1961 saying "I dream of the hour~~
† ~~when the last congressman is strangled to death on the guts of the last preacher—and since the Christians seem to love to sing about the blood, why not give them a little of it? Slit the throats of their children & draw them over the mourners bench and the pulpit and allow them to drown in their own blood, and then see whether they enjoy singing those hymns."~~

~~Come to think of it I guess~~ *≠ his* ~~campaign contributors might be embarrassed if they were identified.~~

~~This is R R. Thanks~~ for listening.

~~Demosthenes would not lack for reasons to be surprised at us.~~ Young Mr. Tyrrell lists all the areas of the world where blood is being shed and lives taken by weapons bearing a Russian trademark. And then adds, "They continue to arm everything on the globe so long as he shows a glimmer of interest in the Marxist whim-wham. Further they rush ahead with gigantic civil defense projects and with a mil. buildup that strongly suggests that they are attempting to achieve nothing less than a war-fighting, war-winning posture in strategic weaponry."

Every Soviet leader up to & including Breshnev has sworn to carry out to the letter the words (~~every one of them~~) of Lenin who said, "It would not matter if ¾ of the human race perished; the important thing is that the remaining ¼ be communist." He also said, "to tie ones hands in advance & to openly tell an enemy who is presently armed that we <u>will</u> fight him and when is stupidity."

Well there's a lot of <u>that</u> around.

This is R R Thanks for listening.

†I didn't have the nerve to say this ❖

Keng Piao
May 4, 1977

Last Jan. the Chinese Information Service in N.Y. ~~hand~~ *released* a report about a commencement address in Peiking that should have had our ears burning. I'll be right back.

With our own counterintelligence capability somewhat hamstrung as it has been recently, it's good to have friends. Intelligence sources in Taipei (the free Republic of China) have made available excerpts of a speech made ~~was~~ by Keng Piao, director of the Dept. for Foreign Liaison, to the graduating class of the "College of Foreign Affairs" in Red China.*

The college is the ~~Communist~~ training institute for diplomats. Kengs speech, like the ~~one~~ *Brezhnev speech* I reported on a few weeks ago, was not for public dissemination—which is a polite way of saying it was SUPPOSED TO BE secret. His topic was, "A Turning Point In Sino-American Relations." It might be well to note that while the name Keng Piao is not exactly a household word in America, he is very much ≠ *a* part of the policymaking process in the Chinese Communist Party.

In his address he was bluntly outspoken about the 2 superpowers, Russia & the U.S. He said both were bent on aggression and therefore the spearhead of Red China's struggle should be aimed at both. The fact that, for the moment, ~~the U.S. is~~ *we are* not being referred to as "U.S. Imperialists," ~~says Keng~~ dosen't mean that Peking has forsaken, or even softened, on Marxist-Leninist principles, says Keng.

*For a news report about the speech attributed to Keng Piao at the time that Reagan was writing this radio commentary see Fox Butterfield, "Peking Is Said to Stress Soviet Over Taiwan," *New York Times,* Jan. 27, 1977.

According to Keng, the Peoples Repub. of China is temporarily caught in a narrow crack between 2 imperialist camps—yes, he calls the Soviet U. imperialist as well as an aggressor. According to Keng, it would be unthinkable for his country to try & deal with the two imperialists at the same time. So, the strategy is to, "temporarily," (and we should ~~keep that word "temporarily" permanently in mind) to~~ PERMANENTLY KEEP ~~IN MIND~~ that word in mind) put their dispute with us aside so as to have one less enemy.

He complained to the graduates that there were some revolutionary hotheads in their people's paradise who don't realize the U.S. for all ~~it is~~ [*its vaunted*] vaunted power has a soft, weak side which they (the communists) can use to their advantage. Ah! To see ourselves as others see us.

Keng explained that Peking while recognizing our imperialism, could at the same time promote—(for it's own purposes)—a friendly relationship with the U.S. In perfect Mao Tse-Tung ~~reasoning~~ language he called this a "policy of duality." ~~In this way it~~ Under this policy they can denounce us for stationing troops in some countries (Taiwan, for instance) and at the same time, with no self-consciousness, endorse our maintaining troops in Western Europe & the Philippines. This ~~is~~ *he* called tactical ~~flex~~ flexibility.

He admitted there was no hurry about taking back Taiwan, ~~as a~~ they simply accept that it belongs to them and they dont mind our taking care of it for them—for awhile. But, he made it plain that normal relations between the U.S. & Red China will ~~only~~ *not* come about ~~if~~ unless we withdraw our Ambassador from Taiwan. On that point he said we haven't lived up to their expectations, ~~Then~~ but then went on to ~~assure~~ *tell* the students, ~~that "Taiwan~~ "Just wait for the opportune day, then we'll tell Uncle Sam to pack up & leave."

Before closing he reaffirmed that the Soviet U. is the primary threat and "detente" is disturbing to Peking. More American leaders he said, ~~would~~ pol., military, & social—~~will~~ *would* be invited to mainland China to keep us quiet & friendly until they can handle, "Soviet revisionist social imperialism." Then it will be our turn.

That's something for us to keep in mind while our touring officials are mastering chopsticks.

This is R.R. Thanks for listening. ❖

Cambodia #1
May 25, 1977

Lets talk of Human Rights and why there has been no worldwide outcry against the appalling inhumanity & violation of human rights in Cambodia. I'll be right back.

~~Somehow the fate of a small South-East Asia Country, (7 mil. population)~~ ~~has been overlooked in the Communist sweep into S.V.N. I'm speaking of~~ ~~Cambodia which in a way was a casualty also of the Viet Nam takeover. A~~ ~~curtain of silence has hidden~~ With our focus on Africa, the Middle East and other world trouble spots few of us have thought to inquire about the fate of Cambodia which fell to the Communists just 2 yrs. ago. Now thanks to a Senior editor of Readers Digest John Barron and Digest ~~editor~~ Far Eastern editor Anthony Paul we have a window ~~on~~ *view of* what has to be one of the most brutal violations *in human history* of all that is decent. ~~in~~ What has happened and is still going on in Cambodia ~~is every~~ *matches or exceeds* in sheer horror everything that Hitler did at his very worst.

Our window is a book called "Murder Of A Gentle Land" published by Readers Digest Press/Crowel Co. N.Y.* Starting in the Fall of 1975 Barron & Paul with the help of 2 other Digest editors began interviewing hundreds of Cambodian refugees mainly in the refugee camps along the border of Thailand. Those they talked to ~~were~~ *represented* a cross section of Cambodian society, the educated, the illiterate, the poor, the affluent, students and professors.

Such a widespread array made it possible to check story against story and thus ~~authenticate~~ *verefy the* tales of horror. It is significant that most of those they talked to had actually ~~greeted~~ *welcomed* the communist conquest because they thought it would bring peace & end the long years of fighting. They were for the most part dis-interested in pol. philosophy & were therefore neither ~~pro~~ for or against communism.

In addition to these personal interviews our ~~experts~~ *authors* & their helpers being experienced journalists & editors monitored radio Phnom Penh ~~the Cambodian Press~~ *as carried by the Foreign Broadcast Assn.* They checked their findings against intelligence reports both foreign & American and sought the counsel of scholars throughout the world who specialized in Cambodia. From all of this has emerged an accurate account of what took place beginning ~~at~~ on April 17, 1975 when the 1st communist troops entered the ~~city of~~ *Capital* City Phnom Penh.

They were greeted warmly as heralds of peace. Within 2 hours however the "heralds of peace" using loudspeakers & going door to door ordered every one of the 3 mil. ~~people in~~ *men, women & children in* Phnom Penn to leave the city. Those who resisted the order or were too slow in obeying were shot where they stood.

---

*John Barron and Anthony Paul, *Murder of a Gentle Land: The Untold Story of Communist Genocide in Cambodia* (New York: Reader's Digest Press, 1977).

The same procedure was being followed at the hospitals. Patients bedridden, some just emerging from surgery, some who were dying were dumped in the streets. Friends & relatives of some who couldn't walk pushed their beds. Those without such help tried to pole their beds with a stick as you would pole a raft through shallow water.

The streets were so jammed that for days the pace was as slow as 100 yds. an hour. Those who had cars only reached the outskirts of the city & there their cars were confiscated. The same scene was being enacted in the other Cambodian cities.

Behind them in the emptying cities books, records, archives of every kind, medical libraries, priceless manuscripts, business & govt. records were being burned. Hospital equipment, automobiles, home furnishings—all were smashed, vandalized and destroyed in an effort to purge Cambodia of it's entire history. This of course included the Temples in the city.

At the same time the killing of former mil. officers, civil servants and their families down to infants & children was going on. They were slaughtered in organized massacres by artillery fire, hand grenades, land mines, machine guns, bayonets and even clubs. I'll take this ⧧ up in the next broadcast. This is RR Thanks for listening. ❖

Cambodia #2
May 25, 1977

Yesterday I reported on a book describing the Communist takeover of Cambodia, it's title "Murder of a Gentle Land." The story isn't pretty but it demands telling.

I'll be right back.

There is no parallel in history for the forced march of mil's. of Cambodians from their town & city homes out into the jungles and fields. All along the line of march communist soldiers goaded them onward & shot them when they couldn't keep up.

There were no provisions for feeding or even providing drinking water and the temperature was a hundred degrees. ~~The authors of this~~ The authors of "Murder of a Gentle Land" tell us the very young & the very old were the first to die. They also quote a Cambodian Dr. who was driven from his clinic with his patients and who spent a month on the highways until he was able to escape to Thailand. He said he passed *by* the body of a child at least every 200 yards. With the living suffering from dehydration and gastro-intestinal afflictions he finally had to face the dread decision of saving his remaining medecines for those he thought had some chance of living.

The fields were littered with the castoff ~~possessions~~ *belongings* of the marchers and with the bodies of the marchers themselves. A few *of the living* were ordered to stay in ~~a fe~~ *certain* villages and only had to endure the march for a matter of days but ~~for~~ most continued on for weeks to unknown destinations in the jungle or to death from cholera, starvation, thirst or sheer fatigue.

There was something of a plan to the horror. Eventually there would be a roadblock and a communist commander would send a group down a jungle trail where they would find they were to create a new settlement in the wilderness—very often with no tools but their hands. ~~Then~~ In these "settlements to be" there would be a meager daily ration of rice.

Out on the road the march would go on. More & more frequently there would be tragic scenes as families would find themselves too weak to carry the old or the children or the sick. Their *heartbreaking* choice was to abandon them or slow down to their pace & be shot with them.

Hear one story of such a choice. A slender young airline stewardess and her husband took turns carrying their 4 month old daughter. The infant was accustomed to canned milk because her mother had not breast fed her & now her body could produce no milk. The canned milk they had brought from Phnom Penh was gone. The young mother whose name was Lon ~~was~~ suffering from dehydration & malnutrition struggled on trying to keep the pace set by the soldiers. She hoped that someplace they would find food for their daughter.

Finally she knew ~~her~~ the end had come for her. In tears she begged her husband to ~~take~~ *save* the baby and himself. *As* He cradled their daughter in his arms the baby smiled & laughed happily. Then through his own tears he said to his wife, "We stay together." ~~≠~~

The friends who witnessed this scene and told it to John Barron & Tony Paul and who had to move on themselves said that of course he really was saying "We die together."

There were probably 4 mil. souls in this tragic march, more than half the total population of Cambodia. By even conservative estimates and after checking with every possible source a safe guess is that possibly ⅓ of the ~~entire~~ Cambodian people died in this murder of a gentle land.

If you are wondering what the purpose *might be* behind this ghastly slaughter the authors provide that also and I'll close this subject on the next broadcast with their explanation.

This is RR   Thanks for listening. ❖

Cambodia #3
May 25, 1977

This is my third commentary on the tragedy of Cambodia as told in John Barron & ~~Tony~~ Anthony Pauls book "Murder of a Gentle Land." I'll be right back.

~~For three days, now—this being the third day of those days~~ I've been reciting the story of what has happened to Cambodia since the communists marched into the capital city 2 yrs. ago.

Today I'll give the reasoning (if one can apply that word to genocide) behind the destruction of Cambodias soc. system and the murder of so many of it's people. At first glance it seems self defeating for the communists themselves to ~~create~~ empty cities & towns, wipe out millions of people ~~with~~ *possessed of* useful skills ~~and talents~~ and to totally destroy the fabric of a people. ~~& culture.~~

In Phnom Penh the U. was turned into a banana farm & pigs rooted in the ~~the~~ *class* rooms. ~~Some~~ Communist ~~cadres~~ *officials* & of course soldiers are the only life in the once flourishing *capital* city. ~~as well as the other cities.~~ In short ~~the~~ *Cambodian* cities have been abolished.

Interviewed in the paper Human Events, Mr. Barron ~~editor of Readers Digest~~ was asked "What is the motivation & philosophy of the communist rulers?" He replied that everything that has been done in Cambodia has been by orders of "Angka Loeu" and I'm not sure I pronounced that correctly but it means the "organization on high" ~~. I suppose it~~ correspond*ing* to ~~what we know as~~ the politbureau in Russia.

~~He described this body as~~ *It* consist~~s~~ing of about a dozen men & women who exercise <u>all</u> the power. They ~~were all~~ *are* from middle class families, educated as lawyers, teachers or economists. All are ardent communists wedded to theory. None ever worked with ~~their~~ *his or her* hands and ~~all~~ *they* spent their adult lives outside of Cambodia.

They are ascetics who believe in the ultimate revolutionary dream of ~~obliterating~~ completely destroying the existing order so that in the consequent vacuum they can create a pure & perfect society. And this is what they ~~undertook to do in Cambodia~~ *have done* without regard to human life or material cost. What a reminder of Lenins line that if ¾ of the world population ~~died~~ *had to die* it would be worth it if the remaining ¼ were communist.

~~Mr. Barron correctly points out~~ These dozen purists moved more swiftly than any other revolutionaries "toward the total obliteration of all that existed²² because in a matter of 2 or 3 weeks the past was eliminated." There ~~were~~ *was* a classless society. All were equal in the jungle & before the soldiers guns. There was no printed word, no money, no religion and everyone was performing the same work.

Even courtship is licensed and to court without permission of the high 12 is punishable by death as are extra-marital affairs. Parents are forbidden to punish their children nor can they order them to do ~~something~~ *anything*. They can only ask. ~~& t~~ *T*he children are encouraged to report their parents wrongdoings. It's pretty heady for a child to know he *or she* has the power of life or death over ~~his~~ mother & father.

They are taught their God is the "organization on high" that their whole life, their every thought, their being must be consecrated to the organization. If they falter the "Wheel of History" will grind them down. There are no schools as such any more but they are indoctrinated with a hatred for anything foreign—especially American. ~~Their life must be dedicated to toiling in the fields.~~

~~The unholy 12 sneer at Russian & Chinese communism & believe they have come the closest to~~ ≠ *to realizing true communism.* ~~What a dream to come true.~~ In the villages ~~the~~ a gong awakes the people at 5 A.M. They work in the fields with only a noon break until evening and on moonlit nights frequently put in 3 extra hours. There are no holidays. ~~and t~~ They work a 7 day week ~~They~~ *and* are only allowed two infractions of rules. On the 3ʳᵈ they disappear. *Women have special privileges—they aren't shot— their throats are cut.* "The Murder of a Gentle land," should be required reading.

This is RR   Thanks for listening. ❖

Korea
August 15, 1977

Is relief that we didn't have a nasty confrontation with N. Korea over the murder of 3 young Americans the only emotion ~~or response~~ *we should* feel? I'll be right back.

In the weeks that have elapsed since ~~N~~ N. Korea shot down one of our helicopters, killing 3 young soldiers the principal editorial reaction ~~was~~ *has* been one of praise for our forbearance, gratitude to N. Korea for accepting our apology & relief that nothing really nasty came of the incident. Of course this mutual conciliation was predicated upon complete*ly* ~~forgetfulness~~ *forgetting how* tragically final the incident was for 3 familys; how drastic *was* the punishment for a simple error in navigation.

Unlike the seizure of the U.S.S. Pueblo 9 yrs. ago in international waters or the shooting down a year later of one of our planes with ~~31 airmen aboard~~ *loss of 31 American lives*—(again over international waters)—our aircraft this time was at fault. It had strayed across the demilitarized zone into N. Korean territory. This we had to acknowledge and did.

It was proper also that we *should* choose our words carefully until we had return of the lone survivor & the bodies of the murdered men. In 1965 the N. Koreans shot down an off course fighter plane and it took a week to get return of ~~the~~ the 1 survivor & the body of the man who was killed. In the case of the Pueblo they held the crew for almost a year and even though we were completely in the right our govt's. conduct shamed us before the world.

In this latest ≠ incident ~~though~~ the N. Koreans after a *single* days delay accepted our apology and we saw the return of our living & dead on the TV news. All across America there was ~~heard~~ heard an editorial sigh of relief. ~~T~~ & it went on for days. The Los Angeles Times referred to the 3 fatalities as "the servicemen who died." As for the, "handling of the matter," the Times said "the tone of the responses on both sides of the line appear to measure a more moderate relationship." *

Well in the 1ˢᵗ place the 3 young men didn't die, they were killed. In the 2ⁿᵈ place why shouldn't the N. Koreans be moderate? They had shot down the inadvertant intruders & we apologized. Again let me say it was proper for our govt., since we <u>were</u> technically in the wrong, to be circumspect until our men living & dead were back in our hands. But enough already of this continued self congratulation as if we'd come through some terrible danger and were safe at last.

It's time to remind ~~the world~~ *ourselves & others* of the difference in culture, in morals and in the levels of civilization between the free world and the communist ant heap. In the years since W.W.II. the Russians have killed more than 100 American servicemen in incidents similar to this. During those years they have violated our air space on occasion. We've kept them under surveillance until they departed, giving them the benefit of the doubt that they were accidentally off course. We never shot them down.

Since 1953 there ~~were~~ *have* been more than 2000 shooting incidents across the zone in Korea. ~~Some 80~~ *Eighty* Americans & almost 500 S. Koreans have been killed. Last year they attacked an American work detail in neutral territory and chopped 2 ~~American~~ *of our* officers to death with axes. Now 4 young servicemen in an unarmed helicopter get off course and are shot down, 3 ~~are murdered~~ *lose their lives* & the 4ᵗʰ ~~escapes with his life~~ *is*

---

* "A Confrontation Defused," *Los Angeles Times,* July 20, 1977.

saved. ~~and t~~ The ~~L.A.~~ "Times" says ~~the we are getting along better~~ *our apology & the N. Koreans acceptance of our apology shows we are getting along better.*

~~But now isn't it~~ *It is* time ~~we wept~~ *to weep* for the men who were murdered. ~~offered~~ *Time to offer* our sympathy to their bereaved families ~~and expressed~~ *but most of all express* our outrage at *a* nation~~s that are~~ so paranoid ~~they~~ *it* behaves like ~~psychopathic killers who~~ *a homicidal maniacs.*

Human rights include the right of ~~a~~ young boys to make ~~an~~ *an* innocent mistake~~s~~ without having to forfeit ~~his life~~ *their lives.* This is RR   Thanks for listening. ❖

Reagan was a vocal supporter of Taiwan. He was first introduced to the country in 1971 when he traveled there at the request of President Richard Nixon to reassure Chiang Kai-shek that the United States remained committed to U.S.-Taiwan relations, even though Henry Kissinger was holding secret meetings in the People's Republic of China. In this commentary, Reagan reports on his second trip to Taiwan.

Taiwan I
May 15, 1978

As they say in the travelogues, "we took our leave of Japan, setting our course for beautiful Formosa"—now known as Taiwan. ~~I'll be~~

I'll be right back.

~~Even though we thought we were prepared for changes in Taipei the capital city of the Republic of China we still were surprised by all that had been accomplished since our 1971 visit.~~ We flew TO TAIWAN from Tokyo in a China Airlines plane and that in itself was an advertisement of what was to come.

Taipei is a modern, prosperous looking city complete with luxury hotels, smart shops and congested rush hour traffic. Industries are flourishing and exports are counted in the billions of dollars. In fact like Japan Taiwan has a surplus in it's balance of trade with us and only recently sent a trade mission to the U.S. to buy $250 mil. worth of American products to reduce the imbalance. Another such mission is planned and for no other reason than to be helpful to us.

Again there were meetings—a dinner with the Foreign Minister, a call on the Minister of Ec. Affairs and a dinner given by the Pres. of the Republic. Always there was *an* undercurrent of concern about what our foreign policy really was. But also there was a feeling of pride and confidence in their own capability. They reminded this American of a quality we once had and which I hope we haven't completely lost.

I renewed acquaintance with Premier Chiang (soon to be Pres.) * the son of the late Generalissimo Chiang Kai Chek. He is a remarkable leader, dedicated to the welfare of his people. Others told me of how this quiet, unassuming man journeyed to the countryside visiting without warning or publicity farmers & workers in their homes. He is utterly realistic about the impossibility of of mixing freedom & communism.

~~We were flown to the Southern tip of the island where an industrial city of more than a million pop. has sprung up.~~ We visited a modern steel mill adjacent to a new shipyard, fully automated and capable of building the largest super tankers. The average age of the workers was 27 in the shipyard and 29 in the steel mill. They were recruited from local high schools, given 2 years training by the companies and provided with new housing & recreational facilities. Incidentally all students in Taiwan start learning Eng. in 7ᵗʰ grade.

Some of those Americans who visit the mainland and return with glowing reports of how much better off the people are under their communist rulers should visit Taiwan. ~~When t~~They justify their enthusiasm about the quality of life in Communist China, explaining away ~~the~~ rationing & scarcity by saying "but the people are so much better off than they were."

Are they? The Communist regime started in 1949 and so did the free Chinese ~~≠~~ *who* retreated to Taiwan. Taiwan had been a Japanese mil. staging area and as such was blasted into rubble by our B-29's. Power plants & railroads had been destroyed. As the Foreign Minister put it they had 5 things— a little brown sugar, some rice, a panniken of tea, an earthquake & a typhoon.

Today one China is totally regimented, there is no personal *freedom* and it cant feed it's people without *importing food*. The other has a prosperous free economy & privately owned farms capable of supplying the peoples every need plus contributing to the nations exports. The roads are jammed with cars & motorcycles, the people watch TV on 3 networks, listen to about 100 radio stations and work in a dozen modern industries.

Their military is superb and of unquestioned morale. Each young man serves 2 yrs. & then is in the reserve for 8 to 10 years. They have 550,000 in uniform & can mobilize 2½ mil. on short notice, realizing they may one day have to fight to keep their freedom.

This is RR Thanks for listening. ❖

*Chiang Ching-kuo.

Reagan is blunt in his criticism of the Carter administration's decision to recognize the People's Republic of China on January 1, 1979. He writes: "They had everything to gain by recognition, we gained virtually nothing we didn't already have."

Taiwan II
January 1979

Today I'd like to talk a little more about the "normalization" of relations with Red China & what it means. I'll be right back.

In the Presidents announcement Dec. 15th that we were ~~opening~~ establishing diplomatic relations with the Peoples Repub. of China on the mainland the inference was given that this was somehow a breakthrough, ~~≠~~ —the result of successful negotiations. This is a little less than accurate. It didn't require any negotiations to do what the admin. has done nor was this any victory as the announcement also implied.

The legitimate govt. of China some 3 decades ago was overthrown by a mil. coup led by Mao Tse Tung. That govt. fled to Taiwan and set itself up as the govt. in exile of China. Mao set up a communist govt. in Peking. Both claimed to represent all of China. The United States continued it's recognition & diplomatic relations with the EXILED govt. ~~of~~ on Taiwan.

In 1972 Pres. Nixon made his historic visit to Peking and opened the door to a relationship with the mainland Chinese. In the discussions & negotiations that followed, trade & cultural relations were established. But the Red Chinese govt. ~~set~~ *made* 3 demands which would have to be met before there could be full diplomatic ~~relations~~ *recognition*. Those demands were, the breaking of our ~~treaty~~ *defense* treaty with Taiwan, cancellation of diplomatic relations & the removal of all Am. military from Taiwan.

For *almost* 7 years this has been the impasse between the U.S. & Mainland China. Neither Pres. Nixon nor Pres. Ford would accede to these demands. We must remember also that Red China was the supplicant. The rulers in Peking wanted full diplomatic recognition, mainly because of their hostile relations with the Soviets ~~U. The~~ They had everything to gain by recognition, we gained VIRTUALLY nothing *we didn't already have.*

The "breakthrough" the Pres. announced on Dec. 15th was, as I said earlier, not a breakthrough at all. We simply gave in to Peking's demands. ~~The price we paid is possibly higher than we know~~
This could have been done anytime in the last 6 or 7 years—~~at any time~~ *whenever* we were ~~ready~~ *willing* to throw a loyal ally ~~out of the boat.~~ *overboard*. During those years poll after poll showed that while ¾ of the Ameri-

can people wanted ~~to~~ to better relations with the mainland, ¾ of them did <u>not</u> want to do this by dumping Taiwan.

Now I believe there are things the Congress can do to lessen the damage that has been done & I'll talk about this on the next broadcast. But one thing cannot be changed; the nations of the world have seen us cold bloodedly betray a friend for political expediency. That memory will not go away.

This is RR   Thanks for listening. ❖

Only a few of Reagan's commentaries are about Western Europe. In this one, he discusses Great Britain. He first met Margaret Thatcher in April 1975 during his visit to London to speak before the Pilgrims of Great Britain on the danger the Soviet Union posed to NATO. Reagan's speech and the meeting with Thatcher foreshadowed future policies as well as an important alliance in fighting the cold war. Below he expresses delight at Thatcher's elevation to the post of prime minister. *

As mentioned earlier, Reagan wrote many of his commentaries while traveling. In a marginal comment here, he notes that he wrote this one on an airplane.

Miscellaneous II
May 29, 1979

It's another one of those days ~~wh when~~ *when* the menu will be a little varied.
† I've been desk cleaning again. I'll be right back.

We can be forgiven ~~if~~ FOR SAYING Washingtons worry about hospital costs sounds a little hypocritical. The Dept. of H.E.W. has ordered the Nations hospitals to adopt a new idea in accounting procedures.

For a number of hospitals the start up cost alone will amount to $100,000. For all of them it will require keeping 2 sets of books—one for the hospital & one for H.E.W. Even without this, ~~reg~~ govt. regulations are adding considerably to the average hospital bill. A recent study ~~of~~ in N.Y. state found that regulations alone added $38.86 DAILY to the patients ~~daily~~ bill.

While on the subject of H.E.W. That agency whose budget is the 3ʳᵈ largest

---

*Reagan's speech and his meeting with Margaret Thatcher were reviewed in the British press. See "Warning that Europe is Main Soviet Prize," *The Times* (London), April 8, 1975; "A Red Alert by Reagan," *Daily Mirror,* April 8, 1975; and "On The Trail of Margaret," *Daily Mirror,* April 8, 1975. Photographs of Reagan's first meeting with Thatcher are in the Peter Hannaford Collection, Box 5. Hoover Institution Archives.

in the world (exceeded only by the Nat. budgets of the U.S. & the Soviet U.) managed to lose an affirmative action plan from the U. of Alabama 3 times. That took some doing since the report was the size of a N.Y. phone book.

When the U. finally managed to get ~~a report~~ *their plan* to the proper desk at H.E.W. they were informed the regulations had been changed and they ~~should~~ *would have to* submit a new plan.

I know I've commented a number of times about our society~~y~~*ies* soft on crime attitude and have suggested ~~our~~ we should have more compassion for the criminals victem. Well here is an outstanding example of what I've been talking about. ~~Virgi~~

Virginia Annables car was stolen a few months ago and driven out on the ice of Longs Islands Great South Bay. There it was set on fire. Miss Annable found her burned out car but before she could do anything about getting it back it had sunk through the weakened ice, coming to rest on the bottom of the bay. Well it was an old klunker worth only about $400—so end of story. Or is it?

The Army Corps of Engineers has informed Miss Annable that her sunken car is a menace to navigation and must be removed from the bay. She will be billed for the removal which the Engineers say will cost $1000. Now wouldn't you think some nice, sensible judge would rule *that* the criminal who stole the car is responsible and tell the Corps of Engineers to find him & collect their $1000.

On a happier note—and I couldn't be happier than I am over Englands new Prime Minister. It has been my privilege to meet and have two lengthy audiences with Margaret Thatcher and I've been rooting for her to become Prime Minister since our first meeting.

If anyone can remind England of the greatness she knew during those dangerous days in WWII when alone & ~~unaffraid~~ UNAFRAID her people fought the Battle of Britain it will be the Prime Minister the Eng. press has already nicknamed "Maggie."

I think she'll do some moving & shaking of Englands once proud industrial ~~community~~ *capacity* which UNDER THE LABOR PARTY has been running downhill for a long time. ~~under the Labor party.~~ Productivity levels in some industrial fields are lower than they were 40 yrs. ago. Output per man hour in ~~some~~ *many* trades is only a third of what it was in the 1930's. Bricklayers for example laid 1000 bricks a day in 1937—today they lay 300. I think "Maggie"—bless her soul, will do something about that.

This *is* RR Thanks for listening.

†(Sorry the plane was bouncing around). ❧

NEGOTIATIONS

In the nine commentaries that follow, Reagan argues that communist states never honor treaties or keep promises, and they always interpret treaties to their unilateral advantage. Making sure that past agreements are abided by should be a precondition for negotiations with such states, he says. Reagan also writes that concluding agreements that are unequivocally in the interest of the United States is not a standard observed by the Carter administration. Informed by the reading of two books by Laurence W. Beilenson, Reagan contends that the historical record shows that the terms of treaties are always violated when state interests change; states that base their armaments policy on treaties never survive; and the interpretation of treaties varies, depending on the language being used. These views form the basis of Reagan's approach to international negotiations.

In the commentary immediately below, Reagan declares that "violating agreements is standard operating procedure for communists." He says that when it cut off assistance to South Vietnam, the U.S. Congress became partly responsible for North Vietnam's violations of agreements with the United States and for the resulting domino effect.

Indochina #2
April 1975

Yes Virginia there really is a domino theory & sad to say it's working right now.—I'll be right back.

Those who ~~dispute~~ *ridicule* the domino theory believed in it when Hitler was picking off small nations in Europe 37 yrs. ago. They just dont believe it applies ~~today in Asia~~ when the enemy is communist & the countries losing their freedom are Asian.

The term domino theory very simply describes what happens to our allies if we back down & let one ally be taken over by the communists because we dont want to be bothered. The enemy ~~feels free~~ *decides it's safe* to go after others;—that we represent no threat to his aggression but even worse our allies no longer able to trust us start making deals.

One can almost hear an echo of the hollow tapping of Neville Chamberlains umbrella on the cobblestones of Munich. This time however the appeasement is taking place in the halls of Congress.

When we withdrew our forces from the long bloodletting in V.N., we did so with the understanding that we would provide weapons & ammunition to enable S.V.N. & Cambodia to resist if the N.Vietnamese violated the negotiated ceasefire. Violating agreements is standard operating procedure for communists—they violated this one 72,000 times in the 1st 12 mo. including the cruel denial of anyword about our 1300 men who are still listed as missing in action. That incidentally was a major point to us in the negotiated ceasefire. So far, they've thumbed their nose at us & refused to allow any of our 31 search teams to set foot on their territory.

We do nothing because the Cong. has taken from the Commander in Chief the authority to take any action at all to enforce the terms of the treaty.

Now that same Cong. with unprecedented irresponsibility has refused to authorize the ~~few~~ money that would permit this great nation to keep its pledged word.

The dominos ~~start~~ *begin* to fall. Three years ago I represented our govt. in Thailand to assure them the Presidents trip to Peking did not mean we would abandon Thailand & close our air bases there (a major part of their economy) Now they tell us they dont want our bases—they're going to do business with Red China.

The Philipines whose hist. & existence as a Nat. is intertwined with ours have announced they are reassessing their relationship with us & are negotiating with Red China.

Japan the great industrial power ~~capable~~ *capable* of modernizing & arming a communist Asia has just opened discussions with Hanoi.

But the dominoes are worldwide. Sec. of St. H. Kissinger returns empty handed from the middle east. A few mo's. ago the power & reliability of the U.S. had brought the Israeli Arab conflict closer to peace than at any time in 50 yrs. Now there is talk of war by summer. The press described Kissingers eyes as wet with tears of frustration.—~~our~~ Our one time power & reliability are no longer believable because of our failure to stand by an ally in far off Indo-China.

Turkey stands aloof—snubbing us. ≠ Greece the southern anchor of the Nato line leans leftward and no longer looks forward to visits by our 6th fleet in the Mediterranean & with Portugal going communist at the other end of that ocean the 6th fleet may soon find it must withdraw or become a model ship in a bottle. Once the dominoes fall we may find ourselves very lonely indeed.—This is RR Thanks for listening. ❖

Vietnam I
November 30, 1976

⧺

Govt. has no greater responsibility than to protect even the least among us whereever he may be in the world if his right to life, liberty & the pursuit of happiness is being unjustly denied. I'll be right back.

A few weeks ago the Los Angeles Times reported that N.V.N.—(although now we are supposed to call it just VN.) and the U.S. were faced with an impasse in the Paris negotiations.* We were trying to get an answer to the question of our men missing in action ~~in the V.N. war~~. A full accounting of these men & the return of all who might still be alive was one of the terms agreed to by N.VN. in the Paris Peace talks which ended ~~the~~ our participation in the war.

The negotiators for VN. in Paris ~~⧺~~ *were* demanding full reparations before they would even discuss the M.I.A's. Reparations is their ~~term~~ *word* for another ~~term~~ term in the Cease Fire agreement. With characteristic generosity the U.S. ~~volunteered~~ had offered (in the Peace Talks) to rebuild & repair the war damage for both N. & S.V.N. if & when they halted the war. Of course the Cease Fire agreement made it plain that each country was to retain it's sovereignty.

We all know that N.V.N. violated every one of the Cease Fire terms and once our forces were withdrawn proceded to conquer & enslave S.V.N. They even murdered in cold blood some of our men & officers who were ~~on grave~~ seeking & identifying American graves—this in accord with another of the Cease Fire terms.

Now ~~they~~ having broken every term of the agreement to which they had given their pledged word they have the nerve to demand that we observe that part of the agreement having to do with our putting up bils. of $ to rebuild their country.

The L. A. Times followed it's news story with 2 editorials castigating the U.S. for vetoing membership in the U.N. for V.N. ~~and~~ They wrote, "We agree with VN. ~~on~~ and it's supporters that the issue" (our M.I.A's.) should not determine either VN's membership in the U.N. or the establishment of bilateral

---

*Don Cook, "Tough Stand Taken in New Viet-U.S. Talks," Nov. 13, 1976; "U.S., Vietnam Open Talks on MIAs, War Damage," Nov. 14, 1976; and "U.S. Vetoes Viet Entry Into U.N.," Nov. 16, 1976.

relations." * Then the editorialist invoked the memory of our Marshal Plan & the rebuilding of Germany & Japan after WWII.

Well I disagree vehemently with the editorials. In the 1ˢᵗ place the U.N. charter specifies that membership in the U.N. is for nations who pledge not to use armed force in the settlement of disputes. N.V.N. is guilty of naked aggression for the purpose of taking an entire nation against it's will. Whatever else anyone wants to say about the war in V.N. it could have ended in a minute any time in those long years if N.V.N. had simply said "O.K. we'll go home & stop trying to conquer S.V.N."

There is no parallel whatsoever to our World War II Marshal plan. The aggressors had been totally defeated,—their aggression ended in failure & we then offered to help them return to the family of nations.

N.V.N. succeeded in its aggression, holds a nation of 19 mil. people enslaved & did so by *force of arms.* ~~violating it's pledged word.~~ For the Times editorials to suggest that we not only overlook this but that we not be "obstinate" (their word) about getting a report on our men, missing in action has the ~~≠~~ *sound* of Neville Chamberlains umbrella tapping on the cobblestones of Munich.

I too am critical of what our state dept. is doing in Paris. We shouldn't be negotiating at all <u>until</u> there has been an accounting of our missing men. ~~The Vietnamese~~ *They* should be told we dont even go to Paris until they keep their word. ~~on that issue.~~ As for letting them in the U.N. maybe they should take our place. This is RR Thanks for listening. ❖

Treaties
October 18, 1977

I hope our Senators will read John Loftons** newsletter "Battleline" specifically the article by Laurence Beilenson before they make a decision on the Panama Canal Treaty.

I'll be right back.

Already we are aware of two provisos in the *Panama Canal* treatys which mean completely opposite things ~~when~~ *depending on whether they are* read by ~~the~~ *a* Panimanian or an American. This alone should alert us to the possibility of other booby traps whether intended or accidental.

---

*"The MIAs in the Shadows," Nov. 17, 1976. A copy of this editorial was attached to Reagan's handwritten draft of this radio commentary.
**John D. Lofton, Jr.

†   Laurence Beilenson a distinguished lawyer and by avocation an historian has written two books which should be required reading for every employee of our state dept. One should be read by all Senators who take seriously their responsibility to advise & consent on treaties. The books are "The Power of Subversion" and "The Treaty Trap." The latter is to my knowledge the <u>only</u> complete history of treaties ever written.

In the article he was invited to write for "Battle Line" Mr. Beilenson turns his attention to the treaties now before the Sen. and writes this telling line, "let us depart from the paper world of making treaties into the real world of performing them." It may come as a rude shock to learn that in spite of the ceremony and dignity with which men sign & have signed treaties back through history most treaties are broken the first time it interferes with the nat. interest of either of the signatories. That is the lesson of "The Treaty Trap." No nation that put it's faith in paper and lowered (as a result) it's mil. hardware has ever survived.

Mr. Beilenson calls attention to the Suez incident. Britain made a treaty with Nasser of Egypt in 1954 by which it would gradually withdraw it's troops (as we are supposed to do in Panama) but would have the right to keep it's technicians & instalations along the Suez *as we are supposed to have in Panama.* By June of 1956 Britain, ahead of schedule, withdrew it's *last* troops. In July Egypt took over the British instalations in violation of the treaty. Egypt was also in violation & still is of the 1888 treaty which guarantys neutrality to all the shipping of the world. Cargo bound to & from Israel is denied access to the canal.

Britain & France sent mil. forces but the U.S. & the Soviet U. charged them with violating the U.N. charter against use of armed force. That charter takes precedence over all treaties including the ones broken by Egypt. ~~They~~ *Britain & France* yielded and withdrew.

If we ratify the Panama treaties we give up all right to sovereignty (which we now have) in the Canal Zone. The United Nations in effect grants nations the right to steal. It recognizes the right of a nation to expropriate *foreign owned* property within it's borders. But the charter denies the country whose property is expropriated the right to use force to repossess that property.

Nowhere, Mr. Beilenson points out in the treaties & protocols accompanying them does the word guarantee ever appear. And he makes the valid point that this omission must be pre-meditated.

Referring to the Protocol to The Neutrality Treaty he asks; "Why *we* should ≠ congratulate ourselves on having won—in words—the neutrality of the canal that we built is puzzling. It seems even more curious that we are crowing about the fact that if we are at war with a nation, it has the same right to use the canal as we have." * For a clincher he points out that Cuba or Russia can become a party to the protocol and have the same right to enforce it that we have.

I hope the Senators will read his article—I hope they'll read his book "The Treaty Trap."

This is RR   Thanks for listening.

†Send copy to Mr. Laurence Beilenson ❖

Human Rights I
January 9, 1978

† ~~Hearing our representatives~~ *at the Belgrade meeting* ~~back away from any~~
Watching our representatives at the meeting in Belgrade on the Helsinki agreement back away from any showdown with Russia on Human Rights is not an inspiring sight.—I'll be right back.

If human rights are denied to a people over a long enough period of time do they then become ineligible for such rights? The answer to that as we listen to the voices raised in Wash. would seem to be, "yes" they do "lose those rights."

~~I turn.~~—We've been meeting in Paris with the representatives of No. ~~Viet Nam~~ *Vietnam*. The announced reason for the meeting is to open the door ~~of~~ *to* friendship between us and to enter into an era of normal relations. The only two sticking points seem to be our demand for an answer as to the whereabouts or the fate of some 2,500 of our men listed as missing in action. And on the No. Vietnamese side their demand for about $3 bil. ~~we~~ they say we promised *in the Paris Peace Accords* ~~for the rebuilding of Vietnam~~ *of the* ~~war torn countries. in the Paris Peace Accords.~~ TO PUT UP THE MONEY TO REPAIR ALL THE BATTLE DAMAGE TO BOTH ~~NATIONS~~. N. *&* SO. *Vietnam*.

Now the~~ose~~ Paris Peace Accords were signed by us, the S. Vietnamese govt. & the present communist regime of No. Vietnam. And it's true we agreed to put up the money. ~~to repair the war damage in both countries.~~ But the accords also called for No. Vietnam to quit trying to conquer S. Vietnam and to immediately give us an accounting of our men.

Haven't our negotiators overlooked what should be the first issue to be settled before there is any talk about friendship or rebuilding any part of Vietnam? There were 2 Vietnams No. & So. They had been separate nations for 1000 yrs. Both became colonial posessions of France in what was known

---

* "An Open Letter to Sen. S. I. Hayakawa Regarding the Panama Canal Treaties," *Battle Line*, 11 (Oct.–Nov. 1977): 15.

as French Indo-China and both were freed after W.W. II when the European nations pressured by the U.S. began liquidating their colonial empires. They returned to their pre-colonial status ~~of~~ as separate nations. The great powers meeting in Geneva set down a plan ~~to~~ *(1)* to allow the people of both countries to move to whichever of the two they chose without interference and *(2)* for an internationally supervised election by the people as to whether they wanted to unite *or* continue as separate nations. ~~& if so what kind of govt. they wanted.~~

The ~~No. Vietnamese~~ *communist dictator Ho Chi Minh of N. Vietnam* refused to hold the election & when a mil. of ~~their~~ *his* people started moving South away from communism UNDER THE TERMS OF THE AGREEMENT his troops ~~set up a~~ barricaded the frontier and halted the mass migration.

The Vietnamese war was *a* plain & simple ~~aggression~~ *effort* by No. Vietnam to conquer So. Vietnam. ~~which w~~ We tried to prevent *this* in a long, bloody war which our govt. refused to win. But now how do we ~~begin negotiations with No. Vietnam~~ *the conquerors unless step one is* ~~without making step one that they free the~~ *negotiate with* No. *Vietnam unless we begin with step one—the release of a* half mil. So. Vietnamese now in concentration camps and ~~withdraw~~ *the* No. *Vietnamese withdrawal* from So. Vietnam leaving it once again a free & independent nation.

For that matter how did we agree to No. Vietnams entry into the United Nations which specifically demands that it's member nations do not take up arms against a neighbor? *Until S. Vietnam is freed—N. Vietnam is* STILL *an outlaw among nations.*

Times up but next air time I'll continue with some other non existent human rights ~~we're not talking about~~ *we've forgotten lately.*

This is RR   Thanks for listening.

†(Put these in the 15 beginning at about the 6ᵗʰ in line—so they'll go on at the beginning of the 2ⁿᵈ week. RR ❖

Treaties
March 13, 1978

In all the debate that has been going on about a couple of particular treaties there hasn't been much time for a ~~general~~ discussion of treaties in general. I'll be right back.

Laurence Beilenson a distinguished Calif. lawyer & scholar authored a book a few years ago that is quite unique. In fact it is, so far as I know, the only history of treaties ~~dating all the way back through biblical times~~ and the observance and lack of observance of ~~those treaties.~~ *same—dating all the*

Radio Treaties

    In all the debate that has been going on ①
about a couple of particular treaties there hasn't
been much time for a ~~general~~ discussion of treaties in
general. I'll be right back.

    Laurence Beilenson a distinguished Calif.
lawyer & scholar authored a book a few years
ago that is quite unique. In fact it is, so far
as I know, the only history of treaties, ~~dating all
the way back through biblical times~~ and the
observance and lack of observance of ~~these treaties.~~ some - dating all
~~the way back through biblical times.~~
One thing stands out sharply — no nation which
put it's faith in treaties ~~but let it's~~ but let it's ~~has~~ mil.
hardware deteriorate stayed around very long.

    The very nature of treaties is such that
more often than not they must be written in
2 languages. The result is that regardless
of the good will of the signatories the different
meaning of words when translated from one
language to another can make for misunderstanding

    Let's take an agreement which while not a formal
treaty was still a joint communiqué between the heads
of state of 2 nations enunciating a policy. I'm talking
about the Shanghai communique that climaxed
the visit of an American Pres. to the Peoples Republic
of China a few years ago. In looking at it one is
apt to be more confused than enlightened.

    The Chinese made a statement ~~with re~~ regard to
our long time ally the Free Republ. of China on Taiwan
that it, quote "opposes the creation of 2 Chinas, an independent
Taiwan or a separate solution "unquote. The U.S in
turn says quote "that it does not challenge this view".
To Americans this was plain English that meant
we neither agreed nor disagreed — we simply avoided
the issue.

Unfortunately it is not that easy & simple.[2] The Chinese translation of the phrase, "does not challenge" is taken to mean that because we ~~do~~ make no objection we agree with China's position. Then there is a sentence to the effect that there should be a peaceful solution to the problem of Taiwan. We would interpret that to mean that Peking ~~doesn't~~ won't launch an attack or try to conquer Taiwan by force of arms. Again Peking denies that this language binds them to seek a peaceful solution.

We have an example ~~to~~ in the Panama Canal treaties that came to light early in the Sen. debate. Senators were proposing amendments to the treaties ~~which~~ apparently didn't disturb the Panamanians — until the Panamanians realized what we meant by amendment. To us an amendment is a ~~binding~~ clause as binding as the original treaty — as witness amendments to ~~our~~ constitution.

To them "enmienda" (amendment) is just a minor change in wording — alright if it is just included in an existing clause but definitely a no-no if it's added as an additional paragraph. Then it becomes serious business.

As we approach the Salt II talks with Russia we should keep in mind that Russian is a far more complicated language than Spanish. Besides which the Russians don't keep their word even when they understand the meaning.

This is RR Thanks for listening.

way back through biblical times. One thing stands out sharply—no nation which put it's faith in treaties ~~& consequently~~ *but let it's ~~hard~~ mil.* hardware deteriorate stayed around very long.

The very nature of treaties is such that more often than not they must be written in 2 languages. The result is that regardless of the good will of the signatories the different meaning of words when translated from one language to another can make for misunderstandings.

Let's take an agreement which while not a formal treaty was still a joint communiqué between the heads of state of 2 nations enunciating a policy. I'm talking about the Shanghai communique that climaxed the visit of an American Pres. to the Peoples Republic of China a few years ago. In looking at it one is apt to be more confused than enlightened.

The Chinese made a statement with ~~≠~~ regard to our long time ally the <u>Free</u> Repub. of China on Taiwan, *that it,* quote "opposes the creation of 2 Chinas, an independent Taiwan or a separate solution" unquote. The U.S. in turn says quote "that it does not challenge this view." To Americans this was plain English that meant we neither agreed nor disagreed—we simply avoided the issue.

Unfortunately it is not that easy & simple. The Chinese translation of the phrase, "does not challenge" is taken to mean that because we ~~hav~~ make no objection we agree with ~~t~~ Chinas position. Then there is a sentence to the effect that there should be a peaceful solution to the problem of Taiwan. We would interpret that to mean that Peking ~~dosen't~~ wont launch an attack or try to conquer Taiwan by force of arms. Again Peking denies that this language binds them to seek a peaceful solution.

We have an example ~~th~~ in the Panama Canal treaties that came to light early in the Sen. debate. Senators were proposing amendments to the treaties ~~with~~ *which* apparently didn't disturb the Panamanians—until the Panamanians realized what we meant by amendment. To us an amendment is a ~~binding~~ clause as binding as the original treaty—as witness amendments to our constitution.

To them "enmienda" (amendment) is just a minor change in wording—alright if it is just included in an existing clause but definitely a no-no if it's added as an additional paragraph. Then it becomes serious business.

As we approach the Salt II talks with Russia we should keep in mind that Russian is a far more complicated language than Spanish. Besides which the Russians dont keep their word even when they understand the meaning.

This is RR   Thanks for listening. ❖

China
April 3, 1978

T'was Bobby Burns the poet who said something to the effect of having the gift to see ourselves as others see us.* I'll be right back.

In this time of doubt & mistrust in ~~our own~~ *the* land when we are ~~fearful of &~~ curbing the ability of our own intelligence machinery to keep us informed, it is especially interesting to note how effective by contrast are the Chinese in the Free Republic on Taiwan. ~~⧧~~ Their record of ~~bringing out~~ *making public* top secret material from the Red Chinese on the mainland is fantastic and I might add very helpful to us.

For example we now have the complete text of a 42,000 word *several hour* speech by Red Chinas Foreign Minister Huang Hua delivered July 30 to all the top level govt. & party functionaries meeting in Peking. It was a complete report on the entire world situation & definitely not for public consumption.** Repeatedly throughout the address Huang cautioned his audience against talking about anything they ~~h~~ were hearing.

Now you know of course I'm not going to give you all 42,000 words. But I thought you might be interested in how we look to the Chinese communists who want ~~us~~ to "normalize relations" with us—providing we'll forget about our friendship with Taiwan.

Huang referred to the Shanghai Communique jointly signed by our two countries as "like other treaties & agreements—merely something on paper." He then went on to say, "The U.S. does not have the strength to deter the resolution of the Chinese people to liberate Taiwan."—We will simply regard ~~thei "(their~~ *their* treaty with Taiwan) "as a scrap of paper." He suggested that it was nothing more than that to us and asked if the American people have the will to share the fate of Taiwan if & when the Mainland govt. sets out to conquer the Free Republic of China. Answering his own question he said, "Go read Am. history, we have not seen such an instance in which the U.S. has had such resolve & courage to sacrifice for others. That is why we dare to conclude that the U.S. is a paper tiger. It can be said that we have the deepest insight into the U.S. and, after having dealt with it for such a long time, we can paint not only it's skin, but also it's bones."

*"To A Louse," in James A. Mackay, ed., *The Complete Poetical Works of Robert Burns, 1759–1796* (Scotland: Alloway Publishing Ltd., 1993), 181–82.
**See "Huang Hua's Report on the World Situation," *Issues and Studies: A Journal of China Studies and International Affairs* 13 (Nov. 1977): 78–84; (Dec. 1977): 76–94; 14 (Jan. 1978): 94–116; and (Feb. 1978): 77–88.

Now that isn't the picture we have of ourselves & history (overall) does not support Huangs image of us. But we should note the examples from recent history he used to support his view; the firing of McArthur* in Korea because he wanted to win the war & our failure to be decisive in Vietnam. He spoke of, "the frailty of the paper tiger that could not withstand a beating" and described us as standing absolutely alone without "a single dedicated fellow traveler."

There is great danger to us in this false image making. It is more often than not the road to war. The Kaiser didn't think we'd fight no matter how great the provocation and Hitler had the same idea. Then there was Pearl Harbor.

Huang said *in effect* China would be patient until it had the relationship it wanted with us and then it would liberate Taiwan and we wouldn't lift a finger. If we really want peace we'd better remind the world of that America ~~they~~ it seems to have forgotten.—We'd better remind ourselves that "paper tigers" ~~get~~ are easily torn up.

This is RR Thanks for listening. ❖

Reagan's political rhetoric is distinctive. He called the Soviet Union an evil empire during his presidency. Below he calls Fidel Castro a liar.

Castro
July 15, 1978

There have been some exchanges lately between heads of state & the words, lie & liar have been heard. I'll be right back.

Several weeks ago the Pres. released intelligence summaries which established pretty conclusively that as long ago as 1976 Soviet & Cuban advisers were asking permission of Angola to go raiding across the border into Zaire. The govt. of Angola is of course Marxist & totally sympathetic to Soviet aims. The intelligence reports stated that Cuban & East Germans trained the raiders for the '77 invasion and that Cubans were involved in the recent massacre at Kolwezi in Zaire.

Down in Cuba Fidel Castro brands all of these reports as lies and implied that the President was lying. He told American reporters: "We may be private about some things. We may be discreet. But we have never lied. We never made use of lies as an instrument of politics." So says Castro.

You know, calling the average man a ~~liar~~ liar is a pretty drastic charge and

*General Douglas MacArthur.

the average man reacts with vehemence when his veracity is so questioned. But calling a communist a liar when he is one is pretty frustrating. How do you insult a pig by calling it a pig? Communists are not bound by our morality. They say any crime including lying is moral if it advances the cause of socialism. That is Karl Marx as interpreted by Lenin.

Fidel says he & his fellow communists never lied. *When he says that* Fidel is a liar & he's been lying on a regular basis since before he seized power in Cuba. In 1958 he said, "we are fighting to do away with dictatorship in Cuba & to establish the foundations of genuine representative govt." A year later in his victory speech he pledged to respect & uphold the countries laws. He also said that if the men in his govt. proved unequal to the task the people could replace them in free elections.

A month later he promised no violation of human rights, no beating of anyone, indeed no one would even be insulted. His former military commander *HUBERTO* Matos in prison now for almost 20 yrs. could attest to the honesty of those promises. And he would have confirmation from the estimated 20,000 pol. prisoners living under the most inhumane conditions.

But here are two Castro statements that make our case. In May of 1958 he made a public ~~statement~~ *declaration:* "I never have been or am I a Communist. If I were, I would have sufficient courage to proclaim it." Now that is a pretty definite statement.

But after he had seized power he asked, "Do I believe in Marxism?" Then answered his own question. "I believe absolutely in Marxism." ~~He said that he believed in it in 1959 when he took over the govt. and back in~~ *believed in it back in* ~~1953 when the attack was made on the Moncada barracks. He said~~ "I am a Marxist-Leninst until the last day of my life." ~~In other words he is & has been for some time an unmittigated liar.~~

~~This is R R Thanks for listening.~~

He added that he was a communist back in 1953 when the Moncada barracks was attacked* and believed in it in 1959 when he assumed the dictatorship of Cuba. Fidel Castro is a liar.

This is RR Thanks for listening. ❖

In this commentary, like the one on Nigeria in the section on Reagan's philosophy, Reagan states that virtue is the defining characteristic of a democ-

---

*Led by Fidel Castro, a group of revolutionaries attacked the Cuban army barracks called Cuartel Moncada on July 26, 1953. Under political pressure, President Fulgencio Batista granted amnesty to many of the revolutionaries, including Castro, who were captured and sentenced. Castro then fled to Mexico to plan the revolution.

racy. The Carter administration sacrificed virtue for political expediency, he writes, when it established formal ties with the People's Republic of China. The administration "broke a treaty without cause" and thereby betrayed Taiwan, "a long time friend and ally."

Reagan mentions General Albert Coady Wedemeyer, commander of U.S. forces in China in the 1940s. Wedemeyer received the Presidential Medal of Freedom from President Reagan on May 23, 1985.

Taiwan I
January 1979

Shouldn't a nation be bound by the moral code of it's people? And can a govt. act dishonorably without ~~dishonoring~~ *bringing dishonor to* it's people? I'll be right back.

Someone once said ~~each~~ *every* form of govt. has a single characteristic which forms the basis for it's ~~being~~ *power;* if that is lost the govt. falls. Monarchy *for example* is based on the affection & respect of the people for the Royal family. When that respect & affection disappears the monarchy falls. Dictatorship is *based on fear, it is* successful ~~because~~ *only so long as* the people fear the dictator. In a Democracy the underlying principle is virtue, when that is lost the democracy ~~is lost~~ *fails &* ceases to exist.

There came a moment in W.W.II. when the Japanese offered Chiang Kai-Shek a separate peace on the most generous terms. He of course knew that the Chinese communists in northern China had an army ready & waiting to seize power—as they subsequently did. The Japanese offer had to be very tempting to the Generalissimo. ~~who~~ *He* could have turned his *FULL* attention ~~& used his army~~ to the red army & guarantyd the continuation of his own regime.

The Japanese of course would have been able to ~~turn~~ *THROW* the entire army fighting on the mainland of China against our forces in the So. Pacific.

Chiang Kai-Shek told our General Wedemeyer of the Japanese offer and of his refusal to make a separate peace. He said that he could not betray his friend & ally, the United States: that he would fight to the end by our side.

In *SPITE OF* all ~~of~~ the platitudinous talk, the reiteration of arguments that the declaration by the Pres. Dec. 15ᵗʰ was simple realization of reality one fact remains very clear: The United States, for the first time in it's history, broke a treaty without cause. We callously betrayed a long time friend & ally which had ≠ refused to betray us. And we did so with a brutal rudeness. ~~The act~~

During the 2 years of the Carter admin. there has been a deliberate snubbing of the govt. on Taiwan.;aAn Asian journey by our Vice Pres. took in virtually every country of the western Pacific except Taiwan. We sent no representative to the inauguration of the Pres. of the Repub. of China, the son of Chiang Kai-Shek. And there was no consultation with the new Pres. warning him of our decision to accept the terms laid down by the Communist rulers in Peking. What our govt. did was entirely lacking in virtue.

My next commentary will continue on this subject.

This is RR Thanks for listening. ❖

Salt II
September 11, 1979

Do arms limitation agreements—even good ones—really bring or preserve peace? History would seem to say "no." I'll be right back.

As the debate rages over whether to ratify or not ratify the Salt II treaty it might be well to look back at that great era of arms limitation agreements that began in 1921. We were in the aftermath of WWI—the war, quote, unquote "to end all wars." Unlike Salt II and Salt I for that matter, the Wash. Naval Treaty of 1922 actually reduced armaments. The three great naval powers scrapped or sank roughly half their battleships & agreed that no new ones would be built for 10 years.

The Wash. agreement was followed by the London treaty of 1930. Battleships had been limited to 35,000 tons, cruisers 10,000 tons & 8 inch guns and limits were placed on other types of vessels. But cruisers at the time were half the size limit in the treaty and mounted 4 & 6 inch guns. With battleships banned there was a rush to build 10,000 ton cruisers with 8 inch guns. And lo & behold the battleship admirals discovered aircraft carriers which they had previously disdained.

Thus the treaties had actually resulted into in improved technology and thanks to the carriers an ability to strike first—as we found out at Pearl Harbor. The treaties also tended to lull the people of our own land & of Great Britain so that Hitlers bu mil. buildup took place with most of us refusing to admit it was happening.

As we debate Salt II we should listen to heed the words of some whose voices are *not* being heard above the clatter. An escapee from behind the iron curtain Lev Navrozov, a Russian exile who recently founded the "Research Center for the Survival of Western Democracies" contends that the original Salt agreement was "based on a mortally dangerous mistake." He identifies that as the 12 years prior to 1975 when we grossly underestimated Soviet spending on armaments. He further contends that Salt II is based on another mistake—the belief that many of the Soviet activities are verifiable when they are not.

Mr. Navrozov refers to an article earlier this year in "Scientific American" in which a U.S. Congressman argued that we could verify the terms of Salt II.* According to the Navrozov many of the Congressmans claims were highly questionable. But adding to his concern was the fact that the editor of that prestigious magazine rejected an offer of an article rebutting the Congressmans claims on the grounds that it wouldn't be suitable for the magazines current needs.

The plain truth is we cannot verify if the Soviets are carrying out the terms of Salt II and it is a falsehood to suggest we can.

In his June 28 column, journalist Ben Stein summed it up very well: "An unrestrained arms race which the U.S. could not possibly lose given our industrial superiority, or a treaty (Salt II) which says that the arms race is over and that we have lost it." And he asks—"which is worse."

This is RR   Thanks for listening. ❖

---

*Les Aspin, "The Verification of the SALT II Agreement," *Scientific American* 240 (Feb. 1979): 38–45.

DEFENSE

The chief defense issue for Reagan is his conviction that the United States has lost military superiority to the Soviet Union. In support of this belief, he discusses weapons projects that have been abandoned; weapons that do not function properly; U.S. troop withdrawals in strategic locations; arms control negotiations that are substitutes for grand strategy; the testimony of respected military officials; and what he believes to be the war-fighting strategy of the Soviet Union. Reagan blames the loss of military superiority on the defense policies of the Carter administration. The loss of military superiority was a major foreign policy theme for Reagan in his 1980 presidential campaign.

To reverse the unfavorable military trend that he outlines in his commentaries, Reagan suggests that the United States undertake an aggressive rearmament program and rid itself of the tendency to make arms control negotiations, instead of military strength, the centerpiece item in its military policy and in its relationship with the Soviet Union.

Invoking the policy assessments of military and foreign policy officials is one of the main ways that Reagan criticizes the Carter administration's defense policy. He does this in the seven commentaries below.

Farewell Speeches
January 19, 1977

When administrations change there are farewell speeches and when high command military officers retire there are farewell ~~speeches~~ statements. I'll be right back.

Shortly before the changing of the guard in the nations capitol the former Sec. of State addressed the Wash. press club. In his address he vehemently denied that we had lost mil. supremacy to the Soviet U. He spoke somewhat harshly of those who claimed otherwise which I had to assume included me. But to tell you the truth he didn't change my mind.

About the same time the ~~retiring~~ just retired ~~head~~ head of Air Force intelligence Maj. Gen. George J. Keegan Jr. gave an interview to the N.Y. Times. He flatly stated that ~~he~~ the Soviet U. has already achieved mil. superiority over this country. "By every criterion used to measure strategic balance," he said, "that is damage expectancy, throw weight, equivalent megatonnage or technology I am unaware of a single important category in which the Soviets have not established a significant lead over the U.S."

The Gen. spoke of the one thing that until recently has not been very much publicized by our side and that is the Soviet emphasis on civil defense, including shelters and stockpiling of food & supplies. He expressed the view that we are probably no longer capable of carrying out our ~~wartime~~ assigned wartime task of crippling the Soviet industrial capacity, nuclear stockpiles & the basic fighting capab*city* of the Russians.

Gen. Keegan expressed his own ~~somber~~ view that the Soviet U. is not only trying for superiority but is preparing for war. He based this somber assessment on a collection of thousands of photographs, pamphlets & documents on Soviet military sites & civil defense projects. In the Times interview he said "In the mil. area alone they have hardened on the order of 35,000 installations. These include 75 underground command posts for the civil mil. leadership within the Moscow Beltway alone." He said "some of these structures were several hundred ft. deep & wide & capable of withstanding 1000 pounds per sq. inch of blast pressure." According to him the hardened sites included headquarters of all the major mil. services, duplicate reserve installations for each & for the entire nuclear chain of command. In addition according to Keegan 10,000 surface to air missile sites have been hardened & 4,500 early warning & ground control intercept radars are in the process of being hardened.

Evidence was given of worker shelters in industrial areas capable of protecting more than 60 mil. workers. Some ¼ of all factory workers are in training programs preparing them "for civil defense leadership roles." ~~And then t~~ The General declared "The implication is that they have quietly and at extra expense taken measures to assure that the essential, civilian-military leadership, the fighting capability and the production capacity can continue to function under conditions of total war." And then he added "that the greatest global conflict in history is likely to occur within the next decade or two unless there is a radical change in United States intelligence perceptions." *

Now I know that Major Gen. Keegan of air force intelligence was giving his own assessment & there are other opinions among the military but only as to degree. The majority opinion ~~about our~~ *among qualified experts* ~~about~~ *as to* the relative strength of the Soviet U. & the U.S. is not on the cheerful side. It's time to ask ourselves if we can afford not to believe them. This is R. R. Thanks for listening. ❖

Korea
May 25, 1977

† It would appear that a double standard exists where ambassadors to the United Nations and Generals of the army are concerned, and the double standard is dictated by the White House. I'll be right back.

A 2 star General who came into the army in W.W.II, *who* served with distinction in that great conflict ~~and~~ as well *as* in the 2 wars since, deserves better from his commander in chief than public humiliation and the destruction of his career.

Major Gen. John K. Singlaub, 55 yrs. of age, ~~was~~ chief of staff of American forces in Korea, is highly respected by his colleagues in the military and is deserving of that respect. ~~He is~~ No longer chief of staff in Korea, he awaits re-assignment. ~~and t~~*T*he consensus among his fellow officers is that he will probably be re-assigned to a ~~post~~ job that will make it plain he is being punished.

In announcing his re-call & reassignment Sec. of Defense Harold Brown said: "Public statements by General Singlaub inconsistent with announced nat. security policy have made it ~~plain~~ very difficult for him to carry out the duties of his present assignment in Korea." The Sec. then went on to say he had directed the Sec. of the Army to take action to that effect.

But calling the Gen. home was not Sec. Browns doing. The order came ~~∉~~ from the Pres. It was public, it was angry and ~~in my opinion~~ *apparently* born of vindictive temper. The Generals associates from buck private to fellow officers knew he was being called ~~in~~ *to* the house for a spanking. In my opinion there ~~was~~ *is* no excuse for this humiliation of a man who has served his country in peace & war with valor, indeed with heroism.

And what was the Generals crime? According to Sec. Brown, "public

---

*David Binder, "Air Force's Ex-Intelligence Chief Fears Soviet Has Military Edge," *New York Times*, Jan. 3, 1977.

statements inconsistent with announced national security policy." * The General has asked no quarter, he simply stated that his remarks expressing his opinion were made in what he thought was background information for a Wash. Post Correspondent & not for quotation. The Wash. Post disputes this, and I'm *not* challenging ~~their~~ that assertion, but, anyone who has been in public life ~~know~~ knows how easy it is for a misunderstanding to take place. All of us have spoken frankly at times in what we thought was an "off the record" session, and found ourselves quoted by a journalist who had not considered the interview off the record.

Gen. Singlaub expressed the opinion that withdrawal of American forces in Korea could lead to war. Pres. Carter has announced his intention of removing those troops. I think the General is right. ~~t~~*T*he S.Korean govt. thinks he's right; ~~t~~*T*he govt. of Japan thinks he's right. ~~a~~*A*nd, most of our top mil. brass think he's right. The war we've already had in Korea was caused by ~~a~~ *the* careless words of an Am. Sec. of State who intimated that we didn't consider S. Korea in our perimiter of defense. *The N. Koreans took that as an invitation & the war was on.*

Admittedly the disciplining of the Gen. is because his statement was ~~counter~~ *critical* of the Presidents declared policy. ~~not because what he said wasn't true.~~ But the Pres. has smilingly apologized for a succession of verbal boo boos ~~by~~ *by* his appointee to the United Nations; outrageous statements that angered & insulted ~~sever~~ ~~*the govt's of*~~ several *of* our allies. Each time like a patient parent the Pres. has explained that Ambassador Young was not correctly stating nat. policy. *He has* ~~murmured~~ *Then, murmuring* a few words about misunderstanding or incomplete communication, ~~and~~ ~~sat back to wait for the next~~ *the Pres. has reiterated his confidence in the Ambassador.*

There is anger & bitterness among our mil. officials who believe Gen. Singlaub expressed what they all feel. Certainly he deserves better from the country he has served so well.

This is RR. Thanks for listening.

†<u>NO 1 to be recorded</u> ❖

---

*Brown's statement is found in Bernard Weinraub, "Carter Disciplines Gen. Singlaub, Who Attacked His Policy on Korea," *New York Times,* May 22, 1977. See also Bernard Weinraub, "Defense Chief Backs Korea Plan, Says the Military Must Support It," *New York Times,* May 23, 1977.

Korea
January 27, 1978

~~Once I sometimes wonder if Washingtons left hand knows what it's right hand is doing & Vice Versa.~~

For a long time now I've suspected our state dept. of being left handed. But now & then they almost seem ambidextrous. It's confusing. I'll be right back.

Last spring Maj. Gen. John Singlaub a most capable soldier with a f distinguished mil. record was abruptly & publicly removed from his post in S. Korea by the Commander in Chief himself. The General had expressed his view in what he thought was a private conversation, that the President's plan to withdraw our 2nd infantry division from Korea could tempt the Communists in the North to have another go at conquering the Republic of Korea.

Arriving in this country the General was summoned to appear before the House Armed Services Comm.* ~~Being the honest man he is~~ He told the Congressmen that our intelligence reports reveal that the N. Koreans have done what the Soviet U. has done—engaged in a massive buildup of military power. And being the honest man he is he said removing our ~~2nd div.~~ *troops* from Korea would seriously weaken S. Koreas ability to defend itself.

Now many months later our State Dept. which from the 1st has supported the President's decision to withdraw the 2nd Division, comes forth with a 12 page report *to Congress* on Korea. And guess what? The report confirms everything that Gen. Singlaub said. It calls the threat to S. Korea serious and stresses the fact that N. Korea has rejected all efforts to ~~stabilize~~ *settle* the pol. issues which divide the the 2 Koreas peacefully.

The report gets very specific regarding the "sizable *military* advantage" the North has over the South and the fact that No. Koreas mil. force is obviously offensive not defensive in nature. In tanks, armored personnel carriers, rocket launchers, artillery etc. the South is outnumbered more than 2 to 1. Their advantage includes jet fighter planes, naval vessels and Russian missiles for use against ships. S. Korea has no submarines but No. Korea builds it's own.

Most significantly the report after stressing the proximity of Seoul to the N. Korean border, makes it plain that S. Korea could survive an attack only

*U.S. Congress. House. Committee on Armed Services. Review of the Policy Decision to Withdraw United States Ground Forces From Korea. 95th Congress. 1st and 2d sessions. May 25, 1977, 3–76.

with our help. They ~~would~~ *will* have to have air, naval & logistic support. The report goes farther and says steps must be taken to "replace the combat capability of the U.S. ground forces we are going to withdraw." We must build up So. Koreas stores of ammunition & equipment, *send* more & better tanks & anti-tank weapons; there must be an increase in ~~the R.O.K.~~ *So. Koreas* capability to utilize sophisticated weaponry and still *with all that* they would need our active participation if war should come.

The report dosen't come right out & say it but it is apparent that it means we'd be better off if the *U.S.* 2ⁿᵈ infantry division stayed *right* where it is. In other words Gen. Singlaub knew whereof he spoke.—*the presence of* ~~The only thing the report dosen't~~ our troops in S. Korea could very well mean the difference between peace & war.

This is RR Thanks for listening. ❧

The Military
September 27, 1977

Does our tradition of civilian control over the military mean that we the people cannot have the benefit of advice & opinion from the mil? I'll be right back.

Evidently reflecting White House unhappiness with public discussion ~~by~~ of strategy by mil. men a memo has gone out to officers of the armed forces which, however it is worded, is a muzzle.

The Army Chief's memo is entitled "Speaking up, Speaking Out." It tries to indicate to the officers that they aren't muzzled and then ends up doing just that. He said the, "unfounded publicity about muzzling the military," could become "a self fulfilling prophecy" if the Generals didn't ~~hol~~ keep their mouths shut. Now anyway you read that it says in effect, "we deny we're not allowed to speak out but if we know what's good for us we wont."

~~Now I~~Let's skip the question of const. right to free speech and whether it even applies here. ~~or not.~~ The question is (and I'll admit it isn't an easy one to answer) how do we the people get the facts we need to ~~express ourselves~~ *form an opinion* on matters affecting our security? Ours is supposed to be a govt. of, by & for the people. Suppose we had a case where the Joint Chiefs of Staff were totally against a defense policy enunciated by the admin. and said as much in a secret meeting with the Pres. their Commander & *in* Chief who then went ahead with his policy. If the Joint Chiefs tacitly went along we would assume the Pres. was carrying out a policy ~~with~~ which had the approval of our mil. experts.

First of all do we want an Army that just follows orders no matter what those orders may be? Isn't that what the Nuremberg trials were all about? Nazi officers charged with crimes against humanity defended themselves on the ground that they had ~~no choice but to obey~~ *simply been carrying out* orders. The court found that no defense and they were convicted.

Right now as a result of 2 ~~cases of~~ officers ~~speaking~~ *publicly* expressing opinions ~~publicly~~ which were contrary *to* or critical of admin. policy ~~they are~~ *the military is* faced with a no win situation. If they go along silently with something they believe is wrong or not in the nation's best interest they appear cowardly and more interested in holding ~~j~~ their jobs than protecting our country. If they resign from the service & make public the reason, they are a one day story and from then on, in no real position to be effective. If they speak up but pledge to carry out the policy in spite of their disagreement ~~they~~ ~~their careers are affected by~~ *cut short* they wind up counting mess kits in camp swampy discredited as having challenged civilian control of the mil.

The Chmn. of the Joint Chiefs has admitted to a comm. of Cong. that the mil. did not want as big a *troop* withdrawal from Korea as the Pres. ordered. Then he expressed ON BEHALF OF THE JOINT CHIEFS support for the Pres's. plan. That dosen't exactly reassure us that reducing our troops in Korea is a piece of brilliant mil. strategy approved by the top brass.

Generals & Admirals shouldn't express pol. opinions but politicians shouldn't express mil. opinions unless the military is given equal time. We've had 2 wars now in which strategy has been dictated by pol. decision—Korea & Vietnam. Our men have never fought more bravely ~~or under greater handicap. We should never ask young Americans to do that again~~ *in any war nor under such ridiculous politically imposed restraints. That must never happen again.*

Is it too much to ask that our mil. experts be allowed to testify in executive session to committees of the Cong. speaking freely with no fear of retaliation? Then at least our representatives can weigh their words against those of the admin.

This is RR   Thanks for listening. ❖

Chiefs of Staff
July 15, 1978

There has been a "changing of the guard" recently at the Pentagon. That of course is just an expression to announce appointment of *a* new Chief of Staff.

I'll be right back.

For more than 200 yrs. our nation has followed a policy of civilian control over the military. The Pres. is the Commander in Chief, ≠ he appoints as Secretary of Defense a civilian and then come the uniformed Admirals & Generals.

The system was designed to guard against military dictatorship and it has served us very well. I'm sure no American, including those in uniform would want to change it. Presidents have the counsel & advice of top military experts in the decisions they have to make with regard to our national safety but ~~they~~ *Presidents* in the final analysis make the decisions.

Several weeks ago we watched on TV as one Chief of Staff, Gen. Brown stepped down. In his farewell remarks the Gen. warned us of danger ahead if we did not add to & strengthen our military capability.

A short time later on the TV screen we saw the Pres. (who was not present at the previous ceremony) announce the appointment of a new Chief of Staff.* He made this the occasion for remarks about our defense stature that were contrary to the warnings of the outgoing Chief.

It is no secret that this Pres. has overridden the advice of the Joint Chiefs of Staff ~~and~~ *or* ignored their opinion on several occasions. What happens if a President using his command authority appoints as Chiefs of the various services men who will tell him what he wants to hear rather than their best considered, military opinion?

We have the case of Gen. Singlaub who was transferred for expressing his opinion against withdrawing American troops from S. Korea. Then later when he expressed a contrary view regarding the Neutron warhead decision he was—quote "allowed" unquote *to take* early retirement.

In the case of the Korean withdrawal he ~~was~~ *had been* informed that ~~the decision had not been made to~~ there was "no announced decision" as yet. Indeed the S. Koreans had been told they would be consulted before any decision was made. In truth they were not.

Now in retirement & free to express himself the Gen. says we weren't honest with the S. Koreans. He also says there was, "no authentic mil. input concerning the decision to withdraw." N. Korea incidentally has a 2 to 1 advantage over S. Korea in artillery, armor & combat aircraft." Their mil. forces are stronger than the combined American & S. Korean forces before we withdrew.

The decision to withhold the neutron weapon was made with no attempt to get military advice. But most telling with regard to the Presidents unwill-

---

*General Brown's successor, General David C. Jones, remained in that post until the summer of 1982, the second year of the Reagan administration.

ingness to take or seek advice was the word to the military regarding the Panama Canal treaties. ~~It was mad~~ The Joint Chiefs were told they could feel free to disagree with the treaties—and resign if they did so.

This is RR   Thanks for listening. ❖

Taiwan's Future
March 6, 1979

We've been told—maybe re-assured is the proper word—that the Repub. of China on Taiwan is so strong that an attack from the mainland is highly unlikely. But is it?

Defense dept. officials including Sec. Brown have told the Senate Foreign Relations Committee that Taiwan could survive any concerted attack by the Peoples Repub. of China—so therefore it's unlikely there would be such an attack for years & years to come ~~&~~ *if ever.*

On the last broadcast I told of the shenanigans in that Sen. committee which will make any resolution of U.S. support for Taiwan so weak as to be meaningless. That is unless Senators attempt to amend some muscle into the committee bill on the floor.

~~And what~~ *Now* about that Defense Dept. testimony to the committee that Taiwan ~~was~~ *is* strong enough to take care of itself? There has been other testimony which was totally unreported by such papers as the N.Y. Times & the Wash. Post—testimony to that same Sen. Foreign Relations Committee. Fortunately a Wash. weekly called "Human Events" has made it possible for us to know about that testimony.*

Vice Admiral Edwin K. Snyder U.S. Navy Retired, told the Sen. Committee that Taiwans defenses would have to undergo a vast modernization program to successfully withstand a sustained assault from the mainland. And it would seem that Admiral Snyders opinion would carry some weight with the Senators. From August of 1974 to August 1977 he was commander of the U.S. Taiwan Defense Command. He was responsible to the Joint Chiefs of Staff for contingency planning for the defense of the Repub. of China including Taiwan & the Pescadores Island.

Just giving Taiwan the weapons presently in the pipeline wont be enough. The Admiral says the R.O.C. wouldn't have a chance if it didn't get such all weather fighter planes as the F-16, Harpoon missiles to stand off the Chinese navy & special anti-submarine equipment. All of this is equipment our 7th

---

*"Ex-Defense Commander Says Taiwan Vulnerable," *Human Events* (Feb. 24, 1979): 4.

fleet would have provided under the mutual defense treaty we are now scrapping.

The admiral further says that without our carrier planes the Taiwan airforce would be neutralized within 2 or 3 weeks. The mainland Chinese navy would pit patrol boats & modern destroyers both armed with surface to surface missiles against 20 old W.W.II destroyers armed with 5 inch guns. And the greatest threat is the Communist Chinese submarine force—almost double the number we have in our whole Pacific ~~navy~~ *fleet.*

Admiral Snyder believes that the island Republic's lines of supply & communications could be disrupted in fairly short order. His message is clear, if Congress fails to make certain that Taiwan receives advanced weaponry ~~it could the Rep~~ the free Repub. of China could be enslaved by the rulers in Peking. And yet it dosen't seem as if the Sen. committee is listening.

This is RR   Thanks for listening. ❖

Soviet Trade
July 9, 1979

Maybe Lenin was right when he said that ~~when the~~ *as* time came to hang the capitalists they would vie with each other to sell the communists the rope.

I'll be right back.

Some years back the Russians built a gigantic truck factory known as the Kama River Truck plant. I say they built it—they couldn't have done more than dig a hole for the foundation without help from the U.S. We gave them a package that included everything from the money they needed to the machinery & technology they didn't have.

Of course this was done with the hope that if they began to have the things free enterprise has provided for us they might become a friend & neighbor. We were careful to point out that a truck plant wasn't like selling them something they could use against us in event of hostilities.

Now we've learned that motors made in the Kama plant are winding up in armored personnel carriers and assault vehicles.

Several weeks ago a Commerce Dept. Official whose job is to monitor the sale of advanced technology to the Soviet U. ~~to~~ so as to guard against giving them something that could be used militarily, blew the whistle on his own dept. He said our system of export controls is a "total shambles."

In testimony to ~~the~~ a closed meeting of the House Armed Services subcommittee on research & development, Lawrence Brady director of the Office of Export Admin. revealed that the Commerce Dept. had not been candid with Congress. He said the system for approving sales to Moscow is in bad shape. This was in direct contradiction to the testimony of his immediate superior Stanley Marcus, Senior Deputy Asst. Sec. for Industry & Trade. Mr. Marcus had told the committee our precautions "are sufficient to insure our nat. security."

A controversy is taking place in the admin. brought on by a debate in Congress over moves to make ~~th~~ it easier to sell advanced American products to the Soviets.

Senior admin. aides including the Sec. of State favor increased trade. Understandably aides in the Defense Dept. & the Nat. Security Council are opposed. Maybe we should remember WWII when a former trading partner returned tons of our scrap iron in the form of shrapnel that killed our young men.

~~This of course~~ What we are talking about today isn't scrap iron. Mr. Brady says that last year only a few hundred of the 7000 requests to sell our products to the Soviet-bloc nations were turned down. We are supposed to insure that nothing we sell can be diverted to mil. use but that is virtually impossible to do. Truck motors turning up in assault vehicles is ~~our~~ proof of that.

Salt II will concern itself with Russias S.S.18 missiles which carry 10 separate nuclear warheads each. Ours carry 3. We didn't think they were within years of learning how to equal us in that dept. Then we sold them technology for making infinitely small & precisely engineered ball-bearings—just the kind needed for multiple warheads on nuclear missiles.

This is RR. Thanks for listening. ❖

ARMS CONTROL

In the commentaries that follow, Reagan launches a far-ranging attack against the SALT II treaty. He invokes statements and testimonies against the treaty made by former military officials, current members of the Congress, and policy experts; expresses concern about the implications for the military balance of not including the Soviet Backfire bomber in the official agreement; opposes the Carter administration's decision to cancel the B-1 bomber program; and contends that the Soviet Union does not believe in "MAD" and does not see nuclear war as unthinkable. He believes that the United States is making most of the concessions in the negotiations; that the treaty does not induce real reductions in armaments and thus does not contribute to "lasting peace"; and argues that the treaty cannot be verified. Finally, he even says that the American public is more skeptical about the treaty than popular public opinion polls suggest.

SALT
November 8, 1977

Too much salt we're told is bad for us—causes hardening of the arteries or something. ~~But w~~We may be getting another kind of salt right now ~~that~~ *and* it could be fatal. I'll be right back.

Recently we've heard optimistic sounds from Wash. about the Salt II talks. ~~with the Soviet U.~~ What is even more disturbing are *the* purring sounds from the Kremlin voicing their belief that ~~≠~~ we have become more reasonable of late.

I'm inclined to believe all of these optimistic noises are bad for our health. From sources in a position to know the word is that ~~any~~ *to* claim ~~that~~ the Russians have made significant concessions ~~in Salt~~ about limiting armaments is simply not true. Any concessions have been by us.

~~We gave too much away in the heralded Vladivostok meeting a few years back & now t~~ The ~~≠~~ PROUDLY ANNOUNCED lowering of the *VLADIVOSTOK AGREEMENT ON* ~~agreed upon~~ number of delivery systems ~~makes things worse. It~~ *only* lowers our total. ~~& raises the Soviets~~ *The Soviets get an increase.* By delivery systems we mean of course the methods of delivering nuclear weapons to *& at* each other.

† For one thing it is reported that we are willing to <u>not</u> count Russias Backfire Bombers in their total but count our B-52's in ours. ~~≠ The Russians ≠~~ INSERT ~~≠~~ The admin. claims ~~that~~ agreement on a limit of 800 multiple war-head, Intercontinental Ballistic Missiles—ICBMs, ~~that~~ will remove the threat to our Minuteman force. Intelligence sources say that within that ceiling ~~that~~ *the* Russians can have 5 to 8 warheads for each of our Minuteman Silos and enough left over—half their total for other targets.

Then there is the agreement with Russias demand for a limit on the range of ship or submarine ~~launched~~ LAUNCHED missiles. It's easy to say "well if both sides are limited to missiles of the same range isn't that fair?" Not when you consider geography.

The agreed upon maximum distance such missles will carry puts all of the population AND INDUSTRY of western Europe & Japan and 69% of the people & industry of the U.S. within range of the Russian weapons. Under the same distance limitation our missiles can only reach 15% of the people & industry of the Soviet U.

The Sept. 24ᵗʰ London Economist ~~also~~ expressed the concern of our allies. "For the U.S. to accept any limits at all on cruise missiles would be a large concession." ~~For the U.S. to~~ The U.S. is in the position of many great powers before it; it has to choose between accomodation with it's adversary & the confidence of its allies." * Simple morality dictates that we deal fairly with our allies.

The Salt II agreement additionally must be accepted on faith. The whole matter of "right to ~~veref~~ verify ~~if~~ *whether* promises are being kept" has been scrapped.

No wonder Gromyko describes negotiations as "businesslike & useful." Translated from the Russian that means "~~we've~~ *Uncle Sam has* been skinned again."

This is R.R. Thanks for listening.

(Insert for P.1)

And what do we *get* from the Russians? A promise that they wont use the Backfire Bombers to attack the U.S. Can anyone possibly believe any country would keep such a promise if war comes?

†Put insert bottom of P. 2. ❧

SALT Talks I
March 13, 1978

How many men with personal experience & first hand knowledge ~~of~~ OF ~~the very inner workings of~~ the highest levels of our Nat. defense establishment must speak out before we'll pay attention? I'll be right back.

~~Preparatory talks meetings~~

Every now & then optimistic reports are given of the progress being made in the talks preparatory to the Salt II negotiations. Usually the optimism seems to be based on what further concessions we'll make once the negotiations begin. We've made some concessions such as cancelling the B-1 Bomber without waiting for the negotiations.

Former members of the highest levels of mil. command ~~≠~~ have uttered warnings about Russias growing might; former mil. Intelligence Chief Gen. Graham, air force intelligence chief Gen. Keegan & Admiral Zumwalt former chief of naval operations to name a few.**

---

*"Cruise for Europe," *Economist* 264 (Sept. 24, 1977): 14–15.

**General Daniel O. Graham, General George J. Keegan, and Admiral Elmo Russell Zumwalt, Jr.

Now writing in Readers Digest former Sec. of Defense Mel Laird says; "The evidence is ~~flagrant~~ *incontrovertible* that the Soviet U. has repeatedly, flagrantly & indeed contemptuously violated the treaties to which we have adhered." He goes on to say; "This evidence has been withheld from the Congress, the press & the public. I believe there is no longer any excuse for denying the Am. people & their representatives facts whose suppression profits only our enemies." *

The former Defense Sec. gives particulars such as the Soviet ~~system~~ deploying of an anti-ballistic missile, the upgrading of medium range missiles to long range weapons & interference in our monitoring efforts—all violations of the Salt I treaty. And, he says, these violations are increasing even as we go forward with plans for another Salt treaty *in* which *we* will rely on the good faith of the Soviet U. ~~f~~For example ~~we~~ having given up the B-1 we're prepared to let the Soviets continue producing their Backfire bomber so long as they dont increase the rate of production. The catch is we dont know what their present rate is & they wont tell us.

Laird says there has been a steady stream of intelligence *reports* about Soviet violations both in the previous admin. & this one but the desire for detente is so great these reports are being kept from Congress & the people.

Sen. Allen** has said that our Salt negotiators apparently feel we could resolve the Back Fire impasse by getting Brezhnev to write a letter promising that the bombers will not be deployed in such a way as to threaten the U.S. That leads to a pretty obvious question; why would they build them if they intended to keep such a promise?

But to get back to the Salt violations, Laird says the Russians aren't hearing a single *PEEP OF* protest from us. They must really be looking forward to the new negotiations—just think they'll have a brand new treaty to violate.

I'll talk more about this on the next broadcast.

This is RR Thanks for listening. ❖

SALT II
March 13, 1978

In these days of highly emotional partisanship in Wash. I ~~dont know about you but~~ I take great pleasure when there is evidence that our representatives are not always bound by party ties. I'll be right back.

---

*Melvin R. Laird, "Arms Control: The Russians Are Cheating!" *Reader's Digest* (Dec. 1977): 98.
**Senator James Browning Allen (D-Alabama).

A Calif. Congressman Rep. Charles Wilson of Calif.—Dem.—has spoken out publicly of his concern about the Salt II treaty being drawn up in Geneva Switzerland. This of course puts him at odds with the admin.

The Congressman visited Geneva in December and observed the negotiators in action. Upon his return he bluntly declared that the treaty now being drawn up threatens our Nat. security. He pointed out that the Soviets will be allowed 2 or 3 times as many nuclear warheads as the U.S. plus the fact that their warheads far exceed ours in power.*

Another hard to understand clause ~~is~~ *provides* that the Russian Backfire bomber which can carry cruise missiles is <u>not</u> covered by the treaty. But the U.S. FB-111 and our B-52's or any other aircraft equipped to carry long range missiles must be counted against the total delivery systems allowed *us* under the treaty.

In very forthright language Congressman Miller stated, "Salt II is an arms control agreement in name only. It would guarantee the Soviet U. strategic superiority for the remainder of this century while doing nothing for U.S. national security." He was equally forthright in declaring that our negotiators seemed more interested in helping Jimmy Carter redeem a campaign promise than in protecting Am. interests.

He described the Soviet team as made up of tough, hard nosed negotiators who've been doing this same job since 1969 when Salt I was passed. By contrast our team has only 2 members with previous experience in any kind of Soviet negotiations. He described our team as wanting a treaty simply for the sake of having a treaty. Our concessions deal with Soviet weapon systems already operative. ~~& deployed.~~ When the Soviets concede at all it is usually with regard to some weapon system we dont have yet.

Then there is the matter of ~~verefication~~ *verification*. Yes our reconnaissance satellites can keep a reasonable count on how many missiles the Soviets have on hand. But there is no way without on site inspection (which the Russians will never agree to) to verify whether the Soviets are indeed complying with the treaty. Satellites cannot tell us whether ~~the~~ the treaty is being violated with regard to new guidance systems, or how many warheads each missile contains.

Summing it up the Congressman says the Salt II treaty the admin. is willing to accept is not in our nat. interest. "In view of a withering bomber force, which will decline in capability during the period, a highly vulnerable ICBM force, & with the Trident & cruise missile programs in doubt within our own govt. <u>no</u> treaty would be preferable to an instrument which would guarantee

*Charles H. Wilson, "Salt II—Blueprint for Disaster," *Reader's Digest* (April 1978): 89–92.

Soviet strategic superiority for the remainder of the century." So says a Dem. Congressman who has been listening in on the Salt II talks.

This is RR   Thanks for listening. ❖

Reagan declares that the Russians do not subscribe to the doctrine of Mutual Assured Destruction, known as "MAD."

SALT Talks
June 27, 1978

A congressman has called on the Pres. to ~~urge~~ *bring* our Disarmament negotiators home from Geneva before they indicate any more concessions in the Salt II treaty being discussed.

I'll be right back.

Apparently some of our team now in Geneva talking reduced armaments with the Russians have forgotten Public-Law 92-448.* This resolve of Congress is still on the books & it has not been altered or diluted since it was enacted.

The law recognizes that the present agreement known as Salt I was an interim agreement offering guidelines for a "more complete strategic offensive arms agreement," which ~~they~~ is ~~referred to~~ *called Salt II*. The law ~~prescribes~~ specifies that any agreement we sign must provide the principle of equality in strategic forces. It also calls for the maintenance of a vigorous research development & ~~p~~ modernization program for U.S. strategic forces. That—it so happens is virtually non-existent.

It's time we looked at that law, at Salt. I & at our understanding of what Salt. II should be. What are the facts concerning the Soviet U? Are they what we thought they were in 1972? Do the Russians subscribe to our belief in "mutual assured destruction" as a deterrent to war? Apparently we think so but just as apparently the Russians do not. We say, "thermo-nuclear war is unthinkable by either side." The Russians have told their own people that while it would be a calamity it is not unthinkable; that it very well might happen & if it does the Soviet U. will survive & be victorious.

Brezhnev (who a recent Am. visitor described as a gentle old man) has admonished the Russian people that "it would be extremely dangerous if the opinion became firmly established in public circles that the threat of war has become illusory."

*Public Law 92-448 is reprinted in Mason Willrich and John B. Rhinelander, eds., *SALT: The Moscow Agreements and Beyond* (New York: The Free Press, 1974), 314–15.

Radio

Salt Talks

A congressman has called on the Pres. to bring our ①
Disarmament negotiators home from Geneva before they
indicate any more concessions in the Salt II treaty being discussed
     I'll be right back.

Apparently some of our team now in Geneva
talking reduced armaments with the Russians have
forgotten Public-law 92-448. This resolve of congress
is still on the books & it has not been altered or diluted
since it was enacted.

The law recognizes that the present agreement
known as Salt I was an interim agreement offering
guide lines for a "more complete strategic offensive arms
agreement", which is called Salt II. The law
specifies that any agreement we sign must
provide the principle of equality in strategic forces.
It also calls for the maintenance of a vigorous research
development & modernization program for U.S. strategic
forces. That it so happens is virtually non-existent.

It's time we looked at that law, at Salt. I &
at our understanding of what Salt. II should be. What
are the facts concerning the Soviet U.? Are they what we
thought they were in 1972? Do the Russians subscribe
to our belief in "mutual assured destruction" as a deterrent
to war? Apparently we think so but first as
apparently the Russians do not. We say, "thermo-nuclear
war is unthinkable by either side". The Russians have
told their own people that while it would be a
calamity it is not unthinkable; that it very well might
happen & if it does the Soviet U. will survive &
be victorious.

Breghnev (who a recent Am. visitor described as a
gentle old man) has admonished the Russian people that
"it would be extremely dangerous if the opinion became
firmly established in public circles that the threat of
war has become illusory."

②

To then Sec. of State Kissinger statement that neither the U.S. or the Soviet U. could escape 100 mil. dead in a nuclear exchange, Russian admiral Shelyag's answer was "Nyet". He said: "In the West it is claimed that humanity, world civilization, would perish in the event of such a war, that everything living on earth would be annihilated. ~~We quite~~ Communists harbor no sentiments of hopelessness or pessimism."

Marshal Krylov denies our concept that in nuclear war there would be no victory. He says: "Victory will be on the side of world socialism." And lest there be any doubt of their unanimity Gen. Altunin in charge of Russia's civil defense program says; the preparation of the country's rear for defense against mass destruction has become without a doubt one of the decisive strategic factors assuring the ability of the state to function in war time and in the final analysis the attainment of victory.

Our own experts write a scenario in which an attack is leveled against Nato at the same time civilians in Russia are evacuated (FROM URBAN AREAS) to prepared positions in the country. In the nuclear exchange that follows they lose 5% of their population — we lost 50% or more.

Needless to say our negotiators are not abiding by Public Law 92-448. Perhaps they should be sent a copy before they say (ANOTHER) good morning to their Russian counterparts.

To then Sec. of State Kissingers statement that neither the U.S. or the Soviet U. could escape 100 mil. dead in a nuclear exchange, Russian Admiral Shelyag's* answer was "Nyet." He said: "In the West it is claimed that humanity, world civilization, would perish in the event of such a war, that everything living on earth would be annihilated. ~~Marxists-Leninists~~ ≠ Communists harbor no sentiments of hopelessness or pessimism."

Marshal Krylov** denies our concept that in nuclear war there would be no victory. He says: "Victory will be on the side of world socialism." And lest their be any doubt of their unanimity Gen. Altunin*** in charge of Russia's civil defense program says; "the preparation of the countrys rear for defense against mass destruction has become without a doubt one of the decisive strategic factors assuring the ability of the state to function in war time and in the final analysis the attainment of victory."

Our own experts write a scenario in which an attack is leveled against Nato at the same time civilians in Russia are evacuated FROM URBAN AREAS to prepared positions in the country. In the nuclear exchange that follows they lose 5% of their population—we lost 50% or more.

Needless to say our negotiators are not abiding by Public Law 92-448. Perhaps they should be sent a copy before they say ANOTHER good morning to their Russian counterparts. ~~again~~ ❖

In the next two broadcasts Reagan cites the defense policy analysis of Thomas C. Reed. Reed was chairman of Reagan's Northern California committee during his first bid for the governorship of California and chairman of the statewide committee for Reagan' reelection campaign in 1970. In 1982–83, Reed was special assistant to the president for national security policy.****

SALT Talks I
July 31, 1978

We may not be too far away from decision time with regard to a new "Salt" agreement ~~with regard to~~ concerning our strategic weapon strength as compared to the Russians.

I'll be right back.

---

*Admiral Vasilii V. Shelyag.
**Marshal Nikolai Ivanovich Krylov.
***Aleksandr T. Altunin.
****A copy of Reed's speech is found in his privately held papers.

You might be interested in some timetables as presented by former Sec. of the Air Force Thomas C. Reed. Tom was part of our Sac. team in the early days & then moved into the Pentagon. By training he is a nuclear physicist. He challenges the concept that "detente" has eliminated the possibility of a nuclear showdown with the Soviet U.

In a presentation to the American Security Council he ~~presented an~~ reviewed recent history beginning with the Cuban missile crisis 16 yrs. ago. It was Oct. 1962 when the world for 6 days hung on the brink of nuclear war. Then the Russians blinked and their missiles were removed from Cuba.

Pres. Kennedy expressed the hope that the govts. of the world could, "turn their earnest attention to the compelling necessities for ending the arms race & reducing world tensions." Unfortunately the Soviet U. turned it's "earnest attention" to a ~~crash~~ *massive* buildup of mil. force. A Soviet deputy foreign minister said: "Never ~~again~~ *will* we be caught like this again." They were caught because we had overwhelming nuclear superiority at the time.

Two years later in 1964 Brezhnev had replaced Khrushchev and begun the work of keeping that deputy foreign ministers promise. He began increasing the resources dedicated to military programs. By 1969 the Soviets had passed us in numbers of ~~IC~~ *(ICBM)* Intercontinental Ballistic Missiles ~~(ICBM)~~ silos. By 1970 with a Gross National Product only half as great as ours they were spending more on arms than we were.

Now follow the~~se~~*is* timetable Tom Reed has put together, remembering that in 1962 we had about an 8 to 1 edge over the Soviets. By 1971 they outnumbered us in tactical aircraft. By 1973 their surface navy outnumbered ours. Also in 1973 they flew ~~the~~ their multiple independently targeted re-entry vehicles (MIRVs). These are the multiple nuclear warheads carried by one rocket which separate in flight and fly on to different targets. We had ~~thought~~ *them* but thought ~~they~~ *the Russians* were years away from catching up. By 1974 they passed us in the number of submarine launching tubes for nuclear missiles. They also added one mil. men to their armed forces. By 1975 their spending on strategic offensive nuclear forces was double ours & seven times as much in the field of ballistic missiles.

Also In '75 they began full scale production & deployment of the Backfire supersonic long-range bomber. They called it a medium range aircraft but it is capable of attacking targets in the U.S. By 1976 they deployed their Delta-~~Class~~ class submarines equipped with a new 4200 mile ~~range~~ missile. We have a comparable submarine system called the Trident.—It wont be on line till 1981. In 1977 they demonstrated a non-nuclear weapon capable of knocking our satellites out of space.

And now it is 1978 and the Soviets are preparing to test their 5th generation of ICBM's while they undergo a massive replacement of existing missiles with a 4th generation system. We completed our last Minuteman Silo in 1967.

This is RR   Thanks for listening. ❖

SALT Talks II
July 31, 1978

What time is it on history's clock for us as a nation? The other day a very noted scholar told me his estimate was—"5 minutes to midnight." I'll be right back.

On the last broadcast I quoted a former Sec. of the Air Force TOM REED regarding the Soviet buildup of mil. ~~force~~ *power* and the dates ~~for~~ by which they had achieved significant mileposts. Today I'd like to continue and start with a future date—1985.

Quite a while ago I did a commentary ~~on that date~~ *which involved* 1985. ~~In~~ Our mil. intelligence had learned that Brezhnev ~~in 1973~~ told a secret meeting of Communist leaders that detente was a strategem to allow the Soviets time to build up their military so that by 1985 they could exert their will wherever they wished.

Former Sec. Reed asks, "what is it about 1985 that captures Brezhnevs attention?" Then he points out that both the CIA & an independent study led by the Mass. Inst. of Technology point to world oil shortages beginning in about 1981. Right now the Soviet U. is supplying oil to it's East European satellites who cant afford to buy ~~oil~~ *it* from the OPEC nations. ~~H~~Tom suggests that the Soviets will not let those satellites starve for energy in the mid 80's and points to the 1500 mile border Russia has with ~~Iran~~ oil rich Iran.~~ ~~Then there is~~ *and the conflicting* interests of Russia & Norway in *the* North Sea oil. ~~He asks~~

To those who think "detente" is working because things seem to be quiet right now Tom says "it's always quiet when you are feeding the alligator—when you throw him an arm or leg every now & then—when you drop Angola or Somalia over the side without much of a splash, when you kill the B-1 & abort the MX missile. Under those circumstances" HE SAYS "things are bound to be quiet—except for the munching & crunching." Will places like Iran or Norway be fed to the alligator when the time comes?

If we started right now to resume production of the B-1, it wouldn't be operational until 1985. If we moved ahead on the MX missiles they couldn't be deployed until 1984.

We are negotiating the Salt II treaty from a position of weakness. Very shortly a proposed agreement will be presented to the Senate for ratification and without doubt that agreement will be flawed and not in our best interest. It would be easy to say we should respond with a flat "no." The answer is not that simple. There should be ~~the~~ *a* most thorough & painstaking study of Salt II particularly with regard to our right to verify whether or not Russia could cheat. If the answer is that Russia could and if the treaty is (as it probably will be) balanced in Russias favor, the Senate should reject it. <u>But</u> at the same time the Congress should be prepared to go forward with a mil. buildup of our own.

Tom Reed reminds us of Somerset Maughams* admonition: "If a nation values anything <u>more</u> than freedom, it will lose it's freedom; and the irony of it is, that if it's comfort or money *THAT* it values more, it will lose that too."

We can have the strategic superiority we had in 1962 if we have the will. ~~Or~~ Or as former Air Force Sec. Reed ~~says~~ *asks,* "will our national leaders ~~in con~~ face the 1980's alone, with nothing but a broad smile & good intentions to protect us in our final days."

This is RR   Thanks for listening. ❖

SALT II
November 28, 1978

As decision time on Salt II draws near, evidence increases, ~~that~~ indicating that we are still being out traded by the Soviets. I'll be right back.

Most of us by now are familiar with the names of weapons systems being discussed in the Salt II talks, ICBM's., Submarine launched missiles, cruise missiles etc. Here is one that has a new sound—"D.T's." No I'm not talking about that "pink elephant on the wall," result of too much imbibing of strong drink—"Delirium Tremens."

The D.T.'s the Russians are talking about are "depressed trajectory missiles." Is that a new one for you? It is for me. Well these are missiles which fly lower than standard ballistic missiles thereby reaching the target in about half the time of the normal ~~hih~~ high trajectory ~~missiles~~ *weapons.*

Such a missile launched from a Submarine—say 100 miles offshore would reach it's target in 4 min's. That dosen't give much warning time even if it is picked up by radar.

The question that has been raised is whether the Soviets will demand a concession from ~~the~~ us if they agree to a mutual abandonment of such a weapon system. It is reported that Pres. Carter leans toward such a mutual

---

*William Somerset Maugham.

abandonment because it would lower the risk of surprise attack & thus make the world a safer place.

The answer to the question is that the Soviet U. will not ask for any new concession from us in return for giving up the D.T. missile. Surprised? Well dont be. You see we are way ahead of them in this particular technology and a mutual abandonment would mean we were already making a concession by giving up something we have and the Russians dont. This seems to be a habit with us. We repeatedly sacrifice the product of our advanced technology—the B-1 bomber, the neutron warhead and now possibly this low flying missile with it's potential for surprise.

The question that should be asked is, what will the Soviets give up if we agree to sacrifice our technological lead? If the object of the Salt II talks is to reduce the possibility of war, what better way is there than to stay so far ahead in weaponry that Russia's imperialistic desires will be inhibited? Inhibited because of their inability to embark on aggression without suffering unacceptable damage.

An Air Force study of fighter aircraft performance in the Korean war provides a convincing answer with regard to the importance of technology. The Russian Mig 15 could perform every maneuver better than our F-86. But the F-86 almost always won in combat against the Soviet plane. At first we *JUST* assumed our pilots were better.—Then an air force study discovered that while the Mig could outperform us on every single maneuver it could not make the transition from one maneuver to another as fast as the F-86.

Giving up our unquestioned lead in our D.T.'s is enough to give a fellow a case of the D.T.'s—the out of a bottle kind.

This is RR   Thanks for listening. ❖

SALT II
December 12, 1978

The script has been written, casting is going on and soon the curtain will go up on the great drama "Please Pass The Salt." I'll be right back.

In view of what I'm about to say let me preface my remarks with a statement. I'm sure all of us would like nothing better than to see the two great superpowers, the U.S. and the Soviet U. agree to a real and effective reduction of armaments, a reduction that would not be one sided, ~~thus increasing~~ *one that would increase* not decreas~~eing the~~ *our* hope for *LASTING* peace.

But as the time nears for submission of a so-called Salt II treaty to the Senate for ratification there is a growing fear among knowledgeable & responsible people that the treaty may be dangerously unbalanced. ~~for~~ Granted no one has seen the treaty, ~~but~~ *nevertheless* leaks have led to a widespread suspicion that restrictions on Russias war, winning ability will be far less than the restraints the treaty will impose on us.

Last June the State Dept. issued a pamphlet called "The Salt Process." * It was designed to sell the people on strategic arms control. Again I say, all of us are agreed on the worth of real strategic arms limitation, but the State Dept. was trying to sell a treaty ~~that~~ which had not even been negotiated.

Now while we await at least a preview of what the negotiations have ~~been~~ accomplished we see a sales campaign being put together in our Capital. Preparations are underway to convince the people that a treaty which has not yet been formulated will be good for us.

A Calif. Sen. Alan Cranston is holding weekly study sessions to educate *Senate* staffers on strategic issues. Key aides to Sen. Gary Hart of Col.** are participating. One cant help but wonder ~~if~~ why, if these two Senators know enough about the treaty to do this they dont just tell their colleagues what they know. Maybe they have told one. Sen. Kennedy has authored several articles praising the treaty. But why then ~~is~~ has a long time Senator, experienced in mil. affairs, Sen. Jackson*** of their own party, come out so strongly against the treaty?

Meanwhile the State Dept. has organized a training program for potential speakers & a series of presentations for community groups. Special briefings have been given organizations such as the Nat. Council of Churches & there are more planned. Key business leaders & others will be invited to the White House for *a* special sprinkling of Salt.

But it is the Senators who must ratify or not ratify the treaty and their decision must be based on one thing alone—is it good for the United States. Why are they *apparently* going to be the last to ~~hear about the treaty~~ *learn what the treaty contains?*

Even the normal, courtesey INFORMATION pipeline from the Pentagon to retired high ranking officers has been shut down. Is it possible the scenario is a repeat of the Panama treaty? Will we be told the treaty is ready? ~~and at the same time it is~~ *Then will it be* initialed in a public ceremony while Congress is in recess? ~~Then of course~~ The Senate ~~will~~ *will of course* be pressured to simply stamp it approved rather than embarrass any of the principle characters involved.

---

*Department of State Publication 8947, General Foreign Policy Series 306, June 1978.
**Democrat.
***Senator Edward Kennedy (D-Massachusetts) and Senator Henry M. Jackson (D-Washington).

Perhaps the Senate should speak first and tell the admin. what ~~will~~ it will & will not accept in a treaty.

This is RR   Thanks for listening. ❖

SALT II—Part I
March 27, 1979

There is one thing most of us dont know about polls & should; many times the result is determined ~~by~~ in advance by the way the question is asked.

I'll be right back.

† At least once a week if not more often we read or hear the result of a*n* *opinion* poll. The majority of pollsters are in my opinion conscientious, honest and pretty dependable. We must realize however that pollsters dont ask questions just to satisfy their own curiosity. They are employed by others and sometimes those others want specific questions asked in a specific way. A simple truth in polling is, "if you ask the wrong questions, you get the wrong answers."

Here is a case in point. Most polls in recent months having to do with U.S. foreign policy and our defensive strength vis-a-vis the Soviet U. have shown a growing concern on the part of the American people. It is safe to say that Americans do not trust the Soviet U. and feel wc are in or close to a dangerous situation.

Now it is possible to say this is borne out by a CBS-N.Y. Times poll regarding the Salt II treaty. The poll shows almost 2/3–63% of the respondents ~~saying, "yes,"~~ favoring such a treaty.

On top of that comes an NBC–Associated Press Poll in which 81% apparently support the Salt II agreement. The tendency is to accept these figures as ~~proof~~ evidence that Americans are worried about our mil. strength or lack of it.

But how do these figures relate to all the evidence that we dont trust the Russians? If there is a lack of trust shouldn't there be a real concern about whether we could depend on the Russians to keep the treaty?

These questions were on the minds of a number of distinguished Americans of both pol. parties who make up the "Committee On The Present Danger." * These are well informed people in the areas of foreign policy & national defense—many of them former cabinet members in both Dem. &

---

*At the suggestion of Richard Allen, a foreign policy adviser to Reagan, the Committee on the Present Danger sent its polls to Reagan on March 14, 1979. See Pre-Presidential Papers, Box 12. Ronald Reagan Presidential Library.

Repub. administrations. They are, as the the name of the group implies, concerned with our present defense policy and dedicated to presenting the truth to the American people.

They decided to look for some answers to the questions bothering them. An inspection of the questions asked in the 2 polls revealed the respondents had been asked simply whether they favored the concept of arms limitation and a limit on strategic ~~mil.~~ (read that nuclear) weapons. It is surprising ~~that~~ *in view of the questions that* the polls didn't get a 100% affirmative response.

Then, and we should be grateful to them, the Committee commissioned it's own poll. The answers were quite different than those offered by CBS–N.Y. Times & NBC–Associated Press. On the next broadcast—tune in same station same time—I'll tell you the ~~que~~ answers they obtained <u>& the questions</u> they asked. I hope our U.S. Senators will see this poll before they vote on Salt. II.

This is RR Thanks for listening.

†Send copy of each of these to Charles Tyroler II—letter attached. RR ❖

SALT II—Part II
March 27, 1979

Today <u>takes</u> off where the ~~last~~ previous commentary <u>left</u> off—the question of polling and what the questions have to do with surprisingly contradictory answers.

I'll be right back.

On the previous broadcast I told of 3 polls & that the answers to the 3ʳᵈ were quite different from those obtained on the first 2.

CBS–N.Y. Times & NBC-Associated Press ~~both~~ *each* took a poll in which the respondents were simply asked whether we should or should not have an agreement with the Russians limiting strategic nuclear weapons. You'd think everyone would say "yes" to such a question and most people did. In one poll the yes vote was 63% in the other 81%.

~~In the face of published data showing that the American people are increasingly suspicious of Soviet intentions and concerned about our mil. strength relative to the Soviet U. The Committee On The Present Danger whic~~

Only the results of the polls—(not the questions) were made public. ~~and~~ *They were* used to ~~support~~ *convey* the idea that Americans are overwhelmingly in support of the Salt II agreement.

This was disturbing to "The Committee On The Present Danger," a bipartisan group of distinguished citizens concerned about our declining defense capability. Knowing that most published data shows the American people are increasingly suspicious of Soviet intentions the committee ~~made~~ made it a point to find out what questions had been asked in the polls. Then they did some polling of their own. There was quite a different result.

A reputable pollster was employed and a series of questions, each one highly specific, ~~was asked~~ *and all dealing* specifically with Salt II were asked of the respondents. The ~~results~~ responses show that the American people are skeptical about Salt II, dont know much about it and are not prepared to support it without additional safeguards.

Less than 10% strongly supported Salt II and a comparable number strongly opposed it. A slightly larger group reluctantly supported it in spite of some misgivings. In other words the vast support the treaty is supposed to have comes down to 20.3%. By contrast 41.7% more than twice as many would have to see more safeguards before they would support it and almost 30% say they dont know enough about it to have an opinion.

There was a true, false question which revealed the people are not only uninformed, they've been mis-informed. Almost ~~half~~ *With the dont knows excluded more than half* said the treaty would require both Nations to reduce defense spending. They are wrong. ~~Almost $\frac{2}{3}$~~ *A full* $\frac{3}{4}$ said the treaty would limit the explosive power of nuclear warheads. They are wrong. ~~Almost 60%~~ *More than* $\frac{2}{3}$ said the treaty would require each side to reduce it's ability to make a nuclear attack on the other. They are wrong. ~~And a like percentage~~ *Almost* $\frac{3}{4}$—71% said the treaty would provide for verification to ~~in~~sure the other side wasn't cheating. They are wrong. And the 68% who thought the treaty would regulate the number of strategic missiles or warheads each side could have are wrong.

This poll ~~proves~~ demonstrates that a searching national debate should be held and that the admin. should give the American people the unvarnished facts about the treaty—what it will & will not do. This the admin. has not done.

This is RR   Thanks for listening. ❖

SALT II
October 2, 1979

Why should there be such a debate as we are having over the Salt II agreement?

I'll be right back

When negotiations began on the 2ⁿᵈ Strategic Arms Limitation Treaty with the Soviet U. 5 specific objectives were named as essential to protect our national interests. They were: To establish equal nuclear capabilities for the U.S. & the Soviet U;—Secure significant Soviet arms reductions, especially in those areas where Soviet offensive forces pose the greatest threat; Stabilize the situation between the 2 countries so that neither would be tempted to strike first during an international crisis;—Reduce the effect of nuclear weapons on world politics;—Enforce <u>verifiable</u> limitations to which both countries must adhere.

Those are reasonable terms and certainly fair to both the U.S. & the Soviet U. Why then should our Senate waste even 5 minutes debating the Salt II agreement? It meets none of the 5 specifics we listed as essential to protect our national interest.

Point one called for equal nuclear capabilities. Note that word, "capabilities." We didn't say equal numbers. The Soviet missiles are far more powerful than ours and the agreement permits them to go ahead with some 300 giant missiles each armed with a number of separately targeted warheads. We are not permitted to have anything similar. Oh we can have the same number of missiles but it's like comparing ~~warships~~ *BATTLESHIPS* to row boats.

Then there is that point about stabilizing the situation so that neither side would be tempted to settle an argument by launching a nuclear first strike. Sec. of Defense Harold Brown has admitted that virtually all our I.C.B.M's, a substantial number of nuclear missile carrying submarines and many of our B-52 bombers would be vulnerable to a Soviet first strike.

Even though some of our European allies express a hope that Salt II will be ratified one cant help but wonder if they are sincere or if they are worried about the Russian Bear sitting right on their borders. Privately they confess to many misgivings. They had counted on the effectiveness of a new weapon, the cruise missile with at least a 1500 kilometer range for their own protection. We ~~barg~~ let the Soviets bargain that down to a 600 kilometer range which puts most Soviet targets beyond it's reach.

Then there ~~was~~ *is* the supersonic Russian Backfire Bomber minutes away from their heartlands. We agreed not to even include those bombers among the weapons to be limited by Salt II. We did likewise with an intermediate range nuclear missile the Soviet SS 20, deployed and able to reach every Capital City in Europe.

And as for verifiability of whether they are keeping their part of the treaty—it just doesn't exist. Salt II allows the Soviet U. mil. advantages which are denied the U.S. Salt II will not increase the chance for World Peace.

This is RR. Thanks for listening. ❖

Reagan weaves a speech by Eugene Rostow into his own analysis of detente, SALT II, and the history of U.S. foreign policy. He devotes more than a week to this subject. Rostow became President Reagan's first director of the Arms Control and Disarmament Agency.

Rostow I
October 10, 1978

For the next few days I'd like to bring you some passages from a memorable speech which may frighten you—in fact it should. I'll be right back.

I know you've heard or seen news reports of warnings by former defense dept. officials, retired mil. personnel and others that our nation is in danger, our defenses ~~weak~~ inadequate and our attitude about Russia unrealistic. I know too that many Americans including members of Cong. dismiss these warnings as coming from advocates of the MIL.-industrial ~~mil.~~ complex & therefore suspect.

But on July 25ᵗʰ ~~of~~ *in* this year of our lord 1978 a man of unquestioned liberal credentials, Sterling Prof. of Law at *the* Yale Law School, former Under Sec. of State for Pol. Affairs under the Johnson admin., Eugene V. Rostow addressed a Conf. on U.S. Security & the Soviet Challenge.

There is no way Eugene Rostow could be called a Hawk or a tool of the mil. interests. That's why his address should be heard by every American. He opened his remarks ~~by~~ saying: "My assignment today is to examine the Salt II agreement now in prospect & to consider whether it is in the nat. security interests of the U.S."

He acknowledged the desirability of having a treaty that abolished nuclear weapons and recalled an episode we should all recall with pride, the 1947 offer of the Baruch plan. That was the ~~offer~~ PROPOSAL we made to put our nuclear weapons and nuclear knowledge in the hands of an international agency ~~to~~ *which would* develope nuclear energy for peaceful uses. We had a nuclear monopoly at the time. We could have commanded the world to do our bidding.

The Soviet U. rejected the Baruch plan, signaling us that ~~they~~ it intended embarking on an Imperial course rather than joining in peaceful, postwar cooperation.

Prof. Rostow then addressed himself to the subject of Salt II & to the pol. & pub. relations experts led by Hamilton Jordan who are trying to explain ~~the~~ Salt II to the Am. people. He referred to them as the "Salt Sellers." And he said, "they claim too much for the agreement. The admin. & it's supporters portray those who question Salt II as monsters of iniquity who oppose arms control and lust for nuclear war with the Soviet U." And he cautioned against *accepting* political mythology.

"For nearly a century," he said, "there has been a current of opinion in the English speaking countries that arms limitation agreements are an IM-PORTANT instrument of peace—and it is tenaciously held, resisting the challenge of contrary experience." He described the arguments in behalf of "Salt" as the same used in behalf of the Wash. Naval Treaty of 1922 when we sank scores of our warships & Britain did the same. Prof. Rostow said: "The Wash. Naval Treaty & it's progeny led straight to Pearl Harbor." He cited several other such post-W.W.I. agreements as helping to bring on W.W.II. Now we are told that without Salt II," he said "we'll bring back the "Cold War."

Well listen to Rostow on ~~that. "T~~ *t*he notion that Soviet-Am. relations have improved in recent years; that the cold war is over:—"The fact is the Cold War is not over. On the contrary it is worse than it has ever been, featured by Soviet threats & thrusts on a far larger scale than those of the simple days of the Berlin Airlift & the Crisis in Greece."

To be continued—This is RR   Thanks for listening. ❧

Rostow II
October 10, 1978

This commentary will be more of the address by Eugene Rostow concerning our security & the Salt talks. I'll be right back.

Eminent, liberal scholar Eugene Rostow in his July 25th ~~address~~ assessment of Salt II which he called "A Soft Bargain, A Hard Sell," said, "we have had a Salt agreement with the Sov. U. since 1972." And he added: "Far from stabilizing world pol's., Salt I has been a part of the most turbulent & dangerous period of the cold war."

What are some of the episodes in this period which was to have been stabilized by that treaty? Well for one, "the Soviet U. defaulted on it's obligations as a guarantor of the peace agreements of 1973 in Indo-China." Those agreements which were so hailed by the world after the long years of bloodshed in Vietnam, that Henry Kissinger was awarded the Nobel Peace Prize, were treated by the Soviets as scraps of paper. As Rostow points out: "The final North Vietnamese invasions of S. Vietnam in 1974 could never have taken place without Soviet equipment & other help."

Another episode was the Soviet promise ~~to Pres. Nixon~~ in May of 1972 to cooperate with the U.S. in seeking peace in the Middle East. Again as Rostow points out; "It violated those promises by supplying, planning, encouraging,

& even participating in the Arab aggression against Israel of Oct. 1973." He goes on to say the intention was, "not only to crush Israel, but also to out-flank Nato, to neutralize Europe and to drive us out of ~~the~~ Europe & the Mediterranean. For the moment, the Soviet plan was to defeated by the brilliant victory of Israel's armed forces, backed by supplies from the U.S." But Rostow adds: "The Soviets patiently pursue their strategic goal."

Sec. of State Rogers testified to our Senate that we had made a number of unilateral interpretations of the first Salt treaty that we should regard any breach of these policies by the Soviet U. as a violation of the "spirit" of the Treaty. All these unilateral interpretations of the treaty were violated by the Soviet U. & we did nothing.

Prof. Rostow says: "The point is obvious and by now beyond dispute. The Soviet U. is engaged in a policy of imperial expansion all over the world, despite the supposedly benign influence of Salt I, and its various commitments of cooperation in the name of detente. The Sov. U. is pursuing that course with accelerating momentum."

He called attention to the most recent manifestations of that momentum in Yemen & Afghanistan—far away places many of us might not be able to locate immediately on a world map. But places of unquestioned importance to anyone bent on world conquest. Rostow says the Soviet moves in those countries result from 2 related forces: "the startling buildup of Soviet strategic & conventional forces during the last 16 yrs., & the paralyzing impact on American politics of our collapse in Vietnam."

I'll continue summarizing Eugene Rostows address in the next commentary.

This is RR   Thanks for listening. ❖

Rostow III
October 10, 1978

Todays *commentary* is a continuation of Eugene Rostows summing up of our position vis a vis the Soviet U.

I'll be right back.

For 2 broadcasts now I've been quoting from an address by Eugene Rostow on the declining position of the U.S. in the face of the growth of Soviet mil. power. That growth over the last 16 yrs. is, "without parallel in modern history. Both our govt. & the British govt." according to Rostow, "have said formally that the Soviet mil. posture and dispositions are offensive in character, & cannot be explained by considerations of defense."

The Sov. mil. budget is 40 to 80% more per year than our own in real terms. Our Sec. of defense ~~is~~ has described the situation as the fable of the tortoise & the hare. We sat back deceived by the belief that we had "overkill" capacity. We cut our mil. budgets by half while the Soviets increased theirs. "Now," as Rostow says, "we are behind in almost every relevant category of mil. power—behind in production; behind in research; and behind in programming." The Am. people are clearly in favor of regaining the mil. position of number 1 but like the hare, officialdom is still sleeping under the tree.

According to the Prof. there is still time to head off a collision between the Soviets & ourselves. It means stepping up our own rearmament and a vigorous, active diplomacy with our allies to restore a pattern of world order based on the charter of the U.N. But this is only possible if we participate as the leader of such an effort. And our nuclear arsenal is as Rostow says "the indispensable foundation for any such program."

He sums up this necessary effort to head off a disastrous collision with this paragraph which I shall quote: "The success of such an effort will depend <u>not</u> upon Salt treaties but upon the reality of the mil. balance and the energy, self confidence, & imagination of our diplomatic campaign. In that process arms limitation agreements with the Soviet U. could play a modest part, <u>if</u> they are genuinely fair, balanced, and verefiable, and are not allowed to induce euphoria about 'detente.' But such agreements cannot significantly alter the cost of our defense programs. We must undertake now to spend quite a lot of money to restore the mil. balance. For years to come, the presence or absence of Salt II would not increase the cost of defense for the U.S. by up to $100 bil. as proponents of Salt claim. Those figures of extra costs if the Salt negotiations fails, or if the Sen. refuses to consent to the treaty, are just as fanciful as the claims of "detente.""

Next broadcast I'll get into Prof. Rostows discussion of nuclear weapons and their role in politics & modern warfare.

This is RR   Thanks for listening. ❖

Rostow IV
October 10, 1978

Today we'll talk of Rostows view of the role of strategic nuclear weapons in modern Po*LITICS*. & warfare.

I'll be right back.

For the last 3 broadcasts I've been excerpting & quoting from an address by Eugene Rostow on our defense posture and the significance of the continuing Salt talks.

It must be understood that strategic nuclear weapons play a role in modern politics and have a bearing on the entire process of world politics. It is often said the goal of our nuclear forces is to deter or make less credible the possibility of war. It is however a mistake to believe that deterrence is also the goal of Soviet nuclear policy.

As Rostow says: "Effective American nuclear deterrence cannot alone keep the Soviet U. from using conventional forces, at least against targets they think we regard as secondary, like Vietnam or Ethiopia. Except for massive attacks on our most vital interests, like Western Europe or Japan defense has to be provided by conventional forces, at least in the 1ˢᵗ instance. But the absence of effective nuclear deterrence would have a disastrous effect, denying all credibility to our conventional force deterrent."

To understand what he means we must review our experience back to 1945 when we had a monopoly on nuclear weapons. In Greece, Turkey, the Berlin airlift, Korea, the Cuban missile crisis, the nuclear weapon was always a decisive ~~weapon~~ *factor* in the background. The Soviets knew that in a nuclear exchange our casualties would have numbered 10 mil. theirs 100 mil. By the middle '60s their buildup had brought us to stalemate. We could no longer hint at the use of nuclear weapons in places like Vietnam.

Now, "there can be no question," says Rostow, "that our position has slipped from stalemate to the borders of inferiority. The strategic force relationship which dominated the Cuban missile crisis will soon be reversed, unless we ~~take~~ *undertake* a crash program immediately—that in the event of a nuclear exchange we should risk <u>100</u> <u>mil.</u> <u>casualties</u> & the Soviet U. <u>10</u> mil."

Rostow correctly points out that if we let such a situation develope: "Our foreign policy & conventional forces would be impotent & we would acquiesce." And of course by acquiesce he means surrender. The end of this great experiment in freedom which has from it's beginning held out hope to a downtrodden mankind all over the world.

"It is the 1ˢᵗ objective of Soviet policy to achieve such a situation"—says Rostow, "Soviet leaders believe it would enable them to determine the future course of world politics."

"This," he says, "is what our nuclear weapons program & the salt negotiations are all about." To those who dismiss the vision of nuclear war as unthinkable, he says, "the vision of Soviet pol. coercion backed by astronomic nuclear & conventional forces is far <u>from</u> unthinkable. No Pres. of the U.S. should ever be put ~~in the~~ into a corner where he would have to choose between the surrender of vital national interests & nuclear holocaust."

This is RR   Thanks for listening. ❖

Rostow V
October 10, 1978

This is number 5 in my summing up of the warnings uttered by Prof. Eugene Rostow with regard to our vulnerability to a Soviet ultimatum.

I'll be right back.

In evaluating the Salt II agreement now being negotiated & the Salt I we've lived under for several years Prof. Rostow points out some frightening possibilities. He raises the question of whether under Salt II we would be able to threaten the Soviets U. with a second strike capability if it should attack us or our allies.

The answer he gives is that the draft of Salt II as we've had indicated in the press deals only with nuclear weapons which could reach the U.S. and that is like a dam across half the river. "We have," as he says, "Vital interests in Western Europe, Canada, Mexico, Japan & other allied nations. It does no good for us to spend 1000's of hours fussing over whether the Backfire bomber can reach the U.S. while it also threatens Western Europe & the Middle East."

"The Soviet U. was allowed in Salt I to have more & larger missile launchers than we because we thought we could stay ahead in Mirving and in accuracy." But 6 fundamental developments have taken place since 1972. The Soviet U. (no.1) has made extremely rapid progress in mirving their missiles. Where ours have 3 warheads, theirs have 8 to 10 and they have greater throw weight ≠ 20 times the destructive power of ours.

Our "Salt sellers" as Rostow calls the admin. spokesmen continue to claim our warheads are the equivalent of the Soviet weapons.—They are not.

The 2nd basic change since 1972 is the Soviet improvement in accuracy of missiles designed to destroy our missiles, planes on the ground & ships in harbor. Hear Mr. Rostow on this: "Soviet Science has achieved a great breakthrough that as a result the Sov. U. is now superior to the U.S. in mil. power; and that the effects of the breakthrough will soon be apparent in world politics."

Thirdly our dependence on submarines now that we've cancelled the B-1 bomber should give us little comfort for the Soviets have made equal breakthroughs in anti-submarine warfare.

Fourth, the Soviet U. has made some of it's Intercontinental Ballistic Missiles mobile. When Salt I was announced assurances were given the Senate that this was not true. Now the admin. confirms it is true.

Fifth, the Soviets now have killer satellites. They can knock from space our communications & spy satellites leaving us blind.

And sixth, there is the Soviet civil defense program. Our leaders continue to tell us that if the Soviets cross certain lines we can kill millions of them without danger to ourselves. This was a plausible answer at the time of the Cuban missile crisis it has "lost long since lost even the appearance of conviction" says Prof. Rostow. He states that, "our fixed site missiles are outclassed in numbers, size, destructive power & survivability by Soviet missiles; we have tossed away our advantage in bombers & our citizen population remains unprotected while the Soviet U. has persevered in air defense, anti ballistic missile programs and in civil defense & evacuation procedures."

Next broadcast the final chapter on Eugene Rostows address. This is RR Thanks for listening. ❖

Rostow VI
October 10, 1978

This is the last of my commentaries on Dr. Eugene Rostows analy *assessment* of Salt II & our position vis-a-vis the Soviet U.—I'll be right back.

Our Sec. of Defense has tried *to* reassure us by saying that a SUCCESSFUL Soviet nuclear strike against our missile silos would be followed by *with* an attack by our submarine launched missiles against Moscow, Leningrad etc. The assumption is that Russia would never launch a 1st strike ≠ and risk our follow up attack. This is hardly a credible assumption since the Russians would have enough nuclear forces to follow up for a second strike against our cities.

Dr. Rostow in the address I've been quoting for the past 5 days sums up our present policy with these words: "Our first new bomber in many years—B-1—has been cancelled. The neutron warhead which might have given Nato a firm shield for 10 yrs. has been remitted to the shades. The U.S. has closed down the Minuteman III production line & delayed the initial operating capability of the missile which was supposed to replace it. MX is on ice for the time being. Furthermore the Trident '(submarine)' prog. has been stretched out." Then he says that while the Pres. assures us our treaty obligations are still firm & we stand behind our allies in the Pacific & Atlantic our former chief of Naval Operations has testified that our navy cant guarantee the sea lanes beyond Hawaii. Sec. of Defense Brown has told the Japanese we cannot assure the naval defense of Japan. We're further reducing our navy, we haven't introduced a new missile system since 1960—the Soviets have unveiled 5. Just what is Salt II supposed to do for us?

Rostow says: "Around the world, people are seriously worried about our state of mind. They wonder whether we have the understanding & will to defend ourselves & our interests in world politics, or whether we are in a mood of suicidal appeasement. As the brilliant leader of a moderate sized country in Asia said recently, "the greatest external threat" (to his nation) "is the weakness of the West. The West is paralyzed & divided."

Our goal is a stable peace. Who has ever met an American who favored war with the Soviet U.? Rostow concludes with the warning that the Soviet rulers will expand their power as long as the risks are not excessive. His closing lines should be heard by every American. "The kind of Salt agreement the Admin. is so frantically trying to sell the country is not a step toward detente or toward peace, but an act of appeasement which can only invite more Soviet pressure & more risk. It would freeze us in a position of inferiority, deny us the opportunity to redress the balance, weaken our alliances, & isolate us.

It would be a step toward war, not peace."

Those are the thoughts of an unquestioned liberal, a scholar who desires peace above all and who finally spoke out because he thinks we could be on the road to war.

This is RR Thanks for listening.

R ❖

WEAPONS

Reagan says that the neutron bomb is the ideal deterrent weapon because it would help the United States be so strong that the Soviet Union would not want to start a war.

War
March 13, 1978

War is an unpleasant thing to talk about. There have been 4 involving the U.S. in my lifetime. I hope and pray there wont be a 5ᵗʰ. I'll be right back.

Several weeks ago on the TV debate I between Bill Buckley* & myself Admiral (now retired) Zumwalt (now retired) presented a case for ratifying the proposed *PANAMA CANAL* treaties. I've been surprised his remarks didn't cause more stir in the press. He said, "we were likelier to lose an *a* nuclear war with Russia, we were likelier to lose a conventional *ground* war in Europe and we were likelier to lose a naval war" in view of the increased size of

---

*William F. Buckley, Jr.

Radio "War

War is an unpleasant thing to talk about. There ①
have been 4 involving the U.S. in my life time. I hope
and pray there wont be a 5ᵗʰ. I'll be right back.

Several weeks ago on the TV debate ~~be~~
between Bill Buckley & myself Admiral ~~former
retired~~ Zumwalt (now retired) presented a case
for ratifying the ~~proposed~~ (PANAMA CANAL) treaties. I've been
surprised his remarks didn't cause more stir in
the press. He said," we were likelier to lose a
nuclear war with Russia; we were likelier to lose
a conventional (ground) ~~war~~ in Europe and we were
likelier to lose a naval war" in view of the increased
size of the Russian fleet. Then his point was
that we'd have a better chance of using the canal
if Panama were friendly toward us.

Now I'm not bringing this up to argue his
final point. I want to talk about ~~this~~ the frank
pessimism he expressed with regard to our strength
vis a vis the Russians.

We want to avoid a war and that is better
achieved by being so strong that a potential enemy
~~is~~ is not tempted to go adventuring. No one
denies that the Russians have ~~amounted a~~ assembled any offensive ~~load~~
force of tanks, mobile artillery, support aircraft & armored
~~this is in nuclear you~~

personnel carriers on the Western front in Europe
superior to our ~~Nato~~ forces. Until recently our
deterrent was nuclear superiority. If the Soviets
attacked Western Europe we could threaten Russia
with nuclear destruction. That of course is no
longer true.

It is at this point that a possible new
weapons system is in a sense discovered by us; one
which can provide the deterrent we need to any
Russian attack. It is the ~~neutron~~ neutron bomb.

Very simply it is the dreamed of death ray [2]
weapon of science fiction. It kills enemy soldiers
but doesn't blow up the surrounding countryside or
destroys villages, towns & cities. It wont even
destroy an enemy tank — just kill the tank crew.

Now some express horror at this and charging
immorality portray those who would use such a weapon as placing
a higher value on property than human life. This
is ~~sheer unadulterated~~ It is harsh sounding but all
~~nonsense~~. war weapons back to the club, the sling & the arrow
are designed to kill the soldiers of the enemy. With
gunpowder & artillery & later bombs & bombers war
could not be confined to the battlefield. And so came
total war with non-combatants outnumbering soldiers in
casualties.

Here is a deterrent weapon available to us at much
lower cost than trying to match the enemy gun for gun, tank
for tank, plane for plane. It isn't unreasonable to believe
that the Soviets will be most hesitant to send those
waves of tanks westward if we have a weapon that
can wipe out their crews at virtually no cost to ourselves.
Indeed the neutron bomb represents a moral
~~enf...~~ improvement in the horror that is modern
war. It just may be that the neutron bomb could
~~be~~ the ideal ~~the~~ deterrent weapon — one that wouldn't
have to be used. This is RR Thanks for listening.

the Russian fleet. Then his point was that we'd have a better chance of using the canal if Panama were friendly toward us.

Now I'm not bringing this up to argue his final point. I want to talk about ~~his~~ the frank pessimism he expressed with regard to our strength vis a vis the Russians.

We want to avoid a war and that is better achieved by being so strong that a potential enemy ~~is~~ is not tempted to go adventuring. No one denies that the Russians have ~~assumed a lead over us in nuclear we~~ *assembled an offensive force of tanks, mobile artillery, support* aircraft & armored personnelle carriers on the Western front in Europe superior to our Nato forces. Until recently our deterrent was nuclear superiority. If the Soviets attacked Western Europe we could threaten Russia with nuclear destruction. That of course is no longer true.

It is at this point that a possible new weapons system is in a sense discovered by us; one which can provide the deterrent we need to any Russian attack. It is the ~~dreamed~~ *neutron* bomb.

Very simply ~~int~~ is the dreamed of death ray weapon of science fiction. It kills enemy soldiers but dosen't blow up the surrounding countryside or destroys villages, towns & cities. It wont even destroy an enemy tank—just kill the tank crew.

Now some express horror at this and ~~portray~~ *charging immorality portray* those who would use such a weapon as placing a higher value on property than human life. This is *sheer unadulterated* nonsense. It is harsh sounding but all *war* weapons back to the club, the sling & the arrow are designed to kill the soldiers of the enemy. With gunpowder & artillery & later bombs & bombers war could not be confined to the battlefield. And so came total war with non-combatant's outnumbering soldiers in casualties.

Here is a deterrent weapon available to us at much lower cost than trying to match the enemy gun for gun, tank for tank, plane for plane. It isn't unreasonable to believe that the Soviets will be most hesitant to send those waves of tanks westward if we have a weapon that can wipe out their crews at virtually no cost to ourselves. Indeed the neutron bomb represents a moral ≠ improvement in the horror that is modern war. It just may be that the neutron bomb could ~~be most~~ *be* the ideal ≠ deterrent weapon—one that wouldn't have to be used. This is RR   Thanks for listening. ❖

Here Reagan expresses his deep concern about the national security implications of President Carter's June 30, 1977 announcement that the deployment plans for the B-1 bomber were being halted.

B-1 Bomber
April 3, 1978

The people of America have a right to know more than we've been told by our govt. about the cancelled B-1 Bomber. I'll be right back.

It has been several months since the Pres. announced his decision to halt production of the B-1 Bomber. I've found, out in the country there is an unease on the part of the people about our *entire* defense posture and the cancellation of the B.-1 is a~~ ~~kind of symbolic of that unease. ~~And~~ Yet we've been given very little information about the plane and only the administrations explanation that it was too expensive and we could easily find less costly substitutes.

Perhaps we weren't told more about the B-1 because the facts reveal the arguments supporting it's cancellation are not true. We are told the B-1 had a price tax of $100 mil. and it was vulnerable to the Soviet Air Defense system. Well no one ~~knows~~ can look with pleasure on a $100 mil. aircraft being knocked down by anti-aircraft fire. First we should know that $100 mil. price tax is figured in 1986 dollars on the basis that inflation will continue. The real price tag is about $65 mil.—still a tidy sum.

It was pointed out that the Air launched cruise missle could be made for $1 mil. and launched by re-fitted B-52's, F-111's or even 747's from outside Russias perimiter. Now this is true—as far as it goes. *But* The 747 modified costs more than the B-1 and of course is (with it's size) extremely vulnerable. The B-52 can only carry half the pay load of the B-1 even though it's almost twice as big & the modification required is quite expensive—especially when you consider you are talking 2 B-52's. to substitute for ~~one~~ *a* SINGLE B-1. The B-1 incidentally travels twice as fast as the B-52 & being so much smaller is less vulnerable because of it's reduced radar image. It shows up on a radar screen about ~~like~~ *the size of* a fighter plane.

The F-111 would have to be stretched and be fitted with the same engines designed for the B-1. It would carry less than the B-52. It would not be as good as the B-1—just cheaper.

Now the ALCM.—(air launched cruise missile) which we were told made it possible to scuttle the B-1. The B-1 was in production and already flying, a war plane so far advanced beyond anything we have that the world would be years trying to match it. ~~The Cruise missile~~ *We* cant start producing cruise missiles until 1981 if then. There have been 4 successive failures in ~~its~~ ~~≠~~ *the* test's so far & finding out why could set back the production date even farther.

The Cruise missiles are limited in range, so many Soviet targets would be out of reach. To extend the range it must be launched from planes flying at great heights which increases vulnerability to Soviet ground to air missiles. The B-1 is designed to go in low beneath radar, penetrating the enemy air defense system before *LAUNCHING THE CRUISE MISSILES.*

If the Pres. has information that the Soviets have a new defense system which makes the B-1 less useful he ~~can~~ *SHOULD* tell us. It wont be a surprise to the Soviets. If not, then we know the Soviets will have to spend more *than the B-1's cost* ~~than we will~~ to ~~find such a defense & that's good~~ *develope a defense against them & what's wrong with that?*

This is RR   Thanks for listening. ❖

Miscellaneous I
May 29, 1979

Here are a few items regarding life behind the Iron Curtain that you might find interesting.

I'll be right back.

With the Salt II treaty coming closer it's interesting to see what the Soviet attitude is. Supposedly we are in the final stages of ~~negotiation~~ *negotiating* the treaty terms and supposedly the Soviets are eager to have the agreement ratified by our Senate.

One cant help but suspect that their eagerness might be because they'll get more ~~of~~ *out* of the treaty than we will. Our President is telling us that Salt II holds out the promise of peace and an end to any *costly* arms race. But what does that do to us if we are the only ones not racing?

Some weeks ago the Soviet U. took off into the wild blue yonder ~~with~~ *testing* a new, intercontinental, *bomber of* supersonic speed. ~~bomber.~~ They already have a bomber called the Backfire which will not be covered by the Salt treaty because the Russians say it's only ~~a~~ *of* medium ~~bomber~~ *range*. Our Air force says it can reach American targets which is the measure of a strategic ~~bomber~~ *aircraft*—still it isn't included in the treaty.

This new plane strangely enough looks remarkably like the American B-1 bomber the President cancelled.

The next Soviet surprise was the testing of an SS18 intercontinental ballistic missile carrying 14 separate ~~nuclear~~ warheads. Apparently Salt II was ready to permit the deployment of this new giant missile with 10 warheads. With this agreed to—why are they testing ~~14~~ *one* with 14? Unless they have no more intention of keeping the terms of Salt II than they did of Salt I and those they violated from the 1ˢᵗ day. Incidentally our CIA & therefore the admin. knew about the 14 warheads for 2 months before the Pentagon learned of ~~it~~ it.

Here is another item *by way of the NAT. REVIEW BULLETIN* from behind the Iron Curtain on an entirely different subject. One thing we know about Communism is that everyone is equal. There is no aristocracy, no ruling class in the workers paradise. Every ~~person~~ *citizen* starts equal to every other citizen and they stay equal.

Well maybe some are a wee bit more equal than others. Take Rumania where the Communist party boss *NICOLAE CEAUCESCU** is President & Commander in Chief. His wife is a member of the Party's permanent bureau and also the pol. executive committee. Their son is sec. of the Union of Communist Youth. They have another son who is a top physicist at the Maghuiele Nuclear Center. Ceaucescu has a brother who is a Major General & lecturer at the Rumanian mil. academy. Another brother is minister of agriculture and a 3ʳᵈ brother is a Senior correspondent of the partys daily newspaper. Would you believe there is a 4ᵗʰ and he runs the Rumanian ec. agency in Vienna? Dont go way—the 5ᵗʰ brother is consul-general in Kiev.

Just to round things out there is a sister who is married to the former Prime Minister. He resigned in March because of ill health. But that's alright because another sister is married to the new Prime Minister.

A nephew is minister of foreign trade and another nephew is deputy Prime minister. Ceaucescus brother in law is state sec. in the ministry of machinery.

And this is RR. Thanks for listening. ❧

As he did in the back-to-back commentaries on a speech by Eugene Rostow, Reagan devotes a series of commentaries to defense. He quotes from an article about the B-52 bomber, which says that despite the Carter administration's statements to the contrary, the B-52 does not have the performance capability of the B-1 bomber.

Defense I
September 11, 1979

Are you as an American ready to accept the truth about our ability to protect this land of the free & home of the brave? I'll be right back.

As debate rages over the ~~me~~ merits or demerits of Salt II how many of us know our situation vis-a-vis the Soviet Union? The Admin. ~~tells~~ told us *FOR*

---

*Nicolae Ceausescu.

EXAMPLE when it cancelled the B-1 bomber that our aging B-52's. were equal to the task & the B-1 wasn't needed. Were they telling us the truth?

The answer to that is N-O- no. The B-1 was designed to go into enemy territory, skimming the tree tops at super-sonic speed, carrying cruise missiles ~~It was~~ guided & guarded by the ultimate in electronic devices. The B-52 is only half as fast and when modified to carry cruise missiles ~~it~~ can only carry half as ~~much pay load and~~ *many*. It was never intended for low level flight. It was meant to go in at extremely high altitudes. And it is old—older than many of the men flying it. When spare parts are needed & they are needed very often these days, they are taken from the few hundred B-52's consigned to the airplane bone pile in the Ariz. desert.

The men flying the 52's have to be the most uncomplaining, gallant heros we've ever had in our armed forces. They know better than anyone how nearly impossible is their task of being part of our quote-unquote "1ˢᵗ line of defense."

Arthur T. Hadley ~~of the Wash. Star~~ *WHO WRITES FREQUENTLY ON MIL. MATTERS* flew ~~a~~ low level ~~mission~~ *in a B-52* across Louisiana, ~~the badlands~~ Okla. & Kansas on a practise mission simulating a penetration of the Iron curtain. His story of the 9½ hour ~~mis~~ flight appeared on the editorial page of the *WASH* Star.* It should have appeared on the front page of every paper in the U.S.

I am going to quote extensively from his article because it contains information the Russians probably already know but Americans dont. And I'll be quoting him on the next few broadcasts.

Hadley approached the flight line at 4:30 in the morning wearing the *SAME* green flame-proof clothes the crew was wearing. Even the name tag is flame proof. ~~Even t~~Though this was a simulated mission everyone was serious at the briefing on the weather. When you fly at 400 *PLUS* miles an hour at 200 ft. in an airplane with a 400 ft. wing spread Mr. Hadley says, "there is no time for fighter pilot maneuvers. Should you attempt to recover too quickly from a mistake the B-52 is as they say in the trade 'apt to exceed it's critical limits.' "

~~This was a~~ By design Barksdale Air Base had no advance notice ~~of~~ that a man named *Arthur* Hadley would be flying this mission but there he was carrying his lunch of sandwiches, junk food, apples & a great deal of fruit juice & milk—like any other crew member. "The plane is 20 yrs. old," ~~Had~~ *HE* writes, "It flew in Vietnam. It has 9994 hours on it. The number 2 engine has

---

* "Our Ever-ready Strategic Forces: Don't Look Closely if You Want to Believe," *Washington Star,* July 1, 1979.

been turning over too slowly. There are serious problems with the instrument lighting system. The pitch & roll instruments on both sides, essential for blind flying are behaving erratically. The forward-looking TV is inoperative in some positions & erratic in others." He sums it up with this line—"no commercial airliner would take off with one quarter of this planes problems."

Next broadcast—we'll take off.

This is RR   Thanks for listening. ❖

Defense II
September 11, 1979

~~On~~ This is take off time for that B52 mission I was talking about on the last broadcast.

I'll be right back.

On the last broadcast I ~~started quoting~~ *quoted* from a Wash. Star article by Arthur T. Hadley former Herald Tribune executive ~~telling~~ *who wrote* of his experience in flying a practise mission in one of our aging B52's. Suited up as a crew member Hadley was privy to the knowledge that the plane had already flown a mission the night before and there had been no mechanics check of several equipment failures which ~~had~~ WOULD HAVE grounded a commercial plane.

The admin. has designated the B52 as capable of the low level missions the B-1 was designed for & which is not now going to be produced. How ~~capable~~ *well equipped* is the high altitude B52 for ground skimming missions. Well just one indicator—it has what is called a wet wing. This means a bullet hole in a wing can set it on fire. In commenting on this the commander of the flight said, "I guess they dont expect these planes to be used more than once."

Hear Arthur Hadleys description of take off. "At 7:10 AM we 8 climb through a small hole in the belly of the aircraft & take our places, mine right behind the 2 pilots. As we begin to check out the plane, the gas runs out on the ground generator. The electric current fails in the plane. The ground crew blames a faulty gauge on the old generator. The pilots guess is that it is part of the mechanic shortage."

"We have some problems starting the engines. . . . number 5 on the right is intransigent. The old plane rocks & shakes as if a herd of moose were stampeding through the cabin. But old 5 wont take hold." Finally, Mr. Hadley tells t us, the mechanics started it the way we do the family jalopy when the battery is dead, they jump started it sticking a couple of wires into it's innards. "Let me know," the mechanic yelled, "when she gets up to 40%." It reached 40 & he pulled out the wires. It took 2 try's to keep it it running.

Several hours later they were skimming the roof tops so low they could read a sign that said "Welcome to Kansas." The purpose of such a mission is to practise being part of our 1ˢᵗ line of defense, which means going in under Soviet radar to escape anti-aircraft fire. Such a wartime mission could be in fog, or darkness. So at 200 ft. ∉ above *the* Kansas countryside they were steer-ing STEERING by a radar probe & a TV screen that sometimes didn't work.

"Suddenly" WRITES MR. HADLEY "the gyro instruments which show how the plane is flying, whether it is upright, or turning, all begin to tumble spin & tumble "on both the pilots & co-pilots side." Writes Mr. Hadley. He HADLEY then describes how the heads pop up into what he calls the real world—meaning they have to steer by looking where they are going instead of depending on instruments. And as he says fortunately they had visibility. He leaves it to the reader to figure out what could happen if they were really in fog or darkness on a real not a practise mission.

Next broadcast I'll tell you the "believe it or not" way in which the tumbling gyros were fixed.

This is RR   Thanks for listening. ❖

Defense III
September 11, 1979

This is the 3ʳᵈ instalment of telling of an eyewitness account of a B52 practise mission.

I'll be right back.

On the last broadcast I was telling you of Arthur T. Hadleys account of flying on an aging B52 bomber 200 ft. above the Kansas countryside. It was a practise mission simulating a low level attack on enemy territory—something the B52 was never built to do.

Like a chapter from the a "Perils of Pauline" serial I left you with the gyros, which tell whether the plane is flying on an even keel, going haywire and starting to tumble. Mr. Hadley assures us in his article that he didn't make up what happened next.

The pilot calmly took a can of juice & drank it down. "This happens all the time" he says. "Then" Mr. Hadley tells us, "he squeezes the can together with his hands & then jumps on it a bit, making of the can a truncated 'V' with a bubble at one end. He takes out his pocket knife and opens up the instrument panel, revealing the pumps for the worthless gyros. He wedges his sculpted juice can beneath the forward edge of the vacuum pump. He ties the can in there with a bandage from the 1ˢᵗ aid kit." Hadley says by this time he felt like he could use a little oxygen from that kit. Then he ~~says~~ *writes,* "the gyros spin back to life. Bruce fits the panel back together with his pocket knife. We return to flying the mission."

At this point in his article Arthur Hadley editorializes as follows. "This is what we plan to throw up against the Soviet U? This aging ~~hunk~~ HUNK of frazzled wires; its radios & radar running on tubes, not transistors; it's wet wing ready to burst into flame. The B52 was designed as a high altitude turbo prop, now it is performing as a low altitude jet flapping it's huge wings at 200 ft. This is our 1ˢᵗ line of defense?"

Mr. Hadley is right to ask those questions for all of us and he goes on in his article to explain why all of us should be asking some questions.

He tells how ground crew informed them they had successfully reached the point where their missiles would have been released & presumably hit within 800 ft. of target. Then still at 200 ft. they headed for their 2ⁿᵈ target where short range nuclear rockets would in a real mission be released. ~~These~~

These are called Srams and the airforce describes them as having a, "range, speed, accuracy & small radar crosssection" which greatly improve our ability to penetrate the enemies sophisticated defense.

On this particular mission there was one drawback; the "srams" didn't work. Even when the radar operator slugged the computer in a spot that usually fires at least one missile—nothing happened.

A couple of months later Hadley was standing at an air base in Minot N.D.—temperature 32° below zero. There was as he describes it "a bit of a ~~flap~~ FLAP." A B52 on a practise run had dropped a whole engine off it's wing somewhere over S.D. They thought they should find it before the Gov. got upset. This is such a common occurrence that we have a regular crew whose job is to find engines & other parts that fall off B52's.

P.S. the Gov. didn't find out.

This is RR Thanks for listening. ❖

STRATEGY

Reagan devotes two commentaries to the national security document, NSC-68, which was declassified in 1975.* NSC-68 was written under the direc-

---

*See "NSC-68: A Report to the National Security Council," *Naval War College Review* 27 (May–June 1975): 51–108.

tion of Paul Nitze, director of the State Department's Policy Planning Staff, and given to President Harry S. Truman in 1950. Reagan quotes passages that sound the alarm of a Soviet military buildup and threat.

Strategy I
May 4, 1977

~~America~~ In all the "show boating" which accompanies a change of administrations, the talk of rebates & then no rebates, energy & the lack of it, have we taken our eye off the biggest game of all? I'll be right back.

Some months ago, American Cause, a bipartisan, tax exempt, pol. ed. org. directed by former Sen. Geo. Murphy, sent out a warning authored by a former ~~writer~~ *editor* with Fortune magasine, C.J.V. Murphy & *James Angleton,* ~~a~~ former chief of Counter intelligence for the C.I.A. ~~Mr. Murphys writing & editing of Fortune *magasine* spanned 34 yrs. and Mr. Angleton was 31 yrs. in counter intelligence beginning with the Office of Strategic Services.~~ ~~What they wrote in Dec.~~ *Their warning* is even more timely today and we should be grateful to American Cause for making it available. They asked ~~some questions that demand answers.~~ *these questions:* "Do Soviet-bloc aims & use of power imperil American security and, if so, what is the nature of the threat? If the danger is real, what should our defense posture be? Can we accept mil. inferiority? Shall we settle for parity or superiority? Are alliances essential? Are we prepared to demonstrate that the Am. leadership can be counted ~~upon for~~ *upon in* a crisis? If the danger is real & must be met with allies, what new direction and stimuli should be imparted to our strategic policies to restore our deterrence to aggression?" *

These questions aren't new. ~~—we've just set them aside since t~~They were first ~~presented to~~ *faced by* Pres. Harry Truman in 1950. In Aug. of 1949, our monopoly on nuclear weapons had ended. The Soviet U. had the bomb. ~~also,~~ In April 7 1950, the Pres. was handed a *very timely* Nat. Security Council paper to be called NSC 68. ~~Sec. of State Dean Acheson was the senior author. The paper was timely.~~ Only 5 yrs. had passed since W.W.II. and Stalin had gathered in Latvia, Estonia & Lithuania ~~His dictators had been firmly established (contrary to his pledged agreements) in Poland, Rumania, Bulgaria, Albania, Hungary & Czechoslovakia.~~ *and implanted dictatorships over the*

---

*Charles J. V. Murphy and James Angleton, *American Cause: Special Reports* (Washington, D.C.: American Cause, 1977), 35. Murphy wrote for *Fortune, Life,* and *Reader's Digest* and wrote campaign speeches for Reagan during his bid for the presidency in 1968.

countries of Eastern Europe. In 2 months he would send the North Koreans against Americans & S. Koreans and launch a new & bloody war.

N.S.C. 68 said "The Soviet U. ~~is~~ animated by a new fanatic faith antithetical to our own <u>seeks</u> <u>to</u> <u>impose</u> <u>it's</u> <u>authority</u> over the rest of the world." It calls for the complete subversion or forcible destruction of the machinery of govt. & the structure of society of non-communist nations by means, both violent & non-violent, & by infiltration & intimidation.

Declaring that even then the Soviet U. had armed forces far in excess of those needed for defense the paper called for the U.S. to have overwhelming atomic capability and conventional forces sufficient to make us not altogether dependent on nuclear weapons. NSC 68 said, "no moral restraints only calculations of practicality, would govern the Kremlins decision whether to resort to a surprise attack—including nuclear." ~~It added that a cardinal requirement in deterring war is to possess sufficient strength in ourselves or in combination with like-minded nations.~~

Then these points were made, "The Kremlin recognizes us as the <u>only</u> threat to it's aims of world domination. We must realize the cold war (which re-writers of hist. today would have us believe was only imaginary) is a real war and the survival of the free world is at stake. With sacrifice & discipline we & our allies would have to achieve a rapid, sustained buildup of ec. pol. & mil. strength. Without superior strength a policy of containment is no more than a bluff. And finally this statement—We stand in greater danger of defeat from lack of will than from any mistakes likely to flow from a show of purpose. "No Nat. ever saved its freedom by disarming itself in the hope of placating an enemy." Those were the ~~guidelines~~ *findings & recommendations* given to Harry Truman 27 yrs. ago. I'll carry on with this tomorrow. This is RR   Thanks for listening. ❖

Strategy II
May 4, 1977

This is going to be instalment 2 of the Special Report put out by American Cause a few months ago, which is more frighteningly timely now than it was then. I'll be right back.

Yesterday I recited the questions faced by Pres. Truman 27 years ago, when our monopoly on nuclear weapons ended & we knew the Soviet U. also had the bomb. ~~And~~ I listed the points given to him in a Nat. Security Council paper called NSC 68 which until recently, had remained secret.

To briefly recap, it stated flatly that Russia ~~was~~ *is* determined to impose its authority over the world; that we ~~were~~ *are* the principal obstacle they would have to overcome, ≠ and if their expansionism wasn't checked or contained soon <u>no</u> <u>possible</u> <u>combination</u> <u>of</u> <u>the</u> <u>remaining</u> <u>free nations</u> <u>could</u> <u>assemble</u> <u>sufficient</u> <u>strength</u> <u>to</u> <u>stop</u> <u>them short</u> <u>of</u> <u>their goal</u>. And that was SAID 27 yrs. ago.

Then were listed the things America must do, ~~with regard to~~ *including* mil. buildup, leadership role among our free world allies, recognition that the cold war was real and that "no nation ever saved it's freedom by disarming itself in the hope of placating an enemy."

Those answers in NSC 68 made clear the resolution of Am. leadership "which though but 5 yrs. after a titanic battle with 3 totalitarian systems, nevertheless was prepared to stand up to a devouring Moscow-run communist imperialism."

What are the answers to the questions of today?—Questions that are even harder? Aleksandr Solzhenitsyn says the Soviet U. has already won the Pol. ~~war~~ side of its war for Europe, the Middle East & the emerging nations of Africa. He says the Kremlin strategists have been, "breaking off piece after piece, country after country." He adds, "you can simply be taken with bare hands." Willie Brandt, a socialist himself, warns that Euro communism in France & Italy is as deadly as the Moscow brand.

But, here in our own country we have a warning we dare not ignore. A group of dozens of well known men & women of both parties; former Sec. of State Dean Rusk, ex-Deputy Sec. of Defense P~~f~~aul Nitze on the Dem. side; David Packard ~~a~~ *former* Deputy Sec. of Defense, Clare Booth Luce & Gordon Gray, members of the President's Foreign Intelligence Advisory Board, on the Repub. side ~~and~~ *also* the General Sec. of the AFL/CIO Lane Kirkland; This group of unquestionable credentials has sounded an alert.

They say, "Our country is in danger & the danger is increasing. The principal threat is the Soviet drive for dominance based upon an unprecedented mil. buildup. The scope & sophistication of the Soviet campaign and its tempo have [*has*] quickened. Encouraging divisiveness among nations new & old, it has been acquiring a network of positions, including naval & air bases, which supports its drive for dominance in the Middle East, the Indian Ocean, Africa & the S. Atlantic. Soviet expansion & world wide deployment of mil. power threaten pol. independence of our allies and access for them, & us, to raw materials & the freedom of the seas."

Then they called for a policy of collective defense just as NSC 68 did 27 yrs. ago. Their summation was that if the present drift continues, the U.S. could find itself isolated in a hostile world with a succession of bitter choices between war & surrender.

Only by mustering a superiority, beginning with a superiority of the spirit, can we stop ~~this latest~~ the thunder of hobnailed boots on their march to world empire.

This is RR Thanks for listening. ❖

In addition to being something of a travelogue of Reagan's visit to Asia in the spring of 1978, the next three commentaries are a statement about Reagan's thinking about the strategic interests of the United States. He discusses why he considers U.S. presence in the Western Pacific to be vital to U.S. security interests and to stability in the region.

Hong Kong
May 15, 1978

I'm still doing a travelogue and today the subject is the British Crown Colony of Hong Kong and Iran. I'll be right back.

Visiting Hong Kong was not really part of the business that had us going around the world. It was intended as a stopover between Taipei and Iran, a one & a half hour flight for an overnight stay. However thanks to the acting British Gov. we had a helicopter tour around the colony and along the Red Chinese border—that barrier to freedom which is penetrated constantly by refugees from the workers paradise. So much so that Hong Kong is bursting at the seams with a population of $4\frac{1}{2}$ mil.

We flew over 3 locations back in the picturesque hills surrounding the city ~~where~~ *to see* 3 new cities ~~are~~ being built from *the ground up*. We also visited the Red Chinese dept. store where luxury items unknown to their own citizens are sold to boost their balance of trade. Hong Kong could of course be swallowed by Communist China in a second but it is a necessary window to the outside world. You cant help but wonder how the Communist bosses can look through that window at the miracle of free enterprise without realizing how stupid they are to stick with the idiocy of Karl Marx.

That night at 11 oclock we climbed aboard a 747 and started our $11\frac{1}{2}$ hour flight to Iran where I learned it is pronounced "I̱ron." We crossed 3 time zones & arrived in Teheran at 8:30 in the morning more than a little sleepy.

Here again we were surprised. Ancient Persia is becoming as modern as tomorrow in an industrial way but still retains much of its cultural heretage. The people are proud, independent and more than generous in their hospitality & courtesy.

We visited the unbelievable beauty of the Mosque at Isfahan, the ruins of Persepolis at Chiraz and the resort areas on the Caspian sea. At the same time we met with govt. officials & their Majesties the Shah & Shahbanou.*

As in the other countries we'd visited the first indication of their modernization was rush hour traffic jams. In Teheran the rush hour seemed to last around the clock. The skyline is studded with huge construction cranes and his majesty told me they were building 300,000 housing units a year.

Iran must receive the worst press of almost any nation. Where have we read of the great effort the govt. is making to upgrade the standard of living & to eliminate poverty? A great reforestation program is turning barren hills & valleys into green forest lands. American industry is encouraged and there is a growing colony of American engineers & technical experts living in the ancient land. An American school is provided for their children.

But above all we should know that Iran has been & is a staunch friend & ally of the U.S. ~~And~~ It has a clear understanding of the *SOVIET* threat to the free world. ~~and~~ *And* It has the 2ⁿᵈ largest border with Russia. ~~and~~ Consequently *it* maintains a top rated, combat ready army & air force as well as naval forces on the Persian gulf. But it too worries about the U.S. and what appears to be a foreign policy based on miscalculation of Soviet intentions.

From Iran we flew to London & then over the Pole to Los Angeles. We found friendship for America in every land we visited and a hope that we would indeed lead the free world in resisting Russian imperialism.

This is RR Thanks for listening. ❖

Japan III
May 15, 1978

If you dont mind I'd like to spend another few minutes talking about our visit to Japan & a widespread worry they have. I'll be right back.

Renewing the acquaintance ~~with~~ *of* Prime Minister Fukuda of Japan, former Prime Minister Kishi,** leaders of the majority party, members of the cabinet and legislature and of course meeting *SOME* govt. officials for the first time was an enjoyable & rewarding experience. On one evening we had dinner with some half a hundred members of both houses of the Diet—the Japanese legislative body.

It was a remarkable experience. We each had a microphone & head set for the lengthy question & answer session so there was instant 2 way transla-

---

*Muhammad Reza Shah Pahlavi and Farah Diba.
**Prime Minister Takeo Fukuda and Prime Minister Nobusuke Kishi.

tion. For many it was unnecessary because they spoke our language. This was true of the other individual meetings also although an interpreter was present for ~~others~~ SOME. In my speaking engagements we simplified the process by providing Japanese LANGUAGE copies of my remarks to everyone present. I'll guaranty you I didn't do any ad-libbing on those occasions. *But I couldn't help but notice how many in the audience were obviously listening & understanding what I said.*

In all these meetings one topic was uppermost in the mind of each person I met. Is the United States withdrawing from the western Pacific? They quoted statements by our leaders, ~~some of which had never~~ *which seemed to indicate such a withdrawal was possible.* They brought up our troop withdrawal from S. Korea, the talk of normalizing relations with the mainland Chinese at the expense of Taiwan & the growing strength of the Soviet Navy in the northwest Pacific.

These were not uninformed citizens worrying about things they had read in the paper. These were ~~the~~ *the knowledgeable* men responsible for 113 mil. people. And since W.W. II totally dependant on the U.S. for their national security. This was the responsibility we assumed in return for their disarming *& disavowing militarism.*

I was to meet this same question in other countries, friendly to us but deeply concerned about a U.S. foreign policy that seems unrealistic & incomprehensible to them.

I tried to tell them of polls showing that Americans want an improvement in our mil. capability, that the Am. people do not support a policy that would abrogate our treaty with the Republic of China on Taiwan and that we intend to maintain a presence in S. Korea. On that last point I had my fingers crossed because frankly I wonder if our govt. does intend to maintain such a presence *or for that matter pay attention to the expressed desire of the people.*

~~One cannot hear the views of these leaders of Asian nations without increasing~~

It was frustrating to hear national leaders *friendly* to the U.S. asking for some assurance that our country has the will to accept leadership of the free world. And they made it very plain there was no other nation with the strength to do so if we abdicated that responsibility.

Our presence in Japan, S. Korea, Taiwan & the Phillipines is absolutely essential to the stability of the western Pacific and actually to peace & freedom in the world. We must be prepared to maintain the 7th fleet at a level of strength capable of keeping the sea lanes open in the northern Pacific & in the Indian Ocean.

This is RR Thanks for listening. ❖

The Pacific
May 15, 1978

Every year the Soviet Union increases the size of its fleet in the Western Pacific by at least one submarine & one surface ship. I'll be right back.

A few days ago I spoke of the concern I observed on my trip to Japan & Taiwan; ~~a~~ *the* uncertainty about our continuing interest in the western ~~p~~Pacific. This was compounded by the growth of Soviet Naval strength in the area.

Here are some of the facts that contribute to Asias decreasing confidence in ~~the~~ Uncle Sam. Sec. of Defense Harold Brown has said there wont be any more reduction in the 7ᵗʰ fleets strength. But defense experts in Japan & some of our own 7ᵗʰ fleet officer corps are concerned about the cuts that have already been made in ~~the~~ *a* fleet that has responsibility for the Pacific from the Kamchatka Peninsula to the Persian Gulf.

Officers who for obvious reasons cant be named say that in a Global war we would have to shift Pacific fleet units to support ~~our mi~~ *our undersized* naval forces in the European theatre. That would reduce ~~the capacity~~ *ability* ~~of~~ our Pacific fleet to maintaining sea lines of communication to Hawaii & Alaska plus some essential military traffic to the Western Pacific. But fleet spokesmen make it plain we wouldn't be able to take an offensive action in the western Pacific and all Commercial air & sea traffic would be halted. This of course is the great concern of Japan & the Republic of ~~Taiwan~~ *China* on Taiwan.

~~This~~ *It* confirms the testimony last Feb. of Admiral Holloway*—chief of naval operations before the House appropriations defense sub-committee that Soviet strength threatens our capability of mounting an offensive in defense of our Asian allies such as the 2 I've mentioned plus S. Korea, The Philippines, Australia & New Zealand. We have defense alliances with all those nations.

Our Ambassador in Japan former Sen. Mike Mansfield told a press conference in Tokyo last March that he had informed the Pres. ~~of the 7ᵗʰ fleets responsibility to ≠ 80% of ≠ the worlds Ocean surface~~ *THAT 70% OF THE EARTHS SURFACE WAS OCEAN & THE 7TH FLEET HAD RESPONSIBILITY FOR PATROLLING 80% OF ~~THAT~~ ALL THAT WATER.* He is firmly opposed to any further reduction in Americas western Pacific forces.

But the Fleet <u>right</u> <u>now</u> is incapable of dealing with more than one re-

*Admiral James L. Holloway III.

gional crisis at ~~at~~ a time. For example trouble in the Indian Ocean ≠ and war in Korea would leave us with having to choose between one or the other. We cant handle both.

Admiral Weisner* commander of U.S. forces in the Pacific has warned that continuation of the present trend including that of the past few years will give the Soviet U. supremacy in the Pacific within a decade. And he adds it will even threaten the U.S. ability to defend itself. Some 7th fleet officers think the balance could tip within 5 yrs. and they say the West Coast is already less than impregnable.

One of Japans leading defense experts say's that in 1976 the Soviet U. fired 2 experimental missiles with a 5000 mile range. This means Soviet Submarines without *EVEN* leaving the sea of Okhotsk can ~~cover~~ *hit* most of the strategic targets in the U.S.

Our allies are nervous. ~~and m~~Maybe we should be a little ~~worked up~~ *uptight* ourselves.

This is RR   Thanks for listening. ❧

MISSILE DEFENSE

Missile defense is not discussed at length in any of the defense policy commentaries, but the Strategic Defense Initiative became one of Reagan's national security trump cards in negotiations with the Soviet Union during his presidency and one of the defense programs to which he was particularly committed. He hinted at the idea of missile defense in his speech before the Republican Convention in Kansas on August 19, 1976, which he then revised as a radio commentary. In the two commentaries below, Reagan criticizes the Anti-Ballistic Missile Treaty of 1972. In signing the treaty, Reagan writes, the United States "bargained that [anti-ballistic missile technology] away in exchange for nothing."

Intelligence
March 23, 1977

Every once in a while something happens that points out how dangerous it is to handicap our counter intelligence agencies as we've done these past few years. I'll be right back.

---

*Admiral Maurice F. Weisner.

In mid-March the Soviet U. warned us that detente would be endangered if American officials continued to criticize violation of Human rights behind the iron curtain. I dont know about you but I didn't exactly tear my hair and go into a panic at the possibility of losing detente.

On Feb. 11 a somewhat liberal newspaper the "Boston Globe" carried a news story that should have been front page in every major paper in the land. So far the only publication I've seen *m aware of* that saw fit to re-print the item was Bill Buckleys magasine "Nat. Review." *

According to the Globe ≠ article British Intelligence, in early 1973, (≠) obtained a speech made by Bre Soviet head of state Leonid Brezhnev at a secret meeting of East European communist rulers in Prague. In their evaluation they *the British* rated this speech as comparable in importance to Kruschchevs 1956 denunciation of Stalin. The British informed our govt. of Brezhnev's speech, but apparently it didn't lessen our desire for "detente."

Mr. Brezhnev told his fellow communist leaders; "We are achieving with detente what our predecessors have been unable to achieve using the mailed fist. We have been able to accomplish more in a short time with detente than was done for years pursuing a confrontation policy with Nato. Trust us comrades, for by 1985, as a consequence of what we are now achieving with detente, <u>we will have achieved most of our</u> objectives in <u>Western Europe.</u> We will have consolidated our position. We will have improved our economy." And then he added the bottom line ≠ which certainly should dictate what our *have guided our own* policy *for these intervening years* beginning like day before yesterday. He said, ". . . a decisive shift in the correlation of forces will be such that <u>come 1985, we will be able to extend</u> our will <u>wherever we need to.</u>"

There was more to his secret speech. He was optimistic about the future of Marxism in France & Italy and now 4 yrs. later we know his optimism was justified. He said Finland was already in the Soviet pocket, ≠ trends in Norway were in the right direction and Denmark was no longer a viable part of Western strength.

Wash. evidently received the news of British intelligence report with less than a wave of excitement. According to the "Globe," then Sec. of St. Kissinger minimized it's importance to say the least. It The only official reference to it came 3 yrs. later (1976) in the "Nat. Intelligence Estimate."

---

*William Beecher, "Brezhnev Termed Detente a Ruse, 1973 Report Said," *Boston Globe,* Feb. 11, 1977, and "Secret Speech: Did Brezhnev Come Clean?" *National Review* (March 4, 1977): 248–50.

Maybe in 1973 there was some excuse such as interpreting Brezhnev's re-marks as a form of campaign rhetoric for in house consumption. But now 4 ~~years later~~ *we can* look back over the 4 year's since the speech was made and see how consistent ~~has been~~ *with his* words Soviet policy has been.

Soviet ~~divisions~~ *forces* on the Nato front have been increased by 54 divi-sions, a 40% increase in tanks to 3 times Natos armored strength. They have developed 6 new strategic nuclear systems and apparently are engaged in a crash program to develope an effective anti-ballistic missile ~~≠~~ system. You'll remember we bargained away our right to have such a weapon for the pro-tection of our ~~eou~~ cities. That was one of our contributions to detente.

Ques.—Why did we keep this info. secret for 3 yrs? And why has the news media ignored it now that the secret is out?

This is R.R. Thanks for listening. ✤

Defense IV
September 11, 1979

For 3 broadcasts I've been relating a frightening story having to do with what is referred to as our 1ˢᵗ line of defense. I'll be right back.

Those of you who happen to have heard any of the last 3 commentaries know that I've been discussing the situation with regard to our aging fleet of strategic bombers. ~~These are the B52's originally built to fly at tremendous heights but which have now been re-directed to extremely low altitude pene-tration of enemy territory.~~

The same writer whose article provided the material for those commen-taries, an article describing his actual flight on a B52 training mission has also visited ~~our~~ a minute man missile silo. ~~This is the 2ⁿᵈ part of our~~ *the* triad ~~upon which our national security is based.~~

Arthur T. Hadley the writer makes clear the 5 story high "minute men" in their silos with their 3 ~~nuclear~~ independently targeted nuclear warheads aren't as old as the B52's. Still they were designed to last 5 yrs.—the oldest are now 14 ~~years old~~—the youngest going on 10 and they will have to last another 10. But that isn't the entire story. The diesels that supply the power to keep the silos at the correct temperature & the computers functioning are much older than the missiles. When we closed down the "Dew" line*

---

*In 1954 President Dwight D. Eisenhower mandated the construction of the Distant Early Warning (DEW) line. The air defense system was to warn of an invasion "Over the Pole" of North America.

in Arctic Canada in the early '60's they were shipped down for duty in the silos.

~~It is~~ These missiles and their threat to the Soviet U. ~~which~~ we're told ~~is~~ *are* a major part of our defense system. Now defense is possibly an erroneous word to use in connection with either the B52 bombers or the minutemen missiles. They are *both* offensive weapons. The truth is there is no defense against a nuclear attack. ~~on us by the Soviets. If they~~

If ~~they~~ *the Soviets* should push the button our magnificent warning system would immediately detect the launch of their missiles. We would know how many were in flight and where they were going to hit us. But there is no defense against them—no way to prevent ~~their destru~~ nuclear devastation of their targets here in the U.S.

There once was the beginning of a defense; an anti ballistic missile system which we had invented and which the Soviets didn't have. We bargained that away ~~actually~~ in exchange for nothing.

Instead of a defense against their missiles we settled for something called mutual destruction. The idea was that if both the Soviets & ourselves knew we could blow each other up then neither of us ~~could~~ could afford to push the button knowing th~~a~~e other side would retaliate.

Today there is reason to question that as an adequate defense. ~~While t~~ The Russians have developed 4 new missile systems which are regularly test fired to the northeast out across the empty stretches of Mongolia toward the Kamchatka Peninsula. We have never test fired a *SINGLE* missile from one of our silos. We cant. They are in the middle of our land *and we dont dare* ~~We can-not~~ risk ~~a mishap~~ sending them out over cities like Portland, Seattle, S.F. & L.A. *ON THEIR WAY TO* ~~toward~~ the Pacific Ocean.

Mr. Hadley finished his article with this question: "When you get out of Wash. & spend time in the shaking airplanes, the freezing missile pads, & falling apart hangars, you begin to wonder if the U.S. is not a paper tiger, but a paper mouse."

This is RR   Thanks for listening. ❖

INTELLIGENCE

Reagan sounds the alarm. He contends that while Communist states have a vast network of spies abroad, the Congress and other entities are tying the hands of the Central Intelligence Agency and the Federal Bureau of Investigation. In the midst of writing his radio commentaries, Reagan was appointed to President Gerald Ford's commission to investigate the activities of the CIA. He discusses the "Team B" report in three of the broadcasts below.*

CIA Commission
August 1975

Having served on the commission investigating the CIA I've been more than a little interested in how our findings have been reported.—I'll be right back.

My own reaction ~~to~~ after months of testimony & discussion during the investigation of the C.I.A. is ~~that~~ "much ado about—if not nothing at least very little." ~~I'll be right~~ Yes we found instances of some wrongdoing with regard to keyhole peeking at our fellow citizens and of course that is wrong. But it did not constitute "massive spying" as had been charged in the press account that actually caused the investigation and ~~most of the breaches~~ *the misdeeds were* scattered over a 28 yr. period. In addition most of them had long since been corrected by CIA itself.

What disturbs me about the witch-hunting mood that came into being almost overnight and the investigations that resulted including most especially the congressional hearings now going on is the inestimable harm that has been done to this Nation's entire intelligence gathering ability. There is no doubt that information sources worldwide have been frightened into silence and certainly our own personnele must be retreating into a "dont stick your neck out" posture.

I've watched very carefully the media's handling of our commission's report. I don't think I'm being unfair in saying that for the most part the media seized upon whatever misdeeds we found & played them up possibly to confirm the earlier charges and possibly because they thought they made for more exciting drama.

One chapter in our report ~~was~~ received very little attention and yet it is vital importance to every American. So if you dont mind—here is the portion of the commissions report you probably haven't seen or heard.
– Insert –

"The number of Communist government officials in the United States has tripled since 1960, and is still increasing. Nearly 2,000 of them are now in this country—and a significant percentage of them have been identified as members of intelligence or security agencies. Conservative estimates for the

---

*See *The Nelson Rockefeller Report to the President by the Commission on CIA Activities, June 1975* (New York: Manor Books, 1975), and Henry A. Kissinger, *Years of Renewal* (Boston: Little, Brown, 1999), 327–28.

Radio   1

Having served on the commission investigating the CIA
I've been more than a little interested in how our
findings have been reported. — I'll be right back.

My own reaction ~~is~~ after months of testimony &
discussion during the investigation of the CIA is ~~that~~
"much ado about – if not nothing at least very little."
~~I'll be right~~ Yes we found instances of some
wrong doing with regard to key-hole peeking at our
fellow citizens and of course that is wrong. But
it did not constitute "massive spying" as had been charged
in the press account that actually caused the investigation
and ~~most of the breaches~~ the misdeeps were scattered over a 28 yr. period.
In addition most of them had long since been corrected
by CIA itself.

What disturbs me about the witch hunting mood that
came into being almost overnight and the investigations that
resulted including most especially the congressional hearings
now going on is the inestimable harm that has been
done to this Nation's entire intelligence gathering ability.
There is no doubt that information sources worldwide
have been frightened into silence and certainly our own
personnel must be retreating into a "don't stick your neck
out" posture.

I've watched very carefully the media's handling of
our commissions report. I don't think I'm being unfair

2

in saying that for the most part the media seized upon whatever misdeeds we found & played them up possibly to confirm the earlier charges and possibly because they thought they made for more exciting drama.

One chapter in our report ~~was~~ received very little attention and yet it is vital importance to every American. So if you don't mind — here is the portion of the commissions report you probably haven't seen or heard.

— Insert —

~~Do you know where the following appeared?~~

"The number of Communist government officials in the United States has tripled since 1960, and is still increasing. Nearly 2,000 of them are now in this country —and a significant percentage of them have been identified as members of intelligence or security agencies. Conservative estimates for the number of unidentified intelligence officers among the remaining officials raise the level to over 40%.

"In addition to sending increasing numbers of their citizens to this country openly, many of whom have been trained in espionage, Communist bloc countries also place considerable emphasis on the training, provision of false identification, and dispatching of 'illegal' agents—that is, operatives for whom an alias identity has been systematically developed which enables them to live in the United States as American citizens or resident aliens without our knowledge of their true origins.

"While making large-scale use of human intelligence sources, the Communist countries also appear to have developed electronic collection of intelligence to an extraordinary degree of technology and sophistication for use in the United States and elsewhere throughout the world, and we believe that these countries can monitor and record thousands of private telephone conversations. Americans have a right to be uneasy if not seriously disturbed at the real possibility that their personal and business activities which they discuss freely over the telephone could be recorded and analyzed by agents of foreign powers.

"This raises the real specter that selected American users of telephones are potentially subject to blackmail that can seriously affect their actions, or even lead in some cases to recruitment as espionage agents."

Close —

That is in Chapter 2 of the commissions report entitled "The Need For Intelligence". The simple truth is Americans are being spyed on massively & continually by a dangerous potential enemy. We need an effective counter intelligence force operating in our behalf.

This is RR — Thanks ---

number of unidentified intelligence officers among the remaining officials raise the level to over 40%.

"In addition to sending increasing numbers of their citizens to this country openly, many of whom have been trained in espionage, Communist bloc countries also place considerable emphasis on the training, provision of false identification, and dispatching of 'illegal' agents—that is, operatives for whom an alias identity has been systematically developed which enables them to live in the United States as American citizens or resident aliens without our knowledge of their true origins.

"While making large-scale use of human intelligence sources, the Communist countries also appear to have developed electronic collection of intelligence to an extraordinary degree of technology and sophistication for use in the United States and elsewhere throughout the world, and we believe that these countries can monitor and record thousands of private telephone conversations. Americans have a right to be uneasy if not seriously disturbed at the real possibility that their personal and business activities which they discuss freely over the telephone could be recorded and analyzed by agents of foreign powers.

"This raises the real specter that selected American users of telephones are potentially subject to blackmail that can seriously affect their actions, or even lead in some cases to recruitment as espionage agents."
Close—

That is *in* Chapter 2 of the commissions report entitled "The Need for Intelligence." The simple truth is Americans are being spied on massively & continually by a dangerous potential enemy. We need an effective counter intelligence force operating in our behalf.

This is RR—Thanks . . . ❖

Intelligence
June 15, 1977

~~Is the cause of justice being served by prosecuting someone for doing things we've~~

The Sen. Select Comm. on Intelligence has published a report that ~~would~~ makes one wonder if they know who really is the enemy. I'll be right back.

In both houses of the U.S. Congress the committees & sub-committees which used to concern themselves with threats to national security by alien & subversive groups have been closed down. There is however a Senate Committee to ride herd on our intelligence gathering agencies to see that they no. 1 operate lawfully & no. 2 effectively. So far they've only concerned themselves with no. 1.

In the committees annual report 38 of its 40 pages are devoted to what the committee has done to make sure ~~the~~ *our* agencies operate lawfully.

Sen. Daniel Moynihan wrote a dissent to the report. in which he said the committee made it sound as if the cheif threat to our liberties was our own intelligence apparatus rather than the enemies that apparatus was supposed to protect us from. In the report there is mention of intelligence activities among us by So. Korea, Chilé, Iran, Taiwan & the Philippines. Has something happened we dont know about? Last I heard all of those countries were friends & allies. Are we to believe the Russian K.G.B., Cuba and others among the communest set aren't doing any snooping?

When I served on the presidential commission looking into the C.I.A. we learned the Soviet U. had quadrupled it's espionage efforts in the U.S. Can we hope that in the next annual report ~~they'll~~ *the Sen. Comm. will* let us know how the enemy is doing now that they are so proud of having brought our own intelligence agencies under control—which means hand cuffed?

This all seems part & parcel of an attitude in Wash. that our liberties will be safe if we can just keep the F.B.I. and the C.I.A. from doing what they are supposed to do.

I've spoken on this program about the indictment of former FBI agent John Kearney by our own Justice Dept. for using wiretaps, mail openings and break ins several years ago against the "Weathermen." When agent Kearney did these things they had been presumed to be legal for 25 yrs. Since then a Sup. Ct. ruling has changed all that and J. Stanley Pottinger head of the Civil Rights Division of the Justice Dept. is plunging ahead not only to get Kearney but apparently to get others in the Bureau among his superiors. Mr. Pottinger is being cheered on by columnists of the N.Y. Times & others—who saw nothing wrong with forgiving draft evaders whose crimes were not presumed to be legal when they committed them. *But as one columnist said "In a free society the police cannot be above the law." No one is suggesting they should be.*

But isn't it time for someone to ask if we aren't threatened more by the people the F.B.I. & the CIA are watching than we are by the FBI & the CIA? What was the situation for example when Kearney was trying to learn the plans of the Weathermen? In the Spring of '68 there were 10 bombings on college campuses; that Fall there were 41. By the next Spring the total was 84 on campus & 10 off. In the 1969–70 school year there were almost 200 on our campuses and in 1970 in the nation as a whole some 3000 bombings—

that is more than 8 a day. Damage was in the millions of dollars and innocent people lost their lives.

Can anyone point to any comparable crimes against the citizens of this country committed by our law enforcement agencies? I think not.

This is R.R. Thanks for listening. ❖

Congressional Committees
September 27, 1977

We used to have Congressional committees with the responsibility for investigating subversion & espionage which might threatened our security. The committees are gone but the threat remains. I'll be right back.

Two years ago by some kind of parliamentary sleight of hand the House Internal Security *Comm.* (once known as the House Comm. on UnAmerican Activities) was made to disappear. It had been a target for years of the Am. Communist party and *for many years*.

At the beginning of the present session the Senate Internal Security Sub Comm. followed the House comm. into oblivion. Executive agencies such as the Subversive Activities Central Board, various police intelligence units etc. have also gone with *the way of the* Buffalo and the Carrier Pigeon. The F.B.I. has been sent back to walking a beat in the suburbs and the C.I.A. is not quite sure what it can or cant do about spies.

Suddenly however Wash. is all aflutter over the possibility that our friend & ally So. Korea might have spread money & favors around the town to influence the thinking of the Congress. Well friend or no friend if improper advances have been made or influence peddling attempted we should know about it.

But how do we figure explain our lack of concern about charges that other not so friendly neighbors have been moving around Wash. with their wolf hides covered by lambskin? No uproar followed the public statements of *by* F.B.I. Dir. Clarence Kelley* & his asst. Ray Wannall that the Soviet Spy Org. the K.G.B. was making an effort to ≠ move in on members & staff of Cong.

This ≠ *was* first brought to light by Sen. Goldwater who revealed that V.P. Rockefeller had told him in 1974 that Sov. agents had actually been planted in *a half dozen* several offi U.S. Senators offices.**

Then there was the case a year ago when Ol Orlando Letelier former diplomat of Chilé (when it was pro-marxist) under Allendé was blown up in

*Clarence M. Kelley.
**Senator Barry Goldwater (R-Arizona) and Vice President Nelson A. Rockefeller.

Wash. by a bomb planted in his car. There was an immediate uproar ~~that~~ over what appeared to be murder of a leftist by someone on the right.

Somehow ~~there was~~ no investigation FOLLOWED even though his undamaged briefcase contained information that he was regularly receiving money from Castros Cuba—some of which appeared to have paid some travel expenses for a member or members of Cong.

Fortunately for us there are some members of Cong. who think that the Soviet spy apparatus and Castros spreading, spider web might be as dangerous as the acts of our friends in S. Korea. Rep's. McDonald *Democrat* of Ga. & Ashbrook *Repub* of Ohio* have co-authored a bill H.R. 48 to reestablish the House Internal Security Comm. The idea is to find out what the Russians & Cubans are doing in Wash. and why the rise of revolutionary violence & bombings all over our country.

The committee if reinstituted would be handed the files of the original committee & given a mandate to look into domestic subversion & terror. So far they have 150 co-signers. You might write your congressman to ask if he has signed on yet. That's H.R. 48—only 68 more *signers* are needed ~~to make it~~ for a solid majority.

I know you PROBABLY haven't read or heard much about this bill. The press has been too wrapped up in the Korea caper. But surely someone in Wash. should be worrying about spies.

This is R.R. Thanks for listening. ❖

Intelligence and the Media
October 31, 1978

The zeal of some to completely shut down our intelligence gathering agencies has led to charges that such agencies are manipulating the news media.

I'll be right back.

Last spring the House SELECT Committee on Intelligence was investigating *alleged* C.I.A. manipulation of the news media. It was all part of the hysteria over the possibility that intelligence gathering agencies & even law enforcement units were threatening the privacy of citizens & freedom of the press.

As a ~~former~~ member of Pres. Fords commission to investigate the C.I.A. I know that the C.I.A. of course sought information from American newsmen & women stationed around the world but this was hardly ~~cloke~~ CLOAK & dagger stuff. Much of intelligence gathering is devoted to evaluations of pub-

*Congressmen Lawrence P. McDonald and John Ashbrook.

lic opinion in various countries, economic conditions and ≠ *characteristics* of public officials. Journalists covering those countries are well informed and able to provide this kind of information—indeed it is the very kind of thing they write for their papers & news services.

One member of the House SELECT Committee with the common sense for which he ~~has~~ is known—Congressman John Ashbrook of Ohio asked Admiral Turner, director of the C.I.A.* to report on *the* Soviet. U's. manipulation of the media. The Admiral was delighted to respond. Just recently the committee received that report. Somehow it hasn't made headlines in the N.Y. Times or many other news dispensaries.

According to the report the primary target for Soviet propaganda—worldwide is the U.S. To carry out that mission the Soviets have created the largest propaganda network in the world. While they deplore Radio Free Europe & Radio Liberty, our ~~programs~~ broadcast efforts aimed at penetrating the Iron Curtain, the Soviets maintain a network broadcasting radio programs in 84 languages, 2000 hours a week. There are also 13 International communist fronts. One of the most effective being the World Peace Council. The Soviets do have a gift for coining nice sounding titles for their burrowing units. That World Peace Council has held a couple of meetings in our country this year.

If you were a listener to any of those broadcasts in any one of the 84 languages you heard that ~~the~~ our C.I.A. was behind the Aldo Moro kidnap-murder.** It wasn't that communist gang at all—they'd never do a thing like that. The Pres. of Zaire—Mobuto*** is engaged in a conspiracy with the U.S., France & West Germany to produce nuclear, cruise missiles in his country. And of course they are still carrying on about the inhumanity of the neutron warhead which Pres. Carter has stalled. Actually it's inhumanity consists of being potentially a most ~~investigative~~ effective ~~weapon~~ *defense* against the 40,000 Soviet tanks lined up on the Nato line.

The only thing lacking in the C.I.A. report that Congressman *John* Ashbrook requested is information about Soviet propaganda in the U.S.—The C.I.A. is no longer allowed to look into such things and I dont know of any other agency in our govt. ~~assigned~~ *with* an assignment to do so.

This is RR Thanks for listening. ❖

---

*Admiral Stansfield Turner.
**Aldo Moro, former Prime Minister of Italy, was captured by members of the Red Brigade on March 16, 1978 and killed two months later.
***Mobutu Sese Seko.

FOREIGN POLICY DOUBLE STANDARDS, HUMAN RIGHTS, INTERNATIONAL ORGANIZATIONS, AND RELIGION

The commentaries below show how Reagan integrates non-military factors into his foreign policy views; his concern about domestic and international assaults on political, social and religious freedom; and his belief that the absence of social equality and political and religious freedom would undermine the Soviet system.

FOREIGN POLICY DOUBLE STANDARDS

For Reagan, the issue of human rights was often treated with a double standard by liberals, who befriended left-wing dictators but opposed right-wing regimes. Speaking before the Foreign Policy Association in New York on June 9, 1977, Reagan said: "If human rights are going to be our principal concern, then we must adhere to a single, not a double standard in our policy." The speech was covered extensively by the media, and Reagan became associated with the double-standard theme. He believed that religious freedom and the right to own property were at the heart of human rights.

This essay praises James Burnham's analysis of foreign policy double standards. On February 23, 1983, President Reagan bestowed the Presidential Medal of Freedom on Burnham. In the ceremony, the president acknowledged Burnham's influence on him: "I owe him a personal debt, because throughout the years traveling the mash-potato circuit [in the 1950s, 1960s, and 1970s giving policy speeches] I have quoted you widely."

Ruritania
August 1975

James Burnham has authored a column ~~that~~ *which* should alert us to the fact that a great many opinion makers ~~are~~ on the watch for any threat from the right have a blind spot to danger from the left.—I'll be right back.

Columnist ~~Mr.~~ Burnham writes an interesting, "what if" story about an imaginary country he calls Ruritania. ~~It reminds one of those old time storys Hollywood used to do about~~

A group of military officers stage a coup and take over the govt. They explain their action as necessary to free the people from oppression by a left wing regime that was headed toward a Soviet style totalitarian dictatorship.

A year later the mil. junta announces it will continue to rule for at least 3 to 5 more years regardless of the outcome of any elections the people might hold.

Naturally they have outlawed the communist & socialist parties and all left wing org's. Leftist & liberal newspapers & publications have been outlawed as have gatherings by liberals. Any attempts to hold such meetings are broken up by right wing militants.

Thousands of people have been jailed without any legal process such as serving warrents and none have been brought to trial. Many thousands of others have fled the country.

Inflation has reached the highest level in the world and unemployment has tripled. Strikes, of course, have been banned as counter revolutionary.

At this point in his story Mr. Burnham asks what the response would be in other Nation's. And here he doesn't have to deal in fancy. There ~~would be meetings~~ *are enough real examples* for us to know that countless meetings would be held, speeches made, organizations formed and demonstrators would march. Student sit-ins would follow editorials, petitions and TV specials denouncing the fascist, military dictators.

Of course the U.N. would get in the act with eloquent speeches thundering through the halls protesting the violation of "human, ~~rights~~ civil & pol. rights of the Ruritanian workers & peasants." ~~T~~

The intelectual community & yes some segments of the clergy would appeal to the conscience of mankind. Burnham describes the Ad-Hoc committees would spring up in a dozen countries demanding sanctions & severance

Radio

(1)

James Burnham has authored a column which should alert us to the fact that a great many opinion makers on the watch for any threat from the right have a blind spot to danger from the left. — I'll be right back.

Columnist

Burnham writes an interesting "what if " story about an imaginary country he calls Ruritania. ~~It reminds one of those old little story Hollywood used to do about~~

A group of military officers stage a coup and take over the govt. They explain their action as necessary to free the people from oppression by a left wing regime that was headed toward a Soviet style totalitarian dictatorship.

A year later the mil. junta announces it will continue to rule for at least 3 to 5 more years regardless of the outcome of any election the people might hold.

Naturally they have outlawed the communist & socialist parties and all left wing org's. Leftist & liberal newspapers & publications have been outlawed as have gatherings by liberals. Any attempts to hold such meetings are broken up by right wing militants.

Thousands of people have been jailed without any legal process such as serving warrants and more have been brought to trial. Many thousands of others have fled the country.

Inflation has reached the highest level in the world and unemployment has tripled. Strikes of course have been

2

banned as counter revolutionary.

At this point in his story Mr. Burnham asks what the response would be in other Nations. And here he doesn't have to deal in fancy. There ~~would be meetings~~ are enough real examples for us to know that countless meetings would be held, speeches made, organizations formed and demonstrators would march. Student sit- ins would fill our editorials, petitions and TV specials denouncing the fascist, military dictators.

Of course the U.N. would get in the act with eloquent speeches thundering through the halls protesting the violation of "human, ~~rights~~ civil & pol. rights of the Ruritanian workers & peasants". ⊕

The intellectual community & yes some segments of the clergy would appeal to the conscience of mankind. Burnham describes the ad-Hoc committees would spring up in a dozen countries demanding sanctions & severance of diplomatic relations. Ruritanian escapees would be offered Professorial chairs on the campuses and their lecture fees would triple.

Then quoting Mr. Burnham — "Murray Kempton, Anthony Lewis, Garry Wills, Harriet Van Horne & Tom Wicker would have a collective fit. A special issue of 'Time' would give in depth coverage of 'Terror in Ruritania.' Jack Anderson would reveal that C.I.A. had financed the Ruritanian Generals" — end quote.

He has drawn a very accurate picture substantiated by actual incidents. But then he explains the reason

③

behind his mythical kingdom story. All that he said about the mil. takeover, the jailing of innocent citizens, the denial of human rights, the ec. tragedy of inflation & unemployment is happening right now. All we have to do is reverse left & right and he is telling the story of Portugal today.

The mil. dictators are left wing, the outlawed parties are moderate or right as are the banned publications. The fiction begins with the description of world reaction. Except for an almost unheard of fringe the usual protest apparatus isn't the least upset about what is happening in Portugal.

As Mr. Burnham says, "The media together with the other reverberators of pub. opinion are so organically and totally biased that they are not aware of their bias. There is one way of responding to acts of the left; another way to the same acts sprung from the right. One simple factor is decisive. Does the regime suppress the Communist Party? If it does it belongs with the bad guys." — End quote.

This is RR - Thanks for listening.

of diplomatic relations. Ruritanian escapees would be offered Professorial chairs on the campuses and their lecture fees would triple.

Then quoting Mr. Burnham—"Murray Kempton, Anthony Lewis, Garry Wills, Harriet Van Horne & Tom Wicker would have a collective fit. A special issue of 'Time' would give in depth coverage of 'Terror in Ruritania.' Jack Anderson would reveal that CIA had financed the Ruritanian Generals"—end quote.

He has drawn a very accurate picture substantiated by actual incidents. But, then, he explains the reason behind his mythical kingdom story. All that he said about the mil. takeover, the jailing of innocent citizens, the denial of human rights, the ec. tragedy of inflation & unemployment is happening right now. All we have to do is reverse left & right and he is telling the story of Portugal today.

The mil. dictators are left wing, the outlawed parties are moderate or right as are the banned publications. The fiction begins with the description of world reaction. Except for an almost unheard of fringe the usual protest apparatus isn't the least upset about what is happening in Portugal.

As Mr. Burnham says, "The media together with the other reverberators of pub. opinion are so organically and totally biased that they are not aware of their bias." There is one way of responding to acts of the left; another way to the same acts sprung from the right." One simple factor is decisive: Does the regime suppress the Communist Party? If it does it belongs with the bad guys."—End quote.

This is RR—Thanks for listening. ❖

Vietnam II
November 30, 1976

Hypocrisy is doing well in the town of Babel on the Hudson and not too bad in the editorial enclaves of some of our leading journals. I'll be right back.

A few days ago I spoke about our negotiations with the North Vietnamese. ~~aggressors who Having wantonly & cold bloodedly violated every condition of the Paris~~ Peace ~~Accords~~ *They* ~~now~~ *are* arrogantly demanding that we kick in with about $3 Bil. ~~If we do so~~ *after which* they say they may possibly give us an accounting of our men still missing ~~in Vietnam~~ *in action.*

In the meantime the U.S. has twice vetoed the N. Vietnam application for membership in the United Nations. For doing so our govt. is being soundly criticized not only by the small in size, large of mouth 3rd world nations in the U.N. ~~by~~ but by ~~our~~ a great many of our own newspapers.

One powerful Eastern paper contends our veto violated ~~one of~~ a, "basic rule of the U.N.—the principle of universal membership by all legit. govts." ~~Now by any standard that charge is based on a false premise. First of all~~ t There is no such U.N. principle or concept as universal membership. The charter welcomes nations ~~that~~ which have renounced force of arms as a means of settling disputes. Article 4 states: "Membership in the U.N. is open to all peace loving states which accept the obligations contained in the present charter and are able & willing to carry out those obligations." ~~One of those obligations is, "to solve international problems of a humanitarian character."~~

~~But~~ And what about that line, "<u>legit.</u> govts."? If someone invades your home carrying a big club, subdues you, & locks you in a closet & squats in your living room does he become the legit. owner of your home?

The N. Vietnamese conquered S. Vietnam by force of arms. *This was no civil war.* They have been ~~civil~~ separate nations for 2000 yrs. Now they hold a *nation* captive just as the Soviet U. holds the countries of Central & Eastern Europe captive.

During all the long years of war N.V.N. fuzzed up the issue by claiming U.S. presence in VN. was the cause of their mil. activity. Their claims were echoed by many papers who now find fault with our UN Vetos. Alright we are no longer in V.N. therefore what reason can the N.Vietnamese have for the mil. occupation of S.VN?

How loud would the editorials objections be if the govts. of S.Korea & the Repub. of China on Taiwan were sending out patrol boats to machine gun makeshift rafts & boats carrying refugees who were trying to escape from those countries? We have learned the N. Vietnamese are doing just that to the conquered people of S.V.N.

We express concern that human rights are being denied to some in Rhodesia, S. Africa & Chilé. But where are the indignant voices protesting the hundreds of thousands of S. Vietnamese, & Laotians & Cambodians who are dying of torture & starvation in ~~cam~~ N. Vietnams concentration camps?

If there is any principle or honor left at all in the U.N. & for that matter in a number of newsrooms shouldn't N.V.N. be told it will be welcome in the U.N. when it has withdrawn to its own borders; when it has once again allowed the S. Vietnamese to govern themselves; when true peace among friendly neighbors has been restored to S.E. Asia and when they've given us an accounting of our men missing in action? We in turn will *THEN* keep our pledge to repair the ravages of war in all their countries. ~~This is R.R. Thanks for listening~~ But that is the only basis upon which there can be any talk of normalizing relations. This is RR Thanks for listening. ❖

Blind on the Left
February 20, 1978

Why is it so many people ≠ alert to any threat from the right are incapable of seeing danger from the left? A remarkable woman who understood this is gone & will be missed.

I'll be right back.

A number of years ago when a concerted, organized effort was made to subvert the motion picture industry & make sure *to a communist* propaganda tool I asked a question which is still unanswered. The question *was* why is it that the many defectors from communism, domestic or International make so little impression on those ~~whose liberalism~~ who had no trouble seeing the menace of Nazism & Fascism. Now ~~let me make it plain~~—for the record—I take 2nd to no one in my detestation of Adolph Hitler & everything he represented. As a matter of fact I'm still mad at the Kaiser. But there are others in the world today as evil as Hitler & guilty of the same brutal, inhuman deeds. When a defector—sometimes one who held ~~high~~ a *fairly high* ~~position~~ *ranks* in the Soviet social order or even a domestic communist party member now dis-illusioned wants to tell us the reason for their defection or dis-illusionment they are dismissed by many liberals as no longer a credible source. And yet very often those same liberals will accept as gospel the complaints of an American who disavows patriotism and proclaims from podium & printed page—"What's wrong with America."

I was reminded of all this not long ago when a very remarkable woman *in* Wash. D.C. died just a few days short of her 80th birthday. It would be impossible to count the lives she touched in Eng. where she was born, in China, Japan, the Soviet U. & here in her adopted home the U.S.

~~In~~ She once described herself as a "premature anti-communist. I told the truth about communism long before the world was prepared to hear it." And Freda Utley knew the truth about communism because as an idealistic young woman in the 1920's she accepted communism. In fact she married a Russian & went to live in Moscow. After he was taken away by ≠ Stalin's secret police she came out of Russia and wrote a book "The Dream We Lost," in which she said: "The just & the unjust enter through the same *revolving* door & the stream pressing in with great expectations is matched or exceeded by the crowd of the disillusioned getting out." *

*Freda Utley, *The Dream We Lost: Soviet Russia Then and Now* (New York: The John Day Company, 1940).

Radio

Blind on the left.

①

Why is it so many people aet alert to any threat from the right are incapable of seeing danger from the left? A remarkable woman who understood this is gone & will be missed.

I'll be right back.

A number of years ago when a concerted, organized effort was made to subvert the motion picture industry to a communist propaganda tool I asked a question which is still unanswered. The question was why is it that the many defectors from communism, domestic or International make so little impression on those who had no trouble seeing the menace of Nazism & Fascism. Now for the record — I take 2nd to no one in my detestation of Adolph Hitler & everything he represented. As a matter of fact I'm still mad at the Kaiser. But there are others in the world today as evil as Hitler & guilty of the same brutal, inhuman deeds. When a defector — sometimes one who held a fairly high ranks in the Soviet social order or even a domestic communist party member now dis-illusioned wants to tell us the reason for their defection or dis-illusionment they are dismissed by many liberals as no longer a credible source. And yet very often those same liberals will accept as gospel the complaints of an American who disavows patriotism and proclaims from podium & printed page — "What's wrong with America".

I was reminded of all this not long ago when a very remarkable woman died just a few days short of her 80th birthday. It would be impossible to count the lives she touched in Eng. where she was born, in China, Japan, the Soviet U. & here in her adopted home the U.S.

She once described herself as a "premature anti-communist I told the truth about communism long before the world was prepared to hear it." And Freda Utley knew the truth about communism because as an idealistic young

woman in the 1920's she accepted communism. In fact she ②
married a Russian & went to live in Moscow. After he was
taken away by Stalin's secret police she came out of
Russia and wrote a book "The Dream We Lost", in which
she said; "The first & the unjust enter through the
same door (revolving) & the stream pressing in with great
expectations is matched or exceeded by the crowd of the
disillusioned getting out".

But many of the intellectuals didn't want to
hear what she had to say. She had impressive
academic credentials but when she came to the U.S.
but publishers and the academy closed doors
against her. She understood all too well; She had
tried communism & learned it's FALSEHOOD. She said
"only those" who have never fully committed themselves
to the communist cause" can continue to believe in it.
Her book "The China Story" which told of how the
Reds were taking over became a best seller — after
China was lost.

It is bone chilling now to read that Soviet
defector Oleg Glagolev former consultant to the Kremlin
on strategic arms is telling our govt. Russia has
the cruise missile already deployed in submarines
off our coasts. Is anyone REALLY listening?

This is RR Thanks for listening.

But many of the intellectuals didn't want to hear what she had to say. She had impressive academic credentials ~~but~~ when she came to the U.S. but publishers and the academy closed doors against her. She understood all too well~~;~~. ~~s~~She had tried communism & learned it's ~~falsehood~~ FALSENESS. She said only those "who have never fully committed themselves to the communist Cause" can continue to believe in it. Her book "The China Story" which told of how the Reds were taking over became a bestseller—after China was lost.*

It is bone chilling now to read that Soviet defector Oleg Glagolev former consultant to the Kremlin on strategic arms is telling our govt. Russia has the cruise missile already deployed in submarines off our coasts. Is anyone RE-ALLY listening?

This is RR   Thanks for listening. ❖

In reviewing the contents of President Reagan's desk in his office in Century City, California on October 4, 2000, Martin Anderson found the typescript of a December 29, 1970 newspaper column by Dartmouth University Professor Jeffrey Hart titled "Reagan." Hart wrote: "First of all, Reagan is extremely intelligent. He is quick, and not easily sidetracked, able to get to the center of a complicated problem almost abruptly. . . . In February of 1971 Reagan will be 60, and perhaps he never will be President; but if not, I hope that we pass a Constitutional amendment enabling him to hold the Senate seats of John Tunney and Alan Cranston simultaneously."

Reagan cites the work of Hart in the commentary below.

Suicide Lobby
March 13, 1978

Anyone in public life who ~~hints~~ so much as drops a hint, he or she might believe in a conspiracy theory is jumping overboard without a life belt.

I'll be right back.

Many years ago during the period called the "cold war," when Americans were very conscious of the threat of subversion, a great Congress of the International Communist movement was held in Moscow. ~~This meeting of world communist leaders adopted~~ The meeting adopted a plan for fighting anticommunism. ~~and didn't make any effort to keep it secret.~~ One part of the plan was directed toward the U.S. and called for a subtle campaign to make anti-

---

*Freda Utley, *The China Story* (Chicago: Henry Regnery Company, 1951).

communism unfashionable. The idea was to use well meaning liberals & others until an anti-communist would be ~~generally looked upon~~ *ridiculed* as some kind of right wing nut guilty of "witch hunting and looking for Reds under the bed." And ~~today we have the fear of even hinting at a~~ *so today most people in pub. life are afraid to hint at a communist conspiracy.*

Prof. Jeffrey Hart of Dartmouth has ~~assembled and~~ documented some facts that reveal a number of ~~the~~ ghosts from the riotous, hatefilled '60s are stalking the land. They can be found in a network of organizations once prominent in the protest against the ~~Viet Nam~~ *Vietnam* war. Today their goal is support of the Salt II treaties & unilateral disarmament by the U.S.

There is ~~an~~ *a Soviet dominated* international org. ~~dominated by the Soviets and~~ known as the World Peace Council. ~~Now~~ You'll have to admit that has a nice sound. Who's against world peace? Last Spring, Prof. Hart says a Council member visited our shores ~~calling for~~ *to set up* a new combine of anti-nuclear ~~development~~ *power plant* people & advocates of disarmament. ~~And before you could even think of "Reds under the bed" there came into being~~ *We now have* M.F.S.—Mobilisation For Survival, based in Phil.

Last Oct. MFS held a conference at Yale U. and the ghosts appeared—in the flesh; Dr. Spock, environmentalist Barry Commoner, Sidney Lens who is hardly on the right side of anything and Daniel Ellsburg* who heroically revealed secret documents he was honor bound to protect. It seems the honor wasn't firmly fastened. ~~Suppo~~

Supporting the conference was the War Resisters League, Am. Friends Service Committee, Women Strike For Peace & others. ~~All these groups were loud & active in their campaign to end resistance to N. Vietnam.~~ They were joined by a new group, The Coalition for a New Foreign & Mil. Policy.

The mobilization has 6 task forces working on Cong. to cut mil. spending, drop all new advanced weapons systems and halt the building of nuclear power plants. Halt them that is in our country. They dont seem bothered that Russia ~~has pulled all stops~~ *is going all out* on it's *own* nuclear power program.

The M.F.S. works closely with the "Nat. Center to Slash Mil. Spending," which is an American arm of the World Peace Council and has in its upper crust a number of veteran members of the U.S. Communist Party. ~~Together~~ They oppose the cruise missile (for us that is) the B-1 bomber (well that's already scratched) & so, *I think,* is the MX mobile strategic missile. ~~I think.~~ They are ~~also~~ against the neutron bomb & anything else new we ~~haven't~~ *might* come up with. ~~yet.~~ They justify Russias huge arsenal on the grounds that the Soviet U. is surrounded by all those hostile nations.

---

*Dr. Benjamin Spock, Barry Commoner, Sidney Lens, and Daniel Ellsberg.

You could call these ~~people~~ *Americans a* suicide lobby—but for heavens sake dont say conspiracy.

This is RR   Thanks for listening. ❖

Desk-Cleaning
April 3, 1978

A little stack of items has collected on my desk again and most of them add up to a tale of weakness in our foreign policy. I'll be right back.

Remember when anti-war protestors and some well known public figures ridiculed the "domino theory"; the idea that if S. Vietnam fell to the communists other S.E. Asian nations would follow?

Well S. Vietnam fell in 1975, Laos shortly thereafter and now Cambodia (already communist) is faced with attack by the N. Vietnamese communists. Cambodia is or was mainly backed by the Chinese Reds & N. Vietnam is of course a Soviet puppet. Cambodia has been adventuring across the border of Thailand *even while it is protesting & resisting the aggression by the Vietnamese on it's other border.*

The Mekong river flowing through Cambodia & southern Vietnam also ~~flows~~ winds between Laos & Thailand. It makes the delta region the rich rice bowl that it is, feeding the whole of S.E. Asia. It follows that control of the Mekong means control of the region. *and after all the ridicule it seems the dominos are really falling.* ~~After the Congress forced our abandonment of S. Vietnam we withdrew our air forces from Thailand.~~

On another front just about the time the campaign warmed up to normalize relations with Cuba we learned of the Cuban troops in Angola—airlifted there by the Soviets. We blustered and made demands unbacked by action. Now Castro has so many ~~mil.~~ troops in Africa that Soviet air force units are flying the air defense patterns over Cuba. That makes it possible for Cuban flyers to fly offensive missions against Somalia—in Russian planes.

Congressman Rudd of Ariz.* has called upon the Pres. to tell the Soviet U. to recall it's mil. personnel from Cuba. He also made the valid suggestion that we should rally our Latin Am. neighbors—most of whom have communist subversion problems—to join us in protesting the Soviet mil presence in the Carribean.

Our state dept. expresses a hope that Cuba will "<u>reduce</u>" the number of troops in Africa so we can go on normalizing (in a friendly way) our relations

*Congressman Eldon Dean Rudd (R-Arizona).

with Cuba. This hardly has the sound of a bold trumpet so it isn't surprising that Cubas top diplomat in Wash. has arrogantly announced that the Castro govt. has no intention of trading it's ties with Africa for improved relations with Wash. Our state dept. will probably react to this by saying "pretty please—with sugar on it." Θ (~~Their~~ *Cuban* sugar which ~~well~~ *might* offer to buy at above the mkt. price.)

One thing has to be said about us—it takes a lot to ~~upset us~~ *make us mad*. We arrested a Vietnamese national DAVID TRUONG several weeks ago on charges of spying.* The Vietnam ambassador to the U.N. YOU'LL REMEMBER was sent home for ~~doing the same thing~~ *his part in the espionage*. Now Congressman Robt. Drinan of Mass. has signed an affidavit in behalf of Truong. Drinan says "he's a fine person, a man with high ideals and thoroughly honest. His sense of responsibility is beyond reproach."

Well you cant quarrel with that last statement. He certainly had a sense of responsibility to his Hanoi bosses. But why dont we let Hanoi sing his praises while we put him in jail?

This is RR   Thanks for listening. ❖

In this broadcast, Reagan declares that the United States ignores the human rights abuses of countries like the Soviet Union but cannot seem to forget the transgressions of "friends and allies back through the years."

Chile
July 27, 1979

Evidence continues to pile up that for some unexplained reason our diplomats have 20/20 vision with regard to the faults of our friends.

I'll be right back.

Let us start with the premise that all of us deplore violation of human rights where ever they take place. Let us agree we dont approve of authoritarian, totalitarian or collectivist govt's. Let us also agree that it isn't our responsibility to change those govts. ~~and~~ *Nor to* impose our tradition of individual freedom on other countries even though the world would be a better place if all people had our freedom.

This must be the philosophy guiding our state dept. with regard to the Soviet U. where totalitarianism & denial of human rights is standard proce-

*See David Binder, "Vietnam Had a Hold on Two Accused in Spying Case," *New York Times,* Feb. 4, 1978.

dure. We continue to seek friendship with the rulers in the Kremlin selling them our technology & our wheat. We even lend them the money so they can buy more. And so it is with any number of other total dictatorships with whom we have diplomatic ~~relationships and~~ *and trade relations.*

But what is hard to explain is our inability to forgive any character flaws at all in those nations which have been our friends & allies back through the years.

I wont attempt a round up of all our friends & neighbors who have felt the sting of our disapproval but would like to take the case of one for examination. Down in S. Am. probably no nation went farther in striving for democracy & individual freedom than Chilé. That is Chilé before the election of Pres. Allende.*

Allende was a Marxist and took Chilé down the road to socialism. Inflation reached 1000%. Businesses of all kinds were nationalized. Journalists who have made an honest effort to talk with the Chiléan man in the street report that there would have been a peoples revolt if the military overthrow of the Allende regime had not taken place. But because of what we see as replacement of a leftist dictator by a military ~~regime~~ *junta* our govt. will have no dealing with Chilé.

Gen. Augusto Pinochet was made Pres. of Chilé. He set out to restore the economy of the nation. He promised to restore democratic rule also and to allow elections. True they haven't taken place as yet but there is reason to believe that if & when ~~we~~ *they* do the Gen. might just be the favorite candidate if he chooses to run.

Since 1975 the govt. of Chilé has employed Gallup to do polling twice a year. Gallup does this under an arrangement which insures there can be no interference by the govt. As of now 67% of the people approve of the present govt. & 70% want no election now. Regarding Pres. Pinotchet, 70% find him decent & humane, 82% find him capable & decisive, 63% find him moderate, 57% find him fair, & 53% consider him suitable for public office and 70% find him likeable.

Maybe those polls are influenced by the fact that prosperity is coming back, inflation has dropped to a fraction of what it was and the food shortages are gone. Sounds like a nice country to be friends with.

This is RR   Thanks for listening ❖

---

*Salvador Allende Gossens.

HUMAN RIGHTS

Reagan opposed President Gerald Ford's signing of the final act of the Conference on Security and Cooperation in Europe, known as the Helsinki Accords, on August 1, 1975, on the ground that it codified the captive nation status of Eastern Europe; that the Soviet Union and other communist states routinely violate human rights; and once again, that such states cannot be trusted to honor agreements.

————

The Soviet Union granted Ida Nudel, a Jewish Refusenik, an exit visa in October 1987. Upon arriving in Israel, she called Secretary of State George P. Shultz in his office at the State Department and said: "This is Ida Nudel. I'm in Jerusalem. I'm home." * President Reagan later declared that the United States rejoiced over the release of Nudel and other Soviet Jews.**

As seen in this commentary, Reagan champions the cause of Nudel before he becomes president.

Soviet Visas
November 30, 1976

In order to leave the Soviet Union a Soviet citizen must have $ 900 Russian Rubles for a visa and more courage than is normally allotted to humankind. Ill be right back.

Russian law and the Universal Declaration of Human Rights fully entitle a citizen of the Soviet Union to an exit visa—meaning permission to leave Russia & live in another country. As a matter of fact that Helsinki pact ~~our gov't. signed~~ *they talked us into signing* contains their pledge ~~by the Soviet Union~~ to let people live where they want to. ~~live. The Helsinki pact like~~ Like yesterdays newspaper THE HELSINKI PACT should be used for wrapping garbage.

Literally thousands of Soviet citizens are in concentration camps ~~simply~~ for trying to obtain an exit visa. ~~Other thousands are trying to survive in a place where the gov't. is the only employer and the~~ For Other thousands the price for seeking a visa is automatic dismissal from ~~your~~ *their* jobs.

*George P. Shultz, *Turmoil and Triumph: My Years as Secretary of State* (New York: Charles Scribner's Sons, 1993), 990.
**See "Remarks at the Welcoming Ceremony for President Chaim Herzog of Israel," November 10, 1987. *Public Papers of the Presidents of the United States: Ronald Reagan* (Washington, DC: Government Printing Office, 1987), 1309.

~~Let me tell you the story of one of those thousands. Her name is~~ *One of the latter is* Ida Nudel, born in Russia in 1931. ~~She is not a defector in the sense of wanting to turn on her native land.~~ She is of the Jewish faith. In a letter to a Soviet official she wrote, "I was born & raised here, I am part of this land. But I am also part of another land as well—a land that is the dream of my people." Ida Nubel wants to go to Israel, wants to be a part of making the ancient prophecys of her religion come true.

When she first applied for a Visa in 1971 she was fired from her job in Moscows Inst. of Planning & Production. The excuse ~~used most often in refusing Visas for exit is that the applicant~~ *for not granting her a visa was that she* is privy to state secrets. ~~of one kind or another.~~ Ida Nubels job was studying the standards of Hygiene in food shops and the control of infection in various foods. She says "the greatest secrets I had access to were where rats & mice build their nests."

For 5 years she has been without a job. In Jan. 1975 she married Yul Brind who had obtained an exit visa before he met Ida. He was forced to leave Russia without her & now lives in Israel.

~~During these 5 years Ida Nubel has been~~ *She is* constantly watched, followed and arrested for no reason whatsoever. In one 15 day period she was arrested 5 times. In Moscow arrests of this kind aren't what you see in Kojack on TV. Over the years she has been forcibly seized, thrown into a dark basement rooms, often disrobed *AND BEATEN* on the pretense of a weapons search, left for days without food ~~& excuse for a~~ *lying on a vermin infested* floor. ~~She has been subjected to beatings & torture.~~

Ida Nubel is 45 yrs. of age, has a history of heart trouble but her medical card has been stamped "Alcoholic" which she is not. In the Soviet U. that is standard practise for anyone they might want to bury in a mental institution.

You'd think her own troubles would be all she has time for but ~~you~~ *then we* dont know this frail, little 45-yr. old lady. She is fondly referred to as "The little angel" by those ~~who~~ imprisoned in labor camps. She sends them soup cubes, vitamens, medicines & letters to boost them physically & spiritually. ~~One P.O. & (that means Prisoner of Conscience)~~ *One prisoner* after his release said, "There is no woman on earth whom we value more."

She has written countless letters to Breshnev and other leaders of the "workers paradise"—not in her own behalf but begging for the freedom of others and their right to leave Russia.

Why don't we write some letters in behalf of Ida Nubel to the Soviet Ambassador—the Soviet Embassy, Wash D.C.? It might worry him a little about "detente" to know how we feel. This is RR   Thanks for listening. ❧

Reagan always believed that the Soviet system was not as durable as many Soviet experts argued. One reason was that it did not adequately provide basic consumer goods. As president, he made similar statements.

Soviet Workers
May 25, 1977

With all the threatening news from Russia *about their tremendous mil. buildup* would you like to hear something encouraging for a change? I'll be right back.

Not too long ago a news item appeared in a few papers that you might have missed. There has been no follow up on it which is puzzling because it was an unusual story with a headline that read; "Discontented Soviet Workers Clamor For Right to Emigrate."

Now I know we are all aware that some of Russias scientists & intellectuals have dared to criticize the Kremlin and some have been allowed to leave. No question but THAT they have shown great courage and I dont mean to detract from their heroism when I point out that they have a certain following, worldwide public opinion on their side & therefore possibly some protection against retaliation. But when a working stiff known only to his family and a few neighbors stands up and says "how do you transfer out of this chicken outfit," that's news.

According to the article, a growing number of wage earners are asking out. Letters have begun reaching people out here in the free world and Soviet dissidents have passed the word that 10's of 1000's of Russian workers are more than a little discontented.

One *remarkable* letter which reached the West was from a shipyard worker. I'm a little surprised & concerned that the story gave his name & where he worked. I keep trying to hope that maybe he used an alias because his letter could put him in Gulag for a long time.

Anyway he asked for international support to help him emigrate to Canada, Australia or the U.S. He's Married & has & *with* 6 children he ≠ officially requested the right to leave Russia more than a year ago but has received no answer.

His reasons for wanting to leave *should* strike a responsive chord in the heart of any *one* of us. He says it ha is impossible to live on his monthly inc. of 194 rubles and he explodes the Soviet fairy tale that they have no inflation. According to him retail prices have risen substantially.—fFruits & vegetables have doubled in price, increases for meat, eggs & lard have been ~~also~~ about 40% and wages have not kept pace with prices.

He is pretty explicit about working conditions too. Frequent revision in norms & pay scales make it hard to earn more than 5 or 6 rubles a day. Operating methods are obsolete & proper tools in such short supply he bought his own. He writes, "That's the way they attempt to draw the maximum out of the worker while paying him the least possible."

Then his letter takes on the social services which of course are supposed to be those free goodies available to all in the "workers paradise." Copies of his letter should go to some of our Congressmen who are trying to get us to go for socialized medicine. ≠ "Ambulances dont come when they are called," he writes. "Doctors are indifferent to their patients. In the hospitals the treatment is bad, the food is bad." Well of course that last one *(HOSPITAL FOOD)* is a kind of universal complaint and no one has ever come up with an answer other than *to* stay well.

But seriously there is a great significance to this letter and what it might be telling us. The Soviet U. is building the most massive mil. machine the world has ever seen and is denying it's people all kinds of consumer products to do it. We could have an unexpected ally ~~in~~ if citizen Ivan is becoming discontented enough to start talking back. Maybe we should drop a few million typical mail order cataloges on Minsk & Pinsk & Moscow to whet their appetites.

This is RR ~~I'll b~~ Thanks for listening. ❖

Olympics
September 19, 1978

A wave is beginning to roll, a worldwide wave and it may just break over the heads of the International Olympic Committee. A great many people dont want the 1980 Olympics held in Moscow. I'll be right back.

On Aug. 8th the Calif. State Legislature—both houses, Assembly & Senate in a rare example of bi-partisanship passed a joint resolution unanimously. In the interest of Human Rights and because of the oppression of S dissidents in the Soviet U., the lack of religious liberty & the inability of the people to emigrate freely they urged the Olympic Committee to remove the 1980 Olympics from Moscow. They further resolved that their resolution should be sent to the Pres. & Vice Pres. of the U.S., to every ~~member of Cong.~~ Calif. Senator & Congressman, to the U.S. Olympic Committee, The International Comm—& to the Soviet Ambassador to the U.S.

Among the "Whereas's" was this one: "The holding of the 1980 Olympic Games in Moscow severely politicizes the ideals of the Olympic games." * Whether they knew it or not the Calif. legislature was part of what seems to be a growing movement worldwide. Formal protests have been filed in Cong. The issue has become a subject of debate in Latin America, Western Europe & even some 3ʳᵈ world countries. The London Times during the Soviet show trials editorialized that a boycott might be in order.** Most of the talk however is not of a 1980 with no Olympics but a transfer *of the games* to another country which does observe human rights.

It might be well to recall the 1936 Olympics which were held in Hitlers Berlin. It was a propaganda tour de force for the Nazi's which dazzled the world and contributed to the belief that surely Hitler wouldn't set the world aflame. But he did—just 3 yrs. later. And now we ~~know~~ know they were building the ovens at Belsen & Auschwitz while the crowds were cheering in the Olympic Stadium.

Our leaders in the Western World have spoken out strongly against the ~~pretense of~~ *pretended* trials ~~for~~ *of* men like Shcharansky & Ginsburg*** who are now rotting in the labor camps—the Soviet Gulag. They'll be rotting ~~in~~ there in 1980 when the Olympic Torch the symbol of sportsmanship & honor is lighted to open the games.

What would happen if the leaders of the Western World told the International Committee & the Soviet U. that torch must be ~~lighted~~ *lit* in some other country unless & until the Soviets honor the Helsinki Agreement?

In a letter to the London Times a former pacifist—a liberal Beverly Nichols wrote: "The West has very few cards ~~to~~ left to play in the shoddy game that now masquerades as international diplomacy. But we still hold the ace of trumps. It may be battered & dog eared, but it is imprinted with the Olympic torch of freedom, and it cannot be outbid. If only someone had the courage to play it." ****

Mr. Nichols has said it all. How would the Kremlin rulers explain the cancellation of the games to their people? And being unable to, what if they would come out of their dark world and agree to ~~host~~ *join* their world neighbors ~~out~~ in the sunlight ~~at least of observing~~ *of* the Helsinki pact which they signed but which they have refused so far to observe?

---

*The August 8, 1978 resolution was adopted by the Assembly and the Senate on August 31.
**"Penalties For Repression," *The Times* (London), July 17, 1978.
***Anatoly Shcharansky and Alexander Ginzburg.
****Beverley Nichols, "Boycotting the Moscow Olympics," *The Times* (London), July 26, 1978.

If they dont and we participate in the games anyway what do we say to our young athletes about honor?

This is RR   Thanks for listening. ❖

Bukovsky
June 29, 1979

Is something going on behind the Iron Curtain that we've been ignoring and does it offer hope for all mankind? I'll be right back.

Vladimir Bukovsky is a 37 yr. old refugee from the Soviet U. who spent half his *ADULT* life in ~~the~~ prison camps and infamous Soviet mental hospitals (call them torture chambers) before finding sanctuary in this country. In 1976 he was exiled from Russia in exchange for the Chilean Communist leader Luis Corvalán.

He has written a book, "To Build a Castle—My Life as a Dissenter." * In this book he tells of his years in prison and of the attempts to destroy his mind when his persecutors would move him from the Gulag into Russias so called mental hospitals.

Far more important ~~is~~ however is what his book tells us about ~~the Soviet U. and~~ the change that is taking place ~~there~~ *in Russia.* ~~In his book he tells of~~ *HE WRITES OF* what was in his mind as the K.G.B. drove him to the airport in Geneva Switzerland where the official exchange for Corvalan ~~would be made & he would be for the 1ˢᵗ time in his life free. He writes,~~ *TOOK PLACE.* "I couldn't rid myself of a strange sensation—as if thanks to a blunder by the K.G.B., I had carried out something very precious, something that should never have been let out of the country." He was referring to his insight into what was happening within the minds & souls of the Soviet people.

All of us in America—that is all of us who view the ~~Soviets~~ U. as a threat to the free world, have some awareness of the Soviet mil. buildup and the Soviet lust for world conquest. Bukovsky tells us of a Soviet U. where dissidents are not skulking in alleys & basements trying to create an underground movement. They are speaking out openly, citing their rights under the Soviet Constitution. (yes there is such a thing). True they are sentenced to prison or sent to the mental hospitals as insane but they are also proving that the 60 years of unceasing propaganda has not made the people a docile mass of willing slaves.

Jews are insisting on their right to emigrate to Israel, industrial workers

---

*Vladimir Bukovsky (trans. by Michael Scammell), *To Build A Castle—My Life As a Dissenter* (New York: Viking Press, 1979).

are forming genuine unions, Ukranians, Tartars and Baltic peoples are talking of nat. independence. "From top to bottom," says ~~Buko~~ Bukovsky, "no one believes in Marxist dogma anymore." He says everyone including the slave masters know ~~that~~ *that* the idea *that* they are building a communist state is a fairy tale.

But here is where his book is important to us.—In the 40's when Stalin was ~~busy~~ burying mil's. & mil's. of Soviet citizens in the torture camps of Siberia there was no word in our press about this. The victems lived in total hopelessness because there seemed to be no awareness of their plight. He makes it plain that beginning in the '60's when the "West" began to realize it's future was somehow tied to what was going on in Soviet prisons the prisoners lived with hope & determination to continue dissenting & resisting. Guards would tell them that Radio Liberty & the BBC had carried stories of their hunger strikes & protests~~.~~ *& thus they were encouraged to carry on.*

Let our state dept. take heed—a little less detente with the politbureau and more encouragement to the dissenters might be worth a lot of armored divisions.

This is RR   Thanks for listening. ❖

Human Rights II
January 9, 1978

Today I'm going to talk about a married couple here in our country who have done more ~~about~~ on their own about Human Rights than ~~our representatives in the Belgrade Conf.~~ *have our diplomats in Wash.*

I'll be right back.

† An American ex-G.I. and his German born wife have made the perilous journey through the Berlin Wall almost a dozen times in the last few years to help people who have no human rights. ~~Most of those they try to help are strangers and the couple I'm talking about~~ *This couple* will have to remain anonymous for obvious reasons. You see they'll be making more trips to E. Germany.

~~Now how long has it been since you've heard a voice raised in our govt. about violation of human rights in E. Germany? Like I said on the last broadcast, when you've been without rights f~~ for a long time we tend to accept it ~~as the normal thing.~~ and are no longer ~~shocked.~~

The wife in our story was a little girl when ~~our~~ *Am.* bombers were flattening the city in which she lived. Her father was ~~a P.O.W.—a German~~ *a* Prisoner in an American ~~P.O.W.~~ *Prison* camp. The war ended, he returned to his family & they watched the Russian tanks roll in. ~~& take over. For 6 yrs. they lived under the communist govt. of E. Germany and then~~ *Six yrs.* later they escaped to West Germany where the little girl grew up and married an American soldier.

Our Mrs. X knew great anguish as she learned of what her country under Hitler had done. She even turned away from God for letting her be born there but that was only for a little while. "Then," she says, "I realized he knew what he was doing when he gave me the life he did." And she explains that her experience fitted her for the missions of mercy she has ~~since~~ undertaken since coming to America. *She & her husband began by making contact with those Germans who had courageously defied Hitler.*

~~She & her husband work with others who are aware that 17 mil. E. Germans live under slave like conditions and are rarely mentioned by those who talk of human rights. She & her husband have~~ *They* learned all the tricks one must know to visit relatives or strangers in E. Germany without bringing the wrath of the ~~govt.~~ *Communists* down on their heads. She says that outside the Soviet U. there is no tighter and more horrible communist govt. than that of E. Berlin. And she adds, "If I remain quiet about what I know I become implicated in the crime in E. Germany just like those who knew what went on under Hitler but preferred to shed the responsibility."

Right now she is trying to help a man named Rolf Mainz & his family. Mr. Mainz held an executive position with a publishing co. Then one day he dropped his membership in the communist party. Several days later he was fired but no one would say why. He can list his credentials in seeking employment but when his name is learned it seems the vacancy has just been filled.

So ~~one day~~ *after 6 months* he wrote a letter to the editor *of a West German paper*—~~a sarcastic~~—*a sarcastic* letter under the heading "Comrades why dont you come live with us?" His letter *TELLING OF HIS EFFORT TO GET A JOB* was printed on the front page. One week later the paper reported he had been arrested 4 days after his letter appeared. He is now serving a 54 month sentence in the worst & most brutal E. German prison. His wife has lost her job & his children are abused at school. Both he & his wife suffer from ill health. Friends *& neighbors* are afraid to even speak to the family let alone offer neighborly help.

Mr. & Mrs. X have helped with money & necessities ~~but~~ *and have contacted the W. German govt. & Amnesty International about ROLF MAINZ. They* say the greatest need *NOW* is for ~~the people & particularly our~~ *our* representatives in Wash. to know about this blatant violation of ~~Human Rights.~~ the Helsinki pact so that hopefully pressure ~~could~~ *might* be put on the E. German govt. to *free Mainz & let him & his family leave*

I hope this helps Mainz & his family & let them leave E. Germany. I hope this helps a little.—Wash. are you listening?

This is RR   Thanks for listening.

†Send copy of this to Mrs. Angela Thompson with attached note. RR ❖

Human Rights III
January 9, 1978

For 2 days I've been talking about violations of human rights in places that dont seem to be of much concern to those in Wash. who talk about human rts.

†   I'll be right back.

Today on the subject of human rights let's get right to to big casino itself—the Soviet U. W In signing the Helsinki pact we gave the Russians something they've wanted for 35 yrs. The pact in effect says that we *virtually accept & legitimize their capture of the We in effect recognize Russias right to hold captive the* Eastern & Central European nations they have held *ruled* since W.W.II. We signed the pact apparently because of one clause which had to do with Human Rights. Those making the decision to sign claimed the Soviet U. by it's signature had agreed to let people have some ≠ if not all of the rights the rest of the us take for granted. They are (for example) supposed to be able to leave the Soviet U. & the captive nations if they choose. The trouble is the *But the* Russians make promises, they dont keep them.

For 40 odd yr's. now we've referred to the iron country curtain countries as the captive nations. Each year we have proclaimed an annual *a captive nations* week to remind the world *& ourselves* that the Soviet U. refuses the right of self determination to the people of these several countries. *holds millions of people in bondage.**

This year as captive nations week drew near there was only silence *no proclamation* from the White House—no proclamation *only silence.* Then representatives of Americans whose heritage is *origin was* one of the enslaved nations

Then Americans of Polish, Hungarian, Czech *Central European* Estonian, Latv Rumanian descent *origin* and all the other captive nations origin *origin—The Polish, Hungarian, Romanian etc.* brought pressure to bear & a weak, meaningless Presidential message *message* was released. It was unsat-

---

*On July 17, 1959, the U.S. Congress, by joint resolution, authorized the president to observe "Captive Nations Week." From then on, it was observed by each presidential administration.

isfactor~~y to everyone except possibly the Russians.~~ *pleased no one but the Russians.*

~~When~~ The U.N. Human Rt's. Commission ~~met~~ in Geneva ⊄ faced an American motion ~~to~~ calling on the U.N. to question the Soviet U. about ~~it's~~ implementation of the human rt's. clause of the U.N. Charter. ~~Then~~ *But then* our chief delegate withdrew the motion before it ~~came~~ *could be brought to* a vote. ~~How serious are we about Human Rt's.?~~

Now comes an act of symbolism which has shocked every American of Captive Nation descent and those of Hungarian ~~ancestry or origin~~ *descent* particularly. I'm talking about ~~the return of~~ the Crown of St. Stephan. The crown was presented to ~~the~~ *an* Hungarian ruler Stephan (now Saint Stephen) by the Pope at a very early time in Hungarian History. It has come to have an aura of mysticism about it with both religious & nationalistic significance to the people of Hungary. Most significant it is symbolic of the legitimacy of ~~govt. in Hungary~~ *Hungarian govt.*

At the end of W.W.II. ~~when~~ we liberated Hungary from the Nazi's but ~~then~~ under the ~~terms~~ *deal made at* ~~Tehran~~ Teheran ⊄ turned ~~Hungary~~ *it* over to the Russians. ~~The only govt. of Hungary at the time was a govt. in exile which had escaped the Nazi's.~~

~~As~~ ~~our~~ *the* ~~U.S. forces were leaving they~~ *Our departing forces* were asked to take the Crown of St. Stephan to keep the Russians from getting it; ~~We were~~ to hold it in trust until *Hungary was* once again *free* ~~there would was a legitimate govt. of a free Hungary.~~ For ~~these~~ more than 4 decades ~~the crown~~ *it* has been kept ~~in~~ ~~at~~ *in the Vaults* at Ft. Knox.

Now the White House has declared this crown which confers legitimacy & the blessings of Heaven upon ~~the govt. of Hungary is rightfully the~~ *Hungarian govt.* ~~to be the~~ *rightful* property of the Godless, communist rulers of that captive land.*

At Teheran We sold ~~the~~ *a* freedom ~~of Hungary which was~~ not ours to sell. Now we ~~confer~~ *give* legitimacy ~~which is~~ not ours to give to ~~the slave masters of Hungary~~ *an illegitimate govt.* Are we really serious about Human Rt's.?

This is RR Thanks for listening.

†Send copy of this one & note attached to Mr. Sworakowski. ❖

---

*Secretary of State Cyrus Vance led the U.S. delegation to Budapest and returned St. Stephen's Crown on January 5, 1978. See Linda Charlton, "Hungary's Ancient Symbol: A Long, Strange Journey," *New York Times*, Jan. 6, 1978, and "Europe: Crown of St. Stephen," *Department of State Bulletin* 78 (Feb. 1978): 29–30.

Helsinki Pact
December 12, 1978

A story in a West German newspaper has brought a SAD sequel to a commentary I did about 2 years ago.

I'll be right back.

About 2 years ago on one of these broadcasts I told of a Calif. couple who have made repeated visits through the Berlin wall to bring aid to East Germans who are being denied basic human rights. They have helped many escape ~~the~~ from slavery into the freedom of West Germany.

Through them I learned of the routine violation of the Helsinki pact by the communist rulers of East Germany. In signing the pact East Germany proclaimed that, "the application for an exit visa to reunite families, will not lead to any change in the rights & responsibilities of the applicant or members of his family."

Many E. Germans learn everyday how false & hollow is that statement and the whole Helsinki pact for that matter. In one town a young girl is barred from school because her mother applied for an exit visa. Neighbors who speak out or befriend such people lose their jobs.

Two years ago I learned ~~of~~ the story of Rolf Mainz who had applied for an exit visa. The couple from Calif. were trying to help him. Rolf had no record as a dissident. Indeed he was a member of the communist party, a commissioned officer in the "National Volksarmee." His brother Klaus, a dentist was a celebrity holding the high jump record & championship in 1953.

Then came the Soviet invasion of Czechoslovakia and the brothers began to think things through. Both applied for exit visas to join their father in West Germany. Rolf resigned *from the party &* immediately lost his job. ~~& was expelled from the party.~~ He wrote a satirical article and sent it to a W. German paper. It was entitled, "Comrades why dont you come live with us," and described life in E. Germany. Four days later he was arrested and so was his brother. Both were sentenced to prison. Klaus the athlete served his term and ~~was finally allowed to leave the country with his family.~~ *his right to leave E. Germany with his wife & children was bought.* His last 9 months were spent in solitary confinement. ~~His~~ *on a* daily food ration ~~was~~ *of* 8 slices of bread, a tiny amount of butter & margarine & a bowl of soup. He suffers from a protein deficiency but is free and has begun to practice dentistry *in West Germany.*

Rolf was sentenced to an additional 5 years. He suffers from a duodenal ulcer the size of a quarter and ~~suf~~ is in constant & excruciating pain. He has lost 44 pounds but ~~he~~ refuses—~~surgical~~ *surgery*. *It seems* that unpopular prisoners have a way of dying on the operating table in ~~his prison~~ BRANDEN-BURG PRISON.

The conditions in Brandenburg ~~prison~~ are beyond description. Almost every day prisoners go on hunger strike in protest of the brutality & inhuman treatment. Their keepers let them go for 8 days then they are tied up & given injections of hypertonic salt solution under the skin. This produces such intense thirst the prisoner can only help himself by eating the bowl of soup set before him.

Rolf is in great danger of losing his life. His diet consists of a saltless watery soup. Many in West Germany and ~~I know~~ our two Californians are trying to help him. Our prayers should go with them.

This is RR   Thanks for listening ❖

Reagan writes that by officially recognizing the People's Republic of China on January 1, 1979, the Carter administration has betrayed Taiwan and those in the PRC who seek freedom. Five years later, during an official visit to the PRC as president, Reagan reaffirmed the United States' "friendship with the people of Taiwan," but declared that "we do not believe that we should involve ourselves in this [PRC-Taiwan relations] internal affair." *

Human Rights
January 1979

Now that we are going to have an embassy in Peking we may have to make some fundamental changes in our foreign policy. I'll be right back.

A few weeks ago on one of these broadcasts I told the story of an entertainer, a juggler in a show ~~troupe~~ TROOP who made a sudden decision to change countries. He was a citizen of the Peoples Repub. of China and the ~~troupe~~ troop he was with was performing in the Sudan. After an evening performance he made his way to ~~the~~ a Sudanese govt. office & asked to be sent to Taiwan. They bought him an airline ticket & he became a free man.

We know of course that literally tens of thousands of mainland Chinese every year make their way to ~~H~~ the British outpost, Hong Kong. Some of these swim through miles of shark infested waters, so determined are they to

---

* "Interview With Representatives of Chinese Central Television in Beijing, China," *Public Papers of the Presidents of the United States: Ronald Reagan, 1984* (Washington, DC: Government Printing Office, 1986), 588.

escape their homeland. And of course a number of them then make their way to Taiwan where there is freedom & the 3ʳᵈ highest standard of living in all of Asia.

I mention this & the jugglers story because it connects with the administrations unexpected move to establish diplomatic relations with Red China. Not too long ago Pres. Carter said "human rights" ~~were~~ *was* the soul of his foreign policy. There are few countries in the world where human rights are more non-existant than in the Peoples Repub. of China. One wonders if the Pres. will address the rulers in Peking through ~~our~~ *his* new Ambassador on this matter of "human rights." Will he for instance bring up the ~~Peoples Republic~~ backing ~~of~~ *by* the Peoples Republic, of the inhumane regime in Cambodia which is practising genocide on it's own citizens. The horror stories from that once happy land top anything in the world for sheer inhumanity.

But within the Peoples Repub. itself the violation of all human rights is confirmed by literally thousands of stories told by ~~the~~ escapees. Visitors to China of course do not see this because visitors are shown only the showcase China. When a U.S. Senator *of Chinese origin* ~~in Peking~~ on an official visit to Peking asked to be allowed to visit the village where his parents had lived he was bluntly refused permission.

I've talked of our betrayal of the 17 mil. Chinese on Taiwan—haven't we also betrayed mil's. & mil's. of Chinese on the mainland who lived with a dream of one day regaining freedom? We have legitimized their slave masters.

This is RR Thanks for listening. ❖

Cuba
June 15, 1977

We continue to move closer to normalized relations with Cuba but have we asked all the questions we should ask? I'll be right back.

A short time ago I addressed the Foreign Policy Assn. in N.Y. giving my views on the International situation. Knowing I'd make reference to Cuba I contacted some noted scholars and asked for the latest information on ~~Cubas~~ Castros political prisoners. Word was returned to me that Amnesty International estimated their number at 80,000. ~~With~~

With confidence in the source I used that figure in my remarks. ~~My~~ It was challenged by a questioner who said his information had also come from Amnesty International and they had put the number of Pol. prisoners in Cuba at 4 or 5000. That isn't exactly the kind of situation a luncheon speaker looks forward too. All I could do was explain how I'd obtained my figure and say I'd re-check with my source—which I did before the afternoon was over.

Let me reiterate the scholars I had consulted are connected with a most prestigious inst. renowned for it's studies on world affairs. They checked with *their* Amnesty International source and learned a typographical error had been made and the 80,000 should have been 60,000. Well that's understanable and ≠ *still left* me in a better position than my questioner. But then came other views all from within Amnesty International. The staff member who said 60,000 was disputed by others in the shop. Finally they came up with something of a consensus that the figure was somewhere between 2 & 20,000. If whoever is in charge in Cuba cant do better than that he must have trouble when it comes to providing meals for the inmates.

But maybe this is our problem when we try to cut through the curtains surrounding communisms closed societies. Not too long ago a slender, soft spoken gray-haired lady addressed a large audience at Dartmouth College. I'm inclined to believe she speaks with greater authority than Amnesty International or those recent visitors to Cuba such as George McGovern who come home warmed by Castros hospitality.

The lady, Anna Galbis once held high positions in the Castro regime. She was studying in Paris (pol. science) when Castro came to power. Returning to Cuba she supported the new govt. enthusiastically, ~~Among the positions she held In the Castro admin. were~~ and served in the Cuban embassy in Wash., also in Peking. Later she held a post in the Ministry of Armed Defense and was a translator & interpreter ~~in~~ at international Marxist Congresses held in Havana.

Yes she is soft spoken but her words aren't soft. Completely disillusioned Anna Galbis likens all of Cuba to a prison except for the "showcases," foreign (make that American) visitors are taken to. Each Cuban is allowed ¾ of a lb. of meat every 10 days, 10 ounces of beans & 3 cans of condensed milk per month. Cubas renowned seafood is processed for shipment to Russia. She makes it plain this diet does not apply to the Party leadership who drive Alfa Romeo cars. ~~According to her there are 50,000 pol. prisoners languishing in 56 prisons, 26 concentration camps & 108 prison farms.~~

~~In 196~~ Her disillusionment came in 1969. She applied for an exit visa and immediately lost her job and became an outcast for 7 years eking out a living by tutoring in Eng. & French. Finally *by way of* relatives in Spain and the fact that she held American citizenship ~~by way of~~ *thru* her father she was able to leave the workers paradise. Anna Galbis says there are 50,000 pol. prisoners languishing in 56 Cuban prisons, 26 concentration camps & 108 prison farms. This is R.R. Thanks for listening. ❖

Cuba
March 6, 1979

One of our congressmen made his own fact finding way to Cuba and came back with a report that definitely does not sound like a tourist ad.

I'll be right back.

Just recently our State dept. said violation of human rights has been erased as a block to normalization of relations with Cuba. Evidently the releasing of a few pol. prisoners was all it took to convince the diplomats in Foggy Bottom that Castro has been reborn as a nice fellow.

Well fortunately we have some representatives in Wash. who like to see for themselves. One of these is Congressman Steve Symms of Idaho.* Steve made a nine day trip touching shore in Jamaica (our newest marxist neighbor), the Dominican Repub. and Cuba. His summation is blunt & to the point. He says the Caribbean is rapidly becoming a Communist lake in what should be an American pond and the U.S. resembles a giant afraid to move.

Describing Cuba as a place where the clock seems to have stopped 20 yrs. ago he says: "There are no new American cars, few new buildings have been erected since the Castro regime took ⧸ over, & the ⧸ buildings that existed before Castro are now in disrepair. The stores are virtually empty with few consumer goods. Milk is available only for children under the age of 7, meat & all other goods are strictly rationed. Commodities we take for granted are not to be found."

Congressman Symms attended mass at one of the few churches still open. People approached him asking for help in leaving the country. They told of waiting as long as 17 years for permission & of having their property & possessions confiscated & being denied employment for all these years because they were listed as wanting to emigrate. Quite simply Cuban citizens have no rights & no freedom. They are constantly under the surveillance of a Soviet style security force.

I would suggest all of this indicates that human rights are not a major consideration in the policies of Fidel Castro. As for normalization of relations Steve Symms urges that we watch Cuba very carefully. And that we keep in mind how much both Castro & the Soviet U. would like the economic help to Cuba that our recognition would bring. Cuba is a heavy load for Russia to bear. It prices out at about $5 mil. a day. For one thing a trade relationship would have a dire effect on our own sugar industry.

*Steven Douglas Symms (R-Idaho).

The Congressman points out that Castro who is a powerful, charismatic leader has a vision that extends beyond the, "walls of his Palm prison in Cuba." His idea of peace is to spread Russian-style communism throughout the world & certainly throughout Latin America & the Caribbean. And Congressman Symms mentioned particularly his influence in Jamaica & ~~Africa~~ Panama.

I'm sure he would agree that the troubles in Nicaragua bear a Cuban label also. While there are people in that troubled land who PROBABLY have justified grievances against the Somoza regime, there is no question but that the rebels are Cuban trained, Cuban armed & dedicated to creating another communist country in this hemisphere.

We should be grateful to Idahos Congressman Steve Symms.

This is R.R. Thanks for listening. ❖

INTERNATIONAL ORGANIZATIONS

Reagan's disappointment in and distrust of international organizations is vividly apparent in these commentaries. He writes that the United Nations does not protect the ownership of private property; encroaches on the political sovereignty of states; can hurt the cause of human rights; failed to play a decisive role in the Vietnam War; and allows member states to stay within the organization even if their dues are in serious arrears. He even suggests that the United States consider withdrawing from the United Nations.

United Nations
May 1975

How much should Americans have to pay for a dream—a dream that didnt come true? I'll be right back.

Probably Only those who lived through the dark horror of W W II can know how much ~~we hoped that we~~ *hope we invested in* the United Nations. The greatest bloodletting man had ever known was finally ended and even the most cynical believed that perhaps we were going to ~~start~~ have a peace that wouldn't lay the groundwork for another war.

~~Most of the world was ravaged by war but~~ *not* ~~our~~ *giant* ~~industrial capacity.~~ We were happy to pay a major share of the funding of the new world organization that would (we hoped) outlaw war. ~~Oh we had a few misgivings about the suspicious attitude of the Soviet Union but we were sure they'd change when they discovered we meant them no harm.~~

U.N.   1

~~How~~ much should Americans have to pay for
a dream — a dream that didn't come true? I'll be right back

Probably

Only ~~those~~ who lived through the dark hours of
WWII can know how much ~~hope~~ we invested ~~that we~~ in
the United Nations. The greatest blood letting man had
ever known was finally ended and even the most
cynical believed that perhaps we were going to ~~start~~
have a peace that wouldn't lay the ground work for
another war.

~~Most of the work was damaged by war but~~ ~~was~~
~~great industrial capacity~~. We were happy to pay a major
share of the funding of the new world organization
that would (we hoped) outlaw war. ~~Oh we had~~
~~a few misgivings about the suspicious attitude of~~
~~the Soviet Union but we were sure they'd change~~
~~when they discovered we meant them no harm.~~

We were just beginning to enjoy peace when ~~the~~
N. Korea crossed the 38th parallel in an unexpected,
unprovoked and outright brutal assault that almost
drove our Americans based in S. Korea into the sea.

This was the 1st test of the United Nations and
they responded. The war in Korea was fought under
the U.N. flag. True Americans did most of the
fighting while Russia took a walk proving that
~~the~~ ideology is thicker than water. Russia didn't
exactly stay out of the Korean action — they just
got involved on the other side. Our airmen fought
against Mig fighter planes and our ground forces
~~fought and~~ were killed by Russian made weapons.

Under the U.N. flag of course it wasn't a war
it was a police action and so it was fought to

2

no conclusion. The aggressor wasn't punished, he first wasn't allowed to win. But then neither were we. It was a new experience for a Nat. that had never lost a war. We didn't lose that one I suppose – just some 50,000 fine young men.

Not too many years later the show opened again in a different theatre – Viet Nam. This time there was a difference. The United Nations wasn't having any. Several times as a member in good standing we suggested ~~that~~ V.N. really was their problem. The answer was "Nyet". So we went it almost alone ~~it was but~~ not quite. Other members of the South East Asia Treaty Organization known as "Seato" took part.

The U.N. never did get around to explaining why this wasn't a legit peace keeping chore for which they had responsibility. Nor have ~~they~~ explained why they turned us down when the N. Vietnamese violated not only the cease fire in 1973 but the Geneva accords concerning the treatment of prisoners. By its charter the U.N. is obligated to "promote universal respect for & observance of fundamental human rights". There is more. Around the 1st of April we asked for UN help in evacuating refugees ~~to the Waldheim~~ ~~refused.~~ Again we were told "Nyet."

Hanoi meanwhile plays a cruel game of cat & mouse. First they denied any knowledge of 1300 Americans missing in action. Then a year ago they returned the bodies of 23 servicemen they admitted had died in their prison camps. Not too long ago they informed Sen. Kennedys office (for some unexplained reason) that they did have a list of the missing after all. And now they've released the names of 3 more they claim were killed in action.

Sen. Domenici of New Mexico has authored a resolution

3

which deserves our support. He says if the
UN cant even perform the humanitarian service of
getting an answer about these missing Americans
it isn't an agency worthy of our dis-proportionite
support. (~~we're still paying that~~ His resolution calls for
the U.N. to produce an accounting of our M.I.A's or we
reduce our payment from 25% of the ᵁᴺ budget to 10%.
~~What's wrong~~ WHY NOT? ~~with that~~? This is RR Thanks for listening.

We were just beginning to enjoy peace when ~~the~~ N. Korea crossed the 38ᵗʰ parallel in an unexpected, unprovoked and outright brutal assault that almost drove our Americans based in S. Korea into the sea.

This was the 1ˢᵗ test of the United Nations and they responded. The war in Korea was fought under the U.N. flag. True Americans did most of the fighting while Russia took a walk proving that ~~the~~ ideology is thicker than water. Russia didn't exactly stay out of the Korean action—they just got involved on the other side. Our airmen fought against Mig fighter planes and our ground forces ~~fought and~~ were killed by Russian made weapons.

Under the U.N. flag of course it wasn't a war it was a police action and so it was fought to no conclusion. The aggressor wasn't punished, he just wasn't allowed to win. But then neither were we. It was a new experience for a Nat. that had never lost a war. We didn't lose that one I suppose—just some 50,000 fine young men.

Not too many years later the show opened again in a different theatre—Viet Nam. This time there was a difference. The United Nations wasn't having any. Several times as a member in good standing we suggested ~~that~~ *V.N.* really was their problem. The answer was "Nyet." So we went it almost alone. ~~We were~~ but not quite. Other members of the South East Asia Treaty Organization known as "Seato" took part.

The U.N. never did get around to explaining why this wasn't a legit peace keeping chore for which they had responsibility. Nor have they explained why they turned us down when the N.Vietnamese violated not only the ceasefire in 1973 but the Geneva accords concerning the treatment of prisoners. By its charter the U.N. is obligated to "promote universal respect for & observance of fundamental human rights." There is more. Around the 1ˢᵗ of April we asked for UN help in evacuating refugees. ~~Sec. Gen. Waldheim refused.~~ Again we were told "Nyet."

Hanoi meanwhile plays a cruel game of cat & mouse. First they denied any knowledge of 1300 Americans missing in action. Then ~~in~~ *a* year ago they returned the bodies of 23 servicemen they admitted had died in their prison camps. Not too long ago they informed Sen. Kennedys office (for some unexplained reason) that they <u>did</u> have a list of the missing after all. And now they've released the names of 3 more they claim were killed in action.

Sen. Domenici* of New Mexico has authored a resolution which deserves our support. He says if the UN cant even perform the humanitarian service of getting an answer about these missing Americans it isn't an agency worthy of our dis-proportionate support. (~~we're still paying thei~~ His resolution calls

*Senator Pete V. Domenici (R-New Mexico).

for the U.N. to produce an accounting of our M.I.A.'s or we reduce our payment from 25% of the UN budget to 10%.

~~What's wrong with that?~~ WHY NOT? This is RR Thanks for listening. ❖

United Nations
November 30, 1976

If you thought the United Nations was a debating society more or less dedicated to *peace* keeping chores (at which it isn't very successful) brace yourself. I'll be right back.

Last June in Vancouver, British Columbia, (which is very nice in June—which is why they met their no doubt) the United Nations held a conference—title: "Habitat: United Nations Conference on Human Settlements." * They'll sell you a copy of the report through their sales section in N.Y. for $10. Before you send off a check give a listen—maybe you'll save $10.

The gist of their findings is a call for complete planning of all land, nation by nation. By a coincidence no doubt, the program they recommend is virtually a restatement of K point 9 in the Communist Manifesto as written by Karl Marx in 1848.

Before they get down to the specific program the report expresses concern with unequal incomes, pollution and a number of other social ills as they perceive them. But then they get down to the business of the aforementioned Point 9, "the gradual abolition of the distinction between town & country by a more equitable distribution of population over the country." I thought that was what some of our environmentalists were objecting to & calling Urban Sprawl.

Well the conference took note of that last & warned against "uncontrolled urbanization." It also was concerned with "rural backwardness" & "rural dispersion." They want to use land planning to encourage "massive shifts in population into specially designed habitats."

Here is the principle as they announced it. "Every state" (that means nation) "has the right to take the necessary steps to maintain under public control the use, posession, disposal & reservation of land. Every state has the right to plan & regulate ~~the~~ use of land, which is one of its most important re-

---

*The conference was held from May 31 to June 11, 1976. *United Nations Conference on Human Settlements: Habitat '76* (Government Printing Office: U.S. Department of Housing and Urban Development, 197), HUD-CPD-138.

sources, in such a way ~~as to~~ that the growth of population centers both urban & rural are based on a comprehensive land use plan."

They use terms that may not frighten them but they sure scare me. For example they describe federal land use planning as a basic step in setting up, "the New International Ec. Order."

Now this was a U.N. conference it's true but somehow burocracy has a kinship and a communications grapevine that crosses all borders. We already have a "new town" program, ~~federally assisted~~ sponsored by our own Dept. of Housing & Urban Developement. There are some 15 cities involved, lured no doubt by Fed. funds. Hud as the dept. is called also has it's own "habitat" division.

I know we dont pay much attention to votes in the U.N. General Assembly but remember that grapevine communications system. When the jungle drums are pounded by one set of burocrats—another set is listening.

Congress will return in Jan. and there will be land planning legis. introduced—re-introduced is the proper word because it was unfinished business when they went home. This time the various permanent employees of Hud and other agencies will appear before the Congressional committees with that U.N. report fresh in mind.

Who was it said, "no mans life, liberty or property are safe when the legislature is in session"?

This is R.R. Thanks for listening. ❖

Human Rights
April 13, 1977

Everyone is for Human Rights. But let's make sure that in promoting Human Rights worldwide—we dont give up our own. I'll be right back.

With talk of Human Rights the latest subject along the Washington cocktail circuit an old threat to our own independence has risen to haunt us. The ~~admin.~~ Pres. in his address to the United Nations promised to "work closely with our Congress" to achieve ~~adoption~~ *ratification* of the Genocide Convention.

Reduced to the simplicity of the that title it would seem that no one could be opposed to our ~~adopting~~ *participation* in such a pact. Genocide,—the wiping out of a people, for whatever reason is of course abhorrent to any civilized being. Our 200 year history makes it plain that the U.S. has never shown even the slightest indication that such a thing would be thinkable.

Unfortunately the Genocide Convention is not as simple as it's title indicates. ~~The U.S.~~ I'll speak to that in a moment but first a little history. When the U.S. agreed to abide by ~~W~~ the World Court in the late '40's, our govt. established—through the Connally Reservation—that the U.S. ~~would~~ reserved the right to decide for itself what cases ~~involving the U.S.~~ *affecting us* would be taken to the World Court. Off & on in these 30 yrs. efforts have been made to scrap the Connally amendment. They have been resisted because without it the World Court could involve itself in our ~~purely~~ PURELY internal affairs.

Now comes the latest effort, the Genocide Convention which in it's article 9 states; "Disputes between the contracting parties relating to the interpretation, application or fulfillment of the present Convention, including those related to the responsibility of a state for genocide or any of the other acts enumerated in Article 3 shall be submitted to the International Court of Justice at the request of <u>any of</u> the parties <u>to the</u> dispute.

Now let your imagination go for a minute. ~~& p~~Picture some of our domestic mischief makers charging any kind of discrimination or unfairness taking their case to an international court which includes jurists from the Soviet Union, ~~Po~~ and other communist & pro-communist nations. Remember once ratified by us this treaty subjects the U.S. to the unreserved jurisdiction of ~~the~~ that International Court. It supersedes all state laws & nullifys all acts of Congress inconsistent with the terms of the Convention.

One of the great watchdogs over the years who stood between us & ratification of this treaty was Sen. Sam Ervin (D.N.C.) recognized as a great authority on our Const. He is now retired but during the many battles over this issue he said things ~~wh~~ we should be remembering now that we are being threatened again.

He said the World Court, "could require the U.S. to go to war to prevent one nation from killing the nationals of another nation." American soldiers could be tried by this international tribunal for killing or wounding the mil. forces of a warring enemy & ~~the the U.S.~~ *the Convention* could authorize calling the U.N. to take action against the U.S.

~~S~~ Former Sen. Ervin says our own public officials & ~~individuals~~ American citizens could be prosecuted & punished for causing mental harm (and who defines what that is) to members of a national, ethnic, racial or cultural group. In short the Pres. in his speech on human rights promised to help Congress ~~≠ short circuit our own Constitutional safeguards~~ *eliminate the guaranty* of our human rights ~~making us subject to an international tribunal with~~ embodied in our own Const.

This is RR Thanks for listening. ❖

Reagan argues that like the United Nations, President Carter does not understand that private ownership of property is one of the most fundamental human rights.

Property Rights
July 6, 1977

The pursuit of an ideal approved by all of us—"Human Rights"—includes the possibility of ambush. We should proceed with caution. I'll be right back.

Speaking on British Broadcasting in early May President Carter pledged anew his commitment to Human Rights. This was re-affirmation of his call on March 17 to the United Nations General Assembly for creation of a Human Rights Division and the creation of a new post in the U.N., "High Commissioner for Human Rights."

So far so good. But on that March day he also announced he would ask Congress for approval of his signing the "U.N. Covenant on Ec. Social & Cultural Rights" & the "Covenant on Civil & Pol. Rights." *

One wonders if the Pres. is aware of what his signing of those 2 covenants would do to ~~Americans~~ one of our most precious rights; *the right to ownership of property.* ~~Both of the U.N.~~ *Both* covenants bar ~~our~~ *that* traditional right. ~~to the ownership of property.~~

In 1973 the U.N. published a review called "United Nations Action In the Field of Human Rights." It covered everything the U.N. has done in that field since 1948 when the General Assembly adopted a "Universal Declaration of Human Rights." That original declaration stated very clearly in article 17 that; "Everyone has the right to own property alone as well as in association with others. No one shall be arbitrarily deprived of his property."

But there have been some changes since 1948. There is now IN THE U.N. a voting ~~block~~ BLOC of 114 nations, most ruled by Marxist or mil. dictatorships. This 3ʳᵈ world bloc has successfully barred the original Declaration of property rights from being included in the 2 covenants. As those covenants are written now it would be contrary to our own const. for Cong. to ratify & the Pres. TO sign them. Our 5ᵗʰ amendment specifically states "no person shall be deprived of life, liberty, or property without due process of law, nor shall any private property be taken for public use without just compensa-

---

*The UN documents Reagan discusses in this broadcast and President Carter's assessment of the documents are found in Peter Meyer, ed., *The International Bill of Human Rights* (Glen Ellen, CA: Entwhistle Books, 1981).

tion." Our 14th Amendment prevents our own states from making any law which abridges those guaranteed rights.

Both U.N. covenants specifically exclude compensation for private property seized for public use. This is in keeping with U.N. Declarations of Permanent Sovereignty adopted in 1962 which the United States strongly objected to. The covenants are of course anti-colonial measures. They are designed to permit expropriation ~~of~~ or nationalization of foreign investment. In short they sanction the right of theft.

Notwithstanding the fact that the covenants violate the 5th and 14th amendments to our const. once ~~we~~ our Congress & Pres. accept them they supersede our const. ~~because~~ We are unique in all the world in that treaties we enter into become the supreme law of the land.

There has been some quibbling about whether the covenants ~~would~~ are recognized as treaties. That however is answered specifically in the U.N. passage on ~~implement~~ implementation where it is stated the covenants are indeed ~~recognized~~ *regarded* as international treaties.

Let us hope that before anyone put's pen to paper they will put in a few hours with a battery of brilliant and persuasive lawyers.

Yes we support the ideal of Human Rights and in our concept of Human Rights ~~our~~ ownership of private property is included. Indeed *it* is basic to our liberty & our pursuit of happiness.

This is R.R. Thanks for listening. ❖

Reagan writes that the United States has little influence over how international banks use its contributions. This is further evidence for Reagan that international organizations cannot be trusted.

Foreign Aid
August 15, 1977

If you were beginning to think Foreign Aid was one of those things—like the weather—that everyone talked about but no one did anything about—you may be wrong. I'll be rite back.

Rep. Bill Young* a congressman from Fla. successfully amended the Foreign Aid appropriation bill and now finds himself ~~lined~~ up against the whole admin. which didn't care for his amendment even a little bit.

In spite of the fact that poll after poll shows the American people increas-

---

*C. W. Bill Young (R-Florida).

ingly disenchanted with Foreign Aid, this yrs. appropriation was almost double last years. ~~a~~And the Sec. of St. says he wants it increased even more in the years ahead.

Congressman Youngs amendment blocked aid *from* going to Uganda, Cambodia, Laos & Vietnam. The White House complained that this hampered efforts to promote American interests around the world. But the part of the amendment that really touched a nerve was language prohibiting indirect aid through international financial institutions over which we have no control. It seems that the Admin. wants to increase our commitments to these multi-lateral org's.

Of the $6.7 Bil. approved by the House about ⅓ $2.1 Bil will be plowed into 6 international funds or banks. Young hasn't been able to get any answers to his questions about where this money goes after it leaves our hands. Exec's. of the banks refuse to testify before Cong. and Robt. McNamara ~~asked to observe~~ *refused to allow the* Congressman to ~~observe~~ *sit in on* a board meeting of the World Bank. We of course are the largest contributor to all of these ~~funds~~ *banks*. And part of our money ~~pays~~ underwrites the payroll of all these banks; ~~w~~Whose employees by the way in many categories are *paid* as much as 57% more than comparable workers in U.S. civil service jobs, besides which they ~~are exempt from paying any inc. tax.~~ *pay no inc. tax on those handsome salaries.* ~~of~~

Congressman Bill Young is calling for a national debate on the whole subject of Foreign Aid. He points out that Americans are unaware of the ~~increasing~~ extent to which foreign aid is being placed in the hands of international org's.*

If the purpose of foreign aid is to further our national ~~objectives~~ *interests* by what ~~ryhme~~ rhyme or reason do we entrust it to international ~~groups who are not~~ *banks* answerable *to* no one but their international charters? And what did our Sec. of State mean when he told the Conference on International Ec. Coop. in Paris last May 30th we must have a "new international ec. syst."?

~~Congressman Young reveals that i~~ *I*n that same week in May the Under Sec. ~~of~~ for Ec. Affairs told a gathering in the State Dept. that *the* international banks should be an "umbrella—a catalyst" for all international finance. ~~H~~ Congressman Young asks what kind of scheme is being proposed for America and shouldn't the Am. people be told about it?

---

*For a review of the legislative outcome of the foreign aid bill see Martin Tolchin, "House Votes to Rescind Its Curb On Loans by International Banks," *New York Times,* Oct. 19, 1977.

One thing we do know—or should know is that some of the "international or perhaps we should call them multi-national banks we *help* finance make what are called "soft loans" to developing countries. Soft loans are 50 yr. loans at no interest—only a slight service charge. But since we *ourselves* are operating on a deficit basis this means we are lending money at no interest which we have to borrow FIRST and upon which we pay the going rate of int.

Calling for a national debate ~~seems~~ on the subject of foreign aid, ~~who~~ how it is distributed and what we get in return for it can hardly be called a radical proposal. Who knows the world might *even* learn ~~that the~~ *how much some* nations ~~most~~ *are* in arears on their dues and contributions to the United Nations and affiliated organizations. This is RR   Thanks for listening. ❖

Guinea
February 20, 1978

What should the United Nation's duty be to people who are subjected to vicious & inhumane torture? I'll be right back.

I have asked a question about the United Nations and must confess I dont know the answer. Perhaps my question should be, what is our obligation, the obligation of each one of us to our fellow human beings who are being denied even a minimal right to life and certainly ~~some~~ *no right* at all to liberty & the pursuit of happiness.

Where the coastline of Africa bulges out into the Atlantic just North of the Equator *lies* a former colony of Spain now SINCE 1968 an independent nation called Equatorial Guinea. It is about the size of the state of Maryland and is ruled by a former civil servant Macias Biyago.*

Dictator Biyago lives in a walled compound in perpetual fear of assassination but dont waste any pity on him. In the 10 years since independence was achieved half the population has fled the tiny country and tens & tens of thousands have vanished without a trace. Those who remain l̶i live in terror.

Western correspondents are barred from the country so ~~ou~~ our information comes from the few remaining diplomats, businessmen, technicians and of course the refugees.

Macias has set up a dictatorship backed by a militia taken from his own tribe plus some Cubans, Russians & Chinese. Incidentally all American diplomats have been expelled from the country. Amnesty International & the London based anti-slavery society have denounced the regime as the most brutal in all the world.

---

*Francisco Macías Nguema.

Death is the penalty for dissent and the method of execution is beating administered by the soldiers of the militia. A former govt. minister now living in exile after escaping through the jungle while the militia combed the countryside looking for him gives an account of life—or perhaps I should say—death in Equatorial Guinea.

From 1971 to 1975 he was kept naked in a cell 7 ft. long & 2 feet wide—his bed the concrete floor. Those dates are just figures and dont really stimulate our imagination to think of 4 years, 24 hours a day in a bare enclosure only 2 ft. wide & 7 ft. long. Oh there was a little diversion. Every Sat. all prisoners were given 50 strokes with a metal rod.

Minister Ekong* said he kept track of the prisoners who were beaten to death in the prison courtyard. Their screams would stop when their backs were broken. Then he would make a mark on the wall. When he escaped there were 157 marks.

~~Another confirmation of the terror that is Equatorial Guinea comes from a former aide to the only Western diplomat still resident in the country the French Ambassador.~~

I know we cant give the inept U.N. the authority to intervene in the internal affairs of nations but it does seem there should be some ~~way~~ supervision ~~of~~ over the transition of former colonies to statehood. ~~After all~~ *especially when* we were all party to the elimination of colonies as a step toward universal freedom. ~~I doubt the people of Guinea feel they have been freed.~~

~~This is RR. Thanks for listening.~~

Come to think of it the Russians & their Cuban stooges say their destiny is to free the downtrodden and they are right there in Guinea at the Dictators elbow maybe we could ask them to take on that chore.

This is RR   Thanks for listening. ❖

No Pay, No Vote
April 3, 1978

Why shouldn't nations, like people, be posted for not paying their dues? Custom and tradition require members of an organization to be paid up or lose voting rights. I'll be right back.

It goes without saying that the U.S. has proven again & again it's generosity. Other nations owe us tens of billions of dollars but they aren't ~~dunned~~ *asked* to pay up. We are first on the scene to bring aid when natural disaster strikes and our Marshal plan & subsequent foreign aid program are

*Pedro Ekong Andeme.

unique in all the history of mans relation to man. We helped allies & erstwhile enemies alike with need the only criteria. All of which ~~qualifies~~ *qualifies* us *now* to make a long overdue move in the United Nations.

A U.N. peacekeeping force in Lebanon is estimated to cost $68 mil. in the first 6 mo. The U.N. is already $166 mil. in debt for other peacekeeping chores going all the way back to 1948 and including ~~such~~ the U.N. emergency force in the Sinai 1956 to 67, the Congo operation in 1960–64 & the current observer force activities in the Middle East.

We've paid our share for all these U.N. undertakings besides which we pay a fourth or more of the entire U.N. budget. The Soviet U. and it's slave states behind the iron curtain have refused to pay some $82 bil. in asessments for ~~there~~ *their* share of these U.N. activities. They claim that since they disapprove of the actions they dont have to pay.

Back in 1964 there was quite a fuss when the U.S. & several Western powers threatened to invoke charter sanctions and deny voting rights to the delinquent nations. Unfortunately we only threatened.

It therefore should come as no surprise to us that the Soviet U. has made plain that it has no intention of supporting the peacekeeping force in Lebanon; that it is opposed to the functions of the force and it believes Israel should be made to pay the entire cost. This should bring the Soviet unpaid bill up to $100 mil. or more. The Soviets even refuse to consider the creation of a permanent U.N. peacekeeping fund.

A U.N. financial expert has been quoted in the press as saying, "If anything brings down the United Nations, I think the financial tangle will." I'll refrain from expressing an opinion ≠ on whether that would be good or bad but one thing does need doing.

If a club member or even in many cases a union member is delinquent in his dues he loses ~~voting~~ *club* privileges including the right to vote until he pays up. Since the U.S. has the unchallenged best record of financial responsibility in the world organization why shouldn't our ambassador officially move that voting rights be denied the Soviet U.? And this time make it stick. If they threaten to pack up and go home—what will have been lost? ~~How~~ Can anyone remember a single instance ~~when they have~~ *in which the Soviet U. has* contributed anything of lasting value? The Korean war, we tend to forget, was fought under the United Nations flag with the Sov. U. lending comfort & aid to the enemy.

If the U.N. would take such an action it might ~~discover it had~~ *acquire* a soul. If it refuses then we could take a walk & discover we still have one.

This is RR Thanks for listening. ❖

Here Reagan finds a rare instance where the United States protects its interests in international negotiations.

Ocean Mining
October 10, 1978

It may not be the shot heard round the world but the U.S. has finally ~~said~~ told the U.N. to stop pushing us around. I'll be right back.

For more than a decade the U.S. has been patiently negotiating with member nations of the U.N. trying to work out a treaty covering the developement of the vast *mineral* riches hidden at the bottom of the sea. But as the years *have* dragged on the U.N. committee on Sea Bed Mining *has* moved closer & closer to *an* ~~treaty~~ international sea bed authority to control & manage the worlds sea beds.

In fact third world nations had moved for a U.N. controlled deep sea mining company called the Enterprise. A private company wanting to explore & mine the sea bottom would be required to get a contract from the "Enterprise" by which the company would have to accept production controls, turn over it's technology to the U.N. & find & evaluate mine sites for Enterprise.

Finally (& this should be an occasion for hoisting the flag) Uncle Sam's patience wore thin. A 39 year old lawyer on our negotiating team Leigh Ratiner *(RA TEEN ER)* declared no nat. interest of ours could justify handing sovereign control of ⅔ of the earths surface *over* to the 3ʳᵈ world. ~~Congress voted~~ *The House of Representatives voted* 312 to 80 to set up a temporary licensing ~~agency~~ *system* whereby private companies can go prospecting in the worlds oceans. The bill is before the Sen. and will undoubtedly pass if it hasn't already. Once the bill is signed into law, consortiums of some 17 American companies are willing to lay ~~#~~ out nearly 1½ bil. dollars to go exploring *in* the Pacific between Hawaii & Mexico.

What they are after are metal-oxide nodules that lie on the ocean floor *as much as 3 miles deep.* They have been photographed & they have been brought to the surface. We know they contain several metals and will run about $100 to the ton. In the Pacific area to be mined the nodules are expected to yield about 30% manganese, 1.4% nickel, ¼ of 1% cobalt and 1.9% copper. We presently depend on imports for most of these metals. Indeed we are totally dependent on import for manganese & cobalt & 90% dependent for nickel. Copper isn't quite as critical, still we import about 15%.

It is estimated the Eastern Pacific alone can provide enough of these metals to last the world for hundreds of years. In other words the U.S. can become self sufficient through deep sea mining.

No one has ruled out the idea of a treaty—one which makes sense—but after ~~the~~ long years of fruitless negotiating ~~when~~ it became apparent that the underdeveloped nations who now control the General Assembly were looking for a free ride at our expense—again. This time, thank heaven, we said, "no." In fact Congress was told by our negotiators we should go it alone whether the 3ʳᵈ world likes it or not. Sea bed mining will go forward with or without a treaty & it was even added—right out loud—"We have the means at our disposal to protect ~~those~~ *our oceans* interests and we <u>shall</u> protect those interests if a comprehensive treaty eludes us."

I wonder why we couldn't have used the same team in the Panama Canal negotiations. There is still time to run them in on the Salt talks.

This is RR Thanks for listening. ❖

RELIGION

There was no belief more central to Reagan's political philosophy than religious freedom. He believed that the absence of religious freedom was one reason that the Soviet bloc eventually would crumble.

The Pope in Poland
June 29, 1979

This commentary is more about Pope John Paul II in Poland and something you didn't see on television.

I'll be right back.

~~A few~~ When Pres. Carter & Leonid Breshnev met at the summit in Vienna, ~~Breshnev~~ BRESHNEV is quoted as saying that God would never forgive them if they failed in their mission. I'm sorry that I can't believe in his sincerity. Indeed I think he was hypocritical and deliberately using the Lords name to curry favor or ~~deceive~~ SOFTEN UP the Pres. who does believe in God as Breshnev does not.

Atheism is as much a part of Communism as is the Gulag. Every kind of roadblock is thrown in the way of religion up to & including imprisonment. Children in Soviet schools are ~~induction~~ indoctrinated from grade 1 with the falsehood that there is no God.

The day after the papers carried Breshnev's quote the Los Angeles Times carried a front page story of another meeting—this one in Poland. It was a report on Pope John Paul II's final appearance on his visit to his homeland. This appearance ~~did~~ *was* not ~~appear~~ seen on TV and until the Times story I dont believe there had been any account of it in the press.

It seems the communist rulers of Poland had barred live TV, press passes were severely limited and at the last minute the agreed upon closed circuit TV had to be cancelled for "technical reasons" ~~just 20 min's. before~~ JUST BE-FORE the meeting began. The meeting was the most significant of the Popes entire visit, significant because it was with the youth of Poland.

The church officials had given out 30,000 tickets but there were 60,000 there. They were a cross section of the countries young people, high school students, University students and working youth. Those without tickets had climbed over 12 ft. walls, helping each other. They had begun arriving while the sun was still high and they sat through the hot hours waiting, passing bottles of water to each other so that no one was left thirsty. They ~~had~~ spread flowers on the path by which the Pope would enter. When he finally arrived they threw thousands more flowers; there was a band and a symphony orchestra.

Then there was quiet and they waited for him to speak. "May I say something to you?" he asked, "I like you very much." Many times he had to hide his emotion as they came in an hour long procession bringing him gifts. And they sang all the old hymns from memory while other thousands of people watched from housetops and windows from as far as the eye could see.

The Pope put aside his prepared sermon and just talked with the thousands of young people, reminiscing of when he was the arch-bishop in that very city. He spoke humorously at times and at others OF the need for high ideals. It was 10:30 at night when he finished speaking. The time had come for the blessing of the crosses, a 12 ft. one brought by one group and the other smaller ones. ~~Wh~~

When he invited the presentation there was movement among the young people and then the meaning of this night for them was revealed; they raised the thousands and thousands of crosses they had brought—many of them homemade.

These young people OF POLAND had been born & raised & SPENT THEIR ENTIRE LIVES under communist atheism. Try to make a Polish joke OUT of that.

This is RR   Thanks for listening. ❖

In this commentary, Reagan worries about attacks on religious freedom at home and abroad.

A Tale of Two Countries
June 29, 1979

The Pope went home to his native Poland and just possibly things may never be quite the same behind the Iron Curtain. I'll be right back.

Once in the days of Stalin he ~~has~~ *is* said to have ~~contemptiously~~ dismissed the Vatican by *contemptiously* asking: "How many divisions does the Pope have?"

Well in recent weeks that question has been answered by Pope John Paul II. It has been a long time since we've seen a leader of such courage and such uncompromising dedication to simple morality;—to the belief that right does make might.

On our TV screens we've seen the reaction to this kind of leadership. Where ever he went in his native land the people of Poland came forth in unbelievable numbers. There were crowds of 400,000, 500,000, *1 MIL. & THEN 5 MIL.* ~~in areas where such crowds meant they had~~ gathered from miles around. ~~They did so~~ even though they dont have the easy means of transportation we have~~, a~~ And they ~~did so~~ *GATHERED* knowing there was every possibility they were risking their ~~live~~ livelihood and even their freedom.

For 40 years the Polish people have lived under 1ˢᵗ the Nazis and then the Soviets. For 40 years they have been ringed by tanks & guns. The voices behind those tanks & guns have told them there is no God. Now with the eyes of all the world on them they have looked past those menacing weapons and listened to the voice of one man who has told them there is a God and it is their inalienable right to freely worship that God. Will the Kremlin ever be the same again? Will any of us for that matter? Perhaps that one man—the son of simple farm folk has made us aware that the world is crying out for a spiritual revival *& for leadership.*

~~This is a tale of two cou~~

Perhaps this should be a tale of 2 countries~~;~~. *For* On the very day that our newspapers reported ~~*that*~~ the Pope had been greeted by the largest crowd in his entire visit, those *same* papers reported that Mrs. Madelyn Murray O'Hare* had launched another attack in our country against our Judeo-Christian traditions.

Mrs. O'Hare who successfully obtained through judicial rulings ~~th~~ a ban on prayer in our public schools has now decided she cant bear the pain of carrying coins which carry the inscription, "In God We Trust."

---

*Madalyn Murray O'Hair.

She cites the Constitutional provision which calls for separation of church & state. Most of her fellow citizens believe the authors of the Constitution simply intended freedom ~~of~~ to worship the God of our choice in the manner of our choosing; that we would not permit the establishment of a state church.

~~The Constitution says the Congress~~

Mrs. O'Hare invokes the 1ˢᵗ Amendment of the Constitution and that is indeed the one which gives her the right to express her views & beliefs. It does not however give her the right to impose her beliefs on others. And it is that same 1ˢᵗ amendment that says Congress, "shall make no laws respecting an establishment of religion or prohibiting the free exercise thereof."

~~The same Founding Fathers who brought the nation into being adopted the~~

Our countries motto is, "In God We Trust." At the rate we're going that motto may be the ~~most valuable thing~~ only thing of value on our coins.

No one is trying to force this woman to believe in God although I'm sure there are many who pray for her soul and even now & then that she'll mind her own business.

This is RR Thanks for listening. ❖

One of the first "openings" in U.S.-Soviet relations during the Reagan administration occurred in 1983, when the two countries quietly negotiated the release of the Pentecostal families who had taken refuge in the basement of the U.S. Embassy in Moscow. Reagan wrote about their plight more than three years before their release.

Vlasenko
October 2, 1979

There are more people than those in boats who need sanctuary in the U.S. and we are being a little less than noble about them. I'll be right back.

~~Yr~~ Yuri Vlasenko a Soviet citizen tried to leave the Soviet U. Yuri Vlasenko is dead.

On March 28ᵗʰ one of our embassy officials went out of the embassy in Moscow and led Vlasenko past the ever present KGB agents into the embassy. Once inside Yuri asked for an exit Visa so that he could leave the Soviet Union. Upon being told that we couldn't do that he revealed a home made bomb and threatened to blow himself up.

Our Ambassador tried to negotiate with him and then turned the matter over to the Soviet authorities who dont negotiate in cases of this kind. They attacked with tear gas & a sharpshooter who got off 2 shots before Yuri Vlasenko detonated his bomb. He died there in the embassy where he had sought refuge.

This tragic story is by way of introduction to the plight of 7 other Soviet citizens who were in the American embassy the day Yuri Vlasenko died. They had been there, living in the reception room since June 27th, 1978.

There are 5 members of one family, 2 of another. All are Christians, members of the largest religious group in Russia & all have other family members outside the embassy who are undergoing the worst kind of persecution.

These 7 made their way to Moscow from Siberia. They had tried in every way to obtain, legally, ~~obtain~~ exit visas from their own govt. Finally in desperation they had sought the counsel of our ambassador. The religious group to which they belong is the largest in the Soviet U. It is also the most persecuted and not one member has ever been allowed to emigrate from Russia.

These seven courageous and desperate people have a promise of sponsorship in America from the Rev. Cecil Williamson Jr. of Selma Alabama. Over the past 10 yrs. they and other members of their families have been imprisoned, tortured, found insane & some have died. Thousands of Americans knowing of their plight have written to them but they haven't received the letters. Our ambassador has ordered that mail to them must go through the Soviet postal service.

Shortly after the Slavenko ~~death~~ killing efforts were made to persuade the 7 to leave the embassy. KGB cars were mysteriously waiting at the embassy entrance. When they refused to give up their sanctuary they were moved to a 20 by 12 ft. room the Marines guards call the dungeon. There for a year now they have lived together in that one room. They are denied embassy food but embassy employees acting like Americans are supposed to act stand for hours in the endless lines and buy food for them in the Russian stores.

Last June the ambassador grudgingly allowed American TV networks to interview them but not to show the room in which they are kept confined. Then another mystery—somehow the interviews were never shown to American audiences.

Détente is supposed to be a 2 way street. Our wheat, and technology can get into Russia—why cant the Vaschenko & ~~the~~ Chernogorsk familys get out?

This is RR   Thanks for listening. ❖

THE THIRD WORLD

Reagan devoted a considerable number of his commentaries on international relations to the Third World. He analyzes many Third World crises in terms of their role as the battleground for superpower disagreements, but is also interested in the internal political and economic progress of developing countries.

AFRICA

In his commentaries on Southern Africa, Reagan argues that Western leaders have mistaken nationalism for Marxist tendencies; cautions that the Soviet threat in the region is growing and has strategic implications for the West; and opposes economic sanctions on South Africa as a means of transforming its political system. Reagan repeated all of these arguments and themes during his presidency. One of his fiercest foreign policy battles occurred in 1986, when his September 26 veto of sanctions legislation was overridden by the U.S. Congress.

Reagan wrote commentaries about countries in other parts of Africa. One on Nigeria is presented in the philosophy section. The final commentary in this set is about political and religious oppression in Sierra Leone.

Rhodesia
February 2, 1977

The Rhodesian conference *that was* being held in Geneva Switzerland has quietly adjourned but I'm sure we'll hear some loud lamenting very shortly. I'll be right back.

Our former Sec. of State, on his mission to Africa, had persuaded the Govt's of Rhodesia & Great Britain and a number of African nationalist leaders to agree to a plan for a temporary govt. of Rhodesia while a transition to majority rule took place. Geneva Switzerland was agreed upon as the site of the conference to iron out details of the majority govt. that would in 2 yrs. take over the reins in Rhodesia.

Now Rhodesia's Prime Minister Ian Smith has announced his govt. will no longer attend the Geneva meetings. Why? What happened? There will be many answers to those questions plus charge & counter charge but there is only one correct answer. Very simply the African nationalists, once they arrived in Geneva, conveniently forgot that they had agreed in advance to every detail of the Kissinger proposal. The representatives of Grt. Britain were willing to let them forget and twas only the Govt. of Rhodesia that escaped the spreading amnesia. And I wasn't aware that ~~ryhmed~~ [*Rymed*] until I said it.

This has prompted a former minister in the Labor Party govt. of Britain, ~~to utter~~ now an independent member of the House of Lords, to utter a few pithy words about what went on in Geneva. Lord Chalfont* says, "the British govt's. attitude toward the Geneva Conference is symptomatic of the desperate paralysis which seems to ~~affli~~ *afflict* the West, confronted by the very f real possibility of strategic disaster in Africa." He says, "if the whole of Southern Africa becomes a Russian colony someone will be on hand to tell us that the communist threat is being disgracefully exaggerated and that African nationalism is stronger than international communism." His Lordship then adds, "I also confidently predict that there will still be people daft enough to believe it."

I'm sure an effort—a herculean effort—will be made to place the blame for the breakdown in negotiations on the Ian Smith regime; to charge that Rhodesia ~~was~~ *is* balking at giving up white rule. That is not the case. The real struggle is between a Soviet backed *black* minority which wants to rule over a black majority.

Two of the African nationalist leaders in Geneva were not chosen by the several tribes in Rhodesia as their representatives. They are self anointed and they have the backing of the Soviet U. They are Robert Mugabe & a man named Nkomo.** They have made it clear that no matter what happened in Geneva their ~~Mar~~ guerrilla troops supported by the Marxist dictator of Mozambique will fight on until there is a socialist govt. in Rhodesia.

*(Arthur) Alun Gwynne-Jones Chalfont.
**Joshua Nkomo.

Radio — Rhodesia

The Rhodesian conference (that was) being held in Geneva
Switzerland has quietly adjourned but I'm sure we'll
hear some loud lamenting very shortly. I'll be right back.

Our former Sec. of State, on his mission to Africa,
had persuaded the Gov't's of Rhodesia & Great Britain and a
number of African nationalist leaders to agree to a plan for a
temporary gov't. of Rhodesia while a transition to majority rule
took place. Geneva Switzerland was agreed upon as the
site of the conference to iron out details of the majority
gov't. that would in 2 yrs. take over the reins in Rhodesia.

Now Rhodesia's Prime Minister Ian Smith has announced
his gov't. will no longer attend the Geneva meetings. Why?
What happened? There will be many answers to those
questions plus charge & counter charge but there is only one
correct answer. Very simply the African nationalists, once
they arrived in Geneva, conveniently forgot that they had
agreed in advance to every detail of the Kissinger proposal.
The representatives of Grt. Britain were willing to let them
forget and t'was only the Gov't. of Rhodesia that escaped
the spreading amnesia. And I wasn't aware that lynched until
I said it.

This has prompted a former minister in the Labor
Party gov't. of Britain, now an independent member
of the House of Lords, to utter a few pithy words about
what went on in Geneva. Lord Chalfont says, "the
British gov'ts. attitude toward the Geneva conference is
symptomatic of the desperate paralysis, which seems to afflict
the West, confronted by the very real possibility of strategic
disaster in Africa." He says, "if the whole of southern Africa
becomes a Russian colony someone will be on hand to tell us
that the communist threat is being disgracefully exaggerated
and that African nationalism is stronger than international
communism." His Lordship then adds, "I also confidently
predict that there will still be people daft enough to believe it."

②

I'm sure an effort — a herculean effort — will be made to place the blame for the breakdown in negotiations on the Ian Smith regime; to charge that Rhodesia is balking at giving up white rule. That is not the case. The real struggle is between a Soviet backed black minority which wants to rule over a black majority.

Two of the African nationalist leaders in Geneva were not chosen by the several tribes in Rhodesia as their representatives. They are self anointed and they have the backing of the Soviet U. They are Robert Mugabe & a man named Nkomo. They have made it clear that no matter what happened in Geneva their guerrilla troops supported by the Marxist dictator of Mozambique will fight on until there is a socialist govt. in Rhodesia.

The London based, Inst. for the Study of Conflict, is quoted as saying "whatever the final outcome of the Geneva Conf. Soviet policy envisions a Marxist revolutionary regime in "liberated Rhodesia."

"Spotlight on Africa" published by the American-African Affairs Assn. asks a question that may cause some sleepless nights in Wash. — what will the U.S. do if a popularly elected, black, majority rule is threatened by a widescale guerrilla war backed by the Sov. U? Spotlight asks, "Congress may well be able to ignore the geopolitical, military & ec. issues at stake in a Southern Africa increasingly falling under Soviet influence but would it be able to avoid providing the only tangible western aid possible to a besieged, black, majority in Rhodesia? That's quite a question.

In the meantime without agreement in Geneva the Ian Smith admin. with the support of the black majority in Rhodesia is proceeding to implement the Kissinger proposal as he said he would. This is RR. Thanks for listening.

The London based, Inst. for the Study of Conflict,* is quoted as saying whatever the final outcome of the Geneva Conf, Soviet policy envisions a Marxist revolutionary regime in, "liberated Rhodesia."

"Spotlight on Africa" published by the American-African Affairs Assn. asks a question that may cause some sleepless nights in Wash.—what will the U.S. do if a popularly elected, black, majority rule is threatened by a widescale guerrilla war backed by the Sov. U? Spotlight asks, "Congress may well be able to ignore the geopolitical, military & ec. issues at stake in a Southern Africa increasingly falling under Soviet influence <u>but</u> would it be able to avoid providing the only tangible western aid possible to a <u>besieged</u>, <u>black</u>, <u>majority</u> in Rhodesia?" ** That's quite a question.

In the meantime without agreement in Geneva the Ian Smith admin. with the support of the black majority in Rhodesia is proceding to implement the Kissinger proposal as he said he would. This is RR. Thanks for listening. ❖

Cuba and Africa
May 4, 1977

A few years ago ~~an~~ a ping-pong game between Americans & Red Chinese gave birth to the expression ping pong diplomacy. Now we're playing basketball in Cuba. I'll be right back.

The ~~2~~ *U.S.* Senators from S. Dak. [*Geo.*] McGovern & [*James*] Abourezk*** have to be congratulated on their ability to hide their disappointment ~~when~~ *while* the U. of S. Dak. ~~lost both~~ basketball team ~~lost 2~~ *was losing 2* games in a row to a Cuban all-star team. As a matter of fact they managed to look ~~pract~~ practically ecstatic.

The game was evidently the result of a meeting between Sen. McGovern and Castro in which the Sen. found the Cuban dictator to be a charming, friendly WELL INFORMED fellow. It sort of reminds you of how we ~~decided~~ *discovered* Joseph Stalin was good old Uncle Joe, shortly before he stole *among other things* our nuclear secrets. ~~among other things~~.

---

*The Institute was founded in 1970. Brian Crozier and Leonard Schapiro were two of the principal founders.

**Reagan's quote varies slightly from the statement in the newsletter. For instance, while he calls the country "Rhodesia," the newsletter says "Zimbabwe." "Congress may well be able to ignore the geopolitical, military, and economic issues at stake in a southern Africa increasingly falling under Soviet influence (as the legislators chose to do during the height of the Angolan civil war) but would it be able to avoid providing the only tangible Western aid possible to a besieged black majority in Zimbabwe?" 10 (Dec. 6, 1976): 2.

***Senator George S. McGovern (D-South Dakota) and Senator James Abourezk (D-South Dakota).

Then the other day one of our leading metropolitan papers editorialized about how wrong it has been for the U.S. to be unfriendly to this island neighbor 90 miles off the Fla. Coast. And how right it is that we should be restoring trade relations. Oh sure, Castro has some 15,000 troops *stirring up trouble in* ~~in~~ Africa and he did visit ~~Mo~~ ≠ *Africa himself* but the fact that his visit coincided with that of Soviet Pres. Podgorny—well it's a small world.

The month was March and Fidel Castro boarded a Russian super-sonic ~~transport plane~~ *plane & flew off*, first to Algeria and then on a tour of Libya, South Yemen, Ethiopia, Somalia, Tanzania and of course Angola. It was also March when military forces armed with Russian made weapons and trained in their use by Cuban soldiers advanced from Angola across the border into Zaire. The invasion was into the Shaba province which is literally a treasure house of Copper, Uranium & Cobalt. ~~the stuff~~

On March 22 Soviet Pres. Podgorny* with a staff of 120 arrived in Tanzania *also* by way of a Russian super-sonic transport. He spent several days in mainland Tanzania & Zanzibar. He then flew on to Zambia & Mozambique. It is unrealistic ~~to~~ for us to fail to recognize the Soviet U. has opened a new stage in it's campaign to achieve strategic dominance over Africa with all it's mineral riches.

Mozambique, a home base for the terrorists who slaughter innocent villagers in Rhodesia has declared itself dedicated to the goal of becoming a Marxist, Leninist state. Angola's conquerors the M.P.L.A. is following suit bolstered by Castros thousands of mercenaries.

Pres. Podg~~orny~~*ony* stood on the bank of the Zambesi ~~river and pro~~ looking toward Rhodesia and proclaimed that "together with the Repub. of Zambia and other progressive African states, the Soviet U. stands on the same side as the peoples of Rhodesia, S.W. Africa & S. Africa." Of course in those latter 3 countries he didn't explain that the people he stands with are not the majority.

In Lusaka he met for several hours with the leaders of the groups carrying on ~~the~~ terrorist, guerilla attacks and pledged the Soviet U., "will permanently support the just struggle of the fighters of Southern Africa."

Castro got back in time for the basketball games, and now we're talking about sending a baseball team to Cuba. That's only part of our response to this Soviet, Cuban assault on Africa. We've removed all obstacles to American travel to Cuba and we are ~~opening~~ negotiating or at least ≠ discussing re-opening of trade & pol. relations with the Cuban govt. And oh yes! We've

---

*Nikolay Podgorny.

ordered a halt to buying Chrome from Rhodesia. It looks like we're going to lose more than a basketball game before the foolishness ends.

This is RR. Thanks for listening. ❖

South Africa
July 6, 1977

A visitor TO WASH. RECENTLY from S. Africa—an official of the govt. of S. Africa called attention to the fact that in the entire hist. of the U.N. S. Africa has never *once* voted once against the U.S.

I'll be right back.

Lets start off by agreeing that apartheid—the separation of the races as practised in S. Africa, is not something with which Americans can be comftorable *comfortable* with. Let's also admit that our discomfort is heightened by our own memories of bigotry, discrimination & prejudice in our own land. We've come a long way toward solving our problem here although no one claims denies the job isn't finished.

But has our own experience made us intolerant and quick to criticize—indeed to punish this other nation without trying to understand complexities we were never faced with? For example is the problem in S. Africa simply one of racial difference? Unfortunately the answer is—no it's not that simple.

The Black majority in S. Africa is made up of several different tribes with long histories of conflict and animosity between them. If majority rule SHOULD COME TO BE in the sense that the black majority came into power tomorrow, there could very easily be outright tribal war as each tribe refused to be ruled or dominated by one of the others.

In coping with this problem, S. Africa has embarked on a plan of setting up separate Republics for each tribe, with self rule & complete autonomy for each. Those most critical of S. African policies have charged this is a subterfuge, an extension of apartheid and that the new Republics will be mere puppet states. But is this true?

But One such state t has come into existence already, the Republic of Transkei. It will celu celebrate it's 1ˢᵗ birthday in Oct. Here are some vital statistics on the baby nation; pop. 2 mil.; larger than Belgium, Israel, Lebanon & more than a score of other nations in good standing in the U.N. Indeed it's pop. is greater than some 30 odd U.N. members. It has a per capita inc. higher than 17 of it's neighbors and a literacy rate higher than 19. Freedom house a liberal group which monitors civil liberties throughout the world finds Transkei providing more civil liberties for it's people than a score of African nations including Angola, Mozambique, Zaire and Uganda—of course.

The United Nations refuses to recognize or admit Transkei to membership calling it a puppet state but it has happily accepted a number of puppets whose strings arc tied to Moscow. If the U.N. can keep a straight face while calling E. Germany an independent nation it has truly reached the ultimate height in hypocrisy.

Is it possible that Transkei is unacceptable because it came into being without bloodshed, or the help of Cuban mercenaries? The new little Republic is pro-western & anti-communist, two characteristics the United Nations does not possess. As a matter of fact we may be *on* the trail of why Transkei is being ostracized by N.Y.'s tower of Babel. Prime Minister of Matanzima* *has* said that developing countries cant afford socialism—and nor ~~developed~~ can other nations for that matter. He has proclaimed that the free market allowed to function is the way to provide the people with ~~food,~~ goods & services & food. ~~And~~ And if that isn't enough to keep him out of the U.N. he is staunchly anti-communist and has an anti-communism clause in the Transkei const.

All of these ~~things~~ may be reasons why Transkei cant get into the U.N. but they sound like good reasons why the U.S. should recognize Transkei and stop ~~act~~ acting foolish.—This is RR   Thanks for listening. ❖

---

*Reagan chastises U.S. Ambassador to the United Nations Andrew Young for meeting with Samora Machel in Mozambique, and is chagrined at the thought of American assistance being given to a "Marxist-Leninist state." Eight years later, on September 19, 1985, President Reagan would have a distinctly convivial meeting with Machel in the White House.***

Mozambique
September 27, 1977

Once again, if human rights are to be any basis for judgement, our country has lined up on the wrong side in Africa. I'll be right back.

On *one of* his Africa trips our U.N. Ambassador visited Mozambique where he got along famously with the dictator of that country, Samora Moses Machel. If memory serves me correctly ~~he~~ the ambassador promised him buckets of money from our endless supply. (Our national debt is roughly

---

*Reagan actually is referring to Chief Kaiser Daliwonga Matanzima.
**This story is recounted in George P. Shultz, *Turmoil and Triumph: My Years as Secretary of State* (New York: Charles Scribner's Sons, 1993), 1116–17.

$725 bil. and it takes 21¢ out of every $ of inc. tax *JUST* to pay the interest) But isn't "Frelimo" worth a little sacrifice on our part.

"Frelimo," that's the name for the liberation movement in Mozambique, ~~≠~~ now about 2 yrs. old. The former Portugese colony is ~~now~~ *today* a typical Marxist-Leninst state—and that is their own ~~name for~~ *description* of it.

Under Portugal there was a great tradition of religion in Mozambique, Catholic & Protestant churches in the South and Muslim Mosques in the North. It was therefore to be expected that the new nations const. would guarant~~yee~~ religious freedom. That const. reads: "The State guarantees it's citizens the freedom to exercise or not to exercise a religion."

It took ~~the liberation ju~~ *movement* "*Frelimo*" just one month to the day to demonstrate the worth of that constitutional right. All hospitals, clinics & dispensaries owned by churches or mission groups were nationalized. All Dr's., nurses and teachers were told to get out of the country bringing to an end a several hundred year old missionary, service-inst.

Machel announced that the people could take the Dr's. places & students would become teachers. Missionaries & Ministers and those associated with health & school units were thrown out of their jobs, their homes & even their automobiles were confiscated.

Very soon 18 large church & private hospitals closed their doors. The 661 Drs. who treated Mozambiques 8 mil. people on liberation day dwindled to 60. Under Portugal the country had boasted one of the finest health programs in all Africa. Now the World Health Org. has declared much of the country a disaster area.

But it is in religion that we can best define human rights in Mozambique. One year after the const. promised religious freedom a govt. spokesman said, "the Socialist state is not neutral in matters of religion & atheism. It is secular because the concepts of nature and of society are opposed to religious and to all spiritual & idealistic concepts."

~~Instruct~~ Religious instruction of children is forbidden and all children over age 5 belong to the state. At 14 they are taken from their parents and sent to Frelimo run camps. One young man served a 6 mo. prison term because he had a religious pamphlet in his pocket.

Ministers & Priests including a number of Americans have been imprisoned with no charges against them. Three Americans were jailed for 13 mo.—no charge & no word from Wash. D.C.

~~Frelimo groups are told to attend churches and demand equal time to point out that worshippers should serve the revolution rather than waste their time in worship. In fact t~~The people have been told that to go to church is to be disloyal to Mozambique. ~~American~~ Religions with an American base seem to get the harshest treatment, although Machel participated personally in the smashing of a Catholic altar while weeping nuns stood by. About 35,000 Jehovahs Witnesses are in concentration camps.

Two days before Christmas last year the govt. ~~p~~ controlled press said "He who believes in God cannot become a member of the party." Some 77,000 religious & pol. prisoners in Mozambique ~~have~~ cry out to the world for help. I guess our U.N. ambassador didn't hear them. This is RR   Thanks for listening. ❖

South Africa
July 15, 1978

We have a lot of people in our land who like to take a hand in creating foreign policy. They are diplomats without portfolio. I'll be right back.

It is the right of every American to have opinions, ~~and~~ *to* express them & when the occasion warrants ~~try~~ to ~~impress those opinions on urge~~ URGE our public officials to take action based on such opinions. We all can criticize our national policies & suggest changes. We can vote against elected officials who refuse to heed our suggestions. But whether as private citizen or pub. servant we cant have our own foreign policy & privately establish our own international relations.

The U.S. maintains trade & diplomatic relations with S. Africa. S. Africans have fought beside Americans in two world wars. It is true however that most Americans find S. Africas policy of apartheid repugnant and hope very much that those S. Africans who share our ~~feelings~~ *repugnance* will strive until they succeed in righting what we perceive to be a great wrong.

Some Americans think we should end our friendship with S. Africa; refuse to allow American businesses to set up branches there and simply ostracize S. Africa until it meets our own standards of racial tolerance. But since we have only recently achieved our present level of tolerance and have a fresh memory of an America where intolerance *bigotry* & prejudice were ~~rather~~ fairly widespread isn't ~~there perhaps a better answer?~~ *it possible that we could be* ~~helpful~~ *more helpful?* ~~Isn't it possible that a~~A friendly America *acting* with understanding & compassion based on our own experience could be of more help in resolving apartheid than we could by turning our back.

A Black journalist, recently returned from a visit to S. Africa told me of American industries there who were showing the way in hiring practises & even in providing employee housing. He said that black employees of Am. firms said it would be terribly hurtful to S. African blacks if the American firms were forced to close up shop.

The other day I came across an item that shows how ridiculous people can be when motivated by prejudice. It seems that the lady in charge of the American Peace Corps is so bitter about S. Africa & it's policies that she wont allow any Peace Corps volunteers to serve in that country. It does seem as though she is making a policy determination that is or should be beyond her authority.

~~But that isn't the incident~~

But never mind that. Recently two young volunteers serving in Botswana, which borders on S. Africa, came down with back ailments. They were not allowed to seek treatment in ~~the~~ *a* nearby S. African hospital. Madame director had them flown to Frankfurt Germany. That is a 14 HOUR flight one way. As one of the young men said, he flew 14 hours, waited another 4½ hours ~~and~~ to spend 20 min's. with a Dr. then flew 14 hours back. ~~The 2 trips cost $3000.~~ And here is the tag line—Madame director, who wouldn't allow treatment in a S. African hospital, sent them to Germany on a plane of S. African Airways. Cost—$3000

This is RR   Thanks For Listening. ❖

South Africa
January 1979

Would the black community in So. Africa be better off or worse off if American Corps. closed *down* their operations in that troubled land? I'll be right back.

While Activism on our college campuses TODAY bears no resemblance to the stormy rioting of the ~~six~~ '60's & early '70's, there is one cause that has caused an emotional ferment among ~~some~~ *our* students. College & U. trustees & regents on a number of campuses have faced demonstrators demanding that the school sell any stocks it may own in companies doing business with So. Africa.

A number of Corporations have received resolutions from some stockholders calling on them to close down THEIR branches in ~~So. Africa.~~ *that country*. The reason, of course, is apartheid and the protesters insist the Corp's. are supporting injustice & exploitation of the black majority by maintaining operations there.

I've pointed out on a number of these broadcasts that we all find apartheid repugnant. I've also pointed out that So. Africa's problem is quite a bit more complicated than our own struggle with bigotry & prejudice.

Now comes a voice from So. Africa itself calling on the protesters to cease & desist. The most popular leader of So. African blacks, the elected ~~leader~~

chief minister of the Zulu homeland, founder ~~of and the~~ *&* Chairman *of* the Nat. Cultural Liberation Movement, Gatsha Buthelezi ~~pleading~~ PLEADS with U.S. firms not to stop doing business ~~with~~ in his country.

Listen to some of his statements. "The uninformed liberals abroad who would like to see a violent confrontation in my country are working for the very thing that everybody here wants to avoid. Our need is for peaceful change, & foreign investment is one of the best agents of that change." Buthelezi then goes on to say that foreign investment creates jobs & brings money to blacks who make up more than 70% of industrial labor. He also says the skills the workers are taught are those they'll need if they are to take their rightful place in So. Africa.

He had few kind words for those visitors to his country who think they can understand ~~So.~~ Africa by spending a few days in Johannesburg. He calls upon them to come to Zulu land and learn of, "the remarkable gains we have ~~met~~ MADE in the last few years"

Buthelezi speaks in warmest praise of American employers in his country. He cites the providing of housing for employees, eliminating discrimination in eating facilities, loans for housing & educational funding. As a result of this & to remain competitive in the labor market local employees have had to adopt the American pay scales & benefits in a number of cases.

This black leader with unquestioned credentials as a respected leader of his people says: "I challenge anyone to prove that the black people themselves are against American investment." This is RR   Thanks for listening. ❖

Namibia I
July 9, 1979

Crime may not pay but terrorism certainly does at least on the African continent.

I'll be right back.

Our govt. and the United Nations among others are very upset ~~with Rhodesia~~ because the terrorist forces of Nkomo & Mugabe were not allowed to impose their rule *on Rhodesia* by force of arms. The Rhodesians by free & open election chose another leader & another more democratic course.

Now we find a sequel in another emerging country, South West Africa known as ~~Nam~~ Namibia. This had been a German colony until W.W.I. after which the League of Nations turned it over to S. Africa.

In 1978 S. Africa accepted a plan drawn up by our country, Britain, France, Canada & West Germany by which ~~Namb~~ Namibia would become an independent nation. This plan was put in effect through the U.N. But, shades of Rhodesia, no sooner had S. Africa given in than the U.N. began changing the plan to which S. Africa had consented.

Last year the U.N. Security Council by a 15 to 0 vote declared that Walvis Bay must be integrated into Namibia.* This was in direct contravention of to the agreement with S. Africa. The bay is one of S. Africas major seaports but what is more significant it has been part of S. Africa since 1884, Namibia was only mandated to S. Africa in 1920.

It now appears that the U.N. and the 5 Western powers changed their minds on Walvis Bay in an effort to persuade Sam Nujoma, leader of a Marx- ist —Leninist *Terrorist* band to accept the U.N. plan. In a sit

In a situation not unlike Rhodesias, Namibia has a terrorist force headed by Nujoma who does not want an ef election to establish a majority rule govt. in Namibia. His group calls itself the Southwest Africa Peoples Organi- zation referred to as Swapo.

As the U.N. sputtered around, unilateraly changing the contract it had signed and postponing an election in Namibia, Nujomas Swapo forces like the bandits of Nkomo & Mugabe in Rhodesia were busily murdering & pil- laging. The govt. of S. Africa decided the only way to settle once & for all who spoke for the people of Nambia Namibia wasould be to hear from the people by way of a free & open election.

Swapo was enraged, the killing increased and one of the leading BLACK moderates who could have won a free election was murdered. Documents were found proving not only that Swapo was responsible for the murder but that other leaders were on a hit list.

Our govt. sent observers to Namibia but their bias was showing, they only met with Swapo leaders. One of our Congressmen who has been con- victed of on 29 felony counts** wanted the DTA that is the moderate party to turn the govt. over to Swapo—apparently without an election. The U.N. has declared Swapo is somehow the only legitimate spokesman for the coun- try. Three U.N. funds *bodies,* the U.N. Commission for Namibia, the U.N. Council for Namibia & the U.N. Fund for Namibia channel mils. of dollars in aid directly to Nujoma the Swapo leader. Unicef & Unesco do likewise.

Chapter 2 on the effort to force *impose* a communist govt. without an election on the people of Namibia will follow—next broadcast.

This is RR   Thanks for listening. ❖

---

*Walvis Bay lies along Namibia's Atlantic shore. Annexed by the Cape Colony in 1884 and later administered by South Africa, Walvis Bay was transferred to Namibia in 1994.
**Congressman Charles Diggs, Jr. (D-Michigan).

Namibia II
July 9, 1979

This is Chapter 2 on the strange case of the United Nations and it's partiality to a pro-marxist band of guerillas in S. West Africa. I'll be right back.

Last broadcast I was talking about the newest emerging country in Africa—Namibia, once under mandate to S. Africa and now freed by that country to become an independent Nation.

S. Africa agreed to terms submitted by the U.S. & the U.N. but immediately ~~thereaffter~~ *thereafter* the U.N. began unilaterally changing the*ose* terms. It is funneling mil's. of dollars to a terrorist leader Sam Nujoma and wants to recognize his TERRORIST band called Swapo as the govt. of Namibia without benefit of a vote by the people. Our own govt. is going along with this in spite of Nujomas declaration that he is a revolutionary and that he isn't fighting for majority rule, ~~he~~ BUT is fighting to seize power.

It isn't red-baiting to call Nujoma a Marxist. He has gone to E. Germany where he signed a compact of cooperation. He visited Moscow where he was promised sophisticated weapons and journeyed to Cuba where he received promises of "unshakable support."

Violence has increased in Namibia. In May all of the people of that country were incensed by the bayonetting of a grandmother & her 2 young grandchildren. The U.N. made no comment about that but vehemently protested S. Africas attempt to capture & punish the murderers.

The interim govt. of Namibia has ~~eliminated~~ *removed* more than 95% of apartheid and has worked hard to achieve a non-racial govt. and complete majority rule.

S. Africa took it's seat in the U.N. and attempted to present it's side of the story. It was their 1ˢᵗ appearance *in the* U.N. in 5 yrs. The ~~U.N.~~ General Assembly voted 93 to 19 to *not accept* their Ambassadors credentials. Even so S. Africa continues to say it will stand by the U.N. proposal it signed in good faith.

It ~~is~~ boggles the mind to think that our govt. believes it is in our best interests to turn Namibia over to a pro-communist govt. when it is obvious that the people of that country prefer a govt. favorable to the West and certainly non-communist.

Namibia is rich in minerals & has great room for expansion with a population of less than 2 inhabitants per sq. mile. A former mayor of it's capital city says; "We believe that the United States has lost sight of what is really happening here. It's support of terrorism is not the policy you would expect from a great power."

No it isn't. And it's hard to understand our agreeing with a demand that Nujomas murderous force be allowed to openly establish bases within Namibia. Possibly we think it is inconvenient for them to have to cross the border from their hideouts in Angola whenever they feel a murder coming on.

The Democratic Turnhalle Alliance ~~is~~ a multi-racial political party called the D.T.A. representing the 11 black, brown & white population groups of Namibia~~. Maybe~~ *continues to strive for free elections. Maybe* we'll be lucky & ~~the D.T.A.~~ *they* will save us from ourselves.

This is R.R. Thanks for listening. ❖

Africa
September 19, 1978

With so much being said about Rhodesia & So. Africa these days it's hard to find news about other African states & that's too bad. I'll be right back.

A citizen of one of the new African states once ~~told~~ *assured* me that Africans believe in one man, one vote—once. The ~~victorious~~ newly elected then make sure there will be no need for another election by eliminating the opposition.

Just recently there was a little news item which I'm fairly confident many of you might have missed. It didn't exactly wind up on page 1.

It seems that Sierra Leone, once considered one of Africas few relatively free nations has verefied that statement about one man, one vote, once. Pres. Siaka Stevens has rammed through a new constitution for his country. It outlaws opposition parties.

The only party permitted henceforth is his All Peoples Congress ~~kno~~ party known as A.P.C. Opposition members of parliament have been given 24 days to change their registration. The leader of the APC party ~~which~~ *who* happens to be Pres. Stevens is the only person eligible to run for Pres. No opposition is permitted. The counterbalancing office of Prime Minister has been eliminated and the Pres. can only be removed for "gross violations" of the new constitution.

There is word from another of the continents new nations which has been LARGELY ignored. Equatorial Guinea, the only Spanish Speaking nation in Africa is or perhaps I should say <u>was</u> ~~Catholic~~ 95% Catholic. It had a population of 350,000, give or take a few when it became independent in 1968. Now there are 90,000 refugees in Spain & ~~≠~~ neighboring African nations and no one knows how many did not escape & were slaughtered.

Some time ago the Pres. of Equitorial Guinea issued an edict that his picture would hang above the altar and that when crossing themselves the citizens would say his name as well as that of God. When church authorities refused the persecution began.

The church has been outlawed, foreign priests expelled from the country, native born priests & nuns are in prison. ~~T~~ News of their fate as well as the extent of the slaughter is not known because the only embassies in the country are those of the Soviet U., East Germany, Cuba, The Peoples ~~Rep~~ Republic of China & North Korea. It is possible that the population has been reduced by half.

Catholics For Christian Pol. Action has called upon all faiths & races to join in protesting this inhumanity. This laymens organization is trying to get information to the public but says it has so far been largely ignored.

It forces us to ask ourselves, when we ~~ask~~ add this to Cambodia and to the ~~lives~~ persecution of the dissidents in the Soviet U. if the world has lost its conscience. The World Council of Churches has given Nkomos guerillas in Rhodesia (these are the forces who shot down the passenger plane) an $85,000 grant.

This is R.R. Thanks for listening. ❖

CARIBBEAN AND CENTRAL AMERICA

On September 7, 1977, President Jimmy Carter and General Omar Torrijos signed a treaty to transfer the Panama Canal to Panama at the end of the century and a treaty that guaranteed the neutrality of the Canal. After intense debate, the United States Senate narrowly ratified the Treaty Concerning the Permanent Neutrality and Operation of the Panama Canal on March 16, 1978, and the Panama Canal Treaty on April 18.

Because of his unrelenting attack on the Panama Canal negotiations during the Ford and Carter years, Reagan was considered one of the leading conservative critics of the treaties. Reagan discusses the treaties in radio commentaries, speeches, magazine interviews, television appearances, and in newspaper columns. As is clear in the commentaries below, Reagan framed his arguments about the Canal negotiations, Panama, and nearby states in terms of his views about defense perimeters and strategic chokepoints, the Soviet Union, treaties, human rights, and his interpretation of the historic mission of the United States in the Western Hemisphere.

Cuba
November 16, 1976

With freedom of speech & press & more worldwide news carried by more outlets than in any other country in the world we can still be victemized by propaganda. I'll be right back.

I think most of us hold to a belief that Russia under the Czars was a land ~~of~~ left behind by the industrial revolution; an almost medieval society made up of masses of illiterate peasantry held in bondage by a thin crust of rich, luxury loving aristocrats.

Coincident with this then is the assumption that bad as conditions are under Soviet rule the people are infinitely better off than they were. That may be true but are they better off than they might have been if the Czars had continued to rule for these last 59 years? A little known fact is that the greatest period of growth in Russia, expansion of industry, production of steel etc. took place between 1900 & 1915. Communism came in 1917 and it took decades for Russia to get back up to some of the production levels of ~~≠~~ 1915.

Wm. Buckley in his magasine "National Review" has recently replied to some present day propagandists who would have us believe Castro's Cuba is a modern version of that Russian ~~fariy~~ fairy tale. We've had some of our more liberal Senators visit Cuba in the interest of normalizing relations between our two countrys. A former aide to McGovern in his campaign is now a kind of agent through ~~which~~ whom American business firms can make contact with Castro. And Frank Mankiewicz has written a book extolling the great advance of Cuba under Castro.*

Now Bill Buckley recounts a ~~stor~~ story that exposes all this make believe. He tells of a young Panamanian banker who had a business of some kind to transact in Cuba. He had arranged through contacts to meet *with* Fidel Castro which was essential to the success of his trip.

The young businessman ~~was~~ spent 2 weeks studying ~~pol~~ the, before Castro Cuba. In addition to this homework he visited *with* Cuban refugees getting all the details he could, figures, places, descriptions of various locales etc.

He had learned also that Castro played games with regard to appointments keeping his visitor guessing as to when the meeting would take place. So he spent his time touring Havana & the countryside visiting medical clin-

---

*Frank Mankiewicz and Kirby Jones, *With Fidel: A Portrait of Castro and Cuba* (Chicago: Playboy Press, 1975).

ics, schools and stores. As Bill Buckley ~~described~~ *tells* it, he tucked all manner of information, facts & figures away in his memory bank.

Castro it seems has a taste for calling a meeting at say 2 oclock in the morning with no more warning than a knock on the door. Our young banker was ready for that. He retired at 8 oclock and sure enough at 2 AM was rousted out of bed to meet Castro & his entire cabinet. But having retired early he was ready.

Castro began the same routine that so impressed some of our Senators. It didn't impress the young Panamanian. Politely but firmly he refuted virtually every claim the dictator made. He had the pre-revolution statistics, he had his own observations from his tour around the city and he challenged everything from the teacher pupil ratio to the availability of food stuffs.

Castro was squirming, his cabinet was helpless. Finally he drew out a copy of Frank Mankiewicz book and presented it to his visitor—who promptly gave it right back. He'd already read it & he could refute that too. I dont know what business the banker was on but I wonder if he'd like to be a Sec. /of State?

This is R.R. Thanks for listening. ❖

Jamaica
July 6, 1977

Should the U.S. heap praise & favors upon a country whose ruler ~~has an-nounced he~~ intends to follow, ~~quote "the rich example~~ *experience* ~~of building~~ the example set by the Sov. U. in, "building a rich new society?" I'll be rite back.

The Prime Minister of Jamaica Michael Manley has been told ~~apparently~~ by a spokesman for the White House & our state dept. that the ~~U.S.~~ *people of America* admires his democratic achchievements; that we want to help in his ~~efforts to~~ *striving* for social & economic justice and that what he is doing has great significance for all the developing world.

Before "we the people" endorse such statements we should ~~know~~ *learn* more about Prime Minister Manleys concept of social & ec. justice. And "we the people" might find ourselves more than a little upset ~~to~~ *with what we* ~~learn as well as~~ with the spokesman who described us as filled with admiration.

Shortly after his election in 1973 Manley began his leftward tilt by flying to the conference of non-aligned nations in Algiers with Fidel Castro in Fidels private plane. Returning from the trip he dubbed Castro the greatest leader he'd ever met. After a follow up visit to Cuba he said, "I walk hand in hand with Fidel Castro to lead our people to a common destiny."

And do you know—he's doing just that. Like Cuba, Jamaica is on the edge of ec. disaster. Tourism once the number one industry has fallen from $400 mil. a year to ¼ of that; inflat. is high and unemployment runs about 30%. Many of the ~~ocean~~ beach front homes and hostelries that sheltered sun seeking spenders are boarded up relics of a bygone way of life.

Manley has organized youth brigades which are sent to Cuba for training as are detachments of Jamaican police. Cuban "technicians" have come to Jamaica. The govt. admits to less than 1000 but Jamaicans put the figure at 5000 and more arriving every day.

Other happenings typical of countries going communist or if you prefer just plain totalitarian have become the new way of life. *But* They are hardly the kind of thing ~~we~~ *one* ~~could~~ *should* say arouses the admiration of Americans. Organized terrorism by gangs of young goons sees beatings of innocent citizens & arson & murder *are* an everyday occurrence. Usually this treatment is directed toward Manleys pol. opponents.

Then & again typical of the totalitarian world, the Prime Minister uses the violence as an excuse to declare a state of emergency (a year ago June). Under emergency regulations arrests have been made, people are held without court order and hundreds are put in detention camps—again mainly *pol. opponents.*

Last December with the state of emergency still in effect the Prime Minister demonstrated his devotion to democracy by calling an election. No public meetings or motorcades ~~w~~ were allowed, no candidate could travel with more than 5 people— ~~≠~~ and roving bands of thugs were a constant threat in neighborhoods where pol. opposition was strong. At vote counting time they moved into ~~the~~ a number of places where the counting was going on and took over.

Manleys govt. owns the only TV station, one of the 2 radio stations and threatens to take over the only independent newspaper left on the island. And shades of Hitler and Allendé of Chile he has his own army. It is called the "Home Guard", 9000 armed, uniformed men which supposedly patrols with the army & the police but which is completely independent of both.

He has ~~begun~~ nationaliz~~ing~~ed the utilities including the phone system and is turning his attention now to banking & essential industries. Rigid controls have been imposed on imports, exports and currency. Yes he walks hand in hand with Fidel Castro but let no one say he has "roused the admiration of the people of our country." This is RR—Thanks for listening. ❖

Panama

August 15, 1977

The secrecy ~~that has surrounded~~ *surrounding* several years of negotiations over ~~the~~ *our* American canal LOCATED in Panama has ended. White House & State Dept. are insisting we must give it away.

I'll be right back.

It would be improper for me to comment on the terms of the agreement reached by the U.S. & Panamanian negotiators until we've all been able to see the treaty & study the terms. It is appropriate however to counter some of the *Wash.* propaganda ~~barrage~~ designed to soften us up by creating a guilt complex over the canal as if it symbolized American imperialism & exploitation of a weaker neighbor. ~~Indeed~~ Nothing could be farther from the truth.

The American people have every right to be proud not only of the great accomplishment in building the canal but of our complete lack of selfishness in all the years of it's operation.

This is not the picture created by our negotiators, Ambassadors Bunker & Ellsworth on ~~TV's~~ "~~m~~Meet The Press." * I'm sure they are honorable men who sincerely believe our national interest would be served by giving up the canal.~~b~~But they left the TV audience with the false impression that we have no ownership rights in the canal and that we have inadequately compensated Panama for our presence there.

Back at the turn of the century When we dealt with the new govt. of Panama which had broken away from Colombia we took over the FRENCH contract ~~the French had~~ had for building a canal. They ~~French~~ had failed completely, largely because of Yellow Fever which killed *the canal* workers like flies. The U.S. paid Panama, ~~& paid Pan~~ *&* Colombia because the original contract was with that country. ~~And~~ Then (and this Mr. Linowitz apparently didn't know when he spoke on TV) we went into what is now the canal zone & bought each piece of privately held land from the individual owners just as any individual would if he were buying a farm or house & lot. We not only have treaty rights—we are the OWNERS OF THE real estate. ~~owners.~~

Then we set out to conquer the dread Yellow fever. Volunteers ~~agreed~~ *allowed themselves* to be stung by ~~the~~ disease carrying mosquitos and some died but we eliminated the killer ~~disease~~ *fever* not only for canal workers but for all of Panama.

---

*The U.S. negotiators were Ellsworth Bunker and Sol Linowitz.

I recently looked at a book of photographs of the construction work, there were no bulldozers then nor heavy earth moving machinery and the obstacles were monumental. No other nation in the world could have built the canal. It ~~was~~ *is* truly one of the great wonders of the world.

There have been more than 50 govt's. of Panama in it's 60 odd years of existence. The present ~~govt.~~ *dictator* took power by a military overthrow of the elected govt. During these turbulent years we have run the canal for the benefit of all the world. We have never made a profit. In fact the original cost of the canal has never been recovered, it still stands as an unpaid debt ~~to~~ *owed* the U.S. Treasury.

We pour about $200 mil. a year into the ec. of Panama giving it a higher standard of living than most of it's Latin American neighbors. We paved the streets of Panama City, built a water system to provide pure fresh water and have negotiated treaty changes over the years to benefit the Panamanians. But until now we have never negotiated our rights of ownership & sovereignty. So we make no profit, we've never recovered the initial investment, we do not exploit the people of Panama—they are better off because of us.

There is an unreality about the whole thing. Wouldn't the logical & honorable ~~thing~~ *course* be for Panama to offer to buy the canal. How do we reconcile yielding to a demand that we hand it over free of charge plus giving them $70 mil. a year for taking if off our hands?

This is RR Thanks for listening. ❖

L.A. Times
September 6, 1977

† Several days ago the Los Angeles Times (on Aug. 29th to be exact) took me to task editorially for opposing the Panama Canal giveaway.* I'll be right back.

The Los Angeles Times has stated that I have "endeared myself to right wing Republicans" by saying I will "work for senate rejection of the new Panama Canal treaties." That raises a question of arithmetic. We are told that only 18% of the electorate is registered Republican. What percentage of these are identified as "right wing" the Times dosen't say but news stories in the Times as in other ~~stories~~ papers must have referred to the national polls which indicate 80% of all Americans are opposed to giving up the canal. As a matter of fact that same Aug. 29 issue of the Times announced that the American Legion & the Veterans of Foreign Wars ~~—6 million ex service~~ *are officially opposed to the new treaties.*

* "Reagan: Appearances Are Deceiving."

But in both the Times editorial and a ~~Times~~ column by Ernest Conine *(SAME DAY)* the principle argument given for ~~signing~~ ratifying the treaties was possibility of riot & bloodshed in Panama & Latin America. Yet the Times says we are not "running from the canal with our tail between our legs,." * ~~and~~ *It* then goes on to say the treaty gives us the right to defend the canal and keep it open even after it is no longer ours.

This raises an interesting question:. If we are so fearful of trouble including actual sabotage of the canal while it is *STILL* owned by us, would we send armed forces against Panama after we have agreed to give it away? if they decided to hasten the takeover?

There are other questions to be asked. Would the Panamanian people or even the present dictator of Panama want to sabotage the canal when it represents 25% of their Gross Nat. Product? A second question could be, does the Times believe the people of Panama are necessarily in agreement with their present ruler who took office at the point of a gun? In a military overthrow ~~he~~ *Gen. Torrijos* ousted ~~the~~ a duly elected President 11 days after he had taken office following a landslide victory. ~~As for~~

One American newspaper the ~~We might~~ Chi. Tribune sent a reporter to Panama several months ago while the negotiations were still going on. He interviewed the people of Panama on the street and in their homes. Even though many admitted the danger in talking to him they expressed their opposition to Torrijos and said giving him the canal would reduce their chances of ~~being free of him~~ *ever freeing themselves* from his dictatorship.

~~As for sabotage~~ One more point regarding the charge that the canal cannot be defended against sabotage. Surely the Germans in W.W.I. who were able to touch off the disastrous "Black Town" explosion in New Jersey ~~wou~~ could have profited by sabotaging the canal. In WWII when our Pacific Fleet had been virtually destroyed at Pearl Harbor our enemys must have wished they could close the canal. And in the Korean & Vietnam wars ~~surely~~ the communists who are the only recognized party left in Panama must have wanted to shut off the supplies we were pouring ~~into~~ through the canal.

The Times says businessmen are fearful that failure to ratify the treaty will set off a wave of violence in Latin America. Of course they are! The State Dept. has been ~~mobilizing~~ *propagandizing* them for almost 2 years to support giving away the canal on the grounds that their business investments in Latin America ~~would~~ *will* be endangered ~~by riots~~ if we dont.

---

* "The Canal: Satisfaction *Not* Guaranteed."

In my next broadcast I'll tell you what some of our greatest mil. experts think about the treaties.

This is RR Thanks for listening.

†This should be the 1ˢᵗ one taped. RR ❖

Panama Canal I
September 6, 1977

Would it shock & surprise you if I did a little talking about the Panama Canal? I hope not because that's what I'm going to do. I'll be right back.

† While we are told the Joint Chiefs of Staff support the giving up of the Panama Canal not enough attention is paid to those men who have led our military in peace & war *the past* who take a contrary view.

The Chiefs are bound by the mil. code to support the policy of the Commander in Chief. Those who have retired from the service are not so bound and we should hear their views on what giving up the canal would mean to our nat. security.

Four great names in modern naval history, all former Chiefs of Navy operations, Admirals Carney, Anderson, Burke & Moorer wrote the Pres. expressing their opposition to the proposed treaty.* They wrote: "As former Chiefs of Naval Operations, fleet commanders and Naval advisers to previous Presidents, we believe we have an obligation to you & the nation to offer our combined judgement on the strategic value of the Panama Canal to the U.S.

Contrary to what we've read about the declining strategic & ec. value of the canal, the truth is that this inter-oceanic waterway is as important if not more so, to the U.S. than ever." Citing their own experiences through 4 wars & the part played by the canal in those wars they said; "As Commander in Chief, you will find the ownership and sovereignty SOVEREIGN CONTROL of the canal indispensable during periods of tension & conflict." They added a line every American should think about, "Loss of the Panama Canal which would be a serious setback in war, would contribute to the encirclement of the U.S. by hostile naval forces, and threatens our ability to survive."

In closing their letter they re-emphasized the importance of the canal to our security and then said "It is our considered individual and combined judgement that you should instruct our negotiators to retain full sovereign

---

*Robert B. Carney, George Whelan Anderson, Jr., Arleigh Burke, and Thomas H. Moorer.

~~rights~~ *control* for the U.S. over both the Panama Canal and it's protective frame, the U.S. Canal Zone as provided in the existing treaty."

Of course such instructions were not given and the negotiated settlement calls for instant giving up of our right to sovereignty. ~~If this treaty is implemented Panama will immediately take over the zone and American employees will no longer be subject to American law.~~

This letter was written on June 6th. On July 22nd Admiral Moorer testified before the subcommittee on the separation of powers, Committee on Judiciary U.S. Senate. ~~As to the~~ As testament to his qualification he went from commander of the 7th fleet in the Western Pacific during the Vietnam war to Commander in Chief of the Pacific, then to ~~the~~ *Commander in Chief* Atlantic, ~~became~~ Supreme Allied Commander of Nato, Chief of Naval Operations and Chairman of the Joint Chiefs of Staff. It is easy to believe him thinking back on the 12 yrs. between 1962 & 74 when he says, "I saw this strategic waterway from many vantage points and under stressful circumstances."

Admiral Moorer told the Sen's. that as Commander of the Atlantic in 1965 & 67 when the war in Vietnam was still expanding he looked to the canal not only as a means of sending support to the Pacific command but in the perspective of the possible need to reverse the flow. There was a possibility of the middle-east situation deteriorating as well as potential trouble closer to home in the Caribbean.

He said "The canal made it possible to pre-position certain types and tonnages but always with the knowledge that the balance could be shifted to meet unforseen situations." And he credited the canal with providing the flexibility to do that.

Believing you should have the benefit of testimony by the Admiral & other mil. experts I'm going to carry on with this in the next broadcast.

This is RR Thanks for listening.

†I think we should start with these as second & third RR ❖

Panama Canal II
September 6, 1977

† This will be the 2nd instalment ~~of~~ reporting on testimony to a U.S. Sen. Committee by mil. leaders now retired who oppose giving away the Panama Canal.

I'll be right back.

Admiral Thomas Moorer former Chairman of the Joint Chiefs of Staff told a Sen. Committee on July 22nd that it is vital to United States interests to retain complete ownership & control of the Panama Canal. He ~~said~~ expressed the gravest concern about surrendering the canal to a leftist oriented govt. allied with Cuba, citing the danger of giving this advantage to a man who might permit Soviet power & influence to prevail by proxy over the canal.

He said, "the ec. lifeline of the entire Western hemisphere would be jeopardized. ~~and the point is: There is~~ no ~~point in surrendering this vital interest.~~ I have yet to see any solid justification advanced as to why the United States should willingly sacrifice the strategic advantages afforded to us by our possession of the Panama Canal." ~~He went on to say those who advocate the giveaway dont take into account that the canal zone could become a satellite base for an adversary.~~

Calling attention to the 8000 miles of added travel in rounding the horn which takes an average of 31 days he said: "If we were denied use of the Canal, we would have to build a much larger navy; much larger storage & harbor facilities on both East & West coasts and provide more merchant ships & escorts." ~~In mil. affairs there is no substitute for ownership of the territory and the ability to control or to deny the waters & the airspace."~~

~~He displayed his knowledge of the canals history when he~~ ~~cited~~ listed ~~the Supreme Ct. decisions—one as recent as 1972 that~~ ~~do~~ ~~uphold our right of ownership & sovereignty.~~

On July 29ᵗʰ Admiral John S. McCain Jr. (retired) appeared before the same Sen. committee. His last active duty was Commander in Chief Pacific 1968–72 during the height of the Vietnam war. Previous ~~duty~~ *experience* included duty with submarines based at Coco Solo in the Canal Zone prior to W.W.II.

Admiral McCain has been a student of sea power in defense of the U.S. and says the Panama Canal is the strategic center for ~~this~~ *the* defense of all the Americas. He called it a, "crucial element of U.S. sea power in the current drive for world domination by the U.S.S.R." He added; "to surrender one square inch of the zone territory, as shown by experience will only lead to future greater demands & eventual loss of the canal itself to a small country that could not possibly stand up against the pressures of stronger powers. Soviet Russia & the communists are making every effort to gain control of the canal."

He concluded his testimony saying, "the U.S. *is* facing the gravest threat in it's history. It has suffered successive defeats all over the world." Predicting that loss of the canal would result in the Caribbean & Gulf of Mexico becoming Red Lakes he said, "It is time for our country to stop cowering, cringing and to act the part of a great & powerful nation with a positive

& constructive program. We have nothing to be ashamed of. Nor need we apologize for all the foreign aid & technical assistance we have given to other nations."

Admiral McCain reminded the Senators that a great student of strategy with canal experience Gen. Thomas A. Lane foresaw the present situation in 1974 when we were already negotiating without the knowledge of the Am. people. Gen. Lane said: "The belief of some officials that U.S. operation & defense of the canal under treaty provisions instead of sovereign authority would eliminate the friction of recent years is a calamitous mis-judgement of the present scene. Marxist-Leninist subversion would be intensified by such a retreat. Friction would mount and the U.S. position would become intolerable. We would be compelled to use force against Panama or withdraw. That is a prospect which <u>no</u> Pres. should impose on his successors." This is RR Thanks for listening.

†Send a copy of this one to Admiral McCain. We have his address in the office. RR ❖

Panama I
October 18, 1977

I hope you are in the mood for a little history ~~which I hope will~~ *intended to* counter some of the more outrageous falsehoods emanating from our State Dept. I'll be right back.

As the debate goes on, to ~~sign~~ *ratify* or not to ratify the Panama Canal treaties, we're being treated to some re-writing of history. It's bad enough to have to counter the claims of the Panamanians but in a way they are being more forthright than our own quote, unquote "diplomats" in the State Dept.

Under the humorous cover of, "Its ours we stole it fair & square," advocates of the "giveaway" are ~~building~~ *trying to build* a fairy tale into an acceptable assumption. We are to believe that ~~number one we~~ *the* U.S. engineered a revolution then slyly took advantage of the revolutionaries & slickered them out of a healthy chunk of real estate.

More than casual mention ~~was~~ *is* made of the convenient & timely presence of U.S. warships off Panama *City & Colon* at the time of the revolution. What isn't mentioned is that U.S. warships ~~off shore were~~ *were frequently* off ~~shore~~ *those shores & with good reason*. We had signed a treaty in 1848 with Colombia ~~giving us the right to build a~~ *under which we built the first transcontinental* railroad across the ~~state~~ *Colombian* province of Panama. Under that treaty we ~~had pledged in perpetuity to~~ *were obliged to* keep the passage across the isthmus neutral & open *in perpetuity*. And this we had done for 50 years.

Eight men were responsible for the revolution—all Panamanians. Panama had made more than 50 attempts in 60 odd years to free itself from Colombia. Our Congress authorized the Pres. to negotiate a *canal* treaty with Colombia or Nicaragua. Colombia rejected the treaty and the 8 Panamanian leaders saw their chance. They seceded from Colombia and avidly sought a ~~treaty~~ canal treaty with us as the only way they could possibly have an independent nation. They were ≠ never encouraged by us to rebel. On Nov. 2ⁿᵈ 1903 Commander Hubbard* capt. of the U.S.S. Nashville received secret & confidential orders ~~via~~ *by way of* the Am. Consul at Colon. The order read & I'll quote it in full, "Maintain free & uninterrupted transit (remember that 1848 treaty) If interruption threatens by armed force, occupy the line of the railroad. Prevent landing of <u>any</u> armed force with hostile intent, <u>either govt.</u> or <u>insurgent</u>, either in Colon, Portobello or other point. Send copy of instructions to the Sr. officer present at Panama on arrival of U.S.S. Boston. Have sent copy of instruction and have telegraphed Dixie to proceed with all possible dispatch from Kingston to Colon. Govt. force reported approaching Colon in vessels. Prevent their landing <u>if</u> in your judgement this would precipitate a conflict. Acknowledgement is required."

The uprising occurred at 6 p.m. Nov. 3ʳᵈ. No pressure had been applied by us, no U.S. troops were landed, some of the Colombian troops joined the insurgents & the bloodless revolution was over. The Panamanians initiated the treaty negotiations and unanimously ratified the treaty almost 3 months before we did. Their 1ˢᵗ Pres. was inaugurated on Feb. 20ᵗʰ 1904.

The treaty granted to the U.S. "all the rights, power & authority which the U.S. would ~~possess~~ *possess* if it were sovereign of the territory—to the exclusion of the exercise by Panama of any such sovereign rights, power or authority." That's very clear yet our st. dept. *says* we have no such rights.

But *in* 1907 the Sup. Ct. ruled "It is hypercritical to contend that the title of the U.S. is imperfect & that the territory does not belong to this Nat."

Tomorrow I'd like to explore some more distortions of truth voiced by the treaty advocates.

This is RR Thanks for listening. ❖

Panama II
October 18, 1977

In it's anxiety to give away the *P.* canal and pay Panama to take it off our hands the admin. is trying to convince us that little would change in the next 23 yrs. I'll be right back.

---

*Commander John Hubbard.

We the people have been given precious little specific information on what would happen, what changes would be made in the running of the Canal if the treaties are ratified. What we have been told is that the application of the treaties would be so gradual we'd all be living in the next century (if we can make it) before any real change would take place.

We'd better understand that the treaty ~~is~~ does not really say that. In the 1ˢᵗ place the original treaty of 1903 would cease to exist. Whatever rights remained to us would be entirely new & limited grants made by Panama to the U.S.

We would acknowledge that Panama is sovereign in the canal zone. All the U.S. citizens including the mil. in what used to be the canal zone would be subject to Panama laws & courts. All police, fire protection, street lighting & maintenance, traffic management & garbage collection will be provided by Panama for which we will pay $10 mil. a year. The Panama railroad & all other land & properties become the property of Panama immediately. ~~We bought~~ *including* the privately owned land in the zone *which we bought* from the owners at a cost of about $160 mil. In addition we pay Panama for our having created the canal.

Of the 14 mil. bases now in the zone we can keep 4 and they will be under direct Panamanian civil & pol. jurisdiction. Signs in Eng. & Spanish will delineate defense sites stating that the sign is erected under the authority of the Repub. of Panama.

We are told by the state dept. & by the Pres. that the U.S. will have the right to Protect & defend the *neutrality of the* canal after the treaty has expired in the year 2000.

The truth? No such right is granted & no such right would exist after the pending treaty expires. Indeed Dr. Escobar Bethancourt* says flatly we would have no right to deny enemy warships use of the canal if we were at war.

If this treaty is supposed to cement friendly relations with Panama why does Escobar Bethancourt the dictators right hand bower incite radical student groups against us with inflammatory slander.

There is nothing *in the treaty* that will prevent the Panamanians from nationalizing the canal as Nasser did with the Suez contrary to the treaty he had signed.

We are told the canal is practically obsolete. If that is true then why dont we just hand it over & not pay $80 mil. a year to them for taking it off our hands? One of the arguments used to bolster the idea it is obsolete is the fact that the giant super tankers cant use it. Well then—why dont we give them

*Romulo Escobar Bethancourt was the chief negotiator for Panama.

N.Y. harbor, S. F. bay, and dozens of others because there isn't a harbor in the U.S. that can take a super tanker. But most of the large (not super) tankers can transit the canal & our Alaskan oil will reach the gulf refineries & the Eastern seaboard by way of the canal.

We have relied on the canal in every serious mil. crisis in this century to aid us to concentrate our fleet in areas of danger.

Tomorrow I'd like to talk about the Soviet threat and where the canal figures in their strategy.

This is RR   Thanks for listening. ❖

Cubans & Russians
March 13, 1978

I'm sure we're all aware of the Cuban & Russian presence in Africa—are we just as aware that they haven't limited their tourism just to Africa? I'll be right back.

Our U.S. Sen. Foreign Relations Committee has had a growing amount of testimony about Cuban & Russian infiltration & influence in Panama. But for some reason is *seems* unwilling to launch a thorough investigation of those tips it has recieved.

A group of Panamanians best described as Civic & educational leaders appeared before the Senate committee and told of witnessing the landing & takeoff of Soviet Planes at the Rio Hato airstrip. This was a U.S. airbase in WWII which we turned back to Panama. The Red Soviet planes come in low over the ocean to avoid radar detection.

The same witnesses told of how a group of Panamanian students every 6 months is sent to Cuba to study. What was it the Russians said about winning just one generation in a country & having that country forever?

Other interesting testimony was that Panamanian students are sent to Russia for 5 yr. study periods. Also that Torrijos has requested Cuban advisors to come to Panama and teach his admin. how to, "set up neighborhood committees to facilitate the govt's. control of the people on a local level." They told the Senators there were agreements between the Soviet U. & Panama to be implemented after the treaties were ratified; construction (by the Russians) of a hydro-electric plant in Panama & establishing diplomatic relations with Moscow among other things.

Lt. Gen. Graham now retired but formerly head of the Defense Intelligence Agency writing in the "Navy Times" said rumors of Cuban operatives in Panama are backed by pretty solid evidence. The Gen. had to be circumspect because of the risk of exposing classified information but he made it pretty clear there were Cuban specialists in guerilla warfare in Panama. Being careful not to put his former colleagues in mil. intelligence on the spot his testimony nevertheless made it clear that a congressional investigation is warranted.

Word in Wash. today is that Americans & Panamanians have met with anti-treaty Senators and talked of Cuban infiltration. Still a pro-treaty Sen. Frank Church complains that if we dont give Gen. Torrijos the canal, Panama will move to the left. Actually Panama hasn't much of a move left to make. In 1976 in the U.N. ~~Cuba~~ out of 21 votes Panama voted 20 times with Russia against the U.S.

Do you suppose the Congressional committees are going to wait and investigate all these reports <u>after</u> we've given the canal away? Anything is possible. ~~in Was~~ The Soviet planes flying over Cuba violate the 1963 agreement between Pres. Kennedy & Krushchev. Our state dept. defends the Russian presence *in Cuba* on the grounds the planes are ~~defensive~~ *there* for defense & the agreement referred to offensive weapons.

This is RR   Thanks for listening. ❖

Canal
April 3, 1978

In all the long Panama Canal debate nothing angered me more than the ~~continued~~ *falsehood* continuously perpetuated by treaty proponents that we have sinned against Panama.

†   I'll be right back.

It's possible that by the time you hear this the long debate in the Senate will have ended & the decision made regarding the Panama Canal. ~~But~~ Regardless, here are some things I jotted down out of sheer frustration while listening to the debates on radio.

In spite of the fact that Panama could never have become a nation without the canal; that we ~~made~~ *gave* a disease ridden, jungle swamp a lower death rate than *our* own & provided the only solid ec. base Panama can count on treaty proponents droned on & on about how we'd taken advantage of this country of ~~1 mil.~~ 1,700,000 people. No mention was made of the fact that ~~Panama~~ *over the* decades we patiently negotiated changes in the *1904* treaty in response to Panamaian complaints. Always the changes benefitted Panama.

Well whether this is after the fact or not here are some ~~f~~ facts the treaty proponents never acknowledged. In 1935 we handed Panama ~~the~~ a housing enclave: 25-2 bedroom homes in a walled area with paved streets and all facilities—cost $300,000. Note that all the cash figures I use are not todays inflated prices but actual ~~cos~~ construction cost. In 1953 they were given a seaside hotel built for $5 mil.

In 1955 there was a treaty readjustment that resulted in the following gifts to Panama; the 300 bed Geo. Wash. Hospital, fully equipped, with all surgical equipment & a one year supply of all hospital needs—cost $15 mil. The railroad stations, yards, yard houses, cargo trucks plus track—$50,000,000. One half of the town of Ancon including the P.O. bldg. & commissary, consisting of 20, two story units—$2½ mil. And the railroad annuity which had been almost doubled in 1936 was ~~&~~ *more than* quadrupled in 1955. That alone ~~will amount~~ *has amounted* to $33 mil. over these ~~next~~ *past* 22 yrs. ~~We~~ *This was done by us even though the 1955 treaty said there was no obligation to alter the annuity.* We also built the Boyd-Roosevelt Highway—50 mil.

In 1963 we made a gift of a Shrimp Fleet—50 trawlers with full equipment—$30 mil.

In 1970 the Thatcher Ferry International Bridge across the canal—$227 mil. and we've been maintaining & painting it every year since at a cost of $700,000 a year.

In 1975 ~~&~~ our State dept. without Congressional Authorization, gave the use of Old France Field (in the Canal Zone) *to* the Free Port Authority of the Panamanian govt. for 15 years, free of charge with an option for another 15 yrs. at the same price. A value of $3,000,000 could be put on this.

On top of these particular items and I dont pretend this is a complete list, ~~there has of course~~ *these just happen to be the ones* I know about, there have been grants in aid & A.I.D. funds totalling ~~550~~ about $550 mil. Adding it all up the donations I've listed come to almost a bil.,$ *actually* $966,500,000. And as I said that isn't replacement cost that is in those real dollars we used to have.

You know giving up the canal itself might be a better deal ~~if~~ if we could throw in the state dept.

This is RR   Thanks for listening.

†This should probably be in the 1ˢᵗ 5. ❖

Guantánamo
August 7, 1978

When the Panama Canal giveaway was ratified by our Senate some of us suggested it might be the first of ~~some~~ other dominoes to fall.

I'll be right back.

Since Spanish, American War days and the freeing of Cuba the U.S. has ~~held~~ maintained a naval base on the island of Cuba at Guantanamo bay. There is nothing imperialistic about this nor does it infringe on Cuban sovereignty the way some Panamanians ~~said~~ thought our canal ~~≠~~ *across* Panama did. The Guantanamo base is on ~~Cuban~~ sovereign Cuban territory leased by us, the lease to run in perpetuity.

I wont get into the strategic importance of this base ~~but~~ other than to point out it's location off the entrance to the Panama Canal and the added range it gives us in securing the So. Atlantic sea lanes. It was key to the Monroe doctrine back when we enforced the Monroe doctrine.

During the long debate over the Panama Canal treaties many opponents of those treaties, particularly men with great experience in naval strategy, pointed to the obvious close relationship between Castro & Panamas dictator Gen. Torrijos. Predictions were made that the Canal, if given up, would only be the 1ˢᵗ of several dominoes & the next dominoe could very well be the Guantanamo naval base. This of course was passed off by ~~the~~ *our* state dept. as having no real basis in fact and we were assured that we were buying the gratitude & friendship of the Panamanians ~~by~~ ~~≠~~ with our magnanimous gesture.

Well the treaties have been ratified and recently Castro ordered a week long celebration of the revolution *by* which he seized the reins of govt. in Cuba. We could also add that he also made Cuba a sattelite ~~nation~~ of the Soviet U. In his speeches during the celebration he brought up Guantanamo using all the phrases which were used so often by the advocates of the Canal treaties. The base was an affront to Cubas sovereignty, it was colonialism, imperialism and of course he wasn't going to stand for ~~it's~~ its' continued presence.

Right on cue those new friends we'd supposedly made in Panama were, "redefining," Panamas foreign policy in a 14 page document. Foreign Minister Nicolas Gonzalez Revilla ~~said~~ *observed* that, the centerpiece of Panamas foreign policy had been the canal. Now that agreement has been reached on that, they can lay the groundwork for a future foreign policy.

Their groundwork covered quite a bit of ground. For example the Torrijos govt. is calling for Israel to yield <u>all</u> occupied Arab lands. Closer to home they want self determination for Puerto Rico. Never mind that Puerto Rico has that already & more than 90% of it's citizens want to stay right where they are—very close to Uncle Sam. Finally Panamas new foreign policy called for the U.S. to give up it's naval base on Guantanamo bay.

Now—will *it* be a surprising coincidence if some of our state dept. types suddenly discover we dont need that naval base & giving it away will win the friendship of Castro?

This is RR Thanks for listening. ❖

Panama
March 27, 1979

~~Did you think~~ The Panama Canal treaty has been ratified, signed ~~&~~ *and* we wont hear anymore talk about Panama—right? Wrong. I'll be right back.

With the Senate debate on ratification of the Panama Canal treaty behind us it's been easy to lose sight of the fact that complex & comprehensive IM-PLEMENTING legislation will have to be passed by both houses of Cong. The treaty is suposed to go into effect Oct. 1ˢᵗ. ~~so a~~A number of bills have already been introduced.

† ~~It's very possible indeed probable that~~ We'll be hearing a great deal about the Panama Canal in the days to come. As a matter of fact the debate has already begun.

None of us who opposed ratification of the treaties wanted to be able to say, "I told you so," but the Panamanian govt. may leave us no choice. It is raising questions about the interpretation of the treaties which were thought to have been fully resolved during the Sen. debate. At least ~~&~~ WE were told they had BEEN by the State dept. & admin. spokesmen.

For one thing the Panamanians now claim they are entitled to possession of all movable equipment in the Canal Zone. There is no mention of this in the treaty but ~~&~~ WHEN OUR Navy started to move about $150 mil. worth of equipment ~~ba~~ out of the zone the order was rescinded. One can only presume in answer to a Panamanian protest.

Of even more serious consequence is a claim that Panama has retroactive jurisdiction over American citizens and businesses in the zone going back—believe it or not—for 7 years. The Panamanians say they intend to collect back taxes from our citizens & more than 140 businesses for that 7 yr. period.

A Congressional committee heard testimony from police officials employed by the Canal Company that they believe they may be prosecuted for actions they took in enforcing the law during ~~the past several~~ *those several* years. ~~And remember~~ Those were years in which rioting & bloodshed took place and the canal & ~~p~~ canal zone property had to be protected.

Another demand not covered by any clause in the treaty would have the U.S. renovate & restore to usable condition all buildings in the zone before ~~Panama takes them over~~ *they are turned over to Panama.* S This would be quite an undertaking. ~~since those are~~ Many buildings ~~that~~ have been deserted & unused for years. ~~& years.~~

You'll remember *we* the taxpayers weren't going to foot the bill for any of the canal giveaway costs. Now it seems the bill is already up to about $4 Bil. Congressmen on both sides of the aisle are more than a little upset. Dem. John Murphy of N.Y, chairman of the Merchant Marine & Fisheries Committee wants the Commission authorized to run the canal during this 20 yr. transition period to come under the control of Congress. The admin. says that would be unacceptable to Panama. ~~MURPHY SAYS IT IS QUESTIONABLE THAT A VALID TREATY EVEN EXISTS.~~

Repub. Congressman Bob Bauman of Maryland has introduced a bill calling for withdrawal of the instruments of ratification until, "their total costs" and "full implications for U.S. citizens," are determined.

Members of a Congressional sub-committee that met with Panamanian officials say there is such a difference in interpretation of the treaty it's difficult to see how it can possibly be implemented. Congressman Murphy says it's questionable that a valid treaty even exists.

Meanwhile Panama has discussed with ~~Ru~~ Moscow the possibility of importing Soviet technicians.

I still dont want to say "I told you so."

This is RR Thanks for listening.

†We should lead off with this one or at least have it one of the 1ˢᵗ to be taped. RR ❖

THE MIDDLE EAST

The politics of the Middle East was not the subject of many broadcasts. In a commentary about Soviet expansionism, Reagan writes that "the real issue in the Middle East has to do with the Arab refusal to recognize that Israel has a right to exist as a nation." In "The Olympics," Reagan sees political motives in attempts to exclude Israel from the games. In "Palestine," he discusses the creation of the state of Israel, and the plight of the Palestinian refugees. The latter issue consumed a great deal of the Reagan administration's foreign policy agenda during the Lebanon war.

Brezhnev
April 13, 1977

There was another part to Mr. Brezhnev's speech on human rights that deserves more coverage than it received from our press. I'll be right back.

On March 21ˢᵗ Soviet Communist Chief Leonid Brezhnev made a speech warning the Pres. of the U.S. to lower his voice on the subject of human rights.* He, of course, received worldwide coverage. Indeed, we could all be excused if we thought that's all he talked about. It wasn't.

He had things to say about the Middle East and frankly, if a man biting a dog is more newsworthy than a dog biting a man then the world press missed the real news in his speech.

In introducing the subject of the Middle East, ~~Mr.~~ Brezhnev sounded as if a re-convening of the ~~Geneva~~ Geneva Conf. on the Arab-Israeli stalemate might be in order. Then, ~~as~~ speaking for the Soviet U. which co-chairs the Geneva Conf, he outlined what his ~~countries position~~ *country considers essential* to a peaceful settlement between Arabs & Israelis. He said, "We hold, in particular, that the final documents should be based on the principle of"— now hear this—"the impermissibility of acquisition of territory by war." He then went on to say that Israel should ~~withdraw~~ WITHDRAW her mil. forces from all the territory she took in the 6 day war back in 1967. And, of course, return that territory to the ~~Arbs~~ Arabs.

This ~~of course~~ *to be sure* is one of the bones of contention in the present stalemate and could ~~have~~ raise among us Americans a question of, "why not?" After all we fought two world wars, were victorious in both and never asked for or took so much as a square inch of anyone elses territory. But we'd be pretty naive if we applied that yardstick to Israel in the present situation.

The real issue *IN THE MIDDLEEAST* ~~is the~~ has to do with the Arab refusal to recognize that Israel has a right to exist as a nation. ≠ To give up the buffer zones Israel took in the 6 day war would be to put cannon on her front walk aimed ~~by~~ *at her front door by* those who have said she must be destroyed.

But let's take a look at those other words of Mr. B. He is telling us the Soviet U. does not believe any nation has the right to hold territory seized by force of arms? Let's play, "what if." What if the U.S. said to Israel, you give back that territory to your Arab neighbors and we'll ~~sign~~ enter into a treaty with you—a mutual aid pact—if you are attacked we come to your aid?

Dont go away! There's more to come if we are playing what if. Then we say to the Soviet U by way of Mr. B. "~~this of course means you get~~ *you, of course, must get* out of Latvia, Lithuania & Estonia which you seized by force of arms." And ~~of course this would include all of Eastern Europe~~ *come to think of it that means turning loose FINLAND* Poland, Czechoslovakia, Hungary, Bulgaria, E. Germany, Rumania, etcetera.

---

*The full text of Brezhnev's speech at the 16th congress of trade unions is in *Foreign Broadcast Information Service, USSR*, March 21, 1977, R1–R17.

As a matter of fact there are some islands north of Japan and some territory in Mongolia ~~the Soviets~~ *you* occupy only because ~~they~~ *you* joined the ~~war~~ *fight* against Japan 20 minutes before the end ~~of WWII~~ *THE WAR*. (I dont think they heard a single shot fired in anger.) And up until then Korea was one country. It only became a North & a South Korea because Russia came in like a squatter and homesteaded *the north* half. Unfortunately, that was during a time when *we* were in that "good old Uncle Joe" mood ~~when we thought~~ *THINKING* Stalin was going to turn out to be the gruff old codger with a heart of gold.

How about that? One sentence by Brezhnev in a speech on March 21ˢᵗ 1977, and if everybody (especially him) did what he said, peace would come to the world. This is RR   Thanks for listening. ❧

The Olympics
September 6, 1977

I'm going to talk about 1980 but dont ~~raise~~ *tune* your political antennae, ~~I'll be talking about~~ *I mean 1980 and* the ~~1980~~ Olympic games. I'll be right back.

Most Americans were angry, frustrated and a little ashamed last year when the young athletes from the free Republic of China on Taiwan were told they couldn't compete in the Montreal Olympics.

If I remember correctly they had made the journey and were on hand when the door was slammed in their faces. The Red Chinese claiming there was only one China had demanded ~~their~~ *the Taiwan* ouster on the grounds that ~~their~~ *the Red* team was the official representative of that one china.

It wasn't the first time an Olympic committee has taken the easy way out under pol. pressure and I'm afraid it wont be the last. The committee should have told the Red Chinese their protest was denied. If they then chose not to compete that would have been their decision. The Olympics are dedicated to sport and by rule & tradition are supposed to ignore politics.

Frankly I would have been ~~delighted~~ *proud* if ~~the~~ *our* young athletes ~~from our country and~~ *and those from* other free world nations had told the weak kneed committee ~~they wouldnt compete unless their contemporaries from Taiwan were allowed to~~ *that Taiwan* would compete or the Red Chinese would be running around the track by themselves. But that didn't happen and the Olympic ~~torch~~ flame seems a little less bright these days.

Now it appears the athletes of another country are threatened with being ousted ~~fr~~ even though the games are 3 years away. The Soviet U. as host of the

1980 games is being a little more subtle ~~in~~ but the goal is the same—ouster of a nation because of politics.

In this case the target is Israel and someone had better start speaking up or Israel will be on the non-competitors list long before 1980 rolls around.

~~App~~ From all that can be learned the Soviet U. is working through the 3ʳᵈ world nations using an ≠ Olympic rule governing eligibility. It seems that a competing nation must belong to at least 5 of the 26 international sports federations to be eligible for the Olympics. If you'll remember the 3ʳᵈ world nations some time ago took advantage of their numbers to pass a resolution in the U.N. general assembly equating Zionism with racism.

Now as the various ≠ international sports federations meet, 3ʳᵈ world nations invoke this resolution to oust Israel on the charge of racial discrimination. So far the manouever has been successful in getting Israel thrown out of 3 federations. If come 1980 Israel does not have membership in the required 5 they just wont be invited to compete. Ineligible dont you know—sorry.

There seems to be a media blackout on this shenanigan and the Olympic committee makes Pollyana noises about Soviet guarantys. You cant help but wonder what would happen if the U.S. Olympic committee just once would say to the international committee "we want to see the guest list now or we aren't coming to the party."

This is RR   Thanks for listening. ❖

Palestine
March 27, 1979

One of the most difficult & complex problems in resolving the middle east situation has to do with the Palestinian Refugees. I'll be right back.

In all the long & involved negotiations leading to peace between Egypt & Israel the most unsolvable problem has always seemed to be what can be done for & with the Palestinian refugees. And it is safe to say this problem concerning the fate of 1½ mil. people is probably the ~~most misund~~ *least by the* American people. Or put another way it is misunderstood the most.

The general assumption is that the refugees (and now they ~~their~~ *have* descendants) were ousted from their homes to make room for the newly created state of Israel. They, their children & their childrens children live in Lebanon in internment camps waiting for the day when they can return to their homeland and <u>again</u> be a nation. I emphasize & underline that word "again" because that is the key to our misunderstanding.

You see the truth is there was no nation called Palestine. Palestine was the

Radio   Palestine   ①

    One of the most difficult & complex problems in resolving the middle east situation has to do with the Palestinian Refugees.   I'll be right back.

    In all the long & involved negotiations leading to peace between Egypt & Israel the most unsolvable problem has always seemed to be what can be done for & with the Palestinian refugees. And it is safe to say this problem concerning the fate of 1½ mil. people is probably the least ~~most~~ ~~known by the~~ American people. Or put another way it is misunderstood the most.

    The general assumption is that the refugees (and now they have ~~their~~ descendants) were ousted from their homes to make room for the newly created state of Israel. They, their children & their childrens children live in Lebanon in internment camps waiting for the day when they can return to their homeland and again be a nation. I emphasize & underline that word "again" because that is the key to our misunderstanding.

    You see the truth is there was no nation called Palestine. Palestine was the name of an area populated by a variety of peoples or social groups – Armenians, Kurds, Maronites, Jews, ~~th~~ Christians etc. And that area was under a British mandate.

    When ~~Israel~~ was created as a nation (carrying out a centuries old BIBLE prophecy) it's borders enclosed less than 20% of the area called Palestine. When the British by a single stroke of the pen created the ~~Kingdom of~~ trans Jordan east of the Jordan river ~~st~~ the new kingdom encompassed ~~the~~ 80% of the former mandate.

    The present refugees include some Muslims who voluntarily left Israel preferring not to be members of the new nation. Some came from Jordan & others from the territories not included in either of the new nations. If there is a bond today we could call nationalism it could be the result of their common plight as refugees. Or possibly it could simply be that having seen the instant creation of Israel & Jordan they have said, "why not us?"

②

There is no common heritage as a people other than their relationship and they were not at any past time a nation. Therefore one has to wonder if nationalism is a strong force among them & how many would choose to live in a new Palestinian state.

The west bank of the Jordan — a territory under U.N. mandate — is proposed as the site of the new nation. But the West Bank is not particularly fertile nor is it blessed with mineral wealth. It is however already heavily populated by Arabs, Jews & Christians and there is a very real question as to whether it could absorb a million & a half people.

The loudest, most persistent voice for a Palestinian state is that of Yassir Arafat head of the P.L.O – Palestinian Liberation Org. He is the leader of terrorist guerilla bands pledged to continued violence & the destruction of Israel. The P.L.O. has already assassinated West bank leaders who might be a threat to Arafats dream of heading up the new nation. No evidence exists that he or the P.L.O. are the choice of the refugees.

Has any effort been made (and if not why not) to canvass the refugees and see where the families & individuals would like to live? About 10% are Christian, 90% are Sunni Muslims. Their language is Arabic, virtually identical to that spoken in Lebanon, Syria & Jordan. What if the Arab states & Israel were to offer citizenship to any who wanted to emigrate? What if all of us helped to fund such emigration? It might eliminate a vexing problem. It might be worth a try.

This is RR Thanks for listening.

name of an area populated by a variety of peoples or social groups—Armenians, Kurds, Maronites, Jews, & Christians etc. And that area was under a British mandate.

When Israel was created as a nation (carrying out a centuries old BIBLE prophecy) it's borders enclosed less than 20% of the area called Palestine. When the British by a single stroke of the pen created the Kingdom of trans-Jordan east of the Jordan river it the new kingdom encompassed the 80% of the former mandate.

The present refugees include some Muslims who voluntarily left Israel preferring not to be members of the new nation. Some came from Jordan & others from the territories not included in either of the new nations. If there is a bond today we could call nationalism it could be the result of their common plight as refugees. Or possibly it could simply be that having seen the instant creation of Israel & Jordan they have said, "why not us?"

There is no common heretage as a people other than their *Arab* relationship as and they were not at any past time a nation. Therefore one has to wonder if nationalism is a strong force among them & how many would choose to live in a new Palstinian state.

The west bank of the Jordan—a territory under U.N. mandate—is proposed as the site of the new nation. But the West Bank is not particularly fertile nor is it blessed with mineral wealth. It is however already heavily populated by Arabs, Jews & Christians and there is a very real question as to whether it could absorb a million & a half people.

The loudest most persistent voice of for a Palestinian state is that of Yassir Arafat head of the P.L.O.—Palestinian Liberation Org. He is the leader of terrorist guerilla bands pledged to continue violence & the destruction of Israel.* The P.L.O. has already assassinated West bank leaders who might be a threat to Arafats dream of heading up the new nation. No evidence exists that he or the P.L.O. are the choice of the refugees.

Has any effort been made (and if not why not) to can *canvas* the refugees and see where the families & individuals would like to live? About 10% are Christian, 90% are Sunni Muslims. Their language is Arabic, virtually identical to that spoken in Lebanon, Syria & Jordan. What if the Arab states & Israel were to offer citizenship to any who wanted to emigrate? What if all of us helped to fund such emigration? It might eliminate a vexing problem. It might be worth a try.

This is RR   Thanks for listening. ❖

---

*Yasser Arrafat.

Part Three

DOMESTIC AND ECONOMIC POLICY

"The campaign trail is no

place for the cynic. I

am more than ever

convinced of the greatness

of our people and their

capacity to determine

their own destiny."

*T*he range of issues that falls under the umbrella of domestic and economic policy is daunting, and necessarily more varied than the issues under foreign and defense policy. Roughly two thirds of Reagan's policy essays were devoted to domestic and economic policy.

When Reagan began to write these essays in early 1975, apparently there was no special plan to cover particular issues. For the next five years he and his small staff wrote week by week, picking topics they thought were important, timely—and sometimes just interesting. The result was nonetheless a blueprint for the policy issues that were important to Reagan from 1975 to 1979.

At the top of the list of essays written by Reagan himself were foreign and defense policy (27 percent) and economics (25 percent). Next was our government, how well it worked, and questions of individual liberty (15 percent). Then came the hot issues of the 1970s—energy and the environment (10 percent). The other major topics covered were education (3 percent), Social Security and health (3 percent), crime (3 percent), social issues (3 percent), and welfare (2 percent). The remaining 9 percent of the essays fell into the categories of religious-inspirational, long quotes, or miscellaneous "desk-cleaning" topics.

In this book over half the essays in the section on "Freedom and Government" deal with the fundamental issue of capitalism vs. communism and socialism, and the conflicts between government and individual freedoms. On topics dealing with "The Economy," over half the essays were on two topics: taxes and regulation (cut the former, reduce the latter).

On economic matters, Reagan clearly leaned toward a relatively pure form of capitalism, with minimum government intervention and regulation. His essays on taxation have a simple theme—the best tax reform is lower tax rates. The goal of his economic policy seems to be a society where the public sector may grow, but at a slower rate than the private sector, resulting in a steadily diminishing role for government.

The essays on government reflect strong beliefs in limiting the growth of government spending, in free trade, and in the kind of regulatory reform that results in fewer, less onerous regulations. He finds the paperwork and bureaucracy of government especially galling, resenting the probing fingers of bureaucrats even in such matters as the questions asked in census taking.

On the questions of our primary energy supplies—oil, natural gas, nuclear power—Reagan addressed the trade-off between our energy needs and the impact of those needs on our environment. Basically, he argued that the goals of ample energy and clean air and water were not mutually exclusive.

The issues of education, Social Security, and health care were not the burning issues in the late 1970s that they would become early in the new century, but Reagan did address them, sometimes in a prophetic way. His education essays speak fondly of his days at Eureka College, and focus on the needs of students as opposed to the bureaucrats who run the public schools. His essays on Social Security argue that it needs to be "totally reformed." A number of the remedies he suggested then are now debated more widely.

The social issues are somewhat surprising. Only 2 percent of his essays dealt with welfare problems, 3 percent discuss crime, and 1 percent drugs. The family, women, and race all received less than 1 percent of his attention. And only one essay—out of a total of 1,044—was written on abortion. Nonetheless, many of his views have gained political support over the years.

There were very few questions of national policy that Reagan did not address. In a larger sense, when you look at the sweep of issues he covered in that five-year period, it was a personal platform. The essays were his vision of where our country should be going, his personal thoughts about what was wrong, what needed to be fixed, and how it should be done.

Reagan's basic economic ideas on spending and taxes and regulation, now often called "Reaganomics," have become far more acceptable than in the 1970s. Today, his views on Social Security are echoed by both major political parties, insofar as they both agree that the system is in danger of bankruptcy and needs reform. Reagan speaks of personal savings accounts as a way to provide a "much better return" than what was being promised by So-cial Security, and many people now are exploring similar options.

Finally, there are a few essays that we have called "Personal Stories."
They are about people he knew, like John Wayne, and the Bible and Christ-mas. They are all inspirational, and many have a moral.

FREEDOM AND GOVERNMENT

Reagan believed, as the first essay in this section makes clear, that America is unique among nations—"the hope of mankind." He felt we had a duty to protect what we had inherited, and to spread the message to the rest of the world like missionaries. In these essays, whether he is talking about the problems of ancient Rome or our voting rules, the national media or public broadcasting—the guiding star is always individual liberty, how lucky we are to have it, and how to preserve and protect it.

The Hope of Mankind
September 21, 1976

Sometimes I think we need to remind ourselves of what it is we're trying to preserve in this country. I'll be right back.

Every once in a while all of us native born Americans should make it a point to have a conversation with one ~~of our fine citizens~~ who is an American by choice. ~~They have a perspective on this country we can never have.~~ They can do a lot to firm up *our* resolve to be free for another 200 yrs.

~~The story is told of~~ *In* a dinner at Mt. Vernon back in revolutionary times, Lafayette ~~said to his~~ *turned to his* host ~~Geo Wash.~~ *and said* "Gen. ~~is you~~ *Wash. you* Americans even in war & desperate times have a superb spirit. You are happy & you are confident. Why is it?" Wash. answered "There is freedom, there is space for a man to be alone & think & there are friends who owe each other nothing but affection." *So simple an answer & so true.*

Now 200 yrs. later ~~it's easy to think that has all changed~~ our self respect as

Radio — Am The Hope of Mankind ①

Sometimes I think we need to remind ourselves of what it is we're trying to preserve in this country. I'll be right back.

Every once in a while all of us native born Americans should make it a point to have a conversation with one ~~of our born citizen~~ who is an American by choice. ~~They have a perspective on this country we can never have~~. They can do a lot to firm up our resolve to be free for another 200 yrs.

~~The story is told of~~ At a dinner at Mt. Vernon back in revolutionary times. Lafayette ~~wrote~~ turned to his host and said, "Here, you Americans even in war & desperate times have a superb spirit. You are happy & you are confident. Why is it?" Wash. answered, "There is freedom, there is space for a man to be alone & think & there are friends who owe each other nothing but affection." So simple an answer & so true.

Now 200 yrs. later ~~it's easy to think that has all changed.~~ Our self respect as a nation has undergone a strain. ~~At~~ At times it has seemed as if the symbol of Am. power has become our departing ambassador, flag under his arm boarding a rescue helicopter.

But there is an awful lot of that other America still around. Like beauty it may be in the eye of the beholder. A few years back a woman who had fled from Poland wrote a letter ~~which was to pointed in a that argument and she~~ said, "Among some of our Am. born friends it is not fashionable to be enthusiastic about Am. There is V.N. drugs, urban & racial conflict, poverty & pollution. Undoubtedly this country faces urgent & serious problems. But we newcomers see not only the problems but also solutions being sought & applied.

I love America because people accept me for what

(2)

I am. They don't question my ancestry, my faith, my pol, beliefs. When I want to move from one place to another I don't have to ask permission. When I need a needle I go to the nearest store & get one. I don't have to stand in line for hours to buy a piece of tough, fat meat. Even with inflation I don't have to pay a days earnings for a small chicken.

I love Am. because Am. trusts me. I don't have to show an identity card to buy a pair of shoes. My mail isn't censored and my conversation with friends isn't reported to the secret police."

On July 5th The "London Daily Mail" filled it's editorial page with an article by Ferdinand Mount in which he sharply criticized his fellow Britons & other Europeans who delight in lambasting the U.S. He said: "What the world needs now is more Americans. The U.S. is the 1st nation on earth deliberately dedicated to letting people choose what they want & giving them a chance to get it. For all it's terrible faults, in one sense Am. still is the last, best hope of mankind, because it spells out so vividly the kind of happiness which most people actually want, regardless of what they are told they ought to want. We criticize," he said, "copy, patronize, idolize, insult but we never doubt that the U.S. has a unique position in the history of human hopes. For it is the only nation founded solely on a moral dream. A part of our own future is tied up in it and the greatest of all the gifts the Americans have given us is hope."

Thank you Mr. Mount — we need that. This is RR Thank for listening.

a nation has undergone a strain. At times it has seemed as if the symbol of Am. power has become our departing ambassador, flag under his arm boarding a rescue helicopter.

But there is an awful lot of that other America still around. Like beauty it may be in the eye of the beholder. A few years back a woman who had fled from Poland wrote a letter ~~which was re-printed in a Nat. magazine. She~~ *and* said, "Among some of our Am. born friends it is not fashionable to be enthusiastic about Am. There is V.N. drugs, urban & racial conflict, poverty & polution. Undoubtedly this country faces urgent & serious problems. But we newcomers see not only the problems but also solutions being sought & applied.

I love America because people accept me for what I am. They don't question my ancestry, my faith, my pol. beliefs. When I want to move from one place to another I don't have to ask permission. When I need a needle I go to the nearest store & get one. I don't have to stand in line for hours to buy a piece of tough, fat meat. Even with inflation I don't have to pay a days earnings for a small chicken.

I love Am. because Am. trusts me. I don't have to ~~carry~~ *show* an identity card to buy a pair of shoes. My mail isn't censored and my conversation with friends isn't reported to the secret police."

~~More~~ recently On July 5ᵗʰ ~~to be exact~~ the "London Daily Mail" filled it's editorial page with an article by Ferdinand Mount in which he sharply criticised his fellow Britons & other Europeans who delight in lambasting the U.S. He said: "What the world needs now is more Americans. The U.S. is the 1ˢᵗ nation on earth deliberately dedicated to letting people choose what they want & giving them a chance to get it. For all it's terrible faults, in one sense Am. still is the last, best hope of mankind, because it spells out so vividly the kind of happiness which most people actually want, regardless of what they are told they ought to want. We criticize," he said, "copy, patronize, idolize, insult but we never doubt that the U.S. has a unique position in the history of human hopes. For it is the only nation founded solely on a moral dream. A part of our own future is tied up in it and the greatest of all the gifts the Americans have given us is hope."

Thank you Mr. Mount—we needed that. This is RR. Thanks for listening. ❖

Free Enterprise
April 16, 1979

It isn't unfair to say that today the world is divided between those who believe in the free mkt. place & those who believe in govt. control & ownership of the economy.

I'll be right back.

Our free mkt. system is usually termed capitalism and by that definition capitalism has hardly been around long enough to deserve all the evil for which it is being held responsible.

Most of us aren't really conscious of how recently the capitalist system came into being. Possibly we look back & think of the extravagant luxury of kings & emperors & see that as capitalism. We have a modern counterpart today in the rulers of Marxist nations. The ruling hierarchy of the Soviet U. live on a scale more akin to royalty than do the heads of capitalist countries.

Maybe our trouble is caused by the term *capitalist* itself. Actually all systems are capitalist. It's just a matter of who owns & controls the capital— ancient king, dictator or private individual. We should properly be looking at the contrast between a free mkt. system where individuals have the right to live like kings if they ~~can~~ *have the ability to* earn that right and govt. control of the mkt. system such as we find today in socialist nations.

We have a very visible example of the contrast between the free mkt. & govt. ownership in a household necessity we take for granted. The invention of Alexander Graham Bell—the telephone offers us irrefutable proof of the superiority of the free mkt.

As recently as 1880 there were only 34,000 miles of telephone wires on the whole N. American Continent. There were dozens & dozens of small telephone companies using several different kinds of equipment and there was no inter-connection between these different ~~count~~ *companies*. The same situation prevailed in all the other so called advanced nations.

If someone had openly advanced a plan to put a phone in every home, on every farm, in every hamlet & city and hook them all together I'm sure someone would have said, "only govt. has the resources to do that."

Now strangely enough in most other countries govt. did take over the telephone system and to this very day the *tele*phones in a great many countries are part of the postal system. In America the govt. wasn't bulldozing it's way into the free mkt. place as it is today. For that we can be grateful. The scattered, competing phone companies were left to the magic of the mkt. place. And that magic worked as it always does.

We take the phone so much for granted it's hard to realize things weren't always this way. We can dial directly to ~~virtually~~ any point in the ~~world~~ country and to a great many outside the country.

With ~~int~~ no intention of insulting anyone ~~it~~ I have to say it only takes a few days trip in many of those other countries ~~to~~ where the telephone is a govt. service to realize there is a difference. ~~Getting~~ A long distance call there can be quite an adventure—so can getting a phone installed.

But here we have them in our cars if we like, in private or corporation owned executive planes & on boats. We bounce long distance calls off privately owned satellites and use telephone lines for network radio & remote broadcasts of sporting & special events.

And all of this came about because private individuals wanting to make a profit for themselves kept thinking of better ~~ways to serve us,~~ *services to offer,* confident that we'd want that better service.

This is RR   Thanks for listening. ❖

Comparisons
March 6, 1979

I'm going to talk figures & statistics today which make you wonder how long communist leaders can hide from themselves the fact that our system is infinitely better than theirs.

I'll be right back.

There are 3 so called superpowers based on size & population in the world, two are communist one is free. If you don't mind trying to follow some figures you'll discover just how superior freedom is to the "workers paradises" that accepted the idiocy of Karl Marx.

In size ~~Ru~~ the Soviet U. is number 1 with 8.6 mil. squ. miles. China is next with 3.7 barely larger than our own country with 3.6.

In population of course China is way out in front with nearly one bil. people. Russia has 262 mil. & we number 220 mil.

We only have estimates for the G.N.P. of Russia & China and they are probably padded but ours is almost twice that of Russia & nearly 5 times that of China. The percentage of our work force engaged in agriculture is only about ⅛ that of Russia & ¹⁄₂₆ that of China, yet both of them have to import food or starve.

We produce 7 times as many automobiles as Russia & more than 600 times as many as China. Those autos travel on more than 3 mil. miles of paved road in the U.S. and only ¹⁄₁₅ of that in Russia, 200,000 miles & in China 161,000.

We outnumber them in telephones 155 mil. to only 22 mil. in all of the vast reaches of the Soviet U. & a mere 5 mil. in China. It makes you wonder what teenagers over there do in their spare time. And don't say they watch TV. We have 133 mil. sets to 60 mil. in Russia & only 700,000 in China. There are more than 11 times as many computers in use here than in Russia & 170 times more than in China.

Now let's get down to some of the differences in daily living. The average wage in our country is $13,400 that is about 4½ times Russia's $3000 and 37 times Chinas $360. ~~Now~~ Perhaps you think ~~theyre~~ THEIR money goes farther than ours. Well not if you translate a purchase into how long you have to work at the average wage to buy something—say a bicycle. An American would only have to work ~~1½ days~~ a day plus 2 hrs. The Russian has to work 7 full days and the Chinese worker PUTS IN 67 days.

When it comes to elbow room in our homes, Americans average ~~145~~ 450 sq. ft. for each individual. In the Soviet U. it's 133 ~~ft~~ and in China they have a confining 30 sq. ft. That is less than half the space we consider minimum in a prison cell.

We aren't too far apart in life expectancy but again we lead with an average of 73 yrs. In Russia it's 69 & in China 65. I'll bet it seems longer ≠ *though* in those countrys—than it does here.

One can't help but wonder if Chinas number 2 man Teng HSIAO PING WHO ~~when he~~ was here recently dosen't remember some of what he saw and question whether his country has chosen the right heros to follow. The plain fact is *followers of* ~~is~~ Marx & Lenin have never come close to achieving what we have and we started with a totally underdeveloped country.

This is RR Thanks for listening. ❖

Freedom Train
November 2, 1976

For about a year now we've celebrated our bicentennial with just about everything & in every way possible. ~~but~~ I'd like to tell you about one of those ways. I'll be right back.

I don't know whether the Freedom Train has come your way yet or not. It's made *well* over 150 stops and traveled more than 25,000 miles and if my schedule is correct it has Georgia, & Florida, to go before years end. In Calif. it played overtime nearly every night to accomodate those who wanted to see the mementos of 200 yrs. of freedom which is its cargo.

The Freedom Train isn't entirely an original idea. We had one ~~in~~ *after* W.W.II to ~~inspire~~ *sustain the war time* patriotism ~~to~~ *as a* help in the ~~war effort~~

cold war. But now in peacetime it is something of a miracle and has proven that while Americans may be fed up with excesses by govt. there is still deep in ~~their~~ *our* hearts a reverence for this blessed land.

~~It~~ *The train* started out in March of 1975 and almost immediately found that even ~~passing by~~ *without stopping* it drew crowds. People gathered at all hours even far into the night *just* to see the big steam locomotive & red, white & blue cars ~~pass pass~~ *roll* by.

When it stops people line up and wait hours in the rain or dark of night to walk through the cars & see the exhibit of freedoms accomplishments; the declaration of Independence, the Const., ~~the liberty bell~~ and the Liberty Bell. There is no end to the variety because ours is a land of variety so there are space vehicles, exhibits having to do with great Nat. heros including those famous in sports & entertainment as well as science & statesmanship.

One little town of less than 4000 population argued so convincingly that the train stopped out in a cornfield while more than 40,000 Americans from miles around visited it in a 2 day period.

In one state a hostile anti-bicentennial group protested the trains appearance as a propaganda tool of big business. They were persuaded to come aboard & see for themselves. When they left the train they were ardent boosters.

More than 5 mil. Americans have gone through the train and it's managers believe this fig. may be almost doubled before it pulls into its final station in December. *There is no counting the people who turned out just to see it go by.*

I said there was something of a miracle in the reaction of people all over America to this particular bi-centennial observance. There is another miracle ~~that~~ in this day of govt. organized, planned and managed activity; a miracle that could maybe only happen in America.

You see the freedom train is privately run on a non profit basis. It has no connection whatsoever with govt. Fed. State or Local. The originator of the idea is a railroad buff; a commodities broker named Ross E. Rowland Jr. He is also the engineer running the train. He raised the funds as well as two steam locomotives from ~~the~~ whatever graveyard old trains retire to. His crew is made up of private citizens who felt the call of duty. One man sold his business to make the trip, another left his photo shop and there are wonderful young people who volunteered because of pride in & love for their country.

Where else but in America could this ~~t~~ happen? Come to think of it how many places are left in the world where there is that much freedom to celebrate?

This is RR   Thanks for listening. ❖

Reagan talks about his personal experiences with Communist sympathizers in Hollywood when he headed the Screen Actors Guild in the 1940s. Reagan believed that communism was a threat at home as well as abroad, as the next two essays demonstrate.

In 1947, testifying before the House Committee on Un-American Activities, he said that "99 percent of us are pretty well aware of what is going on, and I think within the bounds of our democratic rights, and never once stepping over the rights given us by democracy, we have done a pretty good job in our business of keeping those people's activities curtailed. After all, we must recognize them at present as a political party . . . in opposing those people . . . the best thing to do is to make democracy work . . . I believe that, as Thomas Jefferson put it, if all the American people know all of the facts they will never make a mistake. . . . As a citizen I would hesitate, or not like, to see any political party outlawed on the basis of its political ideology. We have spent 170 years in this country on the basis that democracy is strong enough to stand up and fight against the inroads of any ideology. However, if it is proven that an organization is an agency of . . . a foreign power, or in any way not a legitimate political party, and I think the Government is capable of proving that, if the proof is there, then that is another matter."

Communist Conspiracy? #2
October 1975

Back in 1947 Hollywood found itself doing it's biggest battle scene without benefit of stunt men or trick photography. I'll be right back.

Yesterday I talked about a group of writers, advertising people & theatrical folk who have announced plans to radicalize the media. So far those plans consist of ~~a dozen~~ plays, books, films & TV shows purportedly telling the truth about Hollywood back in 1947 when the *film* industry was brought to its knees by a jurisdictional labor dispute. ~~of decided communist origin.~~

Having played a part in that whole affair ~~I've I thought I'd give you a~~ *my own* version ~~that~~ will be somewhat different ~~than what~~ *from the one* you'll see in those ~~dozen~~ shows, plays, books etc. For example I doubt if they'll bother to ~~show how communist~~ *tell how a number* of motion pic. unions & guilds were infiltrated ~~& dominated~~ *& taken over* by communist sympathizers. ~~beginning in the WW II days when~~ *while* ~~many of us were serving in the service~~ *in service in WW II* Or how ~~some of~~ those unions formed a rump organization* outside ~~of the~~ *& apart from their parent group the* A.F.I.. film council then ~~That rump group ordered~~ *engineered* a jurisdictional strike over the question of whether some 350 workers should continue in the union they'd always belonged to or ~~be forced to~~ lose their jobs to ~~another~~ members of another union.

Nor will they explain the real purpose of the strike which was to close down the studios until we were all convinced our own unions were helpless to reopen them. At that point they would propose a great new union including all picture people from producers & stars to prop men & stage hands. And the "they" doing all of this would control that union & the content of pictures which is what the whole fuss was about.

"Tinsel town"—land of make believe in 1947 was for real. The phone would ring at midnight ~~telling you~~ *and you'd be* told where you'd find the bus in the morning that would take you through the massed, rock throwing pickets.

A few tried to drive through on their own but not after ~~their~~ *their* cars were turned over and their arms broken to make them unable to work. Homes were bombed and some members of the striking unions *loyal but* unaware of their leaders true purpose lost their jobs permanently as well as their homes, cars & whatever savings they owned.

The Screen Actors Guild of which I was Pres. unaware ~~of~~ at first of ~~what~~ the truth we would subsequently learn ~~≠~~ volunteered to be the mediator to keep an industry from being closed and 30,000 people from ~~being~~ losing their jobs because of an argument between 2 unions. We began meeting with the rival factions & soon learned who were the bad guys.

~~These~~ *twice-a-day* ~~meetings were to drag on twice a day~~ Those meetings ~~were to drag~~ *dragged* on for 7 months—twice a day—7 days a week. Time after time we'd leave a meeting to get some sleep convinced we had a settlement. The next morning they would walk in with a passle of lawyers & a new set of demands. It was a model for ~~the~~ Pan Mun Jom & the Paris Peace talks yet to come. We'd probably still be meeting if we hadn't said—"enough already—we've kept the studios open without you and the meetings are over."

And that's the way it ended—or did it? ~~I have~~ Why do I have a feeling "here we go again."

---

*The "rump organization" was the Conference of Studio Unions (CSU), led by Herbert K. Sorrell. When the CSU went on strike in late 1946, 3,000 members of the Screen Actors Guild (SAG) voted to cross CSU picket lines, but 350 members signed a petition supporting Sorrell and the CSU.

Tomorrow I'd like to tell you about the Communist fronts and the real Hollywood black list.

This is RR. Thanks for listening. ❖

Conspiracy
February 13, 1979

I suppose this commentary could be seen as taking a backward look, but it will be looking back at an issue that may not go away. I'll be right back.

With all that is happening in these fast moving days we haven't heard too much lately ~~about~~ (at least in front page news) about the recent investigations ~~into~~ of the assassination of Pres. John F. Kennedy. True the testimony about the police radio sound track with it's alleged evidence that a 4th shot had been fired from the "grassy knoll" in Dallas caused a stir. Later evidence however that the radio sound track was from a motorcycle not even in the area at the time of the assassination seems to have left that issue up in the air.

~~Since t~~ This matter will probably come back again & again as witness the modern books purporting to offer new evidence in the assassination of Lincoln. Therefore I'd like to comment on a conspiracy theory in the Kennedy case that seems to have been over looked.

So far the demands for further investigation stem from ideas that Lee Harvey Oswald was not alone in the terrible, bloody deed and that possibly his cohorts were agents of our own govt. *But* why have we hesitated to investigate the possibility that Oswald ~~was~~ *might have been* carrying out a plot engineered ~~≠~~ *by an* international agency? Even the original investigation by the Warren Commission seems to have ignored ~~≠~~ *some* obvious clues and been rather in haste to settle for Oswald as a lone killer.

Former marine, Lee Harvey Oswald gave up his American citizenship and moved to Russia. He had learned the Russian language before he defected. Someone must have helped him do this. Once in Russia he married the niece of a Col. in ~~Russ~~ the Soviet spy organization the KGB. Thanks to that marriage he lived at a level of luxury above that of the average citizen.

~~Accounts have been written~~

While he is supposed to have recanted his favorable views on Moscow, it does seem strangely unlike the Soviets that he was allowed to return to the U.S. with his Russian wife. He was not the usual, disillusioned returnee eager to blow the whistle on his one time associates in Moscow. Indeed he ~~seemed~~ *seems* to have kept his Soviet connection in good working ~~condition~~ *condition.*

The Warren commission was evidently unimpressed by the fact that he was an ~~as~~ enthusiastic member of the *pro-Castro,* "Fair Play for Cuba committee. Nor did the commission find it significant that 2 mo's. before the assassination he went to Mexico to the Soviet embassy there and was seen in the company of 2 known Cuban agents. After his arrest his wallet was found to contain the addresses of "The Communist Daily Worker and the Soviet embassy in Wash.

It has been reported by more than one source that Pres. Johnson & the commission were fearful that evidence of a Communist conspiracy involving as it would the Soviet U. and/or Cuba would anger the American people & lead to a confrontation, possibly even to war.

It is also reported that the F.B.I. files indicated ~~that~~ there might *have been* ~~be~~ a Communist conspiracy involving Oswald but that the commission was unwilling to pursue this. The files further showed that the Justice Dept. & the Warren commission wanted to establish Oswald as alone in the case and to get this conclusion to the *American* people as quickly as possible.

Maybe someday a new investigation ~~might follow that lead~~ *will start down that trail.* This is RR   Thanks for listening. ❖

This essay was written less than two weeks after Ronald Reagan lost the Republican nomination to President Ford. Reagan talks about his plans for the future and the power of party platforms.

Convention #1
September 1, 1976

This is the 1ˢᵗ of what I hope will be a great many chances to ~~talk to~~ *visit with* you ~~about~~ in the days ahead. And I'll begin with where I've been these last 9 mo's.—I'll be right back.

Roughly 9 mo's. ago I signed off on one of these broadcasts ~~because on the following day I announced my can candidacy~~ *and the next day announced I would be a candidate* for ~~the~~ my parties Presidential nomination. For 9 months I've been meeting many of you all over this country, starting in the snows of New Hampshire, through the South, the midwest and the West. The trail ended in Kansas City on Aug. 19.

I have no regrets, only a great feeling of gratitude toward millions of my fellow citizens and memories that will warm my heart ~~for years to come~~ all the years of my life.

~~I believe that~~ In campaigning you meet people in a way that is unique and different. ~~from~~ Just traveling whether on business or pleasure, even out on the speaking circuit ~~cant match~~ doesn't compare to a campaign where people ~~have~~ gather together to exercise their responsibility as citizens. ~~It is a job interview.~~ The candidate is the job hunter, the people are the prospective employers. And you find the great majority take their responsibility very seriously and are truly conscientious. *Only the worlds worst scoundrel could intentionally let them down.*

~~It is no pl~~ The campaign trail is no place for the cynic. I am more than ever convinced of the greatness of our people and their capacity to determine their own destiny. ~~without undue govt. interference.~~

It has been an inspiring experience and at the same time a humbling one. To see young people ~~come from~~ *come to Calif. from* all over the country ~~to Calif.~~ and then at their own expense ride 48 hr's. in ~~trains~~ *busses* to Kansas City with no assurance they can even get into the convention hall simply because they want to help in any way they can. ~~For 4 days~~ They man telephones, drive cars, run errands all for a candidate or a cause they believe in. And then when victory doesn't come ~~to see them shedding tears~~ they stand with tears streaming down their ~~faces~~ cheeks as if somehow they hadn't done enough. You stand looking at those faces & hope you can say something to ease their grief and reward their dedication.

Among the memories will be *those of* landing at airports in the middle of hot, steamy days ~~≠~~ *or* cold, icy nights to find crowds of people young and old patiently waiting to greet you & bid you welcome to their state, their town. Sure there are other memories not so pleasant of some states where machine politics prevail; where delegates to the ~~≠~~ convention ~~tell~~ *say* you ~~they~~ would be their choice but they have to go along with the organization. ~~But~~ There is less of that than ~~there was~~ *in the past* and hopefully less than there will be ~~if todays young people will~~ stay involved *in the future.*

My belief has been strengthened that if govt. would someday *quietly* close the doors; if all the bureaucrats would tiptoe out of the marble halls; it would take the people of this country quite a while to miss them or even know they were gone.

I'm going to continue talking about the issues & problems confronting us. ~~with renewed faith in the ability of all of us to make govt. by the people work.~~ Tomorrow & ~~the~~ possibly the next day I'd like to tell you about the choice ~~we have in~~ the two major parties have given us. ~~a clear cut choice, more so than at any time in the past.~~ I'm not talking about candidates, obviously that wouldn't be proper or permitted. I'm talking about platforms adopted by the parties—two different ways to solve the problems we're faced with.

In the past, platforms ~~werent~~ platitudinous, bland generalities. We've made progress. Today they make specific proposals as they should and I'm going to tell you about them. ❖

Civil Service
February 2, 1977

Is Civil Service ~~for pub. employees~~ a protection ~~of~~ *for* the people against a pol. spoils system or is it a security blanket for pub. employees.

I'll be right back.

My first experience with the multitudinous rules of civil service and the evil they can do came during W.W. II. I was adjutant of an Air Corps instalation under the direct command of Air Corps Intelligence. ~~in the~~ We had approximately 1300 men & officers & 250 civilian employees.

One day a Major doing some significant technical writing came to me & said he couldn't stand it any longer; his civilian secretary "couldn't spell cat." Dutifully I called in the ~~civilian~~ head of the civilian personnel office and told the Major to tell her his story.

She couldn't have been more cooperative. Cheerfully she told the Major she'd draw up the charges for his signature & set the date for a hearing. Suddenly the Major grew wary—"what do you mean—charges?"—he asked. She explained that what would have to take place was similar to our military court martial. The Major would testify to the secretarys incompetence in her presence etc. The Majors reaction was—"not even if we lost the war."

Well I asked the Civil Svc. chief what possible alternatives there were. It was easy as ~~pay~~ pie—she could transfer a very capable girl not ~~now~~ then doing secretarial work to the Majors office & move the offending secretary to another less demanding spot. The catch was that ~~the~~ under civil service rules the incompetent secretary could only be moved by giving her a promotion. And that's how it was worked out. Forgive us there was a war on.

A short time ago a visiting burocrat here in Calif. ~~caused~~ *created* one of those man bites dog stories. He publicly called for reform of Civil Service. S. John Byington Chairman of the Consumer Product Safety Commission referred to Civil Service as, "a rigidly structured—almost fully tenured—burocracy which answers to no one."

He pointed out that when Civil Service was adopted it only covered about 10% of govt. employees. Today the figure is 85%. Now admittedly govt. being what it is there can be no quarrel with some kind of protection for workers who might be capriciously fired for pol. reasons & no one wants a return to the spoils system that gave birth to civil service. But we are denied in the present system the basic tools of management, the ability to hire, to fire & to demote.

That wartime story I told?—had we filed the ~~suggested~~ *required* charges ~~& conducted~~ the hearing could have taken from 6 months to a year f. Mr. Byington is urging that career civil service restrictions be removed from a certain level of management positions.

Maybe it should be pointed out that ~~in recent years~~ *a few decades ago* a great many of those management positions were not civil service only a decade or so ago. Then *an* outgoing admin. turning the reins over to an admin. of the other party would freeze it's appointees into permanency by way of Civil Service. Gradually layers of govt. that were once intended to reflect the policies & philosophies of elected officials began to reflect only their own philosophies. ~~and~~ They have taken to determining policy to a greater extent than any of us know when we cast our votes for legislators & executives.

It shouldn't be impossible to continue the protection & rules of fairness for the bulk of pub. employees while at the same time we determine what layers of management personnel should be appointed by incoming admin's. to help carry out the promises made by the candidates.

This is RR Thanks for listening. ❖

Rome
July 31, 1978

I've been going over some *ancient* history and surprising myself at how modern it really is in spite of the 2000 yrs. that have passed.
I'll be right back.

Back in 1939 an amateur historian, ~~a midwest~~ *H. J. Haskell,* Wash. correspondent for the Kansas City Star, wrote a book called "The New Deal in Old Rome." * The idea for the book came to him when he & his wife were touring ~~Italy~~ *Europe* in pre-World War II days.

They drove over a Roman built bridge in Southern France that ~~towerd~~ TOWERED 165 ft. in the air. ~~and~~ *It* ~~as~~ was ~~typical of the Romans it was~~ also an aqueduct. And almost 2000 yrs. after it's construction that aqueduct was still carrying water.

Haskell wondered how a civilization that could build such wonders could simply disappear into the dustbin of history. And thus a book was born. ~~It is mind boggling to add up the Roman achievements in it's several years hundred year history.~~

*New York: Alfred A. Knopf, 1939.

Rome with a population of about one million received 250 mil. gals. of water a day through 11 great aqueducts for it's several hundred swimming pools, 856 pub. baths & 13,000 fountains. Even though there was no printing press, books were plentiful & Rome alone numbered 28 public libraries. Roman houses had indoor plumbing, with flush toilets.

We can envy a little the Roman postal system that extended north into Europe & south to Egypt and guaranteed safe delivery. Roman justice made possible such things as commercial contracts, property laws, marriage & divorce, wills, trusts, etc.

We've inherited something not necessarily the best of Rome. Quintas, younger brother of Cicero didn't think his brother was a tough enough politician so he wrote a handbook to guide him. He said that, "a flattering manner wrong in other walks of life, was indispensable in ~~pol's~~ seeking public office." And he urged that if possible one should contrive to get a scandal started against an opponent.

But it was in the growth of govt. intervention that we should find a warning. They set interest rates, devalued the currency, created a wheat subsidy & then dumped wheat on the mkt. There were extensive public works like our New Deal–W.P.A.; a welfare system & food stamps. Believe it or not they had a depression & created a Home Loan Corp., an Agricultural Adjustment Admin. which plowed under half the grapes to stop overproduction of wine and their basic coin the Denarius sank lower & lower in purchasing power. They of course didn't have printing press money ~~so they added copper~~ *but they increased the money supply by adding copper* to the silver in the Denarius. It went from 94% silver to only 2/100's of 1% in Romes final days.

They even tried wage & price controls with capital punishment for violators but even then they didn't work as they don't work now. By that time govt. in Rome had brought commerce & industry to a halt with confiscatory taxation & a network of regulations.

In his closing lines Haskell did not attempt to draw a parallel as to the safe limits of modern govt. spending but did ≠ say "it is possible to involve destructive taxation with the dangers of inflation."

This is RR   Thanks for listening. ❖

Census
March 2, 1977

We need to know a great deal more than we do about govt. but how much does govt. really need to know about us. I'll be right back.

The constitution—Article 1 Sec. 2 provides that the govt. shall conduct a head count of all of us at least ~~every~~ *once* every 10 years. The purpose is sound; to make proper allocation of seats in the House of Representatives. This should be noted—the only purpose of the census is to ensure the proper distribution of Congressional representation.

The 1ˢᵗ census was taken in 1790 and the only questions asked were name of the family head and the number of males & females IN THE HOUSEHOLD over & under 16 years of age.

The last census was taken in 1970 and it had grown extensively in size & complexity. That simple head count had become a sociological survey. Free American citizens are now asked—how many marriages, number of children born to the woman of the house—including mis-carriages, value of property, how many bathrooms and on & on. There can be no real reason for these questions other than curiosity and possibly the need to justify an ongoing bureau ~~which~~ *whose* only functions takes place at 10 yr. intervals.

The 94ᵗʰ Cong. just prior to it's adjournment last summer passed a bill giving the govt. the power to ~~have~~ take *a* mid-term census. Which means the snoops will be out every 5 years instead of 10. By way of compensation & thanks to the efforts of Rep. John Ashbrook of Ohio Cong. did eliminate govts. right to put you in jail if you refuse to answer all the questions. They can still fine you up to $500 and institutions, businesses, e religious organizations etc. can be ~~freq~~ fined as much as $10,000.

For some time now there has been an agricultural census every 5 yrs. and it is even a longer more complicated set of questions than are inflicted on the city folks.

Farmers are independent people. On the last go round almost ⅓ of them threw the ~~forms~~ *questionaires* away. This of course led to ~~the~~ an exercise of govt's. coercive power. There were follow up inquiries & threats of prosecution. But even so at last count about a half mil. farmers were still holding out.

When govt. stops respecting the people, the people stop respecting govt. What is happening to all of us is really too bad. We want to respect our govt. but bureaus & agencies carried away with their own purposes are making that extremely difficult.

I'm sure the ~~bur~~ census bureau with it's warehouses full of files takes a pride in knowing how much information, how many facts including trivia the bureau has on all of us. ~~folks a~~ Those employed there probably ~~enoug~~ get a sense of satisfaction in knowing their capability to answer virtually any question about us. But govt. isn't a glorified quiz show. What purpose can it serve for govt. to know how many families have more than one bathtub?

Does knowing such a thing make govt. any better able to serve ~~its~~ *it's* ~~us~~ citizens? The answer of course is no.

Govt. has to know how many of us there are for ~~purp~~ purposes of Congressional representation. I'll even include knowing our ages and the breakdown on HOW MANY ARE male & female, but beyond that they are invading our privacy under threat of punishment if one says it's none of their business. And it is none of their business.

This is RR. Thanks for listening. ❖

Voting
May 25, 1977

It is time for Wash. to hear from the people about the, "instant voter registration plan" ~~that is~~ *now* apparently sailing through Cong. with the wind at it's back and only voter fraud ahead. I'll be right back.

It's funny how sometimes a bill of major importance will take on an invisible cloak and slip through the halls of Congress with very few of the people aware of its passage. The Carter admin. is promoting an election reform bill which I commented on a while back. Without repeating myself I'd like to tell you about one part of that reform which could make a mockery of our entire Dem. process.

The proposal is to allow anyone & everyone to walk into a voting place on election day, show a drivers license, a social security card or some other identification and be instantly eligible to vote. Proponents of the proposal say this will not increase the possibility of voter fraud.

Proponents of the Proposal are either living in a dream world or being cynically dishonest. Voter fraud exists now in spite of the registration laws, provisions to check eligibility and presence at the polls of poll watchers on guard against cheaters. In one Southern State 25 election ~~judges~~ *officials* have been indicted on charges of ~~fra~~ election fraud in the last election. In a challenged congressional election in *yet* another state ~~it has been revealed~~ the winner received the votes of oil stations, warehouses, at least 2 city parks and a few vacant lots. And ~~that~~ *the* idea that a social security card is proof of identity—a woman in Chi. has just been convicted of welfare fraud who had 50 S.S. cards. Soc. Security officials have long admitted that duplicate cards are probably held by ~~several~~ mil's. *of* people.

But about that cloak of invisibility; the Senate rules committee has ~~heard~~ *been given* testimony from the career lawyer who heads the Election Unit of the Justice Dept. Criminal Division ~~that~~ charging that the elec. reform bill has a "tremendous potential for fraud." Then Sen. Thurmond presented a wire to the committee by the chief of the Pub. Integrity Section of the Justice Dept.'s Criminal Div. saying the proposed instant registration would "increase the opportunity for elec. fraud."

~~Then~~ With the issue somewhat in doubt of passage in the Sen. Comm. shenanigans took place. A request to have the Attorney Gen. ~~himself~~ *& others* come before the committee was blocked. ~~Efforts to get other justice dept. officials to appear were blocked by a narrow majority of the comm.~~ And on May 12 the committee sent the bill to the Senate by a 5 to 4 vote. This was done after a comm. member who might have been the 5th no vote was called from the room by the Vice Pres.

Over in the house the Administration Comm. was hearing testimony ~~that~~ *by* elec. experts all over the land from N.Y to Calif. ~~were~~ *who are* frightened of the bill. The head of Chicagos election board (where they know a lot about ~~elec. fraud~~ *cheating*) said, "It will erode the integrity of our elections since it is totally lacking in any safeguards on the front end at the time of registration & voting." He predicted congestion & long lines delaying the voting on elec. day. Similar testimony was given by the Dem. chairwoman of Phil.'s City Commissioner. When other witnesses all Democrats appeared before the comm. to oppose the bill the Dem. members of the comm. were all absent. One staffer when asked why they weren't there laughed & said "they don't want to hear this."

They certainly didn't want to hear Richard Barnett of Chi. a black pol. organizer ~~who said~~ *tell them* the bill would make blacks vulnerable to exploitation by big city machines.

The House Comm. sent the measure to the floor by a 17 to 8 vote. It's time to write your congressman.

This is RR. Thanks for listening. ❖

Electoral College
April 13, 1977

If the electoral college isn't on the endangered species list it should be. At least it should be declared a game bird and given a few months a year when it couldn't be shot at. I'll be right back.

The move is on to revise the election laws.—~~a~~*A*gain! High on the list of changes ~~is the Electoral College~~ which V. Pres. Mondale has proposed ~~elim~~ *is* elimination of the Electoral College. ~~system.~~ *Now* I doubt *if* very many of us could find an excuse for *continuing* the ceremony after each Presidential election in which appointed electors in each state (one for each Sen. & Congressman) go to the state capitol and re-elect the already elected Pres. And maybe some of you think that's all they are talking about doing.

Unfortunately there is more to it than that. The very basis for our freedom is that we are ~~one nation~~ *Nation,* a Fed. of Sovereign States. Our const. recognizes that certain rights belong to the state & cannot be infringed upon by the Nat. govt. This is the guaranty that small states or rural, sparsely populated areas will have a proportionate voice in national affairs.

Those who want to do away with the electoral college really mean they want the Pres. elected in a national referendum with no reference as to how each state votes. Thus a half dozen rural states could ~~each~~ show a majority for one candidate and be outvoted by one big industrial state opting for his opponent. ~~What this kind of popular referendum means is that~~ Presidential candidates would be tempted to aim their campaigns & their promises at a ~~few states with big city populations~~ *cluster of metropolitan areas in a few states* and the smaller states would be without a voice.

If the *would be* executioners of the electoral college are sincere let them eliminate the college but continue to tote up the vote by states. ~~with each states decision giving it~~ *the majority in each state deciding that the state casts all it's votes (one for each Sen. & Congressman) for the winning candidate in that state.* Based on majority rule within each state that states electoral votes, one for each Congressman & Senator, would be given to the winner of the majority vote. The possibility of an appointed ~~electoral going~~ electoral college member voting on his own would be eliminated but everything else would remain the same. Yes it is possible under this system to have a Pres. ~~with less than~~ *elected with a* smaller total vote than his opponent but it has only happened 3 times in 200 yrs. Is that worse than having a Pres. who only carried a dozen out of our 50 states and got all ~~the~~ his votes from big urban areas? Would his programs in agriculture be fair to farmers or would they be aimed at *helping* consumers in big city markets?

The other PROPOSED elec. law changes are equally flawed. The Hatch act would be liberalized so as to allow increased participation in campaigns by pub. employees. There are roughly 15 mil. govt. employees.—~~g~~Grant they each influence one additional vote and ~~that is~~ *you have* a voting block of 30 mil. with a vested interest in high taxes, big govt. & more govt. programs. A congressman or Senator would think twice before launching a crusade to reduce burocracy or govt. revenues.

Then there is a part of the reform calling for easy voter registration. Let the voters walk into the polls on election day ~~and~~ sign up & vote. The idea being that low voter turnouts are due to the present registration rules. Somehow they skip over the fact that mils. of already registered voters don't vote. What's their excuse?

And of course they pooh, pooh the idea that voter fraud might be encouraged. Well in one state right now where they have *such* easy registration the count in the last election of a Congressman has been challenged. So far they've found a half dozen oil stations, several warehouses & empty lots, a cemetery & two public parks *that* voted for him.

This is RR Thanks for listening. ❧

Postcard Registration
January 19, 1977

Is a postcard really the answer to voter apathy or have we opened the door to wholesale voting by tomb stones and empty lots. I'll be right back.

Everyone talks about the weather but no one does anything about it—or so the saying goes. For the last few years maybe not everyone but quite a few have been talking about the number of Americans who don't take advantage of their hard fought right to vote. Unfortunately some decided to do something about it.

In my own state (Calif.) the legislature with great fanfare adopted postcard registration. There are now 14 ~~states~~ out of the 50 STATES in which voter registration can be accomplished by mailing in a postcard. The reasoning behind this is that the low voter turnout is due to the slight difficulty involved in going to a registrar of voters. Of course no one *has* pointed out that the same individual who finds this an insurmountable obstacle might also find going to the Polls too inconvenient.

In Calif. now that you can register by postcard we had 469,301 fewer eligible voters register than in 1972 and 1,005,716 fewer actually ~~voted~~ *voting*. In the 14 states that have adopted this method of registering 8 had decreases in registration—6 had *a* slight increase. But 12 reported a decline in the number who actually voted. In Texas one of the ~~two~~ 2 showing an increase, registration went up by over a million but ~~voter turnout increased by only 1%.~~ *there was no appreciable gain in the number of people who voted.*

In spite of these questionable benefits you can bet that Congress is going to try and pass a national postcard registration plan. The argument of course will be that citizens yearning to vote are prevented from doing ~~it~~ *so* by the ~~insurmountable~~ *horrendous* barrier of having to appear before a registrar. The answer to that is the one the American General gave to the German demand for surrender at the battle of Bastagne in WWII—"Nuts."

It is true that a great many citizens dont register & many who are registered dont vote. Some just cant be bothered but too many are disenchanted with the pol. process. There is a disillusionment with govt.; a feeling that govt. has failed us and that the pol. parties no longer have meaning. Too many Americans feel govt. has grown so big that they as individuals can have no effect on it.

The answer to this and the responsibility of both parties is to show that only by participating can they help change the things that are wrong. Govt. by the people won't work if the people won't work at it.

When Congress tries to present postcard registration as the great solution will they tell us it will *also* be a nightmare leading to another burocratic monster with a cost estimated at $100 mil. & up? I'm sure they won't tell us how much it will open the door to massive vote fraud, always a threat to the Democratic process.

The experience in the states where postcard registration is already in effect gives proof that fraud will be attempted and that there is virtually no protection against it under this system. In one of the 14 states one individual sent in 108 applications and only by accident was the fraud uncovered *but he or she was never identified*. One application turned out to be a city park—hardly a qualified voter. Another was a gas station. There was a boarded up warehouse, a power company, vacant lots & a playground among others.

Why don't we try reverse psychology & make it harder to vote. That might also make it more desirable & attractive. This is RR. Thanks for listening. ❖

In the following essay Reagan takes on a campaign finance issue that remains a matter of contention—contributions to political campaigns from mandatory union dues.

Labor
March 23, 1977

The *new* election laws were supposed to reduce, if not entirely eliminate, the possibility of influence buying through campaign contributions. The new ~~laws~~ *laws* are not an unqualified success. I'll be right back.

I'm going to preface my remarks ~~with~~ by saying that I have the utmost confidence in the rank & file membership of organized labor. I believe in their patriotism & their fairness. They are part of that great body of Americans who pay the freight charge for govt., support good causes and provide the manpower (~~either themselves or their sons~~) when the nation is threatened with war.

I say this so the distinction will be very clear when I criticize as I ~~will~~ *intend to,* the ~~hierarchy~~ *top leadership* of organized labor. ~~In my opinion &~~ ~~without blanket indicting all I still must say~~ Too many of ~~the~~ *THOSE* top leaders ~~subscribe to an elitism in which~~ *that they* believe they know what is ~~better~~ *best* for the rank & file members *better* than do the members themselves.

Victor Riesel* the columnist ~~is probably~~ the best informed commentator on the doings of organized labor ~~He~~ has recently revealed how the leadership is planning to raise additional ~~mils.of $~~ *FUNDS* to influence elections and *get* ~~ensure a govt. subservient to their will. Or perhaps where Cong. is concerned~~ ~~I should say~~ *a Congress* even <u>more</u> subservient to their will.

Already the election laws are *so* rigged *as* to allow the Committee on Pol. Ed. of the A.F.L.-C.I.O. opportunities ~~for giving~~ *not available to the rest of us for* support ~~to~~ *of* candidates. ~~not permitted in~~ *for pub. office.* ~~The head man in COPE (as it's called)~~ *COPE's head man* Al Barkan has come through with a new strategy for raising tens of millions of $. ~~for future campaigns.~~

According to Riesel the plan was unveiled with all the secrecy of a mil. ~~plan move~~ *campaign* at a meeting of top labor officials in Bal Harbour Fla. ~~a few weeks ago. It calls for adding a new dimension to collective bargaining contracts that would have employers~~ *It calls for having management* pay a ~~#~~ modest *per employee* contribution to union-controlled pol. funds. ~~for each # employee of the corp. or firm. Just as the contracts now provide for employers to pay into flower funds, vacation funds, special unemp. benefits etc. they would in the future support labors pol. activities.~~ *This will be a collective bargaining demand & means that in the future the employers will finance labors pol. activities.*

It was pointed out that these contributions could be camouflaged in many fashions. And during the closed sessions the 250 pol. specialists were urged to keep the project quiet ~~& thus away from pol. discussion.~~ *so employers couldn't mobilize & plan against it.* ~~The idea it was pointed out so employers couldn't was to prevent mobilization against the union position.~~

Some of the pol. activists said a checkoff as low as a nickel could result in tens of mil's. of $. ~~The Fed.elec. commission has recently ruled that pol. dues~~

---

*Victor Riesel, a syndicated columnist who specialized in labor matters, died in 1995. Reagan had a copy of Riesel's column as distributed February 22, 1977, titled "Low Visibility Power: Labor's Political Chiefs Devising New Strategy to Raise Scores of Millions for Campaigns," that he forwarded to Peter Hannaford as the source of Riesel's statements.

~~deductions for campaign action are legal~~. Those present made it plain they want the plan in operation in time for the '78 elections. Incidentally, confirming what I said about the leadership not reflecting the desires of the members, the reason for the new plan is found in the carefully guarded financial records of Cope. Right now *the* 14½ mil. members of AFL-CIO are not contributing in any significant way voluntarily. Most of Cope's money is coming from the Unions central treasuries. This is only legal if the money goes for registration drives & for contacting the members themselves. It cant be used to propagandize the public.

As Victor says "the smell of money & powerful pol. machinery being geared up for the next congressional & presidential campaigns permeated the jam packed room." Money means precinct power. Among those *on hand* urging backing for this was Calif's. Sen. Cranston.*

If management gives in to this demand it will ~~be a betrayal of everything they believe in. This is R.R. Thanks for listening.~~ *deserve whatever happens to it for it will be supporting the most powerful special int. group in Am. This is RR   Thanks for listening.* ❖

About the Press
September 21, 1976

I'd like to talk about what happened ~~between Nov. & Aug.~~ to a plane load (sometimes bus load) of press people, campaign staff & a candidate between Jan. & Aug. of this election year. I'll be right back.

I've always believed that a lot of problems ~~are caused by~~ *could be solved by* people talking ~~about~~ *to* each other ~~and the problems~~ *≠ solved instead of* about each other. Now I realize that in a way the job of those who report the news ~~is~~ ~~talking~~ *to talk* about ~~people~~ *the rest* of us. And a lot of us who are or have been in public life do a lot of talking about the press. Usually we are complaining, ~~and~~ sometimes with good reason but maybe we need to have a little more understanding of the other fellows job.

Last Jan. I climbed on one of two chartered busses and began campaigning in N.H. For the next few weeks I alternated between the two busses, riding part of the day in each bus. ~~In addition to camp~~ This I was told was necessary to the happiness and contentment of the traveling press. ~~and~~ Most of the passengers on the busses were just that—the traveling press. The rest of the passenger list was made up of campaign staff, volunteers and one can-

*Alan Cranston (D-California).

Radio   About the press –   ①

I'd like to talk about what happened between Jan. ~to~ to a plane load (sometimes bus load) of press people, campaign staff & a candidate between Jan. & Aug. of this election year. I'll be right back.

I've always believed that a lot of problems could be solved by people talking ~to~ each other instead of ~people~ about each other. Now I realize that in a way the job of those who report the news is to talk about ~people~ the rest of us. And a lot of us who are or have been in public life do a lot of talking about the press. Usually we are complaining, sometimes with good reason but maybe we need to have a little more understanding of the other fellows job.

Last Jan. I climbed on one of two chartered busses and began campaigning in N.H. For the next few weeks I alternated between the two busses, riding part of the day in each bus. This I was told was necessary to the happiness and contentment of the traveling press. Most of the passengers on the busses were just that – the traveling press. The rest of the passenger list was made up of campaign staff, volunteers and one candidate plus wife. Later as the campaign swung out into other states the busses became a chartered 727.

There were network news commentators with names & faces as familiar as those of your next of kin; stars of the print media both magazine & daily paper whose faces were familiar but * whose names were, TV camera crews and photographers. Most of them were representing the Eastern media – I'll confess, to me they were the hostile press. But we were even because to most of them I was that neanderthal reactionary from out west.

I knew many of them had written pre campaign

②

commentaries about me questioning my stomach for the battle, my staying power and whether I was for real. Now we were on tour together through the snow covered hills of N.H. doing as many as 12 towns a day.

In each town the procedure was the same; press off the bus first so they could cover everything from stepping off the bus to greeting the local ~~committees~~ committees etc. Then the town meeting sometimes in an auditorium, sometimes in the fire station, once out ~~door~~ in the snow where I stood and spoke from atop a stack of feed bags and took questions from ~~the~~ the audience. Every so often there would follow a press availability where they could have at me with reference to my ~~answers to questions~~ remarks or reaction to something the opposition had said in their campaigning. In bus & plane between stops we met in one on one interviews.

Over the long several months & thousands of miles you get pretty well acquainted. I saw the ~~actual had seen~~ rough side of their work, the long hours when the day was done for me but they were still filing stories. In some instances with a special feature their producers or editors had called for their work went on through the night ~~and~~ yet there they were on the bus or plane the next morning ready for the days work ahead.

I have to say their ~~my~~ treatment of me was fair. They were objective, they did their job and their pain was real when a shot or a paragraph was cut in the back office which lessened the objectivity of what they had done. More important we parted friends and I'm richer for their friendship. I even think they found the end of the trail not an easy story to write. This is R.R. – Thanks for listening didate plus wife. Later as the campaign swung out into other states the busses became a chartered 727.

There were network news commentators with names & faces as familiar as those of your next of kin; stars of the print media both magasine & daily ~~news~~ *paper* whose faces weren't familiar but whose names were, TV camera crews and photographers. Most of them were representing the Eastern media. I'll confess, to me they were the hostile press. But we were even because to most of them I was that neanderthal reactionary from out west. ~~I used to say they probably thought I ate my young but Nancy made me quit that.~~

I knew many of them had written pre-campaign commentaries about me questioning my stomache for the battle, my staying power and whether I was for real. Now ~~we~~ we were on tour together through the snow covered hills of N.H. doing as many as 12 towns a day.

In each town the procedure was the same; press off the bus first so they could cover everything from stepping off the bus to greeting the local ~~chairpersons~~ *committees etc*. Then the town meeting sometimes in an auditorium, sometimes in the fire station, once ~~stan~~ *out* in the snow where I stood and spoke from atop a stack of feed bags and took questions from ~~≠~~ the audience. Every so often there would follow a press availability where they could have at me with reference to my ~~answers to questions~~ *remarks or reaction* to something the opposition had said in their campaigning. In bus & plane between stops we met in one on one interviews.

Over the long several months & thousands of miles you get pretty well acquainted. I saw the ~~actual~~ ~~hard work~~ rough side of their work, the long hours when the day was done for me but they were still filing stories. In some instances with a special feature their producers or editors had called for their work went on through the night ~~and~~ *yet* there they were on the bus or plane *the next morning* ready for the days work ahead.

I have to say *their* ~~my tre~~ treatment *of me* was fair. They were objective, they did their job and their pain was real when a shot or a paragraph was cut *in the home office* which lessened the objectivity of what they had done. More important we parted friends and I'm richer for their friendship. I even think they found the end of the trail not an easy story to write. This is RR. Thanks for listening. ❖

Public Broadcasting
December 22, 1976

I'll probably be publicly flogged for this but I'm going to talk about quote—public—unquote TV and ~~This is RR~~ who pays for it. I'll be right back.

I suppose I should start with a qualifier. I'm in favor of free speech, oppose censorship and will battle those who would restrict anyones right to speak his or her piece.

Now WITH that settled let me say, nothing about television is free. That of course isn't news to any of you. The "tube" only lights up by way of a considerable outlay of money ~~and we're~~ *as we* all ~~aware of that~~ *well know.* On regular commercial channels the money comes from advertising sponsors and we are reminded of that every time the entertainment is interrupted for a commercial. Incidentally some of the commercials are pretty entertaining & certainly a lot more imaginative than they once were. *But we who view pay in the purchase of products advertised on the air.*

~~But~~ Then there is public television, no crass commercialism and a level of culture some believe cannot be achieved by those who mix enterprise & entertainment. And the general belief is that public TV is free. Well obviously it costs someone something ~~&~~ *but* it is commonly accepted that those who prefer it's cultural level contribute just as private contributors support the symphony, the Opera & the Ballet.

I don't suggest that public TV has fostered this belief or even contributed to it in any way. But truth is public TV has a more steady income than might result from private charity even though it's audience tends to be higher in educational level and income than those who sit through the commercials on regular TV. *This select audience would ~~∌~~* perhaps object to being classed as a special interest group but nevertheless 70% of public TV funding is by tax dollars extracted from the citizenry at large. Therefore it really is "public." ~~There is~~ *A* Public Broadcasting Service ~~which~~ supplies the programs to the local public stations. ~~Now~~ *The* ~~private~~ *commercial* stations are subject to a kind of quality control by the viewers. If we don't watch certain programs the sponsor takes them off the air. ~~We~~ *As* taxpayers *we* have no such control over the programming paid for ~~our~~ *by* our tax dollars on public TV ~~and I don't recall any of us being asked~~ *nor were we ever asked* if this is what we want our tax dollars used for.

If public TV programs can't make it in competition with commercial TV is it right ~~for the~~ *to force the* taxpayer ~~to be for~~ *to subsidize* those programs for an audience that is admittedly more affluent than the average? ~~tax payer?~~ Shouldn't there at least be some way whereby the paying but nonviewing taxpayers could register approval or disapproval of the ~~way t~~ *programs* they are sponsoring?

I won't go into the ~~commonplace~~ *frequency with* which public T.V. indulges in programs which are propaganda for one cause or another but those who pay should have some recourse when there is disagreement with the message. The Pres. of the Farm Bureau Fed. protested about a program on migrant farm workers. The P.B.S. responded in Nov. with an even more blatant ~~propaganda film~~ *program which* even the drama critics described as propaganda for Cesar Chavez & his United Farm Workers. Whatever happened to pay TV? This is RR. Thanks for listening. ❖

Calvin Coolidge was one of Reagan's favorite presidents. Here he explains why.

Images
August 1975

Some day it might be worthwhile to find out how images are created—and even more worthwhile to learn how <u>false</u> images come into being. I'll be right back.

All of us have grown up accepting ~~without~~ with little question certain images as accurate portraits of public figures—some living, some dead. Very seldom *if ever* do we ~~ever~~ ask if the images are true to the original. Even less do we question how the images were created. This is probably more true *of Presidents* in our country because of the ~~extreme~~ intense spotlight which centers on their every move.

~~In recent years we've had some books published aiming at~~

I'd like to talk about 2 Presidents and their images. One was Calvin Coolidge the dry, unexciting New Englander who is more often than not remembered as a lacklustre almost laughable figure who *just* happened to live in the White House for a while.

The other is Dwight David Eisenhower ~~He is~~ remembered with affection, warmth and respect for his great mil. accomplishments in WWII. But for many his image as a President is that of a genial, golf ~~playing President~~ player who didn't stir things up much and who in the main presided over a country that rode at anchor for 8 years. The late John Kennedy *who followed him actually* campaigned on a slogan of, "get the country moving again."

Are these 2 images true or false? I'll list a few facts & you can figure out the answer for yourself.

Calvin Coolidge—the man H. L. Mencken said had been weaned on a pickle. ~~The columnist George F. Will recently~~ *Was he* a kind of do nothing President in one of those ~~historical~~ lulls in our Nations history? If so ~~≠~~ We should have such ~~lulls~~ lulls today. There was better than full employment—jobs were competing for workers. The cost of living went <u>down</u> 2.3%, the

Fed. budget was actually reduced and some of the Nat. debt accumulated in WWI was paid off.

During ~~a~~ silent Cals. presidency the number of automobiles owned by Americans tripled and a great new industry, radio, went from $60 mil in sales to $842 mil. They laughed when Calvin Coolidge said "the business of Am. is business," but we had true peace & prosperity—those things we are promised so often ~~and~~ *but* given so seldom.

Then the "~~Ike~~ *Eisenhower* years"—the era ~~when~~ of the '50s when we are supposed to believe an entire college generation stagnated,—probably because they didn't burn down the library. Well ~~he~~ *Ike* ended a war in Korea that had killed tens of thousands of our young men and for the rest of his 8 yrs. no young Americans were ~~asked to fight and~~ *being shot at anywhere in the world.* He also halted dead in its tracks the advance of communism. Big govt. didn't get any bigger and a citizen could go for an evening stroll in the park without getting bopped over the head. Wages went up steadily but prices remained the same. Steak was 85¢ a lb. and a gal. of gas was only 28¢. You could be well dressed in a $50 suit and $9 shoes. The work day & the work week ~~were growing~~ *grew* shorter and our taxes were reduced. Suddenly more kids were going to college, ~~than~~ more families were buying homes, never had a nation's wealth been so widely distributed and we were so strong that no one in the world even thought about challenging us.

Well as I say you can make up your own mind about the images versus the man but maybe we ought to go back and see what they did that we aren't doing. This is R.R.—Thanks for listening. ❖

THE ECONOMY

After national defense, Reagan's top policy priority was economic prosperity. He often made the point that without a strong economy you could not maintain an adequate defense, let alone pursue all the domestic things an effective government should do.

Reagan majored in economics in college—although he made light of his knowledge. That was before the ideas of John Maynard Keynes dominated economics, and Reagan seems to have learned well the basic principles of classic economic theory. Over fifty years later in the 1980 presidential campaign, when meeting with his top economic advisers—Alan Greenspan, Arthur F. Burns, Milton Friedman, and George P. Shultz—Reagan would listen to advice, but then make the key decisions himself.

Reagan's thinking on the issues that make up economic policy—government spending, taxation, regulation, monetary policy, and technology—are addressed in the forty-one essays below. His main concerns are taxes and regulation, and the number of times he wrote on those issues reflect his interest. The basic policies he favored—lower taxes, effective control of government spending, regulatory reform, and a stable, predictable monetary policy— were clear and never changed.

In "Inflation," the first policy essay he wrote for the radio series, he explores the relation between high prices and government regulations. Peter Hannaford, his assistant, had drafted the first two essays for the radio broad-

casts, but Reagan soon took over most of the writing. See the note at the bottom of Reagan's first essay: "Pete—I thought I'd try one too. Ron."

Inflation
January 8, 1975

Inflation is high prices. Anything that lowers prices legitimately without hurting someone ~~is helpful in fighting~~ helps reduce inflation.

Right now ~~American~~ business is more regulated *in America* by govt. than ~~business~~ *it is* in any other country in the world where free enterprise is still permitted. If we had less regulation we could have lower prices.

Right now small businessmen—meaning those ~~employers of 500 or less~~ *with fewer than 500* employees spend an estimated 130 mil. man hours a year first doing govt. required paper work. This adds about $50 Bil. a year to the cost of doing business. That's $50 Bil. added to the cost of *the* things you buy. Then govt. spends about 15 to 20 Bil. $ finding places to store all that paper & you ~~pay~~ pick up the tab for that in your taxes.

Govt. has grown so big in these last 4 decades that not *even* the office of management & budget in Wash. knows how many boards, agencies, bureaus & commissions there are. But all of them have the power to adopt regulations having all the authority of law. As a matter of fact they have more power in a way. If you are charged with breaking a law you have your day in court & you are considered innocent unless & until you are proven guilty beyond a reasonable doubt.

Breaking a regulation is another matter. The agency enforcing that reg. is judge, jury & executioner & you are guilty as charged unless <u>you</u> can prove your innocence. ~~And~~ Breaking a reg. isn't the hardest thing in the world to do. The Fed. registry which lists all the regs. has almost as many pages as the Encyclopedia Brittanica—which is quite a shelf of books.

One small businessman in our state ran ~~was~~ afoul of one of those regulations. He was ordered to instal separate mens & womens washrooms for his employees.—He only has one employee.—And she's his wife. At home they sleep in the same bed & use the same bathroom.

A baker in Ill. says ~~he~~ even if he understood the forms he was supposed to fill out he couldn't do it. ~~and still have time to bake the bread.~~ He wouldn't have time to bake the bread.

In Conn. a chemical researcher has 5 emps. He ~~fills out 20 forms~~ *Files 37 different reports* for 12 Fed. agencies, 26 sets *of data* for 9 state agencies 25 ~~local~~ *for city depts.* & Now he's just learned he has to make out an environmental impact statement. Probably on why he uses so much paper. The Pres of a small investment house in Ind. spends more than half his time in unproductive minutiae that didn't even exist a few years ago but which now is labeled consumer protection.

A druggist in another state reports it takes more time to do the paper work in connection with a prescription than it does to make up the prescription.

And speaking of drugs & paper work—a few years ago a leading drug firm had to submit about 70 pages of data to the Fed. Drug Admin. to get a drug licensed. Recently the same firm made application for a new drug & sent a truck loaded with 72,000 pages of data to support that application. If penecillin were discovered today it's doubtful if it could get approval.

~~The story goes on through every~~

The story is the same for every kind of business and even worse for the larger corporations. We pay higher prices growing ever higher because Govt. continues to spend more than it takes in and because too much money is chasing too few goods & services. There could be more goods and services available for ~~a~~ us to buy if govt. would lift some of the paper burden from the back of our industrial system. Just a 3% reduction would also save about 12 Bil. $ in govt. costs & that too would serve to slow down inflation.

Pete—I thought I'd try one too.

Ron. ❖

Government Spending

May 25, 1977

Congressional leaders commiserate with us about the ec. slump as if it were a natural disaster like a plague of locusts—and they blame it for the Fed. deficits.

I'll be right back.

A few months ago the new House majority leader* observed that if ~~emp~~ unemployment were reduced to 4½%, the budget would not only be balanced—we'd have a surplus. Just once I wish a member of Congress would turn that around and say, "if the budget were balanced, unemployment would be down to 4½, or maybe *only* 3½%.

We've had deficits for 17 out of the last 18 yrs. ~~starting with a $25 Bil. deficit in 1968. The unemployment rate in '68 was only~~ ~~a~~ %. In the early '70's we had a total *$70 Bil.* deficit ~~for~~ *over* just 3 yrs. ~~of $70 Bil.~~ and unemp.

*Rep. Thomas P. O'Neill, Jr. (D-Massachusetts).

in those 3 yrs. ~~was~~ *averaged* less than 5.3%. In other words, full employment ~~doesn't end~~ *didn't prevent* deficit spending.

We have more people working & paying taxes *this year* than at any time in our history. Yet we are running a deficit of somewhere around $50 Bil.—give or take a few ~~bil.~~ BIL. And that deficit is not caused by unemp. Spending by govt. just rises faster than govt. revenues.

Let's start with ~~that year~~ 1968. Fed. tax revenues were $160 bil. This year they are $365 bil. But expenditures in 1968 were $173 bil. and this year $414 Bil. During those years from '68 to '77 Fed. revenues increased 128%, but expenditures went up 140%. And, we can't blame the cost of ~~living~~ living because that only increased *HALF AS MUCH*—70%.- That period '68 to '77 included good times & bad. In 1968 unemployment was only 3.6%.

The only term we can use is "run away" to describe govt. expenditures over these recent years. Fed. spending on health care increased 261%, interest on the nat. debt—206%, revenue sharing ~~the redistribution~~ 2,367%, Ed. 137%. ~~The one area~~ All of these, plus *many* others, increased far more than the cost of living index. But, strange to say, the one expense targeted constantly for trimming by so many of those who are responsible for the increases in ~~those~~ spending ~~programs~~ — the defense budget has only increased 27% in these last 10 yrs. Which means in constant dollars, ~~it has actually decreased~~ *spending on our* national security has actually decreased.

But the social spending programs, the redistribution of your earnings to others have almost all increased in cost faster—some twice as fast as tax receipts.

It is time that Congress ~~is~~ *be* denied the right to pass off this under-funding as a natural phenomenon spawned by a recession *for* which they ~~also~~ *also* take no blame. Economics may be an inexact science, but it isn't that inexact. The permanent debt ceiling—I'll pause while you laugh—is $400 Bil. but we passed that a long time ago & are on our way to 700 bil. In session after session the Congress meets & solemnly approves a quote—temporary—unquote debt ceiling to cover whatever deficit they have in mind.

What makes this doubly frustrating is that the inflation, caused by these deficits, is then counted on ~~to~~ by those same congressmen to ~~brin~~ bring in extra revenues. Thus they are encouraged to adopt new spending programs. A spokesman for the Congressional budget office predicted these inflation-generated revenues would give us a balanced budget by 1982. Don't you believe it. Those estimated revenues will be earmarked for spending long before they are collected. For every penny added to the cost of living index the govt. will get a penny & a half. Inflation is good business for govt.

This is R.R. Thanks for listening. ❖

The four essays below amplify Reagan's strong view that lower taxes, spending control, and the elimination of inflation are vital.

Economics I
July 31, 1978

We the people need more common sense economics and a lot less demagogery if we are to make or support decisions affecting our welfare.

I'll be right back.

Early in July the leadership of the Calif. AFL-CIO met in convention and made a few decisions that will affect the livelihood of the workers they represent. These leaders of organized labor were more than a little upset about the passage of Proposition 13.* Meaning no disrespect, I feel compelled to say, the remedies they proposed reveal that they believe too ~~much~~ *many* of the ~~pol.~~ economic fairy tales widespread in our land today.

In the first place they must be out of step with their own rank & file members because those members voted <u>for</u> Prop.13 in large & enthusiastic numbers.

But where the ~~ec. fairl~~ ec. fairy tale shows up is *in* the convention's decision to battle for reimposing the property tax Prop.13 cancelled *back* on business & industry. They said it was a $3½ bil. break for business & therefore by their reasoning bad for the individual citizen. If they have their way that $3½ bil. will end up being paid by the very individual citizens they claim they want to help.

~~Labor leaders seem to feel they have to hate the boss~~

Whether it be corporation or corner store, taxes are part of business costs & must be recovered in the price of the product. ~~Lets take that~~ Meaning that all of us as consumers pay those taxes.

Let's take the case of a corner ~~store~~ *grocer* in a nice middle class neighborhood. The store keeper rents ~~his~~ *the* building. Everyone who shops there can understand that he must charge enough to cover the wholesale cost of the things he sells, wages to helpers & his rent plus a fair return for himself so he can make a living. But now supposing he buys the bldg? There is no more rent but there is interest on the mortgage & property tax instead of rent. Obviously he cant stay in business if those costs cant be recovered in the price of the things he sells. And just like his wage earning customers (many of them

---

*Proposition 13 was a state-wide, property tax-cutting initiative in California that passed in June 1978.

union members) he has to make enough gross income to ~~have a living~~ *pay his living costs*—after he has paid his income tax.

What this all adds up to is that govt. can't tax ~~a thing~~ *things like businesses or corporations,* it can only tax people. When it says it's going to, "make business pay," it is really saying it is going to make business help it collect taxes. ~~from the people.~~ Into our corner store comes a regular customer to pick up a loaf of bread on his way home. We've already covered the fact that the grocers mark up includes a share of the property tax on the store. But the truth is the wholesale price the store keeper paid to the bakery included it's taxes, ~~the~~ and more than 150 others going all the way back to the farmer who raised the wheat. If he cant get a price for his wheat that will cover the real estate tax on his farm, he can't stay in business either. *If the trucker who hauled the wheat cant charge enough to cover his license fee & gasoline tax, he can't stay in business.*

Union leaders will serve the men & women they represent a lot better if they'll drop the demagogery & take a simple course in economics.

This is RR   Thanks for listening. ❖

Economics II
July 31, 1978

On the last broadcast I suggested that labor leaders were conducting a kind of class warfare using some very questionable economic theory. I'll be right back.

On my last commentary I criticized the A.F.L.-C.I.O. Calif. convention for *adopting* some resolutions* which were actually ~~helpful~~ hurtful to the men & women they represent. I spoke specifically of the false idea that business can be made to pay a larger share of the tax burden thus relieving individuals. The truth, of course, is that business taxes are part of the cost of operation & must be paid by the customer in the increased price of the product.

But the labor leaders in that Calif. convention made other decisions equally harmful to their rank & file members. For example they raised the old cry (born of demagogery) that *income* taxes should be more progessive, making those with higher earnings pay a bigger share of the tax.

Well right now at ~~around~~ *less than* $10,000 a year (and I don't think many union members earn less) you are in the top 50% of income earners in

---

*The resolutions included a call to repeal that part of a property tax cut (Prop. 13) that went to business and industry, argued that income taxes should be more progressive, and called for increasing the capital gains tax.

the U.S. And ~~that 50% pays~~ *you pay* 94% of the total *income* tax. ~~Oh! But you say *you'll say* "those ≠ we *they* are talking about those *the* really top earners. How top?~~ At a little over $20,000 you are in the top 10% & that 10% pays <u>half</u> the total tax. And if you are talking of the ~~less than~~ *one half of* 1% who earn $50,000 a year *& up*—go ahead, raise their tax to 100%, take every dollar they earn & ~~you can~~ *it will* run the govt. for ~~about~~ less than 3 days.

The delegates to that Calif. AFL-CIO convention I'm sure were well intentioned but they made it clear they did not want a cut in govt. spending. They want more tax revenues to pay for that spending & they don't seem to realize the only source of additional revenue is the great working, middle class which includes their own members. ~~That working, middle class is already working *works* And *which* ~~works~~ WORKS almost 5 months a year to pay ~~their share of the *cost of govt.*~~ for the cost of govt.

Finally the other proposal the convention made was to gain more revenue from the capital gains tax. The delegates ~~echoed~~ *echoed* the Presidents ill considered charge that a reduced capital gains tax constituted a windfall for millionaires. ~~and two bits for the working class.~~ Frankly speaking the President was a little off base.

It's hard to get great numbers of people excited about ~~the~~ *the* capital gains tax. ~~because it isn't something that happens to everyone.~~ Very simply it is the tax one pays upon selling *FOR PROFIT* something one owns. ~~for a profit.~~ It is true it affects *MOSTLY* those who have *SAVINGS TO* invested in stocks, land, or ~~any other assets~~ s*ome other object.* ~~and who then sell that for more than they paid.~~ It is also true that capital investment is what fuels our industry & creates jobs. Our competitors in world trade such as Japan & W. Germany— even Socialist Eng. have no tax on long term capital gains.

But it isn't true to say it affects only ~~the~~ people of wealth. Half of all those reporting capital gains have adjusted gross incomes below $15,000. And more than half of the total amount of capital gains is reported by people with incomes ~~of~~ below $25,000.

In 1969 we virtually doubled the capital gains tax. In 1970 there were 31 mil. investors putting up the capital to increase production & create jobs. Today there are fewer than 25 mil. ~~and we are worried about stagnation in our economy.~~

I wish todays labor leaders had the statesmanship of the Am. Fed. of Labor leaders in 1942 who demanded that the cap. gains tax be reduced if not eliminated because it was preventing the investment of capital needed to create jobs for their members.

This is RR   Thanks for listening. ❖

Money
June 29, 1979

Todays commentary is a collection of items on the subject of money. You remember money? We used to think it was worth something. I'll be right back.

Is the Proposition 13 fever that swept the country last fall & had candidates promising spending cuts beginning to cool down? Or does it just need a ~~boost~~ *reminder* from all of us ~~to remind our elected representatives~~ that another election year is coming up & we still have that fever?

At the height of the fever Sen. Nunn of Georgia introduced an amendment (which was duly passed) calling for a spending limit & ~~a~~ tax reductions over the period 1980 to 82. But as spring fever lulled ~~the~~ *his* economy minded colleagues they reverted to type. By the middle of May it was clear that the Sens. spending limit would be exceeded by $42 Bil. and taxes will go up $68 bil. ~~more than~~ *above* his ceiling. Now this doesn't mean his fellow legislators will raise taxes by that amount. They won't have to. Govt. profits by inflation and as cost of living pay raises move workers into higher surtax brackets the govt. will get that much undeserved income.

Many years ago Nicolai Lenin said a govt. can quietly & unobservedly confiscate the wealth of its citizens thru inflation. Well to make it less unobserved, holders of U.S. Govt. bonds lost $45 bil. in the value of those bonds last year because of the 9% inflation rate.

Harvard Economist Martin Feldstein says our once powerful U.S. economy is slowing down because people are no longer saving money as they once did. It just doesn't pay to save as that ~~figure~~ *loss* on savings bonds indicates. When we save either through insurance or bank savings accounts that money is invested in business & industry to earn the dividends & interest we receive. Without such savings to invest our economy can't grow & provide the jobs our people need.

Prof. Feldstein suggests cutting the tax rates on saving & investment. But as the 1st item indicates Congress is not in a tax cutting mood which indicates some in our Congress need a ~~course~~ *to take* a course in elementary economics.

Two economists with Chicago's Harris bank, Robt. Genetski & Young Chiu have studied the *ec.* growth rate of our 50 states.* Those states that cut taxes had an above average ec. growth. A number of states that sharply in-

---

*Robert J. Genetski and Young D. Chin, "The Impact of State and Local Income Taxes on Economic Growth" (Chicago: Harris Bank, Nov. 3, 1978).

creased their taxes—among them N.Y., Rhode Island, Vermont, N.J. & Mass. suffered an ec. decline. States that neither raised or lowered tax rates went along with lower than average ec. growth.

One last item on money. Citicorp a giant N.Y. bank recently put out ~~an~~ a pictorial document on the hist. of inflation in the U.S. over the last 100 yrs. They did it by picturing stacks of pennies representing the purchasing power of the dollar at various times.

They took the year 1900 as 100 pennies to the dollar & went backward & forward from there. For example in 1894 the dollar was worth 96 pennies. In the war year of 1918 inflation had reduced it to about 55½ cents. It's highest point since then was in 1934 when there were 62 pennies in the stack. A dollar was worth 48 cents in 1942, 27½ cents in 1962 and only 12.8 cents in 1978. It has lost some of that so far in 1979.

This is RR Thanks for listening. ❖

Red Hen
November 16, 1976

A modern day little Red Hen may not ~~sound like~~ *appear* to be a quotable authority on economics but then some authorities *on economics* aren't worth quoting. I'll be right back.

About a year ago I imposed a little poetry on you. It was called "The Incredible Bread machine" and made a lot of sense with reference to matters economic. You didn't object too much so ~~having~~ *having* gotten away with it once I'm going to try again. ~~with~~ *This is* a little treatise on *basic* ec's. called "The Modern Little Red Hen."

THE MODERN LITTLE RED HEN
Once upon a time there was a little red hen who scratched about the barnyard until she uncovered some grains of wheat. She called her neighbors and said, "If we plant this wheat, we shall have bread to eat. Who will help me plant it?"

"Not I," said the cow.

"Not I," said the duck.

"Not I," said the pig.

"Not I," said the goose.

"Then I will," said the little red hen. And she did. The wheat grew tall and ripened into golden grain. "Who will help me reap my wheat?" asked the little red hen.

"Not I," said the duck.

"Out of my classification," said the pig.

"I'd lose my seniority," said the cow.

"I'd lose my unemployment compensation," said the goose.

"Then I will," said the little red hen, and she did.

At last it came time to bake the bread. "Who will help me bake bread?" asked the little red hen.

"That would be overtime for me," said the cow.

"I'd lose my welfare benefits," said the duck.

"I'm a dropout and never learned how," said the pig.

"If I'm to be the only helper, that's discrimination," said the goose.

"Then I will," said the little red hen.

She baked five loaves and held them up for her neighbors to see.

They all wanted some and, in fact, demanded a share. But the little red hen said, "No, I can eat the five loaves myself."

"Excess profits," cried the cow.

"Capitalist leech," screamed the duck.

"I demand equal rights," yelled the goose.

And the pig just grunted.

And they painted "unfair" picket signs and marched round and round the little red hen, shouting obscenities.

When the government agent came, he said to the little red hen,

"You must not be greedy."

"But I earned the bread," said the little red hen.

"Exactly," said the agent. "That is the wonderful free enterprise system. Anyone in the barnyard can earn as much as he wants. But under our modern government regulations, the productive workers must divide their product with the idle."

And they lived happily ever after, including the little red hen, who smiled and clucked, "I am grateful, I am grateful."

But her neighbors wondered why she never again baked any more bread.

This is R.R. Thanks for listening. ❖

In the following essay, Reagan points to the great dangers of continued inflation and expresses the belief that to stop inflation, it may be necessary to endure a period of limited recession.

Recession vs. Inflation
February 27, 1975

Nero fiddled while Rome burned. Congress can't decide which came 1ˢᵗ the chicken or the egg. I'll be right back.

I've talked at some length on these broadcasts about the need to zero in on inflation and not push the panic button because of recession. Now the leaders in Cong. are making it very evident that pol. considerations will determine what they do—not what is good for the country.

Not too long ago Carl Albert*—speaker of the house declared that our problem was 60% recession, 30% inflat. and 10% energy. The simple fact is there would be no recession if it weren't for inflation.

I'm aware that a great many of you are fearful of increasing unemployment & all of us who remember the great depression cant help but react to the doom & gloom being fed to us almost daily in the news. Certainly a recession isn't enjoyable and it's pretty miserable for those who lose their jobs because of it. But a continuation of the inflat. that started to get out of control in the middle sixties can destroy our entire social & ec. system.

Recession must not be allowed to deepen into depression but if inflation is to be stopped we have to sweat out a certain period of recession. Unfortunately *some* politicians overreact to any increase in unemp. and start looking at the next election instead of the next generation. ~~or even the next decade ahead.~~

~~The for~~ Sen. Hubert Humphrey** I'm sorry to say lost sight of the main target recently on a national ~~broadcast~~ television show. He was most vehement in his demand that we start fighting recession like day before yesterday. To hear him you'd never know there was any problem at all about inflat.

Specifically he was calling for the Fed. Reserve Bd. to loosen the purse strings & as he put it make more credit available. Correct interpretation of that is, increase the money supply, print more money and get back on the inflation ~~merry go round~~ *doomsday machine*. The word for it in Wash. ~~where coining words~~ is "reflation"—a handy way to avoid saying <u>inflation</u>. *But as one of our finest economists has said, ~~If The~~ reflation cannot sustain full employment in the long* RUN EXCEPT BY FASTER & FASTER INFLAT.

The Sen. said if the "Fed"—that's Washingtonese for Fed. Res. Syst. doesn't come up with more money Cong. will see that ~~they~~ *it* does. ~~and~~ *It* is

*D-Oklahoma.
**D-Minnesota.

this kind of thinking that got us in this mess in the 1ˢᵗ place. There are signs that we are beginning to control inflat; a drop in interest rates, the rebates on automobile prices, inventory being reduced faster than we'd ~~hoped~~ expected, and a number of others. This is not the time to change our game plan.

Sometimes it seems as if Cong. will do anything to avoid cutting spending or facing reality. Fearful of hard times I know some of you have *probably* written your Congressmen or ~~the~~ Senators urging some kind of action. That's what you'll get—some kind of action. May I suggest that you write & tell them no more tranquilizers we want a permanent cure for what ails us & that doesn't mean printing press money. ❖

Humphrey-Hawkins Bill (Jobs B)
September 21, 1976

No one who grew up in the great depression ~~years~~ can be indifferent to the suffering that goes with wanting to work and not being able to find a job. I'll be right back.

Yesterday when I was talking about the threat to freedom inherent in the Humphrey-Hawkins bill I was aware of the ~~risk~~ danger that I might appear callous *to* the plight of the unemployed. This is definitely not my attitude. ~~I do not suggest an end to unemp. insurance or any of the social reforms that ≠ designed to help the family wage earner through a period of joblessness until he or she can Furthermore~~ I don't question the good intent of Sen. Humphrey or Rep. Hawkins. They mean well and are sincere in their concern for the plight of the jobless.

I hope they and you will ~~grant~~ *credit* me *with* the same ~~sincere concern~~ sincerity & the same *measure of* sympathy for the unemployed. I say this because I'm going to ask some questions about the present unemp. rate and whether *in* ~~in spite of our good intentions, we haven't~~ our desire to eliminate suffering, we haven't in truth added to the problem.

During the recent primary campaign an article appeared in the press quoting a man who was reported to be Pres. of the nations largest employment agency. His agency has more than 500 offices nationwide. ~~and~~ He charges that ~~in this recession & time of unemployment~~ 3 mil. jobs are going begging. ~~He claimed~~ His agency had openings listed for unskilled workers, secretaries, medical personell, file clerks, salesman even marketing specialists and management trainees.

Maybe ~~th~~ his story caught my eye because for some time now I've been keeping count of the number of full pages in the classified section of the L.A.

Sunday Times wherein employers advertise for workers to fill job vacancies. L.A. has an official unemp. rate of around 10% but every Sunday there are some 30 full pages of help wanted ads. *Take a look at your own Metropolitan Sunday paper.*

The Long Beach office of the Calif. State Labor Dept. was seeking applicants for secretarial jobs at $870 a month, 40 cooks at $1000, security guards at better than $3 an hour & craftsmen at $6.50 an hour. The unemployment rate was 10.3 %

To get back to the article, the Pres. of the emp. agency said politicians sounding off about unemp. figures tended to scare job seekers out of looking for a job. He also said we had gone so far in unemp. benefits we've made it too easy not to work & he gave examples.

In Plainfield N.J. a man unemployed for 5 mo's. came to their office. They found him a job at $20 a week better than the job he'd lost—same kind of work. In 90 days his pay would go up another $30 a week. He turned it down. He & his wife were receiving $9,880 a year in unemp. ins. were moonlighting for another $5200 and were eligible for food stamps. At better than $15,000 a year plus food stamps he couldn't afford to take the job *they'd found for him*. In another case a Sec. turned down a ~~$90 a week~~ job saying "I'm going to take a 26 week vacation at $90 a week unemp. benefits *tax free.*"

~~Now let me ask a question—this is not a statement. Would one answer be for unemp. insurance to insist that the insured take a job he or she was capable of doing holding even if it were not the individual's regular work? Then let Unemp. insurance *would* make up the dif. between the lower pay & the full benefit payment while at the same time they were entitled to while making an all out effort to find the proper kind of job?~~

Now let me ask a question. I'm not making this *as* a statement—just asking. Why shouldn't ~~someone~~ *anyone* unemployed <u>have</u> to take any job ~~of~~ which he or she ~~was~~ *is* capable of performing? ~~Let~~ *Why shouldn't* the unemployment check be reduced by the amount of the pay check? ~~for that job. but at the same~~ *In the mean*time *let* the state emp. office ~~as~~ be assigned to find as quickly as possible the right kind of job. Was unemp. Ins. ever intended to fund 26 week vacations? This is RR. Thanks— —❖

Unemployment
August 15, 1977

Englands great Prime Minister Disraeli many years ago said there are lies, big lies and then there are statistics. And so it is with unemployment. I'll be right back.

There are people in America unemployed through no fault of their own, people who desperately want a job with a future. By far the largest group of unemployed are young people. Some want part time work while they continue their ed. Others want to help the family and some are looking for that first toe hold in the job market. The smallest group of unemployed is however the one of greatest concern—the head of household, provider for the family.

I'm not going to get into the subject of what measures could best solve these problems; the effect on teenage employment of the minimum wage; the lack of investment capital to create jobs because of ridiculous tax policies. Both of these are the result of actions motivated by politics not statesmanship. But I would like to point out that our labor dept. statistics on unemployment ~~sound~~ seem to be designed ~~to~~ with the preservation of govt. programs in mind rather than creating full employment. We can't provide answers until we understand who it is we should be trying to help.

Two years ago when N.Y. Cities financial plight was getting so much attention most of us were unaware that Mass. was in about the same shape and the word bankruptcy was heard frequently. Unemp. was at or near the top in all the 50 states (a little over 11%). And of course the cost of the tax free benefits for the unemployed was part of the states financial distress. So even though Mass. as a state has subscribed to all the social reforms of recent years necessity forced it to trim spending wherever & however it could be done.

Unemployment benefits had been hiked and extended in the 1974 repression. Total unemployed had risen in Mass. from about 168,000 in 1974 to almost 300,000 in 1975. So ~~U~~unemployment benefits were attacked as one of the areas in which state spending could be cut. In one year unemployment fell from more than 11% to 7%, a full percentage point below the national average. In numbers roughly 140,000 people were taken off the unemployment rolls. Naturally one has to ask how a state creates 140,000 jobs in less than a year. The answer is—Mass. didn't. There were only 19,000 more jobs in 1976 than in 1975.

The explanation for 120,000 people disappearing from the rolls of the unemployed without getting jobs is that very simply the unemployment figure in America is distorted by the availability of the unemp. benefits. Milton Friedman has said, "a large fraction of our unemployment figure does not constitute a human problem—it constitutes people taking advantage of very good arrangements."

Not only do the tax free benefits lure people to quit jobs more frequently they actually lure people into the job mkt. The effect is an artificial layer of unemployed who don't reflect the ec. situation in the country at all. Right now the U.S. has the highest percentage of it's pop. working than at any time in hist. 41%, but we have a high recession type unemp. figure. Prof. Feldstein* of Harvard a top expert on unemp. says that a possible ¼ of our unemployed represent people who have voluntarily quit their jobs or are people simply moving into the job mkt. because of the generous tax free benefits.

This explains the ec. miracle in Mass. A drive was put on to ensure that benefits went only to ~~people~~ *those* who had legitimately lost their jobs or were seriously looking for work. The disqualification rate on unemp. compensation jumped 200%. Between 74 & 75 Mass. *had* only lost 30,000 jobs but the unemp. rate had gone up by 131,600. In other words 100,000 people simply came out of the woodwork to get on the gravy train. If Wash. would quit playing a numbers game we could bring unemp. down toward 5% with hardship to no one, save bils. of $ and concentrate on the really hard core unemployed who need our help.

This is RR. Thanks for listening. ❖

Reagan was deeply concerned about tax rates and government spending, and returned to those topics in his radio essays again and again. In the following ten essays, he addresses loopholes, spending, the inheritance and capital gains tax, and indexing. The theme that is woven through all these essays is the necessity of lower rates. In November 1978, just before he began his successful run for the presidency, he noted that President John F. Kennedy had cut rates dramatically in the 1960s and that the "result was the longest, sustained economic expansion in the history of our country."

Tax Loopholes
May 1975

Hang on to your pocketbooks *in Wash.*, they're talking tax reform again. I'll be right back.

From time to time I'm going to talk about loopholes in the tax laws and this is one of those times. Pol's. dearly love to make the people believe they have some magic way of extracting taxes from some mysterious "they" who are not now paying their fair share. Under the all embracing subject of tax reform they would have us believe that we'll all be home free—or partly so just

*Martin Feldstein

as soon as they close the loopholes and catch up with that mysterious "they" and make them cough up.

Cong. Corman* of Calif. introduced a bill in Cong. H.R. 1040. He had 43 co-sponsors. The bill states; "Our taxing system is riddled with loopholes that deprive the treasury of bil's. of $ each yr, weakening our competitive, free enterprise syst. & undermining the ~~th~~ morale of the hard working wage earner and small businessman to whom tax loopholes are not available. . . . In 1970 more than 100 Am's. with incomes of $200,000 paid no inc. tax."

That's a pretty strong statement & if it's true we all should be pretty darn mad. ~~Of course~~ *Now* the Cong*mn* is right there in Wash. where he has access to all the facts—~~therefore he should know although~~ *which makes you wonder why* he didn't mention ~~it~~ that in 1970 there were 15,306 individuals who earned $200,000 a year and 15,200 of them (99.6%) pd. an average tax of $177,000 each for a total of $2.7 Bil. The treasury dept. which collects the tax says the 106 who didn't pay had various losses & deductions which amounted to more than their gross inc. but all were being audited.

~~Now it seems that if those deductions were "loopholes"—gimmicks by which they could slip by through somewhat dishonestly *avoid paying taxes* the other 15,200 were pretty silly stupid for for not finding them also.~~

Now it does seem strange that 15,200 people smart enough to make $200,000 a year were too stupid to find the loopholes the other 106 found. Unless, of course, those supposed loopholes are all in the Congressman's mind.

Why is it that so many loophole closing pol's start out by proclaiming they want to lighten the workers load and wind up telling us how much more money govt. will get if the loopholes are closed. Just once I'd like to hear one specify the loophole ~~he'll~~ *he wants* closed and then how much of the citizens tax burden will be released.

Take the 1st one they go after—you might say the showcase loophole, the oil depletion allowance. If it were eliminated totally the govt. would get $1 Bil. *or less* and ~~that w is what~~ the govt. spends *that much* every single day.

The truth is most of what our politicians call loopholes are the legit. deductions the working people depend on to keep their inc. tax from being more intolerable than it is. And ~~ending~~ *eliminating* those deductions would vastly increase govt. revenue. When they talk among themselves here are some of the things they call loopholes & how much ~~they~~ their closing would cost you: deducting the prop. tax on your home & the interest on your mort-

*James Corman

gage $5.7 Bil; making you pay tax on the tax you've already paid to local & st. govts—$5.6 bil.; tighten up on charitable contributions $3½ Bil. (Then of course govt. would have to pick up the tab for those charitable services now paid for by those contributions). Not allowing you to deduct your Dr. bills would mean another $3 bil. out of your pocket.

Anyone ready for a $17.8 bil. tax increase? ~~The next time a pol. sounds off about making someone else pay your share ponder this—If the govt. confiscated all the earnings of those upper bracket people who $50,000 or more a year it would only pay for about 3 weeks.~~ This is RR— —❖

Government Cost II
November 16, 1976

Yesterday I closed my remarks with some figures which might have raised a question or two in your minds. I'll be right back.

In talking about taxes yesterday I tossed in a couple of quick figures at the end about the relative number of taxpayers to tax users. I thought you might be interested in a few more details. Actually the figures reveal a situation that should be disturbing to all of us.

As I've said before, throwing a lot figures at you by radio can be confusing ~~but~~ so I'll try to go slow & hold them down as much as possible. ~~Wm.~~

Wm. Rickenbacker editor of the Rickenbacker report & author of a recently published "Savings & Investment Guide" has pointed out that 28.6 mil. Americans depend on govt. retirement and disability programs. Then you add in recipients of survivor programs—almost 9 mil., unemp. benefits to 6 mil., Military 3½ mil., civilian emps. & dependents and you come up with a total of 81.3 mil. people dependent on tax dollars for their year round living.

All of those tax dollars must come from 70.2 million Americans working & earning in the private sector. Ah! but you say govt. workers pay taxes too. *And* so they do. But all their inc. & therefore the portion ~~pd.~~ *they pay* in taxes comes *originally* from taxes *dollars* so they are just ~~a way station between the taxes pd.~~ returning to govt. tax money already pd. by the ~~em~~ worker in the pvt. sector.

The 70.2 mil. private sector workers have ~~60~~ 62.1 mil. personal dependents so we're talking about a private sector of 132.3 mil. people sharing their inc. with an additional 81.3 mil.

To sum it up roughly 70 mil. Americans provide a living for themselves and ~~an additional~~ 143.4 ~~of~~ additional people.

Now dont take this as meaning there should be no recipients of tax dollars or that all who work in govt. are parasites. Obviously we want to provide for the needy & disabled. Just as obviously we must have & are happy to have in the military those who provide *for our* security. This goes also for police & firemen and all the others providing services we want & need.

The point I'm making is that somewhere there must be a figure beyond which we can't go in the growth of govt. without wiping out those in the private sector who pick up the entire tab.

This is what was behind the Calif. initiative a few years ago to place a figure on the percentage of total gross ~~taxes~~ earnings the state could take in taxes. It was the motivation behind the measure first defeated in Mich.

The plain truth is every effort to slow govt. growth or reduce govt. costs has failed. In the last 20 yrs. corp. profits have risen 105%—wages have gone up 213%—govt. costs have risen 340%. There is one sensible, long overdue answer; fix in the constitution a limit on the share of earnings govt. can take without becoming a drag on the economy.

This is RR. Thanks for listening. ❖

More About Taxes
January 19, 1977

~~Yesterday~~ *The other day* I talked about the unfairness of the Capital Gains tax in this time of inflation. ~~They~~ A bill now in Cong. would add considerably to that unfairness—I'll be right back.

When someone talks about estate or inheritance tax he runs the risk of appearing to be carrying a torch for the downtrodden rich. So let me say in advance I'm going to talk about estate taxes even though I think the wealthy can probably take care of themselves.

We tend to forget that a family farm (and 98% of ~~all~~ *our* farms are family owned) is an estate subject to inheritance tax when the farmer passes on & leaves it to his wife & children. The family owned store on the corner, the repair shop, or small business is the same.

These farms & small businesses are really the backbone of our free enterprise system—millions of individual citizens making their own way, gambling that they can provide a service or product that people need and will buy.

Not too long ago the estate tax was no problem to these private entrepreneurs. The assessed value of the farm or business was low enough that it could be passed on ~~to~~ *with no financial strain to* the sons & daughters who had grown up working with their ~~father~~ *father parents in the* ~~with no strain~~ family enterprise. But then came inflation. The family scale of living did not change or improve but the assessed valuation of the property was vastly increased. Estate taxes following the death of the family head made it impossible for the heirs to keep the farm or business. It had to be sold to meet the demands of govt.

Now a Wisconsin Congressman Henry Reuss* has introduced a bill—H.R. 967 which may well be the final straw on the camels back. Not only will the estate tax continue to be a confiscatory tax grab based on an inflated increase in assessed value which really is nothing more ~~that~~ than the reduced value of our money but a new tax will be added to make sure there will be nothing left.

Let me reiterate—inflation has literally doubled the dollar price of business properties and for that matter the house you live in. But you don't really own twice as much real value, its just a phony paper increase.

~~But~~ H.R. 967 if passed will add a capital gains tax on top of the estate tax. In other words Govt. will tell you IF YOU ARE AN INHERITOR that phony increase represents a profit and therefore *it* must tax what remains after you've paid the estate tax.

Congressman Reuss has an answer for those who say his bill can well mean the end of family owned enterprises. He is quoted as ~~saying~~ suggesting they, "sell out to big corporations or conglomerates." How does that fit in with the anti- big business attitude of the majority in Cong. who ~~are trying to~~ *talk of* breaking up the corporations and conglomerates?

There is one unarguable answer in this time of inflation to the unfairness prevalent in our tax system. It is an answer to the problem of capital gains tax, estate taxes & the inc. tax which moves you up into a higher tax rate when your increase in pay is only enough to match the increased cost of living—it is called indexing. It means adjust the tax rates to reflect the reduced value of the $ due to inflation.

This is R.R. ~~I'll be right ba~~ Thanks for listening. ❖

Indexing
June 15, 1977

Everyone knows what an index is but just possibly "indexing" when it applies to taxes is not so well understood. I'll be right back.

In Calif. the leader of the minority party in the legislature is pushing to have the *graduated* state inc. tax indexed. He is being opposed by the big

---

*Democrat and then chairman of the House Committee on Banking, Finance, and Urban Affairs.

spending majority. Many of you who are listening live in states without an inc. tax or if there is one it is a flat percentage of whatever your inc. happens to be. But all of us are subject to the steeply graduated Fed. inc. tax and here again a few brave souls in Congress like that Calif. legislator are trying to get the Fed. tax indexed.

Very simply indexing means adjusting the graduated surtax brackets to reflect the effect of inflation. As it is now a wage earner who gets a cost of living increase moves up into a higher tax bracket. His pay raise hasn't made him one penny better off as to purchasing power. He's just kept even with the higher cost of living. That is he's kept even until he pays his taxes, then that higher surtax rate takes its bite and he's actually less well off than before the raise.

Here are some examples from Calif. on just the effect of the state inc. tax without figuring in the added chunk Uncle Sam grabs. A family of 4 earning $9600 last year will have to get a $595 raise to keep even with the 6.2% inflat. rate. So this year their inc. is $10,195. But that raise put them in a higher state tax bracket reducing their purchasing power by $70. A family earning $18,300 (about the median inc.) gets a cost of living raise to $19,435 but their taxes go up far more than 6.2%. Add in the Fed. bite on both these examples and you can see why even with the pay raises it still dosen't get easier to pay for those braces on Junior's teeth.

~~Last year~~ *In 1974* the Fed. govt. got an estimated $30 bil. ~~(that's $130 for every man, woman, child & baby in Am.)~~ of undeserved tax because no allowance is made in the tax rates for inflat. That averages out to $130 ~~$520~~ for ~~a family of 4~~ *every man, woman, child & baby* in Am. But don't let that fool you it's a lot more than ~~$520~~ *$130* for the average taxpayer.

Suppose the cost of living index ~~were~~ *was* applied to the tax brackets, then the wage earner would ~~stay in the~~ continue paying the same rate of tax unless & until he got a raise that actually amounted to an increase in purchasing power.

Politicians for the most part dont favor indexing because that would interfere with their spending habits. You see ~~they get~~ *under the* present system inflation is an invisible tax. In Calif. in just the last 3 yrs. state inc. tax collections have increased twice as fast as personal inc. The figure at the national level is probably even higher.

Now the politicians answer is that govt. is also caught by inflat. & must pay higher salaries & prices for things it must buy so indexing would keep it from growing with the economy. Of course govt. costs go up with inflat. ~~and~~ *but* so would tax revenues *even* with indexing. That 1st Calif. family I mentioned would be paying inc. tax on $10,195 instead of $9,600 but the rate would remain the same. Right now for every percentage point of increase in cost of living the govt. gets ~~a penny~~ *one & a half percentage points* ~~of~~ increase in revenue.

Indexing ~~of~~ *of* the Calif. tax would save Californians $345 mil the 1st year. Indexing the Fed. inc. tax ~~would~~ *could* ~~as~~ save ~~Americans~~ *as much as* $30 bil. a year for all of us.

Indexing is an idea whose time has not only come, it is overdue. Several other countries have already done ~~this~~ it. Leading economists endorse it. The American people should demand it in a way Congress can't ignore. Indexing isn't a tax cut, it is a halt to an illicit, hidden increase.

This is RR Thanks for listening. ❖

Taxes
October 18, 1977

~~Our govt.~~ Wash. is talking tax reform which should have us all heading for high ground or burying the family silver in the back yard.

I'll be right back.

When govt. talks tax reform on the eve of an elec. year you can bet whatever they do will be based on the time honored principle of robbing Peter to pay Paul. And the idea is to see that *there are more* Pauls ~~have more votes than the~~ *than there are* citizens named Peter. ~~Govt.~~ *But what govt.* ~~just~~ can't seem to realize *is* that we're all named Paul ~~anymore~~—Peter went bankrupt quite a while ago.

Things are a little complicated this time. The admin. has been talking tax reform for quite a while but ~~do~~ promising a veto of any across the board tax cut. Now however as the promised ec. boom wobbles and wavers a tax cut is suggested as an ec. stimulant but not necessarily a part of the tax reform. From the White House leaks it looks more & more like a case of taking back with one hand what the other hand has given.

The answer is really so simple but unfortunately it doesn't fit the pol. phil. of those in the majority. Economists like Paul McCracken of the U. of Mich., Milton Friedman U. of Chi., Arthur Laffer of U.S.C., Allan Meltzer of Carnegie-Mellon U. & Arthur Burns chrm. of the Fed. reserve board have each made it clear that govt. can increase its tax revenues & create the jobs we need <u>without</u> inflation by lowering the tax rates for business & individuals.

We've tried spending our way to prosperity for more than 4 decades and it hasn't worked. If it did N.Y. City would be the most prosperous spot on earth.

Twice in this century, in *the* 1920's & in ~~1962~~ the early 60's we cut taxes substantially and the stimulant to the ec. was substantial & immediate.

Radio   Taxes   ①

~~Grognt.~~ Wash. is talking tax reform which should have us all heading for high ground or burying the family silver in the back yard.

     I'll be right back.

     When govt. talks tax reform on the eve of an elec. year you can bet whatever they do will be based on the time honored principle of robbing Peter to pay Paul. And the idea is to see that there are more Pauls ~~than there are~~ ~~citizens~~ citizens named Peter. ~~But.~~ But what ~~gvt~~ ~~just~~ can't seem to realize is that we're all named Paul ~~anymore~~ — Peter went bankrupt quite a while ago.

     Things are a little complicated this time. The admin. has been talking tax reform for quite a while but ~~to~~ promising a ~~vote~~ of any across the board tax cut. Now however as the promised ec. boom wobbles and wavers a tax cut is suggested as an ec. stimulant but not necessarily a part of the tax reform. From the White House leaks it looks more & more like a case of taking back with one hand what the other hand has given.

     The answer is really so simple but unfortunately it doesn't fit the pol. phil. of those in the majority. Economists like Paul McCracken of the U. of Mich., Milton Friedman U. of Chi., Arthur Laffer of U.S.C., Allan Meltzer of Carnegie – Mellon U. & Arthur Burns chmn. of the Fed. reserve board have each made it clear that govt. can increase its tax revenues & create the jobs we need ~~without~~ inflation by lowering the tax rates for business & individuals.

     We've tried spending our way to prosperity for more than 4 decades and it hasn't worked. If it did N.Y. City would be the most prosperous spot on earth.

     Twice in this century, in 1920's & in ~~the~~ the early 60 we cut taxes substantially and the stimulant to the ec. was substantial & immediate.

②

Unfortunately the Wash. climate is one in which any tax cut must be for the greater number of people beginning at the lower end of the earning scale and only if it is matched by increases for the lesser number above the average inc.

Should our inc. tax system be more progressive than it is? At present it ranges from 14% to 50% of earnings. Roughly 70% of return on investments. 10% of the workers beginning at 23,000 of inc. pay 50% of the total tax. The other 90% below 23,000 pay the other half. Ah! but what about loopholes? Will the 10% only take 5% of all the deductions allowed by law — 95% of the deductions from so called loopholes benefit the 90% who only pay half the total tax.

Jack Kemp a young congressman from N.Y. who used to quarterback the Buffalo Bills has introduced a job creation bill 5 times in this session and each time he gets more support. The last time 195 votes across party lines. We should help him.

A recent Harris poll finds 70% of the people feel taxes are unreasonable and 66% say they have reached the breaking point. With inflat. every time the price level goes up 1% inc. taxes go up 1.5% due to the graduated scale.

Jack Kemps bill would keep the inc. tax progressive by cutting substantially the inc. tax across the board in every bracket. People would have more of their money to spend as they wish & there would be more for investment to expand our industry. And govt. would reduce the deficit which causes inflat. because the tax base would be broadened by increased prosperity.

This is RR thanks for listening.

Unfortunately the Wash. climate is one in which any tax cut must be for the greater number of people beginning at the lower end of the earning scale and only if it is matched by increases for the ~~fewer~~ *lesser* number above the average inc.

Should our inc. tax system be more progressive than it is? At present it ranges from 14% to ~~70%. Roughly~~ *50% of earnings & 70% of return on investments. Roughly* 10% of the workers beginning at $23,000 of inc. pay 50% of the total tax. The ~~other~~ 90% below $23,000 pay the other half. Ah! but what about loopholes? Well the 10% only take 5% of all the deductions allowed by law—95% ~~are taken by those in the~~ *≠ of the deductions from so called loopholes benefit the 90% who only pay half the total tax.*

Jack Kemp a young congressman from N.Y. who used to quarterback the Buffalo Bills has introduced a job creation bill 5 times in this session and each time he gets more support. The last time 195 votes across party lines. We should help him.

A recent Harris poll finds 70% of the people feel taxes are unreasonable and 66% say they have reached the breaking point. With inflat. every time the price level goes up 1% inc. taxes go up 1.5% due to the graduated scale.

Jack Kemps bill would keep the ~~≠ rate of progressivity~~ *inc. tax progressive* by cutting substantially the inc. tax across the board in every bracket. People would have more of their money to spend as they wish & there would be more for investment to expand *our* industry. And govt. would reduce the deficit which causes inflat. because the tax base would be ~~increased~~ *broadened* by ~~the~~ increased prosperity.

This is RR   Thanks for listening ❖

Taxes Again
June 5, 1978

I try to change the subject but somehow I can't help but talk about taxes every now & then. I don't bring up the subject—Wash. does.

I'll be right back.

By the time you hear this Congress & the Admin. may have reached some agreement about taxes but I doubt that will be good news. Congressmen like Jack Kemp of N.Y. & Wm. Steiger of Wis. with a lot of bipartisan help have been trying to give all of us a real tax break but the White House is arm twisting the leadership in the House & Sen. to block them.

Congressman Steiger wants to encourage more capital investment by rolling the Capital Gains tax back from 50% to the 25% it was before 1969.

Sec. of the Treasury Blumenthal* fresh from addressing business leaders in Fla. where he promised h *to encourage* more investment capital says "no" to Steigers proposal. He claims it will reduce govt. revenues from that tax by $2 Bil. That's kind of funny. In the year before the increase the govt. collected $7.2 Bil. from a 25% Cap. Gains tax. In the 1st year at 50% the govt. only collected $4.7 Bil.

As for general tax relief the White House wants to increase the progressivity of the inc. tax so there'll be little or no relief for anyone making $20,000 or more. This is known as getting the most feathers possible from the fewest geese in order to minimize the squak quacking.

Take a family of 4 with $20,000 earnings—the Presidents plan would give them a $270 inc. tax cut—offset by a $261 increase in soc. security—net tax reduction $9 = maybe. The same family at $25,000 would have a tax increase of $119 & again maybe. *Incidentally at $25,000 they are in the top 10% of taxpayers.*

The "maybes" are because the tax reform they are talking in the White House would involve a a little loophole closing. I doubt that you'd call them loopholes; the deductions you take for local & state taxes including property & special gasoline taxes, and your deduction for medical expenses & casualty for losses not reduced *covered by* insurance—those are hardly loopholes.

But about that progressivity—can we steepen the tax brackets any more than they are without being totally unfair to those who work & earn & make this country go?

Right now the bottom ¼ of all earners only pay less than ¹⁄₁₀ of 1% of the total tax. Indeed the bottom 50% only pay 6% of the total. At $10,000 you become part of the top 50% who are paying 94% of the tax. Forty eight point 6 of that 50% earn between 10,000 & $50,000 a year. where Closing of those so called loopholes would really hurt. They *because you* pay 71% of the tax. The 1.4% who earn $50,000 & up pay almost a ¼ of the total tax—23%.

When the Pres. told his partys platform committee our "tax structure was *is* a disgrace—it must be made more progressive"—he was only right about one thing—it is a disgrace. ❖

---

*W. Michael Blumenthal.

Taxation
November 28, 1978

Congress has finally stewed around with a so-called tax reduction until it got something it could call a tax cut but you & I won't have any extra money to spend. I'll be right back.

We are told by voices from our Mt. Olympus—Wash. D.C. that is—that our taxes have been cut, but don't count on having any extra money to spend. Oh there are one or two parts of the bill that offer some benefit to the economy ~~in the area of~~ *with changes in the* business & capital gains tax; but ~~a~~ an across the board tax cut, it is not.

The Kemp-Roth* bill is supposedly dead, a victim of assassination by those who believe in higher progressivity ~~of~~ in the income tax and that taxation is a method of redistributing the earnings from the most productive to the least productive. Kemp-Roth is not dead,—ideas do not die, it is simply waiting for the wisdom of the people to ~~≠~~ *be accepted by* the majority in Congress.

Andrew Mellon who was Sec. of the Treasury under Presidents Harding, Coolidge & Hoover, in his book "Taxation: The Peoples Business:" explains why the progressive tax idea is really a rip-off, not of the rich but of the worker. He say's: "The history of taxation shows that taxes which are inherently excessive are not paid." And then he explains away the foolish demagoguery of those who want ever higher surtaxes ~~and~~ and label every effort ~~to min~~ *by* individuals to minimize their tax burden as a shameful use of loopholes. Let me ~~read~~ *read* a paragraph from his book.

"The high tax rates inevitably put pressure upon the taxpayer to withdraw his capital from productive business & invest it in tax-exempt securities or find other <u>lawful</u> methods of avoiding the realization of taxable income. The result is that the sources of taxation are drying up; wealth is failing to carry it's share of the tax burden; and capital is being diverted into channels which yield neither revenues to the govt. nor profit to the people. . . . What rates will bring in the largest revenue to the govt., experience has not yet developed, but it is estimated that by cutting the surtaxes in half, the govt., when the full effect of the reduction is felt, will receive more revenues at the lower rates OF TAX than it would have received at the higher rates."

*Congressman Jack Kemp (R-New York) and Senator William Roth (R-Delaware).

Acting on the philosophy expressed in that paragraph Mellon succeeded in getting Congress to cut the highest bracket from the WWI high of 66% to 25%. There were no screams of protest about benefiting the rich and very soon there was such an expansion of the economy & such prosperity FOR ALL THE PEOPLE that we actually made a huge dent in the ~~WWI~~ war debt.

When J.F. Kennedy cut taxes across the board in the 60's, the top marginal rate was 91% & the base 20%. He cut these to 70% & 14%. The result was the longest, sustained, economic expansion in the history of our country. Kemp Roth would further lower the rates to a 50% top & an 8% base. And our most noted economists predict another economic expansion. It is time for Wash. to hear from the people. This is RR   Thanks for listening. ❖

Income Tax
February 13, 1979

It isn't too early to think about spring, that wonderful season of blue birds, budding flowers and the income tax collector. I'll be right back.

Up until a few years ago single people—men & women had a legitimate beef about the income tax laws. They were grossly unfair to the unmarried. Then in 1969 Congress yielded to the growing pressure and took action to end this discrimination. Beginning in 1970 single persons were given a separate tax rate schedule so that none of the singles would pay more than 20% above the married rate.

But as so often happens with govt. Congress didn't quit while they & the people were ahead. Instead they carried on and made some drastic revisions in the rules for married couples.

The option of husbands & wives to file as singles was eliminated. Couples filing separately were required to use the old higher rate schedule the congress had just ~~corrected~~ *reduced* for singles. And couples filing separately and claiming the standard deduction were given maximum allowances that are only half as large as for singles.

With ~~the~~ ½ the wives in America now in the work force Govt. is netting a tidy little ~~bonus~~ *bonus*—$2 bil. last year and growing. A working wife is called a secondary earner and thus her tax rate is automatically the highest surtax bracket ~~her husband is in~~ *of their combined incomes*. An example— hubby earns $20,000 and his wife is picking up $7000 for a total combined inc. of $27,000. Her $7000 is taxed at a full 30%. Incidentally they are both paying social security tax also.

A couple with a combined inc. of $25,000 pays $535 more ~~in~~ inc. tax than a single, $785 more if their inc. is $30,000. If they are both pretty successful and have earnings of $50,000 between them they pay $2,439 more than a single ~~of~~ *with* comparable earnings.

A few years ago some ~~marriage~~ *married* couples developed a practise of flying to the Bahamas during the Christmas holidays for a *vacation in the sun & quick divorce*. After the new year had ~~begun~~ *come in* they would remarry & fly home. The trip was paid for by their tax savings. The practise was so widespread the I.R.S. did what it can do (unfortunately) in this land of the free. They just passed a rule refusing to recognize such divorces.

Today married couples with equal earnings get no benefit from income splitting & filing separate reforms. There are special rules again, quite different from those for single persons and the married couple winds up usually paying a higher tax then if they filed a joint return.

Take it to court you say? Well one couple did and the court even though acknowledging that the tax laws encouraged living together out of wedlock there wasn't anything they could do about it. The Supreme Court refused to review the case.

The admin. in submitting last years tax bill proposed no reform of this inequity even though the Pres. was on record as favoring a reform. The lame excuse was that they didn't want to further complicate the tax structure.

I've only touched on the many inequities. Another one is that a married couple can only deduct half the capital loss 2 singles can deduct and it goes on & on. I believe a Congressional aide has given the real reason why there has been no change. He says the govt. just doesn't want to give up the revenue it gets from the marriage tax.

This is RR   Thanks for listening. ❖

Taxes III
February 2, 1977

This is the 3rd & final instalment of the saga of an audited taxpayer and what he can do if he thinks Internal Revenue has been unfair. I'll be right back.

In the last 2 days I've followed the course of an inc. tax payer who has been told by auditors of Internal Revenue Service that ~~several~~ *deductions he took in* his tax return are being disallowed. Yesterday we had him up to the U.S. Supreme Court, the highest tribunal in our land.

Well first of all the Sup. Ct. accepts only those cases it chooses to hear so it isn't a sure thing that you'll have your day in court. At least in that particular court. But lets cut through all the "ifs" and say the eminent justices found in your favor. You dont owe the added tax, the interest or the penalty. Let's not even talk about whether the cost of all you've done is several times greater than the disputed amount of tax. You've struck a blow for freedom.and A Sup. Ct. ruling will stand as a precedent for years to come sparing all citizens with similar problems from ever having to endure what you've gone through.

Sorry. The ruling you've won applies only to you. The Commissioner of Internal Rev. has the right, a very unique right to non-acquiesce. He has to give you back your money but he reserves the right to go after the next fellow as if the court had never ruled in your favor.

I know most of us believe the Sup. Ct. has the final word in any court case and they do as far as criminals are concerned. But in a sad way—where a tax case is concerned it would seem the Commissioner is more powerful than the U.S. Sup. Ct. But what about the Bill of Rights—my constitutional guarantys.

Well in a case filed Nov. 15, 1976 the authors of the article I've been quoting from for these 3 broadcasts Mr. Green & Mr. Carden tell of a citizen versus I.R.S. who based his case on the Bill of Rights. He refused to answer questions put to him by the Revenue agents invoking the 5th amendment. The Judge overruled him. He then refused on the 4th amendment—his right to privacy. The judge overruled him. Then being a co-plaintiff with his wife he pleaded on the grounds that a married person may not, under law, testify against his or her spouse. The judge overruled him.

The Judges justification is frightening. He stated: "We believe the need for requiring voluntary disclosures of income transcends any personal right to thwart nat. objectives by allowing an undisclosed self-determination of possible self-incrimination to excuse non-compliance with the inc. tax laws." In other words the objectives of the state are more important than the rights of it's citizens. Do you know that is one of the basic precepts of Karl Marx.

Defenses allowed a common criminal are denied a cit. citizen with a tax problem. How far we've come in our inc. tax that once *in 1927* was only 1½% to a top of 5% and now begins at 14% & goes to 70%.

Mr. Green & Mr. Carden suggest the answer might lie in a const. convention which can be called by the legislatures of 38 states to adopt an amendment limiting the percent of earnings subject to tax. There is not limit now. Under the 16th amendment *the* govt. could take 100% of every dollar earned. They also suggest an amendment to limit the size of the nat. debt and to provide *for* paying it off *IN 40 YRS* at 2½% a year. To start with that would be a $15 Bil. payment. Well that makes more sense than adding $50 Bil a year to it.

I'll be right back. This is RR Thanks for listening. ❖

Tax Expenditures
July 27, 1979

If some people in Wash. have their way we may discover we dont own the money tha we earn.

I'll be right back.

I have always believed that govt. has no ≠ right to a surplus; ~~Govt.~~ *that it* should take from the people only the money necessary to fund govt's. legitimate functions. If it takes more than enough it should return the surplus to the people.

In carrying out that policy in Calif. I ran into controversy from some members of the legislature who exemplified the truism that govt. doesn't tax to get the money it needs, it always needs the money it gets. Trying to return ~~the~~ money to the people in the form of a tax rebate was a little like getting between the hog and the bucket. You got jostled about a bit.

The last surplus we gave back amounted to $850 mil. dollars. One angry legislator protested that "giving that money back *TO THE PEOPLE* was an unnecessary expenditure of public funds." ~~In recounting that incident to audiences of taxpayers that line always gets a laugh. I hope we're not laughing too soon.~~

There is a new term being used in Wash. these days, "tax expenditures." If you and I used that term we would be talking about things *UPON WHICH* the govt. spent our tax dollars. ≠ That however is not what govt. means. "Tax expenditures," is the new name govt. has for the share of our earnings it allows us to keep. You & I call them deductions.

The U.S. Govt. claims it is giving up tens of billions of dollars in tax revenues through some 90 deductions we are allowed to take in computing our income tax. And make no mistake about it the govt. has an overpowering urge to shut off those deductions and get that added revenue. One Congressman Sam Gibbons of Fla. says that letting the people take these deductions is the same as if the govt. had written a check ~~and~~ to the taxpayer, subsidizing him. In other words our money is not ours, it is theirs and what we think of as *OUR* after tax earnings is *REALLY* a gift from *THE* govt. ~~to us.~~

A deputy assistant treasury secretary says these "tax expenditures receive minimal govt. control & coordination." Meaning that you & I spend our earnings the way we choose without govt. directing us as to how they should be spent. Indeed the Pres. has proposed a review periodically by Congress to see if deductions should be continued. He told Congress "these programs," (meaning the things we do with our money) "involve spending money for social goals just as much as direct spending programs."

Did you know that your medical expenses, interest on your mortgage, exemptions for dependents etc. were "social goals"? Some of the "tax expenditures" include charitable contributions, property tax on your home, state & local taxes on income & sales, social security benefits, pension plans and a host of others. Congress has already eliminated (starting this year) deduction of state & local taxes on gasoline. ~~taxes~~ In other words we will pay a tax on a tax. That will be an additional $1¼ bil. for Wash.

All told our rich (& wants to be richer) Uncle Sam has an eye on about $170 bil. that we think is ours because ~~we pay it in~~ the Internal Rev. Service says it can be deducted when we compute our inc. tax. It is said Wash. could balance the budget if it eliminated these "tax expenditures." I'm sure it could but it sure would unbalance ours.

This is RR   Thanks for listening. ❖

Constitutional Amendment
February 13, 1979

With Congress back in session and memories of the '78 elections fresh in mind we're going to hear a lot about the process of amending the constitution. I'll be right back.

One of the most frequently asked questions these days has to do with the tax revolt fever sweeping the country. Of course Prop.13 in Calif. is still the best known showcase exhibit but there is plenty of additional evidence that taxes ~~of~~ or more properly the entire subject of govt. spending is very much on peoples minds.

Polls show that 73% of the people support a constitutional amendment to require a balanced Fed. budget "except in times of emergency" such as war. OF COURSE such an amendment won't mean a thing ~~of course~~ unless those emergencies are narrowly & specifically defined. Where govt. spending is concerned a loophole is an ~~inviting opening in Wash.~~ *open door.*

But going on with the poll—two-thirds of the people think it is more important for govt. to cut spending than to cut taxes. Almost 60% felt that cutting govt. spending would be a major step in controlling inflation. My own belief is that cutting taxes will have the effect of cutting ~~taxes~~ *spending* if govt. can no longer run a deficit and that will bring the end of inflation.

Lost in the hullabaloo about Prop.13 is the fact that several states in the

'78 election (helped by a national committee on tax limitation) had ballot measures calling for a % percentage limit on the amount of earnings the state could take in taxes. Most of these passed.

Now a total of 25 states legislatures have passed resolutions calling for a Const. amendment to end Fed. deficit spending. And in Wash. the "Nat. Tax Limitation Committee" made up of business people and such noted economists as Nobel Laureate, Milton Friedman, has unveiled a proposed Constitutional amendment ~~which would require~~ *to control* govt. spending as an alternative to requiring a balanced budget.

I hope we won't lose sight of the main target in a debate over which route we take to amend the constitution. Some want to call a constitutional convention. Others want to go the legislative way with Congress passing an amendment to then be ratified by the states.

~~Voices~~ Among these latter, voices have been raised warning of danger that a constitutional convention would open the door to all manner of proposed amendments. In my view those who warn of this show little faith in our democratic procedures. The Const. provides for both methods and the convention is a safety valve giving the people a chance to act if Congress refuses to.

Frankly I'd prefer the legislative way but maybe it will take the threat of a convention to bring that about. Any number of amendments to end deficit spending have been introduced in Congress and buried in one committee. Why shouldn't that committee learn that unless they let these proposals go to the floor for debate & vote there will be a const. convention?

I might add I think we need both a limit on spending and a ban on unbalanced budgets. One will reduce the inordinate amount of private earnings the govt. is taking & which is a drag on the economy, the other will make sure govt. doesn't evade the limit by running up a debt. Lets hear it for fiscal responsibility.

This is R.R. Thanks for listening. ❖

Reagan describes how he used the line-item veto as governor of California, and why the president of the United States should have the same veto power.

Budget
April 16, 1979

In all the debate over whether a const. amendment should or should not be adopted requiring the Fed. govt. to balance the bud. we are overlooking a much needed amendment.

I'll be right back.

Not many of us are aware that the Fed. budget which is usually announced as the Presidents budget really is a parentless child. For some reason neither the congress or the executive branch has really faced up to the fact that the Fed. budget is the responsibility of everyone & therefore in reality—no one.

When the Office of Management & Budget starts putting the budget together it is faced with programs & spending passed by congress which makes up about 80% of the whole. The executive branch has a "say so" over the other 20%. When completed the budget is sent back to Congress where it is separated into segments & dished out to the appropriate committees having jurisdiction over the various sections of govt. Finally it is returned to the Pres. for signature or veto.

Now it's true that Congress finally after 200 yrs. passed a bill creating a budget committee which supposedly is to weigh the entire budget against estimated revenues. The intent was to create some responsible agency which could possibly think in terms of matching outgo to income. But since the budget has grown $140 bil. in the last 3 yrs.—the largest increase in history—one can hardly say the committee has been a success.

The framers of the Const. must not have had this in mind. They gave the *Pres. the* power of veto over any individual bill including appropriations. And of course the Congress can override a veto but it takes a ⅔ vote. Congress has found a way around this. It can put an absolutely essential spending item into a bill with extravagances the Pres. would like to veto but can't because he'd be vetoing the essential item also.

The answer to this is so simple it has been found by most of our states. Most state const's. require a balanced bud. and most give the Gov. the right of line item veto. *A few Presidents have asked for this.*

Let me use Calif. as an example. The Calif. Const. requires a balanced budget & the Gov. is responsible for submitting such a budget to the legislature. The legislature can remove some things from the budget or reduce *the* cost of some & the legislature can add to the budget.

When it is returned to the Gov. he can by item veto eliminate things the legis. has added to the budget, he <u>cannot</u> put back those things the legis. has removed. To re-increase the budget the legis. must override each veto by a ⅔ vote.

An amendment to the Const. to give an item veto power to the Pres. would eliminate an existing abuse of power by the Cong. The Congress of course would retain the right to override. But the taxpayers would have the protection of a Pres. & a Congress each able to restrain excessive spending by the other. Through this process the Pres. has the responsibility for every dollar spent except in the event of an override of his veto. In that *case* the Cong. must face the people and in effect justify it's increase in the budget.

Does it work? Well in Calif. for 8 years, vetoed spending items totaled $16 Bil.

This is RR   Thanks for listening. ❖

After returning from a trip to Japan in 1978, Reagan argues the case for free trade.

Japan II
May 15, 1978

The Japanese wish us well and are anxious for us to do better than we're doing with regard to our economic problems. I'll be right back.

When we left the U.S. the matter of our unfavorable balance of trade with Japan was an almost every day top item in the news. In a number of circles there was a growing animosity toward Japan, charges of dumping product on our market at less than cost and demands for protectionism—tarriffs, quotas or outright ban on some imports.

Let me give you another view of this problem; how it looks from the other side of the Pacific. I met with *Japanese* business leaders who are also concerned about the trade imbalance even though it is in their favor. They are worried about the voices demanding protectionism and not from the selfish view that it will be directed against them alone. There are Japanese voices demanding protection against our exports to Japan. Protectionism is a 2 way street & *they know that* once started it ends in a demand for retaliation.

Japanese industrialists believe in free trade and they are not building their export supremacy on slave labor wages. While they have not yet reached our own *wage* scale their wages are higher than such other industrial nations as England, France & W. Germany.

Not too long ago if you'll recall they sent a trade mission to our country to BUY several bil. dollars worth of American goods to help reduce our trade imbalance. But they said to me, "Why should we have to do that? Why aren't your businessmen over here trying to sell us these things?" That's a pretty good question.

The truth is they don't see us "Yankee Traders" trying as hard as we once did, aggressively seeking a market in Japan for our goods. Let me give a couple of examples I saw for myself. The Japanese like the English drive on the left hand side of the road. Naturally their automobiles are built with a right hand drive. Now take a look at those Toyotas, Hondas etc. you see every day on our streets. They were built with a left hand drive for American style driving. In Japan when you see a Japanese driving an American car he does so with the inconvenience of a steering wheel on the wrong side for Japanese roads. One of their business leaders said he had asked our auto makers about that & they said it was too much trouble to build cars with a right hand drive.

They make every effort to understand us & our American ways. *What effort* have we *made* to understand the Japanese & their way of doing things? Every graduate of a Japanese high school has had 6 yrs. of English. In our country our students will not only learn no Japanese—a lot of them will have to take a *college* course called bonehead English so they can understand our own language.

The gentlemen I talked with have the friendliest feeling for us and hope desperately that we can solve our energy problem by reducing our dependence on imported oil. Japan is <u>totally</u> dependent on imported oil which should make us skeptical of those who blame *the Arabs for* our falling dollar.

This is RR Thanks for listening. ❖

Reagan often argued that regulations had unintended negative consequences. In the essays that follow, he uses an example of ocean fishing; objects to the constitutionality of other regulation; and objects to the paperwork and bureaucrats that power it.

OSHA
June 15, 1977

Where do we draw the line between what govt. must do to protect us from each other and governments ill advised efforts to protect us from ourselves? I'll be right back.

Summing up govt's. purpose or responsibility in a *single* sentence ~~to~~ risks oversimplification, but if I had to do it I'd settle for this sentence: ~~Quote~~ "Govt. exists to protect us from each other." Brief as it is that ~~covers a lot of territory. It~~ recognizes govt's. responsibility to provide police protection against law breakers; *to maintain* armed forces to keep our land from being invaded and our liberties ~~denied~~ *lost.* ~~by ≠ foreign aggressor. The~~

The sentence also covers govt's involvement in seeing we aren't sold poisoned or contaminated food ~~and~~ *or* dangerous drugs falsely advertised as healthful medicines. ~~It keeps us from being~~ victimized by monopolists, con artists, etc. In other words, *govt's function is to protect us from* all those harmful things that could be done to us by someone else.

I have, however, criticized govt. for not stopping there; for deciding it knows what is best for us and trying to keep us from hurting ourselves. I'm sure many in the various agencies & bureaus of govt. are well intentioned when they do this but what they do can lead to tyranny. An example is the continued effort by govt. to force motorcycle riders to wear helmets. I happen to believe ~~they~~ it's foolish to ride ~~the machine~~ a motorcycle without one *but doing so does not endanger others who are on the highway.* ~~and I agree with govt's. right to see that the machine has proper brakes, lights, rear vision mirror, etc. But all of these protect us~~ *others* ~~when we're on the highway from being injured by the motorcycle rider.~~ The helmet protects ~~him alone~~ *only the rider* & it's his right to ~~take that risk~~ *risk not wearing one* no matter how foolish we think he might be.

Still much of the costly growth of burocracy & the subsequent harassment & interference ~~with~~ *in* our lives is the result of ~~these~~ *well intentioned* pub. servants trying to eliminate all ~~of~~ the hazards of living.

I've been most critical of the Occupational, Safety, & Health Admin., commonly called OSHA, now in existence for ~~6~~ SIX yrs. It came into being to reduce or eliminate job hazards in every kind of business. And ~~while~~ *while* it has inspected, filed charges against employers, *and* written tens of thousands of regulations there has been no reduction in work related injuries or deaths. There has, however, been costly interference and reduction of productivity.

One of OSHA's latest targets, which might explain why I've been critical, is the admittedly hazardous field of deep sea diving. According to the companies in this field there are about *600 commercial* deep sea divers in the whole United States. The hazardous nature of the occupation in indicated by their earnings which run from *$50,000* to *$100,000* a year.

OSHA ~~has~~ is attempting to set standards for practices & equipment that would be required in deep sea diving. OSHA is meeting resistance. For one thing the cost of what OSHA is demanding is greater than the total gross revenue of all the companies in that business.

The companies & the divers do not minimize the hazards of their craft, but they present figures showing that injury & death is not commonplace. When it does occur it is unlikely that a regulation or safety precaution could prevent it: A man hit in the head by a tree carried downstream by the current, another entangled in wire who tore off his helmet in panic & tried to reach the surface.

They are brave men, a breed apart and well aware of the precautions they must take. They have looked at OSHA's proposed standards and to a man say "no thanks." ~~In its magazine "Faceplate~~ *It's easy to see why.* The U.S. Navy IN IT'S MAGAZINE *"FACEPLATE"* has said that to comply with the OSHA standards would *mean* send*ing* the diver underwater weighing 1000 LBs. This is RR. Thanks for listening. ❖

Fish
February 13, 1979

Once again nature must be laughing at us. This time it's the "Fisheries Conservation & Management Act of 1977." That's the act that established the 200 mile fishing limit.

I'll be right back.

A few years ago there was quite a fuss about foreign fishing vessels taking fish ~~off our coasts~~ in American waters, sometimes within sight of shore. Environmentalists expressed fear that overfishing would deplete our offshore fish stocks. The result was a piece of legislation called the, "Fisheries Conservation & Management Act of 1977," which established the 200 mile limit off our coasts. Naturally ~~other~~ *other* nations had & have established similar limits.

I should point out that many in the fishing industry particularly on the East coast supported this measure as a necessary protection. It is also safe to say they no longer feel that way. There is no question but that foreign overfishing has been stopped but so has a lot of American fishing. On top of this we may lose to Canada one of our ~~form~~ finest fishing grounds because the 200 miles is measured straight out from shore. Geography being what it is ~~takes~~ *there* are irregularities along the coast and thus overlaps. One such OVERLAP now being contested by Canada & the U.S. could take from us the northern half of "Georges Bank," which historically has always been considered ours. *But then on our west coast the Canadians have been shut off from their usual salmon fishing grounds.*

The greatest setback however to our fishermen has been caused by the regulations which always follow a piece of well-intended legislation. For example once the act was in effect U.S. fishermen were given a quota of only 10% of ~~what foreigners had been catching the year before~~ *the previous years foreign catch*.

The regional commissions on the East & West coasts set their quotas based on recommendations provided by govt. scientists. These scientists are supposed to be able to count the fish in the sea. Take one region for example, the coast from Maine to S. Carolina: With only 2 boats, 12 scientists are supposed to take a fish census that will determine how many fish the industry can take off that *from the waters* off that entire stretch of coastline. As one exec. of a fishermans marketing assoc. says, "the regional commission itself admits there is no biological justification for their quota levels." But when quotas are reached the Dept. of Commerce simply closes the fisheries. It is admitted even by members of Congress that no one anticipated putting so much power in the hands of the Fed. govt. It's funny how often it ends up that way.

The New England cod & haddock fisheries have been closed down 4 times since the law went into effect. One of these was in mid-summer at the height of the season. For the first time in the memory of man hundreds of workers in processing plants & of course boat crews were laid off in mid-summer.

Almost 2 years after the act the U.S. is importing over 90% of it's fish. New England imported 30 mil. *more* pounds of cod more in the year after the act than it had *did* in the previous year. That does seem like a strange result for an act that was supposed to protect the Am. fishing industry.

While scientists don't seem to be able to count the fish or should I say, find any fish to count, the fishermen say they are thick enough to walk on. One spokesmen for the industry who once supported but now regrets the 200 mile limit says, "We'd rather be fighting the Russians—at least we'd be free."

This is RR Thanks for listening. ❖

In 1977, OSHA claimed the right to inspect private homes. Reagan objects, cites the Fourth Amendment, and calls on Congress to pass legislation to rein in this agency.

Man's Castle
July 6, 1977

A mans home is his castle. We are pretty unique in all the world by reason of the protection against our *because we are protected against* govt's. unwarranted invasion of our homes. I'll be rite back.

One of the most unique features of that document so very unique in itself—the U.S. Const. is the 4th amendment guarantying the sanctity of ≠ our homes. In all the social structures governing man's relation to man prior, to the American revolution, no one challenged *denied* govt's. right to enter a citizens dwelling place to search & to seize.

But here for 200 yrs. "we the people" have declared that officials can not invade our privacy unless they obtain a warrant. And that warrant must show "probable cause." Meaning the magistrate issuing the warrant must be given specific ~~off~~ evidence ~~that~~ which indicates a search is justified in the interest of the public good.

Now suddenly we discover that as bureaus & agencies of govt. have increased in number they have also increased in power. Spawning regulations to make their own jobs easier or just to carry out what they have decided is best for society they increasingly invade, inspect and punish without the formality of a warrant.

Discovery of this was made by Idaho congressman George Hansen. O.S.H.A.—the Occupational Safety & Health Admin. sought entry into a small husband & wife owned business. The wife Mrs Hertzler told the inspector—"not without a warrant." They returned with a warrant but it did not show probable cause so again they were denied entry.

The Hertzlers have a small shop in their back yard. As a courtesy to their 5 employees they let them keep their lunches in the refrigerator which is in the Hertzlers own kitchen. The OSHA inspectors used this as an excuse to demand entry into the Hertzlers home. An arroused Mr. Hertzler ran them off with justified anger.

Learning of this Congressman Hansen who has challenged OSHA's high-handed tactics before inquired of OSHA if they did indeed claim the right to search private dwellings without a warrant. The answer was "yes" OSHA did make such a claim.

His next stop was the solicitors office in the Dept. of labor. There he was blatantly informed by one, Mike Levine that the OSHA act gave the Labor Dept. the authority to conduct such inspections of private homes under Section 8(a) of Public Law 91-596.

~~The consequences of such a statement are staggering~~. Looking at all the areas govt. now claims as within it's jurisdiction and therefore subject to it's regulations the consequences of such a statement are staggering. Your home could be ~~sup~~ subject to search simply because you were hiring a gardener, ~~or~~ having carpet installed or re-doing the kitchen.

Congressman Hansen has called the seriousness of this violation of constitutional principle to the attention of his colleagues. Congress passed the law which gave OSHA it's authority. It is probable that OSHA like so many other agencies has arrogantly gone beyond Congressional intent. But whatever—Congress can undo what has been done and should do so quickly & emphatically.

Daniel Webster said, "Hold onto your const. for if the Am. Const. shall fall there will be anarchy throughout the world."

This is RR   Thanks for listening. ❧

Federal Registry I
September 1975

The French Philosopher De Tocqueville—a century ago spoke of gov't. covering the face of society with a network of small complicated rules until the Nat. is reduced to a flock of timid & industrious animals of which gov't. is the shepherd."—I'll be rite back.

We are indebted to Congressman Ed. Hutchinson of Mich. for compiling some facts & figures ~~that~~ *that* reveal just how close we are to living in a country where everything that isn't compulsory is prohibited.

Not many people in this quote—"land of the free" unquote are aware of a Wash. publication called the "Federal Register." This is a daily publication of the U.S. govt. containing the complete record of the latest rules & regulations put forth by Fed. agencies. It also publishes legal notices issued by the agencies, executive orders & notices of the meetings of Uncle Sams several thousand advisory commissions. All of this means a ~~daily~~ volume of 300,000 to 400,000 words each day. ~~Dur~~

During the '60s you could skim through a one years printing of the Register—just one year mind you—by reading 15,000 pages. ~~That's the equivalent of about~~ Last year it was up to 46,000 *pages* and this year it will be about 50,000. ~~pages. That sh~~ Since the bulk of those pages ~~carry~~ *are filled with* new regulations covering every facet of our lives you can see that we are not exactly footloose free spirits. This years 50,000 pages will contain more than 25,000 separate regulations ~~added~~ on top of all the tens & tens of thousands *passed in* ~~of all the~~ preceding years.

Congressman Hutchison ~~also~~ tells us that if we can't bear the suspense each day of waiting for tomorrows 400,000 words, there is a dial-a-regulation service that will provide you with a sneak preview of ~~the~~ tomorrows regulations.

Just for example ~~there are the regulations of~~ *there is* the Consumer Product, Safety Commission which is only 2 yrs. old but is grinding out regulations with the best of them. They cover everything from tricycles to baseball bats—from gun ammunition to tobacco.

Other agencies are spawning rules on a daily basis covering salad dressing standards, advertising testimonials & prune shipping requirements. Important decisions on how best to do business, how to grow crops, how to shop at the supermarket, how to travel, how to educate your children, in short, ~~the~~ Rep. Hutchison says, "decisions of how to live are being usurped by a govt. which sees <u>no</u> limits to its powers."

Not only does govt. threaten our freedoms it is not equipped to ~~factor in~~ & *take into account or* give consideration to all the unique factors involved in the dealings between 50 sovereign states, 30,000 localities & more than 200 mil. individuals.

The Congressman sums it up thusly; "As each of Washingtons hard & fast regulations proves unresponsive to a new situation, new regulations, exceptions and re-definitions are enacted in a never ending struggle to keep pace with the real world. This is why the Fed. Register is getting bigger and will continue to get bigger until the role of govt. in our society is redefined." Amen!

This is RR Thanks for listening. ❖

Regulations
March 12, 1975

The time has come to regulate the regulators.

I'll be right back.

Back in 1887 the Cong. of the U.S. established the Interstate Commerce Commission to regulate the railroads. It was a noble, well intentioned experiment and probably there was some need for it. But as the ads say, "we've come a long way baby." Fed. regulation now covers every aspect of bus. & industry in Am. ~~In this last bastion~~ In what so many of us think of as the last stronghold of free enterprise bus & industry are more regulated than in any other country in the world where free enterprise is allowed to exist.

Most of us have grown up thinking of govt. regulation as designed to keep big business in its place; to hold it back from becoming an octopus squeezing all of us and robbing ~~of~~ us of our earnings.

That <u>was</u> the original idea. Those who wanted govt. to be our shield & protector assumed that regulatory commissions would be made ~~of~~ up of knowledgeable, objective individuals immune to pol. pressure & dedicated to the pub. interest. They would serve as combination judges, legislators & executives—a kind of new 4th branch of govt. These optimistic hopes have not been realized.

Dr. Paul McCracken former chairman of the Presidents Council of Ec. advisers says, "To anyone willing to look, it is clear ~~enough~~ that—with distressing monotony—regulation has produced sick & arthritic industries." Back in the New Deal when regulation was vastly increased a Presidential commission in 1937 told F.D.R. that the regulatory agencies constituted, "a headless, 4th branch of govt., a haphazard deposit of irresponsible agencies & uncoordinated powers." In 1961 an adviser to J.F.K. recommended a sweeping overhaul ~~OVERHAUL of regulations. In 1971 a Presidential commission found that~~ commissions & agencies were "slow, costly, cumbersome & uncoordinated."

Who pays for ~~the slowness~~ all of that? I don't *just* mean who pays for the administrative salaries & overhead of the commissions. I mean who pays in increased prices—inflation if you will ~~for all~~ caused by unnecessary regulations?

The Bureau of Domestic Commerce estimated 4 yrs. ago that Nat Labor Relations Board anti-competitive policies plus acts by a few other agencies were costing consumers (that's us) up to $3 bil. more in construction, about 1¼ bil. in ~~rail~~ railroading, more than ½ a bil. in printing, & almost as much in supermarkets & trucking. This is just a tiny sample. The Independent Businessmens Assn. estimates their members (small businessmen employing 500 or less) ~~#~~ spend 130 mil. man hours a year just doing govt. required paperwork which adds up to $50 Bil. a year to the prices they must charge. All of this of course is rationalized as protecting the pub. interest.

~~In Cong.~~ There are a host of proposals for more of the same before Cong. right now. There is something else before Cong. The President has asked for a new commission ~~to~~ empowered to focus it's attention on 6 of the independent regulatory agencies & the Consumer Product Safety Commission controlled by Cong. Senate Bill 4145 if passed will create this commission. Special interest groups will lobby against it. You & I should lobby for it. We should demand NOT ONLY its passage BUT that the commission ~~chair~~ be manned by men & women who will determine where the laws of the mkt. place can replace ~~the~~ useless regulations and create real savings for ~~the~~ consumers. Only our indignation voiced out loud will bring this about. ❖

Paperwork and Bureaucrats
September 21, 1976

Sometime's giving a burocrat a new rule is like handing a pyro-maniac a lighted match in a haymow. I'll be right back.

A Congressman from Conn. is upset and properly so. It seems the Dept. of H.E.&W. has told ~~a school district the~~ Wethersfield school officials their all-boy 6th grade choir violates sex discrimination guidelines. Under their rules musical groups can be separated only by vocal range. I hope by the time you hear this the Congressman* has been successful in his fight to restore common sense.

---

*In September 1976 the congressman from the district that included the town of Wethersfield was William R. Cotter (D-Connecticut).

Congressman Charles Thone of Neb. is waging the same fight on another front. He's trying to save paper. If he succeeds a lot of business people & farmers will cut down on tranquilizers.

Congressman Thone co-sponsored the legis. which created the Commission on Fed. Paperwork, a temporary body dedicated to reducing the quantity of forms & reports the Fed. govt. demands of all of us. He tells of the testimony to the commission ~~of~~ by the head of one of our larger ~~≠~~ drug firms revealing that paperwork alone adds 50¢ to the cost of any prescription using his firms medicines.

Just listen to these figures—this firm spends $100 mil a year on research in 5 fields, 2 of which are Cancer & Heart disease. Govt. paperwork requires them to spend more personnel hours than they can invest on Cancer & Heart research.

A medicine for arthritis is on the mkt. only after submission of an application that consisted of 120,000 pages in the original. They had to send 2 additional copies. You don't just drop 360,000 pages in the ~~nearst~~ *nearest* mailbox. Not when you are ~~lu~~ sending over 1 ton of paper. ~~The index to And the the application required a 153 page computer printout.~~

The commission has learned that the Environmental Protection Agency requires a technical data report submitted quarterly. Then for the 2nd quarter you must submit in addition to the 2nd quarter report a copy of the 1st quarter report. And of course in the 3rd quarter you re-submit the reports for the 1st <u>and</u> 2nd quarters. And yes with the 4th quarter report you resubmit the 1st, 2nd, & 3rd quarter reports. These reports to E.P.A. ~~are~~ usually have to do with chemical weed killers and such. They can run 3000 pages ~~to a report~~ *each*.

Now I know that the govt. workers ~~who are~~ responsible for this foolishness aren't evil people. They just get carried away with trying to solve every facet of every problem and believe the country will come unglued if they dont.

The June issue of the American Pol. Science Review published a study done by 2 eminent scholars in 1970. They had interviewed senior employees in 18 Fed. agencies. Regardless of who was Pres. in 1970 he was faced with 83% of all ~~the top~~ supergrade employees who supported & believed in the phil. of big govt. In H.E.W., Hud & OEO* 92% of the top burocrats opposed every effort to reduce the Soc. Svc. agencies. More than 70% wanted to expand them. Of the pol. appointees who were holdovers from the "Great

*Department of Health, Education and Welfare, Department of Housing and Urban Development, and the Office of Economic Opportunity.

Society" era 75% wanted to increase the size of the Fed. govt. & most indicated they wanted a major increase.

Our problem is a permanent structure of govt. insulated from the thinking & wishes of the people; ~~and~~ A structure which for all practical purposes is more powerful than our elected representatives. Only you & I can change that. ~~by sending~~ *We must send* congress a mandate to restore govt. to the people.

This is RR   Thanks for listening. ❖

Drugs and the FDA
May 4, 1977

A bill, to curb some of the burocratic fumbling in the Fed. Drug Admin, defeated in the 94th Cong. has another chance in the 95th. I'll be right back.

Congressman Steve Symms of Idaho has ~~seek the 80~~ 87 cosponsors in ~~Congress~~ the House of Representatives ~~for~~ *on* a bill; "To Expand the medical freedom of choice of consumers by amending the Fed. Food, Drug, and Cosmetic Act to provide that drugs will be regulated under that act solely to assure their safety."

Now, how many of us thought that safety was the only concern of the Fed. Drug Admin. *which from here on* I'll ~~now~~ refer to as the F.D.A.? We have so many laws and we add so many more each year, it's understandable if we failed to note, or to remember that in 1962 the Fed. Drug Act was amended ~~to give the agency~~ *to say that drugs &* medicines should not only be safe—they must be effective.

Sen. Estes Kefauver was chairing the Antitrust & Monopoly Subcommittee which was investigating prices of new drugs. About that time the tragic thalidomide disaster hit West Germany. It had not been licensed in America. It could not have been licensed under our laws as they were then, but it was used to push through, ~~as necessary, a law~~ *in emergency fashion, a bill* granting additional power to *the* F.D.A.

The result of that hasty, ~~emergency~~ *panic*-inspired amendment has hardly benefited the American people. In the first place deciding a medicine is safe to take is one thing, but trying to establish its effectiveness is something else again. Doctors have displayed, over the years, a great ability to sort out medicines which aren't very effective. If aspirin hadn't been approved prior to the 1962 amendment it ~~could~~ couldn't be on the market today. ~~and its very possible we'd be doing without penicillin.~~

~~Sin~~ Prior to the amendment U.S. drug companies added an average of 43 new medicines each yr.—now we're down to 13. It used to take 1 or 2 yrs.

to get a medicine licensed & *at* a cost of about $1 mil. Now it takes 8 to 10 yrs. ~~and~~ at a cost ~~of~~ sometimes as high as $20 mil. The average is about 12.

With all of govt's. concern about eliminating monopoly, the 1962 amendment encouraged monopoly. Only the very biggest drug firms can afford to develop new medicines now. Our govt. almost automatically accepts foreign studies showing a drug is not good. It does not, however, accept such studies if they find the drug is good. Many American discoveries are denied to the American people but are licensed & used effectively in the rest of the world. Three-fourths of new drugs developed in the U.S. are ~~denied~~ *barred to us but sold overseas.*

Take the case of an American ~~development~~ *discovery* arthritis discovery;† it has been given extensive tests in 15 countries, is sold in more than 40 and there have been about 120 mil. "patient hours" of use. It is not available in the U.S. What price have we paid in suffering & death because of the arrogance of officialdom? One F.D.A. official boasted that he had held up for 9½ yrs. any drug for Angina Pectoris and hypertension because, in his opinion, these ~~were~~ *are* symptoms & not diseases.

The Dr. who prescribes the medication is best able to judge it's effectiveness. Congressman Steve Symms says, "the health of Americans should never be subjected to the whims of Congress. The only long term solution is to take away from F.D.A. the power to make the terribly subjective determinations about drug effectiveness." Steve Symms has offered a pro-consumer, antimonopoly bill. It is known as H.R. 54. He could use our help. This is RR Thanks for listening.

†Tell Pete—The arthritis medicine is NAPROSYN developed by Syntex Research Center of Palo Alto. ❖

Reagan's conviction that public employees do not have the right to strike foreshadows his response as president to the strike of the air traffic controllers on August 3, 1981, when he fired those who refused to return to work within 48 hours.

Public Servants
May 25, 1977

When are pub. servants not pub. servants? When they go on strike. This is an issue which must be resolved, and can be, by public action. I'll be right back.

Franklin Delano Roosevelt said "A strike of pub. emps. manifests nothing less than an intent on their part to prevent or obstruct the operations of govt.

until their demands are satisfied. Such action looking toward the paralysis of govt. by those who have sworn to support it is unthinkable & intolerable."

F.D.R. summed it up pretty well. *His words mean that* those who choose govt. employment become a part of the govt. establishment and are sworn to uphold it. Their employers are not their immediate superiors, or even the elected representatives of the people. Their true employers <u>are</u> the people. No amount of rhetoric or reciting clichés such as "2nd class citizens" can change the fact that there is a fundamental difference between private & pub. employment.

In the *fiscal* year that ended in Oct. 1975 some ~~≠~~ 316,000 govt. workers, at all levels, engaged in unauthorized & illegal work stoppages a total of 490 times. They struck for a total of almost 2½ mil. work days in that 1 yr., generally over wages & hours. Tragically, the worst offenders were professional educators, those we trust to implant standards of conduct, concepts of trust and responsibility in tomorrows citizens.

There are almost 10 mil. full time state & local ~~govt.~~ emps. and more than half now belong to employee organizations. ~~Others~~ Some refusing to join such org's. have been forced by a number of govt's. to contribute dues to the organizations they refuse to join.

In my own state, the citizens of Calif. have an opportunity to do something about this situation and the opportunity has been made possible by ~~th~~ a group of their fellow citizens. Teachers, disturbed by a change in ~~state~~ *the* law ~~which recognized giving and~~ *which gave* teacher unions *the* right to bargain for non-members, ~~& which implys the right to strike~~ have formed a "Committee for Individ. Rights." This committee is circulating petitions to put a ~~co~~ proposed const. amendment on the ballot in the 1978 election.

So far they have attracted an impressive array of endorsements from office holders, chambers of commerce and other org's. such as the Professional Educators Group, Nat. Assn. of Prof. Ed's. & the Secondary Elementary Teachers org.

Their proposed amendment would make it "unlawful for any pub. emp. or any emp. org., directly or indirectly, to induce, instigate, encourage, authorize, ratify or participate in a strike against any pub. employer."

The measure continues spelling out what enforcement of this prohibition would entail; "Any violation by a pub. emp. shall result in mandatory dismissal and in the loss of tenure or seniority and in the event that such emp. has both tenure & seniority the loss of both." Anyone dismissed for striking could not be reinstated, but would have to take his, or her, chances of being re-hired as a new emp.

The amendment frees each emp. from obligation to be represented by an org. as a pre-requisite to employment. It also states that dues or fees cannot be imposed as a condition for hiring nor *can there be an* assessment of such fees for pol. purposes. I'll assure you the Nat. Ed. Assn. will come out against this proposal.

But, I hope my fellow Californians will rally round and help provide the 500,000 signatures needed on petitions to put this on the ballot. It is time for the citizenry of all the 50 states to declare that pub. employees cannot strike. This is RR. Thanks for listening. ❖

The next three essays deal with important aspects of unemployment in the late 1970s: plants closing down, foreign workers, and the high unemployment rate among teenagers.

Communications I
April 3, 1978

It's amazing what can happen when diverse groups stop talking about each other & start talking to each other. I'll be right back.

Just recently a meeting took place that revealed how much Americans have been divided by labels and the image making that is all too prevalent in todays society. Congressman Phil Crane of Ill. Repub. and in addition chairman of the Am. Conservative Union decided to try and establish communications with ~~the~~ rank & file Union workers. Obviously he can have contact every day with the hierarchy of organized labor in Wash. Indeed ~~there is~~ a labor lobbyist STANDS in the ~~doorway of~~ *entrance* to the House Chamber ~~who gives~~ *every day giving* a thumbs up or thumbs down signal to Congressmen ~~as they respond~~ indicating how they should vote on legislation when they respond to a roll call. That signal of course reflects the view of organized labor leadership in Wash.

Phil Crane & a colleague, a young Congressman from Okla. Mickey Edwards journeyed to Youngstown Ohio to meet with local labor leaders. Why Youngstown? Because they wanted to hear the views of those ~~men~~ *leaders local* ~~labor~~ LEADERS on the closing of the Youngstown Sheet & Tube Plant which ~~closed~~ *wiped* out the jobs of almost 5000 working men & women in the steel industry.

The locals were understandably edgy about meeting with Congressmen they thought of as the opposition. They insisted on absolute secrecy, no publicity at all and were frankly suspicious that Phil & Mickey might be using them in some way.

The meeting was held on their terms. Congressman Crane asked for their ~~views on~~ analysis of ~~the~~ why the plant closed ~~and~~ as well as the reasons for economic problems in general.

Hear now from the men & women who work on the line not at a desk in the Wash. H.Q's. They told of injury to the investment climate caused by laws passed in Wash. One of them angrily asked if they as Congressmen knew how much it cost to put in a new blast furnace. (This remember was a worker—not a ~~manager~~ *voice for* management.)

They spoke of the inability of management to absorb mounting production costs imposed by govt. regulations. They were eloquent about the lack of a coherent energy policy designed to provide abundant fuel sources to keep industry going. And they told *the* two conservative Congressmen of how inflation was caused by uncontrollable deficit spending by the Fed. govt. They criticized unfair trading practices by some of our foreign competitors *& the harm done by environmental extremists who cared more for fish than people.*

You've heard me on these broadcasts ~~≠~~ *express* the same views. They are solid doctrine in conservative circles. But when Phil Crane asked them to label themselves, *asked* did they think they were liberal or conservative, they unanimously ~~chose~~ *declared* themselves liberal.

Their definition of conservative was the typical stereotype, "spokesmen for big business & bankers, country club set, anti-working people etc."

~~To~~ Next broadcast I'd like to tell you about the follow up to this meeting. This is RR   Thanks for listening. ❖

Apples
November 29, 1977

I don't know whether an apple a day keeps the Dr. away but this year the Labor Dept. did it's best to keep the apples away—from us. I'll be right back.

From time to time on these broadcasts I've discussed the unemployment situation and given evidence that ~~a lot~~ *at least* some of the unemployed prefer ~~it~~ *to remain* that way. It would seem they have an ally in the U.S. Labor Dept.

This last Oct. the apple growers of New England who had seen a late spring snowstorm knock the blossoms off the trees and a Sept. rainstorm do the same to about 10% of the apples ~~(plus making it impossible to pick dur-~~

ing the rain) faced further trouble. The rain had delayed the harvest of the $50 mil. crop until the fruit was ripe & ready to fall but there were no workers to pick the apples.

The U.S. Labor Dept. has been making it harder & harder to emplo bring in foreign labor insisting that the farmers hire unemployed Americans. Now that makes sense providing you can find Americans who'll do the work. And with a 7+% unemployment rate you'd think that wouldn't be too hard *difficult* since a fellow can earn $50 a day picking apples.

But the apples kept on ripening, the growers kept on recruiting and the apples stayed on the trees. The Labor Dept. *itself* staged a recruiting drive in one of N.Y. Citys areas of high unemp. spending $10,000 in the effort. They signed up 75—15 of whom reported for work all *& all* of whom quit the 1st week.

Still the growers had to appear before 5 district courts in 5 states, 2 U.S. courts of appeal & the U.S. Supreme Ct. before they could get permission to hire foreign labor. They were able to prove they had engaged in an intensive recruiting drives among the unemployed in Vermont & in the Eastern cities with high unemployment—Boston, N.Y., etc.

Finally in the last minute nick of time they were permitted to import Jamaicans & Canadians. The crop was saved and the imported laborers seemed pretty happy to get the work. They averaged about $1500 apiece for the few weeks.

In view of the reluctance of Americans to take those jobs it's interesting to see what kind of workers ≠ crossed the border & the Ocean to pick New England Apples. Some of the Jamaicans have counted on this work for a number of years. Their jobs at home have to do with the tourist trade and are therefore seasonal. *They come here, pick apples in New Eng., sugar cain in the South and go home to their seasonal work.*

From Canada come Nova Scotia lobstermen & clamdiggers who go south after their own seasons and then when August—comes to an end in wind up at the end of July. Some of these bring their families down on weekends and make the job a kind of expense paid vacation.

When the Labor Dept. is forced to relent and let these visitors do this work it is of course all legal. But it makes one wonder if how many of our own unemployed are *about the illegal alien fuss. Are great numbers of our unemployed really* victims of the illegal alien invasion or are those illegal tourists actually doing work our own people wont do?

One thing is certain in this hungry world; no regulation or law should be allowed to if it results in crops rotting in the fields for lack of harvesters.

This is RR. Thanks for listening. ❖

Youth Employment
September 6, 1977

A few broadcasts back I made reference to the looting in the N.Y. blackout and the variety of excuses offered by some as explanation. I'll be right back.

Some have said the looting last July in N.Y.* was aggravated by not enough welfare. Others said it was the direct result of 4 decades of *too much* welfare.~~eroding character~~. I myself have deplored a tendency in ed. to ignore teaching moral precepts. Columnist John Chamberlain recognized all these differing views in a recent column** but then came up with what might very well be the best explanation.

Idle hands can get into mischief. Juveniles who can't find summer jobs to keep them busy and to provide pocket money cannot only become bored, & ~~restless~~ they can become resentful toward a society that seemingly doesn't need them.

John called attention to the fact that George Meany*** and Pres. Carter were getting together on the minimum wage. Meany says it should be $3 an hour, the Pres. wanted to go to $2.50. They finally settled on $2.65. How many jobs that teenagers with no experience in the labor mkt. can do have disappeared because possible employers don't think the jobs *they can do* are worth $2.65 an hour?

I remember a meeting I had with a group of youngsters from one of our minority neighborhoods while I was Gov. ~~They were~~ These young people earnestly wanted ~~an~~ an opportunity to work & earn. I expressed the view (backed by some available statistics) that jobs had been eliminated by the minimum wage and that we needed a waiver ~~where~~ *for young* people like themselves. I had thought they might possibly resent the suggestion that they should work below the prescribed pay level. I was wrong. They asked if I would help in trying to get the law changed. I've been trying ever since.

John Chamberlains column reported the findings of U. of Chi. economist Yale Brozen in 2 masterful studies that prove beyond a shadow of a doubt

---

*On July 13, 1977, a few weeks before Reagan wrote this essay, New York City experienced a 'brownout,' which was accompanied by looting in some neighborhoods.
**"New York 'Black Out' Looting May Become Commonplace," by John Chamberlain, appeared in the September 10, 1977 edition of *Human Events*. The newspaper was distributed on September 3, 1977.
***President of the AFL-CIO (American Federation of Labor and the Congress of Industrial Organizations).

that every time the minimum wage goes up teenage unemployment ~~increases~~ *goes right up* with it.

Four Congressmen, Sen's. McClure & Hatch and Rep's. Clarence Brown & John Rousselot were impressed enough by Brozens figures to sponsor ~~as a~~ *an independent* study by Prof. Williams of Temple U. That ~~study~~ is now before the joint ec. committee of Congress.* ~~It confirms Prof. Brozen's findings.~~

Teenage unemp. averages 5X that of the civilian labor force over age 25. And youths between 20 & 24 average 2½ times as much. Young people 16 to 24 are *only* ¼ of the work force, they are ½ *of all* the unemployed. And young blacks have an unemp. rate almost double that of their white contemporaries.

Everyone must feel needed. I've never forgotten an episode a few years ago when one of our winter storms had churned *up* a high tide & rough surf which threatened to undermine & destroy dozens of beautiful beach homes. All day & into the night volunteers filled sandbags & built barricades. ~~Television was covering the battle.~~

It was sometime after midnight when a TV reporter ~~corralled~~ stopped a young man in swimming trunks. It was *so* cold ~~enough~~ *you could* to see his breath. Yes he'd been at it all day. Yes he was cold & tired. Did he live in one of those houses? No. Then why? He was stopped for a second then he said something so poignant, this average teenager, that it should be printed on a billboard. "I guess it's the first time we've ever felt needed."

This is RR Thanks for listening. ❖

Extolling the virtues of American agriculture, Reagan argues that government interference in agriculture does not hold prices down and does not increase farmers' income.

Agriculture
March 27, 1979

In the wake of the tractorcade** to Wash. it might be well to look at the overall farm situation to see what prompted the demonstration. I'll be right back.

Consumerism is a more potent political force than food production. We all eat & therefore buy food but only a few mil. Americans are engaged in producing food. On a sheer vote count it's easy to see which group will capture the interest of govt. as inflat. sends prices skyward.

*James McClure (R-Idaho), Orrin G. Hatch (R-Utah), Clarence J. "Bud" Brown (R-Ohio) & John H. Rousselot (R-California); Walter Williams, professor, Temple University.
**Farmers demonstrated by driving hundreds of large tractors into Washington, D.C.

The housewife is inclined to see inflation as mainly a food problem. Shopping each week in the market she is particularly conscious of the price increases month after month. And it's understandably difficult to convince her that Americans eat better for a lower percentage of income than any other people on earth. Since 1960 food *costs* as a percentage of our ~~income~~ *earnings* have gone down 21%. ~~Incidentally~~ In that same period, *the cost of* govt. has gone up 20%.

Now the farmer & his family *as consumers* buy all the things we buy. ~~as consumers~~ Even the wheat farmer buys bread. As producers the farmers also feel inflation when they meet the payroll, buy tractor fuel, farm machinery, fertilizer etc. I had a personal experience with this on our own ranch. ~~I~~ *We* have a 1953 tractor which I bought 2nd hand MORE THAN 20 YRS AGO for $1200. ~~more than 20 yrs. ago.~~ Just wishing one day I priced a replacement. I was offered $4000 in tradein on the old one which would only leave me $13,000 ~~to pay for a new one~~ *on* TOP OF THAT TO BUY A NEW TRACTOR. I'm still using the old one.

Now maybe this makes the tractorcade more understandable and yet I must say I did not agree with the demand the demonstrating farmers were making. Neither did the majority of their fellow farmers. They were asking govt. to solve their very real problem with a subsidy which of course would increase govt. regulation & control of agriculture. A subsidy is also the govt. way of pleasing the consumer by making it appear that prices are being held down while they take the difference out of your pocket in taxes to pay FOR the subsidy.

We came out of the great depression with a massive program of ~~govt.~~ regulations, controls & subsidies for agriculture. Like most such govt. programs the*re* were scores of conflicting & contradictory programs. I remember one in which the govt. had about half a dozen separate ~~agencies~~ *programs spending mils. of dollars* telling chicken farmers how to increase egg production. A 7th ~~agency~~ *program* spent mils. of dollars buying up surplus eggs.

Then in 1969 we began a move to put farming back into the free mkt. place. The almost 5½ bil. dollar ~~sub~~ farm subsidy dropped to less than $1 bil. by 1975. The subsidies went down by 85%. Net farm income computed in constant dollars went up 16%.

But then we fell into the same old sickness. In ~~the~~ 3 yrs. the farm subsidy rose and last year it was bigger than it was in 1969. The subsidies increased by 725% IN THOSE 3 YRS. Net farm income, again in constant dollars, went down by 14%.

Govt. ~~has~~ interference in agriculture hasn't held down food prices, it hasn't increased the farmers income. They are worse off, we're worse off and govt. costs about $7 bil. more than it did or should. Farm net income in constant dollars was almost twice as great in 1973 as it is now. When will we learn.

This is RR   Thanks for listening. ❖

Admitting a lifelong fondness for riding trains—"I loved every minute of it"—Reagan argues for the abolition of Amtrak.

Trains
July 9, 1979

The sound of a train whistle in the night still is a nostalgic sound to me evoking thoughts of far away places.

I'll be right back.

I suppose I could be called a "train buff." I've never been able to pass a toy store window or model shop without pausing ~~to look~~ if there is a *TOY* train ≠ on display. I longed for an electric train when I was a boy but we weren't up to that spending level so I had to do with the wind up variety.

But it was as a grownup in the years following WWII that trains really became a part of my life. Turning my back on air travel I criscrossed the country on the Super Chief, The 20th Century Ltd., The City of Los Angeles, The Great Northern, Sunset Ltd. and The Lark. I loved every minute of it.

Now all of this is to establish a position for what follows. I wanted you to know of my partiality to trains before bringing up the question of how far our nation should go in subsidizing passenger train travel.

Today Amtrak a semi-public corp. has taken over passenger trains from the Railroad companies. ~~which~~ *They* could no longer run such trains without incurring great losses. The head of one *major* railroad has told me they could run those trains at a profit if the govt. had given them the same relief from unnecessary regulation *it* granted to Amtrak.

Amtrak was launched on the premise of being a profit-making corp. In 1973 it lost $153 mil. Last year the ~~de~~ annual deficit had grown to $587 mil. It has never—repeat—never made money on any of it's routes. Passenger fares only cover about ⅓ of operating costs. Tax dollars make up the balance.

About 2 yrs. ago it was revealed that Amtrak lost enough on the Chicago to Miami run that it would have been better off if it bought each passenger a plane ticket & paid their hotel bill. Fare for the run is $88—cost of operating is $298 per passenger.

The horror stories continue. A study of 10 Amtrak routes revealed they would have lost money if every seat had been filled every trip. On the Chicago to Milwaukee run the govt. loses $32 for every passenger it keeps from buying a $5.50 bus ticket.

Are we subsidizing nostalgia? Do we just like to know the trains are there even though we know we aren't going to ride them? Of course there is the energy argument; that trains are a form of mass transit carrying passengers at a great savings in fuel over the automobile. Not so. Per passenger fuel use on Amtrak is 48 passenger-miles per gal. exactly the same as the average automobile. Buses do 2½ X better than that.

If Amtrak quit and the govt. granted the Railroad Cos. now hauling freight, the right to carry passengers under the same regulations now applying to Amtrak, maybe we could have the trains without the subsidy.

This is RR   Thanks for listening. ❖

Rapid Transit
December 22, 1976

Is Rapid Transit an answer to pollution & congestion or are we being sold a herd of very expensive white elephants? I'll be right back.

In the last election the people of Los Angeles once again voted "no" on a several hundred mile fixed rail rapid transit system. ~~The will of the people was unmistakably clear.~~ But the proponents of such a system didn't get the message. They are still ~~dreaming, and~~ planning with only one change in direction. ~~Since the people of L.A. have said no to funding such a project the planners~~ *They* now seek aid from the Federal govt. Meaning the people of Ill. Iowa N.Y. and all the other 50 states ~~including the people of L.A. will pay~~ *will help pay* for it with their Fed. taxes. ~~And why not? We're paying for "Metro" in Wash. & extension & improvement of rapid transit in other cities across the land.~~

In the 1960's & *early* 70's Wash. spent some $4 Bil. promoting mass rapid transit. ~~systems.~~ Then 2 yrs. ago Congress passed an $11.8 Bil. subsidy ~~to~~ bill. Some $120 mil. of this was spent in Chi. where rapid transit is already ~~an~~ established by way of the famous "Elevated" and where the cities geography is ideally suited to a fixed rail system. The idea was to lure more people out of their ~~ea~~ automobiles and thus ~~relieve~~ *reduce* down town traffic. ~~congestion.~~ The new system attracted passengers but only 8% of them came from automobiles. The rest simply moved to the new system from the "L" as it's called & the buses. In fact it put one bus line out of business.

In Wash. "Metro" an elaborate ~~sys~~ subway system is supposed to have 100 miles of track at a cost of $2½ Bil. That cost figure has already doubled, it is years behind schedule & only 4½ miles *of track* are open for use at a loss of $55,000 a day.

Here in Calif. the pattern remains the same. S.F. much more geographically suited to a fixed rail system than L.A. has been building "Bart" the Bay Area Rapid Transit for several years. The original $1½ Bil. cost estimate has doubled and it is way behind schedule. In 1976 an $11 mil. operating surplus was projected. It *a projected 11 Bil. $ operating surplus* turned out to be a $40 Bil. loss deficit. The number of trips were only half of what had been projected and while a little better than Chi. still the most of the passengers came from busses *not FROM AUTOMOBILES.* Busses incidentally are anywhere from ⅛ to ½ cheaper than Bart. As a matter of fact driving a sub-compact car is cheaper than Bart.

Environmentalists support rapid transit as an answer to air pollution and a saver of energy. There can be no argument that both of these aims would be advanced if rapid transit could replace auto *travel* by private automobile. But at what cost? Even where rapid transit ≠ has been long established it only handles a tiny fraction of the passenger load carried by automobiles.

Most cities of including those of modest size once had rapid transit. The clang of the trolley cars bell was a familiar sound until people abandoned public transportation for their own set of wheels. The automobile gave man one of the more freedom. The freedom to choose his own time table and route of travel on a portal to portal basis. He has shown he does not intend to give up that freedom and govt. has no right to take it from him by a program of deliberately planned congestion.

We need improvement in fuel consumption and the elimination of air pollution, perhaps even a new fuel *energy* source for our cars. How much progress in those directions could we have bought for the $16 Bil. the Fed. govt. is spending on rapid transit which will not appreciably reduce traffic and which apparently the people dont want?

This is RR   Thanks for listening. ❖

Referring to the 1943 speech on the wonders of radio by C. F. Kettering, the director of research for General Motors, Reagan talks of the wonders of science and how so many people, over thousands of years, have contributed to the technological marvels we enjoy in the 1970s.

Kettering
September 6, 1977

Whether you believe the age of miracles is *is or is not* past there is every reason to believe that works of man which seem like miracles still have an unlimited future.

I'll be right back.

Our sons & daughters will *in their lifetime* undoubtedly see things almost impossible for us to imagine. But in my opinion the generation to which I belong will have had an experience they will not know.

There have only been a few ~~moments~~ periods at most in man's history when a single generation presided over a great transition. ~~period.~~ Our generation was one of those. We literally went from the horse & buggy to travel in outer space; to the miracles of communication by which you are hearing my voice. But I don't want to sound like that man back in the late 1800's who wanted to close down the U.S. Patent office because everything had been invented. Nor do I want to sound boastful or smug about the miracles that became ~~com~~ commonplace in our lifetime.

Each generation sees farther than the generation that preceded it because we stand on the shoulders of giants. ~~Back~~

Back in 1943, ~~before TV,~~ when radio had opened a new world to us General Motors had a great Sunday afternoon program of symphonic music. On Oct. 3rd of that year C.F. Kettering a G.M. Vice Pres. & director of Research made a short address on *radio.* ~~that program~~. He called attention to how much we *all* owe the generations that preceded us.

Speaking of how radio could carry the music of the orchestra all over the world he said the elements of radio had been developing over 100 yrs. Then surprisingly this remarkable engineering genius said that in truth the miracle of radio had started 600 yrs. before Christ—2500 yrs. ago.

He made it clear it was only a vague, weak thought at that time when a Greek philosopher Thales of Miletus found that by rubbing amber he produced a force that would pick up straws. Two thousand two hundred years later Queen Elizabeths physician in Eng. Sir Wm. Gilbert did a little playing around with the idea and called the phenomenon he produced, electricity. Sixty years later a German von Gueriche* built a machine that generated sta-

---

*Otto von Gueriche (1602–1686) was a German physicist who, in 1663, invented the first electric generator, which produced static electricity.

tic electricity. A century later B.K Benjamin Franklin identified positive &
negative electricity & proved electricity & lightning were one & the same.

Kettering went on *in* his radio address and told how in 1820 a Dane
named Oersted* proved that electricity would produce magnetism. The idea
was moving faster, Faraday** discovered the principle of the electric motor.
Morse & Bell came along and used the idea to communicate by way of the
telegraph & the telephone. Edison lit *lighted* the world with it and Marconi
& deForest laid the foundation for radio.

Pointing out how these men, unknowing of each other for the most part,
spread *and separated* over 2500 years brought that vague idea to a force that
literally changed the face of the earth. Kettering spoke of how indestructible
an idea is. He also said there have only been a few thousand such thought cul-
tivators in all man's history and without them we might still be living in
caves.

Mr. Kettering had saved his surprise for the last. He said *He closed his
speech saying,* "We might go back 2500 years to 600 B.C. and find out why
the straw *amber* picked up the straws. We don't know that yet." And he
added, "If we did we *I believe we* could open up new fields that might be
quite as important as the elec. light, the telephone or the radio."

This is RR   Thanks for listening. ❖

Telescope I
January 1979

The miracle of the free market place is all around us. It makes you wonder
why we don't have more faith in it. I'll be right back.

† There is a magic in this mkt. place economy of ours that we often forget as
we worry about inflation, the dollars decline and an unfavorable trade balance. The magic is to be found in the way that someone with an idea sees a
problem & comes up with a solution. The motive is of course profit, yet we
all benefit.

For some years now our urban sprawl has been increasingly troublesome
to astronomers & to the colleges & universities offering courses in astronomy. One by one our great observatories are becoming less & less able TO
TRACK THE STARS, as cities pushed their way out to the mountains & hilltops
where the telescopes are mounted. The problem is sky glow from city lights

*Hans Christian Ørsted (1777–1851) was a leading 19th-century Danish physicist, and
played a crucial role in founding electromagnetism.
**Michael Faraday (1791–1867) was an English physicist and chemist.

which vastly reduces visibility. ~~Anyone~~ Moving these observatories would be a very costly business, they are very expensive to build in the 1st place.

Now 2 relatively young men in Atlanta Georgia have seen a need and recognized it as an opportunity. Alan Rand & E. James Grethe, Pres. & V.P. respectively of "The Rand Instrument Corp." have made a scientific breakthrough which will go a long way toward solving the Astronomers problem and at a tremendous ~~cost~~ savings in cost. They & their colleagues at Rand have perfected a mobile observatory. It is a ~~40 inch telescope~~ TELE-SCOPE WITH A LENS SIZE RANGING FROM 16 TO 40 INCHES mounted on a trailer. It can be towed to any location, far from the cities sky glow. Then in a matter of minutes the astronomer can align the polar axis to the celestial ~~poll~~ *pole* and proceed ~~to~~ with deep space research. Rand has also developed the worlds most powerful light amplifier. By light amplification the telescope can reveal instantly galaxies which heretofore could only be seen on a photographic plate after hours of exposure.

There is more—suppose a University is having trouble offering courses in astronomy because sky glow has interfered with it's observatory. A Prof. ~~could~~ *can* take the portable telescope 50 miles away, videotape the heavens and transmit this to ~~the~~ his students in the classroom who would at the same time *be* hear*ing* his *taped* lecture. ~~by tape.~~

To make this portable telescope fully operational Rand offers the means of towing the trailer born scope. It is called "Ramo" which is short for "Rand Astronomical Mobil Observatory." But "Ramo" is more than just a towing vehicle. It ~~is~~ provides living quarters for the astronomers, support instrumentation, dark room facilities, and can be a traveling classroom for as many as 15 students. It is a completely equipped motor home type vehicle and comes in several models ~~of~~ *&* various sizes.

Not only has Rand ~~&~~ Instruments Corp. opened new vistas for astronomers at the same time it solved a vexing problem, there is a spin off which could be of tremendous value to national security. I'll tell you about that on the next commentary.

This is RR   Thanks for listening.

†When typed up—send copies of these 2 scripts & the attached letter to Mr. Grethe (the blue letter). RR ❖

Telescope II
January 1979

~~Yester~~ On the last commentary I talked about a new way of looking at the stars—today it's a way of looking for trouble. I'll be right back.

On the last broadcast I spoke of the breakthrough *in* the field of astronomy the people at Rand Instruments Corp. in Atlanta have made. I don't know whether "spin off," is the right phrase but from their development of a portable telescope has come something called a "Surveillance Network."

If you didn't hear the previous commentary it had to do with Rand's portable telescope mounted on a trailer carriage. ~~making~~ *It is now* possible to escape city sky glow ~~and~~ *THE BANE OF ASTRONOMERS* without having to build great new observatories. Part of the breakthrough is a light amplification system which brings a 40 inch scope up to nearly the power of the largest telescopes. Or as one of the men responsible for this development said, "We can see a man light a cigarette 20 miles away."

And that's the clue to what I called a spin off. Rand has developed a system whereby we can look sideways instead of up. This can be "sideways" across a border, ground to ground, it can be from shore to sea, or ground to air. In other words surveillance against a possible surprise attack is possible day or night with movement of even individuals visible at up to 20 miles.

Five portable telescopes ~~along a line 120 miles long each~~ 20 miles apart can give complete surveillance of a line 120 miles long. What is more important they constitute a network tied into a central command post miles to the rear. There a commander ~~e~~*w*ould instantly see on video screens whatever movement there was ~~on t~~ *20 miles* deep on a 120 mile front. There would be in addition monitoring ~~sh~~ mobile field headquarters controlling the scanners about 100 yards behind each one. It is also possible if there are time problems to simply focus the scope and use it for direct viewing without the video hook up.

One can think of any number of places where such a surveillance system would be invaluable: The Nato line for one. Then there are places like Rhodesia where the terrorists are a constant & murderous threat, or the demilitarized zone between North & South Korea, the Middle East & countless other trouble spots.

The Rand people have not pretended they can solve all surveillance problems 100% or that their surveillance network will prevent war. But if it can reduce the element of surprise by 50% that could mean perhaps 50% less loss of life.

And all of this came to be because 2 men saw a market possibility in the fact that increasing numbers of observatories were being rendered ineffective by the ~~increasing~~ increasing spread of sky glow from city lights. This is RR Thanks for listening. ❖

*The following two essays emphasize the importance of technology to our so-
ciety and warn of focusing so much on some of the negative side effects that
we forget the advantages.*

Technology
August 7, 1978

Is technology really the curse to humanity some would have us believe it is?
Is it the problem or ~~its~~ it just possibly the answer? I'll be right back.

Back in the depression years the ~~smoking~~ *factory* smoke stack belching a
black cloud of coal smoke skyward was a symbol of reassurance that the
good life was still possible. Today it is an evil thing to be deplored and eliminated, symbol of everything that is wrong.

Now I'm not lobbying for air pollution, water pollution or destruction of
the environment in the name of progress. But have we been so busy lately deploring the unattractive byproducts of technology that we've overlooked all
that it can do for us?

It goes without saying that technology has made life easier & more pleasant in a million ways from pre-packaged meals to home entertainment by
electronics, instant *world wide* telephone communication and travel in comfort over thousands of miles in but a few hours time. ~~The list~~

The list could go on & on. Yes I'm aware of the problems accompanying
the benefits but do we throw away the benefits to get rid of the problems or
do we have faith that the technology that gave us the benefits ~~just~~ might just
possibly rid us of the problems?

Right now American industry is stepping up research particularly in the
field of potential shortages in fuel & raw materials. The direction of the research is toward finding catalysts. That isn't a word that means very much to
most of us but catalysts are substances, usually metals that speed up chemical reactions without being altered themselves.

~~Maybe the fact that catalysts isn't a household word is because~~

As an example of what they can mean to you & me, catalysts hold the secret of how to obtain gasoline from coal. The oil industry would be a disaster area without catalysts. An official of one oil company says ~~a~~ catalysts
called "zeolites" more than double the gasoline that can be extracted from a
barrel of ~~oil~~ crude oil.

They make possible reduced prices & use of less-expensive raw materials.
Monsanto chemical company has developed one that allows acetic acid—a
building block for other chemicals—to be made from methanol, a cheaper
material thus cutting costs by 20%.

Radio

Technology

Is technology really the curse to humanity ① some would have us believe it is? Is it the problem or is it first possibly the answer? I'll be right back.

Back in the depression years the ~~smoking~~ factory smoke stack belching a black cloud of coal smoke skyward was a symbol of reassurance that the good life was still possible. Today it is an evil thing to be deplored and ~~eliminated~~, symbol of every thing that is wrong.

Now I'm not lobbying for air pollution, water pollution or destruction of the environment in the name of progress. But have we been so busy lately deploring the unattractive by products of technology that we've overlooked all that it can do for us?

It goes without saying that technology has made life easier & more pleasant in a million ways from pre-packaged meals to home entertainment by electronics instant ~~telephone communication~~ (~~would wreck~~) and travel in comfort over thousands of miles in but a few hours time. ~~The list~~

The list could go on & on. Yes I'm aware of the problems accompanying the benefits but do we throw away the benefits to get rid of the problems or do we have faith that the technology that gave us the benefits ~~first~~ might first possibly rid us of the problems?

Right now American industry is stepping up research particularly in the field of potential shortages in fuel & raw materials. The direction of the research is toward finding catalysts. That isn't a word that means very much to most of us but catalysts are substances, usually metals that speed up chemical reactions without being altered themselves.

~~Maybe the fact that catalysts into a brass stud~~

2

As an example of what they can mean to you & me, catalysts hold the secret of how to obtain gasoline from coal. The oil industry would be a disaster area without catalysts. An official of one oil company says catalysts called "zeolites" more than double the gasoline that can be extracted from a barrel of crude oil.

They make possible reduced prices & use of less expensive raw materials. Monsanto chemical company has developed one that allows acetic acid – a building block for other chemicals to be made from methanol, a cheaper material thus cutting costs by 20%.

Polyethylene the most widely used plastic can now be made by Union Carbide with savings of 50% on capital cost & 75% on energy because of a newly discovered family of catalysts. This translates into bil's. of dollars of savings for consumers in everything from plastic bottles to trash bags within the next few years.

Catalyst technology also will help in the environmental fight. One used in making gasoline will reduce the amount of carbon monoxide in the flue gas at refineries from 20,000 parts per mil. to less than 500.

The word from industry is that recent break throughs have taken place & more can be expected. One spokesman says (believe it or not) that possibly we may produce gasoline one day without oil. In other words the technological genius that gave us our standard of living may very well preserve & enhance it at a lower price.

This is RR. Thanks for listening.

Polyethylene the most widely used plastic can now be made by Union Carbide with savings of 50% on capital cost & 75% on energy because of a newly discovered family of catalysts. This translates into bil's. of dollars of savings for consumers ≠ in everything from plastic bottles to trash bags ~~by~~ within the next few years.

Catalyst technology also will help in the environmental fight. One used in making gasoline will reduce the amount of carbon monoxide in the flue gas at refineries from 80,000 parts per mil. to less than 500. ~~The~~

The word from industry is that recent breakthroughs have taken place & more can be expected. One spokesman says (believe it or not) that possibly we may produce gasoline one day without oil. In other words the technological genius that gave us our standard of living may very well preserve & ~~ien~~-hance it at a lower price.

This is RR   Thanks for listening. ❖

Phone
January 19, 1979

I hear the govt. is ~~suing~~ going to or already has sued the phone company again. It makes you wonder how they the nerve. I'll be right back.

†   Before getting into todays commentary I'd like to add a P.S. to a broadcast of a few days ago. I reminded you of Jim Hendricks the paraplegic cowboy & his horse Calvin & gave his address because many of you had enquired about it & expressed a desire to lend a hand. Well everything in the address was correct except the ~~town~~ name of the town. I ~~was~~ *had been* told it was Bridgetown. It isn't, Jim lives in Beardstown, Ill. B-E-A-R-D-S-T-O-W-N.

Now on with the commentary which has to do with that govt. regulated private monopoly the telephone company & that govt. owned monopoly the post office.

What with busy signals, wrong numbers etc. it's easy to have a grudge against "Ma Bell." Truth is the old girl deserves a big thank you from all of us. For one thing here is a major service none of us feel we can do without, yet in this age of continual inflation that service keeps dropping in cost.

Back in the 1930's a long distance call across country cost $9.50. That was 300 times as much as it cost to send a letter. Now that phone call is only 9 times as expensive as a letter—$1.30 while stamps have gone up to 15¢. And the ratio is even lower if your call only takes 1 minute. Then the price is 54¢. And ~~rember~~ remember 15¢ isn't the total cost of a postage stamp; taxes pay the difference between the price of the stamp & what it really costs to deliver the letter. In 1977 the postal deficit was $1.4 bil.

By contrast Am. Tel.&Tel. ~~Corp. last year~~ *in 1977 paid $6.5 bil. in taxes* & only $2.8 bil. in dividends to it's share ~~owners~~ *holders*.

Not only has the telephone company lowered costs because it has continued to increase productivity, it has offered fantastic improvements that would have boggled the mind of Alexander Graham Bell.

Not too long ago the phone was a pretty hefty piece of machinery mounted on the wall. To call, you removed the receiver from its cradle with one hand, spun the crank handle (which rang a bell) with the other and waited for the operator to ask, "number please." You told her the number and she then plugged a ~~jack~~ *cord* into the proper jack on the ~~swite~~ switchboard and if everything went well your call was completed.

Of course most of us could only afford party lines and we ~~all~~ *each* had a particular ring by which we knew if the call was for us—for example 2 longs & 2 shorts. Everybody on the line knew everyone elses ring and the result was a total lack of privacy because everyone could listen in simply by lifting their receiver.

Today the miracles we already have are going to be topped by video phone; there are recorder gadgets to take phone calls & messages when you are absent and now they talk of electronic mail. If the cost differential continues at the present rate, it is possible the telephone may put the post office out of business within the next 10 or 20 years. Do you suppose that's why the govt. is suing the phone company?

This is RR Thanks for listening

†Make this one the <u>1st</u> to be recorded. RR ❖

ENERGY, LAND AND
THE ENVIRONMENT

In the late 1970s, the energy crisis was in full swing. The price of gasoline and oil was soaring. People waited hours in gas lines and worried about a shortage of heating oil in the winter. Demands for more energy ran up against serious environmental concerns. Over the five-year period, Reagan gave eighty-eight broadcasts on the energy problem and the environment, and we have his handwritten drafts for fifty-five of them.

In the following eleven essays he explores the need for new energy sources, especially oil, natural gas, and nuclear power. He weighs the need for energy against the environmental concerns of producing that energy, often concluding that governmental regulations are overly restrictive.

As president one of Reagan's first actions was the deregulation of the prices of natural gas and oil, to the extent possible by executive order. This action and later, more complete deregulation contributed to reduced energy prices. Soviet reduction in hard-currency revenues from oil and natural gas in the mid-1980s placed their economy under additional stress and hastened their collapse.

Oil I
June 15, 1977

Maybe what I'm about to say could be called; "What we should know about oil." Hopefully it will still some troubled waters. I'll be right back.

I've been out around the country recently in ~~several~~ *a number of* states ~~on~~ filling some speaking engagements. When you do this you usually meet members of the press who have a question or two. Of late those questions have had to do with ~~some of~~ my remarks about the proposed energy legislation and why I ~~apparently~~ don't buy the C.I.A. report quoted by the Pres. which has us running out of oil in about 30 yrs.

Well, it's true I dont buy that report and if the Pres. does then isn't his plea for conservation ~~& sacrifice~~ to reduce consumption by 10% ~~a little~~ *rather* futile? If all the oil is going to be gone in 30 yrs. does it really make much difference if we make it last 33? ~~yrs?~~

~~But let me recite some figures which will explain why~~ I don't believe it will be gone in 30 or 33 yrs. In 1914 the U.S. Bur. of Mines projected future production of Crude oil at 5.7 Bil. Barrels. Since then we've produced ~~in the U.S.~~ 34 Bil. ~~barrels.~~ Incidentally about that same time we were told there was no hope of ever finding oil in Texas or Kansas.

In 1920 ~~our govt. told us we only had a 15 yr. supply left~~ *we were told we'd be out of oil in 15 yrs. Nineteen years later in* 1939 the Dept. of Interior (~~that's 19 yrs. later~~) told us ~~we only had a 13 yr. supply.~~ *we'd run out in 13* yrs. Since ~~1939~~ *then* we have <u>discovered</u> more than the total known oil reserves *we had* at that time.

In 1948 the proven reserves in all of the free world amounted to 62.3 bil. barrels. *Within 24 yrs. there were 9x as many.* ~~By 1972 the fig. was~~ *it was* ~~568.6 bil. barrels—roughly 9x as much. The known reserves in Canada & the U.S. alone had more than doubled. As a matter of fact~~ In 1949 our Dept. of Interior said the end of the U.S. oil supply was in sight. ~~and~~ We increased production in the next 5 yrs. by a mil. barrels a day.

~~And in 1972 free world reserves were 568.6 barrels.~~

~~We increased oil production in the next 5 yrs. by a mil. barrels a day.~~ By 1970 <u>known world</u> reserves were 6x as large as they were in 1950. To digress for a moment this holds true for virtually all the minerals our advanced industrial economy depends on. To give just a few examples known reserves of iron between 1950 & 1970 increased 1,321%, Chrome 675%, Copper 279%, ~~Potash 2,360%~~, & Phosphates 4,430%. To get *BACK* to oil reserves, they had increased 507%.

Significantly & contrary to much of what is being said the amt. of proven reserves is increasing faster than the rate of consumption. ~~In 1948 the known reserves of 62 Bil. barrels were only enough for 20 yrs. at the then rate of consumption. By 1972 the 569 bil. barrels would last 35 yrs. at the rate we were using it.~~

The Nat. Acad. of Engineering explains that U.S. oil reserves discovered to date total 430 bil. barrels but low cost conventional technology will only get ~~about 30%~~ 140 bil. barrels out of the ground. This leaves ~~70%~~ *more than twice that much* 290 ~~bil. barrels much~~ BIL. BARRELS much of which can be recovered by more expensive techniques—~~if~~ & the if is very important, the govt. will allow the price of oil to respond to market demands.

~~Between 1947 & '72~~ For 25 years ~~every 1% rise in price has produced a 4% increase in~~ ~~the supply of~~ *our supply of* gasoline. ~~In 1970 we~~ *Seven yrs. ago we* were producing 9.6 ~~bil.~~ MIL. barrels of ~~crude~~ *oil* a day. ~~Now we are~~ TODAY IT'S only pumping 8.1 ~~and this decline can be laid directly~~ THANKS to ~~restrictions imposed on the industry by govt.~~ BY GOVT. ~~Our govt. has~~ HAVING ~~reduced the production of oil & now offers an answer to the shortage, reducing consumption~~ GOVT. NOW PROPOSES THAT WE REDUCE CONSUMPTION.
~~This is RR. Thanks for listening.~~

Seven yrs. ago we were producing 9.6 mil. barrels every day now we're only pumping 8.1. The decline is caused by restrictions imposed by govt. Having reduced production the govt. now proposes that we reduce consumption. ~~In the~~ For 25 years every 1% rise in price resulted in a 4% increase in the supply of gasoline. Why don't we try the free market again.

This is RR. Thanks for listening. ❖

Reagan wrote the following document listing his sources for the above essay.

Sources for Oil I
June 15, 1977

RONALD REAGAN

Sources for this script.

1. U.S. Bur. of Mines Report 1914

2. Dept. of Int. 1939 & 1949

3. Herman Kahn—Book "The Next 200 Yrs."

4. Council on International Ec. Policy
   Exec. Office of the Pres. Special
   Report, Critical Imported Materials.
   Wash. DC. U.S. Govt. Printing Office
   Dec. 1974

5. Prof. Neil Jacoby U.C.L.A.—"Multinational
   Oil (Macmillan)

6. Prof's. Phillip ~~Gramm~~ GRAMM & Richard Davison
   Wall St. Journal ❖

OPEC
January 19, 1979

It's easy to get mad at the Opec nations when they raise the price of oil—but maybe we should get mad at ourselves. I'll be right back.

The Opec ≠ oil producers have told us the price of oil is going up and our energy agency has informed us that will call for an increase at the gasoline pump. But before we call them greedy monsters, guilty of adding to inflation let me play the devils advocate.

Opec oil is priced in American dollars. In the last few years while our dollar has been going down in value relative to more stable currencies such as the W. German mark & the Japanese Yen—guess what? The actual price of oil for Germany & Japan has been going down.

It's pretty obvious that if $14 will buy a barrel of oil, but 14 American dollars now are only equal to a lesser number of marks or yen, then the Germans & Japanese are getting their oil at a lower price. The Opec nations have to up the ~~dollar price or they are getting a reduced amount of real money~~ *number of dollars they get just to stay even. And it* is we who are responsible for reducing the value of the dollar.

That is only a small part of our foolishness. With some plain common sense we could break up the Opec monopoly. Item number 1, there are vast quantities of natural gas available in the U.S.—if our own govt. regulations did not stand in the way of it being produced. This untapped natural gas would break the back of the Opec cartel.

A deplorable tragedy was preventable & unnecessary in the bitter winter of 1976–77. There was cold & discomfort in homes but even worse was the loss of jobs, production and income as industry had to shut down for lack of fuel.

We had been warned in 1974 that we were in danger of running out of natural gas. Part of the problem is that deeper wells must be drilled. It costs $3 mil. to drill a 20,000 ft. well in Texas. Offshore wells can be drilled for $1 mil. but it takes several years to get them into production. These harder to get at gas deposits cannot be delivered to the pipe lines for the price the govt. allows them to charge. So that gas is neither drilled or delivered. You can't sell a pencil for a nickel if it costs a dime to make it.

Right now in my own state—Calif. a shortage of natural gas exists & it's getting worse. If we substitute coal or oil we aggravate a serious smog problem we already have. It is estimated Calif. could lose 800,000 jobs by 1981 because of reduced gas supplies.

We are currently buying liquefied natural gas from Indonesia for $3.50 ~~a barrel~~ per 1000 cubic feet. A study by the govt's. own Energy, ~~Research~~ RE-SEARCH & Development Agency ~~tell~~ *tells* us that at $3.25 and below there is enough natural gas available for hundreds of years. This study was done in 1974 & nothing has been done about it.

The magic word is decontrol of the well head price. It would take about 5 yrs. lead time to get much of this production underway & we'll have shortages for those 5 yrs. This wouldn't have been true if we'd gotten underway in 1974. But decontrol now and production of the gas available in our own land would literally break up the OPEC cartel. *What are we waiting for?* This is RR   Thanks for listening. ❖

California Gas Shortage
May 29, 1979

It's hard to have a sense of humor when you are sitting in your car for 3 hrs. waiting your turn at the gasoline pump. I'll be right back.

All the world I guess is aware of the Calif. gasoline shortage. Some think we are careless gas guzzlers & it serves us right. Others laugh it off as proof that Californians are pixilated. But Californians sitting in those long lines are angry and to make it worse they aren't certain as to who they should be mad at. Is it the fellow running the gas station? How about the big oil co's? Is there really a shortage & if so who caused it?

One thing we can prove; Calif. drivers aren't to blame as a Wash. Post editorial suggested they were. The average use of gasoline per car in Calif. is 59.7 gal's. a month. In Va. where a lot of Wash. Post subscribers live it is 73 gals. In Maryland it's 66.7.

Calif. has 65,000 oil wells. About 23,000 of them are closed down. Crude oils aren't all the same. Calif. crude is a heavy oil and requires more expensive equipment to refine it. Once upon a time this was reflected in the price for Calif. oil. Since 1973 however the Dept. of Energy has set the price on oil. So when a well in Calif. sands up or a pump breaks down there is no profit incentive in putting it back in operation. At least 15,000 of those closed down wells could be ~~put~~ reopened if the Dept. of Energy would get out of the way & trust the free mkt. to determine the price.

Then there is Alaskan oil—but it's high sulfer oil & Calif. refinerys aren't built to to handle that. Japanese refinerys are. Well then—let's sell the Alaskan oil to Japan & buy the right kind of oil elsewhere for the Calif. refinerys. The govt. won't allow it.

How about changing the Calif. refinerys so they can handle the high sulfer oil? For the last 6 yrs. the Dept's. regulations about how to recover the cost's have made that impossible. That's why in the midst of this shortage Calif. refinerys have only been operating at 80% of capacity.

Just of late the Dept. has made a move to change these regulations—a tacit admission that it has been a road block for 6 yrs. But even this isn't a total answer to the Calif. shortage. There are still price controls on gasoline plus the allocations ~~regulated~~ dictated by the Dept. of Energy. The Dept. has done a little squirming of late & even indicated it's allocation formula might be the reason the roof fell in on Calif. It seems our allocation out here was based on 1972 population figs. We happen to be a fast growing state with mil's. more people & automobiles than we had in 1972. ~~Take~~

The Dept. is updating the formula to 1978 but a tentative effort to let the mkt. determine price has ~~been~~ *been* overruled by the admin.

Have you figured out yet who we should be mad at?

This is RR Thanks for listening. ❖

The two essays below demonstrate Reagan's strong commitment to nuclear power and call into question the rationale of people who oppose it.

Nuclear Power
May 1975

There isn't much talk about energy these days.—Maybe there should be.—I'll be right back.

Once again I'm going to talk about something going on in Calif. because it could happen to all of us.

An overly excited group of Californians have formed a group called "People For Proof" and, if they have their way, we could see a halt to the building of ~~badly needed~~ nuclear power plants which are very much needed to provide us *with* economical, non polluting electrical power.

"People for Proof" wants to put an issue on the Calif. June primary ballot in 1976 which will have the people voting ~~on requiring~~ *to require* proof of safety, beyond any reasonable need, before any nuclear power plants can be built.

Now, everyone is for safety and I'm sure we wish our highways could be 100% safe, that people wouldn't slip in bathtubs and that we'd never have soup spilled down our back in a crowded restaurant. But there aren't any sure things & in life except the old standbys, death & taxes.

Now to start with, 48 Nations beside our own are generating, at low cost, electricity by use of nuclear reactors. So far, there has not been one single accidental death caused by nuclear reactors.

How many tests are <u>too</u> many? ~~There have been~~ The most recent one was made by the Atomic energy commission. It cost $3 mil. and went on for 2 yrs. But ~~if~~ when you count in the number of distinguished consultants who were involved it figures out to 50 man years of effort.

Now if you were at the *race* track and the handicappers told you ~~a horse~~ the odds on a certain horse were 100 to 1 you'd figure his chances of winning were pretty slim.

Well our experts in the nuclear power study have put the odds on a fatal accident occurring ~~because of~~ in a nuclear power plant at 300 mil. to 1. That makes it safer than all the other causes of accidental death put together. Put another way it's about as likely ~~a risk~~ as you being run over by a horse in your bathtub.

Now the leaders back of "People For Proof" know all this which makes you wonder why they're so bent on throwing another road block in the path of getting some badly needed electric power production.

Are they suggesting there must be ~~a~~ *an absolute* guaranty ~~that never~~ of THE complete impossibility of anything ever going wrong? The record so far is one of 100% safety and to repeat the odds again as ~~⅟~~ given by the best experts in the field are 300 mil. to 1. ~~I dont~~ We dont start out in life with odds *that good* on making *our* 3 score & ten.

Now I know this is a Calif. problem—at the moment. ~~b~~But this kind of group is as contagious as the Hong Kong Flu. So I thought you ~~might~~ might like a warning.

This is RR. ~~I'll be~~ Thanks For listening. ❧

Nuclear Power
September 19, 1978

It is rude and ungentlemanly to bluntly call the "anti nuclear power groups" ignorant. They just know a great many things that aren't true. I'll be right back.

§ We continue to be treated to the spectacle of anti nuclear power zealots demonstrating at sites where nuclear power plants are being built or planned or even where they have been in operation. The scene is always the same, a mass rally with speakers warning of a nuclear threat to the human race, then trespass and disruption followed by mass arrests. The arrests ~~f~~ are for misdemeanors and are not taken seriously by the demonstrators, many of whom enjoy clogging the criminal justice system and ~~delight in~~ refusing to leave the jails where they are held.

I'm sure many of these demonstrators are true believers in their cause, sincere in their belief that nuclear power constitutes a great danger to the world. I'm also sure they are unaware that their movement is run by strategists who are cynical & not sincere & who have a motive not announced to the ground troops who go out and get arrested. Indeed some time ago the press carried stories of a coalition being put together to promote unilateral disarmament by the U.S. and opposition to further development of nuclear power in the U.S.

Those two causes aren't as far apart as it might seem at first glance. A study by the ~~h~~Heritage ~~f~~Foundation finds that unless we go forward and fast with the building of more nuclear generating plants we may face the early 1980's with unemployment soaring above the 7 mil. mark & around $90 Bil. a year in lost wages. Our industrial might would be severely crippled by brownouts & power shortages. Where does this tie into disarmament? Well obviously our industrial capacity is the greatest thing we have going for us in the contest with the Soviet U. which is not only going forward with it's military buildup but is plunging full speed ahead in the development of nuclear power. I wonder how many of our demonstrators would like to protest in Russia?

The people of Calif. voted *2 YRS AGO* by a majority of more than 2 to 1 to go forward with nuclear power. So far ~~the~~ Gov. Brown has blocked virtually any such development. The opponents of nuclear energy claim they only want it made safer. In truth ~~it would seem~~ they just don't want it period.

A Congressman from Calif. Bob Badham has called attention to something that has gone unnoticed in all the recent demonstrations in New Hampshire & Calif. The San Onofre nuclear power plant in So. Calif. just passed it's 10th anniversary. In these 10 yrs. it has produced 26 Bil. Kilowatt hours of electricity.~~—that's the energy equivalent of 41 mil. barrels of oil. It has done this operating at 70% of capacity.~~ *Every day it operates it saves 16,000 barrels of oil. And when the 2 new units the demonstrators are protesting go into operation the savings will be 30 mil barrels a year.* ~~But what is~~ *But* most important to those who have built up the false threat of danger is ~~it's~~ *the San Onofre plants* 10 yr. record of perfect industrial safety. Not one employee in all these 10 yrs. has ever experienced a lost time industrial accident.

This is RR. Thanks for listening. ❖

Reagan believes that every one of us is an environmentalist at heart, that tremendous progress has been made in cleaning up the environment, and that one of the chief polluters left is government. In the essays that follow, he also attacks environmental extremism.

Environment
April 13, 1977

Everyone knows that capitalism is responsible for ~~the~~ scarring the earth, polluting the air, ~~&~~ and water, and squandering nature's bounty. I'll be right back.

Virtually every one of us is an environmentalist at heart. Therefore we're all pre-conditioned to accept the idea that ~~industry~~ men in search of profit have torn up the hills, scraped the earth bare, destroyed the forests and dumped their waste in the nations streams & lakes. The motive, of course, pure greed.

Certainly there are evidences that in the past, when our country seemed limitless in it's expanse, capable of bearing the wounds ~~of~~ inflicted by puny humans, there was little regard for nature. Admittedly, too, it was govt. that first sounded the alarm. Pres. Teddy Roosevelt, an outdoorsman himself, led the charge. Of course, there were *also* farsighted individuals who had been crying out against ~~the placer mining~~ *such things as* hydraulic ~~mining~~ *mining* for gold that ripped into hillsides and choked rivers & streams with gravel. *They raised a cry against the* early lumber barons *who* cut down the trees and moved on with no thought of replanting.

But today ~~when~~ so much progress has been made. ~~when~~ *with* The lumber industry ~~≠~~ *is* practically ~~on~~ *on* a sustained yield basis planting as many trees as ~~are cut~~ ~~They~~ *are harvested.* Strip miners ~~replace~~ *replace* the topsoil and stringent ~~rules apply to an~~ *controls limit* air & water pollution by industry. *Now it seems* ~~we find~~ that we, the people, are the despoilers ~~by way of~~ ~~through~~ *through* our own govt. agencies.

The biggest polluter of San Francisco Bay is the city sewer system. In N.Y. City it is the dumping of garbage *in* ~~off the coast that~~ ~~≠~~ *the Atlantic Ocean that* threatens the coast with a tidal wave of toxic sludge. And for a time the nearest stream or body of water ~~to any town~~ *was automatically* the city sewer system.

But *WE ARE DOING SOMETHING ABOUT IT* the present day doom criers notwithstanding, we can all ~~enj~~ feel pretty good about what has been accomplished here in the U.S.A. at both the private & and govt. level. In fact we may be troubled now and then by overkill. Only a few years ago a Gov., of

Radio | Environment ① |

Everyone knows that capitalism is responsible for ~~the~~ scarring the earth, polluting the air, ~~an~~ water, and squandering nature's bounty . I'll be right back

Virtually every one of us is an environmentalist at heart. Therefore we're all pre-conditioned to accept the idea that ~~industry~~ men in search of profit have torn up the hills, scraped the earth bare, destroyed the forests and dumped their waste in the nation's streams & lakes. The motive, of course, pure greed.

Certainly there are evidences that in the past, when our country seemed limitless in it's expanse; capable of bearing the wounds ~~of~~ inflicted by puny humans, there was little regard for nature. Admittedly too, it was gov't. that first sounded the alarm. Pres. Teddy Roosevelt, an outdoorsman himself, led the charge. Of course, there were ᵃˡˢᵒ far-sighted individuals who had been crying out against ~~the place mining~~ ˢᵘᶜʰ ᵗʰⁱⁿᵍˢ ᵃˢ hydraulic ~~mining~~ ᵐⁱⁿⁱⁿᵍ for gold that ripped into hill ~~sides~~ and choked rivers & streams with gravel. ~~early~~ ᵗʰⁱˢ ʳᵃⁱˢᵉᵈ ᵃ ᶜʳʸ ᵃᵍᵃⁱⁿˢᵗ ᵗʰᵉ lumber barons ~~cut down~~ the trees and moved on with no thought of replanting.

But today ~~so~~ so much progress has been made ~~when~~ ~~with~~ The lumber industry ⁱˢ practically on a sustained yield basis, planting as many trees as ~~can be~~ harvested. Strip miners ~~replace~~ replace the top soil and stringent ᶜᵒⁿᵗʳᵒˡˢ ~~limit~~ air & water pollution by industry. ᴺᵒʷ ⁱᵗ ˢᵉᵉᵐˢ ~~it is fact~~ that we, the people are the despoilers ~~through~~ ~~though~~ our own gov't. agencies.

The biggest polluter of San Francisco Bay is the city sewer system. In N.Y. City it is the dumping of garbage in ᵗʰᵉ ᵃᵗˡᵃⁿᵗⁱᶜ ᵒᶜᵉᵃⁿ ᵗʰᵃᵗ ~~off the coast that~~ threaten the coast with a tidal wave of toxic sludge. And for a time the nearest stream or body of water ~~was automatically~~ ~~to was funny~~ the city sewer system.
⸤ ᵂᴱ ᴬᴿᴱ ᴰᴼᴵᴺᴳ ˢᴼᴹᴱᵀᴴᴵᴺᴳ ᴬᴮᴼᵁᵀ ᴵᵀ
But the present day doom criers notwithstanding, we can all ~~say~~ feel pretty good about what has been accomplished here in the U.S.A. at both the private ~~sector~~

②

and govt. level. In fact we may be troubled now and then by over kill. Only a few years ago a Govt. of one of the states fronting on one of the great lakes, announced he was going to halt any industrial thermal pollution that changed the lakes temperature more then one degree. By that he meant no plant could turn clean but hot water into the lake (which would have meant mil. of $ in cooling towers & equipmt) That particular lake undergoes a temperature change of about 40 degrees every year between winter & summer.

But to make us a little proud & optimistic here the story of a Soviet trawler capt. who defected 3 yrs. ago and sailed his ship into a Swedish Port. He has described the fishing operation of those Russian trawlers that seem to be off every coast in every ocean.

They use such fine-mesh nets he says that they catch half grown fish of every kind, the result being that much of the catch rots on board. If the refrigerator vessels cant take what they have, the surplus is thrown overboard polluting the spawning grounds with rotten fish. If they sail into port with their catch and the port facilities cant handle their haul, it is dumped on shore to decay and taken inland later to be burned.

The refugee capt. estimated no more than $\frac{1}{3}$ of the catch ever reaches the consumer as food. That ties in with other information about Soviet agriculture. Their need for imports is not alone the result of drought, crop failure or just plain inefficiency in farming. Like the fish, much of their agriculture out put rots in the field or spoils in storage.

I just thought you'd like to know that now that Spring is here — This is RR Thanks for listening.

~~one of the~~ *a* states fronting on one of the great lakes, announced he was going to halt any industrial thermal pollution that changed the lakes temperature BY more than ~~1°~~ one degree. By that he meant no plant could turn clean but hot water into the lake WHICH WOULD HAVE MEANT MILS. OF $ IN COOLING TOWERS & EQUIPMENT. That particular lake ~~changes it's~~ *undergoes a* temperature *change of* about 40 degrees ~~each~~ *every* year between winter & summer.

But to make us a little proud & optimistic hear the story of a Soviet trawler capt. who defected 3 yrs. ago and sailed his ship into a Swedish Port. He has described the fishing operation of those Russian trawlers that ~~&~~ *seem* to be off every coast in every ocean.

They use such fine-mesh nets ~~that~~ *he says that* they catch half grown fish of every kind, the result being that much of the catch rots on board. If the refrigerator vessels can't take what they have, the surplus is thrown overboard polluting the spawning grounds with rotten fish. If they sail into port with their catch and the port facilities can't handle their ~~hawl~~ *haul,* it is dumped on shore to decay and ~~be~~ taken inland later to be burned.

The refugee capt. estimated no more than ⅓ of the catch ever reaches the consumer as food. That ties in with other information about Soviet agriculture. Their need for food imports is not alone the result of drought, crop failure or just plain ~~lack of farmin~~ *inefficiency in* farming. ~~Much~~ Like the fish, much of their agriculture output rots in the field or spoils in storage.

I just thought you'd like to know that now that Spring is here—This is RR. Thanks for listening. ❧

Endangered Species
July 6, 1977

How much do you miss Dinosaurs? Would your life be richer if those giant pre-historic flying lizards occasionally settled on your front lawn? I'll be right back.

Since the beginning of life on this planet ~~tens of~~ thousands of ~~living things~~ species (plant & animal) have disappeared every century as part of the evolutionary process in an ever changing world.

We as humans share a feeling of guilt because as our numbers HAVE increased we HAVE contributed to the disappearance of some species by destroying their habitat or hunting them down for food, fun & feathers. And sometimes our guilt makes us forget ~~that~~ those thousands of species that simply ~~disappeared~~ *ceased to exist* before men ever appeared in the primeval swamp.

Today we are trying to halt as best we can our contribution to, or hastening of the disappearance of existing plant & animal life. We have identified endangered species and passed laws preventing any act by man which ~~will reduce~~ *might add* reduce their numbers. And I'm sure there is general agreement with this policy. But shouldn't we now & then remember natures part in the ~~process that~~ *≠ elimination ≠ of some* species and separate the serious from the silly in our *own* policy?

Up in Maine a mammoth hydro-electric generating facility was scheduled to be constructed in ~~that~~ a part of our land—(the North East) where power is in short supply. The Dickey-Lincoln dam site was key to this $1.3 Bil. project on the St. John river. Many factors were taken into consideration and a great deal of study went into planning ~~how $1.3 Bil. would be spent~~ *such an expensive project* as you can well imagine.

Then about a year ago someone discovered a clump of wild flowers—about 200 in all in the area to be flooded by the building of the dam.

They were a species of snapdragon, thought to be extinct, called the Furbish lousewart. The $1.3 Bil. Dickey-Lincoln generating facility is halted—stopped dead in it's tracks by ~~our law which says any & all endangered species must be protected~~ *the endangered species act of 1973.*

I'm not a botanist but isn't it possible those plants could be transplanted? I've transplanted wild flowers on the ranch with little or no trouble. I've even gathered seeds and helped the spread of some types to other parts of the ranch. And ~~does~~ *can* anyone really ~~know~~ *say* there aren't other clumps of Furbish-Lousewort hidden in the woods of Maine as this clump was hidden until humans invaded the area to build a dam?

Down on the l̶Little Tennesssee River ~~in Tennessee Valley~~ *the Tennessee Valley* Authority ~~was also going to build~~ *has been building* a dam to produce electricity for about 200,000 homes and I dont know how many industries providing jobs for people in those ~~200,000~~ homes. This project has been going on for about 10 yrs.—$116,000,000 have been spent and the huge Tellico-Dam is 95% complete. Apparently that's as far as it will get. A Fed. court has stopped construction because a school of 3 inch fish called the Snail Darter has been found to spawn in the waters of the Little Tennessee river. This particular "Snail Darter" is an endangered species even though it differs only slightly from the 77 other kinds of Darters found in the rivers of Tennessee.

To date more than 200 projects have been halted to protect among other things an inedible clam, some crayfish, ~~plus~~ freshwater snails etc. And the Fish & Wildlife service announces it is now going to classify as "endangered" some 1700 species of plants.

It is time to ask if some environmentalists & I do mean <u>some</u>, aren't using the Endangered Species Act of 1973 simply to halt construction of projects they don't like. *Which is too bad because* Most of the bil's. of dollars I've mentioned would be in pay checks.

This is RR   Thanks for listening. ❖

Malibu
June 27, 1978

Blackmail is a crime—a particularly nasty crime and it isn't any less nasty when govt. is doing the blackmailing. I'll be right back.

Several years ago the people of Calif. voted for the creation of a commission to come up with a comprehensive plan for coastal development. In the interim while a plan was being studied the commission aided by several regional commissions would have ~~some~~ zoning authority over the entire coast from waters edge to 3000 ft. inland.

† ~~The case for this proposition was presented as one of necessity for such~~ ⚡ ~~before~~ *It was said this was needed to prevent* the beaches of Calif. from being so developed that the public would no longer have access to the ocean. ~~Opposition to the plan was poorly organized & made the fatal mistake of adopting a scare campaign that was patently false. A fair & truthful statement might have reassured the people that there was no threat warranting creation of such a commission.~~

Calif. has 1000 plus miles of coastline *of great* ~~It is of great and various beauty~~ ranging from broad sandy beaches to mountains dropping steeply into the surf, ~~MASSIVE rugged bluffs & cliffs~~ & in the north Redwood forests coming down to the waters edge.

What most Californians weren't aware of was that almost half—some 400 miles of oceanfront was *is* already owned by govt. Cities, Counties & the State own & operate miles of *bathing* beach. ~~and~~

During my own admin. the state added more miles based on projections of population increase. *So much was added that* on any hot, sunny, summer weekend you can find long stretches of state beach ~~virtually empty. Granted there are some beaches with almost a Coney Island look but only because the people prefer them, not because there isn't available space.~~ *with virtually no bathers at all.*

~~Nevertheless~~ *In spite of this* the Coastal Commissions made up of appointees not elected representatives almost ~~immediately~~ *from the very first* assumed dictatorial powers & displayed what can only be described as hostility to any private ownership of ocean frontage.

~~There are clusters of residential development ranging from~~ *Owners of* summer cabins & beautiful year round homes ~~The owners~~ discovered they were greatly restricted as to what they could do on their own property once the commissions came into being. One home owner for example was denied the right to install a Jacuzzi whirlpool ~~bath~~ *plunge* in his yard. *Others have been denied permission to add a room, change a driveway or even lay out a patio.*

~~Under laws as old as the state so far as I know~~

Last winter it was Californias turn to have unusual weather. Roaring Pacific storms brought mountainous waves which at hide tide tore out bulkheads ~~protecting beach homes . and~~ *damaging & undermining beach homes.* ~~Some of the homes were damaged & undermined as beaches were eroded~~ *The level of sand on some beaches was lowered by* as much as 8 to 10 ft. There were round the clock battles as home owners & their friends attempted to sandbag & save the structures. ~~Students~~ *volunteers* from Pepperdine U. worked heroically ~~to~~ *sometimes throughout the night to* save the homes of people they didn't even know.

Now those homeowners have started ~~the work of~~ *to* repair ~~their homes & protect bulkheads~~ *the damage.* The coastal commission says "not without it's permission." But the commission says more; that permission will not be given unless the homeowners agree to give up a strip of their beach front for public use. That is blackmail. The Const. is very clear ~~In the 1ˢᵗ place in the~~ in it's guaranty that govt. cannot take private property without fairly compensating the owner.

If there is a real need (and there ~~isn't~~ *is* NOT) for public ownership of this additional beach frontage govt. should buy it. ~~But govt.~~ *It* has no right to ~~withhold~~ *deny these* homeowners permission to repair storm damage *or* remodel if they choose ~~unless they~~ *in an effort* ~~to confiscate~~ *unless they submit to confiscation of* some of their property. I repeat that is blackmail and like a blackmailer if they get away with it they'll be back for more and ~~no~~ *every* homeowners rights *ocean front or inland* will be endangered.

This is RR Thanks for listening.

†When typed—please send a copy
to ≠ *Mrs. Rob Wolder*—23816 W. Malibu Rd.
Malibu Calif.
(MRS. ROB WOLDER) ❖

Bugs
September 19, 1978

Let's talk about bugs and I don't mean the electronic kind you plant in a phone or chandelier—just the crawly, creepy, flying & stinging kind. I'll be right back.

Our movie screens have been horrifying audiences with stories of monstrous fish biting people, little fish ~~biting~~ *chewing on* people and a variety of things biting & stinging people. Now while the press hasn't really made a big thing of it we learn the movies aren't too far from the truth.

Swarms of locusts & grasshoppers, a plague of crickets, cutworms and ants and swarms of mosquitos are making life miserable & even impossible in many parts of the world. In Calif. pet owners are distressed by an increase in the flea population. In Colorado grasshoppers have swept across a half mil. acres, defoliating trees & munching on crops. In the East one town claims that by official survey 100 mosquitos were landing on each human being every 60 seconds. But that is nothing to what is happening in some of the underdeveloped countries. In India malaria carried by mosquitos killed a million children last year. In Somalia & Ethiopia swarms of locusts numbering in the billions have eaten crops, grassland & forests bringing ~~fa~~ hunger & even famine to the people of those lands.

Some *experts* are treating this as an unexplainable mystery. Actually there is no mystery about it. We can blame it on what I've called pol. pollution. The environmental movement with the best of intentions has engendered pol. reaction by it's demand for action. ~~Pol~~ Pesticides have been outlawed as being more dangerous than the pests they were designed to control.

~~Back i~~ As the decade of the '60's began the insects that carried malaria, typhus, sleeping sickness etc. had been reduced in number by pesticides produced mainly in the U.S. For example ~~DDD~~ DDT had virtually eliminated malaria world wide. In India by 1962 the cases of malaria had been reduced over a 10 yr. period from 100 mil. to 60,000. The locust swarms that had plagued Africa for as long as man can remember were wiped out by sprayings paid for by our Dept. of Agriculture. Then in the late 60's. malaria returned to India. In Ceylon where there had only been 17 cases in an entire year there were 2½ mil. & 10,000 deaths. In Africa the locusts returned to strip the countryside bare.

What happened in that decade of the 60's. to bring back these insect plagues? Well for one thing a talented author Rachel Carson wrote a book called "The Silent Spring." * All of us became alarmed that perhaps we were interfering with nature. ~~Environ~~ An Environmental Protection Agency became a part of the Fed. govt. The most effective pesticide DDT was outlawed but we were told we'd have others as effective but much less hazardous. Unfortunately as fast as the substitutes came on line they were outlawed.

The grasshopper plague in Neb. could have been halted when it began according to Nebraskas agricultural director who said: "We just dont have the chemicals to do the job."

It is ironic that the hearing examiner for EPA back in 1972 said that DDT was harmless to human beings & that properly used it posed <u>no</u> threat to animal, bird or marine life. Yet it is banned by the EPA on the theoretical grounds that it might under some circumstances, someday harm someone or something.

This is RR   Thanks for listening. ❖

Seal Hunt
May 15, 1978

It sometimes seems that we can get more emotionally aroused over mistreatment of animals than we can if the victims are human.

I'll be right back.

A few weeks ago a writer in the Los Angeles Times, Parker Barss Donham, did an article on the 1978 Canadian baby seal hunt. ~~He wrote a~~ *one* ~~line that~~ One line in his article was very thought provoking; ~~He~~ "If seal pups were as ugly as lobsters, their harvest would go unnoticed."

Accompanying his article was a photo that proved his point. It was a snow white *baby* seal with it's black nose & round dark eyes looking like something you'd put in the nursery for the children to cuddle. Add to this, horrifying accounts of men clubbing these cuddly creatures to death in a mass slaughter ~~with~~ *and* WITH the inference that death comes slowly & agonizingly ~~to the seal pups~~ and it's easy to understand the protests & demonstrations every year.

~~Now let me make one thing clear. I'm going against the grain with what I'm going to say~~ NOW FOR THE RECORD, I couldn't hit one of those seals with a club—I couldn't hit a hog with a club and I squirm when I think about lobsters being chucked into that boiling pot while they are still alive. ~~But~~ *Still* I

---

*Rachel Carson, *Silent Spring* (Boston: Houghton Mifflin, 1962). *Silent Spring* is considered one of the most influential ecology books of the twentieth century.

enjoy eating lobster and I love a good steak but I wouldn't want to work in the packing plant.

~~Alright~~ ~~Now that that's said~~ *Now* let me go on with what Mr. Donham had to say about the annual harvest of seal pups. How many of us know how sophisticated the protestors are in their annual crusade against the New-foundlanders who carry on the hunt? There is an international organization which stays in business year round primarily to raise money to protect *against* the seal harvest. A $40,000 a year exec. rides around in the organization's own helicopter. ~~You can't help but think that they'd be out of business if there~~ ~~wasn't~~ *weren't* ~~the annual seal hunt.~~ *All of that would stop if they ever suc-ceded in halting ~~the~~ the seal harvest. It does give you something to think about—particularly if you are one of the contributors to the organization.*

Time wont permit all the facts disclosed by Mr. Donham but here are some that shed ~~some~~ light on what has been portrayed as bloodthirsty bru-tality. In the first place use of the word, harvest is appropriate. The Canadian govt. sets the quota of how many seal pups can be taken. The Harp seal is not in danger of extinction. It is one of the most abundant seal species in the world and the herd is growing not shrinking. Elimination of the seal pup har-vest would have a disastrous effect on the already depleted Atlantic fishing grounds. *The seals consume each year ½ mil. tons of small fish that are a vital link in the food chain for cod, sea birds & whales.*

~~Now~~ So much for that—now for the charge that the seal pups suffer a painful & lingering death. Careful research has been done by the Canadian Fed. of Humane Societies, Soc. for the prevention of cruelty to animals, The Ontario Humane Soc. & the Canadian Audubon Soc. They have studied the best means of killing seals—use of guns, drugs, gas & others. Their final con-clusion is ~~the present so called club,~~ *that clubbing with* a hardwood bat or the Norwegian hokapik is the most humane method & brings on instant death or deep irreversible unconsciousness.

According to these researchers the seal hunt in ~~point~~ terms of humaneness compares favorably with the method of dispatching ~~the~~ domesticated ani-mals which provide us with our daily food supply.

I'm sure Mr. Donham knew he was bucking an emotional tide when he wrote his ~~school~~ *scholarly* article. It took courage but he performed a useful service.

This is RR Thanks for listening. ❖

In this essay, Reagan analyzes the basic conflict between development and preserving the environment, arguing for a balanced approach—"a reason-

able sharing between scenery & the treasures locked up in [Alaska's] untouched wilderness. . . ."

Alaska
November 8, 1977

Will Alaska wind up as our biggest state or will it be our smallest state surrounded by our biggest Nat. Park. I'll be right back.

I'm sure all of us in the other 49 states take pleasure in knowing (even if we never see it for ourselves) *that* there is a vast wilderness of mountains, lakes, rivers, glaciers & tundra where Kodiak bears roam & the great Arctic wolves stalk the Caribou.

All of this is found of course in Alaska, a state which is roughly ⅙ the *total* area of the ~~total~~ United States. It is a place of fantastic beauty with more than 3000 miles of coastline, rushing rivers, trackless forests and great snow covered mt. peaks.

In all of that beauty of course is a richness of natural resources, many of them growing scarce in the rest of our land. There is oil, natural gas, minerals and great stands of timber. These things we need but I'm sure no one wants to treat this ~~great~~ *last American* frontier as we treated the 1ˢᵗ. We are more aware now than we were in an earlier day and we want Americans another 200 yrs. down the road to know there is a place where Kodiak bears, arctic wolves & Caribou live as they always have.

With all of this in mind Congress closed off 80,000,000 acres of Alaska to mining & certain other uses. This is not exactly a city park. It is the size of Maine, New Hampshire, Vermont, Mass., Conn., Rhode Island, New York & New Jersey all put together. And it's close to one fourth of Alaska.

That 1971 law expires at the end of next year. The people of Alaska are beginning to feel like a clay pigeon on a skeet range. All sorts of ideas are being proposed as substitutes for that 1971 law but no one seems to be asking the Alaskans how they feel about it.

Yes they live in all that great beauty and they too want it preserved for their children & their childrens children *and ours as well*. They also want to make a living plus which they know that people must heat their homes in winter & cool them in summer. There must be fuel to drive our cars and lumber & plastic for a thousand different things we use in our daily living.

Right now they wonder why there can't be a reasonable sharing between scenery & the treasures locked up in the untouched wilderness of their state. Environmentalists have persuaded Rep. Morris Udall *of Ariz.* to introduce a bill that would put 145 million acres into federally protected land. Apparently this would be without regard to minerals or oil or gas potential.

This would of course add 65 mil. acres to the 80 mil. now covered by the 1971 law. So *to* the area now equivalent to Maine, New Hampshire, Vermont, Mass., Conn., Rhode Island, New York & New Jersey add Pa., Maryland, Delaware, Virginia & W. Va. Dosen't this seem a little much? Indeed it is environmental extremism. Remember the alternative is not destruction of the natural beauty of Alaska, it is exercise of common sense to have both a great expanse of *permanent* wilderness plus the vast treasures so far untapped in that new frontier.

Udalls bill will surely come to a vote because he's chairman of the House Interior Committee. I hope his fellow Congressmen will overrule the chairman & come up with a less extreme idea.

This is RR Thanks for listening. ❖

The last three essays in this section deal with the use of federal lands, about one third of all the land in the United States. Reagan feels strongly there must be a balance between those who would "pave everything over in the name of progress" and those "who wouldn't let us build a house unless it looked like a bird nest."

Federal Lands
October 10, 1978

I'm tempted to say: "In answer to popular request," todays commentary will again be on Fed. lands.

I'll be right back.

A short time ago I commented on what seems to be the Fed. govts.' determination to acquire even more land than it already owns. In that commentary I gave some rough estimates of the percentage of land in some western states that remains in ~~the~~ Fed. ownership. Since then I've received a few ~~commentaries~~ *querys as* to those estimates & even some ~~expressions~~ suggestions that I might have exaggerated. Actually my estimates were modest by at least a few percentage points.

Anyway here is ~~the~~ an accurate listing of several states. ~~The Fed. govt. owns ⅓ of the U.S.—that would be an area about equal to everything East of the Mississippi.~~ Of Alaskas total acreage, 96.4% is Federally owned, in Nevada it's 86.4%, 66.2% of Utah, Idaho 63.7%, Oregon 52.3%, Calif.

45% & Arizona 43.9%. That of course is only a partial listing. The Fed govt. owns ⅓ of the U.S.—that would be equal to all the land East of the Mississippi river.

In my previous commentary I spoke mainly of those private land owners who were being pressured by burocrats to give up their land thus increasing the Fed. preserve. But there is more at stake than that and all of us have reason to be concerned about Uncle Sam as a land baron.

The Dean of the U. of Arizona College of Mines has written some articles for the Ariz. Daily Star summarizing the situation. He tells us that 50% of all our known energy sources are in these Fed. lands. Yet in 1976 they only accounted for 10% of our total energy production.

According to Dean William Lesher the Fed. govt. has been locking these lands up as fast as new energy sources are discovered on them thereby preventing production which could make us less dependent on foreign sources. In 1968 only about ¼ of Fed lands had been withdrawn from use. Six years later that had become ¾ and no one knows the current rate of withdrawal.

Under the Ford admin. a study was made when it became known that a number of Fed. agencies had been withdrawing such lands piecemeal, not coordinating with each other. That study was made public just before the new admin. took over. It revealed that no one in Wash. knows how much of the Federally owned mineral lands have been removed from use. And it dosen't look ~~like~~ as if we're going to find out because Sec. of the Interior in this admin. Cecil Andrus has suppressed the report.

Now the Bureau of Land Management & the Forest Service under their own interpretations of the Wilderness Act, are trying to lock up an additional 90 mil. acres in Idaho, Montana, Wyoming & Colorado. One of the ~~largest~~ richest natural gas strikes in years was ~~recently~~ *made* within recent months in that area. Why is the govt. so anxious to lock up this land—much of which is barren? Is it a fear that more strikes will be made? Hard as it may ~~seem~~ *be* to believe that—is there any other explanation?

We're so used to calling this ⅓ of our nation, Federal land, isn't it time we remembered that the very term means it belongs to us—to the people of America?

This is RR Thanks for listening. ❖

Land Planning
February 27, 1975

How do we preserve the beauty of nature and our const. right to private ownership of land? I'll be right back.

~~The~~ A majority of us are somewhere in an environmental middle between ~~missionaries~~ those who'd pave over everything in the name of progress and those who wouldn't let us build a house unless it looked like a bird nest.

People are ecology too and most of us are looking for answers that will preserve nature to the greatest extent possible consistent with the need to have places ~~to~~ *where we can* work & live.

The Fed. govt. pushes nationwide land planning which is the greatest threat in 200 yrs. to our traditional ~~≠~~ *right to own* property. Cong. debates a bill which if passed would destroy the right of counties & towns to have local zoning ordinances. And all of this is done in the name of environmentalism.

But what happens to freedom? What happens to ~~≠~~ *your* right to purchase or homestead a piece of land and make it bear fruit if an agency in Wash. can tell ~~you~~ *him* YOU exactly what ~~you~~ YOU can or can't do with ~~your~~ *his* YOUR land including telling you there is nothing you can do but pay the taxes & let it lay idle.

Calif. has a well intentioned coastline protection law that has resulted in ec. disruption and hardship to a great many citizens some of whom just wanted to build a beach house for themselves. There is talk of similar programs for the mountains, deserts and virtually every other area of our state.

Those of us who are neither anti-ecology or environmental extremists seek an answer. How do we protect our const. right to own a piece of this earth at the same time we insure open space & natural beauty for generations ~~not~~ not yet born?

Is it oversimplification to suggest we don't need restrictive laws or govt. land planning but simply the law of supply & demand operating in the free mkt.

Let those who want to live at the beach or in the mountains or desert buy ~~building sites blg~~ bldg. sites in the open mkt. from willing sellers. The vast majority of us through choice or necessity will continue to live in cities, towns and suburbs. However we want to know that when & if the desire strikes us there are ~~places~~ beaches, mountains ~~areas~~ & desert where we can go for an hour, a day or an extended vacation. We don't want to feel that someday private ownership of these beauty spots & natural wonders will shut us out. ~~and The answer~~ OUR ANS. ALSO lies in the open mkt. We the people can collectively (thru govt.) do exactly what the individual can do. We can estimate what we need for our present & future use and then thru govt. buy it. Right now we the people own more than a third of all the land in the U.S. In some of our more scenic states ~~the~~ govt. ownership is as much as 90% of the total state. ~~Calif. owns~~ In Calif. govt. owns 40% of the total coastline.

Much of this publicly owned land is already in the form of parks. Vast areas are Nat. forest land.

If more is needed we should do collectively exactly what we do individually—go buy it. What we must *not* do is give to ourselves collectively in the name of govt. rights we do not posess as individuals. We can have all the open space & recreational land we need. We *do not* have ~~no~~ *the* right to tell someone who owns a beach lot he can't build on it because we like the view as we drive by on the ~~#~~ highway. If the view is that important to us we should buy it. ❖

Property Rights
September 27, 1977

Did you ever think you'd see a time in our country when govt. could invade your property rights without due process or any kind of compensation? I'll be right back.

† I've commented before about the bill before Cong. to add tens of thousands of acres to the Redwood Nat. Park in northern Calif. I'm not only against that bill but think the whole idea of the Nat. park was a fiasco.

Now before you jump to the conclusion I'm some kind of nature hater who wants to pave the country over in the name of progress—hear me out. I will yield to no man *in* my reverence for Gods great out of doors and the beauty which greets us on every hand. To stand in one of the cathedral like groves of Redwoods is a spiritual experience that defies description.

So many Californians felt that way ~~and~~ *in the* past & feel that way today that we have preserved in parks & memorial groves virtually all the superlative Redwoods that make up what are called the Cathedral like groves. ~~The total~~ Redwood parks in Calif. total 283 sq. miles.

Let me point out that Redwoods (which incidentally are a fast growing tree) can be divided roughly into what are called the Superlatives, ~~next~~ *and* the Old growth big trees. ~~and they are mighty impressive.~~ *These latter are in miles &* miles of forests, some surrounding the Superlatives in the parks but most out in the mountains where they are part of our commercial lumber industry.

Several years ago when Cong. yielded to pressure and agreed to a Nat. Redwood park they were informed that ~~the only way~~ there could *only* be such a park if it incorporated one or more of the existing state parks. The Fed. govt. bought 26,000 acres of which 15,600 acres were cut over or non timberland. Only 320 acres were of the Superlatives. But the land was between 2 of our most beautiful state parks. Actually the Fed. purchase amounted to something of a bridge between those 2 parks. So far little has been done to develop it and it's grandiloquent promises of mil's. of tourists worked out to 35,000 visitors ~~a~~ *last* year.

Now H.R. 3813 by Congressman Burton ~~would~~ *could* ~~take some 400 or $500 mil.~~ ~~*according to*~~ *conceivably* cost $1 Bil. to add 48,000 acres to the present park. It would strike a severe blow at the lumbering business of Calif. and wipe out hundreds if not thousands of jobs.

But what is not generally known and what ~~can~~ threatens all of you, ~~whether~~ *no matter where* you live is a little joker tucked away in the proposed park bill. It will give the Sec. of the Interior authority to identify & estab. zones of land outside park boundaries and to regulate use of these lands. ~~And~~ It specifically prohibits govt. from paying anything to owners for loss of the use of their lands. That is about as clear a violation of our constitutional rights as anything can be.

The govt. will be able to keep private owners from using their land, declare a watershed as critical for example and do this without condemnation proceedings or compensation.

This would constitute a very dangerous precedent. It could subsequently lead to regulating land all across the country that happened to border on Nat. Forests, wilderness areas, scenic trails, rivers & parks.

The Congressmans bill should be defeated and the Nat. park should be expanded by working out an arrangement with already existing state parks.

This is RR Thanks for listening.

†Send copy of this to Ms. Hodges (attached letter) ❖

EDUCATION

Reagan wrote a number of essays on what was wrong with American education, and some of his arguments would fit into the discussion still taking place as we enter the twenty-first century—on social promotion, the use of phonics to teach reading, the decline in test scores, and the impact of the teachers' unions. A strong theme running throughout all his writing on education is the desirability of local control and the dangers of interference by the federal government.

Education I
November 16, 1976

"Reading and Writing & Arithmetic" is a fine old song but I'm afraid it's lyrics are as out of date as a nickel cigar. I'll be right back.

I know I've spoken before about the decline in *quality of* public school education as evidenced by college entrance exams over the last 20 yrs. Just recently I read in Washington D.C. newspapers about one of the highest ranking graduates of a D.C. high school—valedictorian of his class who couldn't get a high enough mark on the standard entrance exams to get into Geo. Washington U. The Dean of the U. described the young man as having been conned into believing he'd had an ed.

But it took the news of an interview on a St. Louis TV station to get me back on this subject again. They interviewed a product of the St. Louis public school system, a young man 20 yrs. of age who had gone from Kindergarten through grade 12 and had his high school diploma to prove it. He is a functional illiterate, unable to read or write ~~who is now~~ *presently* enrolled in an adult remedial reading program.

Now lest you think he is ~~in some way~~ exceptional—possibly handicapped in some way let me state for the record he is not mentally retarded. Neither is he stupid. He's just plain untaught. The adult center where he's at last being taught to read says ~~he's~~ he has plenty of company in that one metropolitan ~~#~~ area alone.

Education is compulsory in our land of the free. You can't decide that you'll do without and if you try the law will be knocking on your door asking why isn't Johnny in school where he belongs.

Alright then! But what is our response if little Johnny <u>is</u> in school where he belongs and all that is required of him is his physical presence? If he sits in his assigned seat 5 days a week for 9 months he'll be passed and promoted to the next higher grade.

When I was Governor a black mother during the ~~to~~ height of the controversy over ~~dege~~ desegregation in the schools told me that wasn't nearly as important to her as some of the ed. fraternity would have us believe. She said, "Never mind moving them around to a different school, just teach them where they are." And then she made this request, "stop promoting my son to the next grade just because he's come to the end of the year. Make him stay in the grade he's in until he's learned what he's supposed to know." I'm afraid I thought she was exaggerating when she added, "one day they'll hand him a diploma & he won't even be able to read it."

What happens to a young man or woman who dons cap & gown, is handed a diploma as proud parents & friends applaud; who believes he has qualified to go into the job market and learns he can't even fill out the application for a job?

There have been great innovations in ed. and we're told the old fashioned methods—(phonics as the way to learn to read for example) are no longer approved by educators. Well let them answer one question. It is acknowledged that we have added more to mans knowledge in the last 25 years than in all the previous history of man. Those who did this were brought up in that earlier now outmoded school system; ~~how wrong could it have been?~~ *SURELY IT MUST HAVE BEEN DOING SOMETHING RIGHT.* This is RR. Thanks for listening. ❖

Education (B)
September 21, 1976

Today I'm going to talk a little bit more about ed.—just to get something off my chest. I'll be right back.

~~Yesterday I told the story of a young lady whose ed. began in~~
In this pol. season there has been some talk about the need to increase Fed. aid to ed. Indeed the Nat. Ed. Assn. proclaims a crisis in ed. which can only be met by massive infusions of Bils. of Fed. Dollars.

Well however you define crisis we can at least agree that in the last 20 yrs. the quality of ed. has declined by anyones standard. ~~Ca~~ Scores in College entrance exams have fallen continuously until last year they reached an all time low.

But can this be laid to inflation or reduced spending? In these 20 yrs. inflat. has raised the cost of things 57.2%. The average cost of educating a pupil in the pub. schools has gone up 211%. ~~Enrollment is up 88%.~~ *The* total cost in constant $ has gone up ~~≠~~ *4 X as much as enrollment.* The number of *school* emps. ~~is up 2½ times more than enrollment~~ *has increased 2½ X as much as the increase in enrollment* but significantly the increase in non-teaching emps. administrators et cetera is up 4X as much. There are fewer pupils per teacher & fewer ~~pupils~~ per classroom.

In what has been called the most thorough study of the pub. schools ever made Dr. James Coleman of Johns Hopkins U. says there is no relationship or ratio between the quality of ed. & class size or the number of pupils per teacher or cost or tchrs salary.

Well if the Nat. Ed. Assn. is wrong and ~~scarce~~ *shortage of* money isn't to blame how do we explain the drop in quality? May I suggest the possibility that educators tinkering with the system—their eyes on a brave new world they were going to build right in the classroom just may have tossed out some pretty tried & true fundamentals. We've all been aware of educationists claims that the old fashioned "readin, writin & arithmetic" was no longer relevant. School was going to mould the "now" generation into world citizens free of prejudice, hostility or even a competitive instinct.

Why did we let their theories go without argument? Why did none of us point out that ~~more~~ mankind has made more advances in virtually every field in the last 25 or 30 years than in all of hist. up to the present? It doesn't take a genius to figure out that the men & women responsible for those advances got their ed. in the old fashioned system the educationists are so determined to scrap. Are we to believe ~~everyone~~ *those who* harnessed the atom, took us to the Moon, gave us the miracles of computers, electronics, jet travel, an end to so many crippling & death dealing diseases did all of this in spite of their ed? Someone in those old fashioned schools so despised by ~~the~~ todays elitests must have done something right.

Just let me add a postscript. Yesterday I mentioned the old fashioned McGuffeys readers that were standard in our schools for more than half a century. Fourth graders ~~using them to learn to read were expected to~~ read the sermon on the mount, King Solomon & The Ants by Whittier, Alfred the Great, The History of The United Netherlands. Little Willy could read <u>then.</u> This is R.R. Thanks for listening. ❖

School Days
February 20, 1978

Modern day students in our public schools may have heard their grandparents sing a nostalgic chorus of "School Days"—but they'll never understand it.

I'll be right back.

Think back for a minute to the lines of that old song—"School days, School days—dear old Golden Rule days. Reading & writing & arithmetic, taught to the tune of a hickory stick." To a modern day student that must sound as far out as "Close Encounters of the Third Kind."

Author-Educator Solveig Eggerz has written an essay on "Whatever Happened to the Public Schools & Why." She makes the point that over the past 10 yrs. or so our schools have been drifting away from the traditional concept of teaching toward some idea about shaping the students emotional & cultural attitudes, involvement in social engineering & contemporary fads.

I've been critical of the Nat. Ed. Assn. before in these broadcasts and here I go again. The N.E.A. has published a document entitled, "Curriculum for the Whole Student." It declares "the curriculum must move away from an emphasis on retention of facts to an emphasis on the processes of inquiry, comparison, interpretation & synthesis." There is more but that should be enough to give you the idea.

Miss Eggerz points out that *a* flood of progressive innovations—teaching consumer ed., environment, minority affairs and others heavily larded with cultural relativism have replaced ~~reading~~ *"reading, writing & arith-metic."*

It is this that explains how in our nation's capital an honor student—

straight A's & class valedictorian—was rejected by ~~Georgetown U.~~ *George Washington U.* because of unsatisfactory scores on his College board exams. He was pronounced unfit for college level work. The Dean of Admissions said sympathetically "he thinks he's a real scholar. His parents think he's a real scholar. He's been deluded into thinking he's gotten an education."

Such cases are not so unusual. A few years ago there was a similar one in St. Louis. In several cities law suits have been brought against the school systems alleging they failed to teach the plaintiffs how to read.

Remember how often we've been told that classes are too big, schools need more money etc. Well over the last 14 years spending ~~per student~~ has vastly increased from around $400 per student to $1400. Tchrs. salaries have almost tripled and ~~the~~ *in* just 5 years public school enrollment dropped by more than 50,000 in that Wash. school district alone. Total nat. spending for primary & secondary ed. is 4x what it was in 1960.

In these *SAME* roughly ~~same~~ 14 yrs. the scholastic, aptitude tests—the college entrance ~~tests~~ *exams* called Sat's for short have dropped every year for totals ~~in~~ ranging from 50 points in verbal, ~~+~~ *to* 30 in math. The sponsors of the tests said "the schools are demanding less & less from students & getting it." Yet they are handing out higher & higher grades. Homework has been reduced—heaven forbid ed. should interfere with watching TV. Playing hookey (now called absenteeism) is ignored & text books simplified.

We'd better start singing "School Days" again—to the educators.

This is RR   Thanks for listening. ❖

Bilingual Education II
April 16, 1979

Something has happened to our traditional concept of America being the great melting pot. That something is bilingual ed. I'll be right back.

On the last commentary I spoke of the understanding I had as Gov. of Calif. that bilingual ed. (which was just beginning to be talked about) meant bi-lingual teachers who could help students ~~who of~~ *who spoke a foreign* tongue & were unfamiliar with ~~the~~ English. ~~language.~~ In Calif. & several other South West states where we have a great many Americans of Mexican descent ~~that~~ *language* is a problem in many of our schools.

Apparently my understanding was incorrect. We have bilingual ed. in American schools now. We even have a Fed. Office of bilingual Ed. The director designate of that office has stated that he believes ~~that~~ being taught in one's native language perhaps should be considered a "human right."

Now I'm quite sure that if a native born U.S. child finds himself & his family living in a foreign land he isn't going to be taught in his native tongue. But that seems to be what bilingual ed. means in these United States.

Today our govt. spends $150 mil. a year teaching children of other cultures & languages in their own language. The melting pot tradition in which we taught the foreign born how to fit into our society has been forsaken in favor of teaching them how to be different & remain apart from the mainstream of American living.

Our schools are now teaching students arithmetic, history, geography and such in 70 different languages. There are approximately 290,000 students in our land who are being taught in such tongues as Aleut, Cambodian, Punjabi, Tagalog (the original language of the Philipines *Philipines)* and of course Spanish for that is the native tongue of about 80% of the 290,000. ≠

In 1974 a suit brought in behalf of 1800 eth ethnic students resulted in this verdict—"schools receiving Fed funds must rectify the language deficiency in order to open instruction to students who had linguistic deficiencies."

Well I'm fo all for that and think that's what we should try to do. It seems to me the court ruled that their where the linguistic deficiency was *inability to speak* English they were to be helped to overcome that which means special added instruction in the legal official language of our country. And at the beginning that was the idea. They would be taught in their own language only until they could make a transition to ours.

Today "transition" has been changed to "maintenance." The new goal is to help them maintain proficiency in their original language.

Rep. John Ashbrook of Ohio has declared we are actually preventing children from learning English. The present $150 mil. budget for the bilingual prog. ≠ is slated to go to $400 mil. in the next 4 years.

What is next—traffic signs etc. in 70 different languages? Don't laugh. In San Francisco where they've been debating whether to license self serving gas stations one city supervisor says only if the instructions on the pumps are printed in English, Spanish, Chinese & Tagalog. Incidentally even the Filipinos speak Eng. instead of Tagalog.

This is RR   Thanks for listening. ❖

Sex Education
May 8, 1979

Do you remember when we were told that the increase in the divorce rate & the number of children born out of wedlock were problems sex ed. in the schools could solve?

I'll be right back.

Radio

Sex Ed.   ①

Do you remember when we were told that the
increase in the divorce rate & the number of children born
out of wedlock were problems sex ed. in the schools could solve?

I'll be right back.

Recently a Los Angeles Newspaper, ~~the Times~~
editorialized about "the increasing birth rate among
unwed teenage~~rs~~ mothers," calling it a "personal
disaster for them & their children, & a social disaster
for the country."

The writer then confirmed his opinion by citing
statistics developed in a 2 yr. study by a task force
of the House Select Committee on Population. The figures
are indeed sobering; one mil. adolescent girls get
pregnant each yr. and a third of them have abortions.
Of the 600,000 ~~teen age girls~~ who gave birth last yr.
almost half, 250,000, were under 17 yrs. of age.

About 70% of the pregnant girls do not finish highschool &
90% of those under age 15 drop out of school. In 1976
about half of the public funds expended for "Aid to Families
With ~~Dependent Children~~," 4.6 bil., went to mothers who first
gave birth as teenagers. ~~Other statistics which showed~~
~~give us all power to think most that that~~ Births among
unwed teenagers have more than doubled since 1960,
and the rate of births to girls under 15 has increased
~~in~~ 33% in the last 10 yrs, ~~One last figure~~ 50% of
unwed mothers are in their teens.

The editorial then went on to support ~~the~~ proposals
~~by~~ a member of the congressional committee to increase ~~the~~
funds to extend family planning services to more
teenagers and ~~for~~ for an extension of sex education
in our schools. It was pointed out that these proposals
could lead to a saving of money because so many of
these teenage mothers become dependent on Welfare.

I've never been against saving tax dollars but
I wonder if our first concern shouldn't be the saving

②

these girls from tragedy which could very well color their entire lives. I'm not sure that more ~~sad~~ sex ed., as it is presently taught, is the answer.

Please note that I said, "as it is presently taught." I'm sure all of us are aware of the importance of young people knowing, ~~th~~ as we used to say, "the facts of life." But in ~~the our~~ concern lest "sex ed." in the schools violate religious beliefs have we been teaching sex as a purely physiological ~~function~~ function, like eating ~~a sandwich~~ when you are hungry? Can we completely divorce sex ed., as I'm afraid we do, from any association with moral behavior without implanting in young minds that it ~~has no~~ more significance than eating a sandwich — so why not?

A Calif. scholar has written an essay, "Turning Children Into Sex Experts." The author says; "The 7th grader in my city is advised to set for himself a purely 'personal standard of sexual behavior. No religious views, nor community moral standards are to deflect him from his over-riding purposes of self discovery, self assertion & self gratification." A judge has advocated lowering the age of consent to 13 because youngsters are more sexually active these ~~days~~. ~~schools teach sex only with the parents written~~ Before we accept the congressman's idea that more sex ed. is an answer to teen age pregnancy shouldn't we ask if anyone has done a comparison of ~~that~~ the situation ~~two before~~ such ed. in the schools & after. I've had a report from one district that the venereal disease rate among young people in that district went up 800% in the first few years after sex ed. became a part of the curriculum. Before we do more of what we are doing ~~why dont we~~ find out if what we are doing is part of the problem not the

This is R R Thank you for listening.

Recently a Los Angeles Newspaper, the "Times" editorialized about, "the increasing birthrate among unwed teenagers mothers," calling it a, "personal disaster for them & their children, & a social disaster for the country."

The writer then confirmed his opinion by citing statistics developed in a 2 yr. study by a task force of the House Select Committee on Population. The figures are indeed sobering; one mil. adolescent girls get pregnant each yr. and a third of them have abortions. Of the 600,000 teenage girls who gave birth last yr. almost half, 250,000, were under 17 yrs. of age.

About 70% of the pregnant girls do not finish highschool & 90% of those under age 15 drop out of school. In 1976 about half of the public funds expended for, "Aid to Families *With* Dependent Children, $4.6 bil., went to mothers who first gave birth as teenagers.

Other statistics which should give us all pause to think reveal that Births among unwed teenagers have more than doubled since 1960, and the rate of births to girls under 15 has increased in 33% in the last 10 yrs, One last figure 50% of unwed mothers are in their teens.

The editorial then went on to support the proposals of *by* a member of the congressional committee to increase the funds to extend family planning services to more teenagers and for for an extension of sex education in our schools. It was pointed out that these proposals could lead to a saving of money because so many of these teenage mothers become dependent on Welfare.

I've never been against saving tax dollars but I wonder if our first concern shouldn't be FOR saving these girls from tragedy which could very well color their entire lives. I'm not sure that more sexed. sex ed., as it is presently taught, is the answer.

Please note that I said, "as it is presently taught." I'm sure all of us are aware of the importance of young people knowing, the as we used to say, "the facts of life." But in the our concern lest "sex ed." in the schools violate religious beliefs have we been teaching sex as a purely physiological function function, like eating a sandwich when you are hungry? Can we completely divorce sex ed., as I'm afraid we do, from any association with moral behavior? without implanting in young minds that it is of no *has no* more significance than eating a sandwich?—so why not?

A Calif. scholar has written an essay, "Turning Children Into Sex Experts." * The author says; "The 7th grader in my city is advised to set for himself a purely 'personal standard of sexual behavior. No religious views,

---

*Jacqueline Kasun, "Turning Children into Sex Experts," *The Public Interest* (Spring 1974): 14.

no community moral standards are to deflect him from his overriding pur-poses of self discovery, self assertion & self gratification." *A judge has advo-cated lowering the age of consent to 13 because youngsters are more sexually active these days.*

~~Calif. schools teach sex ed. only with the parents written consent.~~

Before we accept the congressmans idea that more sex ed. is an answer to teenage pregnancy shouldn't we ask if anyone has done a comparison of ~~what~~ ~~what~~ the situation ~~was~~ before *there was* such ed. in the schools & after. I've had a report from one district that the venerial disease rate among young peo-ple in that district went up 800% in the first few years after sex ed. ~~was~~ *be-came* a part of the curriculum. Before we do more of what we are doing ~~we'd~~ ~~better~~ *why dont we* find out if what we are doing is part of the problem not the

    This is RR   Thanks for listening. ❖

NEA
November 29, 1977

It would be wonderful if we could give the National planners, those social engineers who tinker with our social structure a years sabatical. I'll be right back.

Sometimes it seems as if we are walking down a long corridor flanked by closed doors. Then occasionally a voice is raised behind one of those doors loud enough for us to hear a few words. Or a door opens momentarily and we get a glimpse of people huddled deep in discussion. Uneasily ~~th~~ ≠ we re-alize ~~tha~~ from these flashes of sight & sound that we are the subject of all the discussions going on behind those closed doors.

The corridor is the society we live in, the America in which we work and play. Behind those doors is govt. with it's ~~associated~~ camp followers, the pleaders for special interests & causes. And we definitely are the subject of their every utterance.

With all the media that supposedly informs us of everything we should know, flooding & ≠ *inundating* us with words printed & spoken very little information is given us about those planners & their plans until the plans are finalized and we find ourselves obeying a new set of rules at the same time we are billed for the cost of enforcing the rules.

Fortunately a few columnists & publications walk closer to the doors, pause to listen and relay to the rest of us what is being planned. One of our truly great scholars Russell Kirk opened one of those doors for us in the Nov. 11 issue of National Review—a magasine ~~that~~ devoted to quoting the plan-ners and exposing the*ir* plans.

Prof. Kirk's revelation ~~is the~~ *concerns* the lobbying of the Nat. Ed. Assn. which now rivals C.O.P.E.* as a pol. action force capable of electing to office, or ejecting from office congressmen, Senators & even Presidents. Right now ~~the~~ N.E.A. is promoting a separate dept. (cabinet level of course) of Ed. The admin's. response it is suggested will determine whether N.E.A. supports the admin. in the 1980 election.

Russell Kirk with sufficient documentation reveals the dream N.E.A. has which requires the separate dept. if it is to be realized. It is to imitate the collectivist schools of Eastern Europe; to take over functions now traditionally believed to belong to the family.

Quoting the editor of the N.E.A. newsletter Kirk tells us "the day is fast approaching when the schools will be acknowledged as society's agreed upon vehicle for social change. In the school system of the future, all children will be automatically enrolled at birth in an infant & child health program. At age 2 they will become eligible to attend standard day care ~~centers~~ *programs*. School age children will attend from 9 to 5 daily plus optional ~~care~~ custodial care. Curriculum & programs in schools will come more & more to reflect long range planning goals. Thus if the nation adopts 'energy conservation' as a nat. goal there may well be a federally mandated educational program in every pub. school in the nation." And believe me by that time N.E.A. will have done it's best to see that there are only public schools in the nation.— The telling line is, the schools "will become part of a comprehensive human services system which fulfills many of the functions traditionally assumed by the family."

We have been warned. And make no mistake about it the Nat. Ed. Assn. has more lobbying muscle than any of the so called Industrial Empires or big business tycoons we usually think of when we hear the terms special interest & lobbyist.

This is RR   Thanks for listening. ❖

Schools
April 16, 1979

If you believe your local school district is better qualified to run your schools than *is* the Fed. govt. you'd better get ready to do battle. I'll be right back.

I believe a case can be made that the decline in the quality of public school ed. began when Fed. aid to ed. became Fed. interference in ed.

---

*AFL-CIO Committee on Political Education.

Some years back when Fed. aid was first proposed it was offered ONLY on the basis that local govt's. were hard pressed to meet increasing school costs. At the time many educators were fearful that control of the purse strings MIGHT mean control—period and therefore academic freedom would be lost.

Of course the proponents of Fed aid denied they had any intention of interfering with school matters—they just wanted to help meet financial needs. Taking them at their word Sen. Norris Cotton of New Hampshire made a very common sense suggestion. He said if the problem was one of finance alone then why not give to the states a tax source which would be theirs to control & spend. He introduced a bill to turn over to the states the tobacco tax. There would be only one string attached, the proceeds were to be used for education. Of course his bill was defeated which should tell us something about what the proponents of Fed. aid really had in mind.

Last year the Nat. Ed. Assn., which has favored a national school system for a long time, was defeated in it's effort to get a bill passed creating a Fed. Dept. of Ed. The White House is pledged to such a dept. and has gone out of it's way to tell the N.E.A. (now one of the most potent lobbying forces in Wash.) that it will continue to support the idea.

The question is will we who oppose the plan do as we so often do and sit back thinking that last year's victory was the end of the war? If we do we'll have—before the year is out—a bill creating a Dept. of Ed. And that will mean the end of local control of our schools.

The plan is to move fast before opposition can develop. The Sen. Governmental Affairs Committee just recently passed out to the Senate floor by a 16 to 1 vote a bill patterned after the one that was defeated last year. It seems likely that the Sen. will pass it.

If it is to be defeated it will have to be in the House. This won't be easy. Last year the lobbying forces marshalled by H.E.W. were busy fending off tuition tax credits among other things. This year nearly 100 organizations have lined up behind the N.E.A. to flood Congress with letters & postcards. A meeting was held in Jan. to plan strategy with top admin. officials led by the Vice Pres. One of the strategies is to nail down 8 new freshman congressmen before the opposition can get to them. Incidentally samples of the letters & postcards were displayed at the meeting. They hope to put a half mil. of these in the mailboxes of Congress.

One congressman said: "What they want is a central nat. voice for establishing ed. policy." All of us should be aware that the new dept. will be of Cabinet level. We'll be adding a new Cabinet officer and creating a new burocracy of gigantic size to oversee the 1000's & 1000's of public schools now administered by local school districts.

When will we learn the wisdom of the old saying—"if it ain't broke don't fix it."

This is R.R. Thanks for listening. ❖

In these two essays, both Ronald and Nancy Reagan comment on the effectiveness of private schools, and the case is made for preserving their tax-exempt status.

Private Schools
November 28, 1978

Does the ultimate responsibility for educating our children belong with parents or the agencies & depts. of the Fed. govt? I'll be right back.

†   Our nation is blessed with a pluralistic school system reflecting the great diversity of our people. We developed at the local school district level probably the best public school system in the world. Or it was until the Fed. govt. added Fed. interference to Fed. FINANCIAL aid and eroded educational quality in the process.

We have had however an answer to dissatisfaction with this public system; a network of so-called private schools of every description. Some are truly private in the sense that total costs are ~~paid~~ recouped in the tuition paid by those attending. Obviously such schools depend on people of means. There are *however* parochial schools charging tuition but depending in the main on church support.

These schools were born of a desire on the part of parents to have their children educated within ~~an~~ the religious atmosphere of their choice. Of late there have come to be hundreds of privately endowed schools dependent on private citizens contributions offering recognition of ~~religion~~ God in a non-denominational way. *These are a reaction to the ban on prayer in our public schools.*

All these independent or private schools, if you will, have been granted a tax free status, plus tax deductibility for those ~~contributions~~ who contribute to their support. Without this it is doubtful any of them could continue to operate.

Right now hearings are being held which could ~~end~~ *result* in *cancelling* this tax free & tax deductible feature. This is a pocketbook issue threatening every taxpayer because virtually all these independent schools are educating students at a far lower per-student cost than the public schools and usually doing a better job of it.

How can this be happening? Well it's another example of burocracy making it's own law by adopting regulations. ~~The director of the~~ Internal Revenue Svc. Commissioner *Jerome Kurtz* whose job in the treasury dept. is the collection of income taxes has decided to take upon himself additional duties & powers.

With Congress not in session he has decided to issue an edict which will deny the tax exempt, ~~status~~ tax deductible status to pvt. schools that fail to meet an arbitrary quota of minority enrollment & hiring. Pvt. & church supported schools will have to institute minority recruitment, minority hiring programs & provide minority scholarships to increase minority enrollment.

Let me interject that virtually all such schools are presently desegregated & many, many of them do offer scholarships to offset their high tuition rates.

The Commissioner tried to implement his regulation without the present hearings but a number of Congressmen—significantly of both conservative & liberal philosophy descended on him in angry force. Even so he is holding the hearings while Congress is in recess. His obvious intent is to face Congress in Jan. with his edict already established & being enforced.

Chief Justice John Marshall once declared: "The power to tax involves the power to destroy." The I.R.S. threatens the destruction of religious freedom itself with this action. The Commissioner & your Congressman should be hearing from you right now.

This is RR Thanks for listening.

† Schedule so it goes on in the 1ˢᵗ week of Dec. RR ❖

Reagan drafted this radio address for Nancy to deliver, and she edited it. Her edits are shown in brackets.

Nancy
March 6, 1979

I've brought someone with me today who has a heartwarming story to tell about an educational program.

We'll be right back.

† A few weeks ago while Nancy & I were in N.Y. City a friend invited Nancy to visit a school up in Harlem. I was going to tell you about that visit but figured you might like to hear it firsthand. So here she is my wife Nancy.

Thank you Ronnie. ~~I wont take time to tell you about my inner fears and a worry that I might be getting into something like "asphalt jungle." Just let~~

Radio Nancy ①

I've brought some one with me today who has a heartwarming story to tell about an educational program. We'll be right back.

A few weeks ago while Nancy & I were in N.Y. City a friend invited Nancy to visit a school up in Harlem. I was going to tell you about that visit but figured you might like to hear it first hand. So here she is — my wife Nancy.

Thank you Ronnie. ~~I want the ~~ I'll be forever grateful for his invitation. Over the years I've visited many schools and always ~~my~~ ~~and a ~~ ~~something like ~~ ~~biggest jungle~~ ~~just let me say~~ I wasn't prepared for the rooms full of bright, happy children and proud teachers obviously with great affection & love for these children.

The boys were all wearing jackets & neck ties, the girls dressed in plaid jumpers & blouses. They all looked so neat, polite & pleasant

In every class room I visited the students were told by the "Sisters" that I would answer whatever questions they had. These were elementary grade students but the questions would have done credit to a high school. They asked intelligent questions which revealed a knowledge of national issues and what's going on in the world.

Then in one room the Sister asked them if they'd like to tell me about their basketball team. Out of the forest of hands that went up she picked a boy who jumped to his feet & proudly stated, "we've won 7 & lost 2. We have 2 games to go & if we win those we're champions." I asked him if he thought they were going to do that and he said, "Of course". And do you know something — I believe him.

Then they asked me if I'd like to see their cheerleaders and I said yes". By that time I was ready to start cheering myself. A group of girls came forward and did a routine that looked as professional as anything the famed Rockettes might do. I learned they were totally responsible for everything including laying out the choreography.

Made this the 1st to record.

2

I learned there are 56 such schools throughout the inner city, parochial schools once threatened with closing. His eminence Cardinal Cooke of the arch diocese of N.Y. conceived of an idea that these schools could be put to use to help the disadvantaged, the poor. His idea became "The Inner-city Scholarship Fund". It is supported by voluntary contributions & run by a board of trustees made up of New Yorkers of all faiths. This is also true of the students. In the school I visited almost all the students were black & 80% were protestants.

A $370 tuition fee is charged but no deserving student is kept out for lack of money. Ninety two percent of the parents are poor but they'll do anything to keep their children in these schools. Some volunteer to do custodial work. Some of the mothers serve as teachers aides.

One mother with an income of $6300 pays $1100 of that in tuition. She says she does without things, doesn't buy many clothes because education is the most important thing.

By reading & other tests these schools top the N.Y. public schools in educational quality and the total cost per student averages less than $500. Per student cost in the public schools is over $2600.

That was Nancy Reagan — Thanks for listening

me *say [I'll be forever grateful for this invitation. Over the years I've visited many schools and always enjoyed it but I] [think mainly]* I [*just*] wasn't prepared for [*the*] rooms full of bright, happy children and proud teachers obviously with great affection & love for those children. ≠ The boys were all wearing jackets & neckties, the girls dressed in plaid jumpers & blouses. [*They all looked so neat, bright & ale polite & alert.*]

In every classroom I visited the students were told by the "Sisters" that I would answer whatever questions they had. These were elementary grade students but the questions would have done credit to a high school. They asked intelligent questions which revealed a knowledge of national issues and what's going on in the world.

Then in one room the Sister asked them if they'd like to tell me about their basketball team. Out of the forest of hands that went up she picked a boy who jumped to his feet & proudly stated, "we've won 7 & lost 2. We have to 2 games to go & if we win those we're champions." I asked him if he thought they were going to do that and he said, "of course." And do you know something—I believe him.

Then they asked me if I'd like to see their cheerleaders and I said "yes." By that time I was ready to start cheering myself. A group of girls came forward and did a routine that looked as professional as anything the famed Rockettes might do. I learned they were totally responsible for everything, including laying out the choreography.

I learned there are 56 such schools throughout the inner city, parochial schools once threatened with closing. His eminence Cardinal Cooke of the archdiocese of N.Y. conceived of an idea that these schools could be put to use to help the disadvantaged, the poor. His idea became, "The Inner-city Scholarship Fund." It is supported by voluntary contributions & run by a board of trustees made up of New Yorkers of all faiths. This is also true of the students. In the school I visited almost all the students were black & 80% were protestants.

A $350 tuition fee is charged but no deserving student is kept out for lack of money. Ninety two percent of the parents are poor but they declare [*they've said*] they'll do anything to keep their children in these schools. Some volunteer to do custodial work. Some of the mothers serve as teachers aides.

One mother with an income of $6300 pays $1100 of that in tuition. She says she does without things, dosen't buy many clothes because education is the most important thing.

By reading & other tests these schools top the N.Y. public schools in educational quality and the total cost ~~of~~ ~~≠~~ per student averages less than $500. Per student cost in the public schools is OVER $2600.

That was Nancy Reagan—Thanks for listening.

†*Make this the 1ˢᵗ to record.* ❖

Education & Religion
April 13, 1977

~~Some time ago claiming separation of Church & State as called for in the constitution, God was expelled from~~ ~~school~~ *the* ~~classroom.~~

Some time ago on constitutional grounds God was expelled from our public schools. Did we really do this to preserve separation of church & state? I'll be right back.

Having seen the domination of govt's. by *a* religious order and/or those ≠ nations where religious belief was dictated by the govt., the framers of our Const. made sure that our new Nat. would enjoy a separation of church & state. They simply meant that individuals would be free to worship as they chose; that govt. could not favor or discriminate against particular religions or denominations, nor could any denomination assume a role in govt.

~~W~~ I challenge anyone to prove that a clear & present danger to that constitutional protection has ever existed, for *even* one moment, ~~in these~~ *in all the years* since the const. was ratified. And yet a few years ago, egged on by an avowed Atheist, voluntary prayer was banned in our schools. Have we let some among us make Atheism a religion and impose that religion on those of us who believe in our Judeo-Christian traditions?

There is a fundamental dif. between separation of church & state and denying the ~~religious~~ spiritual heritage of this country. Inscribed on the Jefferson Memorial in Wash. D.C. are Jefferson's words, "The God who gave us life gave us liberty—can the liberties of a Nat. be secure when we have removed a conviction that these liberties are the gift of God".

Our coins bear the words "In God We Trust." We take the oath of office asking his help in keeping that oath. And we proclaim that we are a Nat. under God when we pledge allegiance to the flag. But we can't mention his name in a pub. school or even sing religious hymns that are non-denominational. Christmas can be celebrated in the school room with pine trees, tinsel and reindeers but there must be no mention of the man whose birthday is being celebrated. One wonders ~~what~~ *how* a teacher would answer if a student asked why it was called Christmas.

We have gone so far that it almost seems a rule, originally designed to guard against violation of the const., has become an aggressive campaign against religion itself. And *isn't* that ~~is~~ the very ~~violation~~ *thing* we set out to guard against~~?;~~ ~~It is~~ domination of religion by the state. In this case *by* pub. school officials?

Case in point. In an elementary school in St. Petersburg Fla. two teachers came to their classrooms wearing lapel buttons ~~stating~~ *which* read "I Found It." Such buttons, bumper stickers & even billboards are widespread around the whole country. There have even been spot ads on television with people ~~proclaiming~~ *declaring,* "I found it."

At any rate, the school principal inquired what the buttons meant and was shocked to learn ~~it~~ the wearers were simply acknowledging they had found God. ~~It~~ *You* would ~~seem~~ *think* this was a personal thing with each of the two teachers, but the principal didn't see it that way. She said, "I feel if the buttons are worn in the school building and a child asks what they mean, it would be bringing religion into the schools."

Well it would seem that not only is religion lacking in the schools—so is common sense. I wonder what a teacher is supposed to say if a kid asks about those 4 ~~words in fine print~~ *small* ~~letter~~ *words* on a ~~coin~~ *dime*—"In God We Trust." ~~This is RR Thanks for listening.~~—*or maybe that's why they aren't being taught how to read these days.*

This is RR—Thanks for listening. ❖

Regulations Go to College
April 16, 1979

Regulations are like spores of a fungus—they settle anywhere & everywhere and create more spores.

I'll be right back.

More than a century ago a French writer & philosopher Alexis de Tocqueville journeyed to our shores to satisfy himself about how such a great miracle had been performed in such a short time. We were the talk of the world because of our prosperity & industrial growth. He came, he saw & he admired. He admired so much he wrote a book about us.

Even so, ~~however~~ *HOWEVER,* he included in his book some words of warning to us. He said that if we weren't on guard we could find ourselves covered by a network of regulations that would control, "virtually every aspect of human life & behavior."

As you well know I've spoken on these broadcasts a number of times about how unnecessary govt. regulation is slowing our ec. growth and limiting our prosperity.

Today I'd like to tell you about another area you might not be aware of that is in danger of being smothered by the federal govts. spreading regulatory net.

Not too many years back our respect for academic freedom was such that colleges & U's. were exempt NOT ONLY from govt. regulation but even such federally mandated programs as Soc. Security & Workers Unemployment Ins. But beginning in 1964—a time when a few voices were being raised in warnings that govt. was usurping powers it was never intended to have—the federal govt. has increased by 1000% the number of laws pertaining to higher ed.

Today there are 34 congressional committees & 79 sub-committees ~~with jurisdiction over~~ *overseeing* 439 laws affecting higher ed. The Dept. of H.E.W. has declared that if one student on a campus is receiving fed. assistance ~~under~~ such as the G.I. bill or a fed. loan, that college or U., public or private, is subject to federal regulation. Hillsdale college in Mich. is fighting this ~~ruling~~ ruling by the Sec. of H.E.W. in the courts. We can only wish them well.

The regulations cover every aspect of college life, the hiring & firing of faculty—also their promotions; wages, salaries & benefits. ~~Also~~ There are also regulations having to do with building construction, record keeping, financial aid & to some degree educational programs & curriculum.

One Pres. of a modest size independent U. told me the admin. cost of complying with govt. required paper work ON HIS CAMPUS had gone from $50,000 a year to 625,000. There is a study which estimates the total bill for all colleges & U's. has gone to $2 Bil. a year. But brace yourself—modifications to meet energy efficiency standards & requirements of OSHA could ~~add~~ *cost* more than $11 bil. ~~to~~

All of this catches higher ed. at a time when inflat. and erosion of the value of endowments has created an unprecedented crisis. It is doubtful that some institutions can keep their doors open. Fed. aid is hardly an answer to this since it presently costs ~~the cost~~ *some* schools & colleges about 50¢ in admin. costs for every dollar received from the govt. And one way ~~Maybe higher ed. should~~ or another—through taxes for pub. U's. & community colleges or contributions & tuition FOR INDEPENDENT COLLEGES & U's.—we the people ~~foot~~ *pay* these costs in addition to ~~everything else that govt. costs~~ *all the other extravagances of govt.*

This is RR   Thanks for listening. ❖

Academic Freedom
September 1975

Tyranny, like fog in ~~a~~ *the* well known poem, *often* creeps in silently "on little cat feet." I'll be right back.

Samuel Gompers, founder of the Am. Fed. of Labor, was a true labor statesman & a patriot. He was also something of a martyr. When he began crusading for the workers, he was persecuted, beaten & vilified. In those earlier days, the word "goon" was coined as [a] title for "bully boys" employed by management to break up union organizing attempts.

None of this halted Gompers in his crusade but neither did it make him bitter or anti-establishment. He always declared that workers must recognize they are partners of management with a responsibility to maintain the eco[*nomic*] health of their particular industry. He said a strike was a breakdown in communications & that a <u>good</u> labor ~~leader~~ leader would try to remain in negotiations without strikes even if ~~it~~ *he* was ~~to~~ reduced to bargaining for ½ a cent.

Sam Gompers also loved the U.S. of America *with a deep passion*. He was in Mexico when he suffered a fatal illness. He ordered that he be placed on a train and taken to the border so he could die in this country. In his last speech to a labor convention, he made evident his belief in individual freedom. He said, "There may be here & there a worker who does not join a union of labor. That is his right no matter how wrong we think he may be. It is his legal right & no one can <u>dare</u> question his legal exercise of that right."

Now wouldn't you think that statement would have the whole-hearted endorsement of all those in Academia who hold "academic freedom" as the precious right of teachers to be preserved against inroads and encroachment by administrators, alumnae and even parents? If you <u>do</u> think that, you are a little out of step with the campus today.

Mrs. Margaret Ellers, asst. Prof. of engineering graphics at a tax supported inst., Ferris St. College in Mich., has lost her position as a teacher with tenure and ~~with~~ less than a year to go before being eligible for full pension. Now when a faculty member has tenure that means ~~they~~ *he or she* can only be deprived of ~~their~~ *the* job for ~~some~~ moral turpitude or some other terrible offense. Mrs. Ellers' academic record & her private life are above reproach. Her crime (& [*with*] consequent dismissal) was refusal to pay a $160 fee to a faculty union she refused to join.

In late 1973, a teachers union obtained exclusive bargaining rights at Ferris State. The Ferris Faculty Assn. affiliated with the Mich. Ed. Assn. & the

Nat. Ed. Assn. They couldn't make anyone <u>join</u> the union but the administrators of the college rolled over & played dead while a "service fee" was imposed on every faculty member who didn't join. The College Bd. of Control also voted that any faculty member who refused to pay would be dismissed. A number of faculty members refused but only Mrs. Ellers held out to the bitter end. To my knowledge, this marks the 1ˢᵗ such dismissal in the educational world.

Now, some will say that the service fee was fair because even ~~non~~ nonmembers would be getting the benefit of union representation. Some will say that, but it doesn't hold up. Of the $160 fee only $22 covers servicing by the Ferris assn. The balance—$138—goes to the Mich. & the Nat. Ed. Assn. to pay for their lobbying & pol. activities.

Samuel Gompers would have liked Mrs. Ellers. So do I.

This is R.R.—Thanks for listening. ❖

SOCIAL SECURITY AND
HEALTH CARE

In the 1970s, the rapidly rising cost of health care was a new issue. Reagan became a strong opponent of any move toward a national health program run by the government, writing nineteen essays on the issue, and citing the experience of countries with those plans such as Canada, Sweden, and Great Britain.

During the same decade the threat of bankruptcy in the Social Security system was just beginning to loom. Reagan was one of the early voices to call attention to this growing problem, arguing the need to "totally reform" Social Security. In one of his essays he suggests that we consider investing some of the money now paid to the government in Social Security taxes in private savings or insurance, maintaining that individuals could earn better returns than they were now getting from Social Security. He proposed reforms early in his first administration but withdrew them in the face of political opposition, and turned the issue over to a bipartisan commission.

Socialized Medicine I
July 1975

Is there a health care crisis? Probably—but not in the U.S. I'll be right back.

A very fine journalist in the heartland of our country, ~~the mid west~~ M. *STANTON EVANS* recently authored a fine essay entitled "Govt. Can Be Hazardous To Your Health." Mr. Evans made a very telling point not only about the ~~health~~ socialized ~~health~~ medicine argument but also about how those who want more govt. & less freedom have been out manouvering the rest of us.

He points out that the—"secret of winning a debate is to define the grounds on which it is conducted." Having established that he moved on to the ~~whole~~ much debated subject of whether we should have some version of socialized medicine in the U.S. and illustrates how those who want us to give up the best health care system in the world have lured even the Dr's. themselves into playing the other fellows game.

Advocates of Nationalized Health Ins. which is a nice sounding euphemism for socialized medicine have repeated over & over again that our system of ~~the~~ private medical practise is a shame & disgrace & there is a health care crisis in America. And sure enough Congressmen, Senators & Dr's. opposed to the ~~Fed.~~ proposals ~~of~~ for Fed. health care find themselves tacitly ~~agreeing~~ *accepting that* there is a problem. ~~and try~~ but ~~but they just don't like the proposals for solving it.~~ *Then they get into the endless argument over whether the proposals for solving it are any good.* Obviously an argument on that basis means we wind up with some kind of govt. medicine. *The costly tragedy is there is <u>no</u> health care crisis in the U.S.*

~~Then Evans gets down to the wh~~

~~The truth is t~~ Those who've been urging socialized medicine on us for at least two decades have invented a non-existent problem. There isn't a country in the world with govt. medicine programs that can match what we have in the U.S.. Health care ~~in the U.S.~~ *here* is getting better and better & has been made increasingly available to more & more people. In fact where there are problems they are usually caused by ~~our~~ govt. not by the private practise of medicine.

~~M. Stanton~~ Stan Evans cited a ~~rece~~ speech made by the young Mass. Sen.* in 1970 who said, "In spite of the broad agreement that our population has a right to health care the evidence is overwhelming that this right cannot be exercised by most of our people. If we are to avoid the collapse of our health services & the disastrous consequences for 10's of mil. of our citizens we must take action—the cost is increasing but the quality is declining."

He's talking about the country in which polio, tuberculosis, typhoid fever & ~~a number of~~ *many* other diseases have disappeared in our lifetime. Our life expectancy in this century has gone from ~~age~~ 49 years to 70.

We have more Drs. & hospitals in proportion to pop. than any other country in the world. There is one Dr. for fewer than 600 people in the U.S.

*Edward M. Kennedy (D-Massachusetts).

Eng. with In Eng. with it's socialized medicine the ratio is almost double that and we are *for the last 10 yrs we've been* increasing the number of Dr's. 3X as fast as the increase in pop. In even our rural areas hospital facilities are within a 25 mile distance of all but 2% of our pop. & only ¹⁄₁₀ of 1% have to travel more than 50 miles *to find a hospital of at least 25 beds.* On any *On any* given day we probably average about 300,000 vacant hosp. beds & hosp. employees outnumber patients 2 to 1.

The insurance program has kept pace. In 1940 only 12 mil. Americans had health insurance. By 1972 the fig. was 182 mil.—90% of our pop.

Maybe you'd like some more information on just how much *The plain truth is* we don't need Washingtons help in treating our ills. I'll be talk some more about this tomorrow.—This is R.R. ~ ~ ~ ❖

Socialized Medicine
July 6, 1977

We've all heard the admonition—"Physician heal thyself." Maybe it should be paraphrased PARAPHRASED to read, "Physician defend thyself. I'll be right back.

The campaign goes on to bring health care in America out of the free market system and into the protective custody of govt. Those who brought us the postal service and aAmtrack are anxious to provide medical service of the same high calibre.

What is hard to understand—or come to think of it maybe not *be* so hard to understand—is the American Medical Assn's. reluctance to fight back. After decades of sliding from all out war to *against* socialized medicine maybe *is it possible that* war weariness has set in? Heaven knows the determination to put govt. *energy and determination of those who want* have to put govt. in charge of our health has been untiring & persistent.

The A Med. Assn. probably gave in to combat fatigue when it *and* endorsed a nat. health insurance bill which would force all employers to provide health insurance benefits for their employees. Probably such a program looked as if *they* the Assn. *figured* govt. would have a minimum less chance to interfere in the Dr.-Patient relationship under such a program. than if *under* outright nationalization took place. Someplace along the line, however, the troops rallied and *the Assn.* withdrew its support of the bill.

But the defense line—once breached—is hard to restore. The Insurance Industry which <u>should</u> be opposed to govt. medicine is supporting a bill which—just by coincidence I'm sure—calls for a heavy govt. subsidy for the buying of private health insurance.

Much of the ~~defense against~~ *opposition to* govt. medicine has been based on the better quality of medicine we have *here in Am.* ~~because~~ *where* the ~~practice~~ *providing* of health care is still out in the free market.

On these programs I myself have tried to de-bunk the claims of the socialized medicine advocates by citing comparisons between medical quality, availability & cost here & in ~~the~~ other countries. A typical example is an incident told by Congressman Bob ~~Bam~~ BAUMAN.* ~~He was in London on his way to~~ I *On a trip to* England he asked an ~~an attractive~~ English woman *attractive,* (except for some facial scars) what she thought of Englands Nat. Health service. She approved of ~~the system~~ *it* & said —*Quote*—"we all get our medical care free you know." —*Unquote.* This isn't true of course. They are taxed far more heavily than we are and their health service takes a big bite of those taxes.

Then she said,—*Quote*—"It is rather slow. I had to wait 8 yrs. for an appointment with a dermatologist about my face."—*Unquote*—Then she had to wait ~~a~~ *another* year before treatment could begin. ~~But~~ ~~Yet~~ ~~She added~~ *She repeated,* "*But* it is free".

So much for *this kind of case against* socialized medicine. There is another argument ~~against~~ which hasn't been used ~~and~~ *as much as it* should be ~~in view~~ *when you think* of the sense of fair play ~~≠~~ *that* is characteristic of Americans. George Meany of the AFL-CIO is all out for a national health plan. But how would he react if someone proposed ~~telling some of~~ *that* the skilled workers he represents ~~could only~~ *would have* to become govt. employees to practise that skill? Do any of us have the right to tell *some particular* ~~Drs. & Dentists, therapists & nurses~~ *the members of any profession or trade* they must become govt. employees in order to pursue ~~their professions?~~ *their chosen work?*

Of course, we all want to insure that no one is denied needed medical care because of poverty. And we've done ~~a good job~~ *better than* most countries to provide that care. But ~~it would be immoral~~ *wouldn't it violate everything we believe in* to adopt a system based on the idea that the patients have a right to a ~~Drs.~~ *doctor's* services without regard for his right to say how & on what terms those services will be delivered.

This is RR ~~I'll~~ Thanks for listening. ❧

---

*Robert E. Bauman (R-Maryland).

Assembly Line Medicine II
July 9, 1979

This is more about conveyor-belt medical care offered by govt. and why it can't compare with our own system of free choice. I'll be right back.

A former British cabinet minister once said of govt. medicine "the demand for free medical care quickly outruns any possible provision for it."

On the last broadcast I was talking about the Canadian health care system ~~and~~ as described in "The American Spectator" by a Canadian journalist, F. S. Manor. Mr. Manor also touched on a report from Sweden where socialized medicine has been in effect a long time.

In this report an official in the Swedish health service said he was very much against physical check ups. He declared they were "expensive & wasteful since only seldom would a doctor find any pathological condition." But then he went ~~to~~ on to say that if an incipient disease is discovered—"it prompts the patient to insist on expensive modern treatment that will often prolong life for as many as 20 yrs., during which time the patient will continue to make demands upon the state health services."

It is hard to believe but this man—part of the officialdom of govt. health care in Sweden is saying the state prefers that you die young if the alternative is costly ongoing care at state expense.

I have seen other reports from other countries bearing out this same idea that some patients should be left to die if their treatment would be too prolonged & costly to the taxpayers. ~~In those other instances it involved putting patients above a certain age on waiting lists if they were diagnosed as needing costly treatment such as kidney dialysys over a period of years.~~

This ~~would be~~ *is* done by simply putting them on a waiting list until nature takes its course.

Getting back to Canada Mr. Manor cites the increasing number of doctors who leave Canada to practise in the U.S. In Canada a moderately skilled doctor has to see 3 times as many patients each day to earn as much as his American counterpart. But it isn't just ~~earnings~~ pay that prompts his move. His schedule is so heavy that he can only spend an average of 10 to 11 minutes with each patient—that is if they are all on time and passing each other on the way in & out of his office. *Recently the Canadian govt. put pressure on our govt. to halt this migration of doctors to the U.S. and our govt. has now made it difficult for Canadian physicians to move across the border.*

Mr. Manor speaks from some personal experience. One third of every tax dollar in Canada goes to pay for that "free" medical care. He estimates that he has paid about $12,000 over the last 5 yrs. for his so called medical insurance.

Last year he was ~~hit~~ *knocked down* by a hit & run driver. He woke up in a hospital where it was decided ~~benefit~~ without *benefit of* Xrays that he only had swollen legs & multiple abrasions & that he could go home.

Fortunately he has a personal physician who happens to be associated with that hospital, Xrays were taken and a more thorough examination given. He had suffered a concussion, an injured eye and a broken back. Even so there was no room or hospital bed available so he remained on a stretcher in the emergency room. His $12,000 over 5 yrs. hadn't bought him much of an insurance policy.

This is RR   Thanks for listening. ❖

Health Care
October 25, 1979

At least 2 health care plans are now before the Congress. I hope Congress will take a trip to England.

I'll be right back

The advocates of govt. medicine in our country are still at it and one could say probably closer than ever to achieving their goal of compulsory socialized medicine. One can't help but wonder why oh why ~~wont~~ they wont open their eyes and really look at how govt. medicine is doing in countries that already have it.

Our British cousins in the United Kingdom are most often cited as an example of why we should follow their lead and socialize the entire health care field. But what are our British Cousins doing while all this praise is being heaped upon them? They're trying to get back to the kind of private, fee for service medicine we have here in the U.S.—that's what they are doing.

The Electrical & Plumbing Trades Union has just negotiated an additional fringe benefit for it's 45,000 members & their families: Nothing less than a complete package of private health care benefits. And they aren't alone. The automobile assn. will soon be offering it's 5.3 mil. members a new plan guaranteeing private medical care whenever admission to a Nat. Health Service Hospital takes more than 6 weeks. Such a wait, I might add, is rather normal in old blighty. Another firm, I.B.M. has just bought private health insurance for all it's 15,000 employees in Eng.

Now all of this dosen't mean Englands ~~Private~~ massive tax supported

Nat. Health Service is being discontinued. It just means that people ~~will~~ are willing to pay if ~~it~~ they can get treatment more quickly, choose their own Doctors & hospitals and have such *other* amenities as private rooms.

Britain now has 8 private health plans along the line of our own Blue Cross. They have 2½ mil. members and are adding 100,000 a year. It is estimated they'll double their membership in the next 5 yrs. Because of this there has been an expansion of purely private medical facilities. The number of private hospitals is increasing 10% a year. An American company, American Medical International Inc. is investing $85 mil. in 7 new private hospitals in Eng. & Wales. And we can expect even more because the new Conservative govt. of Margaret Thatcher is expected to restore the tax exemption for workers of some $110 mil. in employer ~~health~~ financed health plans. The Labor party had imposed the tax to discourage the growth of private health care.

It's easy to see why private health care is growing even in the face of the so called free govt. care. There are ¾ of a million people on *the* waiting list of the Nationalized Health Program for operations such as hernias, gallstones, hip replacements, varicose veins & even tonsillectomies. Indeed children are waiting as long as 3 yrs. to have their tonsils out.

Britain has had 30 yrs. to make their govt. medical program work. What is happening there is typical of other nations with govt. health plans. ~~Shouldn't this be enough to~~

Shouldn't we profit by their experience & not follow them down the road of Socialized medicine.

This is RR   Thanks for listening. ❖

Social Security
November 29, 1977

Talking about social security is a little like being the messenger ~~who delivered bad news~~ to the king in ancient times. ~~who was~~ *If the message he carried* was bad news his head was lopped off. I'll be right back.

Ready for a little nostalgia? I've just come across a copy of the *1936* notice ~~to all of us back in 1936 about~~ of announcing the beginning of Soc. Security. ~~Bearing an impressive seal~~ It is entitled "Security In Your Old Age" ~~and then ɟ~~ *and is addressed:* "To employees of Industrial and Business Establishments—Factories, Shops, Mines, Mills, stores, offices & and other places of business." Then *it proclaims* "Beginning Nov. 24, 1936 the U.S. Govt. will set up a Social Security account for you, if you are eligible. ~~To un-~~

derstand your obligations, rights and benefits you should r̶e̶a̶d̶ ̶t̶h̶e̶ ̶f̶o̶l̶l̶o̶w̶i̶n̶g̶ ̶g̶e̶n̶e̶r̶a̶l̶ ̶e̶x̶p̶l̶a̶n̶a̶t̶i̶o̶n̶.̶"

T̶h̶e̶n̶ ̶i̶t̶ ̶g̶o̶e̶s̶ ̶o̶n̶ ̶t̶o̶ ̶s̶p̶e̶l̶l̶ ̶o̶u̶t̶ ̶i̶n̶ ̶p̶l̶a̶i̶n̶ ̶&̶ ̶s̶i̶m̶p̶l̶e̶ ̶l̶a̶n̶g̶u̶a̶g̶e̶ ̶t̶h̶e̶ ̶g̶o̶v̶t̶.̶ ̶h̶a̶s̶ ̶p̶a̶s̶s̶e̶d̶ ̶a̶ ̶l̶a̶w̶ ̶t̶h̶a̶t̶ ̶w̶i̶l̶l̶ ̶g̶i̶v̶e̶ ̶w̶o̶r̶k̶i̶n̶g̶ ̶p̶e̶o̶p̶l̶e̶ ̶s̶o̶m̶e̶t̶h̶i̶n̶g̶ ̶t̶o̶ ̶l̶i̶v̶e̶ ̶o̶n̶ ̶w̶h̶e̶n̶ ̶t̶h̶e̶y̶ ̶a̶r̶e̶ ̶o̶l̶d̶ ̶&̶ ̶h̶a̶v̶e̶ ̶s̶t̶o̶p̶p̶e̶d̶ ̶w̶o̶r̶k̶i̶n̶g̶.̶ It explains how employee & employer will pay 1¢ o̶u̶t̶ ̶o̶f̶ *for* each $ of earnings up to $3000 for 3 years. At that point their contributions will increase to 1½ cents a̶g̶a̶i̶n̶ ̶f̶o̶r̶ *for another* 3 years, then 2 cents, a̶n̶d̶ 2½ *&* finally 3 cents. o̶n̶ ̶e̶a̶c̶h̶ ̶o̶f̶ ̶$̶3̶0̶0̶0̶ ̶e̶a̶r̶n̶i̶n̶g̶s̶.̶ This final figure is in the form of a flat out promise, "beginning in 1949, 12 yrs from now you & your employer will each pay 3 cents on each $ you earn, up to $3000 a year. That is the most you will ever pay."

The pamphlet concludes with the guarantee that your money will go into a fund where it will draw 3% interest thus adding 3¢ to every *dollar in the* fund each yr. T̶h̶e̶ ̶f̶i̶n̶a̶l̶ ̶c̶o̶n̶c̶l̶u̶d̶i̶n̶g̶ *And it makes this* promise; i̶s̶ "What you get from the govt. plan will always be more than you have paid in taxes and usually more than you can get for yourself by putting away the same amount of money each week in some other way."

None of these s̶o̶l̶e̶m̶n̶ promises h̶a̶v̶e̶ *has* been kept. Your Soc. Sec. tax is not in a fund earning additional money. It is instead going directly to those now receiving benefits and it is insufficient to do even that. The rate of tax has long since gone beyond 3% and i̶t̶ ̶i̶s̶ the amount of your earnings being taxed i̶s̶ has g̶o̶n̶e̶ *risen* way above the promised ceiling of $3000. The amt. you get back is not more than you paid in nor is it more than you could get by putting your money in t̶o̶ some other plan. Most of you c̶o̶u̶l̶d̶ *with the present tax could* buy in the open insurance mkt. a retirement policy with life protection f̶a̶r̶ ̶g̶r̶e̶a̶t̶e̶r̶ *paying far more* than present soc. security benefits w̶i̶t̶h̶ ̶t̶h̶e̶ ̶t̶a̶x̶ ̶p̶a̶i̶d̶ ̶b̶y̶ ̶y̶o̶u̶ ̶&̶ ̶y̶o̶u̶r̶ ̶e̶m̶p̶l̶o̶y̶e̶r̶.̶

Now the admin. proposes tripling your tax over the next 10 yrs. and the employers tax over the next 2. And this is a temporary expedient only postponing for a brief time a day of reckoning.

During the '76 campaign I called attention to the fact that actuarial experts had estimated Soc. Sec. was e̶n̶t̶i̶r̶e̶l̶y̶ out of balance by from 2 to 4 Trillion dollars. This was vehemently denied. Two well known columnists Jules Witcover & Jack Germond have recently accused me of gross exaggeration.

The governing board of Soc. Sec. consisting of the Sec's of Treasury, HEW & Labor & the Dir. of Soc. Security have just issued the 1977 report. I̶t̶ ̶d̶o̶e̶s̶ ̶n̶o̶t̶ ̶m̶a̶k̶e̶ ̶p̶l̶e̶a̶s̶a̶n̶t̶ ̶r̶e̶a̶d̶i̶n̶g̶.̶ Projected outlays will exceed income (even with the huge increases in the tax) every year for the next 75 years and *Witcover*

& Germond are right the projected deficit is not 2 or 4 trillion.—It is $17 tril-
lion.

Increased taxes are no answer—they only add to inflation & further im-
poverish our people. It is time to totally reform the system ~~before there is~~ *if
we are to prevent* a total collapse.

This is RR   Thanks for listening. ❧

Social Security
January 9, 1978

The new Soc. Security tax bill has been passed by Cong. & Signed by the
Pres. It is the biggest single tax increase in history. I'll be right back.

A couple of months after this years coming election the Soc. security tax
will start climbing until by 1987 it will be three times what it is now for employer & employee. A rate of more than 7% will be applied ~~to~~ *on all earnings*
up to $42,600.

One nice touch I must admit was putting off the actual increase until after
the election. After all you know they must have done that for <u>our</u> benefit.
With our interest centered on the candidates we wouldn't want to be bothered by trivialities such as a tax increase. This could even explain why the cut
in ~~pensions~~ *benefits* from 44% *of* earnings *down* to 41% won't take place
until 1984.

The bill signing ceremony in Wash. was well covered by TV so we saw all
the exchange of congratulations, the backslapping & handshaking. Sure they
were happy—they don't pay any soc. security tax.

This $250 Bil. 10 yr. tax increase will do nothing ~~to~~ but stave off for a few
years the collapse of the Soc. Security system. By it's own admission the program is 17 trillion (yes trillion) dollars out of balance. What happens when
those few years are up? Another tax increase? At what point do we face up to
reforming the system and making it actuarially sound?

Maybe I shouldn't do this but I have a copy of the *official* announcement
of the beginning of Soc. security Nov. 24, 1936. It is addressed to us the citizens & ~~#~~ explains how the program will function, "if you work in some factory, shop, mine, mill, store, office or almost any other kind of business or
industry you will be earning benefits that will come to you later on."

The tax started at 1% of earnings up to $3000. ~~of earnings.~~ And it was ex-
plained how the rate of tax would increase by half a cent every 3 yrs. until it
reached it's ultimate ceiling of 3% but only on $3000 of earnings.

Then came this promise, "That is the most you will ever pay." We were
also promised that our dollars would go into a fund where we were guaran-

teed at least 3% interest. ~~on our~~ *therefore* we would <u>always</u> get back more than we paid in and more than we could get by putting our money into any kind of private investment.

I'm sure they meant those promises but they never kept them. Right now more than half the people presently paying into Soc. Security will get less than they pay in—possibly as little as half. For more than half the work force the social security tax is bigger than the inc. tax and remember it is not deductible for inc. tax purposes—you pay a tax on a tax.

Truth is if we could invest our & our employers share of the Soc. Security tax in savings or insurance we could ~~do better~~ *double the* return promised by Soc. Security.

It was <u>never</u> going to cost more than 3% on $3000. Now it's going to *cost* more than 7% on $42,600 and ~~still~~ it's *still* bankrupt.

This is RR   Thanks for listening. ❖

Pensions
September 6, 1977

Erisa sounds like an exotic foreign name—actually it is E.R.I.S.A. ~~the~~ standing for "Employee Retirement Income Security Act." I'll be right back.

† All of us should be more aware ~~of~~ than we are of the Employee Retirement Income Security Act of 1974. This is particularly true if we're participants in a non governmental pension fund. One man has tagged that set of Initials E.R.I.S.A. as standing for "Every ridiculous idea since Adam."

The purpose ~~behind the~~ *underlying* passage of the act was worthwhile and in the concept of govt's. responsibility to protect us from each other. Many workers have seen pension plans they were counting on in anticipation of their non earning years wiped out in bankruptcys, company failures or ~~just~~ just by faulty planning or management ~~of the pension fund~~. When that happens it is a tragedy of major proportions. Therefore the passage ~~of~~ by congress of the 1974 act to protect employees pension rights.

But as in so many things govt. attempts to do with good intent, the solution to the problem *has* become the problem. Commissioner of Internal Revenue Jerome Kurtz recently told a House Subcommittee as many as 30% almost ⅓ of the nations half mil. private pension plans may have gone out of business since "Erisa" was born in 1974. A subcommittee aide said the total is about 5 times the number previously believed to have ~~folded~~ closed up shop. Let me hasten to say this doesn't mean 30% of the nations workforce have lost their pensions. Most of the plans *that failed* were in small companies so about 5% of the workers have lost their retirement security.

~~This figures, because~~ The reason for dropping the plans is the 1974 act. Small pension plans have been driven out of existence ~~because~~ by the complex & cumbersome financial & reporting requirements. Small businesses are far less able to handle the paperwork and meet the financial requirements ~~of~~ & regulations ~~which dont~~ than are large corporations with computerized operations, large legal staffs & auditing dept's.

After hearing the testimony one congressman told Kurtz, "This is an alarming development. By passing the act, we may well have driven out 100,000 or 150,000 plans." An idea of the *SIZE* problem they were trying to solve and the subsequent overkill is indicated by ~~an~~ *the* asst. sec. of labor for labor-management problems who said the labor dept. disposed of 1370 pension fund investigations last year—(remember there ~~are~~ *were* some 500,000 pension plans). They found *only* 642 violations—all but 4 were settled out of court.

It's ironic that Wash. should be in the business of trying to regulate private pension ~~funds~~ *plans* in view of their mis-handling of Soc. Security. Significantly Fed. employees managed to exempt themselves from Soc. Security and set up for themselves instead a most generous pension program which hangs over future taxpayers as an unfunded liability of bils. & bils. of dollars.

Just recently a columnist for the Boston Herald Am., a specialist in ec. affairs revealed some startling facts about the Soc. Security Disability Program & the disability pensions for Fed. emps. This year the govt. (meaning us) will shell out $32 bil. for disability pensions & that does <u>not</u> include our disabled mil. veterans.

The Fed. govt. pays it's disabled emp's. 75% of their full time salary & it's tax free. ~~A~~ It isn't surprising that 12% of the total civilian Fed. work force are living on disability pensions. In soc. security, disability pensioners have increased 45 times as fast as the increase in pop. and the cost has gone up almost 2000%. Which explains why the Soc. Sec. Disability fund will be gone by 1979.

Congress should give "Erisa" a quiet burial *and Soc. Security immediate 1ˢᵗ aid.*

This is RR Thanks for listening.

†SEND A COPY OF THIS TO—~~MAN~~ ED. KING—ATTACHED LETTER. ❖

SOCIAL ISSUES

In later years the so-called social issues played a major role in Republican politics, some would say a dominant role. Yet in the five years from 1975 to 1979, these issues took a backseat in Reagan's essays. Of seven of the important social issues that would later be much discussed—drugs, family values, abortion, gun control, gay rights, school prayer, and immigration—we can find only a trace in his writings. In all he devoted less than 3 percent of his radio addresses to these questions. The topic that received the most attention, drugs, had eight essays—all on the potential dangers of marijuana. A few were written on gun control laws; none on gay rights; one on immigration. Only one essay concerns abortion.

The Family
June 29, 1979

I'm sure all of us feel that the family is the basic unit in our social structure. And some of us ~~worry that~~ *are worried* about the strength of that basic unit.
    I'll be right back.

Many people are concerned today about what seems to be an erosion of the family structure. Articles have been written suggesting that the rising incidence of crime, the drug culture and the increase in illigitimate births is evidence of the FAMILY'S deterioration ~~of the family.~~
    I only mention that by way of introduction to todays topic which has to do with the nomination of a Fed. judge. The Pres. has submitted the name of

Patricia Wald as his appointee to the U.S. Circuit Court for the District of Columbia.

This particular judicial post is considered by many to be the most influential Fed. tribunal besides the Supreme Ct. itself. And since judicial rulings often become what is known as "case law," it is interesting to note some of the expressed views of the nominee to this important bench.

Ms. Wald in a 1974 article on the rights of youth suggested that childhood has been seriously compared to slavery. Now I'll admit to remembering a few hot summer afternoons when my father had reminded me it was my turn to mow the lawn (my brother & I shared that task) that I could have been persuaded ~~I suffered~~ *I was the victim of* enforced bondage. But from my present vantage point that & other chores like carrying out the ashes seem little enough in return for what my parents had to put up with.

Some of Ms. Walds suggestions for removing the slave chains ~~of~~ from our children would do very little to restore the family as a unit in our social fabric. True, she proposes that every young child has the right to be consulted & informed about critical decisions in his or her life. I think many of us as parents will admit to sometimes not involving our children AS MUCH AS WE SHOULD in discussions about things affecting them. But I also think most parents know that ~~after the~~ *when we do, after the* discussion IS OVER the final executive decision is ~~theirs~~ *ours* to make.

Ms. Wald however dosen't see it that way. She ~~argued~~ *argues* or at least did in 1974 that, "the child's interests deserve representation by an independent advocate before a neutral decision-maker."

That does evoke a warm family picture. Dinner is over, Mom & Pop are in the living room and the door bell rings. Junior says, "that's my advocate about this summer camp business." He lets him in, the parents introduce themselves and then present their case. The advocate listens and ~~then~~ proposes (maybe) a compromise solution acceptable to his client—their little boy.

According to the President's nominee for the judgeship; "A youth ought to be able to seek legal advice or help to redress his grievances against family, school or others who adversely affect him. . . . A child or youth should have access to free or paid legal services on a confidential basis to discuss his personal grievances. . . ."

To top it off IT is ~~a proposal~~ *proposed* that adolescents should be able to seek medical or psychiatric care on their own. "This option," she says, "will become economically possible," when we have a nationalized health program. That's good because it will be Mom & Pop who'll need ~~the shrink~~ *to visit a shrink.*

This is RR   Thanks for listening. ❖

Day Care Centers
March 23, 1977

It has been said a baby sitter is a teenager acting like a parent while the parent is out acting like a teenager. Govt. sees it as something much more grandiose. I'll be right back.

Day care for *children of* welfare mothers so they can get jobs and stop being a burden on the taxpayers sounds like an unassailable idea. After all how much can taking care of a little child cost? ~~And,~~ if a little subsidy will get mama off the welfare rolls and on to the taxpayers rolls with the rest of us, it's a good investment. Or, it would be if govt. didn't ~~spend so~~ *insist on* acting like govt.

Last Fall the state of N.Y., through it's welfare admin., told the insolvent city of N.Y. *it* should *reduce* it's average day care cost from 75 to $65 a week. Now $65 is about $3250 a year per child. That's a little high just to get someone a job—particularly so if there is more than one child in the family. Incidentally, the swank, upper crust nursery schools caring for the children of *even* the very rich only charge $75 a week.

In N.Y. state, outside the big town, day care runs $40 a week—that's $2000 per child per year. There really is no way to estimate a nat. average on this, because the truth is dozens of govt. agencies in several govt. depts. all have a piece of the action under a variety of titles—"child care", "child development" etc.

We start out with what seems like a practical idea, if a mother of small children can't get a job because she has to take care of her children find a way to care for the kids while she's at work. A lot of women who aren't on welfare & never were are working, how do they handle the problem? Well some of them do pay private nursery schools or day care centers. In those swank $75 a week establishments the staffing level is 1 teacher for 10 children. When govt. gets into providing the day care *however* the staffing standards are a little different. For children up to 6 wks. of age it's 1 employee per child. From 6 ~~wks.~~ weeks to 3 yrs. 1 to 4, 1 to 5 for ~~3 & 4~~ 4 *& 5* yr. olds. ~~& then of course they've reached kindergarten age at 5.~~ *But 5 is kindergarten age and there are usually about 20 kids for each kindergarten teacher.* ~~I know~~ *I know* these Fed. staffing standards are for the benefit of the child but one gets an uneasy feeling they might be for the benefit of the staff.

To get back to those mothers who've solved the problem themselves, most of them don't use the $75 nursery schools at all. There is grandma, or a *housewife* sister with kids of her own or a neighbor who happily watches after the children for a few $'s. Still the professional day care idea has a powerful lobby, far better organized than the great majority of mothers who think mothers are supposed to take care of their *own* children, if they can.

The lobby has professionals ~~vocalists~~ who say they, the professionals, can develope the child better than an amateur who just happens to be a mother. Then there are those in the feminist movement who say the state should raise the kids ~~because it~~ *so they wont* interfere with mamas ~~won't be hinderd hindered in their careers~~ *seeking a career.* One question is avoided by the day care lobbyists; if there is such a crying need & such a demand for institutionalized child care, how come the private sector hasn't moved into the field to supply the needed service for a profit? Now the lobbyists are promoting day care for ~~vacation~~ school age children after school & during vacation—staffing level 1 employee to 15 children age 6 to 10, one for 20 from 10 yrs. to 14.

In the meantime Stanford Research, the Urban Institute and even ~~Bro~~ liberal Brookings have found that most women who need day care can find it and that private care is as good as public & at a lower cost. Still on Capitol Hill, people like V.P. Mondale,* say child developement is too important to be left to chance—meaning—to the parents in the home.—This is RR. Thanks for listening. ❖

Basketball
November 28, 1978

On our sports pages we are used to reading groups of initials like N.B.A.—N.C.A.A.—AAU & N.F.C. We may be getting a new set—H.E.W.—I'll be right back.

Just a few years after James Naismith invented basketball, High School girls in Dubuque Iowa were playing the game. The year was 1898. Today Iowa ranks 2ⁿᵈ in the nation in the number of girls participating in interscholastic basketball. The box office draw is greater for the girls state highschool tournament than for the one ~~to~~ WHICH decides the boys state championship. ~~team.~~ And because the game is taken so seriously, ~~≠~~ Iowa is a prime recruiting area for colleges & Universities. Or didn't you know that athletic scholarships are given to girl basketball players?

There are several other states where girls basketball ~~is flourishing but it~~ *is very big. Even though it* isn't nationwide as *is* the boys game ~~If it's big~~ IT'S POPULAR in such diverse states as Tenn. Okla & N.Y.

*Walter F. Mondale

If you haven't seen the "coed" game let me tell you ~~of~~ how it differs from ~~the boys game:~~ BOY'S BASKETBALL; there are 6 players not 5 on each team, 3 guards & 3 forwards and only the forwards are allowed to shoot. And there you have the reason for this dissertation on girls basketball. The Dept. of Health, Ed., & Welfare is troubled ~~by this~~ that perhaps in some way there is a sex discrimination issue in the matter of guards in THE girls ~~basketball game~~ not being allowed to shoot.

A girl in Tennesee found a Fed. judge who was willing to hand down a decision declaring the 6 player game violated the equal protection clause of the Const. Which only proves we should do a better job in appointing Fed. judges. His decision *I'M HAPPY TO SAY* was overturned~~,. I'm happy to say, and~~ H.E.W. should ~~consider very carefully the wisdom of~~ *give careful thought* TO JUST butting out. The next thing you know we may have a govt. regulation that baseball players get to take turns pitching, or a football lineman MUST have ~~an~~ equal ~~right~~ OPPORTUNITY to carry the ball.

Some Iowa girls who play basketball summed it up best in a letter to *the* Sec. of H.E.W. They asked: "Is it true that you are pushing 5 girl basketball?" And they added, "if so why?" Then they informed him the girls game was faster, had better teamwork and if he'd ever seen a girls game he'd know that.

There is no question but that the better athletes play forward but then that ~~provides~~ *makes* it possible for girls of lesser ability to participate and more girls get a chance with 6 instead of 5 on a team.

One lady who is active in wanting H.E.W. to intervene and outlaw the 6 girl ~~type of~~ team proclaims with great assurance that the girls of Iowa & their parents will ultimately realize the change was for their own good. That is the, "govt. knows best," kind of arrogance, that has a lot of Americans really frustrated.

Surely we can find some violations of human rights going on in the world where we won't have to convince the victims ~~that~~ they are being badly treated.

Very soon now the Iowa Girls State Basketball Tournament will take place and everyone will have a lot of fun—including the 3 guards on each team who don't shoot baskets and aren't complaining.

This is RR   Thanks for listening. ❖

This is Reagan's only radio address on abortion, although he briefly mentioned the 1976 platform plank on abortion in a 1976 radio address.

Abortion Laws
April 1975

An unborn childs property rights are protected by law—it's right to life is not. I'll be right back.

Eight years ago when I became Gov. I found myself involved almost immediately in a controversy over abortion. It was a subject I'd never given much thought to and ~~in a sense~~ one upon which I didn't really have an opinion. ~~In other words~~ ~~As~~ *But now I was* Gov. *and* ~~it turned~~ abortion turned out to be something I couldn't walk away from. A bill had been introduced in the Calif. legislature to make abortion available upon demand. The pro & anti forces were already marshalling their troops and emotions were running high. Then the author of the bill sent word down that he'd amend his bill to anything I felt I could sign. The ball—to coin a cliché—was in my court. Suddenly ~~the it had become necessary for me to take a position & on a subject I'd never before given~~ *as I said on a* ~~+~~ *matter I'd never really ever given any thought to* I had to have a position on abortion.

~~To shorten this down~~ I did more studying, ~~researching~~ & soul searching ~~on this matter~~ than *on* any thing that ~~faced~~ *was to face* me *as* Gov. ~~in all my~~ ~~those 8 years in office.~~ I discovered that neither medicine, law or theology had ever *really* found *a common ground on the subject.* ~~a com.~~ *any* ~~consensus on the~~ ~~Views ranged from those~~ ~~On one hand there were those who~~ *Some* believed an unborn child was ~~like some kind of~~ *no more than a* growth on the body female & she should be able to remove it as she would her appendix. Others felt a human life existed from the moment the fertilized egg ~~attached itself to the ovary wall~~ *was implanted in the womb.* ~~I now~~

Strangely enough ~~Calif. had a law passed almost unanimously by~~ the same legis. that ~~was so divided on th this~~ ~~on this~~ ~~subject~~ *couldn't agree on abortion had unanimously passed* ~~had passed~~ *by a* ~~virtually unanimous vote~~ a law making ~~anyone liable~~ ~~guilty of murder~~ *it murder* to abuse a pregnant woman. ~~to the extent that~~ ~~when so doing to~~ *so as to* cause the "death of ~~the~~ *her* unborn child." ~~I found further that an unborn child (called a fetus by those who support abortion) has property rights.~~ *Another inconsistency— the unborn have property rights protected by law.* A man can will his estate to his wife & children & any children yet to be born of his marriage. ~~Now a law is being proposed that~~ *Yet the proposed abortion law* would ~~let one person for whatever reason take the life of the~~ *that* ~~unborn child.~~ *deny the unborn the protection of the law in preserving its life.*

I went to the lawyers on my staff and ~~verified this property right~~ *right of* abortion   Radio

An unborn child's property rights are protected by law —
it's right to life is not. I'll be right back.

Eight years ago when I became Gov. I found myself
involved almost immediately in a controversy over abortion.
It was a subject I'd never given much thought to and ~~in~~
~~since~~ one upon which I didn't really have an opinion.
~~I who~~ But ~~now I was~~ Gov. ~~and found~~ abortion turned out
to be something I couldn't walk away from. A bill had
been introduced in the Calif. legislature to make abortion
available upon demand. The pro & anti forces were already
marshalling their troops and emotions were running high.
Then the author of the bill sent word down that he'd
amend his bill to anything I felt I could sign. The
ball — to coin a cliché — was in my court. Suddenly
~~the~~ I had to have a position on abortion. ~~it had become necessary for me to take a position~~
~~as I said on a subject I'd never really ever given any thought to~~
~~on a subject I'd never before given.~~

~~To shorten this down~~ I did more studying, ~~researching~~
& soul searching ~~and this matter~~ than any thing that ~~was to face~~ on
me ~~as former~~ ~~those~~ ~~2 years in office.~~ I discovered that neither
medicine, law or theology had ever ~~really~~ found ~~a common~~ common ground
the subject.
~~on the views ranged from those~~ ~~On one hand there was those~~
~~some~~ believed an unborn child was ~~the sacred~~ no more than a growth
on the body female & she should be able to remove it as she
wanted her appendix. Others felt a human life existed from
the moment the fertilized egg was implanted in the womb. ~~could itself to the wemal.~~
~~Now~~ Strangely enough ~~Calif. had a law passed almost~~
~~unanimously by~~ the same legis. that ~~would devote an abortion~~ couldn't agree on abortion
abortion had ~~subject had passed~~ unanimously passed ~~entirely unanimous voted~~ a law making
it murder to abuse a pregnant woman ~~to react that~~
~~anyone state guilty of abortion~~ woman ~~her is doing to~~
so as to cause the "death of ~~the~~ her unborn child". ~~If found~~
~~further that an unborn child (called a fetus by those~~

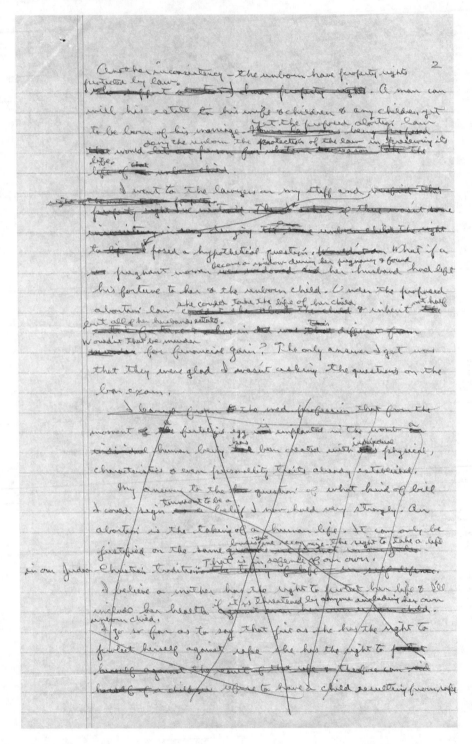

2

Another inconsistency — the unborn have property rights protected by law. A man can will his estate to his wife & children & any children yet to be born of his marriage. Yet the proposed abortion law would deny the unborn the protection of the law — in preserving its life.

I went to the lawyers on my staff and I posed a hypothetical question. What if a pregnant woman became a widow during her pregnancy & found her husband had left his fortune to her & the unborn child. Under the proposed abortion law she could take the life of her child & inherit not half but all of her husbands estate. Wouldn't that be murder for financial gain? The only answer I got was that they were glad I wasn't asking the questions on the bar exam.

I learned from the med. profession that from the moment of the fertilized egg is implanted in the womb a human being has been created with its physical, characteristics & even personality traits already established.

My answer to the question of what kind of bill I could sign turned out to be a belief I now hold very strongly. An abortion is the taking of a human life. It can only be justified on the same grounds one recognize the right to take a life in our Judeo-Christian tradition. That is in self defense.

I believe a mother has the right to protect her life & I'll include her health if it is threatened by anyone including her own unborn child.

I go so far as to say that just as she has the right to protect herself against rape she has the right to refuse to have a child resulting from rape

3

There is a quite common acceptance in medical circles that the cell — let's call it the egg — once it has been fertilized is on it's way as a human being with individual physical traits & personality characteristics already determined.

My answer as to what kind of abortion bill I could sign was one that recognized an abortion is the taking of a human life. In our Judeo-Christian religions we recognize the right to take life in defense of our own. Therefore an abortion is justified when it is done in self defense. My belief is that a woman has the right to protect her own life or health against even her own unborn child. I believe that just as she has the right to defend herself against she can protect herself against a child resulting from that violation of her person. So she should not be made to bear a child resulting from that violation of her person and therefore abortion is an act of self defense.

I know there will be disagreements with this view but I can find no evidence what so ever that a fetus is not a living human being with human rights.

the unborn ~~to own property~~ I've mentioned. ~~Then I asked if there wasn't some inconsistency in deny~~ denying the *same* unborn child the right to life. I posed a hypothetical question. ~~Wouldn't an~~ What if a ~~wo~~ pregnant woman ~~were widowed and~~ *became a widow during her pregnancy & found* her husband had left his fortune to her & the unborn child. Under the proposed abortion law ~~couldn't she abort the child~~ *she could take the life of her child* & inherit *not half but all of her husbands estate.* ~~the entire fortune & wherein did was that~~ *this* ~~different from murder~~ *Wouldn't that be murder* for financial gain? The only answer I got was that they were glad I wasn't asking the questions on the bar exam.

~~I learned from D the med. profession that~~ from the moment of ~~the~~ *a* fertilized egg ~~was~~ *is* implanted in the womb ~~an~~ *a* ~~individual~~ human being ~~had~~ *has* been created ~~with its~~ *individual* physical characteristics & even personallity traits already established.

~~My answer to the~~ ~~his~~ question of what kind of bill I could sign ~~as a~~ *turned out to be a* belief I now hold very strongly. An abortion is the taking of a human life. It can only be justified on the same ~~grounds we permit in our Judeo-~~ *basis that we recognize the right to take a life in our Judeo-*Christian tradition. ~~the taking of a life in self defense~~ *That is in defense of our own.* ~~I believe a mother has the right to protect her life & I'll include her health against even her own unborn child~~ *if it is threatened by anyone including her own unborn child.* ~~I go so far as to say that just as she has the right to protect herself against rape she has the right to~~ ~~protect herself against the result of that rape & therefore can rid herself of a child or~~ refuse to have a child resulting from rape.

There is a quite common acceptance in medical circles that the cell—let's call it the egg—once it has been fertilized is on it's way as a human being ~~whose~~ *with individual* physical traits & personality characteristics ~~have~~ already ~~been established~~ *determined.*

My answer as to what kind of abortion bill I could sign was ~~a bill~~ *one* that recognized an abortion ~~was~~ *is* the taking of a human life. In our Judeo-Christian religion we ~~accept that each one of us has~~ *recognize* the right to take life in defense of our own. Therefore an abortion is justified when ~~it is~~ done in self defense. My belief is that a woman has the right to protect her own life ~~& I'll~~ & ~~include~~ health against even her own unborn child. ~~I also~~ *I* believe *also* that just as she has the right to defend herself against ~~a rapist~~ *rape* ~~she can protect herself against a child resulting from that violation of her person.~~ rape she ~~does~~ *should* not ~~have~~ *be made* to bear a child resulting from that violation of her person and therefore abortion is an act of self defense.

I know there will be disagreement with this view but I can find no evidence whatsoever that a fetus is not a living human being with human rights. ❖

Martin Luther King
November 29, 1977

A very questionable ~~honor~~ *holiday* proposal has been ~~proposed~~ *made* ~~in ma to honor the of~~ *for* a holiday to honor slain civil rights leader Martin Luther King Jr. Somehow I doubt that he would consider it an honor. I'll be right back.

Perhaps by the time you hear this Gov. Milliken* of Mich. will have signed into law a new additional holiday for Michigan's state employees. I hope not and I'm not against holidays.

Michigans state Sen. has voted to change the *official* observance of Dr. *Martin Luther* Kings birthday from the ~~nearest~~ Sunday *nearest* to Jan. 15th to *a working day* the ~~nearest~~ Monday nearest that date. This would apply to state courts and banks. It seems that in our increasingly *govt.* controlled economy, banks in Mich. are subject to unusually tight controls. It is a natural assumption in the Wolverine state that the holiday would apply to other state employees as well.

One Senator Jack Welborn** stood alone in opposition to the plan. It took courage because obviously he would appear as a callous individual opposed to the idea of honoring the slain Rev. King. This of course ~~would~~ *could* lead to the ~~cha~~ additional charge of ~~racism~~ racism.

Well Sen. Jack Welborn is neither callous nor racist but ~~he probably had in mind~~ *what he had in mind was* something *far* more suitable as a memorial than a paid holiday for public employees. ~~who f~~For the most part *they* average *getting a* higher pay rate than the taxpayers who provide their salaries. The additional holiday for state employees would (or maybe by now—will) cost the state of Mich. more than 4½ mil. dollars. But it *wasn't the money that caused* ~~Jae~~ Jack Welborn ~~voted~~ *to vote* no. What he proposed instead was something in the nature of a living memorial to the victim of an assassin's bullet.

He offered 2 programs which would cost roughly the same as the proposed holiday. One would be in the form of Martin Luther King scholarships

*William Milliken.
**State senator (R-Kalamazoo, Michigan).

for disadvantaged students. The other would be an institute to study <u>non</u>-violent–(put the emphasis on <u>non</u>) protest activities *so that maybe one day we can find an answer to senseless & tragic killings.*

The value of the first is obvious and certainly the second is appropriate considering the manner in which Dr. King lost his life. Welborn also pointed out that ~~middle~~ *middle* class state employees vacationing at the expense of hard working citizens, some of whom ~~were~~ *are* low-income laborers ~~was~~ *is* hardly a fitting way to honor someone who gave his life in the cause of social justice for the disadvantaged.

State Sen. Jack Welborn was alone in his no vote against the holiday. He was alone in his proposal for the scholarships and the study program. He was also alone among his colleagues in the Mich. State Senate in the exercise of common sense. It seems to me that just possibly—Dr. King ~~might agree~~ would approve of Jack Welborns vote & his proposals.

This is RR   Thanks for listening. ❖

Indians' Plight
August 1975

Before we circle the wagons & send for John Wayne we'd better pause to see if it's really us against the Indians again or has someone got us all shooting at each other? I'll be right back.

Is there a "pale face" among us who dosen't feel the need to go back about ¾ of a century and do a better job of ending the Indian wars? During these ~~¾ of a century~~ past 4 score and several years we've tried govt. paternalism that was well intentioned but solved nothing and only proved that as a foster parent govt. is a colossal failure. The Bureau of Indian Affairs means well but it seems to be trying to outnumber the Indians it's supposed to be caring for.

When a tragedy like the happening at Wounded Knee* takes place it seems as if the players on both sides are "good guys" and we don't know who we're supposed to be for or against. Murder has been done. Good men Red & White have died, children have been orphaned & women widowed. It's time for someone to turn up the lights and say "don't anyone leave this room."

I think maybe someone has. Unfortunately he had to do it in a letter to the

---

*On December 29, 1890, on the Pine Ridge Indian reservation in South Dakota, about 200 Sioux men, women, and children were massacred by U.S. troops. In 1973 some 200 members of the American Indian Movement took the area by force, making demands during a 69-day siege in which two Indians were killed, and one U.S. marshal seriously wounded.

editor and that isn't exactly the way to get national attention. ~~Nevertheless his letter merits attention.~~ The writer of the letter is ~~Dick Wils~~ the President of the Oglala Sioux tribe in Pine Ridge S.D. where much of the trouble has taken place. Listen to what he has to say.

(Insert letter as edited)—then add—*(Close)*

"Once again our Pine Ridge Reservation is in the news, and once again there is a great deal of confusion about what it is that is going on here. . . . Our reservation was invaded in 1973, at the time of the Wounded Knee occupation by a bunch of outsiders, both Indian and non-Indian, and it is again being invaded by a bunch of outsiders.

"There is something very strange about these outsiders. . . . They drive fancy cars, better cars than our people. They . . . seem to have money to spend on airplane trips. . . . And . . . they carry powerful weapons, which makes them able to outshoot the FBI.

"A lot of us . . . are asking: . . . Where are they getting their money and their weapons? . . . Who are these people who invade our reservation? How are they getting by without holding down jobs? Who is paying them? Who is supplying them with their fancy weapons?

"And why do the newspapers and television stations fall for the false stories that are being put out by the groups supporting these invaders? When an Indian got killed in the shootout with the FBI, the story that was put out by these outside groups was that his name was Joe Kills Right. That was to make it sound like he was a Sioux. . . . His name was Joe Stuntz and . . . he was from Idaho. The one person who has been arrested so far comes from Oklahoma. He's another outsider.

"What are all these people doing on our reservation? . . . They are not brave enough to come into the towns where there are able-bodied people. They go out into the country and terrorize some poor old folks. And when they cause trouble that makes news, some church organizations rush in to 'mediate.' What is there to mediate? What we on this reservation want is a chance to live in peace and for our people to improve their lot. We don't want these outsiders to create trouble and give our reservation a bad name.

"There is a lot that has to be done to improve the life of our people. Our people need jobs, better educational opportunities. We have to end the misery and boredom which affects our young people. We have to give them a real chance in life.

"We want to build up our reservation communities and provide a decent life for everyone. For that we need help and support and the interest of a well-informed public. But to get a well-informed public we need newspapers that print the facts as they are."

You can't tell the players without a program. It's time for some good investigative reporting to properly identify the good guys & the bad guys. Come to think of it weren't there outsiders with personal axes to grind who got us fighting each other 100 yrs. ago? This is R.R.—Thanks for listening. ❖

A Gift
March 13, 1978

Gifts to public office holders have become a pol. no-no associated with chicanery & wrongdoing. But aren't there gifts an elected official <u>should</u> accept out of kindness? I'll be right back.

During my own terms in office I was aware of the gifts one couldn't accept ~~But there~~ no matter how well intentioned the donor. But there were gifts that couldn't be refused without doing a great unkindness. The handmade gift from a class of school children, the knitted afghan from an elderly woman who proudly recreated the state seal. To have returned such gifts would have been too hurtful to good & sincere people who were asking nothing in return.

Today a 78 yr. old man lies in a hospital far from his Okla. home. He can no longer speak so we have no way of knowing the depth of his hurt but it is reported that he is despondent.

The man is Chief Redbird of the Cherokee nation. For more than 60 years he has presented to each Pres. of the U.S. a ceremonial headdress. In the beginning they were made with the traditional eagle feathers. Later as we learned *of* the need to protect these handsome birds, turkey feathers were used. But whichever—they were beautifully made in the ancient manner and we can only partially understand the significance of *giving* these spectacular headdresses to the ~~white~~ "pale face" chief in Wash.

Chief Redbird's first presentation was to Woodrow Wilson who recieved it with dignity & appreciation as did other Presidents ~~who~~ who followed. They were Warren G. Harding, Calvin Coolidge was on virtually every front page wearing his. Then came Herbert Hoover, Franklin D. Roosevelt, Harry Truman, Dwight D. Eisenhower & John F. Kennedy who could hardly be forced into a hat. But respecting the dignity of the Chief he donned the headdress. Lyndon Johnson & Richard Nixon also received the Chief & his gifts.

Though ill & far from home Chief Redbird made & sent to Pres. Carter his symbolic gift, his way of invoking the great spirit of his people to watch over the Chief in the White House.

The staff returned the symbolic gift to the Chief telling him the Pres. did not accept gifts from the public. A spokesman for the Chief said "This bonnet is not a gift. It's a symbolic tribute to the nations chosen leader."

Obviously Chief Redbird wasn't asking anything for himself or his people. Certainly no one would have thought the Pres. was taking advantage of his high position or obligating himself in a way not in keeping with his trust.

A good & gentle man lies ill, his kindliness & loyalty rejected and a tradition he started as a youth now broken—possibly forever. because ⧸

Yes he is despondent—he must also be somewhat bewildered by the ways of the white man.

This is RR   Thanks for listening. ❧

Welfare Program #2
April 1975

Yesterday I spoke of the 62 Congressmen D. & R. who are sponsoring a program of welfare reform at the Nat. level and suggested that they need our help. No right thinking person questions our OUR responsibility to lend our less fortunate neighbors a hand but we cannot cannot ignore any longer the harm we are doing to the very people we are trying to help.

We can look to history for what might happen if we don't recognize what we are doing and where we're going. Eng. embarked on it's 1st welfare program in 1547. By the end of the 17th century nearly ⅕ of the Eng. Nat. was receiving aid at least part of the time. (The mayor of S.F. has just announced that 1 out of 4 in that city are on wf.) In Eng. the dole had was often 3X as much as the laborer could afford for himself & his family. By the end of the 18th century at a place called Speenhamland decided that wages below a certain level should be supplemented according to the price of bread & the number of children in the family. (sound familiar?) In the next 20 yrs. the cost of the prog. doubled & redoubled until it was ⅙ of the total Nat. expenditure. Some local govts. went bankrupt (that's what the our mayors are crying about). Labor was demoralized, riots & fires swept the countryside.

In 1832 a Royal Commission was appointed to study the prob. At the end of 2 yrs. the commission reported—"the worker need not bestir himself to work." So they recommended that relief should not be made more attractive than the pay for the most menial of jobs. They said "We do not believe that a country in which every man whatever his conduct or character is insured a comfortable living can retain its prosperity or even it's civilization." In commenting on the social workers they said, "Their feelings are all on one side. Their pity for the pauper excludes any for the taxpayer." They saw the problem as "How to afford the people relief without injury to their diligence or their providence."

History does repeat itself. In 1969 the House ways & means comm. discovered the highest factor determining the size of the caseload was the size of the grant. When grant levels are too high there is no incentive to work. Not only have we accepted the QUESTIONABLE premise that WF is a right, we have carried that to the extreme of believing certain types of jobs are more disgraceful than W.F. It is time to disabuse ourselves of the idea that any job is somehow disgraceful or dishonorable.

~~A couple of years ago~~

Some time back a Rutgers U. Prof. discovered what that Eng. Royal commission learned 150 yrs. ago. He said, "The bils. of $ that are being spent on the urban poor by all levels of govt. go mainly to support a growing WF burocracy of tchrs. aides, youth workers, clerks, supervisors, key punchers, & peoples lawyers. The buroc. is sustained by the plight of the poor, the threat of the poor, the misery of the poor, but it yields little in the way of loaves and fishes to the poor. When the old programs demonstrably fail, they are re-baptised and refunded."

Sixty two Cong. are proposing a way to change this. They need our help.

This is R.R. Thanks for listening. ❖

Welfare
December 22, 1976

The American people are the most generous people on earth. They can also be the most angry people on earth when they feel they are being cheated. I'll be right back.

Back in 1971 when Calif. completed the first & up til then the only major reform *of welfare* ever attempted we discovered the rewards ~~are~~ *were* astounding. First off we halted an annual increase in the welfare rolls that was *a* staggering ~~and~~ 40,000 cases a month and replaced it with an 8000 a month decrease. The truly needy benefitted because we were able to increase their grants 43% ~~and the~~ *at the same time we saved the* taxpayers $2 Bil. over a 3 yr. period.

The one question I've heard all over this land in these past many months is "what can we do about welfare?" Well as usual when things reach a certain point in this country the people begin to stir and action follows.

Four years ago in Elizabethtown Pa. a woman named Dorothy Forney led in the formation of the "Nat. Welfare Fraud Assn." I feel a little smug because she says Calif. was the inspiration. Now in St. Clair Co. Ill another woman 29 yr. old Roza Gossage—assistant St's Attorney has become probably the most productive welfare fraud prosecutor in the U.S.

Roza worked her way through the U. of Ill. & DePaul U. Law school. She has no fondness whatsoever for free loaders. In just 2 yrs. she has filed charges against 350 suspected welfare cheaters and has a near perfect record of convictions. She says, "the cheating was so blatant I could hardly believe it." And she described the cheaters as "leeches who drink up the resources of those who need welfare assistance."

She found as we had in Calif. there were those with unreported inc. & others with multiple addresses collecting several welfare checks. One of her finds was a county supervisor collecting welfare under her maiden name. Another owned a tavern which she hadn't reported & was selling it to another welfare recipient. One woman not only had a full time job—she won $10,000 in the state lottery which she didn't report. Finally just pulling a file at random she showed a Wall St. Journal reporter the case of a woman who had reported her husband as deserting her ten yrs. ago but they still have a joint checking account, co-signed for a small business admin. loan & paid $13,000 for a fish market.

When a legis. committee asked Mrs. Gossage how ~~all~~ so many people could get on the rolls illegally she said "Its easy. They just lie." Now Ill. is sending teams into other counties. In Mich. the state expects to ~~recover~~ *save* $50 mil. this year just by turning up absent husbands & fathers whose families have been getting welfare.

Politicians in Wash. keep saying something must be done and many of them say turn welfare back to us in Wash. Don't you believe it. Welfare varies from state to state but pretty generally it is run by the counties, under a state welfare office which in turn is subject to rules & regulations of H.E.W. in Wash. Much of what is wrong can be ~~cleared~~ corrected if we will at the county level tell ~~our~~ county govt. we want them doing what Mrs. Gossage has started doing in St. Clair Co. Ill. As the exec. director of Nat. Dist. Attorneys Assn. says, "too many prosecutors ~~dont~~ ignore welfare fraud because you have to put on your hat & coat & go out & find it."

This is R.R. Thanks for listening. ❖

Poverty
January 19, 1977

Washington is having an argument about how many people live below the poverty line in America and we all have quite a stake in the outcome. I'll be right back.

Our govt. has set a level of inc. below which ~~all who~~ *everyone is* to be considered as living in poverty. Incidentally that inc. level is 800% higher than the worlds average inc.—not the worlds poverty level—it's average inc.

~~Recently~~ *Last Fall* the census bureau released figures indicating that in the war on poverty, poverty is winning. The Bureau said that in spite of the bils. & bils. of $ we take from the workers & producers & ~~benef~~ redistribute to those below the poverty line there are more poor people than there were a year ago. The present total according to the census bureau is roughly some 25.9 mil. of our fellow citizens.

Now comes a different figure from a different source. *According to the N.Y. Times t*he Congressional Budget Office (which I will refer to for the rest of this broadcast as the C.B.O) says the Census Bureau only uses cash inc. in arriving at it's figure of 13.8% ~~living~~ of Americans living in poverty. But in the last 10 years non cash help—fringe benefits with a definite cash value have gone up from less than $2½ Bil. to more than $40 Bil. So adding in food stamps, housing aid, medicare & medicaid etc. CBO says that <u>after</u> <u>taxes</u> only 6.9 not 13.8% of Americans are living below the poverty line. That figures out to just half the number of poor the census bureau found or just under 13 mil. people.

There is an interesting point which prompted me to use the term a few seconds ago about "<u>after</u> <u>taxes</u>." CBO found that the poverty ~~level was~~ total was only 6.7% of the pop. before subtracting taxes. It jumped to 6.9 after taxes were paid. ~~Somehow~~ *The prin. tax paid by the poor is the Soc. Security tax. Somehow* it seems that one of the aids to the truly poor would be to exempt them from ~~a tax~~ giving *that* money to govt. which govt. ~~would~~ then returns to them in the form of grants. But that's probably too simple a solution for govt. to think of.

But to get back to the main point—roughly 13 mil. Americans living below the poverty line are helped by govt. funds either in direct cash, food stamps, pub. housing, medical care etc. The total bill for this govt. help is *according to the report* roughly $200,~~000,000,000~~ *Bil.* Now lets do a little arithmetic. We are spending $200 bil. to bring 13,000,000 ~~men, women, young people, children & babies~~ *people* up to at least the poverty line which is $2800 for a single individual, $5500 for a family of 4 and ~~on up~~ *proportionately higher* for larger families.

Divide 13 <u>mil.</u> into 200 <u>Bil.</u> and we come out with ~~more than~~ *about* $15,500 for every ~~individual~~ man, woman, young person, child & baby. That would be $62,000 for the average family of 4.

Well we know of course that those who need help aren't receiving anything like ~~that~~ $15,500 a year so there is only one conceivable answer. Like so many other things done by govt. there ~~is~~ *must be* an unconscionable administrative overhead. What would govt. have to say if it were discovered that a private charity was taking in ~~15,000~~ more than $15,000 for every 2 or 3000 it gave to the needy? This is something to think about when Congress talks of federalizing welfare or forcing us all into a govt. run health insurance plan. This is RR Thanks for listening. ❖

Food Stamps
July 6, 1977

We all expect the kids to rush for the doors on the last day of school. In fact we think it's cute. Somehow it dosen't seem the same when legislators do it. I'll be rite back.

As the U.S. Congress began watching the clock on the last day before the Memorial day recess the people took something of a beating. Rushing to adjourn the Sen. passed & sent to the house ~~a~~ *the* "Food & Agriculture Act of 1977. Included in the act was a 2 yr. extension of the Food stamp program.

Now I for one have advocated a thorough overhaul of the food stamp caper for some time; even had a task force work on a plan for reform my last year as Gov. But what I had in mind was somewhat different than the changes the Senators made.

The Welfare lobby with the Presidents blessing ended the requirement ~~to~~ *for* purchasing food stamps. They are now free. In the past there was some effort to recognize the extent of need. Some people received stamps free, others paid on a sliding scale based on their inc. & need. But even at the top of the scale ~~they~~ *the stamps* were a bargain. Now they are ~~a~~ *more than a* ~~free~~ bargain THEY ARE FREE for everyone but the taxpayer.

Sen. McGovern has long advocated doing away with the purchase part of the program as a quote—1st step—unquote toward a guaranteed annual inc.

The Senators didn't change that part of the program that made strikers and college students eligible for food stamps. I remember ~~when we learned of~~ a student at one of our state U's. who had quite a deal worked out. He was ~~eligible~~ allowed to buy $25 worth of food stamps for 50¢. Another convenience in the program was recognition that you couldn't always make your food stamp purchases come out to an even $25 so the stores could give a small amt. of ~~change~~ cash for the unused stamps. In his case it amounted to 47¢. The first week of each month he'd buy $25 worth of stamps—get $24.53 worth of supplies & 47¢ change. The 2nd week he'd put 3 cents with the 47 & repeat. ~~Doing the same the 3rd week~~ By the end of the 3rd week he'd have *a total of* $73.59 worth of groceries plus *another* 47¢. Putting in his 3 cents *again* he'd make his 4th week buy of food stamps which he *then* sold to friends for $15. ~~For~~ A monthly investment of 59 cents ~~gave him~~ *his take each month was* $15 in cash ~~each month~~ plus $73.59 worth of food. When I ~~heard~~ *first learned* about him I didn't know whether to stop ~~him~~ *what he was doing* or hire him as state finance director. Now of course he doesn't even need the 59¢.

~~The bill is~~ *Free food stamps are intended* for the poor but in establishing whether a recipient qualifies they use net, not gross inc. Therefore the real cutoff point for a family of four ~~can be as~~ *is about* $10,600 and for larger families much higher.

If ~~this hasn't irritated you try so far~~ *you aren't irritated yet*—try this on for size. Sen. Carl Curtis* proposed an amendment to at least halt or reduce chances for fraud. He wanted the Dept. of Agri. to issue I.D. cards containing the recipients photo, set up an earnings clearance system to check reported inc. with ~~their~~ employers and a cross ~~checking~~ to ~~keep~~ prevent recipients from picking up more than one set of food stamps.

On May 24th the Curtis amendment to prevent outright cheating was defeated *in the Senate* 57 to 37. ~~hardly a # I doubt if the day will be hailed as # marking~~

This must go down in the records as a sad day for those who toil & pay taxes—indeed for America.

This is RR   Thanks for listening. ❖

Welfare
January 9, 1978

We'd all better know a little bit more than we do about welfare reform as it's presently being discussed in Wash. I'll be right back.

For some time now we've been told the Carter admin. will present a plan for welfare ~~return~~ *reform*—possibly in the session of Cong. beginning in Jan. While there have been leaks here & there as to the direction *in which* such reform would take us we've had little in the way of an outline or summary.

Now thanks to Rep. Charles Thone of Neb. we have some factual information. I doubt that it will rouse our enthusiasm for the proposed reforms.

To begin with I'm convinced ~~f~~ in view of our own experience with welfare reform in Calif. that a primary goal of reform should be to ~~ref~~ reduce the

*Carl Curtis (R-Nebraska).

welfare rolls. ~~In Calif.~~ Our caseload was increasing by 40,000 people a month. We reversed that and achieved an 8000 a month reduction in the rolls for more than 3 yrs. This doesn't mean we callously threw needy people into the streets nor is this what I'm suggesting at the Nat. level. It is true there were some freeloaders who did not belong on welfare and some I call paper people—names on paper of nonexistent people ~~enabling some in-dividuals to~~ *which meant some clients were* collecting more than one welfare check. ~~Ou~~

Our reforms tightened eligibility procedures but mainly we directed our effort to salvaging human beings & making them self supporting. The proposal for welfare reform in Wash. will ~~add~~ *put additional* people ~~to~~ on the dole says Congressman Thone.

Our reforms reduced the overall cost in this one state alone by $2 bil. in 3 yrs. The ~~Fe~~ admin. proposal will increase the *annual* cost by almost $15 bil., about $12 bil. more than the admin. said it would cost. ~~a year.~~ That estimate is based on the present value of the dollar but the reform wouldn't go into operation until 1981. If inflation continues that $15 bil. estimate will have to *be* increased considerably.

Even that dosen't tell the whole story. The program is designed to provide govt. jobs for all who can't find private employment. The ratio now ~~of~~ *for* public employees is one for every 4½ in the private sector. Or try this one on for size—there are about 73 mil. people in the country working & earning in the private sector. They are the only source govt. has for tax revenue. Their taxes are supporting 81 mil. *other* Americans who are totally dependent on tax dollars for their year round living. That should be a convincing argument against making govt. the employer of last resort.

The admin. has projected this program will put 1.4 mil. people to work by 1981. The pvt. sector created more jobs than that in just 2 months and it didn't take a single tax dollar to do it.

Welfare can be reformed by using common sense. The objective should be to care for those who can't help themselves, give temporary aid to those who can while you get them back into the ~~free mkt~~ *private industry* job market. This is not the objective apparently of the Admin. proposal.

This is RR   Thanks for listening. ❧

In several radio addresses Reagan argues that marijuana is a dangerous drug and opposes legalization. But while emphasizing that young people should be made aware of the risks involved, he also says, "If adults want to take such chances that is their business."

Marijuana
August 1979

There is more evidence in on marijuana and it should ring an alarm bell particularly for parents.

I'll be right back.

From time to time I've used these commentaries to report an update on the continued research into marijuana. Medical Science has come a long way since the 1972 report by the Nat. Commission on Marijuana & Drug Abuse which gave the weed a relatively clean bill of health.

Everyone who had the urge to light up a joint somehow became aware of that report and could recite it as a litany—exhaling smoke on every line. Strange to say however (or maybe not so strange) the confident & happy pot smokers overlooked a follow up report by members of the same commission which in effect said ~~opp~~ "Oops we overlooked a few things in the 1ˢᵗ report."

Further research has continued to repudiate that first report, research by increasing numbers of scientists here and abroad. And yet none of these subsequent findings seem to have caught the attention of the estimated 16 mil. regular users in our land—4 mil. of whom are between the ages of 12 & 17.

Those who have no axe to grind except to report the scientific facts they have uncovered say that marijuana has a far greater potential for harm than was previously believed.

The toxic ingredient which ~~is~~ provides the effect pot smokers want ~~is~~ has a jawbreaker name which I may not pronounce correctly—Tetrahydrocannabinol which I will henceforth refer to as T.H.C. This THC lodges in the bodies fatty tissues and that includes the brain & the reproductive organs. Now for those hard to sell souls who liken a joint to a martini the difference is our body eliminates the martini in 24 hours. THC stays in the body for a month. A person who only lights up a couple of times a week is keeping his most essential bodily organs permanently soaked in this toxic drug.

Does this have an effect? You can bet on it. Science now knows that it reduces the ability of the brain to transfer information from short term to long term memory in adition to other adverse & irreversible effects on the mental processes.

It slows the bodys production of the white blood cells which play a major role in fighting infection. And it lowers the male hormone & sperm count in men which if I may be blunt leads to sterility.

But there is another effect, which in this day & age ~~when we print~~ *of* warnings on cigarette packages about the danger of cancer from smoking to-

Radio

Marijuana

①

There is more evidence in on marijuana and it should ring an alarm bell particularly for parents.

I'll be right back

From time to time I've used these commentaries to report an update on the continued research into marijuana. Medical Science has come a long way since the 1972 report by the Nat. Commission on Marijuana & Drug Abuse which gave the weed a relatively clean bill of health.

Everyone who had the urge to light up a joint somehow became aware of that report and could recite it as a litany — exhaling smoke on every line. Strange to say however (or maybe not so strange) the confident & happy pot smokers overlooked a follow up report by members of the same commission which in effect said "oops we overlooked a few things in the 1st report."

Further research has continued to repudiate that first report, research by increasing numbers of scientists here and abroad. And yet none of these subsequent findings seem to have caught the attention of the estimated 16 mil. regular users in our land — 4 mil. of whom are between the ages of 12 & 17.

Those who have no axe to grind except to report the scientific facts they have uncovered say that marijuana has a far greater potential for harm than was previously believed.

The toxic ingredient which provides the effect pot smokers want has a jawbreaker name which I may not pronounce correctly — Tetrahydracannabinol [tetra-hydra-cannabinol] which I will henceforth refer to as THC. This THC lodges in the bodies fatty tissues and that includes the brain & the reproductive organs. Now for these hard to sell souls who liken a joint to a martini the difference is our body eliminates the martini in 24 hours. THC stays in the body for a month. A person who only lights up a couple of times a week is keeping his most

2

essential bodily organs permanently soaked in this toxic drug.

Does this have an effect? You can bet on it. Science now knows that it reduces the ability of the brain to transfer information from short term to long term memory in addition to other adverse & irreversible effects on the mental processes.

It slows the bodys production of the white blood cells which play a major role in fighting infection. And it lowers the male hormone & sperm count in men which if I may be blunt leads to sterility.

But there is another effect, which in this day & age ~~when we print~~ of warnings on cigarette packages about the danger of cancer from smoking tobacco, should give any pot smoker pause to think. The smoke from burning marijuana contains many more cancer causing substances than tobacco. And if that isn't enough it ~~leads~~ leads to bronchitis & emphysema.

If adults want to take such chances that is their business. But surely the communications media and public figures whose ~~voices~~ words get some attention should let 4 mil. youngsters know what they are risking when they light up a "joint" and pass it around because they think it's the in thing to do.

This is RR Thanks for listening.

bacco, should give any pot smoker pause to think. The smoke from burning marijuana contains many more cancer causing substances than tobacco. And if that isn't enough it ~~causes~~ leads to bronchitis & emphysema.

If adults want to take such chances that is their business. But surely the communications media and public figures whose ~~names~~ *words* get some attention should let 4 mil. youngsters know what they are risking when they light up a "joint" and pass it around because they think it's the in thing to do.

This is RR. Thanks for listening. ❖

Punishment
May 4, 1977

It isn't always the judges fault when lawbreakers get off easy. Sometimes it's the law & we can do something about that. I'll be right back.

I've been as critical as anyone about lenient judges who are reluctant to impose severe sentences, or who ~~sentence & then~~ send the guilty back to the street on probation. Sometimes, however, the judge has no choice under state statutes and those can be changed if enough of us will make our wants known to our legislators.

A few weeks ago a ~~Calif.~~ judge of the *Calif.* Sup. Ct. Harry V. Peetris sent me a copy of his remarks *made* in open court as he sentenced a convicted murderer. He explained that it was the obligation of the court to deter the convicted man from committing crimes in the future, to deter others ~~from committing such crimes~~ *and to protect society.*

The Judge told me he was frustrated in achieving these goals by ~~the~~ *California's* New Sentencing Act of 1976. ~~in Calif.~~ The man before him had served 2 prison terms for armed robbery & burglary & an extra term for parole violation. Now after a 4 month trial he had been found guilty of 4 cold blooded, deliberate murders, one of them for hire. His victims were a man, ~~&~~ a 15 yr. old boy and 2 women.

In describing the crimes, Judge Peetris said ~~the~~ *a* woman & her son were seated in their living room. The murderer placed a gun deep in her ear and fired. The boy begged for his life but was killed in the same manner, because, in the words of the killer, he couldn't leave an eye witness to the first ~~crime~~ *murder.*

His 3rd victim was his cocaine supplier who also begged for his life. This time the weapon was a sawed-off rifle and the victim was stuffed in a plastic, garbage bag and buried in the Forest.

~~Victim~~ He was hired to kill victim number 4, a woman. Using a hand gun he shot her in the head 4 times. Miraculously she lived but was partially paralyzed. Two months later for an additional fee he returned & finished the job saying, "This time she's really dead."

In passing sentence, Judge Peetris said the only appropriate punishment would be death in the gas chamber. But the people of Calif., who voted better than 2 to 1 to reinstitute capital punishment several years ago, are still waiting for the legislature to pass the implementing legislation. The next proper sentence would be life imprisonment without parole but under Calif. law such a penalty doesn't apply to first degree murder. And, the New Sentencing Act of 1976 forbids the judge from passing sentence for each of the 4 murders and having them run consecutively.

All the Judge could do is sentence ~~the convicted~~ *this cold-blooded, professional* killer of 4 people to prison with the knowledge that he would be eligible for parole in 5 yrs. & 10 months.

Judge Peetris said, "The sentence that the law allows me to render also fails to provide protection for the witnesses who in this case came forward under threats of death from the defendant." There were 4 women who couldn't hide their stark fear while they were on the witness stand. They will live with the knowledge that in less than 6 years, the man they helped to convict ~~will b~~ might possibly be free to carry out his threat on their lives.

The law properly provides for a judge to be lenient when the case calls for leniency. It does not provide for his being severe when that is called for in order to protect society. Only the people can make their legislators change the law. This is R.R. Thanks for listening. ❖

Crime
December 22, 1976

A sociological ~~≠~~ theory which may just be a sociological fairy tale is quote—poverty causes crime—unquote. I'll be right back.

A ~~≠~~ short time ago I talked about crime on this program and suggested there might be a simpler answer than some of the sociological theorizing we've been hearing for so long. Well now I have company.

A number of top scholars from the halls of Academia have been working on this problem with some astonishing results. They are Prof. Paul Erlich of the U. of Chi. Prof. James Q. Wilson of Harvard & Prof. Gordon Tullock of Va. Polytechnic Inst.

In my opinion they lay to rest once & for all the theory that poverty causes crime. I myself have remarked many times that we had possibly the lowest crime rate in our history at a time when poverty was most widespread during the years of the great depression. But now these scholarly gentlemen have put it in a test tube and come forth with fact & figure.

In the ~~last~~ 15 yrs. from 1950 to 1975 ~~crime~~ we reduced the number of people living below the poverty line by more than half. It was the greatest decline in poverty in our history. In that same period violent crime increased by 2½X & property crimes by 2¼. Put in percentages poverty dropped by 55% crime increased by 160% & 124%.

In their research the Prof's. went beyond bare figures and found substaniation by seeking out high crime areas and poverty pockets. For example the 15 lowest-crime-rate states in the nation are ~~substa~~ all below the median inc. level. The most impoverished ethnic communities are among the lowest in crime rate. By contrast several of the highest crime rate ~~cist~~ cities are "rich" communities with very small poverty areas.

Thank Heaven they didn't ~~ju~~ stop with finding out what dosen't cause crime. They carried their research into what does cause it. And the answer is indeed rather simple. In the main increase in crime is proportionate to the decrease in punishment.

Those States which have the best law enforcement, the highest percentage of convictions and the longest prison sentences, have the lowest crime. And generally in recent years a permissive philosophy has led to a reduced penalty for crime. The conviction rate for burglary in our land is less than half what it was in 1960. For murder it is 30% less.

Nationwide in the 10 yrs. between 1960 & 1970 we had 139% increase in crime but our prison population went down 8%. In other words an offenders chance of going to prison was about twice as great in 1960 as it was in 1970.

To wrap up their research inquiries were made in Canada & England where it was confirmed that punishment does ~~cut down~~ reduce crime.

There is reason to hope. In some of our cities including N.Y. special teams of police & prosecutors are zeroing in on repeaters, bringing them to quick trial, and going after stiff sentences—no plea bargaining. Word is it's paying off. This is RR Thanks for listening. ❖

Crime I
November 30, 1976

Is it possible that with some of our problems we are ignoring obvious answers and ~~lookin~~ looking for solutions as complex as the problems seem to be? I'll be right back.

More years ago than I like to remember—let's just say a couple of decades Before TV when radio was still exerting it's magic spell I was witness to an incident which had something of a lesson for all of us.

In those days an important part of any radio drama was the sound effects man; ~~He was~~ an ~~+~~ *inventive* fellow ~~with a box like chest on wheels filled with~~ *equipped with a trunk full of gadgets*. *There were half* coconut shells for the sound of horses hooves; a wooden train whistle; ~~and~~ celophane which ~~by crumpling~~ *when crumpled* in his hands ~~he~~ could be either a cozy campfire or a raging inferno, a limitless array of just things & stuff with which he could improvise.

The incident I mentioned had to do with a radio drama being rehearsed for airing on WHO Des Moines where I was a sports announcer. During the several days of rehearsal the sound effects man was trying everything to get the sound of water falling on a board. He tried rice on a drum, dried peas on cardboard and all sorts of other combinations without success. Then in desperation he tried water on a board & believe it or not it sounded *just* like water on a board.

Sometimes I think govt. should try "water on a board" instead of ~~some of~~ the social experiments which are tried in good faith but which fall short of results. During the war on poverty back in the '60's there was a Fed. program designed to reduce the number of high school dropouts. Money was provided for schools to hire STUDENTS WHO WERE PERCEIVED AS potential dropouts. They were paid to stay after school and clean up classrooms, wash blackboards and that sort of thing. Then an order went out that the jobs ~~should only be given~~ MUST BE GIVEN SOLELY to kids who had gotten in trouble. It only took about 7 min's for a good kid to realize he had to toss a brick through a window, snatch a purse or something of the kind to be eligible for some easy after school money.

Watching the TV news the other night I was reminded of "water on a board." A Los Angeles lady ~~78 yrs. of age~~ was asking the County Bd. of Supervisors, "What have we done to our country?" She had been beaten and her purse snatched by 3 young people 2 boys and a girl. A witness a kindly black lady WHO had come to her aid, ~~she~~ told the police the three ~~thief~~ assailants had gone into a nearby house. ~~The police were so~~ *They were found* ~~them~~ hiding in a closet.

The victim said, "My arm was broken. I spent the night in jail. Now I have no nerves in that arm. I am 78 yrs. old. I raised 3 children by myself—put them through college. I never asked for a penny from anyone." Now she lives in perpetual terror. She said, "I never open my door after 5 oclock at night. I'll have to move. We used to have a great country." And then she asked "What have we done with it?" The county hearing answered her question with a chorus of, not enough money, a need for more facilities, training programs—all the usual reform ideas for a type of crime that grows more prevalent day by day. That is rice on a drum or dried peas on cardboard.

The young man who knocked her down & stole her purse got 1 week in jail and a years probation. It is *past* time ~~for~~ TO TRY water on a board. ~~Why not~~ *Let's just start* treating 17 yr. old muggers, robbers, rapists & murderers like muggers, robbers, rapists & murderers? This is RR. Thanks for listening. ❖

Polls and Guns
August 7, 1978

Polls & poll taking have become a standard bit of Americana, but maybe we should know a little more than we do about how the questions are asked.

I'll be right back.

The great statesman Disraeli once said, "there are lies, expletive deleted lies, and statistics. Now I'm not going to be that forceful about polls. But we should know more than we do about how the questions are phrased by the pollsters and whether a certain public relations result is the goal of the organization or individual paying to have the poll taken.

~~For examp~~ A few years ago in a Wash. economic conference a lady who heads up a large financial house put her finger on ~~it~~ the matter of polling. She said, "ask a citizen if he'd like govt. to provide a certain service for the people and the answer will probably be yes." But then she said, "give the citizen a $100 bill and ask him if he'd like the service if it meant giving up the $100."

What brought all this to mind was the widespread press given to a poll in which apparently 84% of Americans favor stringent hand-gun control & registration. A third of those polled would even ban the manufacture of such weapons.

Now frankly I dont support this kind of gun control and I've never before seen evidence that the Am. people are that up in arms about arms if I may coin a phrase. At any rate I did a little checking.

This particular poll was conducted by a reputable firm so I'm not inferring that pollsters are guilty of falsification. But the sponsor of this poll was the "Center for the Study & Prevention of Handgun Violence and it was taken on the occasion of the 10th anniversary of the tragic ~~anniversary~~ *assassanation* of Robert Kennedy.

A little more than a year ago another reputable pollster was commissioned by the Second Amendment Foundation which defends our right under the 2ⁿᵈ amendment to bear arms. Their poll found that 54% of Americans believe the answer to violent crime lies in stiffer punishment. Only 10% would outlaw handguns. In fact when the question was asked: "Do you think gun controls have helped to reduce crimes committed with guns?" 67% said no.

Possibly we need to augment polling with some more comprehensive research. A U. of Wis. sociologist in a 1975 study found that, "gun control laws have no significant effect on violence beyond what can be attributed to background social conditions." Spoken like a true sociologist. But he also found that gun controls laws do not limit access to guns by those who intend *doing* violence.

Much more recently a survey of 6000 law enforcement officers found that 80% feel gun control laws have no effect on crime and 83% believe criminals would benefit more than citizens from the banning of hand-guns. In other words the laws would make it hard for the law abiding to get a gun but not the criminal.

Maybe the only poll that's really reliable is the one taken in liberal Mass. in 1976. A referendum to ban ownership of handguns was on the ballot in the November election. The voters of Mass. defeated it 3 to 1.

This is RR   Thanks for listening. ❖

New York
September 1975

Maybe it's a good idea to hold the Nat. Pol. Conventions in N.Y. next year. It could be very educational.

I'll be right back.

As a Californian I wouldn't want you to think I begrudge N.Y. City *rather than L.A.* getting the Dem. Nat. Convention. As a matter of fact perhaps those who help shape nat. policy <u>should</u> t̶a̶k̶e̶ live in & inspect at first hand what the "new economics" of the past few decades have done for "Fun City" or w̶h̶a̶t̶ *in the words of* Mayor Beame* r̶e̶f̶e̶r̶r̶e̶d̶ ̶t̶o̶ ̶a̶s̶ the "Big Apple."

Seriously I don't believe any American where ever in the land he may live takes pleasure in the plight of our greatest city. N.Y. for more years than I've lived a̶s̶ has been the very symbol of Americas greatness. a̶ ̶c̶i̶t̶y̶ fFinancial capitol of the world, center of art, the theatre, publishing & style.

Today it is prostrate, facing default of its bonds which will have nation

---

*Abraham Beame

~~wide~~ if not world wide repercussions and dying the slow & painful death of bankruptcy. It's leaders cry out for help, asking the state & the nation to bail it out. But why should the people of Peoria, St. Louis or rural America be taxed to save this city of such great wealth?

If we were talking about a natural disaster, Americans would *mobilize,* as they always have, to help their neighbors. Even neighbors 3000 miles away. But N.Y. is not the victim of some calamity of nature or of unavoidable economic troubles. N.Y. is an example of what can happen to this entire country if we don't re-chart our course and restore common sense & fiscal responsibility to the handling of public affairs.

~~Sad~~ Cruel as it may sound, it would be foolish to tap our national resources to bail N.Y. out of its troubles when no one in the city seems moved to correct the policies which led to its present disastrous plight. It's bankruptcy is not the result of recession. There was no falling away of revenues. As a matter of fact real property values, inc. taxes and sales taxes have held up better than in most cities and N.Y. has probably the highest rate of taxation in the country.

The problem lies on the spending side. A whole army of politicians & city leaders past & present thought they could promise anything & everything and never face a day of reckoning. Tax revenues have been increasing 8% a year in N.Y.—but spending has gone up 15% a year.

That one city has almost 4X as many employees as the state govt. of Calif. the most populous state in the Union. There are 49 municipal workers for each 1000 residents. Most other cities run between 30 & 35. New York spends $151 a year per person on health and hospitals; most other cities are at $50 or below. Only one city in America of more than a million population spends more than $20 a year per person on welfare; New York is $315. It's city university is larger than virtually any state university in the land and not one student, regardless of means, pays a penny in tuition.

One last point. New York's swollen payroll is augmented by the most generous fringe benefits in government. For many employees, they equal 50% of base pay.

The sad fact is, New York City must face reality and save itself and we'd all better watch and learn.

This is RR   Thanks for listening. ❖

San Francisco
November 2, 1976

In the recent campaign season, "help for the cities," was kicked around quite considerable & the demagogery was ankle deep. I'll be right back.

When politicians at the Fed. level bleed for the inner city and ~~proclaim~~ *demand* that Fed dollars be funneled into the skyscraper walled canyons to stave off disaster some obvious questions go un-answered. For example 75% of the ~~people~~ tax paying citizenry live in the cities. ~~Are th~~ Is it being suggested that the other 25% be taxed to help the majority? Or if all the cities are in trouble does it really make sense for Wash. to extract taxes from the city folk & send it back as somehow new & additional financing?

There might be more than one answer to ~~these~~ *those* questions. Obviously the quarter of our people in rural America can't underwrite the cities. Just as obviously two cities in trouble can't help each other by exchanging tax dollars taken from their own inhabitants. It is true that part of our ~~troub~~ troubles stem from Washingtons confiscation of tax sources which should properly be left at State & local levels but more money is not as good an answer as less spending by the cities themselves.

While Roger Boas a three ~~term~~ term commissioner in San Franciscos combination city-county Gov. was up for ratification as ~~appointee~~ the cities chief administrative officer a few weeks ago that "less spending" answer was frankly confirmed. What makes this news~~worthy~~ WORTHY is that Roger Boas was and note I speak in the past tense an enthusiastic big spender during his time in govt. as a legislator. He says, "I was just like all the giveaway artists".... Labor would come along with some proposition ... and it was probably brought in by fellows who had been hanging your house signs during the campaign. It usually got through and was put on the ballot and nobody could understand it including the people who had put it on. We're paying for that now."

But times have changed. Boas says "Im very conservative now. I think it's the only way to survive." He gives figures that are probably typical of many if not most big cities which are crying for someone to bail them out. San Franciscos general expenses have increased 193% in the past 11 yrs. The breakdown of ~~those~~ *that* cost increase is more shocking. Pension *Payroll* costs have risen 528%, the municipal railway 409% and health & hospitals 312%.

Boas says "before there was a recognition that the cities were in *financial* trouble there wasn't too much thought given to containing what were often excessive demands from labor" and he adds "I voted for every one of them." He describes some demands as tremendous greed & crazy and says there should be "no give at all in financial matters." "Equitable, yes. Fair, yes. But no featherbedding."

San Francisco with a gross receipts tax on small business and excessive labor costs has seen an exodus of small business from the city. The story is probably typical of many cities faced with the problem Boas describes as "avoiding bankruptcy and still giving citizens decent services for their money."

Now if we can just have a few more converts. This is R.R. Thanks for listening. ❖

Mail
September 19, 1978

Everyone I'm sure has a story about mail delivery or non-delivery and they usually end with the line, "what can we do about it?" I'll be right back.

If prices in general had gone up at the same rate postal rates have climbed we'd probably be marching on Wash. Certainly it would be cheaper to eat our money than to buy groceries with it.

But Americans aren't complaining as much about the skyrocketing cost of stamps as they are the nosediving quality of service. Already substitutes *of various kinds* are popping up as alternatives to the post office. Every time however that one of those substitutes involves itself with first class mail,—delivery of letters or post cards, the law is invoked by postal authorities ~~closing down~~ *and* each such operation is closed down.

I reported to you some time ago about the young house wife in Rochester N.Y. who built a thriving business delivering business letters in downtown Rochester for 10¢ each, delivery the same day guaranteed. The Post office obtained an injunction and halted this invasion of it's monopoly on 1ˢᵗ class delivery even though it cant match price or delivery time.

Now we get a story that suggests the Postal authorities can truly see the sparrows fall. Millions of Americans grew up in this land getting their first lesson in free enterprise by mowing lawns, selling lemonade on the sidewalk or running errands. That may be going the way of the buggy whip and the village smithy.

In Charleston S.C. there is an enterprising young 14 year old named Kenny Maguire. He was learning *in* that old fashioned way about working & earning but now he's had a lesson in the arrogance of big govt. Congressman Eldon Rudd of Ariz. has brought the story of Kenny Maguire to light and I'm grateful to him for doing so.

Astride a bycycle Kenny earned $10 delivering 80 wedding invitations. ~~Now he's out of~~ That was the begining & the end of his delivery service. Postal authorities jumped in & grounded him for interfering with their legal monopoly over mail delivery. Kenny did the job faster than the post office can do it and he was certainly less expensive—by $2 ₵ for 80 invitations.

Does this mean that Mom can't ask Johnny to run next door with a note to a neighbor or a recipe? Congressman Rudd says that Congress should break the Postal Service monopoly, so that *not only* youngsters like Kenny but enterprising Americans of any age can provide the American People with the mail service they have a right to expect & which they are not getting.

About 35 or 40 years ago you could make a phone call across the country for about $25.70. And for that amount of money you could send almost 1300 letters from one coast to the other. Now you can make that phone call for 54 cents or thereabouts and for that amount of money you can only send 3 letters. ~~And~~ So the govt. keeps checking on & even suing the Bell System because they charge it's a monopoly.

This is RR   Thanks for listening. ❖

PERSONAL STORIES

Every now and then Reagan would write a radio essay on something of special personal concern to him. Below are half a dozen examples, including his thoughts on a new translation of the Bible, stories about acts of charity by T.K.E. (Tau Kappa Epsilon), his fraternity house at Eureka College, his friend John Wayne, and Christmas. The last essay is Reagan's final radio address, broadcast the day he announced his candidacy for the 1980 presidential nomination. In it he tells for the first time how he wrote these essays.

The Bible
September 6, 1977

What would you say if someone decided Shakespeares plays, ~~or~~ Charles Dickens novels or the music of Beethoven could be rewritten & improved? I'll be rite back.

Writing in the journal "The Alternative" Richard Hanser author of "~~Jesus the book~~" "*The Law & The Prophets*" *and* "Jesus: What Manner of Man is This?" has called attention to something that is more than a little mind boggling. It is my understanding that the Bible—(both the old & new testaments) has been the best selling book in the entire history of printing. ~~But more than that; back over the centuries~~ *years* ~~when the people were in the main illiterate~~

Now another attempt ~~is going to be~~ *has been* made to improve it. I say another because there have been several fairly recent efforts to—quote "make ~~it~~ *the bible* more readable & understandable"—unquote. But as Mr. Hanser so eloquently says, "For more than 3½ centuries its language and its images have penetrated more deeply into the general culture of the English speaking world, and been more dearly treasured, than anything else ever put on paper." He then quotes the irreverent H. L. Mencken who spoke of ~~it~~ it as purely a literary work and said it was, "probably the most beautiful piece of writing in any language."

They were, of course, speaking of the ~~King James~~ *authorized* version, the one that came into being when the England of King James was scoured for translators & scholars. ~~at a time when the English language~~ It was a time when the English language had reached it's peak of richness & beauty.

Now we are to have "The Good News Bible" which will be in, "the natural English of everyday adult conversation." I'm sure the scholars and clergymen supervised by the American Bible Society were sincerely imbued with the thought that they were taking religion to the people ~~in~~ *with* their "Good News Bible" but I cant help feeling we should *instead* be taking the people to religion ~~by~~ *and* lifting them with the beauty of language that has outlived the centuries.

Mr. Hanser has quoted from both the St. James version & the "Good News Bible" some well known passages for us to compare. A few thousand years ago Job said "How forcible are right words!" The new translators have him saying "Honest words are convincing." That's only for openers. There is the passage, "For in much wisdom is much grief: and he that increaseth knowledge increaseth sorrow." Is it really an improvement to say instead, "The wiser you are, the more worries you have; the more you know the more it hurts."

In the New Testament—Mathew, we read "The voice of the one crying in the wilderness. Prepare ye the way." ~~Now In t~~The Good News version translates that, "Someone is shouting in the desert. Get the road ready." It sounds like a straw boss announcing lunch hour is over.

The hauntingly beautiful 23rd Psalm is the same in both versions, for a few words "The Lord is my shepherd" but instead of ~~the following~~ *continuing* "I shall not want" we are supposed to say "I have everything I need."

The Christmas story has undergone some modernizing but one can hardly ~~called~~ call it improved. The wondrous words "Fear not: for, behold, I bring you good tidings of great joy" has become, "Don't be afraid! I am here with good news for you."

The sponsors of the "Good News" version boast that their bible is as readable as the daily paper—and so it is. But do readers of the daily news find themselves moved to ~~say~~ wonder, "at the gracious words which proceeded out of his mouth"? Mr. Hanser suggests that sadly the "tinkering & general horsing around with the sacred texts will no doubt continue" as pious drudges try to get it right. "It will not dawn on them that it has already been gotten right."

This is RR   Thanks for listening. ❖

Missing Person
April 3, 1978

I've had an opportunity to be on several campuses lately and the contrast with the riotous '60s makes it a happy experience. I'll be right back.

Having had ~~el~~ intimate contact with some ~~of~~ of *the* most violent of our Universities during the days of anti-war and anti-almost anything demonstrations it's a joy to be invited to a campus today. The students are courteous to visitors, aware of world happenings, and have inquiring not closed minds.

The contrast aroused many memories of that different time a decade ago and one EXPERIENCE in particular I'd like to share with you. As Gov. I was automatically a member of the board of regents of the U. of Calif. The ~~bord~~ *board* met monthly, ~~Each *each* time on a different campus~~ rotating the meeting place to each of the 9 campuses.

As the governing body of the U. the board was of course a legitimate target for the dissidents. Some would even travel from their own campus to the meeting place to make sure we would receive a proper reception.

The incident that continues to haunt me occurred on the campus ~~of~~ at San Diego. ~~When~~ I arrived there on one of those GREY Calif mornings. ~~where with a high fog overhead makes for a grey dreary day. I was met by a security detail that told me a special~~ *Anyplace else you'd say it was a cloudy day. In Calif. it is a high fog but it still makes for a dreary day. It wasn't brightened any when the advance security detail told me a special* reception had been planned for my arrival.

It seems the meeting was being held in a building deep in the campus requiring about a 200 yd. walk. ~~But they assured~~ The demonstrators had decided on a kind of silent vigil. The walk to the entrance of the bldg. was flanked by grass covered sloping embankments on which the students had gathered several deep leaving only a narrow path thru which I would have to march while they stared silently down at me.

Security had another idea not knowing whether the vigil would remain silent (and inactive) for the whole 200 yd. walk. They said they could drive me to the rear of the building & smuggle me in through a back door.

Frankly I'd had it by this time with the riots, & the pickets & the ~~van~~ *vandalism* and I refused. The~~re~~ir silent vigil wasn't going to keep me from going in the front door. So I started down the narrow path.

It's pretty hard not to appear self conscious with more than a thousand HOSTILE YOUNG people ~~stand~~ —most of them almost near enough to touch watching your every step & expression. It was a long 200 yards.

I was almost to the end of the ~~crowd~~ *ordeal* when ~~an~~ *a rather small,* attractive, blonde girl stepped out of the crowd & stood on the walk facing me. I thought "Oh Dear Lord what have they planned for me now. But she put out her hand and ~~said~~ spoke ~~and~~ *her* voice ringing like a bell in *all* that *deep* silence. She said "I just want to tell you I like everything you are doing." I took her hand but I couldn't thank her, there was a baseball-size lump in my throat. ~~I went on into the building~~ I've never forgotten that moment and her courage. I could go on into the building she had to stay out there with her peers. I never found out who she was. How I wish I could. I'd like to tell her what her bravery meant to me. I'd like to say thanks.

This is RR. Thanks for listening. ❧

John Wayne
June 29, 1979

This commentary will be a few minutes of remembering a friend. You probably think of him as a friend too.—I'll be right back.

† It is still difficult for me to realize that John Wayne is no longer here~~,~~. ~~larger than life and very much a part of our lives.~~ If you don't mind I'd like to share some memories with you.

~~I was out on the road—the mashed potato circuit—when the news came and I found I was not alone in my sorrow. Virtually every one I met—people who had never known Duke except as they saw him on the screen were saddened and wanted to talk about him. Most asked what was he really like?~~ Many people in these last few weeks have asked *what was he really like?*

~~The answer is,~~ *Well* he was just about what you saw on the screen. He stood up for what he believed was right, he placed a high premium on honor and he had a rare sensitivity. Nancy & I can bear witness to that.

There are 2 other men in Nancys life—both alike in many ways and yet different—John Wayne ~~or Duke~~ & Jimmy Cagney. Now I'd better explain this although I don't think any of you had any wrong ideas.

Some years ago before either of us knew Duke really well there was a time of labor trouble in Hollywood. As Pres. of the Screen Actors Guild I was up to my neck in it. I'd leave the house in the morning on my way to another of the meetings that filled my day. Nancy would be left with the trade papers & the movie columns in the newspapers.

~~Very often~~ Emotions ran high and very often I'd come in for ~~som~~ a pretty rough going over. Nancy hadn't developed *as she did later in Sacramento* the ability to read such attacks without getting upset.

On one particularly bad day she received a phone call right after she'd read the papers. It was John Wayne. He told her he just thought she might like to hear a friendly voice and then proceeded to tell her why she shouldn't let these stories get her down. A few minutes later she had another call, this time from Jimmy Cagney who said about the same things Duke had said. From then on every morning when the press was bad she'd get those two calls.

Then there came a time when a mass meeting had been called at which I'd have to preside. Nancy dreaded the thought of being there but wouldn't stay home. This time she received a call in the afternoon. It was Duke. He asked her if she'd feel better if ~~sh~~ he were there. The answer was "yes" of course. When it came time for me to go to the podium she was escorted to a place in the audience by Duke—dressed in a dinner jacket. He'd left a dinner party to be there.

A few years ago several of us were talking about a friend who was terminally ill. The question arose—would you rather know or not know if you were about to die. Duke said with no hesitation he'd want to know and in typical Wayne fashion added, "So you could throw your Sunday punch."

Several weeks before he left us he threw his Sunday punch—he told the Dr's. to use him in any way they could to learn if they could, anything that might one day help someone else. Then in the last hours of his pain he refused sedatives so he could be with his children & grandchildren.

Goodbye & God Bless You Duke.

†This should go as Number 1.

RR ❖

T.K.E.
May 8, 1979

Now why would 5 young men want to roll an empty beer barrel across the U.S. from coast to coast? I'll be right back.

† The largest Greek Letter College fraternity in the U.S. is Tau Kappa Epsilon, known on the campuses as T.K.E. It's members are referred to as Tekes.

On March 31ˢᵗ *in Boston Mass.* 6 Tekes from 6 different colleges, Missouri Valley College, U. of Wis., Newberry College of S. Car., James Madison U. of Va., ~~and~~ Ashland College of Ohio & Drake U. of Des Moines Iowa started rolling an empty beer keg. Their destination Los Angeles Calif. 3,300 miles away.

Now if nostalgia grips you and you think it's a return of old ~~time~~ fashioned spring time jinks like panty raids or swallowing goldfish hear me out. These young men and their fraternity brothers in more than 300 chapters are engaged in one of the largest public service projects ever undertaken by a fraternity.

By the time they arrive in Los Angeles they will have gone through 16 states. Arrival in L.A. is scheduled for June 12ᵗʰ. All across the country local college chapters are notified when the barrel rolling team is in their vicinity and various celebrations are held.

What would make these young men set out on such a journey? Well I said it was a public service project. They are crossing the country raising money for St. Judes Childrens Research Hospital. They have the blessing of the Grand Council ~~of TKE {~~ the board of directors } *of TKE* and the undying gratitude of one of their own fraternity brothers.

St. Jude hospital was founded in 1962 by a Teke named Danny Thomas. Yes that is <u>the</u> Danny Thomas who has brought so much laughter to audiences in theatres, on TV, the screen & night clubs. Through his efforts over the years he has also ~~brought~~ helped bring ~~heal~~ life & health to uncounted thousands of children. St. Jude hospital has been Dannys cause, his hobby & his avocation. His ways of saying thanks to the Lord for the blessings that he himself has known.

St. Jude Hospital is the only institution solely dedicated to conducting basic & clinical research in the catastrophic diseases of children. ~~The research hospital~~ *It* is located in Memphis Tenn. One of it's most frequent & welcome visitors is Danny Thomas.

If the barrel rollers are on schedule they should be somewhere in New Mexico by now. Their goal is one mil. dollars. They should be in Ariz. the last few days in May & early June crossing into Calif. at Earp on June 7ᵗʰ. And as I said, reaching L.A. June 12ᵗʰ 3324 miles ~~later~~ from Boston.

The other night I saw a TV movie about Fraternity life. It was the old stereotype about snobbish young men & women living selfish lives, ~~in which they lookeding~~ *LOOKING* down on non-members and being pretty useless & obnoxious in general. Maybe that was true in a long dead past but not any more. They're too busy doing things like helping children.

Would you forgive me if I told you I'm a Teke.

This is RR Thanks for listening.

†Due to the schedule make this the 1ˢᵗ broadcast.

RR. ❖

Christmas
February 20, 1978

Someone sent me a Christmas item I thought you might like to hear. It is the nativity according to Marx & Lenin. I'll be right back.

In these few months since ~~Christmas~~ *the holidays* I've told a couple of Christmas stories on these broadcasts and as a result received one in return. Or possibly it was because of a broadcast about the Ukraine. Whatever the reason I'm grateful for it.

When the Ukraine was free and not ~~in~~ *under* Soviet bondage Christmas was of course the religious day that it is in the Western World. A favorite Ukrainian carol was "Nova Radist' Stala"—"The Joyous News Has Come to Us." A Ukranian now teaching at the U. of Utah has written an article ~~showing~~ *about* the evolution of Christmas under communism—at least as it applies to this Carol.

In the good days of freedom the people of the Ukraine sang these verses: "The joyous news has come—Which never was before, Over a cave, above a manger, A bright star has lit the world, Where Jesus was born—From a Virgin Maiden, Clad in raiment poor Like a peasant baby. The shepherds with a lamb Surrounded the child, And on flected knees They him glorified: We beg you, our King, We pray to you Today: Grant happiness & joy To this family."

Now of course this was neither fitting nor permitted under communism, ~~but~~ still the Commissars were a little leery about an outright ban. They chose to allow the song after some rewriting, in fact they provided the Ukrainians with two versions neither of which could actually be said to have made the Ukrainian hit parade.

Here is the first version; "The joyous news has come—Which never was before, A Red star with 5 tails ~~hH~~as brightly lit the world, (See they only changed one ~~line in that verse) The~~ line in that verse—but wait) The Altars have crumbled, And all the Kings have fallen. Glory to the working people, To shepherds & the ploughmen! Glory to our host And to his fair hostess! May their friendly household Know only happiness. May all their family, Especially the children, Grow up to be strong & happy, So's to fight the rich men." ~~(Can't you see the childrens happy faces in that last line)~~ *You know our own kids could probably get away with singing that one in the classroom)*

The second version is a little meatier even though the got ~~this~~ the Christmas story down to 2 verses instead of 4. "The joyous news has come—Which never was before, Long-awaited star of freedom—Lit the skies in

October. ~~W~~ (If you're wondering what happened to ~~≠~~ December—the revolution took place in October) "Where formerly lived the Kings—And had the roots their nobles, There today with simple folks—Lenins glory hovers."

The people of the Ukraine both in & ~~out of~~ *outside* the Iron Curtain were so carried away by these verses they added one of their own. They sing it but carefully refrained from putting it in the song books.

It goes; "We beg you our Lord, We pray to you today: Grant us freedom, return glory—~~t~~*To* our mother Ukraine!" I guess we all hope their prayer is answered.

This is RR   Thanks for listening. ❖

Miscellaneous and Goodbye
October 25, 1979

For the last time I'm cleaning up my desk with a few items you should hear. I'll be right back.

Believe me, my friends I speak to you today with mixed emotions and maybe it's fitting that I make it the final desk cleaning day.

The first item is, in my opinion, very serious for all of us and another indication of how far we are straying from the very basics of our system.

The Mountain States Legal Foundation has filed a suit with the Fed. govt. claiming that constitutional rights of several states are being violated. When Congress voted to extend the time for states to ratify the Equal Rights Amendment it refused to allow several states to change their position and rescind the approval they had given ~~several years ago~~ *earlier.*

† A few weeks ago the U.S. Dept. of Justice, which should be the defender above all of constitutional rights, filed a motion with the ~~Idaho~~ Idaho court where the case is being heard. The motion was to disqualify the judge appointed to hear the case.

Now hear this! The Justice Dept. wants him disqualified because ~~he is a member~~ *of his religion.* He is a member of the Mormon church. I leave it to you ~~what sue~~ *to imagine* what ~~that~~ such a precedent could do to our entire system of justice if judges can be either assigned or disqualified on the basis of religion.

These next few items may ~~cause you to~~ *make you laugh* but you'll hurt a little too. A former Calif. Supt. of Ed. Dr. Max Rafferty has uncovered a few items having to do with extremes in the battle of the sexes.

H.E.W. has discovered that in one public school more boys than girls were being spanked. If the school dosen't want a mil. dollars in ~~≠~~ Fed. aid to be withheld it will henceforth spank girls & boys in exactly equal numbers.

Radio

Miscellaneous & Goodbye

This must be last broadcast

①

For the last time I'm cleaning up my desk with a few items you should hear.

I'll be right back.

Believe me, my friends I speak to you today with mixed emotions and maybe it's fitting that I make it the final desk cleaning day.

The first item is, in my opinion, very serious for all of us and another indication of how far we are straying from the very basics of our system. The Mountain States Legal Foundation has filed a suit with the Fed. govt. claiming that constitutional rights of several states are being violated. When Congress voted to extend the time for states to ratify the Equal Rights Amendment it refused to allow several states to change their position and received the approval they had given earlier.

A few weeks ago the U.S. Dept. of Justice, which should be the defender above all of constitutional rights, filed a motion with the Idaho court where the case is being heard. The motion was to disqualify the judge appointed to hear the case.

Now hear this! The Justice Dept. wants him disqualified because of his religion. He is a member of the Mormon church. I leave it to you to imagine what such a precedent could do to our entire system of justice if judges can be either assigned or disqualified on the basis of religion.

These next few items may make you laugh but you'll hurt a little too. A former Calif. Supt. of Ed. Dr. Max Rafferty has uncovered a few items having to do with extremes in the battle of the sexes.

H.E.W. has discovered that in one public school more boys than girls were being spanked. If the school doesn't want a mil. dollars in Fed aid to be with held it will henceforth spank girls & boys in exactly equal numbers.

In Woonsocket R.I. the City Council has ruled that from now on those metal covered holes in our streets we've long called "man holes" will hence forth be known as "person holes." And in Missoula Montana a "Peeping Tom" ordinance is now a "Peeping Person" law.

Well that's all the desk clearing for today and as I indicated when I began it has been my least such chore. This is my final commentary. I'm going to miss these visits with all of you. I've enjoyed every one. Even writing them has been a lot of fun. I've scratched them out on a yellow tablet in airplanes, riding in cars, and at the ranch when the sun went down.

When ever I've told you about some mis-fortune befalling one of our fellow citizens you've opened your hearts & your pocket books and gone to the rescue. I know you have because the individuals you helped have written to let me know. You've done a great deal to strengthen my faith in this land of ours and it's people. You are the greatest.

Some time later today if you happen to catch me on television you'll understand why I can no longer bring you these commentaries.

This is RR. And from the bottom of my heart — thanks for listening.

In Woonsockett R.I. the City Council has ruled that from now on those metal covered holes in our streets we've long called "manholes" will henceforth be known as "person holes." And in Missoula Montana a "Peeping Tom" ordinance is now a "Peeping Person" law.

Well that's all the desk cleaning for today and as I indicated a moment ago when I began it has been my last such chore. This is my final commentary.

I'm going to miss these visits with all of you. I've enjoyed every one. Even writing them has been a a lot of fun. I've scratched them out on a yellow tablet in airplanes, riding in cars, and at the ranch when the sun went down. W

Whenever I've told you about some mis-fortune befalling one of our fellow citizens you've opened your hearts & your pocketbooks and gone to the rescue. I know you have because the individuals you helped have written to let me know. You've done a great deal to strengthen my faith in this land of ours and it's people. You are the greatest.

Sometime later today if you happen to catch me on television you'll understand why I can no longer bring you these commentaries.

This is RR. and from the bottom of my heart—thanks for listening.

†This must be last broadcast ❖

Part Four

OTHER
WRITINGS

"I believe it is our pre-ordained

destiny to show all mankind that

they, too, can be free without

having to leave their native shore."

OTHER WRITINGS
NOV. 6, 1925–NOV. 5, 1994

This is a selection of Reagan's writings from the earliest one we have—a short story written when he was fourteen years old—to his final public communication, the letter on his devastating illness, Alzheimer's disease, written when he was eighty-three. They are arranged chronologically.

In one of the dozens of stories about Reagan as movie actor that appeared in various popular magazines over the years, a reporter writes in 1947 that "In private life, Reagan is most interested in writing." Indeed, whatever else he was doing, he wrote. Our selections barely touch on the vast quantity of correspondence, both personal and issue-oriented, he carried on with a wide variety of people over many years. Even in the White House he regularly read and answered letters from citizens every week.

The two stories that follow were written as English assignments in Dixon High School, the first when Reagan was fourteen years old and the second when he was sixteen. *

Hallowe'en
November 6, 1925

"Twas the nite of Hallowe'en, but nothing was still." The good people went to sleep that <u>memorial</u>[*able*] * * Saturday night with the sounds of laughter,

---

*Both are in the Pre-Presidential Papers, Special Collection. Ronald Reagan Presidential Library. First discovered by Edmund Morris.
* *Apparently a teacher's correction.

running feet, and muffled shouts ringing in their ears. Then were they peaceful, and only then, at twelve oclock a gasping, panting roar awakened the town.

The northbound passenger was waiting on the siding. The freight due from the north was vainly fighting to get over a hundred foot stretch of greased track. These trains were only held a mere matter of an hour and a half by the evidence of a stirring juvenile populace.

But the next morning a greater shock came. The city was transformed, but less beautiful. The telephone poles were artistically draped with porch furniture, signs, and various parts of buggys and wagons. The streets looked like rummage sales, while schools and stores found their doorways piled with representatives of the last nights ≠.

But alas! Except for an occasional chair on a telephone pole, the scene was soon shattered by the respective owners of the collected articles. ❖

[B+] *

Yale Comes Through
November 17, 1927

Mark had with an air of mystery and promise, insisted that I dine with him. And here we were, in one of those little cafes tucked in a cranny just off broadway, a place without the elegance of ~~famous~~ famous places, and without the soiled squallor of the bowery, a place that defied any attempt to classify it. A place where people from all walks of life seemed to lose their air of the commonplace. I was agog with interest as Mark, conscious of this perfect setting, leaned toward me and, spoke in a hoarse, strained whisper.

His opening remark stunned me into silence. "Listen to these two men next to us, I have been noticing them for two days." His eyes glittered as he spoke, "There is some gigantic robbery ~~plan~~ being planned."

He motioned for me to cover my surprise. I tried to act bored and disinterested, as I gazed around the room. The two men next to us, had their heads close together over the table, they seemed to be in the midst of a heated discussion.

One was a tall dark man with glittering black eyes, and a lean hard jaw. His companion who seemed to do most of the talking was a swarthy, dark haired man, short and stout with a pointed Van Dyke beard, and a pointed waxed mustache.

Suddenly we heard the talkative man hiss, "Fool! bombs are too

*Reagan's grade

bungling, gas is smooth and silent." My heart suddenly cross blocked my liver, and my adams apple drop-kicked a tonsil.

The conspirators soon left, and so did we. As we passed their table Mark snatched a piece of paper from the mess of dishes. We paid our checks, and climbed into Marks, "sweetheart of Yale flivver."

Several moments later we were still gazing at each other with horror struck eyes. The paper he held was an accurate map of the United States Treasury building at Washington. The word gas seared through my brain like a hurtling meteorite. For outlined in red ink on the map was the complete ventilating system of the treasury building.

By the notes etc. we found that on the chosen day, a hired murderer clothed in a specially constructed gas mask would empty hundreds of cannisters of gas into the ventilating tubes. And all over the building, clerks, bookkeepers, and marines guarding the vaults, would be killed like rats in a trap. The poison would creep through the tubes, fanned on by the strong air currents, filling the corridors and vaults, strangling the marines with poisonous, slimy fingers, like creeping tendrils of some giant vine writhing, and crushing. The thieves would then enter, protected by masks, and plunder at will, while the air was still murky with floating clouds of death, and while men lay in sprawled heaps of twisted agony.

We were speechless, it did not seem possible that two mere undergraduates of Yale should stand alone between this gang of maniacs, and the horrible tragedy outlined on that soiled paper.

But being two members of the much discussed, and ofttimes cursed, younger generation we went into immediate action. We rattled, and clattered down to the nearest police station, where we were well known, and welcome. We spluttered, and splurged, and finally told our story, and showed our little map. The sergeant went into action also. And soon we were speeding through the city, in a big police car. Mark having followed the men, the day before, we soon reached their place of abode, and here events moved so swiftly that it left me a confused blur of shouts, crashing doors, and feeble protests.

Soon we stood before the two criminals who were rocked by gales of laughter. The seargeant looked at me very disgusted. "What splendid advertising," said the tall man "to think that our scenario should get such recognition." "What do you think of that," said Mark dangerously calm.

"Sock," he sent the would be author sprawling and seized a torn sheet of news paper. The men cried out in protest, and then sprang for the door. They were seized by several burly policemen however.

"I'm sorry sergeant," spoke up Mark, "but these men are wanted even if they cant rob the government."

He held before our startled eyes a screaming headline, "Lunatics escape." "Reward." Beneath these startling words were photograps of our new found friends. So the honor of "old Eli" was upheld. ❖

This poem, written by Reagan when he was seventeen years old, was printed in the Dixonian, *his high school yearbook, in 1928.*

Life*
1928

LIFE

I wonder what it's all about, and why
We suffer so, when little things go wrong?
We make our life a struggle,
When life should be a song.

Our troubles break and drench us,
Like spray on the cleaving prow
Of some trim Gloucester schooner.
As it dips in a graceful bow.

Our troubles break and drench us
But like that cleaving prow,
The wind will fan and dry us.
And we'll watch some other bow.

But why does sorrow drench us
When our fellow passes on?
He's just exchanged life's dreary dirge
For an eternal life of song.

What is the inborn human trait
That frowns on a life of song?
That makes us weep at the journey's end,
When the journey was oft-times wrong?

Weep when we reach the door
That opens to let us in,

---

*Dixonian 1928 yearbook; copy in Pre-Presidential Papers, Special Collection. Ronald Reagan Presidential Library.

And brings to us eternal peace
As it closes again on sin.

Millions have gone before us,
And millions will come behind.
So why do we curse and fight
At a fate both wise and kind.

We hang onto a jaded life
A life full of sorrow and pain.
A life that warps and breaks us,
And we try to run through it again.

R.R., '28. ❖

This short story from his college years was written just after he turned nineteen.

Squall*
February 24, 1930

The wind sweeps down the river with a siren ~~like~~ roar as it bends the trees on either shore like a hand pulled across the bristles of a hairbrush. Closer it comes, the sullen water shakes its gray back like a bear awakening from a nap. Oily ~~waters~~ rollers appear; Swifter, higher they climb,—white crests break at the peak of each swell. The canoe rises on the first few nervously, gingerly as your dipping paddle hurls it forward.

Then like an avenging pack the wind is upon you, battering, pulling the paddle from your grasp, screaming in your ears. The whitecaps fling themselves up under your prow, up—up you hang motionless then down with sickening speed, crashing into the next wave with a shuddering blow that racks every rib. The next wave catches the prow still down, the lowered head takes the shock and rises drunkenly as water pours in on the gun'nles.

Up again, up-up—the wind catches the high curved prow and swings it over, the low stern slides into a trough. Over you heal—over until you must hang far out over the upper gun'nle, all your weight on the paddle. Slowly at first then with a swift pivot the canoe heads into the wind again. Desperately you paddle now, dip-pull, dip-pull—your shoulders ache your throat swells it seems as though your very heart must be torn out.

*Pre-Presidential Papers, Special Collection. Ronald Reagan Presidential Library.

A massive gray wall towers ahead of you. Up goes the prow—up—it hangs, then heals over—you have lost! The canoe is off that absolute hairline of wind heading.

Over, over, until you are standing on your gun'nle, with a sick lurch you slide into the trough broadside. You wheel out of the trough and go scudding before the wind. The stern drops from under you—then up it comes on the crest and you surge forward borne on the very wave that has just defeated you.

Quickly the wind dies, the waves smooth out and you must wait for another squall to renew the feud. ❖

Reagan wrote the following essay for a college course on romantic literature.

*Return to the Primitive**

Spring 1930

Although Wordsworth was the main impetus in the Romantic movement that swept through the worlds literature, the mutterings of such a movement began softly and generally among many writers before him.

One of the earliest traces of this new literature was a renewed interest in primitive life and "the noble savage." This interest took form in many ways. Some writers wrote of the simple life and its virtues others took to glorifying early man, and many merely touched it in a renewal of nature study.

In the glorifying of ancient man, poets found a glamour in the primitive ≠ savage—especially those Americans who had the fierce Indians before them. Others took to painting the rustic peasant type with a romantic glamour. An interest and turning to America is noticed after this as we can see in "Berkeleys"—"Verses On the Prospect of Planting Arts and Learning in America."

> "The Muse, disgusted at an age and clime
> Barren of every glorious theme,
> In distant lands now waits a better time,
> Producing subjects worthy fame."

This stanza shows the growing disgust with all the classic subjects so worn out in Europe. The last stanza of this poem shows in what direction the

---

*Used with the permission of Eureka College, Eureka, Illinois, where the original is on display.

poets interest was turning, lured no doubt by the simplicity & romantic adventure of frontier life and exploration.

> "Westward the course of empire takes its way;
> The four first acts already past,
> A fifth shall close the drama with the day;
> Times noblest offspring is the last.

From Henry Brooke's "Universal Beauty," we have such titles as "Nature Superior To Civilization",—"The Splendor of Insects" and "Moral Lessons From Animal Life." These alone show the content of his verses and to what he owes his subject matter.

In Joseph Warton's "Enthusiast," we have the author offering lifes *worldly* glories to himself and choosing rugged nature instead. In a dozen places he expresses the enthusiastic return to nature.—

> "Happy the first of men, ere yet confined
> To smoky cities; who in sheltering groves,
> Warm caves, and deep-sunk valleys lived and loved,
> By cares unwounded; what the sun and showers,
> And genial earth untillaged, could produce,
> They gathered grateful, or the acorn brown
> Or blushing berry; by the liquid lapse
> Of murmuring waters called to slake their thirst,
> Or with fair nymphs their sun browned limbs to bathe;
> With nymphs who fondly clasped their favorite a youths,
> Unawed by shame, beneath the beechen shade,
> Nor Wiles nor artificial coyness knew.
> Then doors and walls were not; the melting maid
> Nor frown of parents feared, nor husbands threats;
> Nor had cursed gold their tender hearts allured:
> Then beauty was not venal. Injured love,
> Oh! well wither God of raptures, art thou fled?"

Then too we have him later in the same poem expressing the new rebellion against the staid classic rules of poetry that dominated what we term the preromantic age.

> "What are the lays of artful Addison,
> Coldly correct, to Shakespeare's warblings wild?"

In the poems and stories about Robin Hood we find a praise of the simple life, indeed most of these poems such as "Robin Hood & Guy of Gisborne," almost make the reader want to take a bow and arrow and live in the "Greenwood."

Henry Brooke also glorifies the simple life in his "The Conventional Child and The Natural" from "The Fool of Quality." It is a story of two sons the elder is loved so much by his mother that the younger brother is sent to a peasant woman to be reared as her own son. Naturally the petted older son grows up temperamental and spoiled. While his little brother grows sturdy and healthy and with many wise and good qualities. Even at the age of five years Brooke has Harry the younger wise enough to disdain convention and the artificialities of aristocratic society to say nothing of having a well developed sense of justice etc.

But I'm not discussing this to criticize, merely to show the growing romantic tendency towards glorifying nature and the simple life of man. ❖

Reagan abhorred war and said so throughout his life. Here is a glimpse of his thinking at age twenty.

Killed in Action*
May 7, 1931

James Edwards dropped the evening paper in his lap and stared thoughtfully into the blazing fire. "David Bering" he said softly, "David Bering of the A.E.F. suicide club."

Slowly the book lined walls receded. His comfortable arm chair was the yellow slime of a shellhole as he crouched, shivering from the damp chill that "issue blankets" and army ponchos could not keep from eating into the very bones of a man. Ten feet away his companion loosened the top on an ammunition box, prying it up with a trench knife. Edwards rose wearily and pulled a torn canvas over the machine gun to protect it against the drizzling rain.

There was a slopping noise from behind them and *Sergeant* Riley ~~the Sergeant~~ slid from the communication trench into the shellhole. "Cozy place you got here boys," he grinned through a weeks growth of beard. "Sure the waters fine," growled Edward. "Hows the ammo holding out," asked Riley. The *bent* figure ~~bent~~ over the box straightened up "Fine, we got plenty," he said, "but we cant eat the d—n stuff, the lead gets in our teeth." "Out of

*Pre-Presidential Papers, Special Collection. Ronald Reagan Presidential Library.

grub, eh? Well, the brasshats must think we left our bellys back in training camp. There isn't a kitchen within ten miles of the front," answered Riley. He fished around in his pack for a moment then tossed over a mouldy half loaf of rye bread, "Here you guys can have a banquet on that. If a work out-fit stumbles in I'll send some hot grub up. But you wont be needing food in a little while. We've got info that the 'Jerrys' are coming over at noon, its 8:10 now, so tighten your belts and hang on til then." He turned back into the trench. "See you later," he called, "I hope." They could hear him laughing as he splashed through the mud.

"Cheerful devil," said Bering as he looked after the departing officer. David Bering was a good looking youngster about 22 years old. Still young and unspoiled ~~by~~ after two years of army life, one of them spent in the trenches.

"Why not be cheerful," demanded Edwards with a bitter laugh, "this is a noble work we are doing, you know. Making the world safe for democracy." "Poor old Jim," grinned Dave, "after a whole year of glorious combat you're still a cynic." "That's just it," the older man said seriously "we are a bunch of hams and we know it. You know this whole mess is a mistake as well as I do. Why what in Gods name have any of us got against those Heinies? Not a thing. We're heros now, but when we get it in the neck and the fracas is all over we'll be ~~≠~~ tramps."

"When its over," Bering repeated softly "Gee, it'll be worth fighting for."

"What will," asked Edwards more to keep the conversation going than from any desire to know about Daves private life. "Well I'll have one more year to go at Harvard and then the city and a job. There's a girl in my home town and—well we've planned things together from then on."

Edwards was not old himself, but his thirty years had robbed him of some of Berings optimism, ~~of~~ *his* idealism and youth. A lump came to his throat as he listened to the boy talk of sacrifice and glory and heroism and he cursed mentally at a world so ordered that once every generation it must be bathed in the blood of youth like this one.

They were silent for a while as Dave opened cartons of cartridges and Jim pulled down his last Y.M. Fag. It was 11:30 when the fireworks started. The Boche laid down a curtain barrage behind our front line and then proceeded to flatten the trenches. For thirty minutes the bombardment continued until the very heavens seemed shaken by the blasts. A whistle rising to a shrill scream, then an earsplitting crash rocked the earth.

At 12:00 sharp the thunder stopped so suddenly that the silence hurt ones ears. "Here they come," cried Dave, leaping to the gun. Edwards glanced above the sand bags as he ~~dove~~ pulled the canvas covering aside. A gray wave was crawling slowly across the mud a scant hundred yards away.

The allied artillery came into the fight with a barrage laid in front of the advancing troops. It didn't seem possible for a fly to come through that wall of flaming steel alive, but the Heines did. Straight through that inferno, closing in as ~~the~~ gaps opened in their ranks. The stuttering "tac tac" of machine guns could be heard now above the roar of the big shells. Bering was crouched over the gun gripping the jerking butt as it spouted a stream of death. Edwards fed the belts to the greedy breech swiftly. The barrage had lifted and was now leveling the German trench to prevent the moving forward of replacements. Slowly the Yank fire drove them back. Suddenly Edwards straightened up his face blank, then he crumpled forward over the smoking gun. Bering uttered an oath and quickly dragged him ~~back~~ down to the bottom of the pit. He rolled him over on his back and loosened his tunic. There was an ugly wound in his left shoulder and he was losing blood fast. Dave quickly fashioned a pad and bound it to the wound, after which he rigged a sling ~~out of a gas mask~~ *from his belt* and propped Jim up ~~aga~~ in the shelter of the sand bags.

~~Jim~~ *The wounded man* had begun to come around before the operation was finished, but when Dave lifted him a wave of nausea overcame him and he fainted again.

Several hours later Riley came up with a relief crew and found Edwards babbling deliriously ~~while~~ *as* Bering endeavored to hold him in the shell hole. Riley and Bering carried him ~~through~~ back ~~and he was sent to a base hospital~~ *to the trench. An hour later he was taken to a base hospital.*

When he was finally released the armistice had been signed and he was an ex service man with an honourable discharge and a twisted shoulder. He had traced the old outfit in an effort to find his buddy. But all he could learn was that Bering had been gassed a week before the armistice and sent home. All further attemps to find him had been in vain.

Thirteen years. James Edwards picked up the paper again and glanced at the obscure news item.

:: A tramp, David Bering met his death today beneath the wheels of a fast Santa Fe freight.

Bering an ex service man had been gassed in the war and was bumming his way to the Speedway *veterans* hospital for treatment. He attempted to board the moving train and lost his footing. He was thrown under the wheels when he fell.

Notices have been ~~sent~~ broadcasted but no relatives or friends have claimed the body. He will be buried in the potters field. ❧

Less than two weeks after signing a movie contract with Warner Bros. and arriving in Hollywood, the twenty-six-year-old Reagan began writing a weekly series of articles about his career for the Des Moines Sunday Register. *They show a young Reagan who is effusively happy with his new life, interacting with some of Hollywood's stars, complete with many photos. Many years later, when asked if the studio helped him write the series, he replied, "No, I wrote 'em, and I never got paid." * The newspaper chose the headlines for the articles.*

This is the first of seventeen articles he wrote.

The Making of a Movie Star**
June 13, 1937

[*Dutch Reagan, former sports announcer for radio station WHO, Des Moines, is now in Hollywood where he has a contract with Warner Bros. He is now at work on his first picture. And he has agreed to write a letter to the folks back home every week, telling them all about what happens to a newcomer to the movies. These letters will be published every Sunday in The* Des Moines Sunday Register. *Here is the first one.*]

HOLLYWOOD, CAL.—Not so long ago the gentlemen who run the Des Moines Register and Tribune would have grinned cheerfully while they slit my throat—at least I had that impression when I was broadcasting over WHO—and here I am, telling the home folks through their generous columns how it feels to be a male "Alice in Wonderland."

I guess it's all a part of the crazy pattern which my life has become since a few weeks ago I was introduced to Max Arnow, Warner Bros. casting director, invited to make a screen test and suddenly woke up with a movie contract in my fist.

Hope my friends don't think I've suddenly gone nutty and already have the idea that I'm pushing Clark Gable, Dick Powell and the other boys around for a place in the spotlight because of the title on this series.

"The Making of a Star" is Basil Walters' idea, not mine, and personally I think the managing editor is taking an awfully lot for granted.

As a matter of fact, I feel very humble and not a little bit scared at the present writing. However, this isn't getting on with the story.

Edmund Morris, DUTCH: A Memoir of Ronald Reagan (New York: Random House, 1999), p. 133n.
***Des Moines [Iowa] Register.*

I left Des Moines in a cloud of dust and with every intention in the world of taking things easy. There was no particular hurry to get to Hollywood, although the studio did intimate that it would be just as well not to stop off to feed the bears in Yellowstone on my way out.

But I got a cramp in my foot, and somehow or other couldn't get it off the gas pedal and at the end of the first day looked up to discover I was in Cheyenne, Wyo., 650 miles from home.

Ever since I had signed the contract and committed myself to at least a brief whirl at the movies, I'd had the same sort of a feeling that a man must have in death row at Fort Madison. He knows he has to walk up the scaffold and take it in the neck, and is anxious to get it over with as quickly as possible.

That must be why I made 600 miles the second day, from Cheyenne to Nehi—a town about 100 miles west of Salt Lake City, Utah. I was flagged down by a motorcycle cop in the Mormon capital. He told me I'd been doing 60 miles an hour in a 25 mile zone.

"Sergeant," I told him—that's a trick I learned when I was a police reporter, always to call any cop without stripes a sergeant, because it flatters them—"I've just come from Iowa where they have no speed limits and I'm not used to looking for signs."

"Where are you going, buddy?" he demanded.

"Hollywood," I answered, proudly. "I'm an actor."

"I oughta lock you up," he growled, slightly sore. I guess he thought I was kidding him.

But I fished my contract out of my pocket and showed him that I was going to get paid for acting, anyway, and he shook his head in bewilderment and waved me on.

From Nehi to Los Angeles is one awful ride, especially crossing the hot desert in the middle of the day. Last summer in Des Moines was like zero weather by comparison.

I only knew of one hotel in Los Angeles and finally found it, the Biltmore. I'd stayed there before when I was out here with the Cubs. I was so tired I could hardly wobble, having made 640 miles that day, but after a shower and change of clothes I felt like I might live and went downstairs to the Biltmore Bowl.

I really would rather have gone to bed, but I had a job to do and I was going to do it if I passed out on my feet.

I would have been lower than the underside of a snake if I hadn't hunted up Joy Hodges the very first thing, and personally expressed the thanks I'd already given for the part she played in getting me into pictures.

You see it was Joy—who started her career singing over WHO—who had introduced me to George Ward, the agent. Ward suggested I might have screen possibilities and before I could close my mouth to say no, he'd called up Max Arnow and made a date for me to meet him. Which brought the screen test and my job.

Joy is now starring with Jimmy Grier's orchestra in the Biltmore Bowl, and she was so happy I'd taken at least the first step up the ladder that she could hardly sing. While she was at the microphone I got to thinking about Des Moines and all the people I know, and the next thing I knew someone was shaking me.

"Hey, Dutch!" Joy was yelling. "You can't sleep here. You'd better go up-stairs and climb into the hay. Besides, the bowl of soup doesn't make a very good pillow."

I shook myself awake and staggered out, expecting to sleep like the well known log. But I was so excited with what I had to face the following day and from the after-effects of my hard drive that I tossed about all night.

Bright and early the next morning, dressed in my best bib and tucker, I was at Warner Bros. studio out in Burbank ready to report to Mr. Arnow.

I had confirmed in my bedroom mirror the fact that I looked pretty snappy before I left. My white sport coat, tailored to my measure and never before worn, would show Hollywood that I knew a thing or two and read Esquire regularly. Especially, in combination with my new blue slacks.

I smiled my prettiest for Mr. Arnow as I walked into his office and helped myself to a chair.

"Where in hell did you get that coat?" he demanded, giving me a fishy-eyed once over. While I was stuttering he went on: "You can't wear that out-fit. The shoulders are too big—they make your head look too small."

Disappointed and crestfallen, I tried to explain that the shoulders weren't padded, that my shoulders are broad and I had bought the coat as the very latest cut in sports wear.

"Sports my eye," Arnow grunted and pushed a couple of buttons. A young man burst into the office.

"Yes, Mr. Arnow," he said, before he was asked.

"Take him over to the wardrobe and see what the tailor can do with this outfit," the casting director ordered. "He looks like a Filipino."

"Yes, Mr. Arnow," the young man answered, and led me out.

I hate to tell you what that tailor did to my beautiful coat. All the tucks and pleats, all the looseness was ruthlessly whacked out while I sat by and saw murder done. He altered the shoulder lines to make them look narrow.

When I put it on it felt like a strait-jacket, but Mr. Arnow nodded his approval when he saw me and I knew I was hooked. He sent the pleasant young man with me to the makeup department, and there I was turned over to the tender mercies of Perc Westmore, famous for making people look like they ain't.

Westmore stood up in the middle of the floor, and while I fidgeted, walked around me, squinting from all angles. I felt just like a prime steer must feel when it's shown in the prize ring at the stock pavilion.

"That Arnow guy must think I'm Houdini," I heard Westmore mutter, not too far under his breath. "Some of the mugs he signs up!"

A vision of the great American desert flashed across my mind. Also the long hours I'd spent behind the wheel of my car getting here, and I could see myself doing the same thing all over again, but pointed in the opposite direction. This time, I decided, I'd take it easy—say 30 miles an hour.

When Westmore finally sighed, and suggested that perhaps he might be able to make me look human, I felt like I'd been reprieved on the scaffold.

"Come in tomorrow for some tests," he said, and I beat it out of there in a hurry, only to bump into Mr. Arnow outside.

"Come on, we're going to look at your screen test," he said. I entered the projection room with all the eagerness of a hobo getting a free meal, and came out like a whipped dog with its tail between its legs.

The test, made when I was broadcasting the activities of the Cubs out here training, was TERRIBLE. It only lasted a few minutes, but I was scrooched down so far in my chair that I was almost on the floor when it finished.

"Why," I whispered to Mr. Arnow, "why did you hire me?"

He laughed so hard I thought he was going to rupture a blood vessel. ❖

This handwritten letter replying to a critic of one of the General Electric Theatre presentations provides some perspective on those years.

Letter to the Editor of The Catholic Reporter*

c. 1962

Dear Sir

I am very late with this but the March 30 ~~Column~~ edition of your paper has just been brought to my attention. In that issue your TV critic Chris Con-

---

*Hoover Institution Records, Box 994; Ronald Reagan Biography, GE & Borax, 1954–65. Hoover Institution Archives. *The Catholic Reporter* was located in Kansas City, Missouri.

don reviewed our G.E. Theatre presentation based on the real life experiences of ~~Mis~~ Mrs. Marion Miller.

It is not normal practise with me to answer critics or protest unfavorable reviews. In this case however Mr. Condon didn't exactly confine himself to criticism of our dramatic quality, his main concern was with our ideology. In fact his concern was so great he suggested the networks or the govt. should take steps to prevent this ~~type of program from happening again.~~ *sort of thing.*

General Elec. was accused of using the program to promote its "reactionary Laissez faire theories." This accusation was made with out supporting evidence or documentation in a style that is becoming more & more familiar these days. The inference ~~is~~ *being* that the charge is so much a matter of common knowledge no proof need be furnished. *Well first of all, what reactionary theories?*

~~In reply I can only answer with the line, "Name one." Meaning of course name one~~ ≠

And second with regard to the show for eight years G.E. Theatre has been characterized by variety ~~we have ranged~~ *ranging* from adventure to fantasy, from Opera ("No Room in The ~~In~~ Inn") to musical comedy.

During the last few seasons we tried to do topical stories touching on problems of the day. Many ~~people~~ viewers were generous in their comments about plays we presented dealing with alcoholism, teenage marriage, juvenile delinquency, school dropouts and the tragedy of the retarded child. In none of these ~~I might did we try to~~ *I might add did we* pontificate or pretend we had solved the problems for all who'd listen.

It was only natural *that* we should explore the great ~~problem~~ ideological conflict besetting the world today. We were amazed at how few stories were available on this subject. We could have done a show on the "Nazis" every week but no one was writing about ~~the~~ Communism.

~~In doing Mrs. Miller's book we attempted the near impossible—~~ ≠ ~~five years of~~

Before commenting on the play itself Mr. Condon dismissed Jeanne Crain & myself as being cast because of our activity in "Right wing circles." Jeanne (Mrs. Paul Brinkman) is a mother of several children and has found time to participate in several reputable charitys as well as church activities (She is Catholic) I have no personal knowledge of ~~any other~~ political ~~activities~~ participation beyond the normal duties of voting & paying taxes.

My own "Right Wing Circles" must include membership in three A.F.L. Unions covering stage, Screen & TV and the fact that I served as a dir. & officer for one of these Unions twenty years or more. During that time ≠ ~~forced~~

the Communists made an all out effort to take over the Mot. Pic. Industry resorting to force & violence ≠ including street riots & bombings. I suppose those of us who resisted & prevented this takeover could be termed ≠ Right wing depending on your viewpoint. I cant believe Mr. Condon meant to imply my campaigning in 1960 for Mr. Nixon was proof of Right Wing activity because then he would have to ~~term~~ *classify* me as "left wing" during all those years prior to 1960 when I was a very active & militant Democrat.

Finally his review came to the subject of our G.E. play Mrs. Marion Miller and he said her adventures were outdated now because such Communist hi-jinks only happened in the '30's. ~~and cant happen~~ This is terribly ungallant of Mr. Condon because Mrs. Miller was a small child in the '30's. Her adventures continue today or dosen't Mr. Condon think harassment, constant police protection etc are adventurous?

Mr. Condons impatience with the theme of anti-communism indicates there is a real need for more ~~not less~~ TV exposure of this problem not an FCC ban on the subject.

Sincerely ❖

Although Reagan's handwritten annotation on this document, which was typed on his personal stationery, says, "Written around 1962," he mentions that Marshal Sokolovsky's book, Military Strategy: Soviet Doctrine and Concepts, *has been translated into English. The English translation of the revised edition was published in 1963, and thus we use this date. The handwritten original is lost. The typewritten version is printed here without editing. It is an unvarnished statement of the strategy for dealing with the Soviet Union that he would follow, some twenty years later, as president.*

"Are Liberals Really Liberal?" *

c. 1963

Liberals traditionally defend the right of the individual to pursue unpopular beliefs and causes. It is the Liberal who disavowed communism yet defended the communist on the domestic scene against exposure, identification and questioning, even by duly constituted authorities. It is the Liberal today who bravely insists we can afford to provide public forums on our campuses for

*Ronald Reagan Subject Collection, Box 1; Speeches and Writings Pre-1966. Hoover Institution Archives.

communist functionaries to speak and appeal to our students—this of course in the name of academic freedom.

I'm sure you can understand then why it is disturbing to me to learn this magnanimous defense of 'freedom to speak' isn't exactly of a blanket nature. Shortly after I had campaigned for candidates of my choice in the 1960 election, the St. Paul Minnesota Teachers Federation passed a resolution demanding that my appearance in a St. Paul high school be cancelled because, according to the teachers, I was a controversial personality.

Now I've read in the press that the Committee On Political Education of the A.F.L.-C.I.O an organization known as "Cope" has patronized a strange new arrival on the research scene whose principal product is a one hundred dollar book giving all the lowdown on Right wing extremist speakers. According to what I read "Cope" urges this book on labor councils all over the country, with the added urging that said councils use the book to head off and prevent the appearance in their communities of speakers listed in the book. Failing in this, they are to contact civic leaders, clergy, newspaper editors, etc. and expose the speaker prior to his appearance, thus rendering him ineffective.*

Even though I spent more than twenty years in labor as an officer and director of a union, even leading that union in a strike that secured a pension and welfare fund I am, according to the news story, included in the book's "verboten list". Since I supported political candidates opposed by "Cope," and oppose much legislation endorsed by "Cope," my presence in the book is to be expected. But how do Liberals explain the presence in the book of a Liberal Democratic Senator whose voting record is almost one hundred percent liberal, pro labor and welfare states? As a matter of fact the Liberal wing of the Democratic party has slated Senator Dodd** for elimination in 1964. One can only assume that his liberalism isn't enough to offset his strong, intelligent and thoroughly responsible anti-communism.

Today our Government openly pursues a policy of accommodation with the Soviet Union and is supported almost one hundred percent by the liberal establishment of both parties. According to the articulate advocates of this answer to the bomb threat, they have evolved the only (and you can underline only) method for avoiding a nuclear holocaust.

The theory goes something like this: As time goes on the men in the Kremlin will come to realize that dogmatic communism is wrong. The Russian peo-

---

*The Minnesota high school and COPE stories are recounted in Ronald Reagan with Richard G. Hubler, *Where's the Rest of Me? The Ronald Reagan Story* (New York: Duell, Sloan and Pearce, 1965), 270–271.
**Thomas J. Dodd (D-Connecticut).

ple will want a chicken in every pot, and decide some features of decadent capitalism may make for more plentiful poultry, while their system hasn't even provided a pot. By a strange paradox us decadent capitalists will have discovered in the meantime that we can do without a few freedoms in order to enjoy government by an intellectual elite which obviously knows what is best for us. Then on some future happy day Ivan looks at Joe Yank, Joe looks at Ivan, we make bridge lamps out of all those old rockets, and discover the cold war just up and went away. To bring all this about it is of course necessary that we whittle the back edge of our heels round so we can lean over backwards in an all out effort to prove to Ivan that we aren't mad at anybody.

Now don't get me wrong. I am sure the people who advocate this policy and who believe in an eventual mellowing of communist rulers, are sincere and dedicated to the cause of world peace. It would be nice if they in turn recognized that many who question their program are as nobly motivated as themselves. After all, we couldn't send "Other people's sons to war," without sending our own too.

I am more than willing to admit that I can't prove this accommodation routine won't work, but none of the accommodators can prove it will, so we are talking about a very "iffy" thing. The soul chilling thing is we are being talked into betting the house and lot, including the wife and kids on this great big "if." What do our liberal friends give as reasons for backing their horse? Has communism retreated one foot anywhere in the world? Has Nikita said, "You are right about self-determination, I'm letting the Poles, Czechs, Hungarians and all those other fellows hold elections"? Did he tell the Chinese they were unruly savages for suggesting war, or did he tell them "Don't rock the boat, I'm getting what we want the easy way"? About the only thing offered is that Nikky K. is smiling more and hasn't said anything about burying us, at least where we can hear it, since he set up shop on our side of the hedge. (He still is in Cuba, isn't he?) Two thousand year's ago, standing in the Athenian market place, Demosthenes asked, "What man would let another man's words rather than his deeds tell him who is at peace and who is at war with him"? Mr. Khrushchev is speaking softly, but American mothers are weeping softly as they receive the telegrams from Korea and VietNam that begin, "The defense department regrets to inform you—."

A somewhat liberal man, the late Al Smith, used to preface a debate by saying, "Let's look at the record." With no desire to be hostile or snide I'd like to call attention to the liberal record where communism is concerned. Every time an individual has been brought to public view by a charge of communist affiliation, the liberal establishment has risen in wrath, not against the person charged but against those they term witch hunters and red baiters. Almost without exception the responsible investigating agencies of government and the courts of our land have upheld the charge and confirmed that the individual is indeed guilty of betraying his own country to the advantage of the Soviet Union. Yet to this day with no admission he was wrong in the past, the liberal rises up to defend each new quarry of the "witch hunt" as he defended Harry Dexter White, Lauchlin Currie and Alger Hiss. A glaring example of this dual standard involves two officers of our Army. It is not my purpose to go into the guilt or innocence in either case, but simply to point out the difference in reaction. General Walker* allegedly uttered some intemperate remarks at a cocktail party associating people prominent in and out of government with communism. He was undeniably strong in his own anticommunist feeling. The hue and cry was immediate and ended with the General retiring to civilian life. Not too long ago another General, and let me make it clear, one who is well thought of by the liberals, testified before a U.S. Senate committee and told that committee of an incident in the Korean war that was either outright treason or a most amazing coincidence. The only company of an American combat division to be captured in toto by the enemy was surrendered by it's Captain, who was suspected by his fellow officers of being a communist. My point is that in one case intemperate cocktail talk became a front page story while a possible case of treason and betrayal to the enemy was passed over without mention.

Continuing to look at the record it becomes painfully clear that our foreign policy today is motivated by fear of the bomb, and is based on pure conjecture that maybe communism will mellow and recognize that our way is better. Now a few questions: If we relieve the strain on the shaky Russian economy by aiding their enslaved satellites, thus reducing the danger of uprising and revolution, and if we continue granting concessions which reduce our military strength giving Russia time to improve her's as well as to shore up her limping industrial complex—aren't we perhaps adding to the communist belief that their system will through evolution catch up and pass ours? Then accepting without question that accommodation does not envision ever letting the enemy conquer us by peaceful means don't we face reaching the eventual point at which he understands this? When this day arrives he will be stronger thanks to us, and then perhaps we'll learn how similar accommodation and appeasement are. The latter doesn't give you a choice between peace and war—only fight or surrender. A book by a high ranking

*Edwin A. Walker

Soviet officer has been translated into English, "Military Strategy: Soviet Doctrine and Concepts" by Marshal Sokolovsky.* The Marshal is very blunt in his statement of the why and wherefore of the Russian military, "it's sole mission is to fight and win World War III." He's equally blunt in explaining that W.W.III isn't inevitable—it can be avoided if the Soviet achieves it's goal of world domination by other means.

Now more questions: If we truly believe that our way of life is best aren't the Russians more likely to recognize that fact and modify their stand if we let their economy come unhinged so that the contrast is apparent? Inhuman though it may sound, shouldn't we throw the whole burden of feeding the satellites on their slave masters who are having trouble feeding themselves? While we have a power edge (which means no one in Russia is about to pull a trigger) shouldn't we do what honor and morality demand, and set Cuba free, insist that the U.N. take up the problems of Russian colonialism and call off the unhealthy brainchild of our diplomacy the coalition government we forced on Laos? If you say in answer that doing these things is no guaranty against war, I agree because unfortunately it only takes one nation to make a war, and the only sure way to avoid war is to surrender without fighting. But accommodation is based on wishing not thinking, and if the wish doesn't come true the enemy is far stronger than he was before you started down that road. The other way is based on the belief (supported so far by all evidence) that in an all out race our system is stronger, and eventually the enemy gives up the race as a hopeless cause. Then a noble nation believing in peace extends the hand of friendship and says there is room in the world for both of us.

We can make those rockets into bridge lamps by being so strong the enemy has no choice, or we can bet our lives and freedom on the cockeyed theory that if we make him strong enough he'll learn to love us. ❖

This brief statement, written on the notepad provided each governor at the 59th Annual Governors' Conference, United States Virgin Islands, October 16–24, 1967 (and so monogrammed), was apparently jotted down before he spoke at the meeting.

---

*The book is edited by Marshal V. D. Sokolovsky with an introduction by Raymond L. Garthoff. (New York: Frederick A. Praeger, Inc., 1963).

Speech*
October 1967

Time—realized what we mean by equality & being born equal. We are equal before *God* & the law with a guaranty that no acquisitions of property during our lifetime or achievement no matter how exemplary should give us more protection than ~~any of~~ those of less prestige nor should it exempt us from any of the restrictions imposed on all of society by law.

But let there be no mis-understanding about the right of man to acheive above the capacity of his fellows. We are all richer because of a Shakespeare & a Tennyson a Beethoven & a Brahms. Would the world be better if Big League baseball was so organized that every citizen who wanted to had a turn at playing Willy Mays position? We live—yes even the so called poor— with conveniences beyond the wildest dreams of a King a hundred years ago because an individual thought of a horseless carriage, an ice box & later a refrigerator, radio, T.V., and machinery that lifted ~~the~~ burdens from our backs.

Why did so much of this develope so far & fast in America? Because we unleashed the underlined{individual} genius of man, recognized his inherent dignity and guarantyd reward commensurate with ability & achievement.

Now suddenly we are told we've been following a wrong track we should turn back and pay heed to those of *the* 19th century who stressed ~~the~~ collective humanity, minimizing the individual—Rousseau, Fourier and Marx.

We are faced with a choice; either we go back to this collective "we" as the supreme power with the "state" it's agent—supremely powerful and unlimited in authority; ~~o~~Or we continue on the high road accepting man as a unique individual ~~with~~ a creature of the spirit with abilities and capacities God given master of not servant of his own creation the state.

The time has come to reclaim our rights ~~to~~ our inalienable rights to human dignity, self respect, self reliance to once again be the kind of people who once made this Nat. great. ❖

Reagan responds to criticism of his part in the dedication of a field house at Eureka College. It is one of many letters in which he deals with issues, not the purely personal.

*Pre-Presidential Papers, Box 21. Ronald Reagan Presidential Library.

Speech

Time - realized what we mean by equality & being born equal We are equal before God the law with a guaranty that no acquisition of property during our life time or achievement no matter how exemplary should give us more protection than any those of less prestige nor should it exempt us from any of the restrictions imposed on all society by law.

But let there be no mis-understanding about the right of man to achieve above the capacity of his fellows. We are all richer because of a Shakespeare & a Tennyson a Beethoven & a Brahms Would the world be better if Big League baseball was so organized that every citizen who wanted to had a turn at playing Willy Mays position? We live - yes even the so called poor - with conveniences beyond the wildest dreams of a King a hundred years ago because an individual thought of a horseless carriage, an ice box & later a refrigerator, radio, T.V. and machinery that lifted the burdens from our backs.

Why did so much of this develope so far & fast in America? Because we unleashed the <u>individual</u> genius of man, recognized his inherent dignity and guaranteed reward commensurate with ability & achievement

Now suddenly we are told we've been following a wrong track we should turn back and pay heed to those of the 19th century who stressed the collective humanity, minimizing the individual. Rousseau, Fourier and Marx.

We are faced with a choice; either we go back to the collective "we" as the supreme power with the "state" it's agent - supremely powerful and unlimited in authority; Or we continue on the highroad accepting man as a unique individual a creature of the spirit with abilities and capacities God given master of not servant of his own creation the state. (over)

59TH ANNUAL GOVERNORS' CONFERENCE
UNITED STATES VIRGIN ISLANDS
OCTOBER 16-24, 1967

GOVERNOR RONALD REAGAN
CALIFORNIA

The time has come to reclaim our rights our
inalienable rights to human dignity, self respect, self reliance
to once again be the kind of people who once made this
Nat. great

Letter to the Editor of the Pegasus*
March 31, 1971

To the Editor

The Feb. 16 issue of the Pegasus has just reached me. I'm sorry to learn that some members of the college community were distressed by ~~the~~ my part in the recent dedication of the field house. Perhaps they can find some solace in the fact it was named for two of us and can mentally block out one Reagan & think only of my brother.

Apparently ~~ther~~ their distress results from a mistaken belief concerning my attitude toward higher education and more particularly academic freedom.

Personally I believe in acad. freedom but oppose limiting it to any one segment of ~~the~~ academe. The teacher who interprets it as *covering* only the teachers right to teach is ignoring the students acad. freedom and the right of parents to have some say as to what their children are learning. Then there ~~are~~ *is the academic freedom of* those who finance the whole operation and have some beliefs about the kind of schooling they wish to make available with their contributions—*All these are entitled to some share of academic freedom.*

The Feb. 16 article quoted from two speeches of mine found in a book entitled "The Creative Society."** Three paragraphs from one speech were given as evidence of my "radically right wing reaction to happenings at the cradle of revolutionary youth movements in America, the U. of Calif. At Berkeley." I'll not quibble over the choice of words in describing the Berkeley campus as a "cradle of revolution." Let me just say the phraseology conveys a ~~very~~ *rather* inaccurate parallel to the doings at Independence Hall in Phil. some years back.

~~My main point of difference or rather my question has to do with how the reading of~~ I AM AT A LOSS AS TO *how one reads into my remarks* "right wing radicalism?" ~~into my remarks.~~ The first speech quoted was made in 1966 before I was Gov. and while I was still making my living in Hollywood. (I just slipped that latter point in hoping you'd be reminded that Hollywood is not exactly a symbol of prudishness or sheltered living.)

---

*Letters to the Editor, Eureka College *PEGASUS*, Eureka, Illinois, March 31, 1971. *PEGASUS* is the school newspaper. Original in Pre-Presidential Papers, Box 20E. Ronald Reagan Presidential Library.
**Ronald Reagan, *The Creative Society: Some Comments on Problems Facing America* (New York, Devin-Adair Co., 1968).

The speech was made in response to an incident on the Berkeley campus which had ~~Calif.~~ shaken Calif. more than ~~an 8 pt. earthquake on the Richter scale~~ A MOVEMENT OF THE SAN ANDREAS FAULT. A Coalition of New Left groups had been granted permission to hold a fundraising social event in the Universities Pauley ballroom subject to all the rules covering such events. As it turned out all the rules were broken including a refusal to end the evening at the prescribed hour. This however was of minor importance compared to the affair itself.

Great numbers of *young* high school age ~~young~~ people attended as guests of the sponsoring groups who proceded to mix psychedelic lights with pornographic films projected on the walls. Drugs replaced the traditional punch and the halls & stairways were cluttered with the prone figures of those who were in a stupor from indulging.

On the dance floor girls stripped to the waist and some couples found intercourse more entertaining than dancing possibly because of the attention they attracted. There was of course vandalism, property ~~destruction~~ damage and general use of the ballroom as a toilet.

What *actually* brought all of this to public attention was the refusal of many in the U. admin & faculty to find anything wrong ~~in~~ WITH this innocent ~~evening of~~ fun & frolic. Granted educators have repudiated "en loco parentis" as a part of their duty they surely must admit to some responsibility as adults.

~~My speech It was in reference to this happening I spoke and attempted to point out that adults be they plumbers or Professors have should conduct themselves in such a manner as to provide examples for emulation by the young.~~

Confusion was ~~confounded~~ compounded when I found the balance of the article on ~~Page 4~~ ANOTHER PAGE (you had neglected to print ~~the word~~ "continued on p. 11") Here you take two paragraphs ~~from a speech~~ of mine, one of which makes it obvious I'm opposed to teachers indoctrinating students and somehow you come to the conclusion I advocate indoctrination. I do not. In our U. of Calif. we've had instances (too many to be termed isolated) of faculty basing grades on the pol. viewpoint of the student. ~~as expressed in papers and exams.~~ On one campus students have learned that wearing a letter sweater in class can lead to discrimination by ~~the Prof. That is so Mickey Mouse it would be laughable if it weren't so reprehensible~~ FACULTY MEMBERS WHO HAVE DECIDED THEIR THING IS DISCOURAGING ATHLETICS.

Professors should teach you how to think not necessarily what to think. If a Prof. for some reason does impose his personal bias on his students then he should at the same time urge them to find someone of a contrary opinion, hear his reasoning & having heard both sides ~~make the student should~~ form his own opinion. I assume we still do accept that most issues have more than one side.

Now strangely enough some of those who demand the right to indoctrinate, under the name of academic freedom, have falsely charged that I seek to apply a political saliva test to balance liberal leaning ~~faculty~~ faculty with an equal number of conservatives. Again—not true. My complaint is that apparently such saliva tests are already being applied in the hiring of faculty & it should be stopped.

Finally with a sureness that almost amounts to arrogance the author of the article describes my generation of Eureka students as some kind of Rover boys gaily playing pranks ~~and naturally of course totally different from todays young people especially in our willingness to be~~ *BETWEEN CLASSES IN WHICH WE SUBMITTED CHEERFULLY TO BEING* spoon fed the customs and morés of the past. *NEVER HAS THE PAST BEEN SO OPEN TO QUES. AS IT WAS IN THAT LONG AGO TIME.*

We came to college age in the midst of a social and economic upheaval, the great depression, ~~that~~ *which* was for real. Never was there so much questioning of previously accepted rules & precepts. Life was a very grim business, but somehow we managed to keep a sense of humor, which I have difficulty finding, ~~on~~ *at least on our* Calif. campuses *today*.~~at least~~ And we have presided over the greatest econ. & social revolution the world has ever seen.

You protest what you say is an old fashioned idea of mine that ed. should preserve an outmoded traditionalism. Again you have mis-judged *what* ~~and True~~ *my beliefs are.*

True ed. is societys attempt to enunciate certain ultimate values upon which individuals & hence society may safely build. When men fail to drive toward a goal or purpose but only drift the drift is always toward barbarism. You have every right to ask the reason befind the morés & customs of what we refer to as civilization. Challenge we can afford. You have no right & it makes no sense to reject the wisdom of the ages simply because it is rooted in the past. Challenge—but weigh the answers to your challenge very carefully.

We prize as the greatest of freedoms the freedom to choose. But we are not really free to choose until we become sufficiently disciplined to know what the results of our choices will be. ~~Niagara Falls might look like a great ride & a lot of fun to a surfer but he's in for an unhappy surprise if he tries it.~~ Therefore a teacher must not teach the young only what they want to learn. The experience of the human race must be offered. We must learn for example the price of just getting by.—that we get from life exactly what we put in—no more—no less. That privileges & obligations come out even.

Before we burn down the schools because they aren't relevant (which I sometimes suspect ⧧ *means* because they aren't sufficiently pleasant baby sitting facilities) we'd better figure out what they must be if each generation is to grow up as complete human beings capable of exercising freedom of choice. They must be institutions designed to impart sound discipline based on moral standards which will become self discipline in the individual student. I know from my own ~~study of~~ memory the easy question of why study history—whats so important about where we've been. At your age you are interested in where you are going. But we must study mans achievements as well as his failures. The problems we must solve today are the result of errors of the past. True freedom is the freedom of self discipline—the freedom to choose within acceptable standards. Take that framework away & you lose freedom.

I hope I haven't read your generation wrong. ~~I hope~~ AND THAT you still find freedom precious.

Sincerely,

R.R.

Send a copy to Pres. Ira Langston, Eureka College *with note*

Dear Ira

Enclosed is *copy of* a reply to the article quoting me in the Feb. 16 Pegasus. I thought you might like to see it in case the editor chooses to keep it to himself. *I really am getting to be an old grad.*

Best Regards

Ron ❖

This speech, delivered by telephone to young conservatives at the Young Americans for Freedom Convention in Houston, Texas, is an overview of contemporary American history that weaves together Reagan's analyses of domestic and foreign policy.

Speech on phone to YAF Convention in Houston, Texas*
September 5, 1971

† Since you've been so kind as to grant me these few moments for greetings & salutations, perhaps you'll not take it too unkindly if I impose further on your time. As representatives of Y.A.F., you are political independents. Still you've found in your pol. activism an affinity for the Rep. party, rejecting the

*Pre-Presidential Papers, Box 20. Ronald Reagan Presidential Library.

albumin brained soc. engineers who would set mass above man *and* who think soc. progress is superior to individual action or choice, group compulsion *is* the only road to Utopia, & Ec. security *is* a more desireable goal than personal freedom.

When I think of the Phil. prevalent in so much of the intellectual community, I marvel at the way you have obtained an ed. yet remained steadfast in your beliefs, resisting the zeitgeist—the wind of our times.

Poll after poll reveals that a most persistent myth is the acceptance of the Dem. party as the most efficient & reliable in times of Ec. stress. Evidence of this is the rush to register Dem. by so many of your newly enfranchised peers. These are the same young people who have been so stridently vocal in their denunciations of the estab., and who find govt. too big, impersonal and oppressive.

I suppose the myth of Dem. ec. capability had it's beginning in the fact that a Rep. Herbert Hoover was Pres. at the time of the crash & depression which began in 1929. The Demos. came to power in the elec. of 32, and for almost 40 years they have been applying a variety of nostrums from their social medicine chest.

In just one two-year period—1953–54—has there been a Rep. Congress, and curiously enough that is the only time in all the 40 years that the dollar remained stable.

When Herbert Hoover left the White House, there were 230 Americans for every Fed. Employee. When Richard Nixon entered the White House there were only 67 citizens for each Fed. emp. And what prosperity did such a growth in govt. bring us? In 1939, after 7 years of New Deal programs costing bils. of dollars, 25% of the labor force was still unemployed. But then in 1939 we became the arsenal of Democracy; full employment & prosperity were on their way & so was W.W. II.

Following the war, as we began to catch up with the shortages of consumer goods, unemp. began to increase. bBut then came war again, this time in Korea, and once again we had full emp. A Rep. pres. ended that war and led us through the longest period of peace we've known since W.W.II. Also during that time of peace we had virtually no inflation. Peace was not the result of appeasement. At one point Red China threatened ~~peace~~ *war* and an invasion of Taiwan. Pres. Eisenhower said, "they'd have to climb over the 7th fleet to do it," and there was no war.

Then came Camelot and 3 years of unemployment averaging higher than the unemp. we have now in this time of ec. hardship. Somehow the communications media was unaware of it, and in the many Presidential press conferences of those 3 years no reporter ever asked Pres. Kennedy what he intended doing about unemployment.

It was from Camelot the first American combat troops went to V.N. And soon we had another Dem. Pres., the great society ~~and,~~ full scale war in V.N., and of course full employment & prosperity on the home front, but no sacrifice. The war was conducted on a guns & butter basis, which brought on runaway inflation. The 1939 dollar *had* lost 61¢ of purchasing power by 1968. One has to wonder at the ~~persistent~~ staying power of the Dem. myth.

Now a Repub. Pres. is bringing this 4ᵗʰ war in our century to a halt. In the transition from a war to a peacetime ec., some 2 mil. defense workers & mil. personnel have been thrown on the job market. There is unemployment and, of course, ec. dislocation. There is also the inflation he inherited and which neither his predecessor nor George Meaney had the guts to tackle. He is confronted by a hostile Cong. and a burocratic jungle peopled by permanent govt. employees determined to carry on the discredited soc. tinkering of the past 40 years.

There is more. John F. Kennedy announced the discovery of a missile gap in 1960. After the elec. he admitted no such gap existed, so in 8 years the Demos. created one. And the present Demo. Congress has made it plain they have little stomach for any rebuilding of our deteriorated defense structure.

Summing it up,—there have been 4 major wars in my lifetime, all under Demo. Presidents, and we've only achieved full emp. & prosperity during & because of those wars.

Now our opponents would lead the Nat. again, shedding crocodile tears over the present ec. distress, and professing absolute innocence over having anything to do with it. Somehow they remind me of the wide-eyed blonde in the tabloids who has just bunched 6 shots from a '38 in her boyfriends bread basket, and says she didn't know the gun was loaded.

And what do they have in store for us if they get back in charge? Well, 6 would-be-Presidents now in the Sen. have, between them, introduced more than $143 bil. in new social welfare programs. The Dem. Party Council has declared open season on taxpayers. The council has called for, "a shift of financial resources from Pvt. to govt. chanels to meet the growing needs of health, welfare, employment & other domestic problems." They call for a "vigorous tax prog." and we learn the wage earning citizen who averages working 5 mo. out of the 12 to pay for the cost of govt. should be denied such legit. tax deductions as interest on his home, mortgage or instalment payments ~~prop~~ *or* his property tax, as well as a limit imposed on charitable contributions. It is time to ask ourselves seriously if this Nat. can survive 4 years of what they have in mind.

I know something of your discomfort *&* your unhappiness ~~wh~~ with what you feel has been the present administration's abandonment of some Repub. principles. At the same time, I have been the beneficiary of your ~~friendship~~ friendly approval, warm commendation, & generous words. I was terribly tempted tonight to limit myself to simply expressing my personal gratitude, and I am grateful—humbly grateful—to all of you. But you are too important—too vital to this country's very existence for me to indulge in what would be a cop-out.

Perhaps we have all been at fault. We've forgotten that a Pres. lives in a liberal community. That the heritage of these 4 decades ~~has~~ is a constant pressure in the Nation's capitol from the left. We who think of ourselves as Conservatives have sat back critically observing, but doing no pressuring in behalf of our own views. Be critical, be vocal and forceful in urging your views on the Pres. He needs that input to counter the constant pressure from the opposite side; he needs the arguments you can provide. In all of this we've fallen short.

Let me take the one issue of the announced China visit and ask you to consider a few points that might have been overlooked in your deliberations.

I've heard staunch Republicans say if Hubert Humphrey were Pres. and had announced such a visit we as Republicans would be horrified & united in our opposition.

Of course we would, & why not? Look at the track record. A Dem. Pres. brought back the bitter fruit of appeasement from Yalta & Potsdam. A Dem. Pres. snatched defeat from the jaws of victory in Korea. A Dem. Pres. scaled the heights of statesmanship in the Cuban missile crisis and then lacked the courage or wisdom to take the final step to the summit. A Dem. Pres. disgraced this Nat. at the Bay of Pigs, & a Dem. Pres. faltered & was unwilling to exact a price for the thousands of young ~~men~~ Americans who died in the jungles of V.N. A Demo. Pres. made possible the Godless, inhumane tyranny of Mao Tse Tung's Red China. Yes, we'd be horrified, & with good reason, if Hubert Humphrey was representing us in talks with China.

But it is a Repub. Pres. who has said he's willing to talk. He has been blunt in his declaration that we will not under any circumstances desert an old friend & ally, Chang Kai Shek. There is no indication that he'll give anything away or betray our honor. If I am wrong & that should be the result—time then for indignation & righteous anger. But in the meantime, let us remember that this Am. Pres. who has said he'll go to China is the same man who as a

Vice Pres. went to Moscow and there in the glare of the television floodlights, surrounded by microphones, heard Nikita Khruschev threaten ~~the U.S.~~ ACTION BY THE SOVIET U. against the U.S., and he replied, "Try it & we'll kick *the* h—l out of you."

Young Ladies & Gentlemen, remember your very title—you are Young Americans for freedom. That is your mission above all ~~over~~ others. You are most important in this particular moment of history, because so many of your peers have listened to false prophets & demagogues. Consider very carefully the long hard struggle that lies ahead, and how far we've traveled together to reach this moment of hope for all the things we believe in. Weigh the alternatives, and use your strength wisely & well.

God Bless you in your deliberations, & grant you wisdom & courage & strength.

†CC: Lyn N.
      Press
      EM
      MD
      Bob Walker
      John Mitchell
      Jerry Martin ❖

This letter is a feisty response to a "yes or no" questionnaire in which Reagan explains Keynes and defends then President Nixon.

Letter to Dr. McDowell *
late 1971 or early 1972

† Dear Dr. McDowell:

I appreciate your letter and your generous words about me & my efforts, Also your kindness in trying to make my reply brief & easy.

Unfortunately, I don't believe it is possible to answer your questions on a yes or no basis, any more than you could give BY MAIL a complete diagnosis of illness on a similar basis. ~~by mail.~~

First of all, it seems to me your questions ignore completely the circumstances of a Pres.—the 1st in 48 yrs. *to not* have IN at least one house of the Cong. A MAJORITY of his own party on the day of his inauguration. More than that, he must depend ~~on~~ *for* implementation of his admin & exec. orders on a burocracy ≠ almost totaly opposed to his policies & which is be-

*Pre-Presidential Papers, Box 20; Miscellaneous. Ronald Reagan Presidential Library.

yond his control to fire or replace. I have had 1ˢᵗ hand experience with a similar situation. ~~And~~ *Is* no consideration ~~is~~ *to be* given to the mood of the people, who were so divided that he was elected by less than half ~~of~~ the electorate?

Tak~~eing~~ *under* ques. one—your sub questions A & B. Does a remark quoted by a reporter that "he guessed he was now a Keynesian" make the Pres. an advocate of Keyensian Ec's? My own degree happens to be in ec's. I am not a follower of Keynes, but neither were the New Dealers, Fair Dealers & new ec's zealots of Camelot & the Great Soc. Keynes advocated deficit spending when the economy was in trouble & paying off the debt when times were good. The Demos. perverted this to permanent deficits in good times & bad. Could the Pres., in the ec. dislocation that accompanied his anti-inflat. fight & the transition from a war to a peace-time ec., shut off spending by the world's biggest buyer of goods & services (the U.S. govt.) without risking a full scale depression?

The deficits he agreed to were within a frame-work his ec. advisors ~~advised~~ *said* were controllable, in that outgo did not exceed what income would be if the country ~~was~~ *were* running at full employment. Johnson's policy of guns-&-butter ran deficits when we were already at full employment, & by 1969 we had an inflat. rate ~~at~~ *of* more than 6%.

A number of ~~us~~ ~~g~~Governors were breifed by the Pres. during his 1ˢᵗ yr. in office. We learned then of what he had inherited and how imminent ~~was~~ and great was our danger from inflat. ~~as well~~ with the accompanying loss of foreign markets. Since then he has walked the thin line between runaway inflat. & ec. collapse, taking the blame for high prices & unemp. at the same time.

Devaluation forced our trading partners abroad to make their own money honest and quit taking an unfair advantage of us in the mkt. place. Controls, in my opinion, were window dressing—a kind of shock therapy because our people were in a recession frame of mind & unnecessarily holding back on normal purchasing. None of this represents a change in the Presidents Republicanism. He has referred to deficits & controls as bitter medicine which must not be institutionalized, but must be eliminated as soon as the patient shows signs of recovery. That time is near, the plus 6% inflat. rate of 1969 was down to 2.8% as of Aug. 1971. Workers whose pay increases had netted no increase in purchasing power prior to 1970 ~~have now had~~ now enjoy a 6% increase in their ability to buy.

As for "C,", I'm sure you know of my own opposition to the "Family Assistance Plan." The President's own idea was similar to my own—work or else. What ~~his~~ H.E.W. came up with as a means of attaining that end was something else again. I doubt we'll ever see it in operation. In the meantime, Calif. has acheived a reform in welfare which is pleasing to the Pres. &, I'm sure, ~~the~~ *to* people like yourself.

Subhead "D", The Pres. has not allowed our defenses to become 2$^{\underline{nd}}$ rate. He endorsed and got, by the skin of his teeth, approval of the B1 Bomber. He got ABM by one vote. Congress is dead set against any mil. spending. But be assured we are not 2$^{\underline{nd}}$ rate. We were on the way if the Russian buildup could not be halted. The aim of the present agreement ~~was~~ *is* to interrupt that buildup. M.I.R.V. is the margin of difference on our side and it is a satisfactory margin.

Regarding E, there is widespread propaganda that Red China is the drug source. All I know is that an equally firm belief exists among those knowledgeable & active in the field ~~to~~ that this is not so.

F. It must be obvious that a great international chess game is being played, and our player (the Pres.) has the disadvantage of a divided pub. opinion, a peace at any price bloc in Cong., and the need for time & elbow-room. We might as well get into "G" on this one too. He didn't delay 4 yrs. ~~on~~ *in* taking "easy & obvious" steps in V.N. He's only been there 3 yrs & 5 mo. ~~But~~ And for almost 2 years he has been following a game plan that will put the ground war back where it belongs, in Asian hands. And since when is S.V.N. or Cambodia falling? I think the N. Vietnamese are getting their fannies kicked for the 1$^{\underline{st}}$ time. But what easy & obvious steps could he have taken? Have we forgotten Kent U. & all the other riots? Did he have pub. support 3 yrs. ago for an attempt to escalate the war & try for victory? I'm afraid not.

As for questions 2 & 3, I don't think we should confuse principle with tactical necessities. As the man said, "when you are up to your keister in alligators it is hard to remember your original purpose was to drain the swamp." I think his principles are still solid.

And finally, if enough of us stay home we'll d—n well find out how far a left-leaning Demo. Pres. can take us down the wrong road. Sen. McGovern has made it pretty plain that your profession will be socialized completely, earnings ~~will be~~ of all workers will be redistributed, and "land planning" will be revealed as the end of property ownership. Of course when he gets through disarming us—none of the above will matter.

I'm sorry I couldn't get all this into the check list.

Best regards,

RR

†(The Doc. has a stamped letter attached. So look what we can do & still save 8¢.) RR ❖

This is the only newspaper column we have found written in Reagan's own hand. He expresses concern about the outcome of the elections in Portugal and about the implications of a Communist presence there for the country and for other parts of Europe.

On Portugal *
May 12, 1975

The elections in Portgual have taken place & some of our media have immediately jumped to a conclusion they obviously wanted to believe before the elections even took place; namely that everything ~~now~~ is rosy in Portugal. Well if rosy is used ≠ as a descriptive term with regard to color they are right. Everything in Portugal is rosy—Red.

It is true the Communists only got 11 or 12% of the vote. The rest was divided among several other parties who have one thing in common—they are all left of center. They are just different denominations of the same religion—socialism. You see all the pol. parties to the right of center ~~were~~ have been outlawed by the young mil. ~~leaders~~ *officers* who seized power & who are maintaining a mil. dictatorship.

They allowed the election to take place only after telling the people it was meaningless and would make no difference in the way the country was run. It was in all practical terms a pacifier to keep the public quiet. So Portugal ~~is~~ has simply had a large pub. opinion poll with those of one pol. & ec. philosophy banned.

There is no doubt many of those whose parties were outlawed participated in the elec. by voting for whichever socialist group they considered the least of the evils.

In the meantime the Soviet U. pours an estimated 10 to 12 mil. $ a month into support the small but well organized communist party which now controls (with the blessing & permission of the mil. dictatorship) the press. The banks & insurance industry have been taken over by the govt. and more businesses & industries will follow.

The free world is faced with a choice—like one of those good news, bad news stories. Only in this case it's a bad news, bad news choice. One—the Russians will repeat a kind of Czechoslovakia takeover & make Portugal a Russian satelite. That would be bad—but not as bad as *the* second choice, the one they'll probably make. Portugal will continue to operate as an independent country with a left wing mil. dictatorship. ~~w~~Which for some reason

*Pre-Presidential Papers, Box 20. Ronald Reagan Presidential Library.

never seems to offend some ~~of~~ Americans as much as a right wing mil. dictatorship.

Communists have already been appointed to all the key govt. posts. Behind the scenes the Soviet U. will "stage manage" the show. On stage Portugal acting independent will remain in Nato (the free worlds 1ˢᵗ line of defense) only it will be there as an ally of the enemy not the U.S.

This will have a profound effect on a very shaky Italy already ~~beset by~~ *harboring* a large & powerful communist party. Spain could possibly ~~ungo~~ undergo a change and eventually France.

Meanwhile in the present climate here in the U.S. nothing will be done to encourage the majority of Portugese who dont want to be communist. ❖

This handwritten draft of a major insert for Reagan's stump speech in his 1976 presidential campaign is a statement about social and economic policy in California and the nation.

Stump Speech Insert*
January 22, 1976

~~Last Sept.~~ I *have* proposed that half a dozen funcs. now being performed by the Fed. Govt. should be transferred back to st. & loc. govts. for admin. & control. I suggested they were not properly ~~tasks~~ the province of the Nat. govt. and could be more efficiently & ec. handed at levels of govt. closer to the people.

In making this proposal I made it very clear that such a transfer should be systematic, ~~orderly~~ & phased in over a period of time possibly in some cases even years. I also made it plain that with the transfer of authority *there* should also ~~go~~ be a transfer of resources—meaning the Fed. taxes presently used to fund these services.

The half dozen programs were ed., housing, community developement, manpower training, revenue sharing & welfare.

I predicted at the time that we could expect to hear screams of anguish from the carpeted ante-rooms in Wash. Burocracy is adept at protecting its nest. It also has a built in instinct for preservation *reproduction* of its own kind. Dr. Parkinson** in his book wrote that govt. employs a "rat catcher" & ~~the~~ one day finds he has become a "rodent control officer." *He has no intention of getting rid of the rats—they have become his reason for being.*

*Pre-Presidential Papers, Box 21. Ronald Reagan Presidential Library.
**Cyril Northcote Parkinson.

~~My prediction was based on exper~~

My prediction of course has come true. A well orchestrated chorus of doom criers ~~have~~ their voices amplified in this pol. season, have ~~been~~ predicted every disaster but a plague of ~~locust~~ locusts. ~~since I made my proposal.~~ ~~Depression and fiscal disaster at the local level,~~ Increased local taxes, the needy thrown out in the snow to die, and ~~∦~~ fiscal disaster & depression are just some of ~~the~~ what they say we can expect if we reduce the size & power of the ~~Fed.~~ Wash. burocracy.

I've heard it all before. A few years ago in Calif. we were faced with the kind of "welfare mess" we are still faced with in Wash. For 4 yrs, we tried to halt the ~~ever~~ runaway increase in ~~cost~~ caseload & cost but nothing seemed to work. We were frustrated by Fed. regulations, court orders obtained by "welfare rights groups" using govt. paid lawyers from O.E.O. and a liberally oriented Dem. majority in the legis.

Finally we appointed a task force—some ~~fam~~ members of ~~our~~ ~~∦~~ ~~official~~ ~~family~~ our admin. and a number of public spirited citizens who were willing to give of their time & talent. They ~~worked for 7 months, studying~~ STUDIED the Congressional acts, the Reg's. (which they found in many instances were contrary to Cong. intent) and our own state reg's. Prior to this we had been dependent on the welfare professionals for information and all they had told us were the things we <u>couldn't</u> do. *What we <u>could</u> do according to them was accept things as they were.*

At the end of 7 mos. ~~they~~ *our task force* handed us the most comprehensive ~~WF~~ proposal for WF reform ever attempted in this co. Some of the provisions were administrative and could be implemented immediately. But much of the reform depended on legis. and some on waivers from H.E.W. in Wash. By this time our caseload was increasing by 40,000 *people a mo.*

~~Our legislature refused to even allow me to present the proposed reforms~~ ~~to a joint session. I dont know that any govt. has ever been refused~~ *turned* ~~down in~~ denied a requested

The legis. of course was totally ~~opposed to~~ *against* any of the measures we proposed although (and this has a familiar ring) they too said there should be welfare reform. It was just our welfare ~~tha~~ reform that wouldn't work. Their chorus of doom proclaimed that we would simply shift the burden of welfare to County general relief ~~& the~~ *which would increase* property taxes at the local level, ~~would have to be raised.~~ The needy would be turned out in the street and we'd wind up with a state deficit of $750 mil. Sound familiar?

~~Well~~ *Unable to even get the legis. to listen to our proposals* we took our case to the people. ~~and~~ We told them of recipients WHO WERE earning more than the median inc. ~~who were~~ *were* *yet were* legally drawing welfare, medicaid & food stamps. One county ~~with~~ *had* 194 full time co. emps. drawing welfare, some of them wf case workers acting as case workers for each other. Hundreds of checks were being sent to families who had gone abroad to live—one family was receiving its check in Russia. *Intrigued by our story the news media sent reporters out to see if they could get on W.F. They found they could sometimes more than once under different names.*

The people heard the facts and were outraged. They made their feelings known to the legislature and ~~pretty soon afterward~~ *after having been delayed almost* half *a* yrs ~~delay~~ we got our reforms.

The 40,000 a mo. *increase in* case load ~~increase~~ became an 8000 a month decrease. No one died in the streets. Co. General relief went down in caseload *not up.* ~~as fast as the drop in welfare.~~ Forty three of our 58 co's. were able to reduce their property tax rates 2 yrs. in a row and the second year 2 other counties joined them. Oh Yes! ~~And~~ that $750 mil. deficit turned out to be an $850 mil. surplus which we returned to the people in the form of a one time tax rebate. —One Sen. who had opposed us said he considered giving that money back to the people an unneccessary expenditure of pub. funds.

Now I feel like I'm seeing *& hearing* a re-run ~~of~~ *on* the late, late show. Wash. is filled with talk about the welfare mess & everyone says something should be done about it. The only proposal the burocracy could come up with was the "Family Assistance plan" which ~~would have~~ died aborning (thank Heaven) because it would have added 12 mil. to the W.F. rolls at a cost of tens of bils. of $ a year.

A lib. Sen. *now a Presidential cand.* recently charged that WF by any standard of measurement is a dismal & utter failure. He describes it "as a ship at sea without rudder or compass (and I'll swear ~~he took the~~ *I had that* line ~~from~~ *in* one of my speeches) it has no basic goal except to perpetuate itself, creating new generations of wf. recipients and new generations of welfare burocrats." He termed it the "Root cause of inflation" & so it is. He *too* demanded reform but offered no plan.

The truth is no one in Wash. knows how many people ~~in W~~ *in this co.* are on welfare. They only know how many checks they're sending out. ~~Under the present syst.~~ In Chi. a woman used 80 names, 30 addresses, & 15 tel. numbers in collecting food stamps, soc. security, *welfare* & Vets benefits ~~from~~ from 4 deceased but non-existent husbands. ~~Her as well as welfare.~~ Her tax free—cash inc. alone was $150,000 a yr.

In Calif, we reduced the rolls by almost 400,000 in 3 yrs, saved the taxpayers $2 bil. and raised the grants to the deserving needy ~~by~~ an average of 43%. ~~In St~~ *By making* able bodied wf recipients work *at useful community projects* in return for their grants we funneled 57,000 *of them* thru those projects into pvt. enterprise jobs in just the last 6 mo. of '73 & the 1ˢᵗ 6 mo. of '74 when *the recession was deepening &* unemp. was increasing.

In St. Johns Township Ind. they began an experiment with their "tTemp. rRelief pProg." something similar to our co. general relief. They made recipients work for their grants. Cost of the program had been averaging $5000 a month. In SEPT. the 1ˢᵗ mo. of the experiment the cost dropped to $1200. In Oct. it was $900, Nov. 800 & in Dec. $300.

I still propose *that* welfare be administered

One last footnote on welfare.—A judge in Cambridge Mass. found a woman guilty of ~~fraud~~ Welfare fraud. He ordered her to repay $1,511.64 to the welfare dept. at $15 a mo.—~~Then~~ *but* he ordered the dept. to increase her grant $15 a mo. so she could pay off the debt.

~~I still propose that~~ *For the sake of the people we are trying to help & for the taxpayers* welfare SHOULD be administered at the state & local level without the benevolent hand of Wash. laying a finger on it.

~~≠ what they ≠ shortage ≠ so far they've destroyed 3.2 dwelling for every one they've built and the score reads a net loss of 314,000~~

Food stamps are as out of control as welfare. ~~Some~~ A few years ago a journalist in an Eastern paper wrote of ~~an incident involving~~ a welfare recipient ~~& food stamps. The man~~ *who* worked part time on a farm. One day he stole a ham from a farmers smokehouse and sold it to a grocer for $27.

With 20 of the $27 he bought $80 worth of food stamps. He ~~bought the ham back for $29~~ *worth of stamps and bought and $51 worth of groceries. Then he bought* ~~worth of groceries returned it to the smokehouse then purchased~~ *used the stamps to buy back the ham for $29 plus $51 worth of groceries.* ~~The journalist~~ *Then he returned the ham to the smokehouse. The journalist* concluded his item saying, "the farmer got his ham back, the grocer made a profit & the man on welfare had $7 in cash and $51 in groceries—with no one the loser."—~~No on~~ *That's the kind of arithmetic that got N.Y. in trouble.*

Food stamps are of course welfare but they are administered by the dept. of agriculture. ~~not H.E.W.~~ Sec. *of Agri.* Butz* ~~of agri.~~ has tried to have this program transferred *to the WF agencies* ~~over.~~ The truth is if someone had set out to design a welfare program that wouldn't work he couldn't do better than ~~the~~ food stamps ~~program. The Fed. govt.~~ *You probably figure that way when you stand in the check out line with hamburger while the guy ahead is buying T Bone steaks with food stamps. The Fed. govt.* makes the rules and then orders the states to go out and FIND people who can be ~~added to the rolls~~

*Earl L. Butz.

of those considered eligib eligible to receive stamps. And they've found them. In 1965 there were fewer than ½ mil. Ams. drawing food stamps at a cost of only $36 mil. today last year there were 19 mil. & the cost was $5 Bil. and more than 57 mil. are declared eligible at least 1 mo. out of the year. *Advertisements right now tell you to check because even at incomes of $16,000 a year you too may be eligible.*

What do you do when you are a Gov. and a call comes in from an irate father in another state who declares he's making $100,000 a year, sending his son to college in your state and wants *demands* to know why you are putting his son on welfare. Well it turns out his student son was getting food stamps & we had to tell the man that under the rules if his son asked for food stamps we had to give them to him. We had a young woman *in Calif.* receiving stamps as a student—and she was studying to be a witch.

In many counties of one major state where U's. & Cs. are located 20% of the food stamp recipients were are students. Stan College papers print detailed instructions on how to obtain them *stamps*. Santa Clara Co. where Stanford U. is located has 15,000 recipients *students getting food stamps. Tuition at Stanford is ___.*

There is no minimum age limit—a teen age high school boy left home, moved in with friends and paid his way with free food stamps.

No limit is placed on the value of a home, auto or pers. property. In fact ownership of an expensive home can actually help qualify you. A Louisiana recipients home was robbed of $3700 in jewelry, $240 in cash & $500 worth of food stamps. The exec. city editor of a metropolitan paper reported that he was told by the loc. welfare dept. he could purchase food stamps even though he informed them his salary was $400 a week, he owned a $40,000 home, a 3 acre lot, & 2 late model cars *and his salary was $400 a week.*

Taxpayers finance strikes by way of food stamps. The Wharton *(WHARTON)* School of Finance & Commerce estimates that major strikes in 1969–71 cost the taxpayers *public* $240 mil. in stamps for strikers.

The Nat. Ed. Assn. has notified its 1 mil. 1.7 mil. *tchr.* members that to apply—that they are undoubtedly eligible *& to apply.*

Graft is rampant in the admin. of the program and food stamps are easily counterfeited. Two men in Calif. were arrested who had 1.3 mil. $ worth of counterfeit stamps. A man in Texas is alleged to have accepted $300 in food stamps for performing car repairs & painting, 300 for a used car & 250 for a mini-bike.& $300 worth for $150 cash.

Does anyone doubt that transfering this program to states & loc. govts would be an improvement? In Calif. we completed a task force study of this program too late in our admin. to do anything about it but much of what *a* *number of our* recommendations have been included in a reform bill authored by Sen. James Buckley.* The bill would reduce costs by $2 Bil. while it increased help to the truly needy by 29%.

Washingtons record in activities not it's proper province is discouragingly consistent. Years ago they set out to build low-cost housing for the poor. So far they've destroyed 3½ dwellings for every one they*'ve* built. Their net loss ~~in~~ BY 1968 WAS 314,000 housing units. But of those they *have* built almost ½ ~~can only be~~ *aren't low-cost. They can only be* afforded by upper middle class renters.

~~Washingtons plan to curb urban decay has created urban slums.~~

F.H.A. has lost $1.4 Bil. on resale of houses taken in mortgage foreclosures~~.~~ *&* There have been major scandals in 20 large cities in the last 4 yrs. *The rate of foreclosure is 7X what it is in the pvt. sector.*

When he was Sec. of H.U.D. George Romney ~~showed~~ *proved to* a Congressional committee that under the rules they had laid down the govt. could not provide housing for less than 20% above the ~~cost of such~~ *price charged* by pvt. ~~ent~~ builders. ~~In Wash. un~~ *At the time* housing for the poor in Wash. was being built at a cost of $56,000 per unit.

Right now H.U.D. is out advertising that ~~⅓ of~~ *under present regulations* ⅓ *of* the families in Am. are probably eligible for a rent subsidy ~~and under present regulations~~ and everyone should run down to their nearest friendly burocrat to check on this. It seems if your inc. is ~~only~~ 80% ~~of~~ *or less of* the median inc. in your neighborhood you are eligible. In some areas that means ~~an inc of~~ *people with inc's. of* around $15,000 *can have part of their rent paid by their neighbors.*

In recent years ~~there has~~ we've all been concerned because little Willy dosen't seem ~~to know how~~ *able* to read. In Calif. our *St.* U's. have added a FRESHMAN course dubbed "bonehead" Eng. for students who have entered the U. (and they had to be in the top 12% of their class to enter) but who haven't learned enough grammar in high school to take Freshman Eng.

Over the last 10 year pd. the scores on entrance exams for college have been nose diving and last year were the lowest we've ever known. ~~By coincidence the~~ *By some quirk or coincidence the* decline in ed. quality has been in direct proportion to the increase in Fed. financial aid. The General Accounting Office in reviewing the results of ~~the~~ TITLE 1 OF THE Fed. Aid to Ed. Act of 1965—(the reading program) finds ~~the gap~~ *that* between the educationally deprived children *who were supposed to be helped* BY THE PROGRAM *&* THE

*Rep., New York.

~~& that of~~ average children ~~in the prog. in 14 states has~~ the gap has widened *in 14 states.*

Former Congresswoman Edith Green of Oregon when she was chairman of a Cong. subcommittee on ed. said: "I have come to realize with much pain that many bil's. of Fed. tax $ have not brought the significant improvement we anticipated. There ~~may~~ *are* even ~~be~~ signs we may be losing ground. Programs never seem to phase out, even after the prob. has been solved or after the program has shown very disappointing results."

She went on to describe the committees experience ~~when it went over to visit~~ *in visiting* the dept. dispensing the ed. ~~aid~~ grants. She said: "A Fed. agency consists of an upper echelon of pol. appointees and a vast underlay of permanent civil service burocrats.—The lower level burocracy runs the show. This means regulations and guidelines are issued, laws are interpreted, contracts are let & grants are made by 3rd & 4th rank officials who are immune to constituency complaints." By that last sentence she meant—the burocracy dosen't have to be beholden to the people. They cant be voted out of their jobs.

She described what ~~the comm.~~ *they* found as complete ~~chaos~~ chaos. No one knew to whom the grants were given, for what purpose or what were the results. And then ~~she said~~ *added,* "We cant tolerate more centralization & Fed. control."

Some years ago when Fed. aid to ed. was 1st proposed a group of distinguished college & U. Presidents went to Wash. They expressed a fear that Fed. funds would be followed by Fed. rules ~~and~~ *THUS ENDANGERING* Academic Freedom. ~~would be endangered.~~ As an alternative they suggested a plan whereby the tax paying citizen would be allowed to ~~contribute~~ *subtract* a ~~certain~~ *prescribed* portion of his inc. tax ~~to~~ *and send it to* the ed. inst. of his choice.~~and send a receipt for the contribution in lieu of~~ *the* ~~money to the Internal Rev. Svc.~~ The govt. would set the ~~percent~~ *amount* of tax which could *THUS* be contributed. This would *IN FACT* be Fed. aid but it would be ~~One of~~ given directly by the people ~~and a healthy~~ *not in the form of Fed. grants. Also a* competitive feature would be introduced; ed. inst's. would have to do well to attract contributors *and there is nothing wrong with that.*

One of the U. Presidents ~~in~~ *who attended* those meetings told *me* how for days they argued with Francis Keppel Dir. of ed. He insisted ~~the Fed. govt.~~ *there was no threat to academic freedom that Wash.* had no intention of interfering with ed. policy.—There would be no strings attached to the grants of money. The Presidents kept asking—then why wouldn't their proposal work. Finally he blurted out—"because under such a syst. the govt. wouldn't be able to achieve it's soc. objectives."

And soc. objectives there are! The Carnegie Foundation surveying 132 schools describes conditions as ~~did the Congress woman~~ *woman Green as—* "confused & chaotic—full of contradictory guidelines, enforced by agencies that are often feuding with each other." ~~They say~~ *The foundation says* the very survival of some of the schools is threatened because of the excessive cost of required paper work.

Dartmouth an independent college of prestige & rich tradition was hiring a new dean. They knew who they wanted to hire but ~~had~~ *were ordered* ~~to ad-~~ ~~vertise first in Nat.~~ *couldn't until they had advertised first in a number of Nat.* publications. Last summer the U. of Wash. was required by H.E.W. to present statistical ~~≠~~ info. on its 15,000 faculty & staff in a new format that cost $50,000. One middle size independent college had govt. paper work costs go from $2000 to $166,000. The Am. Council on Ed. has found the cost of complying with Fed. progs. ~~has~~ increased in 10 yrs. to ~~10 &~~ as much as 20X what it was. Some schools which have never taken a penny of Fed. funds are now being told they come under H.E.W. regulations because a few of their students are on Fed. scholarships or loans. *B.Y.U. in Salt Lake City has been told it can no longer enforce it's own* STUDENT *dress & appearance code*—~~it's against H.E.W. regulations~~ ~~H.E.W. dosen't like it.~~ *H.E.W. in Wash. has decided there shouldn't be such codes.*

Public *grammar* schools are being forced to fill out forms if pupils are punished ~~for any reason~~ *stating the reason for & kinds of punishment administered.*

~~The Fed. govt's.~~ Washingtons handling of job training is a twin to the confusion & chaos Congresswoman Green found in Fed. aid to ed. ~~One program~~ ~~r~~Right there in the Capitol City ~~spent~~ $71,000 was spent on a job training prog. ~~from~~ which ~~only 1 person~~ *resulted in only 1* person finding employment.

From the beginning Wash adopted a policy of paying people, (even those on W.F.) to take job training. The result was predictable. Many took job training only for the pay they received for doing so, moving from one program to another *upon completion of each course.* One such program in a low inc. area in L.A. a few years ago paid the enrollees to learn dishwashing. The training slots were filled ~~by~~ but those taking the training good naturedly joked that dishwashing was ~~the~~ *the* one ~~of the~~ job~~s~~ they could always get without ~~any~~ training.

In 1968 C.O.R.E. the Comm. On Racial Equality* said: "Handouts are demeaning. They do violence to a man, strip him of his dignity & breed in

*Congress of Racial Equality (CORE).

him a hatred of the total syst. Poor men want the same as the rest of us. Poor men want to be independent. Poor men want jobs, ownership, control over their own destiny. Welfare is no answer but there is an answer. We seek to harness the creative energy of pvt. enterprise to achieve a solution to Americas crisis. We look to Am. independence of spirit to recognize opportunity & to take advantage of it. We look to the vitality of Am. initiative to transform the underdeveloped parts of this Nat. It has happened in the past—it can happen again."

No one can quarrel with that statement but in the years since it was spoken what have we had under the majority leadership in both houses of the Cong? *Certainly not a revival of our independent spirit nor development of the creative spirit of free ent.* ~~Last year costly paper work required of~~ *the* ~~#~~ ~~independent bus. man & woman increased by 20%. Jobs in Pvt. enterprise declined by~~

~~For one thing~~ We have had *instead* a massive build up in the staff & budget of Cong. itself. ~~Cong.~~ *It* has increased in everything but it's output of legis. There has even been a 60% *increase* in the number of words spoken on the floor of the house. If ~~only~~ we could harness that ~~that energy~~ *fuel source* we wouldn't have to turn the thermostats down. ~~Staff that once numbered 4500 is now around 35,000 & the cost of running the show is 8X what it was.~~ THE STAFF OF CONG. *has increased by 256% &* THE *bud. by 681% in* just a couple of decades. ~~or so ago.~~ One of the items in their bud. is $40,000 to fold copies of Senators speeches.

I mentioned energy—we've heard promises that our goal was to become independent of outside imports. Wash. somehow refuses to learn that the best thing it can do is to do nothing. In 1958 there were 58,000 new *oil* wells being drilled, then Cong. got into the act with price controls & regulations. By 1973 we were only drilling 27,000. Frightened by the ~~crunch a couple of years~~ embargo and the consequent shortage of ~~fuel~~ *oil* they freed new oil discoveries from price controls. ~~and~~ In just 2 yrs. ~~there~~ we were up to almost 39,000 new wells. ~~So now~~ *But they wouldn't leave well enough alone. Now* we have a new energy bill and already *the drilling rigs are closing down by the hundreds.* ~~that fig. is going down and imports are increasing~~ *going up.* In a few years we'll be dependent on imports for 50% of our oil. ~~&~~ What if we have an embargo then?

Cong. has met the problem of recession by treating the symptoms, passing emergency job creation programs. The jobs are all in the field of govt. and they must be new jobs. So when N.Y.C. with its troubles laid off 260 policemen & 150 firemen *at the same* they hired (with Fed. funds) 400 new employees in the dept. of mental Hygiene.

The Dir. of the Hill-Burton project—the program in which the govt. subsidizes hospital construction turned back *almost* $300 mil. he didn't need because there is now an excess of hosp. beds in the country. The house appropriations sub. comm. refused to let him save the money—it had to be spent. When Cap. Weinberger* was Sec. of H.E.W. he wanted to turn back $17 mil. in student aid funds for which there were no applicants. Cong. ordered him to ~~send out~~ find & persuade students to take the money.

But ~~govt. tries~~ *Wash. does try* to protect us. The Fed. trade commission rules it is misleading to the consumer to call a Fake fur—a fake fur. A company is not allowed to say its product is better than another—but it can say it's the best.

Think of all the tragedy we've been spared by the Consumer Product Safety Commissions *timely* warning to mothers that sharpened pencils & shiny scissors can bring howls of pain from children if they aren't used with care.

A Rutgers Prof. has written, "that the bils. of $ that are being spent on the urban poor by all levels of govt. go mainly to support a growing w.f. buroc. of tchrs. aides, youth workers, clerks, supervisors, key punchers & peoples lawyers. The buroc. is sustained by the plight of the poor, the threat of the poor, the misery of the poor, but it yields little in the way of loaves & fishes to the poor. When the old programs fail they are re-baptised & refunded." ❖

Attached to this speech is a note from Reagan to Martin Anderson: "Marty— I decided just to totally re-write so our friend Khachigian could get an idea of my way of saying it. Here is his draft, & mine. Incidentally I'm grateful to him. It sure is easier for me than starting from scratch. Ron"

Speech on Agriculture**
December 8–9, 1979

We live in what has been called the age of technology. All of us are aware of the miracles *of electronics, ~~and~~ communication & transportation* that have taken place in ~~our~~ *the* lifetime of a single generation. ~~b~~But very few, even among the best informed, ~~are~~ know that the greatest miracle has been the technological revolution in agriculture which had it's beginning here in the heartland of our Nat.

The American farmer has made our country the envy of every other in-

*Caspar Weinberger.
**From a private collection.

dustrialized nat. in the world and the provider (directly or indirectly) for nearly all the world.

Am. Agri. is a modern miracle story. In this century there has been an almost mass migration of people from farm to city and yet the increase in per man hour productivity of those who remained on the farm & ranch exceeds that of virtually any other industry.

† Three decades ago Americans spent ~~22%~~—almost a ¼—22% of their disposable inc. on food. Today in spite of double digit inflation only 17% of disposable inc. is required to put food on ~~the~~ *Americas dinner* table. And not only do 3½ mil. farmers feed 220 mil. Ams. but the produce from nearly 1 out of 3 acres is exported BEYOND OUR BORDERS to a hungry world. This year farm exports will total $30 bil. which will pay for some 60% of the oil we have to import. Without this our imbalance of trade would be disastrous.

While I believe in the free market place and an absolute minimum of govt. interference in the market, govt. could ~~be~~ & should be of help in seeking new & expanded ~~markets~~ overseas farm markets. It would be my goal to do this; ~~≠~~ to demand that the U.S. be treated with the same fairness in international trade that we extend to other nations, particularly with regard to our agricultural exports.

The record of the Carter administration ~~is not one in farm policy~~ in agricultural policies is not one that demonstrates understanding of farmers problems or for that matter much concern over those problems.

The administrations handling of energy has made planting & harvest seasons a high stakes game of chance. Those who labor from sun up til late in the summer evening must now put up with govt. paper work growing out of multitudinous *& unnecessary* regulations reflecting the whims of burocrats in a distant capital. Inflat. has made the farmer the greatest victim of the cost-price squeeze. And *farm folk* ~~he's~~ ha*dve* had all the lip service, double talk & meaningless rhetoric FROM WASH. they need.

When I became Gov. of Calif. (the number one agricultural state in the Union) the farmers voice had not been heeded in Sacramento for some time. I take great satisfaction from knowing that we changed that. I would like to do the same thing in Wash.

Possibly the greatest failure of the Carter admin. has been it's handling of the economy. Inflat. which was 4.8% when he took office is now 3 times ~~as grea high~~ *that much*. And yet net farm income is $3 bil. less than it was 6 yrs. ago. Last month (Nov.) the Dept. of Agriculture predicted that net farm inc. in 1980 will drop 19% because of inflat.

‡ ~~During the years that Earl Butz was Sec. of Agriculture we learned that farm subsidies dropped from $5½ bil. to 800 mil. But net farm inc. rose by~~

16%. Under this admin. the subsidies have risen to $6 bil. and net ~~farm inc. has fallen by 14%.~~

In the face of skyrocketing land prices, high interest rates, the cost of machinery, fuel & fertilizer how do the sons & daughters of farmers follow their parents into farming today? How does the family farm remain in the family when estate taxes make no allowance for inflat. and force the sale of the farm in order to pay those taxes. This is also the problem for thousands of family owned stores & other businesses. A change in the estate tax would be one of my first priorities in much needed tax reform. But above all, inflat. must be controlled and since Govt. is the cause of inflat. Govt. alone can end inflat. and I would like to do just that.

All of us have a stake in the, "energy crisis." None higher however than the American farmer. Just last Spring you faced uncertainties over fuel supplies. I was in a plains state at that time when they were within 2 weeks of being too late to plant and ~~govt.~~ *the* Dept. of Energy had not yet approved an allocation for fuel for tractors. In dealing with an energy shortage it makes no sense to shut off the resources that sustain <u>human</u> energy—food, the most fundamental of them all.

The trouble with our energy policy is that this admin. dosen't have one. We cannot solve fuel problems by merely allocating shortages. Nor will we solve them by creating additional govt. bureaus on top of the one which spends 12 bil. tax $ a year without producing one quart of diesel oil or gasoline.

The answer is development of domestic energy sources to make us independent of foreign oil & natural gas. And the energy industry free in the market place, unhampered by govt. is best able to do that. *Just as you are best able to produce food and fibre when you are free from govt. interference.*

~~I would~~ As Pres. I would consider it the height of folly to let bureaucratic clumsiness prevent the allocation of essential fuel supplies to farmers.

Another hazard to agriculture which is within our power to eliminate has to do with transportation. Last ~~summer September~~ Sept. a massive financial loss involving mil.'s of tons of commodities was only narrowly averted. We can no longer neglect as this admin. has the overtaxed, overregulated and progressively outdated commodity transportation system. There must be immediate attention given to the need for upgraded road beds; more rail cars & improved water transportation.

I've referred to regulations several times. Am. industry, the shopkeeper, professionals, entrepreneurs & farmers—, virtually all of us, have found ourselves increasingly bound by regulations having the power of law. ~~There is EPA & FDA, DOE & ICC~~ In charge of enforcing these regulations are almost countless depts., agencies, bureaus & commissions known by their initials, FDA, & *and* IRA, & EPA & DOE. & ICC and everyones favorite OSHA. However well intentioned *in* their beginning they have given *our* govt. a hostile, adversary relationship with it's own bus. & farm community.

The choice is not, as some would have us believe, between regulation or no regulation. Govt. has an obligation to protect us from each other. Therefore certain sensible, reasonable regulations are in order. Unreasonable, nit-picking regulations carried to absurdity, harassing & financially crippling the economy are unneccessary.

The law regarding pesticides, for example, provides for taking into account not only the hazards in their use but also the economic, social & environmental benefits. EPA ignores this part of the law and ~~bases~~ *enforces* it's regulations on a, "no risk" basis.

I cannot & would not tolerate the "arrogance of officialdom" that has made govt. overbearing & interventionist in it's attitude toward those it was created to serve. I would certainly support the reasonable request of farmers to speed up regulatory procedures in order to eliminate uncertainty caused by burocratic footdragging. ~~Admin. of Govt. regulations should be administered with reason & proportion and~~ And I would see that legitimate grievances rec'd. a fair & sympathetic hearing. But most of all I would do my utmost to see that conflicting, unfair, unreasonable & unneccessary regulations ~~would be~~ *are* eliminated.

†† I have never met a farmer who wouldn't prefer ~~the~~ a freedom from govt. agents stalking his property, measuring each acre of production, hovering over paper work and the implementation of complex rules. I believe farmer & rancher alike want to produce at their greatest capacity, leaving it to their abilities to make a living. During the years that Earl Butz was Sec. of Agri. farm subsidies dropped from $5½ bil. to 800 mil. But net farm inc. rose by 16%. Under this admin. the subsidies have gone back up to $6 Bil. and net farm inc. has fallen by 14%.

It would be my ~~intention~~ strong intention to work closely with farm organizations & leaders; to listen not lecture; to place in the Dept. of Agri. people who believed local farmers know more about their own concerns than does Wash. It is time to stop pitting farmer against city-dweller; producer against consumer with a politically inspired "cheap food" policy.

I know there are many other issues of key interest to the agricultural community—conservation, rural development and fundamental agricultural research, to name a few. All of these should receive proper consideration.

But I also know that farmers do not limit their interests to just their own special concerns. ~~They~~ *You* are concerned about the same issues as ~~their~~

YOUR fellow citizens living in town & city. Farmers too must buy groceries at costs inflated by short sighted govt. policies. (The wheat grower especially is frustrated when he pays 45¢ for a loaf of bread that only contains a nickel's worth of wheat.) ~~Their~~ *Your* homes will be just as cold & dark as the city dwellers if we lack ~~fuel~~ *home* heating oil & fuel for our utility plants. ~~Their incentive to work & produce is just Today~~ *You* are just as penalized as the rest of us by unjust & unreasonable taxes. ~~They~~ *You* too are disturbed by our waning strength and declining prestige in the world.

I have come to this great heartland of America to seek your support—not because I believe I can solve all your problems but because I believe you can if *only* someone will get govt. off your back. ~~and~~ I believe I can do that—I want more than anything to try.

Shortly after W.W.II., in the Christmas season of 1948, I was in England. One evening after spending the day touring the countryside I stopped in a little country inn. The proprietors were an elderly couple. As the lady was serving ~~us~~ *me* she said; "You're American aren't you."~~?~~ I said I was and she said; "I knew it. I can tell. We had a great many of your chaps stationed just down the road from here. They used to come in at night and they'd have songfests." By this time her voice had softened and she was looking past me—remembering. "T'was one Christmas eve," she said, "Me and the old man was alone here. They called ~~to~~ me Mom & they called him Pop. All of a sudden the door burst open and in they came with presents for both of us." Her voice was very soft now as she said, "Big S strappin lads they was—from a place called Ioway."

Neither those "big strappin lads" nor their sons & grandsons need govt. ~~how to~~ to tell them how to bring food for a hungry world from the blue, black soil of this heartland.

†*Check figures*

‡~~CHECK THESE FIG.~~

††*check these fig's.* ❖

This speech draft for the 1980 presidential campaign is a comprehensive statement of Reagan's foreign policy views. It calls for a grand strategy based on economic and military strength, credibility abroad, and strong alliances. Parts of the document—several pages at the beginning and at the end—are entirely in Reagan's own hand and parts are Reagan's editing of a typewritten draft. The typed portions of the document are shown in brackets, and Reagan's editing of these portions is shown with strike-throughs and italics.

*"State of the Union" Speech**
March 13, 1980

If I were delivering a state of the Union address and doing my utmost to present our situation ≠ as accurately & comprehensively as I could; I would have to tell you that inflation and interest rates are possibly higher than at any time in our history. Our per man hour rate of increase in productivity, once the very foundation of our industrial might is now less than half that of most of ~~our industrial~~ the nations ~~who compete~~ *competing* with us for world markets and less than one third ~~of~~ what it is in Japan.

Our energy policy is a web of burocratic confusion in which THE COST OF one Fed. agency alone—(the Dept. of Energy) ~~adds a dime to the cost of we pay for each gallon~~ *is equal to almost 10¢* FOR EACH ~~prize~~ GAL. of gasoline we buy. We live in an energy rich nation but our govt. tells us we can only reduce our dependence on foreign oil imports by turning down the thermostats & driving less, driving slower or not driving at all.

Well so much for the good news. The bad news is that the Soviet Union, an imperialist power whose ambitions extend to the ends of the earth, has now surpassed us in virtually every type of weapon. The Soviets arrogantly warn us to stay out of their way and we respond by finding human rights violations in those countries which have been ~~his~~ historically our friends & allies. Those friends feel betrayed and abandoned and in several specific cases they have been.

A Soviet slave state has been established 90 miles off our coast; our embassies are targets for terrorist attacks; our diplomats have been murdered and half a hundred Americans are captives going into the 5th month ~~in~~ now in our embassy in Iran. All of us have been dishonored, our credibility as a great nation compromised to ≠ say the least. ~~and o~~*Our* shield *has been* tarnished.

We are a proud people with much in our history to be proud of. But in our national capital, pride in our country & our heritage seems to be out of fashion. That is not true of our people. All over America I have found the people hungering to be told the truth about our situation and ready to respond to a legitimate call to duty. The American people are not ready to consign the American dream with all that it means to oppressed people everywhere to the dustbin of history. ~~just another great civilization.~~

*From a private collection. Reagan delivered this speech before the Chicago Council on Foreign Relations on March 17, 1980. A typed version of the speech is found in Citizens for Reagan Box 7, and Peter Hannaford Box 5. Hoover Institution Archives.

May I suggest an alternate path this nation can take; a change in foreign policy from the vacillation, appeasement and aimlessness ≠ of present policy?

That alternate path ~~must offer~~ *must offer* three broad requirements. <u>First</u> it must be based on firm convictions, inspired by a clear vision of, and belief in Americas future. <u>Second</u>, it calls for a strong economy based on the free market system which gave us an unchallenged leadership in creative technology. <u>Third</u>, and very simply we must have the unquestioned mil. ability to preserve world peace and our national security. And let me make ~~it~~ plain this can only be done if we will eliminate the foolishness that has reduced almost to the vanishing point our intelligence gathering capability. We cannot afford for example ~~to take~~ having 8 congressional committees overseeing all covert intelligence operations.

When I say our *foreign* policy must be based on our convictions I ~~mean~~ mean our belief in the principles and ideals which make this nation what it is. We ~~must~~ must take the lead in pointing out to 3rd world nations the superiority of our system. Our state dept. for too long has seemed apologetic if not downright hostile about American capitalism. We must use our neglected ability at communications—Radio Free Europe, The Voice of Liberty, The Voice of America to call attention to those nations that once were poor but now enjoy a standard of living far above that of their neighbors who put their faith in communism. We can point to a Singapore, a Taiwan or a South Korea.

Our diplomats speak with a sense of guilt about the gap between the rich & poor nations. Well poverty ~~was~~ *is* not imposed ~~by~~ on poor nations by those called rich. They are poor precisely to the extent they have ignored or turned away from free market capitalism and yes to the extent they have placed their faith in marxist-controlled economies. Cuba is a classic example. It once enjoyed the highest standard of living in all of Latin America. Today it is little better than a penal colony of the Soviets with rationing, *extreme austerity and scarcity of even simple necessitys.*

We have been a generous people we should continue to be. We have contributed more than any other nation to the political, social & ec. betterment of the world. A few years ago a Prime Minister of Australia said: "I wonder if anybody has thought what the situation of the comparatively small nations of the world would be if there were not in existence the U.S.—If there were not this giant country prepared to make so many sacrifices."

Who in the world today would say this of us? Just as our foreign policy lacks a sense of direction so does our effort to help others. We turn dollars made available by American taxpayers over to the United Nations & other international organizations who make no effort to separate the deserving from the undeserving. And in so doing we often find ourselves underwriting those who call us imperialist ~~and they~~ *while* THEIR pursuit OF ~~marxism~~ marxism *is* literally *≠* subsidized by American capitalism.

The Carter admin. invited Castro to establish a diplomatic mission in Wash., sent our diplomats to Havana and encouraged Am. business men to expand trade with Cuba. Cuba responded by sending Cuban mercenaries to Africa & the middleeast under the command & sponsorship of the Soviet U. *and by becoming a mil. base in this hemisphere for the Soviets.*

We have not helped those who want to be free of Soviet & Cuban domination nor have we countered the hate America propaganda spewing forth from Havana. We have not tried to get our message directly to the Cuban people.

Coming to the second of our broad requirements, we cannot meet our world responsibilities without a strong ec. policy which is effective at home & in the world mkt. place. We cannot go on ~~with~~ allowing govt. to spend beyond it's means while our currency depreciates in value literally by the day & week.

The admin. explains away much of our inflation as caused by the need to import oil. We import less than ½ of what we use. W. Germany imports 96% & Japan 100% but their inflation rate is only a fraction of ours. As a result their workers save a MUCH higher percentage of their earnings than Americans do. Their industry invests more in capital equipment and research and their govts. *only* take ⅔ ~~as much of~~ *the percentage of* total output in taxes as does ours.

~~[consumption to investment, and redirecting manpower and ≠ from non-essential overhead and services to producing things the rest of the world wants.~~

We have lost out in international economic competition not only because we have become overgoverned, overregulated and overtaxed, but because ~~the]~~ *our* [method of taxation has discouraged investment risk and enterprise, and the results of overtaxation have siphoned people and their work from the private sector which accounts for our production, to the public sector which is not only the least productive segment of our economy, but devotes much of its activity to impeding production and stimulating consumption.] *Today only about 79 mil. Americans work & earn in the productive private sector. About 82 mil. get their income from govt.*

[An unbalanced administration of the anti-trust law has led to compulsory licensing of new technology that benefits foreign competitors. ~~Also, American firms are denied the economies of scale which modern technology~~

often requires, while] O[ur foreign competitors are free to pool their resources so as to drive American business out of foreign markets. Hence, the application of o]O[ur anti-trust policies—designed to foster competition in the American market—needs to be re-evaluated to avoid making American firms uncompetitive abroad.] *are applied to American firms in the world market in such a way as to make them non-competitive with other industrialized nations.*

[Since our foreign policy lacks a sense of direction, so inevitably does our foreign assistance.

Since we seem to be unable to tell friend from foe, we turn over our taxpayers' money to the United Nations and other international organizations to let them distribute our foreign aid. We should not only use foreign assistance frugally, but we should control where it goes. And such assistance ought to be combined with a vigorous program to make the case for America and for the capitalist system that has made America great.]

We must put our ec. house in order so we can once again show the world by example that ours is the best system for all who want security and freedom. [by contrast, work day and night to make the poorer nations of the Third World believe that they must choose Marxism and live under a Soviet-style dictatorship in order to succeed.

Until the tragic and disgraceful events in Iran, the Carter Administration used to boast that it knew how to improve our relations with the countries of the Third World. But in fact, we have courted these countries with a campaign of meekness, apologies and concessions. This has only provoked our enemies to become more extreme. But our friends have been taught the bitter lesson by the present Administration that the more they support the United States, the more likely they will be treated badly by us.

Communism is good at guaranteeing life-time jobs to dictators, but it is terrible for economic development. This is the fact that we have to get across to the people in the poorer countries. The American success story used to be a shining example, something that other people aspired to.—the American dream. Yet, because of our own intellectual confusion and because of our unwillingness to answer Marxist propaganda, the American dream is now seen by many as America's guilt.] *It was & can still be the American dream. But the world must see that we still believe in* it *that dream.*

[But] *(and this brings us to* POINT III*)* [the best foreign policy cannot preserve the peace and protect the realm of freedom unless it is backed up by adequate military power.

We are in such a dangerous situation today because t The Carter Administration and the Democrat-controlled Congress have neglected our military strength~~.~~ & ~~They~~ cut back our defense programs while the Russians were building ~~up~~] *theirs to an extent never before seen in the world.*

[Since the Soviet invasion of Afghanistan~~, Mr. Carter has been trying to convey~~] *and the Presidents discovery that the Soviets cant be trusted he has now indicated* [that he now recognizes the importance of a strong defense. ~~But the new image is deceptive. Despite Mr. Carter's admission that he has now discovered what Soviet policy is all about, he clings to the flawed SALT II treaty.~~]

He called for a mil. bud. increase which allowing for inflation leaves us ~~somewhere~~ totally unable to match THE *Soviet build up. He sternly announced the suspension of action on the Salt II treaty—for awhile. Now he has called again for it's ratification. The President at the same time however declares*

[~~The lack of political conviction leads to a debasing of language, as in the case of the President's declaring~~ that he will keep the United States "~~second to none in military strength." Now, the Administration is proposing a defense program which will let the Soviet Union move ahead of us in strategic arms and further surpass us in conventional ones.~~] *2ⁿᵈ to* NONE IN MILITARY STRENGTH. *How can he keep us where we are not? We are already 2ⁿᵈ to <u>one</u>, namely the Soviet U. and that is a very dangerous position in which to be. Besides* [Soviet investment in strategic arms will continue at a rate nearly three times as large as ours, their investment in conventional arms will be nearly twice as large~~—given the proposed program.~~ So what we have been told is simply untrue.

There are no easy solutions, and I do not believe in deceiving the American people. To rebuild our military strength will take] DETERMINATION, PRUDENCE & [a sustained effort ~~and *determination and* require prudence.~~ We simply have to face the harsh fact that ~~we must turn around these deteriorating trends in the military balance.~~

Our defense policy has to be invigorated across the board.

~~First~~, ~~t~~To prevent the ultimate catastrophe of a massive nuclear attack, we urgently need a program to preserve and restore our strategic deterrent. The Administration proposes a costly new missile system~~. that will not be deployed~~] *But we can't complete that* [until the ~~late 1980s.~~] *end of this decade.* [Given the rapidly growing vulnerability of our land-based missile force, a faster remedy is needed.

~~Without any quid pro quo from the Soviets, the B-1 bomber was cancelled and with a shrinking fleet of old B-52s, while the Soviets keep producing a highly capable multi-purpose bomber. Clearly, this situation must not continue.~~

~~Second,~~ ~~w~~We have to maintain a superior navy. ~~Since~~ ~~w~~We are a nation with vital interests and commitments overseas, our navy must stay ahead of the Soviet build-up. This means commissioning the ships and developing the technology that will enable the United States to command the oceans for decades to come.

~~Third,~~ ~~w~~We must ~~end the deterioration of our~~] *restore an active* [Ready Reserve ~~forces~~] *force* [and provide the necessary incentives to retain ~~the~~ skilled men and women in the armed forces. ~~people who have been trained at great cost. The case of a typical Maintenance Petty Officer who takes care of the expensive F-14 aircraft illustrates what I have in mind. Such an officer now makes about nine thousand dollars per year. He cannot even hold two jobs—like many enlisted men now do—because for at least six to eight months a year he is at sea. Even though~~ h] *I believe we can make a volunteer mil. force work. But we cant when we force men to serve at a pay scale lower than welfare.* ~~We put a~~*A non-commissioned officer on a carrier is put in charge of a $25 mil aircraft.* ~~He~~ *H*[e often works sixteen hours a day. He ~~makes~~] *EARNS* [less than a cashier at a supermarket. ~~Small wonder~~] *Is it any wonder* [the Armed Forces are losing two-thirds of their trained personnel. To me, it makes far more sense to fix this urgent problem of personnel retention and to restore the strength of the Reserves, than to debate now whether we should hire hundreds of bureaucrats to compile a gigantic roster of young men and women] *for a possible future draft.*

[~~Fourth,~~ ~~w~~We have to take full advantage of the contributions that American science and technology can make to the defense of the United States and to the protection of peace. ~~This requires a vigorous expansion of our research and development efforts. The United States first sent a man to the moon; let us use~~

~~Fifth,~~ ~~w~~We must once again restore the United States intelligence community. A Democratic Congress, aided and abetted by the Carter Administration, has succeeded in shackling and demoralizing our intelligence services to the point that they ~~cannot~~] *no longer* [function effectively as a component part of our defenses. With all the military and terrorist threats confronting us, we need a first-class intelligence capability, with high morale and dedicated people. We have the means to regenerate our intelligence organizations, and I would surely employ those means.]

~~The 3rd of our broad requirements of our foreign policy is the need to re-build what one Pres. called, "the great arsenal of Democracy."~~

But while we do all these things and ~~they~~ ~~it~~ they are essential, we must above all have a grand strategy; a plan for the dangerous decade ahead. We must be prepared with contingency plans for future Irans and Afghanistans. It is painfully apparent that we have been ~~caught~~ *surprised* repeatedly and faced with situations we have never anticipated and for which we have no ready plan of action.

When it was learned the Soviet U. had added to it's airforces & submarines in Cuba (all of which we meekly accepted as within their rights) a combat brigade of ground ~~forces~~ *troops,* Pres. Carter said this was unacceptable to the U.S. He has since accepted the unacceptable with no further protest.

[Totalitarian Marxists are in control of the Caribbean island of Grenada where Cuban advisors are now training guerrillas for subversive action against other countries, such as Trinidad-Tobago, Grenada's democratic neighbor.

~~And we know that~~ iIn El Salvador, Marxist-totalitarian revolutionaries, supported by Havana and Moscow, are preventing the construction of a democratic government.

Must we let Grenada, Nicaragua, El Salvador all become additional "Cubas," eventual outposts for Soviet combat brigades? ~~If so,~~] *Will* [the next push of the Moscow Havana axis ~~will~~ be northward to Guatemala and thence to Mexico, and South to Puerto Rico and Panama?

~~There are other important examples of how our foreign policy suffers~~ ~~from a lack of conviction.~~ In the United Nations—where we pay the lion's share of a bloated budget—~~we have tolerated shameful proceedings in which~~ ~~the United States is pilloried and insulted. Repeatedly, in the chambers of the~~ ~~United Nations,~~ Puerto Rico and Guam are alledged to be instances of colonialism, yet hardly a single speech is being given, hardly a word is said about the vast and expanding colonial empire of the Soviet Union.

Recently, the Administration took great pride ~~when the United Nations~~ ~~voted~~] *& hailed as some kind of victory* a U.N. [resolution condeming the invasion of Afghanistan, ~~but~~] *even though* [that ~~very~~ resolution did not even mention the Soviet Union by name.

These humiliations and symbols of weakness add up. The unwillingness of the Carter Administration to make our case is pervasive. We apologize, compromise, withdraw and retreat; we fall silent when insulted and pay ransom when we are victimized.

~~If I become President, I assure you, our diplomats will be instructed to re-~~ ~~spond whenever and wherever our country is insulted. We will once again~~ ~~speak up for America.~~

~~In the defense of freedom, there is and can be no substitute for American~~

power. ~~This means that we will have to spend more money to rebuild our military strength. We can afford to do this; during the Eisenhower Administration, when the rate of inflation averaged only one percent per year, we spent about twice as much of our gross national product for defense as we do today. That is why I stress the proper management of our economy as a precondition for a sound foreign policy.~~

~~We also should have learned the lesson that we cannot negotiate arms control agreements that will slow down the Soviet military buildup, as long as we let the Soviets move ahead of us in every category of armaments. Once we clearly demonstrate to the Soviet leadership that we are determined to compete, arms control negotiations will again have a chance. On such a basis, I would be prepared to negotiate vigorously for verifiable reductions in armaments.~~

~~This is how we shall find peace through strength.~~

IV

Confronted by so many pressing crises, we would all like to find quick solutions. What can be done, tomorrow, ~~you may ask, t~~ To free our diplomats in Teheran? What can be done now to turn back the Soviet invasion of Afghanistan?

We can neither solve these present crises, nor cope with graver, future ones, unless we ~~rebuild our strength—our political strength and convictions, our economic strength, our military strength. Once we~~ regain a reputation of reliability toward our allies. ~~we will not be rebuffed—as the Administration recently was with its offer of aid to Pakistan. And once we reestablish a sense of trust, our allies will more effectively work with us.~~ This means avoiding what we did to Taiwan, or what we did to Korea with the mistaken plan for withdrawing troops, or to the German Chancellor with the incredible flip-flop on the "neutron bomb," or to Israel with the recent scandal in the United Nations.]

Our grand strategy must recognize those areas of the world which are necessary to any plan for preserving world peace. Here in our own hemisphere I have urged a North American Accord to bind the 3 great nations of ~~N~~ this continent closer together. I have already spoken of Central America and of the Caribbean and certainly we must regain the friendship & ~~support~~ trust of the nations of S. Am.

In the middle east our alliance with Israel must be continued for both our sakes. Israel ~~is~~ a stable democracy sharing our own values maintains with it's combat trained & experienced military a deterrent to Soviet expansion in that troubled part of the world.

We must continue efforts to win the friendship & trust of the other Nat's.

of the middle east but we must <u>not</u> attempt to impose our solution to the problems there. This can be said of the trouble in Lebanon where we should offer our help but without dictating terms. The same thing applies to the tragedy involving 2 of our Nato allies over Cyprus.

We never sought the leadership of the free world but no one else can provide it. And without our leadership there ~~will~~ can be no peace in the world. It is time we purged ourselves of the Vietnam syndrome that has colored our thinking for too long a time.

Speaking at ~~N.D.~~ Notre Dame U. 5 months after he had assumed office Pres. Carter said; "we are free of the inordinate fear of communism which led to the moral poverty of Vietnam."

Possibly Vietnam was the wrong war, in the wrong place at the wrong time. But when 50,000 Young Americans make the ultimate sacrifice to ~~to~~ defend the people of a small defenseless country against the Godless tyrany of communism that is not an act of "moral" poverty. It is in truth ~~an act~~ a collective act of moral courage.

It is time we recognized that the veterans of that war fought as bravely & effectively as any American fighting men ever fought in any war and did so with one hand tied behind their backs by ~~o~~ their own govt. It is time we told them that never again will we allow the immorality of asking young men to fight & die in a war our govt. is afraid to let them win.

One parting note. For years now we have witnessed the starving Cambodian men, women & children;—the agony of refugees from S.E. Asia—struggling ashore in Maylaysia from leaky boats after a horrid passage across the So. China Sea. Many dont make it but on all those boats there could be written "this is what happens to friends of the U.S."

If there is one message that needs to be sent to all the Nations of the world by the next Pres. it is this: "There will be no more Taiwans, & no more Vietnams. Regardless of price or promise—Be it oil from Arabia or an Ambassador sitting in Peking—there will be no more ~~betrayal~~ abandonment of friends by the U.S. of Am.

I want very much to send that msg. ❖

In Reagan's view, peace was the first purpose of American foreign policy. In this speech to the Veterans of Foreign Wars, he discusses why he thinks American foreign policy has been working against peace and how that trend could be reversed. World peace was a major theme of Reagan's 1980 presidential campaign.

PEACE*
August 18, 1980, Chicago, Illinois

~~I have always found it strange that those like yourselves~~ *that you* who have ~~known the agony of war are often singled out by those who shout shout~~ ~~"peace" the loudest as being somehow responsible for war.~~

It has always struck me as odd that you who have known at first hand the ugliness and agony of war are so often blamed for war by those who parade for peace.

I think the answer is obvious. Having known war, you are in the forefront of those who know that peace is not obtained or preserved by wishing and weakness. You have consistently urged maintenance of a defense capability that provides a margin of safety for America. There is no such margin today.

But because *of* your support for military preparedness, there are those who equate that with being militant and desirous of war. Back in the '20's, Will Rogers had an answer for ~~pacifists~~ *those* who believed ~~a strong military~~ *that strength* invited war. He said, "I've never seen anyone insult Jack Dempsey"—~~world~~ (world heavyweight champion at the time).

About 10 days ago, ~~the~~ *our new* Sec. of State addressed a labor convention. He took me to task. Indeed, he denounced me for urging that the U.S. should seek to achieve military superiority. Actually, I've called for whatever it takes to be so strong that no other nation ~~would~~ *will* dare violate the peace. If that means superiority, so be it. But the Sec. was downright angry. ~~with me.~~ He charged that such a policy would lead to an all-out arms race & even war. Well, I have a message for the Sec.—we're already in an arms race but only the Soviets are ~~racing~~ *racing*. They are outspending us on ~~defense~~ total military by 50% and more than double, SOMETIMES TRIPLE, on strategic nuclear weapons.

One wonders if the Sec. of State or the Pres. for that matter sees any threatening pattern in the Soviet presence by way of Cuban proxies in so much of Africa, which is the source of minerals absolutely essential to industry in Japan, Western Europe, and the U.S. We are self sufficient in only 5 of the 27 minerals ~~vital~~ *important* to ~~our~~ *us* industrially & strategically.

Then there is the Soviet takeover in Somalia, Ethiopia, So. Yemen, and now Afghanistan. ~~which~~ THIS LAST moves them ~~to~~ 500 miles closer to the oil-rich ~~middle east~~ ARABIAN GULF. And is it just coincidence that Cuban &

*Reagan-Bush 1980 Campaign: Papers, 1979–80, Box 949, Ronald Reagan Presidential Library.

Soviet-trained terrorists are bringing civil war to Central American countries in close proximity to the rich oil fields of Venezuela & Mexico?

World peace must be our number one priority. It is the first task of state-craft to preserve peace so that brave men need not die in battle. But it must not be peace at any price; it must not be a peace of humiliation and gradual surrender. Nor can it be the kind of peace imposed on Czechoslovakia by Soviet tanks just 12 years ago this month. And certainly it isn't the peace that ~~has come~~ *came* to ~~So. East~~ [*Southeast*] Asia with our signing of the Paris *Peace* accords.

Peace must *be* such that freedom can flourish and justice prevail. Tens of thousands of boat people have shown *us* there is no freedom in ~~Viet Nam~~ *the so-called peace in Vietnam*. The hill people of Laos know poison gas not justice, and, in Cambodia, there is only the peace of the grave for at least ⅓ [*one-third*] of the population slaughtered by the Communists.

For too long, we have lived with the "VietNam Syndrome." Much of that syndrome ~~was~~ has been created by the No. Vietnamese aggressors who now threaten the peaceful people of Thailand. Over & over they told us for nearly 10 years that we were the aggressors bent on imperialistic conquest. They had a battle plan. It was to win on the city streets of America & in our news media what they could not win on the field of battle. As the years dragged on, ~~they~~ we were told that peace would come if we would simply stop interfering.

It is time ~~that~~ we recognized that ours was, *in truth,* a noble cause. A small country newly free from colonial rule sought our help in establishing self-rule and the means of self defense against a totalitarian neighbor bent on conquest. We dishonor the memory of 50,000 young Americans who died in that cause WHEN WE GIVE WAY TO FEELINGS OF GUILT AS IF WE WERE DOING SOMETHING SHAMEFUL, and we have been shabby in our treatment of ~~the~~ *those who* returned. ~~veterans~~ They fought as well and as bravely as any Americans ~~fighting men~~ have ever fought in any war. They deserve our gratitude & our respect. ~~We~~

~~We owe it to them~~

There is a lesson for all of us in ~~that tragic war~~ VIETNAM; if war does come, ~~you~~ *we* must have the means & the determination to prevail or ~~you~~ *we* will not have what it takes to secure the peace. And while we are at it, let us tell those who fought in that war that we will never again ask young men to fight & possibly die in a war our govt. is afraid to let them win.

Shouldn't it be obvious to even the staunchest believers in ~~dis~~ unilateral disarmament as ~~a~~ THE SURE road to peace that peace was never more certain than in the years following W.W. II when we had the mightiest mil. force in the world and a monopoly on nuclear weapons?

True, there was the Korean tragedy, but even that bolsters the argument. There is no question but that North Korea's attack on So. Korea followed an injudicious statement from Wash. that our sphere of interest in the Pacific and our defense perimeter did not include Korea. Then followed our first "no win war," a PORTENT OF MUCH THAT HAS HAPPENED SINCE.

But reflect for a moment how, under U.S. leadership the free nations joined together to rebuild *a* war-ravaged Europe. Our will & our capacity to preserve the peace were unchallenged. There was no question about our credibility and our welcome throughout the world. Our erstwhile enemies became close friends and allies.

When John F. Kennedy demanded the withdrawal of Soviet missiles from Cuba and the tension mounted, it was Nikita Krushchev who backed down, and there was no war.—maybe because oOur nuclear superiority over the Soviets was about 8 to 1.

But, then, in the face of that *such* evidence that the cause of peace is best served by strength not bluster, an odd thing happened. Those responsible for our defense policy ignored the fact that some indication *evidence* of aggressive intent on the part of the Soviets was *surely* indicated by the placement of missiles in Cuba. to begin with No attention was paid to the declaration of *by* the Soviet foreign minister that they would see *make sure they* never had to back down again. No one could possibly *mis*interpret his statement. as anything He was announcing the inten*tion* of the Soviet U. to begin a military buildup.

Our policymakers, however, decided there the Soviet U. would not attempt to catch up, that, for some reason, they would be satisfied with the status quo and accept 2ⁿᵈ place as their proper place *position*. Sometime later, in 1965, Sec. of Defense McNamara, was positive in his assertion *in an interview in U.S. News & World Report, stated unequivocally* that the Soviets were making no moves whatsoever to enhance their nuclear capability vis-a-vis ours.

Fifteen years have gone by since that exercise in positive thinking. When AT THAT TIME we led the Soviets in some 40-odd mil. categories according to the Nat. Defense Council. Today they lead us in all but 8 and, according to the Council, will surpass us in those in the next few years if present trends continue.

Someone in the United Kingdom once described four stages or periods of thinking that led to W.W. II. He said that when warnings came of a military buildup by *in* Hitler's Germany, they THOSE WARNINGS were greet greeted with disbelief. Then when there was no denying the evidence of Hitler's rearming, the response was "we're too strong; he can never match us so what's to worry about." Stage 3, ~~found~~ when the Nazi ~~buildup~~ *forces had* achieved equality, was greeted by the English with pleasure. They said; ~~we have~~ "GOOD. THERE IS a balance of power, & that has always brought peace." The buildup continued until the Nazi superiority was plain for everyone to see—stage 4, and the response was, "we mustn't try to catch up; it would be provocative & might cause war."

Is there a parallel? Are we in stage 4? Is that why the Sec. of State became so angry THE OTHER DAY at the ~~suggestion~~ idea that we should improve our defensive capability?

Soviet leaders talk ~~of~~ arrogantly of a so-called "correlation of forces" that has moved in their favor, opening up opportunities for them to extend their influence. The response from th~~is~~e admin. in Wash. has been one of weakness, ~~vacill~~ inconsistency, vacillation & bluff, or so it seems. A Soviet combat brigade is discovered in Cuba; the Pres. goes on TV to declare its presence 90 miles off our shore is unacceptable. The brigade is still there. Soviet troops mass on the border of Afghanistan. The Pres. issues a stern warning against any ~~action~~ *move* by those troops to cross the border. They cross the border, execute the puppet Pres. they themselves had installed, and carry out a savage attack on the people of Afghanistan. Our credibility in the world slumps further. ~~He~~ THE PRES. *proclaims we'll protect the middle east by force of arms and 2 weeks later admits we dont have the force.*

Is it lack of a coherent policy? Is it vacillation and indecision? There is another more frightening possibility—the possibility that this admin. is being very consistent, that it is continuing the McNamara doctrine that we have nothing to fear from the Soviets—if we just don't provoke them.

Well, ~~war~~ W.W.II came about without provocation. Firmness based on strong defense capability is not provocative. Weakness can be provocative simply because it is tempting *to a nation whose imperialist ambitions extend to the ends of the earth.*

We find ourselves increasingly in a position of dangerous isolation. Our allies are losing confidence in us, and our adversaries no longer respect us.

There is an alternative path for America which offers a more realistic hope for peace. We must take a stand against terrorism in the world and combat it with firmness, for it is a most cowardly and savage violation of peace. We must regain that margin of safety I spoke of both in conventional arms & the deployment of troops. And we must allow no weakness in our nuclear deterrent.

There is something else. We must remember our heritage, who we are &

WHAT WE ARE, and how this nation, this island of freedom, came into being. And we must make it unmistakably plain to all the world that we have ~~the will~~ no intention of compromising our principles, our ~~beliefs~~ beliefs or our freedom. That we have the will & the determination to do as a young Pres. said in his inaugural address 20 years ago, "bear any burden, pay any price." Our reward will be world peace; there is no other way to have it.

For more than a decade, we have sought a detente. The word means relaxation. We don't talk about a detente with our allies; there is no tension there that needs relaxing. We seek to relax tensions where there are tensions—with potential enemies. And if those potential enemies are well armed and have shown a willingness to use ~~action~~ *armed force* to gain their ends (ends that are different than ours), then relaxing tensions is a delicate & dangerous business.

Detente has meaning only if both sides take positive actions to relax the tensions. When one side relaxes while the other carries out the greatest military buildup in the history of mankind, the cause of peace has not been advanced.

Arms control negotiation can often help to improve stability but not when (like with detente) the negotiations are one-sided. And they obviously have been one-sided and will continue to be so if we lack steadiness and determination in keeping up our defenses.

I think continued negotiation with the Soviet U. is essential. We need never be afraid to negotiate as long as we keep our long term objectives (the pursuit of peace for one) clearly in mind and dont seek agreements just for the sake of having an agreement. It is important, also, that the Soviets know we are going about the business of building up our defense capability pending an agreement by both sides to limit various kinds of weapons.

I have repeatedly stated that I would be willing to negotiate an honest, verifiable reduction in nuclear weapons by both ~~countries~~ our countries to the point that neither of us represented a threat to the other. I cannot, however, agree to a treaty—specifically, the Salt II treaty, which, in effect, legitimizes a nuclear arms buildup.

We have an example in recent history of our ability to negotiate properly BY keeping our objective clearly in mind until an agreement is reached. Back in the mid 50's, at the very height of the "cold war," Allied & Soviet military forces were still occupying Austria in a situation that was virtually a confrontation. We negotiated the Austrian State Treaty calling for the removal of all the *occupying* forces, Allied & Soviet. If we had negotiated in the manner we've seen these last few years, Austria would still be a divided country.

The American people must be given a better understanding of the threat

~~confronting~~ *hanging over* us and of the need for effort &, yes, sacrifice to turn the situation around. Our govt. must stop pretending that it has a choice between promoting the general welfare & providing for the common defense. Today they are one & the same.

Let our people be aware of the ~~various ways that threat hanging over us could can~~ be implemented ~~by~~ *several objectives of* the Soviets in this decade AND THE THREAT THEY ARE TO CONTINUED PEACE. An attempt will be made to separate our ~~NATO~~ *NATO* allies from the U.S. Nations like W. Germany & France are already being approached by the Soviets, carrot & stick in hand. Another I've already mentioned is an increase of Soviet influence in the Persian Gulf—(the Arabs ~~prefer~~ would rather we call it the Arabian gulf).

Not much attention has been given to a 3rd move, and that is the encirclement and neutralizing of Communist China. Much closer to home is Soviet-inspired trouble in *the* Caribbean. ~~There is Cuba of course and now~~ Subversion & Cuban-*trained* guerilla bands *are* targeted on Jamaica, Honduras, *El Salvador,* & Guatemala. ~~#~~Leftist regimes have already taken over in Nicaragua & Grenada. ~~And of course the Soviet U.~~

A central concern of the Kremlin will always be ~~their~~ *the Soviet* ability to handle a direct confrontation with our military forces. ~~Paul Nitze~~ in a recent address, [*Paul Nitze*] said; "The Kremlin leaders do not want war; they want the world." For that reason, they have put much of their mil. effort into strategic nuclear programs. Here the balance has been moving against us & will continue to do so if we ~~continue on~~ *FOLLOW* the course set by this admin.

The Soviets want peace & victory. We must understand this and what it means to us. They seek a superiority in nuclear strength that, in the event of a confrontation, would leave us with ~~the~~ *a* choice ~~between~~ of surrender or die. ~~We could have the peace of a~~ *Surrender would give us peace allright; the peace of a* Czechoslovakia or an Afghanistan. ~~or peace on our terms~~ *But* if we have the will & the determination to build a deterrent capability ~~of such strength~~ we can have real peace because we will never be faced with a Soviet ultimatum. Indeed, the men in the Kremlin could in the face of such determination decide that true arms limitation makes sense.

For a nation such as ours, arms are ~~only~~ important only to prevent others from conquering us or our allies. We are not a belligerent people. Our purpose is not to prepare for war or wish harm to others. When we had ~~the~~ great strength ~~at~~ *in* the years following W.W.II, we didn't use ~~it~~ *that* strength for territorial gain. Our foreign policy ~~then~~ should be ~~our~~ *TO SHOW BY* example ~~of~~ the greatness of our system and the strength of American ideals. The truth is we would like nothing better than to see the Russian people living in freedom & dignity instead of being trapped in a backwash of history *as they are.*

The greatest fallacy of the Lenin-Marxist philosophy is that it is the "wave of the future." Everything about it is as primitive as tribal rule; compulsion in place of free initiative; coercion in place of law; piracy in place of trade, and empire-building for the benefit of a chosen few at the expense of the many. *We have seen nothing like it since* FEUDALISM.

Where have people given a choice freely chosen Communism? What other system in the world has to build walls to keep its people in?

Recently Academician Andrei Sakharov, one of Russia's great scientists [*and*] presently under house arrest, smuggled a statement out of the "Gulag"—the prison which is the Soviet U. It turned up in *the* N.Y. Times Magazine of June 8. Sakharov wrote: "I consider the United States the historically determined leader of the movement toward a pluralist & free society, vital to mankind."

He is right. ~~of course~~. We have strayed off course many times [*and*] been careless with the machinery of freedom bequeathed to us by the Founding Fathers, but, somehow, it has ~~survived~~ managed to survive our frailties. One of those Founding Fathers spoke the truth when he said, "God intended America to be free."

We have been a refuge for the persecuted & down-trodden from every corner of the world for 200 yrs. Today some of us are concerned by the latest influx of refugees, the ~~boat~~ boat people from ~~S.E.~~ [*Southeast*] Asia & from Cuba—all ~~are refugees from~~ *fleeing from the inhumanity of* communism. We worry about our capacity to care for them. I dont believe we should turn them away.

But let's do a better job of exporting Americanism. Let's meet our responsibility to keep the peace at the same time we maintain without compromise our principles & ideals. ~~Let it be our destiny to strive for a world in which people can live in freedom in their own homeland without~~

I believe it is our pre-ordained destiny to show all mankind that they, too, can be free without having to leave their native shore. ❖

This is the first economic speech by President Reagan—just sixteen days after he became president. Even then, with all the White House speechwriters and the resources of the federal government at his disposal, he was still writing for himself.

Economic Speech—Address to the Nation*
February 5, 1981

Good evening:

I have asked for this time tonite to give you a report on the state ~~of the~~ *of our* nation's ECONOMY. A few days ago I was presented with a report I had asked for—a comprehensive audit if you will of our economic condition. You wont like it, I didn't like it, but we have to face the truth and then go to work to turn things around. And make no mistake about it, we can turn them around.

I'm not going to subject you to the jumble of charts & figures and economic jargon of that audit but rather will try to explain where we are, how we got there & how we can get back.

First however let me just give a few "attention getters" from the audit. ~~The total deficit for~~ The Fed. budget is out of control and we face runaway deficits, $80 bil. for ~~the~~ this ~~year we're in~~ BUDGET YEAR THAT ENDS OCT. *1.* That deficit is larger than the entire *Fed.* budget in 1957 and so is the $80 bil. we NOW pay in interest on the nat. debt every year.

Twenty years ago in 1960 our Fed. govt. payroll was less than $13 bil. Today it is 75 bil. During those 20 yrs. our population has only increased by 26.3%. The Fed. budget has gone up 529%.

We have just had 2 years of back to back double *digit* inflation, 13.3% in 1979—12.4% last year. ~~This hasn't happened *to us* since W.W.I.~~ *The last time this happened was in W.W.I.*

In 1960 mortgage ~~rates~~ interest rates averaged about 6%. They are 2½ times as high now 15.4%. The percentage of your earnings ~~that govt.~~ the Fed. govt. took in taxes in 1960 has almost doubled. And finally there are 7 mil. Americans caught up in the personal indignity and human tragedy of unemployment. If they stood in a line—allowing 3 ft. for each person, the line would reach from the Coast of Maine to Calif.

Well so much for the audit itself. Let me try to put this in personal ~~≠~~ terms. Here is a dollar such as you earned, spent or saved in 1960. Here is a quarter, a dime & a penny—36¢. ~~That's~~ *Thirty Six Cents is* what this 1960 dollar is worth ~~in purchasing power today~~ TODAY. *And if the present inflation rate should continue a couple of more years that dollar of 1960 will be worth a dime.*

What has happened to that American dream of owning a home? Only 10 yrs. ago a family could buy a home ~~for a little~~ *and the monthly payments av-*

*From a private collection.

eraged little more than a quarter—27¢ out of each dollar earned. Today it takes 42¢ out of every dollar of income. So, fewer than 1 out of 11 familys can afford to buy a home.

Regulations adopted by govt. with the best of intentions have added $666 to the cost of an automobile. It is estimated that all together regulations ~~of~~ of every kind, on shopkeepers, farmers and major industries add $100 bil. to the cost of the goods & services we buy. And then another 20 or 30 bil. is spent by govt. handling the paper work created by those regulations.

I'm sure ~~that~~ you are getting the idea that the audit presented to me found govt. policies of the last few decades responsible for our economic troubles. We forgot or just overlooked the fact that govt.—any govt. has a built in tendency to grow. We all had a hand in looking to govt. for benefits as if govt. had some ~~other~~ source of revenue *other* than our earnings. Many if not most of the things we thought of or that govt. offered to us seemed attractive.

In the years following the 2ⁿᵈ World War it was easy (for awhile at least) to overlook the price tag. Our income more than doubled in the 25 years after the war. We increased our take home pay ~~more~~ in those 25 yrs. by more than we had amassed in all the preceding 150 yrs. put together. Yes there was some inflation 1 or 1½% ~~but it~~ THAT didn't bother us. But if we look back at those golden years we recall *that even then* ~~that~~ voices ~~were~~ *had been* raised warning that inflation like radioactivity was cumulative and that once started it could get out of control. Some govt. programs seemed so worthwhile that borrowing to fund them didn't bother us.

By 1960 our nat. debt stood at $291 bil. Congress in 1971 decided to put a ceiling of 400 bil. on our ability to borrow. Today the debt is $931 bil. ~~and I have to ask for~~ SO CALLED temporary increases IN THE DEBT CEILING have been allowed 21 times in these 10 years and now I must ask for *another* ~~an~~ increase ~~to~~ IN THE DEBT CEILING or the govt. will be unable to function past the middle of Feb. and *Ive only been here 2 weeks.* We face in the near future a public debt ~~in excess of~~ THAT COULD EXCEED a trillion dollars. *This is a figure literally beyond our comprehension.*

~~W~~ We know now that inflation is the result of ~~this~~ *all that* deficit spending. Govt. has only 2 ways of getting money other than raising taxes. It can go into the money market & borrow, competing with it's own citizens & driving up interest rates *which it has done,* or it can print money AND IT'S DONE THAT. ~~Both~~ Both methods are inflationary.

† We're victims of language, the very word "inflation" leads us to think of it as high prices. Then of course we resent the person who puts on the price tags forgetting that he or she is also a victim of inflation. Inflation is not high prices it is ~~reduced~~ *a reduction in the* value of *our* money. ~~When the money~~

supply is increased and *but* the goods & services available for buying are not, we have too much money chasing too few goods.

Wars are usually ~~characterized~~ ACCOMPANIED by inflation. Everyone is working or fighting but ~~the~~ production is ~~not for~~ *of* ~~consumer goods it is for weapons & munitions.~~ *of weapons and munitions not things we can buy & use.* ~~Again~~ *So* we have a healthy payroll but a limited supply of product for sale.

One way out would be to raise taxes so that govt. need not borrow or print money. But in all these years of govt. growth we've reached—indeed surpassed, the ability of our people to bear an increase in the tax burden.

Prior to W.W. II taxes were such that on the average we only had to work between 5 or 6 weeks *each year* to pay our total Fed., State, & local tax bill. Today we have to work between 5 or 6 <u>months</u> to pay that bill.

Some say shift the tax burden to business & industry but business ~~cant~~ *doesn't* pay taxes. Oh dont get the wrong idea, business is being taxed, so much so that we are being priced out of the world market. ~~You see~~ *But* business must pass it's costs of operation & that includes taxes, onto the customer in the price of the product. ~~or service In short~~ Only people pay taxes—all the taxes. *Govt. just uses business* IN A KIND OF SNEAKY WAY *to help collect the taxes.* ~~in a kind of sneaky way.~~

Today this once great industrial giant of ours has the lowest rate of gain in productivity of virtually all the industrial nations with whom we must compete ~~for~~ *in the* world market~~s~~. We cant even hold our ~~domestic~~ *own* market *here in America* against ~~foreign imports of~~ ≠ FOREIGN automobiles, steel and a number of other products.

~~The Japanese worker produces~~

‡ Japanese production of automobiles is 20 times as great—per worker as it is in America. The Japanese steelworker out produces his American counterpart by about 35 %.

This isn't because they are better workers. I'll match the American working man or woman against anyone in the world. But we have to give them the modern tools & equipment that workers in the other industrial nations have.

We invented the assembly line & mass production, but punitive tax policies and excessive & unnecessary regulations ~~have~~ plus govt. borrowing have prevented us from ~~modernizing~~ updating plant & equipment. When capital investment is made it is usually for some unproductive alterations demanded by govt. to meet various of it's regulations.

Excessive taxation of individuals has robbed ~~them~~ *us* of incentive & made overtime unprofitable.

We once produced about 40% of the worlds steel. We now produce 19%.

We were once the greatest producer of automobiles, producing more than all the rest of the world combined. Today the big 3, the major auto companies in our land have ~~posted~~ sustained ~~great~~ *tremendous* losses in the past year and have been forced to lay off thousands of workers.

All of you who are working know that even with cost of living pay raises you cant keep up with inflation. In our progressive tax system as you increase the number of dollars you earn you find yourself moved up into higher tax brackets, paying a higher tax rate just for trying to hold your own. The result?—The standard of living in our country is going down.

Over the past decades we've talked of curtailing govt. spending ~~so that~~ *SO THAT then* we can ~~then~~ lower the tax burden. Sometimes we've even taken a run at doing that. But always we held that taxes couldn't be cut until spending was reduced. ~~You know~~ *Well* we can lecture our children about extravagance until we run out of voice & ~~breath~~ breath. *OR* We can ~~also~~ cure their extravagance simply by reducing their allowance.

It is time to recognize that we have come to a turning point. We are faced with an economic calamity of tremendous proportions and the old business as usual treatment cant save us.

Together we must chart a different course. We must increase productivity and that means putting Americans back to work. That means making it possible for industry to modernize & make use of the technology which we ourselves invented. That means *ABOVE ALL* bringing govt. spending back within govt. revenues which is the only way ~~we can~~ together with increased productivity that we can reduce & yes eliminate inflation. ~~And that means reducing tax rates over a period of time to make govt's. share of gross national~~

In the past we've tried to fight inflation one year and then when unemployment increased ~~we'd~~ turn *THE NEXT YR.* to fighting ~~that~~ *UNEMPLOYMENT* with more deficit spending as a pump primer. ~~of~~ *SO AGAIN* up ~~would go~~ *GOES* inflation. ~~again.~~ It ~~wont~~ *HASN'T* worked. We dont have to choose between inflation & unemployment—they go hand in hand. It's time to try something different and that's what we're going to do.

We've already placed a freeze on hiring replacements for those who retire or leave govt. service. We have ordered a cut in *govt.* travel, reduced the number of ~~govt.~~ ≠ consultants to the govt. & stopped the buying of office equipment & other items. We have put a freeze on pending regulations and set up a task force ≠ under V.P. Bush to review existing regulations with an eye toward getting rid of ~~unnecessary~~ as many as possible. ~~But it will take more, much more.~~ We have decontrolled oil which should result in more domestic production & less dependence ~~over time~~ on OPEC. And last we have eliminated the ineffective wage & price program of the Council on Wage & Price Stability.

But it will take more much more and we must realize there is no quick fix. At the same time however we cannot delay ~~in~~ in implementing an ec. program aimed at reducing tax rates to stimulate productivity & reducing the rate of increase in govt. spending to ~~do away with~~ reduce unemployment & inflation.

On Feb. 18th I will present *IN DETAIL* an economic program to Congress embodying the features I have just stated. It will propose budget cuts in virtually every dept. of govt. It is my belief that these actual budget cuts will only be part of the savings. As our ~~Dept. heads~~ *Cabinet Secretarys* take charge of their depts. they will search out areas of waste, *≠* extravagance & costly administrative overhead which could yield substantial reductions.

At the same time we are doing this we must go forward with a tax *RELIEF* package. I shall ask for a 10% ~~a year~~ reduction across the board in the personal inc. tax for *EACH OF* the next 3 years. Proposals will also be submitted for accellerated depreciation allowances for business to provide ~~for~~ necessary capital *SO AS* to *≠* create jobs.

Now here again in saying this I know that language as I said earlier can get in the way of clear understanding of what of our program is intended to do. Budget cuts can sound as if we are going to reduce govt. ~~programs~~ spending to ~~less~~ *A LOWER LEVEL* than was spent ~~last year,~~ *THE YEAR BEFORE.* ~~that some worthwhile &~~ *≠ essential* ~~programs will be eliminated or cut drastically below their present level.~~ This is not the case. The budgets will increase as our population increases and each year will see spending increase to match our growth. Govt. revenues will increase as the economy grows but the burden will be lighter for each individual because the ec. base will have been expanded *by reason of the reduced rates.*

Let me show you ~~some~~ *a* charts I've had drawn to illustrate how this can be. Here ~~is the first one~~ you see 2 slanting lines. The bottom line shows the increase in tax revenues. The *red* ~~top~~ line *on top* is the increase in govt. spending. Both lines turn sharply upward reflecting the giant tax increase *ALREADY* built into the system for this year 1981 & the increases in spending built into the '81 & '82 budgets *and on into the future.*

As you can see the spending line rises at a steeper slant than the revenue line and does so increasingly toward the end. That ever widening gap between these lines measures the constant deficits we've been running ~~& at the end is the~~ *including this years* $80 bil. deficit. ~~I've already mentioned.~~

Now on ~~this 2nd chart you'll see what we are confident will be the result of~~ *the dotted lines represent the reduced rate of increase that will follow if Con-*

gress accepts our ec. program. Both lines continue to rise allowing for *necessary* growth but they dont rise ~~so~~ *as* steeply and ~~at the end~~ the gap narrows as spending cuts continue over the next few years until ~~Spending continues. And~~ finally the 2 lines come together meaning a balanced budget and the end of inflation. We think that will happen by 1983 and at that point *tax* revenues in spite of ~~the~~ reductions ≠ ~~plan will increase~~ *will be increasing* faster than spending which means we can have ~~further~~ further reductions in the tax rates.

In all of this we will of course work closely with the Fed. Reserve system toward the objective of a stable monetary policy.

Our spending cuts will not be at the expense of the truly needy. We will however seek to eliminate benefits to those who are not really qualified ≠ ~~not in actual need of help~~ *by reason* OF NEED.

~~Our basic system is sound, we can meet our responsibility to those who through no fault of their own need our help. We~~

As I've said before, on Feb. 18th I'll will present this ec. package of budget reductions & tax reform to a joint session of Cong. & to you in full detail.

Our basic system is sound, we can, with compassion continue to meet our responsibility to those who through no fault of their own need our help. We can meet fully the other legitimate responsibilities of govt. We cannot continue ANY LONGER our wasteful ways at the expense of the workers of this land or our children.

†*Keep this in if you think it's OK*
‡*Check this with Marty or Murray Wiedenbaum* ❖

On Saturday, March 19, 1983, President Reagan wrote this arms control memorandum at Camp David, instructing his National Security Advisor William Clark, "Bill, please place this into the system." While this document speaks for itself, Clark points out that its importance rises when considered with the following critical U.S.-Soviet events occurring in the February/ March 1983 time frame:

On January 27, 1983, U.S.-Soviet INF talks had resumed in Geneva; U.S. negotiators stress the Reagan Zero Option ideal, but emphasize flexibility. On February 8, the Soviets successfully test their new ICBM. On February 15, Ambassador Dobrynin concedes the Soviets expect U.S.-European missile deployment to succeed. Later in February, National Security Decision Directive #75 on soviet policy adds the new plans for influencing the internal policies of the U.S.S.R., termed "Rollback." On March 6, the Kohl "deployment" coalition is victorious in West German elections. On March 8, President Reagan delivers his "Evil Empire" address in Florida (the Soviet press

*denounces the event, saying "Reagan exhibits pathological hatred of social-
ism and communism"). On March 23, only four days following his Camp
David INF memo, the President resolutely announces his Strategic Defense
Initiative against missile attack, and offers to share that technology with the
Soviets. On March 26, Chairman Andropov charges President Reagan
"seeks to disarm the Soviet Union." On March 30, President Reagan proposes his compromise INF "interim solution," and begins to look forward to
the anticipated Summit with Chairman Andropov.**

I.N.F. Negotiations**
March 19, 1983

I believe we must announce our intention to offer an interim plan for reducing the number of I.N.F. missiles before the negotiations recess. I say this
with one qualifier—have we discussed this with the people at the table—
namely Paul Nitze? No one can have knowledge of the nuances and the flavor unless they've been present during the negotiations.

Having said that let me suggest that we tell our allies and our team to that
we intend to continue trying to persuade the Soviet representatives of the
wisdom and mutual benefit of eliminating this entire family of weapons. (Before they eliminate the family of man)

So our ultimate goal remains the same but we are willing to negotiate an
equitable & verefiable interim reduction—when the sessions resume in June.

The Soviet team at one point indicated a willingness to reduce the number
of S.S. 20's to 162 but at the same time predicated this on Nato remaining at
zero. This of course would have left the situation virtually unchanged from
what it is at present. True they would have reduced their warheads from
around 1300 to 486 but they would retain a monopoly on Intermediate
range missiles targeted on the Nato nations who in turn would have no deterrent force at all. And this is what is at issue—both nations should have a
deterrent NUCLEAR force or as we have urged—no such force *at all* in order to
stabilize the situation on the continents of Europe & |Asia.| ?

We will finalize the details with regard to proposed numbers and means of
verifiability as quickly as possible and after consultation with our allies present an interim plan to the Soviet U. *prior to resuming negotiations in June.*

If agreement can be reached as to the number of weapons we will begin
our phased deployment on schedule up to the number agreed upon while the
Soviet U. dismantles weapons down to meet us. If no agreement can be

---

*Interview with William Clark, October 23, 2000.
**From a private collection.

I. N. F. Negotiations

I believe we must announce our intention to offer an interim plan for reducing the number of I. N. F. missiles before the negotiations recess. I say this with one qualifier – have we discussed this with the people at the table – namely Paul Nitze? No one can have knowledge of the nuances and the flavor unless they've been present during the negotiations.

Having said that let me suggest that we tell our allies and our team that we intend to continue trying to persuade the Soviet representatives of the wisdom and mutual benefit of eliminating this entire family of weapons. (Before they eliminate the family of man)

So our ultimate goal remains the same but we are willing to negotiate an equitable & verifiable interim reduction – when the sessions resume in June.

The Soviet team at one point indicated a willingness to reduce the number of S.S.20's to 162 but at the same time predicated this on Nato remaining at zero. This of course would have left the situation virtually unchanged from what it is at present. True they would have reduced their warheads from around 1300 to 486 but they would retain a monopoly on Intermediate range missiles targeted on the Nato nations who in turn would have no deterrent force at all. And this is what is at issue – both nations should have a deterrent NUCLEAR force or as we have urged – no such force at all in order to stabilize the situation on the continent of Europe & [Asia] ?

We will finalize the details with regard to proposed numbers and means of verifiability as quickly as possible and after consultation with our allies present an interim plan to the Soviet prior to resuming negotiations in June.
If agreement can be reached as to the number of weapons we will begin our phased deployment on schedule up to the number agreed upon while the Soviet U. dismantles weapons down to meet us. If no agreement can be reached we will have to continue deployment to the level necessary to provide a believable deterrent.

reached we will have to ⨯ continue deployment to the level necessary to provide a believable deterrent. ❖

*Soviet Foreign Minister Andrei Gromyko usually attended the United Na-
tions General Assembly debate in New York in the fall and then traveled to
Washington to meet with the American president at the White House. Such
high-level U.S.-Soviet contacts came to a virtual halt in the aftermath of the
Soviet invasion of Afghanistan in December 1979.*

*Breaking the post-Afghanistan sanction against the Soviets, President
Reagan agreed to receive Soviet Foreign Minister Andrei Gromyko at the
White House on September 28, 1984. On the Monday morning before the
meeting the President called Secretary of State George Shultz and asked him
to come to the White House. "George," he said, "I've looked over your talking points, and they are very good. But I've been thinking about this all
weekend up at Camp David, and I've written my own talking points, and I'm
very satisfied with them. You can look them over if you want.* **

*The following document, which Reagan kept in his desk in Century City,
California, long after he left the presidency,* ** *contains these talking points.
The document expresses his desire to eliminate nuclear weapons; sets out all
elements of what became known as "the four-part agenda"—U.S. commitment to arms control, regional security, human rights, and trade and bilateral
contacts; states that peace is the goal of U.S. foreign policy; and separates
what Reagan considers the symptoms of the cold war from the sources of it.
Soviet imperialism, Reagan writes, is the source of the tension; the arms race
is a symptom of the conflict, and would be easier to control if the source of
mistrust were removed. The themes and ideas in Reagan's talking points also
are found in the "Peace" radio broadcast that he wrote in early 1975 and in
his March 13 and August 18, 1980, campaign speeches.* ****

*Public accounts of the Reagan-Gromyko meeting indicate that Reagan
did indeed use his own talking points on that important occasion.* *****

*George P. Shultz, *Turmoil and Triumph, My Years as Secretary of State* (New York: Charles
Scribner's Sons, 1993), 482.
**At Nancy Reagan's request, on October 4, 2000, Martin Anderson examined the papers in
Reagan's desk and found this document.
***The radio commentary and speeches are included in this book.
****See Andrei Gromyko (translated by Harold Shukman), *Memories* (London: Hutchin-
son, 1989), 304–309; John Newhouse, "The Diplomatic Round: Talk About Talks," *The
New Yorker,* December 31, 1984, 40–52; and Dan Oberdorfer, *The Turn: From the Cold
War to a New Era. The United States and the Soviet Union, 1983–1990* (New York: Posei-
don Press, 1991), 87–93.

"Mr. Minister"
September 23, 1984

~~Mr. Minister I've looked forward to this meeting and wish it could have taken place 3 or 4 years ago. I very much want to hear your views but if you dont mind I'd like to begin by expressing a few thoughts of my own, hoping that I can persuade you that I dont eat my young.~~

There are differences between our 2 pol. & ec. systems and I dont think either one of us will change. But we do have to live in the world together and we do have some things in common. We are both superpowers as viewed by the rest of the world and the rest of the world knows that the fate of all mankind is in our hands: that a war between us could literally wipe out all humankind.

Mr. Minister ~~I tell you with all sincerity~~ the U.S. will never start such a war. Now you may say you have nothing but my word for that but I ask you to look at the record. When W.W. II ended—a war in which we were allies, we were the only nation whose industry was intact,—not ravaged by war. Our military strength was at it's greatest & we alone had the ultimate weapon, the nuclear bomb.

We could have dictated to the world. We didn't. Instead we set out to help not only our allies but *ALSO* our erstwhile enemies to rebuild their economies & their industrial strength.

† *At the same time* We dismantled our military and today have only 2/3 as many nuclear weapons as we had in 1967. We have in these last ~~few~~ *several* years removed 1000 nuclear weapons from Europe & will have removed another 1400 by 1988. —*(INSERT 1)*

Yes we are rebuilding our depleted strength now because your own massive *MILITARY* buildup, the greatest in world history, is far beyond any defense needs and we feel it is a threat to us. From Lenin through Brezhnev your leaders & others high in your govt. have repeatedly proclaimed their dedication to world revolution & the eventual one world communist state. There were missiles in Cuba, continued expansion in S. East Asia & Africa as well as in Latin America.

Let me make it clear I'm citing some of the reasons why we feel you are a threat to our security and why we are determined to acquire sufficient strength to deter hostile action *AGAINST US* by you. We are not out to achieve superiority but we do not intend to become vulnerable *to an attack* or to an ultimatum in which our choice would be surrender or die. ~~or to outright attack.~~

Now you have expressed a belief that we are the aggressor and while I've already listed some reasons why we dont think there is any substance for such a belief let me take that a step further. We are well aware of the great losses you suffered in W.W. II. We know also that history records invasions of Russia going back over the centuries. Can we not take steps to clear the air of these suspicions? Would not arms reductions be an easy problem to solve if we could prove to each other that ~~we~~ neither of us has any aggressive intent?

We both know that other countries have turned to nuclear weapons and more are quietly working to achieve that goal. The danger of ~~some~~ such proliferation is the possibility of accidental war brought on by neither of us but triggering a conflict that could ultimately involve us both. But what if we who have the power to destroy the world should join in saving it? If we can reach agreement on reducing and ultimately eliminating these weapons we could persuade the rest of the world to join us in doing away with all such weapons.

~~Your country has proposed the beginning of negotiations to limit weapons in outer space. We are ready for such negotiations but we also want to begin negotiations for the reduction of offensive nuclear forces. We think there is an inherent relationship between these 2 classes of weapons. We believe a first objective could be, conclusion of an interim agreement that establishes on the one hand immediate constraints on space weapons & on the other begins the process of reductions in offensive nuclear arms.~~

We have shown each other that we can make some progress on bilateral issues. We have come to agreement on ~~some~~ *several* matters beneficial to us both. Maybe one of the things we should consider with regard to arms negotiations is the presence of senior levels in addition to the technicians. Another idea is a back channel which allows us to explore problems and solutions and to exchange ideas informally without commitments. We are ready to begin such a process with you & Ambassador Dobrynin* if you think such an idea has merit.

Mr. Minister I know you feel we are invading your sovereignty ~~rights~~ when we get into the area of human rights. I hope you've noticed that we would prefer quiet diplomacy on this subject but let me point out why we are concerned. Ours is a nation of immigrants. We are made up of the bloodlines of all the world and ~~we~~ OUR PEOPLE retain a loyalty to the countries of ~~our heritage.~~ THEIR ORIGIN. A man does not forget his mother because he has taken a wife. We also have a governmental system responsive to public opinion. It is easier for us to arrive at agreements with you if segments of our so-

*Ambassador Anatoly Dobrynin.

ciety are not upset by what they feel is a violation of human rights in the land of their ancestry. May I point to ~~an example~~ *your handling* of the matter of the pentacostal familys in our embassy. We have not, nor will we indicate in any way that this was anything other than a generous action by your govt. Your handling of that matter made such things as the grain ~~embargo~~ *agreement* easier for us to achieve.

I know some of your colleagues with less knowledge of our system than you have possibly think an American President can simply make decisions & they become policy or law. We have an elaborate system of checks & balances which as you know makes a President's life not quite that simple.

Mr. Minister the people of both our countries if asked would, I know, say peace was their greatest desire. If we really are worthy ~~to be~~ *of being* their leaders shouldn't we provide them with what they want above all else. And have we any right to lead if that is impossible for us to deliver?

†*Insert 1*

During these same years—since the Salt I agreement was signed the Soviet U. has added 6000 warheads, 3800 of those since the signing of Salt II. Since 1972 we have built only 2 systems—you have built 31. ❖

Reagan's Goodbye
November 5, 1994

My Fellow Americans,

I have recently been told that I am one of the millions of Americans who will be afflicted with Alzheimer's Disease.

Upon learning this news, Nancy & I had to decide whether as private citizens we would keep this a private matter or whether we would make this news known in a public way.

In the past Nancy suffered from breast cancer and I had my cancer surgeries. We found through our open disclosures we were able to raise public awareness. We were happy that as a result many more people underwent testing. They were treated in early stages and able to return to normal, healthy lives.

So now, we feel it is important to share it with you. In opening our hearts, we hope this might promote greater awareness of this condition. Perhaps it will encourage a clearer understanding of the individuals and families who are affected by it.

At the moment I feel just fine. I intend to live the remainder of the years God gives me on this earth doing the things I have always done. I will continue to share life's journey with my beloved Nancy and my family. I plan to enjoy the great outdoors and stay in touch with my friends and supporters.

Unfortunately, as Alzheimer's Disease progresses, the family often bears a heavy burden. I only wish there was some way I could spare Nancy from this painful experience. When the time comes I am confident that with your help she will face it with faith and courage.

In closing let me thank you, the American people for giving me the great honor of allowing me to serve as your President. When the Lord calls me home, ≠ whenever that may be, I will leave with the greatest love for this country of ours and eternal optimism for its future.

I now begin this journey that will lead me into the sunset of my life. I know that for America there will always be a a bright dawn ahead.

Thank you my friends. May God always bless you.

Sincerely,

Ronald Reagan

APPENDIX

"This is Ronald Reagan

Thanks for listening."

RONALD REAGAN'S
RADIO ADDRESSES
1975–79

Of more than 1,000 radio addresses taped by Ronald Reagan and distributed by O'Connor Creative Services, handwritten drafts by Reagan have been found of 670 of them. O'Connor used batch numbers (such as 75-01 and 75-02) to identify sets of radio addresses. The 1976 series begins in September 1976, when Reagan returned to broadcasting after the 1976 presidential primary election campaign, and continues for a year. Thus, batches 76-08 through 76-19 were distributed in calendar year 1977, and the next batch is 77-20. In 1978 and 1979, O'Connor's batch numbers match the calendar years. A few O'Connor distribution lists are missing.

The radio addresses for which we have handwritten drafts by Reagan are indicated by bold type in the Title column and a document description in the Handwritten Draft column. For example, 14-2 is legal-size paper, two pages; 11-3 is letter-size paper, three pages. Sometimes the color of the ink is noted; p indicates pencil. The "ldt" designation means that a line was drawn through the document by a secretary indicating it had been typed. Usually this was not done. Where someone else is known to have written the initial draft, the author's name is shown in the Handwritten Draft column.

Almost all the documents were found in the Pre-Presidential Papers in boxes 12, 14, 15, and 21, located at the Reagan Presidential Library in Reagan's private collection. A box number (B) is indicated only where the handwritten draft and typescript are in different boxes; a "pc" indicates that the draft is in a private collection. A process is underway to prepare for public use the documents in the Pre-Presidential Papers that are presented in this book. The completion of this process will produce new box numbers, and a new index that correlates the numbering system that was used at the time we wrote this book with the new numbering system.

Various collections in the Hoover Institution Archives (see Introduction) have copies of the typed radio addresses that Reagan used when recording them (double-spaced, and sometimes including handwritten changes) and single-spaced copies of the addresses as recorded, which were prepared by O'Connor Creative Services and distributed to radio stations with the records or tapes. The O'Connor distributions do not include Reagan's introduction to each broadcast or his sign-off line: "This is Ronald Reagan. Thanks for listening."

Where a taping date indicates only a month and year and not a specific day, the taping date is estimated. Addresses taped on a particular date usually went out in the next O'Connor distribution, but were sometimes held for a later distribution.

The radio addresses were usually distributed to radio stations on two-sided records; sides A and B. Where no side is indicated, the addresses were distributed on tape. The Book Page column is the page number in this book where a typescript of the handwritten draft can be found.

O'Connor Number	Title	Side/ Number	Taping Date	Handwritten Draft	Book Page
75-01	Food Stamps	A1	1/8/1975		
	Consumer Protection	A2	1/8/1975		
	Inflation	A3	1/8/1975	9-4 B12	255
	Boondoggle	A4	1/8/1975		
	Cuba	A5	1/8/1975		
	Unemployment (1)	B1	1/8/1975		
	Unemployment (2)	B2	1/8/1975		
	Unemployment (3)	B3	1/8/1975		
	Bureaucrats	B4	1/8/1975		
	Civil Service	B5	1/8/1975		
	3 R's	B6	1/8/1975		
	Postal Service	B7	1/8/1975		
	Fair Trade	B8	1/8/1975		
75-02	Inflation Fighting	A1	2/1/1975		
	Supply and Demand	A2	2/1/1975		
	Surprise Tax Bills	A3	2/1/1975		
	Energy Problems	A4	2/1/1975		
	Rocky's Story	A5	2/1/1975		
	Public Employees	B1	2/1/1975		
	Viet Nam Policy	B2	2/1/1975		
	Capitalism-Socialism	B3	2/1/1975		
	Volunteerism	B4	2/1/1975		
	Incredible Bread Machine	B5	2/1/1975		
	Red China	B6	2/1/1975		
75-03	Federal Budget	A1	2/14/1975		
	Detente	A2	2/14/1975		
	Peru Revolution	A3	2/14/1975		
	Mozart vs Sibelius	A4	2/14/1975	Peter Hannaford	
	The Delta Queen	A5	2/14/1975		
	A Cuba Documentary	A6	2/14/1975	14-2 B 21	
	Farm Facts	B1	2/14/1975	14-2 B 21	
	Tax Plan #1	B2	2/14/1975	14-3 B 21	
	Tax Plan #2	B3	2/14/1975	14-3 B 21	
	Tax Plan #3	B4	2/14/1975	14-3 B 21	
	Arms Limitations	B5	2/14/1975		
	Crisis of Democracy	B6	2/14/1975		
75-04	**Unemployment #1**	A1	2/27/1975	14-2 B21	
	Unemployment #2	A2	2/27/1975	14-2 B21	
	W. Germany/Inflation	A3	2/27/1975		
	National Debt #1	A4	2/27/1975		
	National Debt #2	A5	2/27/1975		
	Congress & Security	A6	2/27/1975		
	The Work Ethic	B1	2/27/1975		
	Land Planning	B2	2/27/1975	14-2 B 21	338
	Price of Beef	B3	2/27/1975	14-2 B 21	
	Private Government	B4	2/27/1975		
	N.H. Senate Contest	B5	2/27/1975		
	Recession vs Inflation	B6	2/27/1975	14-2 B 21	264
75-05	Southeast Asia	A1	3/12/1975		
	Energy Sources	A2	3/12/1975		
	Capital Punishment	A3	3/12/1975		
	Vacation Exchange Program	A4	3/12/1975		
	The Superintendent's Dilemma	A5	3/12/1975		
	Oil Talk	A6	3/12/1975	14-2 B 21	
	Tiffany & Company	B1	3/12/1975	14-2 B 21	
	Cold Beer	B2	3/12/1975		

O'Connor Number	Title	Side/ Number	Taping Date	Handwritten Draft	Book Page
	Regulations	B3	3/12/1975	14-2 B21	294
	Federal Retirement Pensions	B4	3/12/1975		
	Easy Voting	B5	3/12/1975	14-2 B 21	
	The Money Supply	B6	3/12/1975		
75-06	Portugal #1	1	March-75		
	Portugal #2	2	March-75		
	Energy #1	3	March-75		
	Energy #2	4	March-75		
	Campaign Law	5	March-75		
75-07	**Indochina #1**	A1	April-75	14-2 B 15	
	Indochina #2	A2	April-75	14-2 B 21	48
	Satellites	A3	April-75		
	Utility Subsidies	A4	April-75		
	Postal Feedback	A5	April-75		
	Patent Proposals	B1	April-75		
	The New Congress	B2	April-75		
	Abortion Laws	B3	April-75	14-2 B21	380
	Welfare Program #1	B4	April-75	14-2 B21	
	Welfare Program #2	B5	April-75	14-2 B21	389
	Welfare Program #3	B6	April-75	14-2 B21	
75-08	London #1	A1	April-75		
	London #2	A2	April-75		
	London #3	A3	April-75		
	Regulations—New Wave #1	A4	April-75		
	Regulations—New Wave #2	A5	April-75		
	Farm Workers Union	A6	April-75	14-2 B21	
	No Time to Confuse	B1	April-75		
	Vietnam	B2	April-75	14-3 B21	
	Land Use	B3	April-75		
	Peace	B4	April-75	11-3 B 21	4
	Government: Big vs Small #1	B5	April-75		
	Government: Big vs Small #2	B6	April-75		
75-09	The Amazing DeBolts	A1	May-75		
	The Washington Media	A2	May-75		
	Italian Bureaucracy and the U.S. Treasury	A3	May-75		
	United Nations	A4	May-75	14-3 B 21	159
	Red Sea	A5	May-75		
	Nuclear Power	B1	May-75	14-2 B 21	323
	Recession's Cause	B2	May-75		
	Portugal	B3	May-75		
	Government Computers	B4	May-75	11-2 B 21	
	Adoption	B5	May-75	11-2 B 21	
75-10	Agency for Consumer Advocacy	A1	May-75		
	George Meany and Economics	A2	May-75	14-3 B 21	
	Communism, the Disease	A3	May-75	14-2 B 21	10
	Soviet Superiority	A4	May-75		
	The EPA Strikes Again	A5	May-75		
	Panama Canal	A6	May-75		
	Boondoggles' Foe	B1	May-75		
	Radical Chic Revisited	B2	May-75		
	Falling Dominoes	B3	May-75		
	Truth in Spending	B4	May-75		

O'Connor Number	Title	Side/ Number	Taping Date	Handwritten Draft	Book Page
	Congress vs Local Government	B5	May-75	14-2 B 21	
	Tax Loopholes	B6	May-75	14-2 B 21	268
75-11	Is This the Land of Our Fathers?	A1	Jun-75	Maureen Reagan (recorded by MR)	
	Is Government Our Big Brother?	A2	Jun-75	Maureen Reagan (recorded by MR)	
	Seen Your Doctor Lately?	A3	Jun-75	Maureen Reagan (recorded by MR)	
	Big Mo	A4	Jun-75	14-3 B 21	
	Inflation as Tax	A5	Jun-75	14-3 B 21	
	Cost Overruns	A6	Jun-75	11-2 B 21	
	Gun Control #1	B1	Jun-75		
	Gun Control #2	B2	Jun-75		
	Gun Control #3	B3	Jun-75		
	Button Button	B4	Jun-75		
	Letters to the Editor	B5	Jun-75	14-2 B 21	15
	Business Profits, Myths & Realities	B6	Jun-75	14-2 B 21	
75-12	Free Enterprise	A1	Jun-75		
	Law and Order	A2	Jun-75	14-2 B 21	
	Job Hunting	A3	Jun-75		
	Budget "Uncontrollables"	A4	Jun-75		
	Aquaculture	A5	Jun-75		
	Stopping Vandalism	A6	Jun-75		
	Mariana Islands	B1	Jun-75		
	Congressional "Perks"	B2	Jun-75		
	Samizdat	B3	Jun-75		
	M.I.A.	B4	Jun-75		
	Pacific Legal Foundation	B5	Jun-75		
	Polls on Government	B6	Jun-75		
75-13	Chile	A1	Jul-75	14-2 B 21	
	UNICEF	A2	Jul-75	14-2 B 21	
	Socialized Medicine I	A3	Jul-75	14-2 B 21	364
	Socialized Medicine II	A4	Jul-75	14-2 B 21	
	Community Work Experience Program	A5	Jul-75		
	Phu Quoc	A6	Jul-75	14-2 B 21	
	Welfare Reform Corporations I	B1	Jul-75		
	Welfare Reform Corporations II	B2	Jul-75		
	Welfare Reform Corporations III	B3	Jul-75		
	Do Away with IRS?	B4	Jul-75		
	Turtles and Aquaculture	B5	Jul-75		
	Somalia	B6	Jul-75		
75-14	Equal Rights Amendment—Pro	1	Aug-75	Maureen Reagan (recorded by MR)	
	Equal Rights Amendment—Con	2	Aug-75		
	Soviet Life	3	Aug-75		
	World Affairs Report	4	Aug-75		
	"Why don't they ___ ?"	5	Aug-75		
75-15	Oil and the Shah of Iran	1	Aug-75		

O'Connor Number	Title	Side/ Number	Taping Date	Handwritten Draft	Book Page
75-20	Economic Planning	A1	Oct-75		
	The Russian Wheat Deal	A2	Oct-75	14-3 B21	26
	Secret Service	A3	Oct-75	14-3 B21	
	Detente	A4	Oct-75		
	Some Thoughts on Unemployment	A5	Oct-75		
	Samizdat	A6	Oct-75		
	Common Situs Picketing	B1	Oct-75		
	New Gasoline Lines?	B2	Oct-75		
	The Superintendent's Dilemma	B3	Oct-75		
	The Incredible Bread Machine	B4	Oct-75		
	A Break for the Handicapped	B5	Oct-75	Julie Nixon Eisenhower (recorded by JNE)	
	Welfare Abuses	B6	Oct-75	Julie Nixon Eisenhower (recorded by JNE)	
75-21	Clearcutting	1	Nov-75		
	Government Pay	2	Nov-75		
	Letter to Employees	3	Nov-75		
	Panama Canal	4	Nov-75		
	Welfare Letter	5	Nov-75		
	National Land Use Policy #1	6	Nov-75		
	National Land Use Policy #2	7	Nov-75		
	National Land Use Policy #3	8	Nov-75		
	The Trouble with New York City	9	Nov-75		
75-22	Crime	1	Nov-75		
	What Would You Do If You Woke to Find a Burglar in Your Home?	2	Nov-75	William F. Buckley (recorded by WFB)	
	Is Gerald Ford Ganging Up on New York City?	3	Nov-75	William F. Buckley (recorded by WFB)	
	Should Ex-CIA Employees Be Treated as Second-Class Citizens?	4	Nov-75	William F. Buckley (recorded by WFB) William F. Buckley	
	How Do You Talk Back to Eric Sevareid?	5	Nov-75	William F. Buckley (recorded by WFB)	
	Should We Really Give Away the Panama Canal?	6	Nov-75	William F. Buckley (recorded by WFB)	
	Women in Government and Politics #1	7	Nov-75	Julie Nixon Eisenhower (recorded by JNE)	
	Women in Government and Politics #2	8	Nov-75	Julie Nixon Eisenhower (recorded by JNE)	
	Women in Government and Politics #3	9	Nov-75	Julie Nixon Eisenhower (recorded by JNE)	
76-01	**Convention #1**	A1	9/1/1976	14-2 B 21	235
	Platforms A	A2	9/1/1976		
	Platforms B	A3	9/1/1976	14-2 B 21	
	Platforms C	A4	9/1/1976	14-2 B 21	
	Panama Canal	A5	9/1/1976		
	Getting Back at the Bureaucrats A	A6	9/1/1976	14-2 B 21	
	Bureaucrats B	B1	9/1/1976	14-2 B 21	
	Congress' Automatic Pay Raise	B2	9/1/1976		

O'Connor Number	Title	Side/ Number	Taping Date	Handwritten Draft	Book Page
	Women's March	B3	9/1/1976	14-2 B 21	
	China	B4	9/1/1976		
	Shaping the World for 100 Years to Come	B5	9/1/1976	14-2 B 21	9
	Tax Reform	B6	9/1/1976	14-2 B 21	
76-02	The Median Is the Message	A1	9/21/1976		
	Panama's Press	A2	9/21/1976		
	Mao's China	A3	9/21/1976		
	About the Press	A4	9/21/1976	14-2	247
	Education (A)	A5	9/21/1976	14-2	
	Education (B)	A6	9/21/1976	14-2	344
	Herman Kahn, Futurist	A7	9/21/1976		
	Paperwork & Bureaucrats	B1	9/21/1976	14-2	295
	Institute for Contemporary Studies	B2	9/21/1976		
	Humphrey-Hawkins Bill (Jobs A)	B3	9/21/1976	14-2	
	Humphrey-Hawkins Bill (Jobs B)	B4	9/21/1976	14-3	265
	FORBES on "Full" Employment	B5	9/21/1976		
	President Coolidge	B6	9/21/1976	14-2	
	Nuclear Wastes	B7	9/21/1976		
	The Hope of Mankind	B8	9/21/1976	14-2	224
76-03	The Ford Strike	A1	10/18/1976		
	Election Day, November 2, 1976	A2	10/18/1976		
	Vietnam	A3	10/18/1976	11-3	
	Reporters, Sources & Laws	A4	10/18/1976		
	The Fate of 14 (b)	A5	10/18/1976		
	The Speedy Trial Act	A6	10/18/1976		
	Welfare	A7	10/18/1976	11-2	
	Running Fence	B1	10/18/1976		
	"Bread Machine" and Janeway	B2	10/18/1976		
	Soviet TV and America	B3	10/18/1976	Peter Hannaford	
	Government Forms	B4	11/28/1978	11-2	
	Milton Friedman #1	B5	10/18/1976		
	Milton Friedman #2	B6	10/18/1976		
	Sweden 1	B7	10/18/1976	11-2 B 14	
	Sweden 2	B8	10/18/1976	11-2 B 14	
76-04	Diamond Lanes	A1	11/2/1976		
	Tax Reform I	A2	11/2/1976	14-2	
	Tax Reform II	A3	11/2/1976	14-2	
	Hoover's America Plan	A4	11/2/1976		
	Africa	A5	11/2/1976		
	Freedom Train	A6	11/2/1976	11-3	230
	Glomar Explorer	A7	11/2/1976		
	Katyn Forest	B1	11/2/1976	14-2	31
	Big Government and the Cities	B2	11/2/1976		
	San Francisco	B3	11/2/1976	14-2	406
	Berkeley's Street Tax	B4	11/2/1976		
	The Politics of the Federal Government	B5	11/2/1976		
	The Alaska Gas Pipeline	B6	11/2/1976		

O'Connor Number	Title	Side/ Number	Taping Date	Handwritten Draft	Book Page
	The Communes	B7	11/2/1976	11-3	
	New Directions	B8	11/2/1976		
76-05	Centralized Planning	A1	11/2/1976		
	Bureaucrats Revisited	A2	11/2/1976	14.5	
	Inflation and the Property Tax I	A3	11/2/1976		
	Inflation and the Property Tax II	A4	11/2/1976		
	Land Use Planning	A5	11/2/1976		
	Education I	A6	11/16/1976	14-2	342
	Education II	A7	11/16/1976	14-2	
	Campaign Reminiscence	B1	11/16/1976	14-2	
	Citizen's Choice	B2	11/16/1976		
	Liberals	B3	11/16/1976	14-2	
	Red Hen	B4	11/16/1976	1/8p. intro	262
	Government Cost I	B5	11/16/1976	14-2	
	Government Cost II	B6	11/16/1976	14-2	270
	Solar Energy	B7	11/16/1976		
	Britain	B8	11/16/1976	14-2	
76-06	Unemployment & Inflation I	A1	11/16/1976		
	Unemployment & Inflation II	A2	11/16/1976		
	Unemployment & Inflation III	A3	11/16/1976		
	Unemployment & Inflation IV	A4	11/30/1976		
	Unemployment & Inflation V	A5	11/30/1976		
	Cuba	A6	11/16/1976	14-2	195
	Terrorism	A7	11/16/1976	14-2	
	United Nations	B1	11/30/1976	14-2	164
	Vietnam I	B2	11/30/1976	14-2	50
	Vietnam II	B3	11/30/1976	14-2	134
	Pardons	B4	11/30/1976	14-2	
	Child Services Act	B5	11/30/1976	14-2	
	Socialism	B6	11/30/1976	14-2	
	Soviet Visas	B7	11/30/1976	11-3	144
	Human Rights Double Standard	B8	11/30/1976		
76-07	Postal Profits	A1	11/30/1976		
	Special Parents; Special Kids	A2	11/30/1976		
	Update on Social Security	A3	11/30/1976		
	Crime I	A4	11/30/1976	14-2	401
	Crime II	A5	11/30/1976	11-3	
	America's Strength	A6	12/22/1976	11-3	12
	Crime	A7	12/22/1976	11-3	400
	Public Broadcasting	B1	12/22/1976	11-3	250
	Welfare	B2	12/22/1976	11-3	390
	Tricentennial	B3	12/22/1976		
	The Family . . . and Other Living Things	B4	12/22/1976		
	Milton Friedman and Chile	B5	12/22/1976	11-3	
	South Vietnamese Boat People	B6	12/22/1976		
	New Hampshire & Vermont	B7	12/22/1976		
	Memo to a Liberal	B8	12/22/1976		

O'Connor Number	Title	Side/ Number	Taping Date	Handwritten Draft	Book Page
76-08	Strategic Stockpiles	A1	1/19/1977		
	Farewell Speeches	A2	1/19/1977	14-2	64
	Campaign Law Violated?	A3	1/19/1977		
	Panama	A4	1/19/1977	11-1	
	Television	A5	1/19/1977	11-2	
	Korea	A6	1/19/1977	11-3	
	People Power	A7	1/19/1977		
	Tax Limit	B1	12/22/1976	14-2	
	Televisions & Profits	B2	12/22/1976	14-2	
	Health Care	B3	12/22/1976	14-2	
	Rapid Transit	B4	12/22/1976	14-2	307
	Junk Food	B5	12/22/1976	11-3	
	Building Codes	B6	1/19/1977		
	OSHA	B7	1/19/1977	14-2 B20 misc	
	More About OSHA	B8	1/19/1977	14-2 B20 misc	
76-09	The Real China?	A1	1/19/1977	14-2	
	Capital Gains	A2	1/19/1977	14-2	
	More About Taxes	A3	1/19/1977	14-2	271
	Postcard Registration	A4	1/19/1977	14-2	244
	Poverty	A5	1/19/1977	14-2	391
	Amnesty	A6	2/2/1977	14-2	
	Foundations	A7	2/2/1977	14-2	
	Conservation	B1	2/2/1977		
	China	B2	2/2/1977	14-2	
	Tom Wolfe's New Book	B3	2/2/1977		
	Torrijos, Human Rights and Money Lenders	B4	2/2/1977		
	IBM	B5	2/2/1977	14-2	
	Congress	B6	2/2/1977	14-2	
	Civil Service	B7	2/2/1977	14-2	237
	Rhodesia	B8	2/2/1977	14-2	179
76-10	Minimum Wage	A1	2/2/1977	14-2	
	Taxes I	A2	2/2/1977	14-2	
	Taxes II	A3	2/2/1977	14-2	
	Taxes III	A4	2/2/1977	14-2	281
	Agriculture Day	A5	3/2/1977	11-2	
	Update on Cuba	A6	3/2/1977		
	Cuba II	A7	3/2/1977	14-2	
	England	B1	3/2/1977	14-2	
	Seabrook	B2	3/2/1977	14-2	
	Germany	B3	3/2/1977	14-2	
	Added Inflation	B4	3/2/1977	14-2	
	Census	B5	3/2/1977	14-2	239
	Sports and Religion	B6	3/2/1977	14-2	
	Amtrak	B7	3/2/1977		
	Free Press and Property Rights	B8	3/2/1977		
76-11?	Economic Plan	1	3/23/1977	14-2	
	Equal Rights Amendment	2	3/23/1977		
	Taxes	3	3/23/1977	14-2	
	Intelligence	4	3/23/1977	14-2	117
	Saccharin	5	3/23/1977		
	National Review	6	3/23/1977	14-2	
	Chile I	7	3/23/1977	14-2	
	Chile II	8	3/23/1977	14-2	
	Chile III	9	3/23/1977	14-2	
	Labor	10	3/23/1977	14-2	245

	Murphy's Law	11	3/23/1977	14-2	
	Day Care Centers	12	3/23/1977	14-2	377
	Charity	13	3/23/1977	14-2	
	"Argo Merchant"	14	3/23/1977	14-2	
	Government by the People	15	3/23/1977	14-2	
76-12	Redwoods	A1	4/13/1977	14-2	
	Capital Punishment	A2	4/13/1977	14-2	
	Electoral College	A3	4/13/1977	14-2	242
	Panama	A4	4/13/1977	14-2	
	Brezhnev	A5	4/13/1977	14-2	212
	Gasohol	A6	4/13/1977	14-2	
	Coal Tar	A7	4/13/1977		
	Human Rights	B1	4/13/1977	14-2	165
	Jamaica	B2	4/13/1977	14-2	
	Recyled Theater	B3	4/13/1977		
	Environment	B4	4/13/1977	14-2	326
	Education & Religion	B5	4/13/1977	14-2	359
	Miranda	B6	4/13/1977	14-2	
	Student Letter	B7	4/13/1977	14-2	
	Arson	B8	4/13/1977	14-2	
76-13	FBI	A1	5/4/1977		
	A Renewable Source	A2	5/4/1977	14-2	
	Rhodesia	A3	5/4/1977	14-2	
	Lawnmowers	A4	5/4/1977	14-2	
	Cuba & Africa	A5	5/4/1977	14-2	183
	Kidco	A6	5/4/1977	14-2	
	Keng Piao	A7	5/4/1977	14-2	35
	Punishment	B1	5/4/1977	14-2	399
	Drugs & the FDA	B2	5/4/1977	14-2	297
	Lord Chalfont	B3	5/4/1977	14-2	
	Recycled Streamliner	B4	5/4/1977		
	Strategy I	B5	5/4/1977	14-2	110
	Strategy II	B6	5/4/1977	14-2	111
	Bill Niehouse	B7	5/4/1977	14-2	
	Postcard Registration	B8	5/4/1977		
76-14	Korea	A1	5/25/1977	14-2	66
	FBI	A2	5/25/1977	14-2	
	Voting	A3	5/25/1977	14-2	241
	Public Servants	A4	5/25/1977	14-2	298
	Cuba—Trouble in Paradise	A5	5/25/1977		
	National Review	A6	5/25/1977	14-2	
	Cambodia #1	A7	5/25/1977	14-2	36
	Cambodia #2	B1	5/25/1977	14-2	38
	Cambodia #3	B2	5/25/1977	14-2	40
	Soviet Workers	B3	5/25/1977	14-2	146
	Why Government Costs Money	B4	5/25/1977	14-2	
	Marijuana	B5	5/25/1977	14-2	
	Government Spending	B6	5/25/1977	14-2	256
	Inflation	B7	5/25/1977	14-2	
	Russians	B8	5/25/1977	14-3	33
76-15	Privacy Bureau	A1	6/15/1977	Peter Hannaford	
	Vietnam	A2	6/15/1977	14-2	
	Oil I	A3	6/15/1977	14-3	318
	Oil II	A4	6/15/1977	14-2	
	Cuba	A5	6/15/1977	14-2	156

O'Connor Number	Title	Side/ Number	Taping Date	Handwritten Draft	Book Page
	Episcopal Controversy	A6	6/15/1977	Peter Hannaford	
	Intelligence	A7	6/15/1977	14-2	124
	OSHA	B1	6/15/1977	14-2	288
	DNA Research	B2	6/15/1977	Peter Hannaford	
	Indexing	B3	6/15/1977	14-2	272
	Force Account Work	B4	6/15/1977	Peter Hannaford	
	Common Sense Bureaucrats	B5	6/15/1977	Peter Hannaford	
	Economic Fairy Tales	B6	6/15/1977	14-2	
	Health Costs	B7	6/15/1977	14-3	
	Names	B8	6/15/1977	14-2	
76-16	Private Property	A1	7/6/1977	14-2	
	The Hatch Act	A2	7/6/1977	14-2	
	South Africa	A3	7/6/1977	14-2	185
	Food Stamps	A4	7/6/1977	14-2	393
	Man's Castle	A5	7/6/1977	14-2	291
	Jamaica	A6	7/6/1977	14-2	196
	Endangered Species	A7	7/6/1977	14-2	329
	Socialized Medicine	B1	7/6/1977	14-2	366
	The Principal's Principles	B2	7/6/1977		
	Property Rights	B3	7/6/1977	14-2	167
	Cambodia	B4	7/6/1977	14-2	
	Bulletins	B5	7/6/1977	14-2	
	Spending	B6	7/6/1977	14-2	
	Government Cost	B7	7/6/1977	14-3	
	Quiz	B8	7/6/1977	14-2	
76-17	Food Stamps	A1	July-77		
	Neutron Bomb I	A2	July-77		
	Neutron Bomb II	A3	July-77		
	Ukraine	A4	July-77		
	Tax Shift	A5	July-77		
	Drunk Driving	A6	July-77		
	Korea I	A7	July-77		
	Korea II	A8	July-77		
	Korea III	B1	July-77		
	Laxalt	B2	July-77		
	Human Rights	B3	July-77		
	Snail Darter	B4	July-77		
	Busing	B5	July-77		
	NEA	B6	July-77		
	Porpoises and Tuna	B7	July-77		
	Small Business	B8	July-77		
76-18	Panama	A1	8/15/1977	14-2	198
	Cover Up	A2	8/15/1977	14-2 ldt	
	Justice Department	A3	8/15/1977	14-2 ldt	
	Unemployment	A4	8/15/1977	14-2 ldt	266
	Medical Care	A5	8/15/1977	14-2 ldt	
	World Research	A6	8/15/1977	14-2	
	TRIS	A7	8/15/1977	14-2 ldt	
	Montage	B1	8/15/1977	14-2 ldt	
	Dream World	B2	8/15/1977	14-2 ldt	
	Tom Hayden	B3	8/15/1977	14-3 ldt—gr [green]	
	Business	B4	8/15/1977	14-2 ldt—gr bl [blue]	
	Inflation	B5	8/15/1977	14-2 ldt—gr	
	Korea	B6	8/15/1977	14-2 bl.	41
	Rhodesia	B7	8/15/1977	14-2 gr.	
	Foreign Aid	B8	8/15/1977	14-2 ldt bl.	168

O'Connor Number	Title	Side/ Number	Taping Date	Handwritten Draft	Book Page
76-19	L.A.Times	A1	9/6/1977	14-2	199
	Panama Canal I	A2	9/6/1977	14-2 note from RR	201
	Panama Canal II	A3	9/6/1977	14-3	202
	The Bible	A4	9/6/1977	14-2	409
	Kettering	A5	9/6/1977	14-2	309
	Government Costs	A6	9/6/1977	14-2	
	Cuba I	A7	9/6/1977	14-2	
	Cuba II	B1	9/6/1977	14-2	
	Youth Employment	B2	9/6/1977	14-2	303
	The Olympics	B3	9/6/1977	14-2	214
	Government Can Cost Less I	B4	9/6/1977	14-2	
	Government Can Cost Less II	B5	9/6/1977	14-2	
	Pensions	B6	9/6/1977	14-2	373
	Blackout	B7	9/6/1977	14-2	
	Furbish Lousewart	B8	9/6/1977	14-2	
77-20	Pot	A1	9/27/1977	14-2 ldt	
	Rhodesia	A2	9/27/1977	14-2 ldt	
	Carter Welfare Reform #1	A3	9/27/1977		
	Carter Welfare Reform #2	A4	9/27/1977		
	The Stalinoids	A5	9/27/1977		
	Hospital Costs	A6	9/27/1977	14-2	
	Mozambique	A7	9/27/1977	14-2	186
	Olympics	B1	9/27/1977	14-2 ldt	
	Tax Limitation	B2	9/27/1977	14-2 ldt	
	Air Bags	B3	9/27/1977	14-2 ldt	
	Camps	B4	9/27/1977	14-2 ldt	
	The Military	B5	9/27/1977	14-2 ldt	69
	Property Rights	B6	9/27/1977	14-2 note re letter	340
	Congressional Committees	B7	9/27/1977	14-2 ldt (ink)	126
	The Myth of the Medicare Millionaires	B8	9/27/1977		
77-21	Energy	A1	10/18/1977	14-2	
	Carter Welfare Reform	A2	10/18/1977		
	Treaties	A3	10/18/1977	14-2	51
	Panama I	A4	10/18/1977	14-2	204
	Panama II	A5	10/18/1977	14-2	205
	Panama III	A6	10/18/1977	14-3	
	Steel	A7	10/18/1977	14-2 dark	
	Land	B1	10/18/1977	14-3 dark	
	Taxes	B2	10/18/1977	14-2 dark	274
	Energy I	B3	10/18/1977	14-2 dark	
	Energy II	B4	10/18/1977	14-2 dark	
	Equal Time	B5	10/18/1977	14-2	
	Items	B6	10/18/1977	14-2	
	Investigative Agencies	B7	10/18/1977	14-2	
	Drugs	B8	10/18/1977	14-2	
77-22	SALT	A1	11/8/1977	14-2 gr	75
	Pushers	A2	11/8/1977	14-2	
	Kearney	A3	11/8/1977	14-2	
	Alaska	A4	11/8/1977	14-2	336
	Good News	A5	11/8/1977	14-2	
	Youth and Crime	A6	11/8/1977	14-2	
	Free Enterprise	A7	11/8/1977	14-2	
	Aid to Vietnam	B1	11/8/1977	14-2	
	The Individual	B2	11/8/1977	14-2	
	Taxation	B3	11/8/1977	14-2 dark	

O'Connor Number	Title	Side/ Number	Taping Date	Handwritten Draft	Book Page
	Energy	B4	11/8/1977	14-2	
	Restitution	B5	11/8/1977	14-2	
	Freedom	B6	11/8/1977	14-2	
	An Angry Man I	B7	11/8/1977	14-2	
	An Angry Man II	B8	11/8/1977	14-2	
77-23	Superintendent's Dilemma	A1	11/21/1977		
	Capitalism/Socialism	A2	11/21/1977		
	Socialism	A3	11/21/1977		
	Inflation and the Property Tax I	A4	11/21/1977		
	Inflation and the Property Tax II	A5	11/21/1977		
	Public Employees	A6	11/21/1977		
	Red Hen	A7	11/21/1977		
	President Coolidge	B1	11/21/1977		
	Education	B2	11/21/1977		
	Christmas 1977	B3	11/21/1977		
	Bread Machine and Janeway	B4	11/21/1977		
	The Incredible Bread Machine	B5	11/21/1977		
	People Power	B6	11/21/1977		
	Button, Button	B7	11/21/1977		
	America's Strength	B8	11/21/1977		
77-24	Snail Darters	A1	11/29/1977	14-2 gr dark	
	Nicaragua I	A2	11/29/1977	Peter Hannaford	
	Nicaragua II	A3	11/29/1977	Peter Hannaford	
	Visas	A4	11/29/1977	14-2	
	National Security	A5	11/29/1977	14-2	
	National Health Insurance I	A6	11/29/1977	14-2	
	National Health Insurance II	A7	11/29/1977	14-2	
	Social Security	B1	11/29/1977	14-2	370
	Martin Luther King	B2	11/29/1977	14-2	385
	Coffee	B3	11/29/1977	14-2 gr dark	
	Automobiles	B4	11/29/1977	14-2 gr dark	
	NEA	B5	11/29/1977	14-2	351
	Kidco	B6	11/29/1977	14-2	
	Apples	B7	11/29/1977	14-2 gr bl	301
	Herman Kahn, Futurist	B8	11/29/1977		
78-01	Salt II	A1	1/9/1978		
	Christmas	A2	1/9/1978	14-2	
	American Farm School I	A3	1/9/1978	14-2	
	American Farm School II	A4	1/9/1978	14-2	
	Human Rights I	A5	1/9/1978	14-2	53
	Human Rights II	A6	1/9/1978	14-2	150
	Human Rights III	A7	1/9/1978	14-2	152
	Taxes	B1	1/9/1978	14-2	
	Our Country	B2	1/9/1978	14-2	
	Crime	B3	1/9/1978	14-2	
	Miscellaneous	B4	1/9/1978	14-2	
	Welfare	B5	1/9/1978	14-2	394
	Healthy Competition	B6	1/9/1978	John McClaury	
	Pot	B7	1/9/1978	14-2	
	Social Security	B8	1/9/1978	14-2	372
78-02	Big Mo	A1	1/27/1978	14-2	
	Panama	A2	1/27/1978	14-1 red	
	St. Stephan's Crown	A3	1/27/1978	14-1	

O'Connor Number	Title	Side/Number	Taping Date	Handwritten Draft	Book Page
	Korea	A4	1/27/1978	14-2	68
	Oil	A5	1/27/1978	14-2	
	"Independents" vs IRS	A6	1/27/1978		
	Regulation	A7	1/27/1978	14-2	
	Welfare Reform	B1	1/27/1978	14-2	
	Miscellaneous	B2	1/27/1978	14-2	
	Looking Out a Window	B3	1/27/1978	14-2	18
	Jobs	B4	1/27/1978	14-2	
	Miscellaneous	B5	1/27/1978	14-2	
	Pity the Middle Class	B6	1/27/1978		
	Miscellaneous	B7	1/27/1978		
	Father & Son	B8	1/27/1978	14-1	
78-03	Panama Canal Debate	A1	2/20/1978		
	Spaceships	A2	2/20/1978	14-2	
	Redwoods	A3	2/20/1978	14-2	
	Swordfish	A4	2/20/1978		
	Farm Day	A5	2/20/1978	14-2 bl	
	Tax Limitation 1978 Style	A6	2/20/1978		
	Steel	A7	2/20/1978	14-2	
	Labor	B1	2/20/1978	14-2	
	Economy	B2	2/20/1978	14-2	
	Neighborhoods	B3	2/20/1978		
	Cuba	B4	2/20/1978	14-2	
	Treaties	B5	2/20/1978	14-2	
	Neutron Bomb	B6	2/20/1978		
	Bakke	B7	2/20/1978	14-2	
	Blind on the Left	B8	2/20/1978	14-2	136
78-04	Canal	A1	3/13/1978	14-2	
	Treaties	A2	3/13/1978	14-2	54
	Salt Talks I	A3	3/13/1978	14-2	76
	Salt Talks II	A4	3/13/1978	14-2	
	Cubans & Russians	A5	3/13/1978	14-2	207
	Salt II	A6	3/13/1978	14-2	77
	Two Worlds	A7	3/13/1978	14-2	
	War	B1	3/13/1978	14-2	99
	Suicide Lobby	B2	3/13/1978	14-2	139
	Budget	B3	3/13/1978	14-2	
	Mineral King	B4	3/13/1978	14-2 gr	
	Local Control I	B5	3/13/1978	14-2	
	Local Control II	B6	3/13/1978	14-2	
	A Gift	B7	3/13/1978	14-2	388
	Items	B8	3/13/1978	14-2	
78-05	Canal	A1	4/3/1978	14-2	208
	Tax Time	A2	4/3/1978	14-2	
	Crime	A3	4/3/1978	14-2	
	China	A4	4/3/1978	14-2	58
	Bill Simon	A5	4/3/1978	14-2	
	Missing Person	A6	4/3/1978	14-2	411
	Three Martini Lunch	A7	4/3/1978	14-2	
	Government	A8	4/3/1978	14-2	
	Spies	B1	4/3/1978	14-2	
	No Pay, No Vote	B2	4/3/1978	14-2	171
	B-1 Bomber	B3	4/3/1978	14-2	103
	Farm	B4	4/3/1978	14-2	
	Regulators	B5	4/3/1978	14-2	
	Miscellaneous	B6	4/3/1978	14-2	

O'Connor Number	Title	Side/ Number	Taping Date	Handwritten Draft	Book Page
	General James	B7	4/3/1978	14-2 dark	
	Desk-Cleaning	B8	4/3/1978	14-2 dark	141
78-06	Guinea	A1	2/20/1978	14-2	170
	Christmas	A2	2/20/1978	14-2	415
	Do Right	A3	2/20/1978	1/2	
	Life & Death	A4	2/20/1978	14-2	
	School Days	A5	2/20/1978	14-2	345
	Government Security	A6	3/13/1978	14-2	
	Sports	A7	3/13/1978	14-2 dark	
	Fighting Cal Graham	B1	3/13/1978		
	Greensville County Elections	B2	3/13/1978		
	Snails & Signboards	B3	3/13/1978		
	Nit Picking	B4	4/3/1978	14-2	
	Communications I	B5	4/3/1978	14-2 dark	300
	Communications II	B6	4/3/1978	14-2	
	Soviet Consumer	B7	4/3/1978		
	Air Cargo Deregulation	B8	4/3/1978		
78-07	Japan I	A1	5/15/1978	14-2p	
	Japan II	A2	5/15/1978	14-2p	287
	Japan III	A3	5/15/1978	14-2p	114
	Taiwan I	A4	5/15/1978	14-2p	43
	Hong Kong	A5	5/15/1978	14-2p	113
	Women	A6	5/15/1978	14-2p	
	Education	A7	5/15/1978	14-2	
	Alger Hiss	B1	5/15/1978	14-2	
	Rhodesia	B2	5/15/1978	14-2	
	The Pacific	B3	5/15/1978	14-2	116
	Seal Hunt	B4	5/15/1978	14-2	334
	Dulles Airport	B5	5/15/1978	14-2	
	Castro's Prisons	B6	5/15/1978	14-2	
	Miscellaneous	B7	5/15/1978	14-2	
	Health Care	B8	5/15/1978	14-2	
78-08	Taxes Again	A1	6/5/1978	14-2	277
	National Security	A2	6/5/1978	14-2	
	Hearst	A3	6/5/1978	14-3	
	Spending	A4	6/5/1978	14-2	
	Energy	A5	6/5/1978	14-2	
	Oil	A6	6/5/1978	14-2	
	Russia	A7	6/5/1978	14-2	
	Planes	B1	6/5/1978	14-2	
	Drugs	B2	6/5/1978	14-2	
	Foolishness	B3	6/5/1978	14-2	
	Money	B4	6/5/1978	14-2	
	New Talk from a Labor Leader	B5	6/5/1978		
	Salaries	B6	6/5/1978	14-2	
	Davis-Bacon Act	B7	6/5/1978		
	Education	B8	6/5/1978	14-2	
78-09	U.S.-China Relations	A2	6/27/1978		
	Normalization	A1	6/27/1978		
	District of Columbia	A3	6/27/1978	14-2	
	Fraud	A4	6/27/1978	14-2	
	SALT Talks	A5	6/27/1978	14-2	79
	Cities	A6	6/27/1978	14-2	
	Stamps	A7	6/27/1978	14-2	
	Asia	B1	6/27/1978	14-2	

O'Connor Number	Title	Side/ Number	Taping Date	Handwritten Draft	Book Page
	Asia II	B2	6/27/1978	14-2	
	Free Press	B3	6/27/1978	14-2	
	Alex. Solzhenitsyn	B4	6/27/1978	14-2	
	Alex. Solzhenitsyn II	B5	6/27/1978	14-2	
	Inflation	B6	6/27/1978	14-2	
	Mailbu	B7	6/27/1978	14-2	331
	Miscellaneous	B8	6/27/1978	14-2	
78-10	Government	A1	7/15/1978	14-2	
	Mirages	A2	7/15/1978	14-2	
	Lumber	A3	7/15/1978	14-2	
	Freedom of Speech in Russia	A4	7/15/1978	14-2	
	Stanley Yankus	A5	7/15/1978	14-2	
	Charity	A6	7/15/1978	14-2	
	School Busing	A7	7/15/1978		
	Wedding	B1	7/15/1978	14-2	
	South Africa	B2	7/15/1978	14-2	188
	Cuba	B3	7/15/1978	14-2	
	Castro	B4	7/15/1978	14-2	59
	Walter Knott	B5	7/15/1978		
	Trains	B6	7/15/1978	14-1	
	Chiefs of Staff	B7	7/15/1978	14-2	70
	Proposition 13	B8	7/15/1978	14-2	
78-11	SALT Talks I	A1	7/31/1978	14-2	82
	SALT Talks II	A2	7/31/1978	14-2	84
	Employment	A3	7/31/1978	14-2	
	Economics I	A4	7/31/1978	14-2	258
	Economics II	A5	7/31/1978	14-2	259
	Paperwork	A6	7/31/1978	14-2	
	Religious Freedom	A7	7/31/1978	14-2	
	Miscellaneous	B1	7/31/1978	14-2	
	Rome	B2	7/31/1978	14-2	238
	South Seas	B3	7/31/1978	14-2	
	Prisoner Exchange	B4	7/31/1978	14-2	
	Local Government Center	B5	7/31/1978		
	Alternative Energy and Uncle Sam	B6	7/31/1978		
	A Refugee Success Story	B7	7/31/1978		
	Accidents	B8	7/31/1978	14-2	
78-12	Income Tax	A1	8/7/1978	14-2	
	British Health Care	A2	8/7/1978	14-2	
	History	A3	8/7/1978	14-2	
	Brainwashing I	A4	8/7/1978	14-2	
	Brainwashing II	A5	8/7/1978	14-2	
	Tax Revolt	A6	8/7/1978	14-2	
	Left & Right	A7	8/7/1978	John McClaury	
	The Average Man	B1	8/7/1978	14-2	
	Polls and Guns	B2	8/7/1978	14-2	403
	Guantanamo	B3	8/7/1978	14-2	209
	Government Cost	B4	8/7/1978	14-2	
	Pay Raise	B5	8/7/1978	14-2	
	Miscellaneous	B6	8/7/1978	14-2	
	Two Worlds	B7	8/7/1978	14-2	13
	Technology	B8	8/7/1978	14-2	313
78-13	Mexico's Oil	A1	9/19/1978		
	Olympics	A2	9/19/1978	14-2	147
	Prop. 13 Fallout	A3	9/19/1978	14-2	

O'Connor Number	Title	Side/ Number	Taping Date	Handwritten Draft	Book Page
	Terrorism	A4	9/19/1978		
	Land	A5	9/19/1978	14-2	
	Pot	A6	9/19/1978	14-2	
	Nuclear Power	A7	9/19/1978	14-2	324
	Needed—Better Use of National Forests	B1	9/19/1978		
	Mail	B2	9/19/1978	14-2	407
	Africa	B3	9/19/1978	14-2	193
	Utilities	B4	9/19/1978	14-2	
	Bugs	B5	9/19/1978	14-2	333
	Government Payroll	B6	9/19/1978	14-2	
	Free Enterprise	B7	9/19/1978	14-2	
	Miscellaneous	B8	9/19/1978	14-2	
78-14	District of Columbia	A1	10/10/1978	14-2	
	Amtrak	A2	10/10/1978	14-2	
	Bi-Lingual	A3	10/10/1978	14-2 dark	
	Federal Lands	A4	10/10/1978	14-2	337
	Ocean Mining	A5	10/10/1978	14-2	173
	Rostow I	A6	10/10/1978	14-2	92
	Rostow II	A7	10/10/1978	14-2	93
	Rostow III	B1	10/10/1978	14-2	94
	Rostow IV	B2	10/10/1978	14-2	95
	Rostow V	B3	10/10/1978	14-2	97
	Rostow VI	B4	10/10/1978	14-2	98
	End of an Emergency	B5	10/10/1978		
	Argentina	B6	10/10/1978		
	Environment	B7	10/10/1978	14-2	
	Soviet Nuclear Power	B8	10/10/1978		
78-15	Letelier I	A1	10/31/1978		
	Letelier II	A2	10/31/1978		
	Intelligence and the Media	A3	10/31/1978	14-2	127
	Welfare	A4	10/31/1978	14-2	
	The Escalator	A5	10/31/1978	14-2	
	Nuclear Power I	A6	10/31/1978	14-2	
	Nuclear Power II	A7	10/31/1978	14-2	
	Crime	B1	10/31/1978	14-2	
	Waste	B2	10/31/1978	14-2	
	Nuclear Carrier	B3	10/31/1978	14-2	
	Pensions	B4	10/31/1978	14-2	
	Self-Help in the Neighborhoods	B5	10/31/1978		
	Chinese Libertarians	B6	10/31/1978		
	Davis-Bacon Act	B7	10/31/1978		
	Miscellaneous	B8	10/31/1978	14-2	
78-16	Private Schools	A1	11/28/1978	14-2	354
	Toys	A2	11/28/1978	14-2	
	Hope for the Cities	A3	11/28/1978	Peter Hannaford	
	Basketball	A4	11/28/1978	14-2	378
	Horse & Rider I	A5	11/28/1978	14-2	
	Horse & Rider II	A6	11/28/1978	14-2	
	China	A7	11/28/1978	14-2	
	SALT II	B1	11/28/1978	14-2	85
	Jokes	B2	11/28/1978	Peter Hannaford	
	An Accurate Thermometer	B3	11/28/1978	Peter Hannaford	
	Miscellaneous	B4	11/28/1978	14-2	
	Wood I	B5	11/28/1978	14-2	

O'Connor Number	Title	Side/ Number	Taping Date	Handwritten Draft	Book Page
	Wood II	B6	11/28/1978	14-2	
	Bilingualism	B7	11/28/1978	Peter Hannaford	
	Taxation	B8	11/28/1978	14-2	279
78-17	Christmas Day	A1	12/12/1978		
	SALT II	A2	12/12/1978	14-2	86
	Panama Canal	A3	12/12/1978	14-2	
	Gambling on the Dollar	A4	12/12/1978		
	The Checkoff Ripoff	A5	12/12/1978	John McClaury	
	Gas	A6	12/12/1978	14-2	
	Taxes	A7	12/12/1978	14-2	
	Keep Off the Grass	B1	12/12/1978	14-2	
	Helsinki Pact	B2	12/12/1978	14-2	154
	Bread	B3	12/12/1978	14-2	
	Business Tax	B4	12/12/1978	14-2	
	ERA	B5	12/12/1978	14-2	
	Miscellaneous I	B6	12/12/1978	14-2	
	Miscellaneous II	B7	12/12/1978	14-2	
	Textbooks	B8	12/12/1978	14-2	
79-01	Taiwan	A1	January-79		
	Taiwan I	A2	January-79	11-2	61
	Taiwan II	A3	January-79	11-2	45
	Taiwan III	A4	January-79	11-2	
	Jim Henricks	A5	January-79	11-2	
	Patent Medicine I	A6	January-79	14-2	
	Patent Medicine II	A7	January-79	14-2	
	Human Rights	B1	January-79	11-2	155
	Health Insurance	B2	January-79	11-3	
	Telescope I	B3	January-79	11-2	310
	Telescope II	B4	January-79	11-2	311
	Miscellaneous I	B5	January-79	14-2	
	Miscellaneous II	B6	January-79	14-2	
	Miscellaneous III	B7	January-79	11-2	
	South Africa	B8	January-79	11-2	189
79-02	Phone	A1	1/19/1979	11-3	316
	OPEC	A2	1/19/1979	11-2	321
	Federal Trade Commission	A3	1/19/1979	11-2	
	The Official Rules	A4	1/19/1979	John McClaury	
	Anti-Poverty Abuses I	A5	1/19/1979		
	Anti-Poverty Abuses II	A6	1/19/1979		
	Wind Energy in Denmark	A7	1/19/1979	John McClaury	
	Counterintelligence	B1	1/19/1979	11-3	
	Australia I	B2	1/19/1979	11-2	
	Australia II	B3	1/19/1979	11-2	
	Peace Corps	B4	1/19/1979	11-2	
	A Policeman	B5	1/19/1979	11-2	
	Miscellaneous 1	B6	1/19/1979	John McClaury	
	Miscellaneous 2	B7	1/19/1979	11-2	
	Regulations	B8	1/19/1979	11-2	
79-03	Proposition 13 and the Post Commission I	A1	2/13/1979		
	Proposition 13 and the Post Commission II	A2	2/13/1979		
	Deregulation	A3	2/13/1979		
	Dishonest Environmentalists	A4	2/13/1979		
	Fish	A5	2/13/1979	14-2	290
	Constitutional Amendment	A6	2/13/1979	14-2	284

O'Connor Number	Title	Side/ Number	Taping Date	Handwritten Draft	Book Page
	Pot	A7	2/13/1979	14-2	
	Saying "No"—Part I	B1	2/13/1979	14-2	
	Saying "No"—Part II	B2	2/13/1979	14-2	
	Conspiracy	B3	2/13/1979	14-2	234
	Lawrence Welk	B4	2/13/1979	14-2	
	Income Tax	B5	2/13/1979	14-2	280
	Hamburgers	B6	2/13/1979	14-2	
	Long Walk	B7	2/13/1979	14-2	
	Miscellaneous	B8	2/13/1979	14-2	
79-04	Nancy	A1	3/6/1979	14-2	355
	Lettuce Strike	A2	3/6/1979		
	Taiwan's Future	A3	3/6/1979	14-2	72
	POW	A4	3/6/1979	14-2	
	Cuba	A5	3/6/1979	14-2	158
	The 100 Club	A6	3/6/1979	14-2	
	CIA	A7	3/6/1979	14-2	
	Miscellaneous	B1	3/6/1979	14-2	
	Inflation	B2	3/6/1979	14-2	
	Human Rights	B3	3/6/1979	14-2	
	Comparisons	B4	3/6/1979	14-2	229
	Nuclear Power I	B5	3/6/1979	14-2	
	Nuclear Power II	B6	3/6/1979	14-2 gr bl	
	Higher Standard of Living	B7	3/6/1979	14-2 gr dark	
	Student Economists	B8	3/6/1979		
79-05	Panama	A1	3/27/1979	14-2	211
	Small Business I	A2	3/27/1979	14-2	
	Small Business II	A3	3/27/1979	14-2	
	Scared Straight	A4	3/27/1979		
	Palestine	A5	3/27/1979	14-2	215
	Miscellaneous	A6	3/27/1979	14-2	
	Agriculture	A7	3/27/1979	14-2	304
	Rhodesia	B1	3/27/1979	14-2	
	District of Columbia	B2	3/27/1979	14-2	
	Miscellaneous II	B3	3/27/1979	14-2	
	Rural Renaissance	B4	3/27/1979	John McClaury	
	Washington Weather	B5	3/27/1979	14-2	
	SALT II—Part I	B6	3/27/1979	14-2	88
	SALT II—Part II	B7	3/27/1979	14-2	89
	Miscellaneous III	B8	3/27/1979	14-2	
79-06	New England Energy Barriers	A1	4/16/1979	John McClaury	
	Land Use: The California Precedent	A2	4/16/1979		
	The Real Impact of Inflation	A3	4/16/1979		
	Real Estate Signs	A4	4/16/1979		
	Jonestown	A5	4/16/1979	14-2	
	David & Goliath	A6	4/16/1979	14-3	
	Schools	A7	4/16/1979	14-2	352
	Budget	B1	4/16/1979	14-2 p	285
	Food Stamps	B2	4/16/1979	14-2	
	Bilingual Education I	B3	4/16/1979	14-2	
	Bilingual Education II	B4	4/16/1979	14-2	346
	Regulations Go to College	B5	4/16/1979	14-2	360
	The Salcido Family	B6	4/16/1979	14-2	
	Miscellaneous	B7	4/16/1979	14-2	
	Free Enterprise	B8	4/16/1979	14-2	228
79-07	T.K.E.	A1	5/8/1979	14-2	413

O'Connor Number	Title	Side/ Number	Taping Date	Handwritten Draft	Book Page
	Three Mile Island I	A2	5/8/1979	14-2	
	Three Mile Island II	A3	5/8/1979	14-2	
	Whistle Blowers; Poverty's Causes	A4	5/8/1979		
	Parable of the Talents— Updated	A5	5/8/1979	William Gavin	
	McCarthy	A6	5/8/1979	14-2	
	Miscellaneous	A7	5/8/1979	14-2	
	Grove City College	B1	5/8/1979	14-2p	
	I'm Only 17	B2	5/8/1979	14-1p	
	Oil	B3	5/8/1979	14-2p	
	Fluid Flame Burner	B4	5/8/1979	14-2p	
	Disaster Area	B5	5/8/1979	14-2	
	Sex Education	B6	5/8/1979	14-2	347
	Graffiti	B7	5/8/1979		
	Banned Words	B8	5/8/1979		
79-08	California Gas Shortage	A1	5/29/1979	14-2	322
	Oil	A2	5/29/1979	14-2	
	Sex Education	A3	5/29/1979	14-2	
	People's Park I	A4	5/29/1979	14-2	
	People's Park II	A5	5/29/1979	14-2	
	Free Trade vs Protectionism	A6	5/29/1979		
	Political Bestiary	A7	5/29/1979		
	Marijuana	B1	5/29/1979	14-2	
	The Delaney Amendment	B2	5/29/1979		
	Miscellaneous I	B3	5/29/1979	14-2	104
	Miscellaneous II	B4	5/29/1979	14-2	46
	Investment Lag	B5	5/29/1979		
	Crime	B6	5/29/1979	14-2	
	Vietnam War	B7	5/29/1979	14-2	
	Operation Get Smart	B8	5/29/1979		
79-09	John Wayne	A1	6/29/1979	14-2 dark	412
	Double Standard	A2	6/29/1979		
	The Pope in Poland	A3	6/29/1979	14-2	174
	Nuclear Power	A4	6/29/1979	14-2	
	Oil Profits	A5	6/29/1979	14-2 dark	
	Miscellaneous	A6	6/29/1979	14-2	
	Money	A7	6/29/1979	14-2	261
	A Green Lawn	B1	6/29/1979	1/3	
	Bukovsky	B2	6/29/1979	14-2	149
	Molecules	B3	6/29/1979	14-2 dark	
	A Tale of Two Countries	B4	6/29/1979	14-2	176
	Joan Baez I	B5	6/29/1979	14-2	
	Joan Baez II	B6	6/29/1979	14-2	
	The Family	B7	6/29/1979	14-2	375
	Corruption	B8	6/29/1979	14-2	
79-10	Busing Amendment	A1	7/9/1979		
	Sen. Jackson on SALT II	A2	7/9/1979		
	Soviet Trade	A3	7/9/1979	14-2	73
	Trains	A4	7/9/1979	14-2	306
	Nigeria	A5	7/9/1979	14-2	16
	Assembly Line Medicine I	A6	7/9/1979	14-2	
	Assembly Line Medicine II	A7	7/9/1979	14-2	368
	Namibia I	B1	7/9/1979	14-2	190
	Namibia II	B2	7/9/1979	14-2	192
	The MSHA Test	B3	7/9/1979		

O'Connor Number	Title	Side/ Number	Taping Date	Handwritten Draft	Book Page
	Free Speech for Business?	B4	7/9/1979	14-2 dark	
	Energy-Saving Computer	B5	7/9/1979		
	Project Match	B6	7/9/1979		
	Miscellaneous	B7	7/9/1979	14-2 dark	
	Elementary Energy Lessons	B8	7/9/1979		
79-11	Congressional Promises and Performance	A1	7/27/1979		
	Income Tax Indexation	A2	7/27/1979		
	Chile	A3	7/27/1979	14-2	142
	International Year of the Child	A4	7/27/1979		
	Tax Expenditures	A5	7/27/1979	14-2	283
	Another Side of the U.N.	A6	7/27/1979		
	A Different Watergate Story	A7	7/27/1979		
	Miscellaneous I	B1	7/27/1979	14-2	
	Neoconservatives	B2	7/27/1979		
	Common Sense from a Neighbor	B3	7/27/1979		
	America	B4	7/27/1979	14-2	
	Miscellaneous II	B5	7/27/1979	14-2	
	Free Speech	B6	7/27/1979	14-2	
	Showcase U.S.A.	B7	7/27/1979	14-2	
	Miscellaneous III	B8	7/27/1979	14-2	
79-12	What to Expect from the Soviet Succession	A1	Aug-79		
	Thank You, Chairman Brezhnev	A2	Aug-79		
	Better Representation for Skilled Tradesmen	A3	Aug-79		
	Government Housing Programs	A4	Aug-79		
	Alaskan Anger	A5	Aug-79		
	Waiting in Line	A6	Aug-79		
	Citizen vs Chicago Transit Authority	A7	Aug-79		
	Tax Revolt Going Strong	B1	Aug-79		
	The Magic Money Machine	B2	Aug-79	14-2	
	Administration Report Clears Oil Companies	B3	Aug-79		
	Marijuana	B4	Aug-79	14-2	396
	Voting Records	B5	Aug-79	14-2	
	Power	B6	Aug-79	14-2	
	Food Stamps	B7	Aug-79	14-2	
	Living Dangerously . . . Sometimes	B8	Aug-79		
79-13	**Defense I**	A1	9/11/1979	14-2	105
	Defense II	A2	9/11/1979	14-2	107
	Defense III	A3	9/11/1979	14-2	108
	Defense IV	A4	9/11/1979	14-2	119
	Talking Back	A5	9/11/1979	14-2	
	Miscellaneous I	A6	9/11/1979	14-2	
	Ships	A7	9/11/1979	14-2	
	SALT II	B1	9/11/1979	14-2	62
	Miscellaneous II	B2	9/11/1979	14-2	
	Miscellaneous III	B3	9/11/1979	14-2	
	Miscellaneous IV	B4	9/11/1979	14-2	

O'Connor Number	Title	Side/ Number	Taping Date	Handwritten Draft	Book Page
	In Business	B5	9/11/1979		
	How to Handle Dissident Bureaucrats	B6	9/11/1979		
	Local Energy Solutions	B7	9/11/1979		
	Temperature Restrictions	B8	9/11/1979		
79-14	Vlasenko	A1	10/2/1979	14-2	177
	Six Lies on Energy	A2	10/2/1979		
	Department of Education	A3	10/2/1979	14-2	
	SALT II	A4	10/2/1979	14-2	90
	Hollywood East	A5	10/2/1979	14-2 B pc	
	Defectors	A6	10/2/1979	14-2 B pc	
	In Defense of Success	A7	10/2/1979		
	Coal	B1	10/2/1979	14-2	
	California	B2	10/2/1979	14-2 B pc	
	The Draft	B3	10/2/1979	Martin Anderson	
	Red Tape	B4	10/2/1979	14-2 B pc	
	Radioactivity	B5	10/2/1979	14-2 B pc	
	The Golden Fleece	B6	10/2/1979	14-2 B pc	
	Gadgets	B7	10/2/1979		
	Land	B8	10/2/1979	14-2	
79-15	Cuba Overseas	1	10/25/1979		
	Cuban Conditions	2	10/25/1979		
	Israel I	3	10/25/1979		
	Israel II	4	10/25/1979		
	Salt	5	10/25/1979		
	Health Care	6	10/25/1979	14-2	369
	Miscellaneous and Goodbye	7	10/25/1979	14-2	416

ACKNOWLEDGMENTS

This book *is* Ronald Reagan.

Over the years he spent thousands of hours sitting on airplanes, in the back seats of automobiles, on trains, at a desk at his home, and at the ranch in the mountains at Santa Barbara—writing. Most of the words in this book are his.

Many people were links in the chain of events that transformed the unsorted stacks of legal size yellow pages, stored in old cardboard boxes, into this handsome volume. We will try to acknowledge them all.

First and foremost is Nancy Reagan, who recognized the historicic importance of these papers and gave us permission to examine them. For many years she watched Reagan study and write and wanted others to understand him as she does.

George Shultz, who was at Reagan's side for six and a half years as his secretary of state when the Cold War was won, gave us counsel and support, and wrote the Foreword.

The scholarly resources of the Hoover Institution, and the strong support and encouragement of John Raisian, the Director, and Charles Palm, the Deputy Director, were vital to the project. Carnegie Mellon University, where Kiron Skinner is an assistant professor, similarly provided strong support for the book, as did the Office of the Dean of the Faculty and the Office of the President at Hamilton College, the Olin Foundation, and the Council on Foreign Relations.

The archivists at Hoover were especially helpful in providing access to the many Reagan documents in the collections of the Hoover Institution—Elena

Danielson, Archivist; Linda Bernard, Assistant Archivist; Carol Leadenham, Aparna Mukherjee, Natalia Porfirenko, and Remy Squires, Audio Visual Specialists.

A special note should go to Mark Burson, the executive director of the Ronald Reagan Presidential Foundation, and to Joanne Drake, chief of staff to Ronald Reagan, who were both instrumental in facilitating access to the private papers stored in the Ronald Reagan Presidential Library in Simi Valley, California. Mark Burson also provided valuable assistance in preparing our book contract, and his strong recommendation that the words "In His Own Hand" should be part of the title played a key role in the selection of the title we are using.

Anne Hawkins and John Hawkins, our agents, were suggested to us by one of our colleagues at the Hoover Institution, Bruce Bueno de Mesquita. They have played an important role in the complex negotiations that were necessary for this project to proceed and have been a wonderful source of keen advice and inspiration throughout the entire process.

The Free Press has been a terrific publisher. We owe a special debt to Paul Golob, our first editor, who instantly saw the book's potential and, with the support of Paula Duffy, then publisher of The Free Press, offered us a contract. Both Paul and Paula left before the book was complete, but their successors, Bruce Nichols, Vice President and Senior Editor, and Bill Shinker, Publisher, have been superb. Carol de Onis, the Copyediting Supervisor, oversaw the uniquely difficult job of copyediting this book with both skill and tolerance.

Bruce Nichols was our main editor. His organizational suggestions and editing have greatly improved our original manuscript. At every step in the crafting of this book, from the jacket copy to the jacket design to the proofing, his advice and counsel have been invaluable.

We are deeply appreciative of publisher Bill Shinker's understanding of the nature of this book, his full support, and his promotional ideas and leadership.

The archivists at the Ronald Reagan Presidential Library were uniformly helpful and did much to make our many days of research in the files productive and enjoyable. We want to express our thanks and appreciation to archivists Diane Barrie, Kelly Barton, Steve Branch (audio-visual), Greg Cumming, Dennis Daellenbach, Mike Duggan, Sherrie Fletcher, Lisa Jones, Cate Sewell, and Jenny Sternaman for their professional support.

While writing the book, we conducted numerous interviews, especially with the very small number of people who were physically with Ronald Reagan during the times that he wrote, and who worked with his papers after he had finished writing them. They included Peter Hannaford, Harry O'Connor, Ed Meese, Michael Deaver, David Fischer, Dennis LeBlanc, Elaine Crispen Sawyer, and Helene von Damm. Peter Hannaford was especially helpful in describing how he worked with Reagan, for almost five years, in producing the radio commentaries that are in this book.

We also want to express our thanks to all those, some of them unnamed, who contributed wonderful examples of handwritten documents by Ronald Reagan from their private collections. Without their efforts, much of this material would have been lost forever.

Anthony Glass, Eureka College Archivist and Technical Services Librarian, and Jeff McSweeney, Director of Alumni Relations, helped find the Eureka College documents. A special note of thanks to Irv Letofsky, a for-mer editor of the *Los Angeles Times* and the country's foremost collector of Ronald Reagan movie posters, who tracked down the seventeen articles that Reagan wrote for the *Des Moines Sunday Register* newspaper in 1937.

The essence of this book is the selection of handwritten essays that Ronald Reagan wrote. Brenda McLean, Assistant to Martin Anderson, and Susan Schendel, Assistant to George Shultz, did the difficult, painstaking work of transforming the handwritten drafts into print, showing all of the editing that was done in the original. The handwriting of Ronald Reagan is clear and easy to read, but not so with the editing. Often, while editing, he did such a thorough job of crossing out words that it is difficult, and sometimes impossible, to discern his first thoughts. He also used many abbreviations in these handwritten drafts, depending on his secretaries to flesh out the words in the script he used to record from or in the copy sent to people who requested a transcript.

But Brenda and Susan did a superb job of untangling those edits and abbreviations so that, in most cases, we can easily follow the flow of his words. In addition they both provided comments and suggestions that often found their way into the book.

Sergiy Kudelia, our research assistant throughout the project, carefully checked many facts and conducted other projects assigned to him. Jong Lee, Alex Porfirenko and Phyllis Villec also conducted research on this project.

As the book entered its final stages a number of people read the very rough manuscript and provided us with useful comments and criticism. They included Richard V. Allen, Arnold Beichman, William P. Clark, Robert Conquest, R. Dan McMichael, Edwin Meese, Thomas C. Reed, Byron Skinner, and Lowell Wood. At the end, Romayne Ponleithner did a first draft of an index that we hope will be appreciated by the readers of this book.

A number of people helped in many ways, from commenting on specific policy points in the draft to offering general advice and counsel. They are: Patricia Baker, Anne Burnham, James Burnham, Alan Cafruny, W. Glenn Campbell, Otto Toby Davis, Robyn Dawes, Bobby Fong, Karen Green, Grace Hawes, William Keech, Steven Klepper, Claudia Mitchell-Kernan, Molly Molloy, Juanita Nissley, Raymund Paredes, Rita Ricado-Campbell, Condoleezza Rice, Steven Schlossman, Ellana Schwartz, Thomas Schwartz, Gloria Skinner, Ruby Skinner, Eugene Tobin, Linda Wheeler, Tom Winter and Dawn Woodward.

And finally, one last word. This book could never have been done without its three authors, each one of them contributing—in equal measure—necessary components. They collaborated throughout every phase of the project and, now that it is completed, they are still good friends—probably the greatest achievement of all.

INDEX

Looking Outa window. ①

It's nightfall in a strange town a long way from home. I'm watching the lights come on from my hotel room window on the 35th floor.

I'll be right back.

I'm afraid you are in for a little bit of philosophying if you don't mind. Some of these broadcasts have to be put together while I'm out on the road traveling what I call the mashed potato circuit. In a little while I'll be speaking to a group of very nice people in a banquet hall.

Right now however I'm looking down on a busy city at rush hour. The streets below are twin ribbons of sparkling red & white. Tail lights on the cars moving away from my vantage point provide the red and those coming toward me the white. It's logical to assume all or most are home ward bound at the end of a days work.

I wonder why some social engineer hasn't tried to get them to trade homes. The traffic is equally heavy in both directions so if they all lived in the end of town where they worked it would save a lot of travel time. Forget I said that & dont even think it or some bureaucrat will try do it.

But wonder about the people in those cars, who they are, what they do, what they are thinking about as they head for the warmth of home & family. Come to think of it I've met them — oh — maybe not these particular individuals but still I feel I know them. Some of our social planners refer to them as "the masses" which only proves they don't know them. I've been privileged to meet people all over this land in the special kind of way you meet them when you are campaigning. They are not "the masses," or as the elitists would have it — "the common man." They are very uncommon.